Money, Currency and Crisis

Money is a core feature in all discussions of economic crisis, as is clear from the debates about the responses of the European Central Bank and the Federal Reserve Bank of the United States to the 2008 economic crisis.

This volume explores the role of money in economic performance, and focuses on how monetary systems have affected economic crises for the last 4,000 years. Recent events have confirmed that money is only a useful tool in economic exchange if it is trusted, and this is a concept that this text explores in depth. The international panel of experts assembled here offers a long-range perspective, from ancient Assyria to modern societies in Europe, China and the US.

This book will be of interest to students and researchers of economic history, and to anyone who seeks to understand the economic crises of recent decades, and place them in a wider historical context.

R.J. van der Spek is Professor Emeritus of Ancient Mediterranean and West-Asian History at the VU University (Vrije Universiteit) Amsterdam, the Netherlands.

Bas van Leeuwen is Senior Researcher at Utrecht University and the International Institute of Social History, Amsterdam, the Netherlands.

Routledge Explorations in Economic History

Edited by Lars Magnusson, Uppsala University, Sweden

72. Natural Resources and Economic Growth
Learning from History
Edited by Marc Badia-Miró, Vicente Pinilla and Henry Willebald

73. The Political Economy of Mercantilism
Lars Magnusson

74. Innovation and Technological Diffusion
An economic history of early steam engines
Harry Kitsikopoulos

75. Regulating Competition
Cartel registers in the twentieth-century world
Edited by Susanna Fellman and Martin Shanahan

76. European Banks and the Rise of International Finance
The Post-Bretton Woods era
Carlo Edoardo Altamura

77. The Second Bank of the United States
"Central" banker in an era of nation-building, 1816–1836
Jane Ellen Knodell

78. War, Power and the Economy
Mercantilism and state formation in 18th-century Europe
A. González Enciso

79. The Western Allies and Soviet Potential in World War II
Economy, Society and Military Power
Martin Kahn

80. Money, Currency and Crisis
In Search of Trust, 2000 BC to AD 2000
Edited by R.J. van der Spek and Bas van Leeuwen

For a full list of titles in this series, please visit www.routledge.com/series/SE0347

Money, Currency and Crisis

In Search of Trust, 2000 BC to AD 2000

Edited by R.J. van der Spek and Bas van Leeuwen

LONDON AND NEW YORK

First published 2018
by Routledge
2 Park Square, Milton Park, Abingdon, Oxon OX14 4RN

and by Routledge
711 Third Avenue, New York, NY 10017

Routledge is an imprint of the Taylor & Francis Group, an informa business

British Library Cataloguing-in-Publication Data
A catalogue record for this book is available from the British Library

Library of Congress Cataloging-in-Publication Data
A catalog record has been requested for this book

ISBN: 978-1-138-62835-9 (hbk)
ISBN: 978-1-315-21071-1 (ebk)

Typeset in Bembo
by Deanta Global Publishing Services, Chennai, India

Contents

Figures

Maps

Tables

Appendices

Contributors

Dirk J. Bezemer, Professor of Economics of International Financial Development, University of Groningen.

Kevin Butcher, Professor of Classics and Ancient History, University of Warwick; Fellow of the Royal Numismatic Society and the Society of Antiquaries of London.

Juan Castañeda, Director of the Institute of International Monetary Research, Lecturer in Economics, University of Buckingham.

Jan Gerrit Dercksen, Lecturer in Assyriology, University of Leiden.

Dennis O. Flynn, Professor Emeritus of Economics, University of the Pacific, and President/Director of the Pacific World History Institute.

Peter Foldvari, Lecturer, University of Amsterdam/International Institute of Social History.

Oscar Gelderblom, Professor of Financial History, University of Utrecht.

Panagiotis P. Iossif, Deputy Director, Belgian School at Athens.

Joost Jonker, Associate Professor of Economic History, University of Utrecht; NEHA Professor of Business History, University of Amsterdam.

Michael Jursa, Professor of Assyriology at the University of Vienna.

Kristin Kleber, Professor of Ancient Near Eastern Studies at the Vrije Universiteit Amsterdam.

Jan Lucassen, Professor Emeritus of International and Comparative Social History at the Vrije Universiteit Amsterdam and Honorary Research Fellow at the International Institute of Social History at Amsterdam.

Nicholas Mayhew, Professor Emeritus of Numismatics and Monetary History, Ashmolean Museum, Oxford.

John M. Mooring, Senior Operational Risk Manager at NN Group NV, The Hague; PhD student at Vrije Universiteit Amsterdam.

Alessandro Roselli, Visiting Fellow at Cass Business School, City University, London, and at the University of Buckingham.

Pedro Schwartz, Fundación Rafael del Pino Research Professor at the Universidad Camilo Jose Cela, Madrid.

R. J. (Bert) van der Spek, Professor Emeritus of Ancient Mediterranean and West-Asian History at the Vrije Universiteit Amsterdam.

Bas van Leeuwen, Senior Researcher, Economic and Social History at Utrecht University.

Richard von Glahn, Professor of History at the University of California, Los Angeles.

Yi Xu, Associate Professor of Economic History, Guangxi Normal University.

Jaco Zuijderduijn, Senior Lecturer Economic History at Lund University.

Preface and acknowledgements

This book originates in a conference held at the Vrije Universiteit Amsterdam on 12 and 13 December 2014 on the theme: 'Coins, currency and crisis from c. 2000 BC – c. AD 2000. On silver, paper and trust in historical perspective.' The conference was organized on the occasion of the retirement of one of the organizers, Bert van der Spek, as professor of Ancient Mediterranean and West-Asian History. The subject reflected his fascination for silver that has been used as a unit of account and means of payment for over four millennia all over the world. The conference may be considered as a spin-off of an earlier research program of the editors (in collaboration with Jan Luiten van Zanden) that resulted in another book in the series Routledge Explorations in Economic History (no. 68), *A History of Market Performance from Ancient Babylonia to the Modern World*, edited by R.J. van der Spek, Bas van Leeuwen and Jan Luiten van Zanden (London and New York: Routledge: 2015). The present volume focuses on the long-run development of the monetary economy and its interaction with real economic development. It is again an inspiring cooperation of ancient historians, Assyriologists, economic historians and economists, and thus an example of what we may call 'historical economy'. This research is embedded in the work of the research group 'Impact of Empire' of the National Research School in Classical Studies in the Netherlands (OIKOS; coordinators Olivier Hekster and Rens Tacoma) and in CLUE+, Research Institute for Culture, Cognition, History and Heritage, Vrije Universiteit Amsterdam.

We thank all those who helped us in organizing the conference and facilitating the publication of the book. The conference was funded by the Dutch Economic History Archives (Nederlands Economisch-Historisch Archief, NEHA), the Clio Infra project (Project leader: Jan Luiten van Zanden) and the Faculty of Humanities of the Vrije Universiteit. We thank the contributors for their input in the conference, for their preparedness to rework their papers in a tight schedule to fit them into the framework of this book and, last but not least, for their patience in waiting so long for the final publication. We also thank the publishers for their patience and their excellent work in producing this volume. Finally, we thank the anonymous peer reviewers for their support, suggestions and critical remarks. We hope everybody will be pleased by the final result.

Bert van der Spek
Bas van Leeuwen

1 Money and trust

R.J. van der Spek and Bas van Leeuwen

Feasts are made for laughter; wine gladdens life, and silver (money) meets every need.

Ecclesiastes 10: 19

Introduction

The idea for this book was born during the time that our Vrije Universiteit Amsterdam research team on *Market Performance from Ancient Babylonia to the Modern World* (see Van der Spek, Van Leeuwen, Van Zanden [eds.] [2015]) was studying the prices of many different periods and regions. Nearly all these prices were recorded in silver, from Ancient Mesopotamia and China to modern Europe. That raised several questions. First: why does humankind put so much trust in a commodity (it is, after all, a commodity) that may shine finely, but that cannot feed, clothe or house anyone. The answer is most often sought in it being considered beautiful, shining, rare and durable. It can be fractioned, and it can be used for luxury goods, an important feature in a society in which gift exchange is important (apart from exchange through trade). It should be noted that the first coins (fine objects with some distinguishing mark) had that function. But the fact remains that people put their trust in a nice and shiny but ultimately useless material.

It remains fascinating that people accepted silver for products such as grain. This applies also to the modern economy. Even though financial intermediaries (such as states) used people's trust to expand the stock of money by issuing more coins, debasing these coins or issuing money in paper or digital form, the role of silver and gold remains important, even following the abolishment of gold and silver standards. Until 1967, gulden coins (guilders) in the Netherlands were struck in silver. Furthermore, in the face of the economic crisis, in December of 2014 Dutch newspaper readers learned that the Netherlands kept a reserve of 612 tonnes of gold, of which only 11% is in the Netherlands and 61% is in the US. In a secret operation, the Dutch National Bank shipped 130 tonnes of gold from the Unites States to Amsterdam. By this operation, the reserve in Holland has since grown to 31%. A similar measure was taken recently by Germany. The Islamic State has now issued their own coinage: coins in gold, silver and bronze.

It is clear from the above that even though (precious) metals played an important role in the stock of money, this role nonetheless declined over time. First, because the intrinsic value of coins and specie started to differ from their nominal value, e.g. because of debasements (Zuijderduijn, Chapter 10), introduction of banknotes, etc. Second, in the course of history, other types of money, such as ledgers from merchants and bank deposits, were introduced. This distinction between cash and other, more complex, types of money is also reflected in the various definitions of the stock of money. For example, M0 consists of notes and coins, M1 consists of the former plus demand deposits and M2 consists of the former plus saving deposits. Obviously, M0 and, to a lesser extent, M1 have dominated throughout history until our present centuries, and they are the types mostly discussed in the following chapters in this volume.

This brought us to the second question: what is the actual role of money in the economy? The straightforward answer given in many textbooks is that money fulfils three functions, serving as a store of wealth, unit of account and means of exchange.[1] As is discussed later in this book, the first two functions are the ones that caused a rise in the use of currency, but they were also the ones that suffered first once trust in that currency got lost. In the same way, throughout history governments as well as private institutions have tried to use monetary expansion to finance less than economically beneficial activities, something that at times could also undermine trust in the currency. Indeed, trust in financial intermediaries, or even in precious commodities, is not evident. The state may follow a policy of monetary expansion by bringing more silver (or silver coins) into circulation, or by printing more money; silver coins may be debased by the state or other intermediaries, be of low quality, become abundant on occasion and scarce on another or they may easily be stolen. There are well-known periods in history when the trust in silver decreased, as in the later Roman Empire after Constantine the Great introduced a gold coin, the *solidus*. The *solidus* remained the standard coin far into the Middle Ages, when the silver coinage lost trust and the market economy was at a low ebb. Yet silver is usually the basic means of exchange, and when a society goes over to gold as the standard, this is usually a sign of weakness of economic performance (see Kleber, Chapter 5; Butcher, Chapter 7; Xu and Van Leeuwen, Chapter 13).

Yet trust is not necessarily based on the intrinsic value of the money substance or guarantees by the state. Some people have proposed to leave it instead to the market. In this vein, we see the introduction of e-coins, such as the bitcoin. The system on which the original bitcoin was based was introduced online in a paper written by Satoshi Nakamoto (presumably a pseudonym) in 2008. In this paper, titled 'Bitcoin: a peer-to-peer electronic cash system', it was stated that one of the main reasons for introducing a bitcoin system was to enhance trust. With such a system, financial mediators would be no longer necessary. More importantly, since any payment was guaranteed to be unique, double spending would become impossible. Or, as put forward by Nakamato

(2008), the bitcoin is 'an electronic payment system based on cryptographic proof instead of trust, allowing any two willing parties to transact directly with each other without the need for a trusted third party'.

The origins of money

This quest for 'trust' has to start from the creation of money in ancient times. Scholars have often sought for *the* origin of money, but we need not assume that money was invented in one place. Money probably had different sources in different cultures. In many societies, this origin is related to the acceptance of silver (or other commodities) as money. Silver was used as a medium of exchange, unit of account and store of value in the third millennium BC in Mesopotamia, and it remained so for millennia. We observe that in many languages the words for silver and money were interchangeable. In Sumerian logograms, it is written as KÙ.BABBAR. The sign KÙ (or: KU_3) was used in the late fourth millennium BC in documents from Uruk, southern Mesopotamia. The meaning of the word is both 'shining' and, as substantive, 'shining metal'. BABBAR means 'white'. 'Gold' is rendered as KÙ.GI = 'yellow shining metal' (Krispijn 2016). In Akkadian (the Semitic language that emerged in Mesopotamia next to Sumerian and was the language of the Old-Akkadian Empire, Assyria and Babylonia), the word for money and silver was *kaspu*.

This can be observed in many expressions, such as *ana kaspi nadānu*, 'to give for silver; to sell' and *ana kaspi mahāru*, 'to receive for silver; to buy'. In ancient and modern Hebrew, it is *kesep* or *kesef*. The word *kesef* is translated as both 'silver' and 'money'.

In Ancient Greek, there are several words for money, some of them related to 'silver'. The word *ho argyros* (from *argos*, 'shining') means both silver and money. Greek *to argyrion* means 1) coin; 2) money. *Argyrion katharon* = 'hard cash', lit. 'pure silver' (Theocritus 15.36). Other words reveal another attitude to silver: money is also indicated as *chrēmata*, 'things that are needed (from *chrāsthai*, 'to need, to be in want of, to use'); assets, things, money'. It appears that money was seen as a commodity. But there is also an abstract term: *nomisma,* referring to coinage. It means 'anything sanctioned by current of established usage, custom'. The word is explained by Aristotle as follows: 'but money has become by convention a sort of representative of demand; and this is why it has the name 'money' (*nomisma*), because it exists not by nature but by law (*nomos*) and it is in our power to change it and make it useless' (Aristotle, *Nicomachean Ethics* 1133b 1).

Latin has two words for money: *pecunia*, possibly derived from *pecus* (genitive *pecoris*, 'cattle', thus originally property in cattle, apparently an important indicator of wealth in early Rome[2]). But the Romans also used *argentum* (silver) as a term for money, although in Rome the earliest specie was bronze, at first in uncoined form, *aes rude* (rude bronze). The bronze was weighed; *stipendium* (military pay) is derived from the Latin verb *pendere*, 'to weigh'. The name of the later coin *as* is probably derived from *aes*, 'bronze'. In the third century,

Rome introduced silver coinage, the *denarius* (derived from plural tantum *deni*, 'together ten' *asses*). The *denarius*, which was the main silver coin of Rome for over four centuries, was probably introduced in 211 BC and produced in enormous quantity from the silver looted in the sack of Syracuse the year before. The coin represented 10 *asses*, hence the word *denarius* (from *deni*, 'tenfold').[3]

In China, the word for money, *qian* (钱), referred in ancient times to farming tools, which were used for monetary exchange in much the same way as cattle was used in the Roman Empire. When the first money was created, it was cast in the form of these tools (cf. Von Glahn, Chapter 12). This use of the object for primitive exchange can also be seen in the word for shell (*bei*, 贝). These shells were used from the Shang dynasty (1600–1046 BC) to the Spring and Autumn Period ca. 500 BC. Afterwards, the character was added to all kinds of concepts related to value, such as wealth (财) and capital (资) (if you look closely, the character *bei* is part of the characters for wealth [see left side] and capital [see bottom side]).

So in many cases the word 'money' refers to the commodity used in exchange. But this is not always the case. The word money in Germanic languages has a completely different origin. The German and Dutch *Geld*, related to English *yield*, literally means 'recompense', for instance, in the context of repayment as penalty for injuries. We see the term in composite terms, such as *wergeld*, 'compensation for man (*wer*) slaughter'. The German *vergelten* and Dutch *vergelden* both mean 'to requit', 'to retaliate'. So, paying something back, i.e. some sort of loan or debt.

This discrepancy between the meaning of money we can also find back in the modern languages. Besides the German *Geld* and the Dutch *geld* being derived from Germanic languages, the French words for 'money' and 'silver' are the same: *argent*. The English 'money' and 'mint' are both derived from Moneta, the epithet of the Roman Goddess Juno Moneta, in whose temple the mint was established (*monēta*). *Nummus* is the word for 'coin', derived from Greek *nomos*. Italian and Spanish words for money (Sp. *dinero*, it. *denero* or *soldi*) are derived from Roman coins, from the silver *denarius* and the late Roman gold *solidus*.

It is clear from the above that, even though in many cases the meaning of the word 'money' was derived from silver or other precious goods, in other cases, like in Germanic languages, it may be more like a debt (or credit). This links directly to a debate on the nature of money in which two approaches come to the fore. The traditional idea is that money was a commodity which replaced or facilitated barter. This is the orthodox view advocated by Adam Smith, Heichelheim and others. Since the beginning of the twentieth century, this idea has been under attack. Some, such as Mitchell-Innes (1913; 1914) and Goodhart (1989; 1998), have argued that there is no evidence for a society where trade was simply barter exchange, and that debt was the origin of money.[4] Hence, it was not the value of the money (e.g. silver) that mattered, but the right of the creditor to receive payment, or the requirement of the debtor to pay. This latter view is advocated in this book by Dirk Bezemer (Chapter 3), who argues that debt notes and tallies preceded coinage by far. It is true indeed that money as a unit of account was present from the earliest times in Mesopotamia, especially in an institutional context. Debts (or credits) held in the institutional books were owed from/to individuals with entitlements from or obligations to the institutions, as well as by other institutions, and these debts and credits were transferable. Yet various authors (e.g. Coggan 2011) have also taken a less hardline stance, actually arguing that money can only be considered credit in fiat money systems where the intrinsic value of the money is lower than the nominal (i.e. metal) value. Dennis Flynn (Chapter 2) advocates a new approach by disaggregating 'tangible' (commodity based) and 'intangible' monies.

Even though the question whether money is a commodity or not in itself is not an issue (in the end, all monies are commodities to a certain extent), this discussion is nevertheless more than just an academic debate, as it affects the trust in money as well as monetary policy measures (see the following sections).

Trust

It is clear that the difference between intrinsic and nominal value has increased over time. An interesting question is thus where money derives its value from. Basically, it is a mental construct by which everyone accepts money. As pointed out by (Harari 2014), '[t]rust is the raw material from which all types of money are minted'. Yet it is equally clear that commodity-type monies are in a better position than debt/credit types. Indeed, possession of silver or cash gives more confidence, and thus pleasure, than debt notes because of the intrinsic value. In times of crisis, people go to the bank to get cash money instead of leaving their money in bank accounts. One might imagine that in times of famine, people who run to the bank to demand their bank deposit would even prefer grain to cash money or silver. So intrinsic value can create confidence, but even silver or grain can, at times, lose value, while debt notes and the like can gain trust in various ways, such as by government backing. Roselli (Chapter 15, this volume) maintains that government backing is a precondition for any money.

But rather than generating new ways to gain trust, over time one witnesses an increase of financial instruments, such as cash, shares or bonds, often related to monetary easing. Since these instruments relied less and less on an intrinsic content, this created an increasing quest for trust. Some authors (among others, Udovitch 1979) have argued that the rise of financial instruments was caused in response to increasing financial demand caused by economic growth, while others have argued that these financial inventions were the ones causing economic growth (e.g. Tracy 1985). But no matter the causal relationship, in all cases the argument is that the aim of inventing new financial instruments was related to an improvement of the three functions of money (a medium of exchange, unit of account and store of value).

The question of how these instruments developed and how this impacted trust is dealt with in various chapters. For example, in Chapter 12, Von Glahn shows that during the Mongol Yuan dynasty in China (1271–1368), the integration of fiscal units and currency lent trust to the system, which allowed the state to issue paper notes. But whereas this system broke down in China in the early Ming dynasty, in Holland an opposite trend is witnessed, with money being created by borrowing from private lenders by cities in Holland (Zuijderduijn, Chapter 10). The resulting money stock was artificially increased by setting repayment in silver coins and subsequent debasements of these coins by the sovereign. Consequently, it was generally held that these debasements became a standard policy by the government until the moment this system broke down. But Gelderblom and Jonker show in Chapter 11 that these events also occurred in private society in subsequent centuries. They document that, among other things, new bookkeeping practices resulted in more trust, and hence opened up the possibility of an expansion of the settlement of debts and payment by 'ghost money', which in turn resulted in an expansion of the money stock. Hence, trust followed from different sources in China and Western Europe, leading to very different development paths.

Monetary institutions

Obviously, with the rise of more complex financial instruments, the role of institutions also grew in importance. This has three reasons. First, the institution (mostly the state) can help to provide confidence in a money, as was the case in China during the Yuan dynasty. Second, the state can use the money for stimulating the (real) economy. Third, via money, institutions are capable of gaining control and profit.

The first point is best illustrated by the State Theory of Money (Knapp 1905). This theory argues that money comes into existence thanks to the fact that it is issued and guaranteed by the state. What Knapp called 'the state money stage' begins when the state chooses the unit and names the substance accepted in payment of obligations to itself. The final step occurs when the state actually issues the money material it accepts. In (almost) all modern developed nations, the state accepts the currency issued by the treasury (in the US, coins), plus notes issued by the central bank (in the US, Federal Reserve notes), plus bank reserves (again, liabilities of the central bank). The material from which the money issued by the state is produced is not important (whether it is gold, base metal, paper or even digitized numbers at the central bank). No matter what it is made of, the state must announce its nominal value (that is to say, the value at which the money-thing is accepted in meeting obligations to the state) (Wray 2004a).

The State Theory of Money certainly has value, but it is not universally true. As we refer to coinage, in most cases coins were issued by some government authority: Lydian kings (but possibly also local warlords), Greek city-states, Persian kings and satraps, the Roman senate. But there are also examples of private persons minting coins themselves (see for China, Peng 2015). Likewise, in China and parts of the Near East, bullion was also used in exchange. In addition, in economies of the Near East where silver bullion was used as currency, the state (or similar authority) did not *issue* currency. Silver circulated and was an object of trade, and it was used as means of payment. Yet the state (or, in some cases, the temple) had a role in stabilizing the currency market both in China and the Near East. In the latter region, for example, the state tried to obtain silver by conquest, booty, tribute and trade, and they brought it into circulation by payments to labourers. Merchants acted in co-operation with the state. The Assyrian *kārum* (commercial office) in Kanesh played a role in obtaining good conditions for trade (see Dercksen in Chapter 5, this volume). Old Babylonian merchants went on expeditions backed by investments by the king (Leemans 1960; Stol 2004). Debt notes were accepted as money, though probably on a limited scale (cf. Jursa in Chapter 5, this volume). But the most important point is: who set the standard measures? Who decided that 8.3 grams of silver constituted a shekel? Though we do not possess proclamations of the sort, it is clear that the metrology was set by the authorities (temple or king) (cf. Hudson 2004[5]). There were several different standards in the beginning, but the standard set at the end of the third millennium BC (empire of Akkad, king Naram-Sin) was still valid at the end of the first millennium (Powell 1989–1990). There was a standard in the Old Babylonian period (and after) that equated 1 shekel of silver to 1 GUR (*kurru* = 300 litres, later 180 litres) of grain = 1 monthly wage (see Chapter 5[6]).

Whatever the case, the government plays some, or perhaps a decisive, role. We know expressions as 'the measure of the king' or 'the cubit of the king', but apparently competing systems existed within one society. In Assyria, after 714 BC silver was measured 'in the mina of Carchemish'. We see this in the Bible as well. In Genesis 23:16, Abraham buys a tract of land for 'four hundred shekels of silver, according to the weights *current among the merchants*'. A *shekel of the sanctuary* we find in Exodus 30:13, Exodus 38:25 and Numbers 7:13 and 85, all regarding payments due to the temple. Finally, a shekel is mentioned in II Samuel 14:26 '*by the weight-stone of the king*' (*be 'even ha-melek*) in the hilarious description of the hair of the handsome prince Absalom, son of Solomon, that was so beautiful and heavy that he had to cut it every year (!), and which weighed 200 shekels by the weight-stone of the king.

The second use of money is for stimulating the real economy. In the past, injection of money into circulation by governments has taken place, but hardly for engaging in economic politics. It was simply done to meet expenses. Nevertheless, these injections of course had impact, either for the good if these led to investments, or for the bad when they was used only for consumption or, even worse, for destruction in warfare. It also depended how it was done, i.e. with high trust money (with high intrinsic value) or with debt-notes or treasury bills.

The core areas of the Assyrian, Babylonian and Persian empires profited much from the silver imports by booty and tribute. This silver was used for the building of palaces, cities and irrigation canals. A good case in point is the economy of classical Athens (fifth century BC). A great part of the prosperity of Athens can be explained by the availability of silver, first thanks to the finding of silver in Laurium in Attica, second by the collection of tribute in silver. The silver of Laurium enabled the Athenians to build ships, with which they withstood the Persians in 480 BC at Salamis, and which provided work and a living for hundreds of carpenters, shipwrights, rope-makers, etc.; thus, the Athenians were able to create an empire, which caused the influx of more silver thanks to the contributions of the allies in the Delian League (established 477 BC). The expansion of the Roman empire benefited greatly from the influx of silver coming from the East, as the Hellenistic empires had succumbed to the Romans. When a lot of silver, some of it ultimately originating from the treasury of the Persian empire captured by Alexander the Great (cf. Van der Spek 2011), flowed into the Roman Treasury, it ended up in the pockets of rich land-owners and politicians. It is one of the explanations of the economic boom in the first two centuries of our era.

In later periods, the same is true. The imports of silver from South America in the sixteenth and seventeenth centuries had a double effect. Inflation was one of the results, but even so it led to building projects, new enterprises and all kinds of investments that stimulated growth far into China. But increasingly the monetary expansion had a lower intrinsic value, such as paper cash or digital money. In such a situation, standard classical economic theory says that money is neutral, at least in the long run. That is, a rise in the stock of money will only increase the nominal variables, such as prices and wages, but will not allow one to buy more goods or services, as people know the rise of money stock and hence will not buy more. This will be less the case if money has a high intrinsic value (e.g. silver), since that value remains more stable, suffering less inflation. It is also less likely if the money is invested in capital-generating projects that have a positive effect on the long-run structure of the economy.

In monetarist theory, neutrality of money is true only in the long run, whereas in the short run people will react since they do not know if a rise is caused by a monetary or real shock. In neoclassical economics, this last point is conceded, but since people are well aware of the policy they can distinguish between real and nominal shocks; hence, nominal shocks cancel out, even in the short run. Only in Keynesianism we see there can be both short- and long-run effects (Keynes 1930). Especially in post-Keynesianism it is argued that money today is not created by the central bank, but by borrowing from banks (either private or government). That implies that the money multiplier does not exist, and the lending by banks is directly necessary for the economy. A related argument is that of Werner (2003), who basically states that credit availability should be increased by the central bank by purchasing low-performing assets and lending directly to government and private companies. Also, the government should directly borrow from banks. Such a system is supposed to remove bad debts and bring money directly into the economy.

The third factor regarding institutional involvement in the currency is control, for example, in the form of taxation, debasements, etc. In the ancient Near East, states had the power to increase the amount of silver (money) by conquest, booty and state-supported trade. After the invention of coinage, they had the possibility to manipulate the currency by lowering the weight of the coins and decreasing the silver content by alloys with other cheaper metals. The introduction of bronze coinage was in many respects the introduction of fiat money. Coinage itself led to profit when the coins had higher value than bullion of the same weight. For example, Xuyi and Van Leeuwen (Chapter 10) show that from the seventeenth century onwards other metals were increasingly added to copper coins in China. The issuing of paper money in later periods was a major example of such debasement. Even today, with the bitcoin, we see various government attempts to control the coin which, besides regulating criminal affairs, is often related to tax matters.

Structure of the book

The present volume deals with a major element in society: money. Though we all deal with it every day, it is actually difficult to understand what money really is and what its role in economic life really is. Many studies on the essence of money have been written over time (starting with Aristotle), with the recurring point being trust. Whatever the nature of money, it a) must fulfil the functions of money (i.e. unit of account, medium of exchange and store of value) and b) must be accepted by society.

Both aims of money may often contradict each other. After all, an increase in economic development requires more money, e.g. for means of exchange, but this may lead to an expansion of the stock of money by reducing its intrinsic value. In order for this money to keep its value, more trust is required. This continuing contradiction will run as a red line through this book.

So, what money is made of (silver, bronze, paper, bits and bytes) is less important than the trust that is being generated, while the amount of trust, in turn, is imperative to what one may do to influence money (monetary policy). This is the focus in the theoretical treatises in Chapters 2 and 3. In Chapter 2, Flynn takes one side in the debate when he stresses the aspect of money as commodity and the difficulty of pricing this commodity, while in Chapter 3 Bezemer argues that at least part of the money stock is derived from debt and can, hence, be reinvested profitably in high-quality assets in order to prevent debasements.

Obviously, the use of this discussion about trust and policy hinges on who actually uses money. In certain times and societies, money was only available in such large denominations that ordinary shopping or salaries could not be paid. This obviously limits both the demand for trust as well as its function for monetary policy. Therefore, in Chapter 4, Lucassen introduces the concept of 'deep monetization' to indicate how the use of money has spread through society. This concept is also used in several other chapters.

The following chapters deal with the role of money (monies) in different societies over time. Van der Spek, Dercksen, Kleber and Jursa give an overview of the role of (uncoined) money in Mesopotamia from c. 2000 to 330 BC (Chapter 5); Mooring, Van Leeuwen and Van der Spek (Chapter 6) discuss the origin of coinage in Greece, the Near East and China, why it was successful in Greece and China but not the Persian empire and how it gained full acceptance in the East only with Alexander the Great. Van Leeuwen, Iossif and Foldvari (Chapter 7) make an estimate of the measure of monetization in the Seleucid Empire and compare this with the diffusion of the Euro. In Chapter 8, Butcher examines the role of the government in the Roman Empire, while Mayhew in Chapter 9 gives an overview of the role of silver and money in England from the Middle Ages to the nineteenth century.

Over time, we clearly witness an increasing divergence between nominal and intrinsic value, including attempts to generate more trust. This truly takes a leap in the Middle Ages and Early Modern times. For example, Zuijderduijn (Chapter 10) explores monetary policy, public debt and default in Holland, c. 1466–1489, while Gelderblom and Jonker (Chapter 11) go into the vexed phenomenon of 'ghost money', i.e. the use of currency without tangible coins for the following centuries. Von Glahn (Chapter 12) shows that, even though China was initially more advanced in enlarging the stock of money, given the early introduction of paper money in Song-Yuan China (AD 960–1386), it lost that position to the West in the following centuries. This is confirmed in Chapter 13 by Xu and Van Leeuwen, who evaluate the role of silver in China, especially its effect on stagnation and growth (1430–1935).

The rise of more paper money, lowering of intrinsic values and increasing international trade in goods and services, but especially capital, poses many challenges in the twentieth and twenty-first centuries. Castañeda and Schwartz (Chapter 14) present a case study on twentieth-century Spain and the impact of monetary policy on financial crises, while Roselli (Chapter 15) gives an overview of the role of money and monetary policy in the long twentieth century. Finally, the editors (Chapter 16) try to come arrive at a conclusion on humanity's search for trust in a major element and sometimes engine of the economy: money.

Notes

1 Note that Dennis Flynn (Chapter 2) makes a distinction between tangible and intangible monies and holds that there are three more requirements for defining the different moneys: standard of value, link money and measure of relative values.

2 At least the ancients thought so: Varro, *De Re Rustica* (2.1.11); *De Lingua Latina* (5.92); Cicero, *De Republica* (2.9); Ovidius, *Fasti* (5.280–1).

3 For a recent discussion: Burnett (2012).

4 Innes was wrong in assuming that barter was not the precursor of trade with the aid of money. As a matter of fact, even long after the invention of money, barter continued to play an important role in exchange (see e.g. Chapter 5). Goodhart (1998) incorrectly ridicules the use of silver bullion as money, as it was effectively the main money substance in the Near East for 2,000 years. For the view that money originated in debt, see now also Graeber (2011). For Mesopotamia see Hudson (2002: 16).

5 Note that the metrology was not well understood by Hudson. He takes the measure of capacity of 1 GUR to be 30 kur (Hudson 2004: 112) and 60 kur (ibid. 114), which is inconsistent and incomprehensible, as Sumerian GUR is the same as Akkadian *kurru*.

1 GUR/*kurru* consisted of 30 BÁN/*sūtu*. The *kurru* was originally 300 litres, but by the first millennium it was 180 litres.

6 Stol 2004: 861; cf. however: Codex Hammurabi §§ 257 and 261: wage set at 8 GUR per year for farmers and herdsmen; CH 258: 6 GUR per year for the cowman. Interest rates also seem to be established by the state: CH 88: 'If a merchant has given corn on loan, he may take 100 litres of corn as interest on 1 GUR (= 300 litres); if he has given silver on loan, he may take 1/6 shekel 6 grains as interest on 1 shekel of silver.'

References

Burnett, A. (2012). 'Early Roman coinage and its Italian context', in Metcalf (ed.) (2012): 297–314.

Coggan, Philip (2011). *Paper Promises: Money, Debt and the New World Order*. London: Penguin Books.

Goodhart, Charles A.E. (1989). *Money, Information and Uncertainty*. Cambridge, MA: MIT Press.

Goodhart, Charles A.E. (1998). 'Two concepts of money: Implications for the analysis of optimal currency areas', *European Journal of Political Economy*, 14: 407–432.

Graeber, David (2011). *Debt: The first 5,000 Years*. New York: Melville House.

Harari, Yuval Noah (2014). *Sapiens: A Brief History of Humankind*. London: Penguin Books.

Hudson, Michael (2002). 'Reconstructing the origins of interest bearing debt', in Hudson and Van de Mieroop (2002): 7–58.

Hudson, Michael (2004). 'The archeology of money: Debt versus barter theories of money's origin', in Wray (2004b) : 99–127.

Hudson, Michael and Van de Mieroop, Marc (eds.) (2002). *Debt and Economic Renewal in the Ancient Near East*. Baltimore, MD: CDL Press.

Keynes, John Maynard (1930). *A Treatise on Money*. Volumes I and II (1976), New York: Harcourt, Brace & Co.

Kleber, Kristin and Pirngruber, Reinhard (eds.) (2016). *Silver, Money and Credit. A Tribute to Robartus J. van der Spek on Occasion of his 65th Birthday on 18th September 2014*. PIHANS no. 128. Leiden, the Netherlands: Nederlands Instituut voor het Nabije Oosten.

Knapp, Georg Friedrich (1905/1973). *The State Theory of Money*. Clifton, NY: Augustus M. Kelley.

Krispijn, Theo J.H. (2016). 'Early silver: Thoughts about the sign KU_3 in the earliest documents from Uruk', in Kleber and Pirngruber (eds.) (2016): 1–10.

Leemans, W.F. (1960). *Foreign Trade in the Old Babylonian Period, as Revealed by Texts from Southern Mesopotamia*. Leiden, the Netherlands: Brill.

Metcalf, W.E. (ed.) (2012). *The Oxford Handbook of Greek and Roman Coinage*. Oxford: Oxford University Press.

Mitchell Innes, Alfred (1913). 'What is money?', *Banking Law Journal* 30.5: 377–408 (reprinted in Wray (2004b): 14–49).

Mitchell Innes, Alfred (1914). 'The credit theory of money', *Banking Law Journal*, 31.2: 151–168 (reprinted in Wray (2004b): 50–78).

Nakamoto, Satoshi (2008). 'Bitcoin: A peer-to-peer electronic cash system', obtained 15 Feb. 2017, https://bitcoin.org/bitcoin.pdf.

Peng, Kaixiang (2015). 'Money supply and the price mechanism: The interaction of money, prices and wages in Beijing in the long nineteenth century', in Van der Spek *et al.* (eds.) (2015): 442–69.

Powell, Marvin A. (1989–90). 'Masse und gewichte', *Reallexikon der Assyriologie*, 7: 457–517.

Stol, Marten 2004. 'Wirtschaft und Gesellschaft in altbabylonischer Zeit', in Charpin, D., Edzard, D.O. and Stol, M., *Mesopotamien. Die altbabylonische Zeit*, Fribourg, Switzerland: Academic Press/Göttingen: Vandenhoeck & Ruprecht: 641–975.

Tracy, James D. (1985). *A Financial Revolution in the Habsburg Netherlands. Renten and Renteniers in the County of Holland 1515–1565.* Berkeley, CA: University of California Press.

Udovitch, Abraham L. (1979). 'Bankers without banks. Commerce, banking and society in the Islamic world of the Middle Ages', in Lopes, R.S. (ed.), *The Dawn of Modern Banking*, New Haven, CT: Yale University Press: 255–273.

Van der Spek, R.J. (2011). 'The "silverization" of the economy of the Achaemenid and Seleukid empires and early modern China', in Archibald, Z.H., Davies, J.K., Gabrielsen, V. (eds.), *The Economies of Hellenistic Societies, Third to First Centuries*, Oxford: Oxford University Press: 402–420.

Van der Spek, R.J., Van Leeuwen, Bas and Van Zanden, Jan Luiten (eds.) (2015). *A History of Market Performance from Ancient Babylonia to the Modern World.* London: Routledge.

Werner, R. (2003). *Princess of the Yen: Japan's Central Bankers and the Transformation of the Economy*. London: Routledge.

Wray, L. Randall (2004a). 'Conclusion: The credit money and state money approaches', in Wray (2004b): 79–98.

Wray, L. Randall (ed.) (2004b). *Credit and State Theories of Money: The Contributions of A. Mitchell Innes.* Cheltenham, UK: Edward Elgar.

2 Six monetary functions over five millennia

A price theory of monies

Dennis O. Flynn

Disaggregation of monies in global history

Roles of monies have always been hotly debated. Not only have discussions centered on monetary outcomes (e.g. the economic effect of monetary expansion), but also on the nature of money, which changed from the time when four main monetary substances – silver, gold, copper, and cowry shells – were traded globally during the sixteenth through eighteenth centuries,[1] evolving into digital monies that are common today. Aggregation problems have persisted for both tangible and intangible monies, however, throughout centuries of evolution of the nature of monies, as well as interactions with non-monetary items.

Beginning with tangible monies since AD 1500, silver mines were concentrated in Spanish America and in Japan. The most prominent end-market for silver was China, and trade routes worldwide connected silver-production regions with silver-end-market regions. Meanwhile, the pattern for African/Asian/American gold production was different; indeed, *China systematically exported* gold to Japan, Europe, and the Americas *in exchange for silver* (1540s–1640, and again in 1700–1750).[2] The Maldives islands dominated cowrie shell production, most of which gravitated to Asian end-markets, but up to a million pounds of Maldivian cowries traversed European ports annually en route to West African end-markets. The world's leading copper producer during the late seventeenth century was Japan, with perhaps double Sweden's output. Chinese end-markets again predominated, but end-markets in Europe absorbed Japanese copper too. In conclusion, geology determined locations of production of each major monetary substance, while end-market demand was unique for each monetary substance, thereby determining distinct intermediary trade routes.

Over the most recent 150 years or so, concerns have developed over inability of commodity monies to sufficiently accommodate population growth and economic expansion. Hence, expanding monetary stocks were facilitated through creation of new monies that were increasingly de-linked from limitations inherent in production of commodity-based monies. For digital currencies today, de-linkage from commodity monies is virtually complete.

Aggregation of various monetary types into a singular label 'money' throughout history, as mainstream theory instructs, is a mistake. Indeed, even aggregation *within* a subset category, such as 'silver monies', is a mistake. For example, Irigoin (2013) points to substantial Chinese imports of Mexican pesos after early nineteenth-century Mexican independence, but one particular coin, the Carolus peso, was specifically preferred. Inferior non-Carolus coins from certain Mexican mints were rejected, melted, or significantly discounted within China.[3] Moreover, silver *bullion* (*sycee*) was *exported* from China, while silver Carolus coins were simultaneously *imported* into China. Hence, given that silver objects were both exported and imported simultaneously, and that specific Mexican pesos commanded a premium vis-à-vis other pesos, disaggregation of silver 'money' is an historical necessity, a problem exacerbated further by aggregation across silver coins and non-silver coins (e.g. Kishimoto 2011; Kuroda 2008; 2013; Von Glahn 2011).

Aggregating monies: Some historical examples

Aggregation across distinct commodity monies is one problem, but a second problem concerns aggregation of tangible and intangible monies. Indeed, many monies are not tangible. This is perhaps best illustrated via historical examples.

Assyriologists and historians of antiquity state that the earliest known forms of writing consisted of lists of things owned and debts owed. Bookkeeping was necessary to track individual/group economic performance. Long before coins appeared, construction of coherent accounting systems presented formidable challenges. First, heterogeneity of items owned/owed required bookkeepers to utilize a single accounting unit to express diverse holdings/obligations. Second, the market value of a monetary standard varied over time. Third, objects containing the monetary-standard substance decayed, and they also differed in quality. Ancient bookkeepers sometimes chose foods (e.g. barley or dates), and also fine silver weights as accounting units for expression of values of things owned/owed. As today, ancient accountants preferred monetary standards anchored to objects of relatively stable value over time. Silver often served as Monetary Standard (see Chapters 1 and 5, this volume).

The shekel (Hebrew corruption of Babylonian *shiqlu*), *representing* c. 8.33 grams of silver (refined to seven-eighths fineness in Neo-Babylonian and Persian periods), was a Mesopotamian unit-of-accounting-money from the third millennium BC. This unit-of-accounting-money shekel was *intangible*. The shekel *represented* a specific weight in fine silver; *shiqlu* means 'weight'. The weight measure *shiqlu* should be distinguished from *shekel* coins introduced in places such as Phoenicia, Judah, and Carthage during the Persian and Hellenistic periods. No shekel coin was used in Babylonia.

The shekel of silver was an intangible unit of accounting. In conjunction with a 'link-money', the shekel helped translate diverse transactions into grams of pure silver in accounting terms.[4] Silver was not always exchanged, but it facilitated exchange. If 90 litres of barley and 180 litres of dates were valued equally in terms of shekels, it meant that in actual practice 180 litres of dates could be bought for 90 litres of barley. Of course, if parties agreed and silver was available, barley or dates could also be bought for 8.33 grams of silver bullion. As a matter of fact, thanks to increased monetization of Babylonian society in the first millennium, physical silver was used in many transactions (cf. Jursa in Chapter 5, this volume). In such cases, marketplace discussion could arise about quality of the silver, in the same way as quality of barley and/or dates. Thus, documents often specify silver as 'refined' or 'in good condition' or 'with 1/8 alloy' or similar. But even then parties might quibble about fineness, silver content, and quality.

Silver was tangible, as were barley and dates. Prices of barley and dates were expressed in silver; the problem is, prices of silver cannot be expressed in silver. Wide acceptance of silver representation as (intangible) unit of account and physical silver as (tangible) means of exchange must have helped stabilize the value of silver, but clearly value fluctuations existed. Concern for the purchasing power of silver in many Mesopotamian texts (see Van der Spek in Chapter 5, this volume) is telling in this respect. Ancients were well aware that an influx of silver diminished the purchasing power of silver (Van der Spek, ibid.). If we read in texts that a shekel could buy 360 litres in one year and only 60 litres a year later, then either barley's market value rose six-fold or silver's market value fell to one-sixth its previous value (or some combination of the two). If causation emanated solely from the silver market (fall in silver value), then commodity prices (in shekel-weight) across the board would have risen 600%. If the 600% price rise was mostly concentrated on barley's value, on the other hand, then barley market forces were responsible for this price spike. Empirical evidence must determine which hypothesis to reject, or whether compound forces generated this episode of price inflation. When studying the rise of prices in the sixth century BC, we must look for instruments to detect causes of price developments. Simultaneous increase in many commodity prices leads Jursa *et al.* (2010: 749) to conclude that inflation toward the end of the sixth century BC was 'caused by a rapid increase in the quantity of [silver] money'. This conclusion is sensible, yet the *price* of silver is the key, rather than the '*quantity* of money'.

Conquest of Babylonia by Alexander the Great in 331 BC brought about an important change in monetary exchange. Alexander introduced Greek coinage (drachmas, didrachms, and tetradrachms), mostly according to the Attic (Athenian) weight standard. So, silver (and later bronze) coins replaced silver bullion. However, in Babylonian cuneiform texts prices were still expressed in shekels, perhaps due to conservatism of the people who continued to write in Akkadian cuneiform, as Aramaic and Greek had replaced Akkadian in daily transactions. From this practice, we might infer that coins were weighed, but a rule soon emerged such that a didrachm coin (8.6 grams) was viewed as equivalent to one shekel (8.33 grams). This means that when we read prices in shekels we must assume that the author had Greek coins in mind. Thus, there is a huge difference between the meaning of 'shekel' in the time before Alexander (meaning a weight measure of 8.33 grams) and the time after Alexander (meaning a Babylonian rendering of a Greek coin, the didrachm, actually weighing 8.6 grams). Counting of money may have replaced weighing money (cf. Van der Spek 2017 and Chapter 6, this volume). This does not mean, however, that weight did not matter. We observe confusion in a pricelist from the early Parthian period (c. 138 BC), where it is stated that two shekels of silver in staters of Demetrius buy 84 litres of barley, while in staters of Arsaces one gets only 72 litres.[5] This can only mean that the point of reference here (two 'shekels' of silver) is not the intangible measure of 8.33 grams, but rather the tangible stater = tertradrachm coin. The weight of the Demetrius stater was simply heavier than the Arsaces stater. It is for good reason that some texts specify what kind of coins were expected or allowed, such as a coin issued by the reigning king (i.e. at least its equivalent in weight), an elephant stater, or a lion stater. As is usual in coin transactions of all times, users of coins took the value of the coins into account. They look at silver content, weight, legenda, issuing authority; all these features help to assure trust. Although the price of a good may be assessed as one shekel = two drachmas, it mattered if the coin exchanged was a lion stater, a stater of king Antiochus, or any other tetradrachm. It also mattered if e.g. a tetradrachm or didrachm coin lost weight due to wear and tear. Bronze coins could be accepted as long as the recipient was sure that the government and/or market participants were ready to accept bronze at a certain standard in relation to silver.

There is also a long-term analytical issue: The market value of silver changed over historical time. As Standard of Value, silver functioned as a benchmark against which to compare relative values of all non-silver commodities. Supply and demand forces determine silver's market value, yet the price of silver is expressible in terms of what money? As observed above, changing silver value cannot be expressed relative to silver itself, so the accounting-money shekel is disqualified.[6] For any Monetary Standard – silver, dollar, yen, euro, or others – there remains the perplexing issue of explaining change in market value of the Monetary Standard over time. The Price Theory of Monies confronts this challenge (below) via application of a sixth monetary function: *Measure of Relative Values*. Prior to discussion of the *Measure of Relative Values* monetary function, however, we turn to the mostly forgotten *Link-Money Function* utilized in Europe (and earlier in Mesopotamia).

Indeed, in the Netherlands neither Guilder nor Stiver (English spellings) coins were minted between the 1570s and 1681, yet Dutch bookkeeping entries were expressed in conceptual non-coin Guilders and non-coin Stivers. Einaudi (1953) dated such 'Imaginary Monies' back to Charlemagne, yet Dutch accounting monies served the same Unit-of-Accounting function as the Mesopotamian shekel. Both Unit-of-Accounting monies expressed market values as fine-silver-weight equivalents. Dutch/VOC accounting policy specified an ideal Rixdollar coin to which intangible Guilders/Stivers were 'linked'.[7] The ideal Rixdollar, a 'link coin' arbitrarily declared equivalent to 47 Unit-of-Accounting Stivers in 1606 CE, *represented* 25.7 grams fine silver; thus, each Stiver *represented* .5468085 grams (= 25.7/47) fine silver, and each Unit-of-Accounting Guilder *represented* 10.93617 grams fine silver (20 times more). As with didrachm coins in Mesopotamia, tangible Rixdollar coins contained less than 25.7 grams fine silver due to wear and tear and coin adulteration. Yet, intrinsic content of the *ideal* Rixdollar coin was fixed at 25.7 grams fine silver. Dutch Guilder/Stiver accounting entries in effect expressed all transactions in specific fine-silver-weight equivalents. In both Mesopotamian and Dutch cases, an intangible link-money connected (a) to an intangible unit-of-accounting money and thereby (b) represented a tangible quantity of fine silver (Silver Standard). Such bookkeeping unity was necessary because actual Dutch/VOC transactions involved numerous distinct exchange media (none suitable as an accounting unit). Silver fulfilled the Monetary Standard function. In sum, silver continued to function as a *relatively stable* monetary Standard of Value, *but silver was still not a perfectly stable* Standard of Value.[8]

Six monetary functions over five millennia

Many intangible unit-of-accounting monies carried names of physical coins that existed previously and/or subsequently (e.g. guilder). Even though a unit-of-accounting and a tangible coin could be called by the same name (see e.g. Gelderblom and Jonker, Chapter 11), they were fundamentally different. Unit-of-accounting monies are necessarily intangibles irrespective of whether (a) the intangible money preceded tangible coins that adopted the same name later on (e.g. shekel), or (b) the intangible money sequentially followed a physical coin that had existed before (e.g. guilder). The Mesopotamian shekel *represented* 8.33 grams fine silver; the intangible Dutch guilder *represented* 10.93617 grams fine silver. Shekel coins did not exist at the same time as tangible pieces of silver of defined quality in the pre-Alexander period, even while didrachm coins served medium-of-exchange and store-of-value functions. No guilder or stiver coins were issued between the 1570s and 1681 either, so other tangible monies fulfilled Medium-of-Exchange and Store-of-Value functions in that case.

Given that money can thus exist in various forms, both tangible and intangible, we are presented with a problem: Monetary history contradicts modern monetary theory's requirement that three monetary functions – unit of accounting, medium of exchange, and store of value – be satisfied simultaneously in order for anything to qualify as 'money'. Besides all kinds of aggregation problems outlined above, nothing could qualify as 'money' because unit-of-accounting requires intangibility, while the other two conventional functions require tangibility. Simultaneous tangibility and intangibility is impossible, so mainstream 'money' cannot exist. A 'link-money' function – as well as (tangible) Standard-of-Value and (intangible) Measure-of-Relative-Values functions – must also be included (in addition to the three standard functions indicated by asterisks in the numbered list). The Measure-of-Relative-Values function is necessary because it is not possible to express value of a tangible money relative to itself:

Historical functions of monies (Price theory of monies)

1 Unit of accounting* (intangible)
2 Medium of exchange* (tangible)
3 Store of value* (tangible)
4 Standard of value (tangible)
5 Link-money (intangible)
6 Measure of relative values (intangible)

It is obvious that these six functions cannot be fulfilled simultaneously because some functions require tangibility while others require intangibility.

How do these functions work in mainstream economic theory?

Micro and macro theory

Adding three *additional* monetary functions has various implications for policy-related aspects of mainstream monetary economics. First, price *ratios* require application of an intangible money (Function 6 above). This follows from microeconomics whereby prices of wine and bread – each expressed in terms of an intangible 'ratio' dollar – are expressed in terms of a 'relative price' ratio that cancels all intangible 'ratio' dollars; the result is x loaves of bread per bottle of wine. This expression of prices in relative terms is sensible, yet this commonplace procedure is incompatible with standard macroeconomic theory, since fulfillment of conventional monetary functions (see above) requires tangibility. Microeconomic price ratios are created, on the other hand, via an intangible money. Second, whereas microeconomic quantities are explicitly expressed as time-dimensioned flows, macroeconomic monetary quantities are tangible, point-in-time stocks that have accumulated, which is why monetary quantities cannot be accommodated within microeconomics. Look at your own personal holdings of various coins and paper bills. Each displays the year of minting or printing. Inventory stocks of tangible monies are survivors from past production (rather than current flows).

Third, starting with the work of Keynes (1920s–1930s; cf. Keynes 1964 [1935]), mainstream economists settled on 'the interest rate' as textbook 'rental price of money' (Figure 2.1). Yet *the* interest-rate transmission mechanism conventionally claimed to connect 'monetary' and 'real (i.e. non-monetary)' sectors creates yet another obstacle for monetary historians; it is not possible to construct a general production theory for tangible monies while postulating the interest rate as a rental price of money.

Nevertheless, this interest-rate channel at least furnished a patchwork route for inclusion of monies in policy debates. Indeed, worldwide focus on interest rates for monetary policies today reflects dominance of Keynesian prescriptions, leading to relentless pursuit of monetary policy stimulation of investment

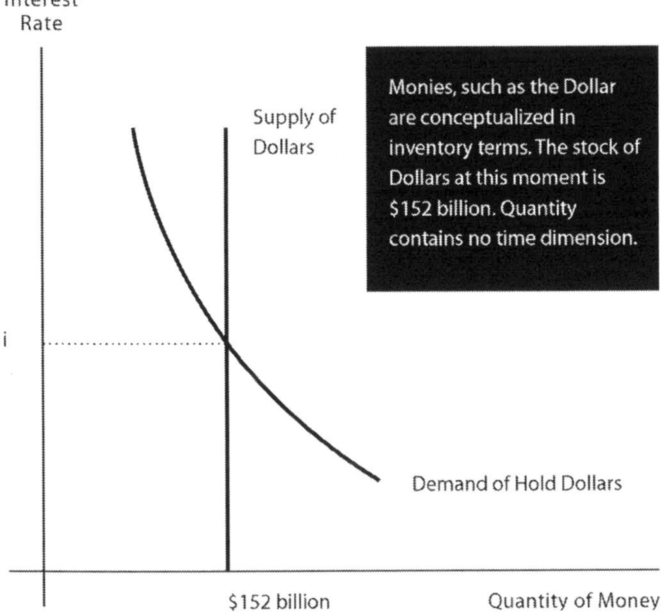

Figure 2.1 Money supply and money demand in macroeconomics.

through low interest rates (Figure 2.2). This worldwide strategy *appears to have been effective* over recent decades, but unprecedented global debt escalations prompt many today to ponder whether mounting debt regimes are sustainable, particularly in context of dramatic wealth concentrations (e.g. Piketty 2014).[9] Nonetheless, prominent policy makers worldwide exude confidence in global financial solidity. Incompatibility between monetary theory and historical evidence, however, indicates misplaced confidence. This morning has already faded into history. Inventory stocks are historical artifacts that deserve center stage in any realistic economic analysis.

Open-market operations and interest-rate manipulation

Mainstream economists accept as canon the fact that money supply expansion, all other things equal, lowers interest rates as described by textbook models. Recent experience seems to confirm this view, since expansionary monetary policies coincide with historically low interest rates. But monetary expansion *itself has not caused* target interest rates to decline over recent decades. Rather, specific institutions make expansionary monetary policy *appear to* depress interest rates, while no such money–interest-rate relationship existed throughout monetary history. Indeed, open Market Operations increase stocks of base monies – as in textbook sketches – via purchase of debt instruments (e.g. U.S. Treasury Bills), and

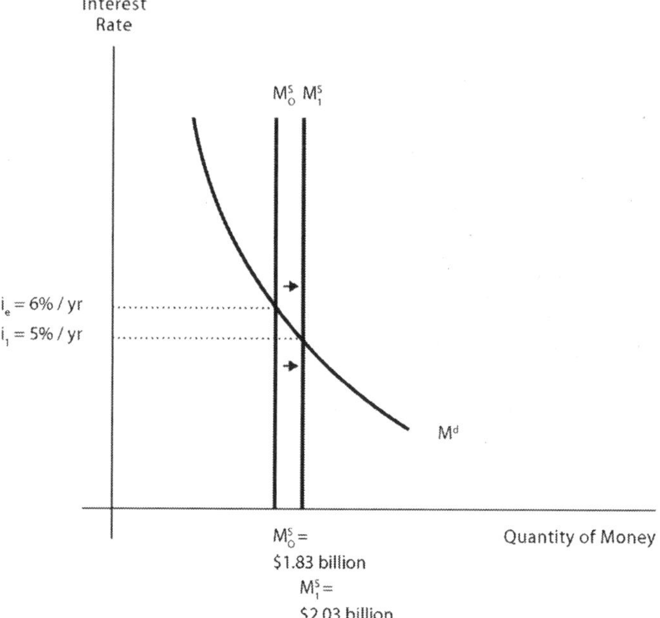

Figure 2.2 Central bank manipulation of *the* interest rate.

massive T-Bill purchases do raise T-Bill prices. Yet any government asset (e.g. oil reserves or government lands) could alternatively be exchanged in purchase of T-Bills (rather than Fed checks), thereby also raising T-Bill prices. T-Bill prices rise due to enhanced T-Bill purchase – thereby forcing interest rates down – irrespective of what particular asset is exchanged for T-Bills. Yet no economist would argue that the interest rate is therefore the rental price of, say, government oil, so why should the interest rate be considered the 'rental price of money'? The interest rate (percentage divided by time) is not the 'price' of anything.

Interest rates have changed throughout history without alteration in monetary stocks, and vice versa. Monetary expansion today could also be achieved without purchase of debt instruments. The Federal Reserve could build oil reserves through the purchase of oil directly via written check, for instance, thereby augmenting Base Money without involving credit instruments. Oil prices (not bond prices) would rise. This sort of monetary expansion would impact energy markets, not interest rates. Changing monetary stocks need not involve credit markets.

Valid monetary theory should apply under diverse institutional arrangements. Alternative institutional arrangements throughout history have not involved manipulation of interest rates. Mainstream monetary models are myopic, contradict millennia of empirical evidence, and also provide false confidence for financial experts worldwide.

A price theory of monies

A description

Thus far it has been argued a) that functions of money can either be tangible or intangible, b) that incorporation of all monetary functions requires adoption of a Measure-of-Relative-Values money that is intangible (allowing conversion of all prices expressed in intangible dollars to be converted into ratios of tangible quantities), and c) this implies that tangible monies are themselves valuable in the manner of other goods. This has various practical consequences (further discussed in Flynn 2015b). Laws of Supplies and Demands represent a 'Unified Theory of Prices' in the sense that prices of all goods and services – including tangible monies – are expressed in the same intangible-ratio dollar (ir$) routinely displayed throughout microeconomics. All goods are treated as inventory stocks, however, including tangible monies. While conventional money supply and money demand are already couched in Inventory Supply and Inventory Demand terms, mainstream labeling of axes contrasts sharply with labeling under the Price Theory of Monies.

Conventional monetary axes are labeled 'the interest rate' and (aggregate) 'money stock' (Figure 2.2).[10] Price Theory of Monies labels differ fundamentally. Each tangible money's price (e.g. the USD one-dollar bill, Figure 2.3) is expressed relative to intangible-ratio dollars (ir$). The quantity-axis label pictured in Figure 2.3 refers to accumulated USD one-dollar bills at an instant in time.[11] Price is not 'the interest rate', but rather the exchange value at which tangible USD one-dollar bills could be *purchased/sold*. Market price of the USD one-dollar bill (P_{USD1} = ir$100/USD1) is arbitrarily posited in Figure 2.3.

The price of a hypothetical brand of red wine is likewise determined by interaction of Inventory Supply and Inventory Demand. If there exist 52,132 bottles of x-red-wine at market price ($P_{x\text{-red-wine}}$ = ir$1000/bottle x-red-wine in Figure 2.4), then division of the ir$ -wine price by the ir$-US dollar price

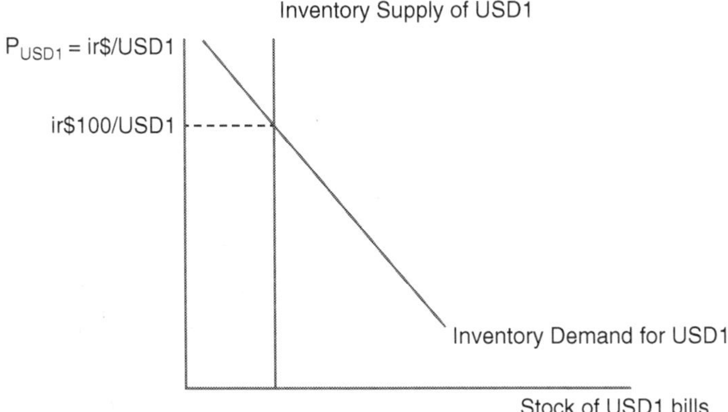

Figure 2.3 Determination of the ir$-price of a one-dollar bill.

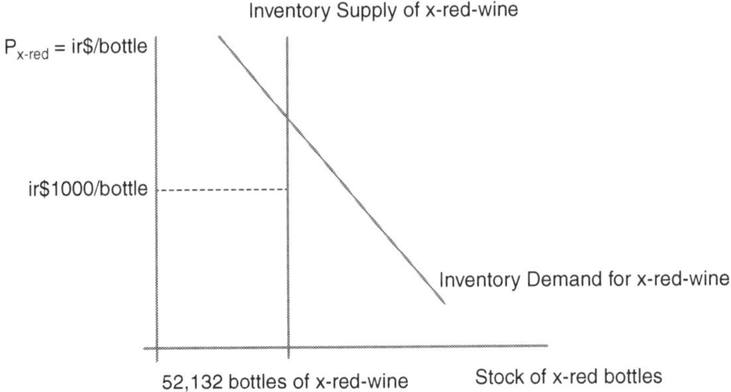

Figure 2.4 ir$ Price of x-red-wine.

cancels intangible-ratio dollars (ir$), yielding tangible price of 10 USD1/bottle of x-red-wine. This exchange rate is 10:1.[12] A non-economist would (accurately) state that this wine's price is ten bucks/bottle. While this presentation of price determination may appear uncontroversial, it is unconventional. First, Inventory Supply and Inventory Demand determine the wine's price; wine price is *not* determined by intersection of 'production supply' and 'consumption demand' as depicted in conventional (flows-only) microeconomic analysis. Second, conversion of intangible-ratio-dollar wine price (= ir$1000/bottle) into a ten *tangible* one-dollar-bill price per bottle is achieved through simple division of the ir$ wine-price by the ir$ USD1-price. Conventional microeconomic wine-price is expressed as ten *intangible ratio-dollars/bottle*, whereas Unified Theory wine-price is expressed as ten *tangible dollars/bottle* (via a ratio of intangible ratio-dollars). In sum, physical/tangible dollars and physical/tangible non-monetary goods are united within Laws of Supplies and Demands. Conventional isolation of monetary aggregates within a macroeconomics silo – divorced from disaggregated 'real goods' within a microeconomics silo – is unnecessary. The Unified Theory of Prices accommodates all goods and services. Tangible inventory stocks of monetary goods and non-monetary goods come into unified focus.

Price theory of monies applied to twenty-first-century institutions

Do the above-mentioned statements also apply to digital monies of the twenty-first century?

Yes, Laws of Supplies and Demands apply to commodity monies and fiat monies alike, irrespective of time period or institutional peculiarities. In the same sense that no modern scientist restricts Laws of Gravity or Laws of Thermodynamics to particular times, places, or institutional arrangements, Laws of Supplies and Demands also apply to all tradable monetary goods at all times.

Commodity monies are obviously tangible, yet *fiat* monies are also tangible. It is useful to distinguish fiat *currencies* vis-à-vis fiat *digital deposit* monies at commercial banks. Fiat currencies contain *negligible* intrinsic value, whereas fiat bank deposits contain *zero* intrinsic value, yet both monies are tangible. Ability to stock/inventory implies tangibility; by definition, intangible items cannot be stocked. The Price Theory of Monies recognizes tangibility of each fiat money.

Intangibles are impossible to hold in inventory stocks, including the historical intangible monies discussed in previous sections. Since *stocks* of digital monies are recorded and tracked through time these days, they must be considered tangible goods. Digital balances are physical entities that should *not* be described as 'virtual monies'. Creation and tracking of digital monies requires expenditure of energy via computer hardware, software, labor, and other materials.[13] Computerized zeros and ones exist physically, so digital monetary balances are stocks of tangible monies.

Personal possession of valuable assets has always been dangerous. Commercial currency storage developed in response to risk of currency loss. When access to currency was restricted to its owner, the owner/customer paid a commercial storage rental fee (e.g. bank deposit boxes today). The currency owner received a receipt (or deposit box key) in proof of currency ownership. Given sufficient trust in a respected deposit facility, a reputable stored-currency owner might conveniently transfer currency ownership without moving it. If a transfer of ownership receipt involved a normal purchase, then a currency-ownership receipt could be swapped for a non-monetary-good ownership receipt, thereby fulfilling the conventional 'medium of exchange' function of money. Neither the monetary good nor the non-monetary good (e.g. wheat) need be physically moved. This exchange of receipts – perhaps involving mere receipt endorsement – involves no lending/borrowing, so no economic/financial credit is involved. Ownership transfer via mere currency-deposit-receipt endorsement need not involve 'credit money'. Money and credit have existed independently for thousands of years. In sum, a storage facility's promise to store, return, or transfer ownership of tangible items (whether monies or not) need not involve credit. Indeed, credit need not necessarily involve monies, as illustrated when a seed grain loan at the onset of growing season requires repayment of more grain after harvest (including accumulated interest). Lending/borrowing need not require money. While money and credit have no doubt become increasingly intertwined due to innovations in financial institutions in recent times, money and credit must nonetheless be considered distinct entities. A future research agenda devoted to disentanglement of complex, evolving relationships among monies and credit instruments over centuries is to be encouraged, but conflation of tangible monies and credit instruments must be avoided from the outset.

Monies, credit instruments, and interest rates

As pointed out, money and credit, even though intertwined at certain times, are fundamentally unrelated. This conclusion influences relations between monies and the 'real' economy, since mainstream monetary theory today treats the interest rate as the primary transmission mechanism connecting money supplies to 'real sectors' of economies. Given institutional frameworks today, this view is understandable because manipulation of monetary stocks via central bank purchase/sale of credit instruments is commonplace. For instance, Federal Reserve Open Market purchase of US Treasury Bills does indeed inject base-money dollars into markets. Moreover, commercial banks do create rounds of monetary deposits through subsequent loans under fractional reserve banking rules (i.e. 'money multiplier'). Since bond prices move opposite bond interest rates, bond prices rise in response to Fed bond purchases, thereby reducing bond interest rates. Lower interest rates stimulate investment spending, elevate aggregate demand and thus Gross Domestic Product. In short, central bank interest-rate manipulations do indeed connect 'monetary' and (non-financial) 'real' sectors.

This money → interest rate → real-sector narrative, however, is inapplicable to millennia of monetary history. First, historical evidence demands maximum conceptual disaggregation of monies, in contrast to conventional aggregation of discrete monies as 'money'. Second, melting coins into non-monetary commodities (and, vice versa, minting) depended upon individual coin price vis-à-vis bullion price, an issue modern monetary theory ignores.[14] Third, profit (seigniorage) from minting specific coins (e.g. a Mexican peso with a particular date/mint-mark combination) depended upon coin market price vis-à-vis cost of its mint production. That is, coin production was endogenously determined throughout most of history, as opposed to the exogenous policy variable portrayed in macroeconomic theory.[15] Fourth, commodity monies throughout history flowed persistently beyond borders (indeed, hemispheres), so textbook focus upon 'national' monetary stocks conflicts with historical realities. Robust monetary theory must apply to myriad historical institutional settings.

Imagine a commercial bank reserve requirement of 100% along with zero Open Market operations. The Federal Reserve could expand US dollar stocks through currency or check issuance while purchasing goods and services. The (single-entity) Federal Reserve Treasury could, for instance, bolster national oil reserves via purchase of, say, two billion barrels of oil in exchange for USD $100 billion in new Federal Reserve notes. Global oil prices would likely rise, and the market value of Federal Reserve notes would decline. Interest rates would be unaffected, or nearly so: changing monetary stocks need not necessarily affect interest rates. Current Federal Reserve interest-rate manipulation occurs, *not because of augmented US$ inventory stocks*, but because current policy *augments inventory demand for credit instruments*. Institutional purchase of debt instruments is but one possible link. The interest-rate channel could be avoided via alternative transmission mechanisms, yet textbooks portray credit market intervention as the sole option, thereby inappropriately conflating monies and credit instruments. Evolution of specific monetary institutions this past century is a complicated topic deserving focused analysis.[16] Portrayal of 'the interest rate' as 'price/rental price' of any money, however, is misleading.

Unit-of-accounting divided by product quantity (e.g. ir$/unit of x) involves price dimensions. Interest-rate dimensions are percentages divided by time (%/time), so interest rates are prices of nothing. Application of the intangible-ratio dollar (ir$), indispensable in microeconomic analysis, is required for proper expression of tangible money prices.

Accounting concepts: Distinctions among credits, debits, credit, and monies

As indicated earlier, transplantation of accounting concepts into monetary theory enhances historical understanding. Consider fictitious loan applicant John Doe (Table 2.1). Doe *owns* $486,500 in 'assets', expressed in unit-of-accounting US dollars. Doe *owes* $219,500 in 'liabilities', also expressed in ia$ (intangible accounting dollars). His net worth on 1 August 2016 is $267,000, defined as assets *owned* minus liabilities *owed*.

A balance sheet is enhanced via accounting 'credit'. Thus, Doe's receipt of a $1,000 cash gift on 2 August 2016 increases cash holdings from $500 (Table 2.1) to $1,500 (Table 2.2), while Net Worth also rises by $1,000 to $268,000. Doe is wealthier due to receipt of this gift.

A balance sheet deteriorates with an accounting 'debit', negatively impacting Net Worth/Wealth. Table 2.3 reflects loss of $5,000 worth of uninsured

Table 2.1 John Doe balance sheet on 1 August 2016

BANK OF XYZ			
Personal financial statement for John Doe			
1 August 2016			
Assets (A)		*Liabilities* (L)	
Cash	$ 500	Credit card balance	$ 2,000
Checking account	$ 2,000	Mortgage balance	$ 200,000
Savings account	$ 3,000	Automobile loan	$ 10,000
Stocks	$ 30,000	Signature loan	$ 2,500
Bonds	$ 20,000	TOTAL LIABILITIES =	$ 219,500
Retirement account	$ 95,000		
Real estate owned	$300,000	**Net worth (= A – L) =**	**$ 267,000**
Furniture	$ 15,000		
Automobiles	$ 12,000		
Miscellaneous assets	$ 9,000		
TOTAL ASSETS =	$ 486,500		
Monthly income		*Monthly expenditures*	
Salary	$ 4,000	House payment	$ 1,500
Interest earned	$ 10	Utilities	$ 200
Miscellaneous	$ 300	Taxes	$ 200
		Food	$ 800
		Wine and beer	$ 1,000
		Entertainment	$ 100
TOTAL INCOME	$ 4,310	TOTAL EXPENSES	$ 3,800

Table 2.2 John Doe balance sheet on 2 August 2016

BANK OF XYZ			
Personal financial statement for John Doe			
2 August 2016			
Assets (A)		*Liabilities* (L)	
Cash	$ 1,500	Credit card balance	$ 2,000
Checking account	$ 2,000	Mortgage balance	$ 200,000
Savings account	$ 3,000	Automobile loan	$ 10,000
Stocks	$ 30,000	Signature loan	$ 2,500
Bonds	$ 20,000	TOTAL LIABILITIES	=$ 219,500
Retirement account	$ 95,000		
Real estate owned	$ 300,000	**Net worth (= A – L)**	**=$ 268,000**
Furniture	$ 15,000		
Automobiles	$ 12,000		
Miscellaneous assets	$ 9,000		
TOTAL ASSETS =	$ 487,500		
Monthly income		*Monthly expenditures*	
Salary		House payment	$ 1,500
Interest earned	$ 4000	Utilities	$ 200
Miscellaneous	$ 10	Taxes	$ 200
	$ 300	Food	$ 800
		Wine and beer	$ 1,000
		Entertainment	$ 100
TOTAL INCOME	$ 4,310	TOTAL EXPENSES	$ 3,800

furniture due to burglary on 3 August 2016. Doe's furniture assets decline from $15,000 to $10,000, and Net Worth drops from $268,000 to $263,000 (Table 2.3).

'Credit' in economics refers to lending/borrowing, while accounting 'credit' could reflect receipt of a gift. A gift raised Doe's cash holdings and Net Worth by $1,000 (Table 2.2), for instance, yet this development is unrelated to economic/financial 'credit markets' because no loan was involved. Accounting 'credit' does not imply an economic/financial 'credit transaction'. Similarly, the $5,000 accounting debit due to furniture burglary (Figure 2.3) involved no lending/borrowing, so no economic/financial 'debt' is involved.

Next, consider a $1,000 rug purchase via Doe check that reduces his checking balance from $2,000 to $1,000 (Table 2.4). A simultaneous $1,000 credit raises miscellaneous assets from $9,000 to $10,000 (Table 2.4); total assets, liabilities, and Net Worth are unaltered. Composition of Doe's assets was remixed, yet no loan took place, so economic/financial credit is not involved. Accounting 'credit' and economic/financial 'credit' refer to different things, as do accounting 'debit' and economic/financial 'debt'. When store clerks ask, 'Cash or credit?' cash payments and credit transactions are clearly considered *alternatives*. Economic/financial credit borrowing appears under (right-side) 'Liabilities', whereas gifts and cash purchases appear under (left-side) 'Assets'. Remixing of assets does not involve economic/financial credit.

Table 2.3 John Doe balance sheet on 3 August 2016

BANK OF XYZ					
Personal financial statement for John Doe					
3 August 2016					
Assets (A)			*Liabilities* (L)		
Cash	$	1,500	Credit card balance	$	2,000
Checking account	$	2,000	Mortgage balance	$	200,000
Savings account	$	3,000	Automobile loan	$	10,000
Stocks	$	30,000	Signature loan	$	2,500
Bonds	$	20,000	TOTAL LIABILITIES =	$	219,500
Retirement account	$	95,000			
Real estate owned	$	300,000	**Net worth (= A – L) =**	**$**	**263,000**
Furniture	$	10,000			
Automobiles	$	12,000			
Miscellaneous assets	$	9,000			
TOTAL ASSETS =	$	482,500			
Monthly income			*Monthly expenditures*		
Salary	$	4,000	House payment	$	1,500
Interest earned	$	10	Utilities	$	200
Miscellaneous	$	300	Taxes	$	200
			Food	$	800
			Wine and beer	$	1,000
			Entertainment	$	100
TOTAL INCOME	$	4,310	TOTAL EXPENSES	$	3,800

Intangible unit-of-accounting monies today

Viewing dollars in Tables 2.1–4 as tangible is tempting because conventional monetary theory implicitly assumes all monies to be tangible. Tangibility is certainly required of medium-of-exchange and store-of-value functions, yet unit-of-accounting (Tables 2.1–4) dollars are intangible (as were accounting shekels long ago). Acknowledgement of *intangible* accounting dollars, however, implies that zero monies exist today, according to conventional theory. Monies have existed for thousands of years, of course, but no money can perform all required monetary functions when some require tangibility while others require intangibility.

Consider Table 2.4 below. Company stock certificates possess an estimated market value of $30,000 because sale of all shares that day would have yielded $30,000. But shares were *not* sold that day. They were held, and future stock-sale net proceeds are unknowable. Similarly, estimated market value of Doe's automobile that day is $12,000, but its actual future sales price is unknowable. The same applies to net-proceed estimates from sale of bonds, real estate, and other assets. Balance sheet asset evaluations are often contested, which is why lenders require independent appraisals of real estate and other big-ticket items; moreover, banks assign little credence to smaller, customer-evaluated

Table 2.4 John Doe balance sheet on 4 August 2016

BANK OF XYZ					
Personal financial statement for John Doe					
4 August 2016					
Assets (A)			*Liabilities* (L)		
Cash	$	500	Credit card balance	$	2,000
Checking account	$	2,000	Mortgage balance	$	200,000
Savings account	$	3,000	Automobile loan	$	10,000
Stocks	$	30,000	Signature loan	$	2,500
Bonds	$	20,000	TOTAL LIABILITIES =	$	219,500
Retirement account	$	95,000			
Real estate owned	$	300,000	**Net worth (= A – L) =**	**$**	**263,000**
Furniture	$	10,000			
Automobiles	$	12,000			
Miscellaneous assets	$	10,000			
TOTAL ASSETS =	$	482,500			
Monthly income			*Monthly expenditures*		
Salary	$	4,000	House payment	$	1,500
Interest earned	$	10	Utilities	$	200
Miscellaneous	$	300	Taxes	$	200
			Food	$	800
			Wine and beer	$	1,000
			Entertainment	$	100
TOTAL INCOME	$	4,310	TOTAL EXPENSES	$	3,800

asset values. Independent appraisers furnish conflicting market values. Even valid bank balances are open to challenge, as claimed account balances may in fact belong to someone else. One job of bank underwriters is to investigate neglected liabilities and co-signatures. Checking and savings balances are often assumed to be convertible into hard currency on demand, but recent depositors in Greece and elsewhere have cast doubt upon banks' promises to deliver currency. Even personal currency holdings could be stolen. Lawsuits could be pending. In sum, unit-of-accounting dollars are abstract, intangible, subjective estimates of market valuations. Only the destitute have a solid idea of personal net worth. Conversion of assets into tangible after-tax dollars occurs only through liquidation, while liabilities can be negotiated. Bottom line: Net Worth expressed in intangible unit-of-accounting dollars is quite different from tangible dollars held. All unit-of-accounting monies are intangible, which means it is impossible for any money to fulfill all three functions specified in conventional monetary theory: (1) intangible unit-of-accounting, (2) tangible medium-of-exchange, and (3) tangible store-of-value. Moreover, conventional monetary theory does not even acknowledge existence of three remaining monetary functions: (4) monetary standard, (5) link monies, and (6) measure of relative values.

Trust and disaggregation

Introduction

Tangible monies are ultimately goods held in inventories, values of which can be demonstrated via the intangible ratio dollar. Trust in the values of tangible monies is often relatively straightforward. Yet there are various routes through which such trust can be lost. Trust is required of any business, including banks. Confidence that $1,000 in pocket currency is equivalent to a $1,000 bank deposit requires trust in the promise that $1,000 currency will always be delivered by the bank on demand. When numerous customers lose confidence in this promise, a 'run on the bank' occurs. Currencies and bank deposits are both tangible, yet they are *imperfect* substitutes. Holding cash is risky, and it includes the danger of having received counterfeit currency. Currency trust must be balanced against bank deposit trust. The promise to deliver currency is distinct from actual delivery of currency, which explains why the Federal Deposit Insurance remains a crucial institutional innovation. Currency monies and deposit monies should not be aggregated. Trust in bank promises varies around the world, however, and worries about the sustainability of worldwide debt spirals are *far from* irrational.

Credit theory of money

Some scholars claim that money is an instrument of debt, rather than monies as goods, a belief that would significantly alter how one approaches the 'search for trust' issue. Indeed 'Credit Theory of Money' advocates claim that monies originated from debt instruments, and hence all monies are *inherently* credit instruments. Economist Michael Hudson (2004) argues: (a) that money emerged from public sector activities, not the private sector (p.108); (b) that [third millennium BC] '*What is true for today's paper money thus was true of silver. Its value was established by public institutions accepting it as payment*' (p.108); (c) that lack of domestic silver mines necessitated silver imports into Mesopotamia (p.111); and (d) that 'in antiquity there were no banks engaged in credit creation. The debt problem did not involve a monetary problem in the modern sense of the term' (pp.124–125).

I agree with the general conclusions of Hudson, Bezemer, and others who claim that escalating debts threaten the sustainability of twenty-first-century global economies, and that monetary authorities exacerbate debt spirals. Yet, the Credit Theory of Money claims that money originated from debt instruments are unconvincing. Hudson acknowledges that Mesopotamian exports (e.g. textiles) were necessary for silver imports, given that they had zero domestic silver mines. Imported silver performed monetary functions: Public institutions 'gave value to silver' (Hudson 2004: 107) and 'were the ultimate guarantors of the value of silver' (Hudson 2004: 116). Yet silver's market value must have pre-existed beyond Mesopotamian borders; otherwise, what determined terms of trade between Mesopotamian exports vis-à-vis silver imports? One cannot 'give value' to a good that already possesses value elsewhere. Moreover, silver imports due to arbitrage tend to augment silver stocks and thereby *depress* silver's value in recipient markets.[17] Also, how could Mesopotamian officials 'give value to' and 'guarantee value of' silver without acknowledging that people/institutions beyond Mesopotamia therefore must have 'given value to' and 'guaranteed value of' Mesopotamian textile exports? Silver contains no mystical qualities that warrant special models applicable to it alone. I acknowledge Hudson's criticism of ideological free-market myths, and his claim that public entities may have influenced market mechanisms. But no entity today can determine/guarantee the market value of silver, and I know of no evidence to suggest anything different for the long-past Mesopotamian silver trade c. 3000 BC. Conventional Laws of Supply and Demand are indeed woefully inadequate for accurate description of market forces, but our Laws of Supplies and Demands offer many additional descriptive tools.

Hudson fails to distinguish accounting 'credits' and economic/financial 'credit' as discussed above. One can accept Hudson's (2004: 107) statement that many 'credits due to the public institutions' may have been economic/financial credit devices, but elsewhere he conflates accounting 'credits' and economic/financial 'credit': 'The public institutions seem to have spent this [imported] silver and provided other metals to the population in exchange for crops. There are a few hints that royal distributions on ceremonial occasions also may have played a role' (Hudson 2004: 108). Yet, public purchase of crops with silver simply remixes goods on the Asset side of balance sheets (as in Table 2.4); likewise, a gift (Table 2.2) leaves Liabilities unaltered and thus has nothing to do with economic/financial credit. Debts were settled in silver, but debts were also settled in barley and dates. Is Hudson willing to argue that dates and barley therefore originated from credit instruments?[18] Barley and dates are foods. Utilization of foods for unit-of-accounting and medium-of-exchange functions implies nothing about foods originating from credit instruments. Credit documents specify interest payments and due dates. Hudson's purchase and gift examples involve neither interest payments nor due dates, and they do not involve economic/finance credit instruments.

Conclusion: Appraisal and outlook

Six separate monetary functions have been identified, including three functions specified in mainstream monetary theory. Three of the six functions – medium-of-exchange, store-of-value, and monetary standard – require monies that are tangible. The other three functions – unit-of-accounting, link-money, and measure-of-relative-values – require monies that are intangible. Conventional monetary theory acknowledges just three functions – unit-of-accounting, store-of-value, and medium-of-exchange – while ignoring the other three. Moreover, standard theory states that all three *acknowledged* functions must be simultaneously satisfied in order for an item to qualify (among others) in an aggregate called 'money'. This mainstream requirement forces us to conclude that 'money' has never existed (and cannot exist in principle) because unit-of-accounting monies – from the Babylonian shekel in the third millennium BC up to today's accounting dollar (ia$) – are *intangible* monies. It is impossible for an intangible-unit-of-accounting money to simultaneously satisfy tangible-medium-of-exchange and tangible-store-of-value functions. Tangibility and intangibility are mutually exclusive, so requirement of simultaneous satisfaction of all three mainstream functions involves logical contradiction. Moreover, monies that fulfill only one monetary function are ubiquitous in the historical literature. Thousands of distinct monies have existed throughout history; indeed, invention of new monies continues into the twenty-first century. Teams of economists at central banks today regularly calculate monetary aggregates (such as M1, M2, … M_n) in order to estimate 'the money supply' of a nation. These 'money supply' aggregates are mythical theoretical constructs without counterparts in reality, however, because constituent components are incommensurate in terms of function and tangibility. Distinct monies require separate analyses. Monies should be conceptually disaggregated to the maximum extent possible. Doing so implies jettisoning the basic microeconomics–macroeconomics dichotomy.

Trust is a central theme throughout the collected essays of this volume. Trust in specific commodity monies has long depended upon belief in stability of their respective market values. Market value of a tangible particular money would be maintained if change in Inventory Demand for it were matched proportionately by change in its Inventory Supply: This is an essential message of the Price Theory of Monies proposed herein. No commodity-money substance enjoyed greater popularity over vast distances throughout the last five millennia than did silver, in large part due to relative stability in the white metal's market value. Durability of silver contributed mightily to maintenance of its value. Since annual loss (including wear and tear) was typically no more than 1–5% of existing silver stocks, inventories of silver accumulated through generations. (These accumulations are labeled 'Inventory Supply' in this essay.) Abundant stocks of silver imply relative stability of Inventory Supply because typical additions and subtractions tended to comprise small fractions of accumulated stocks. During times when Inventory Demand for silver was relatively stable, market value of silver deviated little because interaction of stable Inventory Supply and stable Inventory Demand rendered price stability. In short, trust in commodity-money silver depended in large part on relative stability of its market price; market price depended, in turn, upon relatively stable Inventory Supply and Inventory Demand.

Countless economic convulsions – due to climate change, soil exhaustion, war, and other factors – have of course jolted economies into disequilibrium throughout history. Famine associated with significant reduction in Inventory Supplies of grains, for instance, could destabilize an entire region. A world region (perhaps Mesopotamia) undergoing such a severe economic contraction would generally experience steep decline in wealth, forcing an economic scramble among those living in the affected region. Collapse of demand for non-grain assets would normally accompany a general plunge in wealth. Existing supplies of many non-grain assets, however, would not necessarily fall initially in response to famine. Immobile assets such as immovable homes, for example, could experience drastic reductions in market price, since depleted inventory demand could encounter fixed inventory supply. A drastic plunge in market price of commodity-money silver would be unlikely, however, because decline in Inventory Demand for silver would set in motion automatic mechanisms leading to reduced Inventory Supply of silver. Local silver price might drop some, but silver markets frequently extend far beyond a particular region in crisis. Individuals would not necessarily have to sell silver locally at an extreme price discount, however, because local and foreign silver merchants would be expected to exploit temporary arbitrage opportunities. Local silver sellers would be attracted to both local and foreign merchant buyers seeking to export silver, thereby mitigating against an otherwise more drastic fall in silver price. Arbitrage simply refers to purchase of a product at low price in one market in order to re-sell it elsewhere at a higher price. Collapse of a local economy would not normally have much impact on silver's price in the rest of the world, so the 'world price' of silver would remain relatively unaffected. In consequence, relatively high foreign silver prices establish arbitrage possibilities through exportation of silver from the weak region. Silver exports reduce domestic Inventory Supply, other things equal, until domestic silver stocks eventually fall to the level of (reduced) Inventory Demand within that region. When this process has played out, the local silver price essentially matches silver price elsewhere. Wealth in the traumatized area is lower than what it was before famine, and Inventory Demand for silver (among many other goods) would inevitably decrease. Less silver is eventually held in the region, but the price of silver nonetheless maintains stability. Inventory adjustment mechanisms (for portable goods) are important in terms of generating long-term trust in durable objects, because automatic mechanisms tend to preserve market values of highly durable, widely traded goods such as silver. Trust in durable, transportable, and popular commodities, such as silver, is fortified by relative price stability generated through impersonal market mechanisms. Trust in price stability due to market forces is, of course, quite distinct from trust attributable to personal or institutional reputation and integrity.

Wealth is composed of things owned (net of debts). Things owned occupy physical space. People of modest means tend to store belongings where they live. Off-site storage can be advantageous for those who can afford to pay for it, of course, and commercial storage has existed for thousands of years. Commercial storage of tangible monies requires payment of rent. Receipts furnish proof of ownership. A receipt implies claim of ownership, a matter distinct from the issue of loans. In other words, stored monies need not involve debts. Storage companies are caretakers (not borrowers) of stored items, which is why they receive rent rather than pay interest. Trust is crucial for the success of commercial storage facilities, some of which also offer (trustworthy) insurance coverage for items stored (for an additional fee).

To recapitulate, intrinsic content generates trust in commodity monies, since market value of bullion exists independently of monetary form. Fiat monies contain little intrinsic content by definition, on the other hand, so establishment of trust must be based upon different considerations. Trust can be established through the credible guarantee of fixed-rate exchange of fiat money in favor of commodity monies upon demand. Once again, intrinsic content provides assurance of value stability, but in this case credibility of the guarantor is required for maintenance of trust. Risk of guarantor default must be balanced relative to the risk that commodity monies themselves might be counterfeit, substandard, difficult to transport, or involving other problems. Guarantor trust is central in the case of fiat monies.

Commercial lending of stored monies raises an additional set of issues involving trust. First, monies stored at banks must normally be fungible in order to facilitate lending. That is to say, depositors cannot insist upon return of the exact same monies originally deposited in the bank (monies must be considered interchangeable). Even then, a new form of risk arises, because storage facilities (banks in this case) that lend out OPM (other people's money) typically do not maintain reserves equal to 100% of deposit balances. Fractional reserve banking has provided a mechanism for tremendous expansion in loan capacities, to be sure, but risk of inadequate reserves arises whenever a 'run on the bank' materializes. Not only is trust in a bank's reputation required, depositors must also consider the integrity of bank borrowers. There are countless examples of breakdowns in the evolution of credit monies throughout history. Thus, financial panics became intertwined with monetary history as increasingly complex credit monies evolved. Establishment of the US Federal Deposit Insurance Corporation (FDIC), and similar backstop financial institutions in other countries, has obviously been important in terms of building widespread trust. In essence, the entire financial strength of a federal government serves as lender-of-last-resort in the event of commercial bank failure. Since the 1930s, depositor trust is largely based upon federal government guarantees.

All federal governments are not perceived financial equals, of course, as depositors in Greek (and other) banks were recently reminded. Aid from international agencies such as the International Monetary Fund now exist, but assistance is contingent upon stringent economic controls vis-à-vis government spending, unemployed citizens, damaged businesses, and burdens of heavy taxation for current and future generations. Near meltdown of the US financial system in 2007–2008 suggests that major economic powers are also not immune to concerns regarding trustworthiness. Private, business, and government debt-accumulation issues have spiraled upward throughout the world over recent decades. Surely there must exist an upper limit to debt sustainability, but who knows the ultimate credit ceiling? I hope and *trust* that experts in monetary and financial matters will adopt historical perspectives in order to elucidate perplexing roles of monies and credit instruments that appear to be propelling national, regional, and global economies along paths vaguely understood.

Notes

1 Flynn and Giráldez (1997) for elaboration.
2 For a comparative study of the role of silver in international trade in antiquity and the early modern period, see Van der Spek (2011).
3 Refusal of payment in sub-standard silver was also common thousands of years earlier in Babylonia (Jursa *et al.* 2010: 483–484).
4 Cf. Flynn (2015a: 56) for the concept.
5 Slotsky and Wallenfels (2009: 83–97, text 6 r. 12'–15'). For the weight of the coins cf. commentary on p. 94, n. 65. See also Mooring *et al.* (chapter 6).
6 This common-sense conclusion is correct. Inadequacies in conventional Laws of Supply and Demand are detailed below.
7 Calculations based upon discussion of Dutch link monies in Wolters (2008).
8 When I say: 'silver served as Monetary Standard', I mean the market value of prescribed weight/quality of silver served as a benchmark against which all non-silver market values were calculated. For a summary of bewildered attempts to define the term 'monetary standard', see Mason (1963).
9 I agree with Bezemer (Chapter 3, this volume) and others who emphasize dangers, including central banks' responsibility for escalating debts worldwide.
10 Textbooks sometimes label quantity 'real balances' (M/P), a monetary aggregate divided by a weighted Price Index. The Price Theory of Monies insists upon disaggregation of individual monies considered inherently 'real' (obviating need for any divisor).
11 Monetary quantities are counted like non-monetary items, eliminating need for 'real balances' as in M/P.
12 Van der Spek (2016: 139) correctly refers to Babylonian price lists as 'exchange rates' vis-à-vis a quantity of silver.
13 Production of intangible services also requires stocks of inputs. Yet, aside from deposits and withdrawals, a bank balance maintains its inventory stock; accountants correctly list such bank balances assets (i.e. inventory stocks) and not services.
14 Minting and melting mechanisms are discussed further in Flynn (2015a).
15 A notable exception, Findlay and Lundahl (2002) explicitly treats the money supply as endogenous during an era of European history that unfolded over centuries. Aggregation techniques constrain Findlay's argument, in my view, but sound instincts accompany his appreciation of historical complexities.
16 Distinction between nominal and real interest rates must be kept in mind. I refer here to impacts upon real interest rates. To the extent that a money loses value, price inflation could raise nominal interest rates expressed in terms of that money. This matter is distinct from the core money-versus-credit issue emphasized here.
17 For a discussion of vanishing silver-value premiums in Chinese markets vis-à-vis markets in the rest of the world (1540s–1640 and 1700–1750 periods), see Flynn and Giráldez (2002).
18 Speaking of temple wool sales at Eanna, Jursa *et al.* (2010: 559) write: 'The temple almost always intended to receive silver also from buyers with low income of cash who purchased small quantities of wool. Other means of payment (like barley or sesame) were rare. Clauses in credit purchase contracts stipulating barley instead of silver, in case the deadline could not be met, contained punitive interest. The barley payment was thus not an alternative means of payment'. Note that normal interest was paid in silver, while 'punitive interest' was paid in barley.

References

Einaudi, L. (1953). 'The theory of imaginary money from Charlemagne to the French Revolution' (translated by George Tagliacozzo), in Lane, F.C. and Riemersma, J.C.

(eds.), *Enterprise and Secular Change: Readings in Economic History*, London: George Allen and Unwin: 229–261.

Findlay, R. and Lundahl, M. (2002). 'Towards a factor proportions approach to economic history: Population, precious metals and prices from the Black Death to the price revolution', in Findlay, R., Jonung, L., and Lundahl, M. (eds), *Bertil Ohlin: A Centennial Celebration (1899–1999)*, Cambridge, MA: MIT Press: 495–528.

Flynn, D.O. (2015a). 'Link-unit-of-account versus ratio-unit-of-account moneys: Seventeenth-century Dutch mint policy', in Leonard, J.K. and Theobald, U. (eds.), *Money in Asia (1200–1900): Small Currencies in Social and Political Contexts*, Leiden, the Netherlands: Brill: 41–70.

Flynn, D.O. (2015b). 'Silver in a global context, 1400–1800', in Bentley, J.H., Subrahmanyam, S., and Wiesner-Hanks, M.E. (eds.), *The Cambridge World History*, Vol. VI, *The Construction of a Global World, 1400–1800 CE*, Part 2, *Patterns of Change*, Cambridge, UK: Cambridge University Press: 213–239.

Flynn, D.O. and Giráldez, A. (eds.) (1997). *Metals and Monies in an Emerging Global Economy*, Aldershot, UK: Ashgate/Variorum Press.

Flynn, D.O. and Giráldez, A. (eds.) (2002). 'Cycles of silver: Global economic unity through the mid-18th century', *Journal of World History*, 13/2: 391–427.

Hudson, M. (2004). 'The archaeology of money: Debt vs. barter theories of money's origins', in Wray L.R. (ed.), *Credit and State Theories of Money: The Contributions of A. Mitchell Innes*, Cheltenham, UK and Northampton, MA: Edward Elgar: 99–127.

Irigoin, A. (2013). 'A Trojan Horse in Daoguang China? Explaining flows of silver in and out of China'. Working Paper 173, Department of Economic History, London School of Economics.

Jursa, M., Hackl, J., Janković, B., Kleber, K., Payne, E., Waerzeggers, C.A.H., and Weszeli, M. (2010). *Aspects of the Economic History of Babylonia in the First Millennium BC: Economic Geography, Economic Mentalities, Agriculture, the Use of Money and the Problem of Economic Growth*. Münster: Ugarit-Verlag.

Keynes, J.M. (1964 [1935]). *The General Theory of Employment, Interest, and Money*. New York: Harcourt, Brace & World.

Kishimoto, M. (2011). 'Foreign silver and China's domestic economy', paper presented for session 'The World Upside Down: The Role of Spanish American Silver in China during the Daoguang Reign Period 1821–50.' Third European Congress for World and Global History, April 14–17.

Kuroda, A. (2008). 'Concurrent but non-integrable currency circuits: Complementary relationships among monies in Modern China and other regions', *Financial History Review*, 15/1: 17–36.

Kuroda, A. (2013). 'Anomymous currencies or named debts? Comparison of currencies local credits and units of account between China, Japan, and England in the Pre-industrial era', *Socio-Economic Review*, 11: 57–80.

Mason, W.E. (1963). *Clarification of the Monetary Standard: The Concept and Its Relation to Monetary Policies and Objectives*. University Park, PA: The Pennsylvania State University Press.

Piketty, T. (2014). *Capital in the Twenty-First Century*. Cambridge, MA: The Belknap Press of Harvard University Press.

Slotsky, A.L. and Wallenfels, R. (2009). *Tallies and Trends. The Late Babylonian Commodity Price Lists*. Bethesda, MD: CDL Press.

Van der Spek, R.J. (2011). 'The "silverization" of the economy of the Achaemenid and Seleukid empires and early modern China,' in Archibald, Z.H., Davies, J.K., and

Gabrielsen, V. (eds.), *The Economies of Hellenistic Societies, Third to First Centuries*, Oxford: Oxford University Press: 402–420.

Van der Spek, R.J. (2016). 'KI.LAM = *nadānu*, "exchange rate": More evidence from the price lists', *Nouvelles Assyriologiques Brèves et Utilitaires*, 2016/3: 139–141 (no. 83).

Van der Spek, R.J. (2017). '*Manûtu ša Bābili* = the Babylonian subdivision of the mina', *Nouvelles Assyriologiques Brèves et Utilitaires*, 2017/1: 33–37 (no. 20).

Von Glahn, R. (2011). 'Money demand and silver supply in 19th-century China', *Empires, Systems, and Maritime Networks: Reconstructing Supra-Regional Histories in Pre-19th Century Asia*. Working Paper Series 05, Ritsumeikan Asia Pacific University, Beppu, Oita, Japan, 67–85.

Wolters, W.G. (2008). 'Heavy and light money in the Netherlands Indies and the Dutch Republic: Dilemmas of monetary management with unit of account systems', *Financial History Review*, 15.1: 37–53.

3 Unproductive debt causes crisis

Connecting the history of money to the current crisis

Dirk Bezemer

Introduction

In this paper I will connect the historical debt nature of money to financial crisis. The causes of the latest crisis have been sought in a large variety of factors, but a fundamental cause still remains underappreciated: debt growth. My argument proceeds in five steps.

First, money, and by extension all forms of finance, are forms of debt. This can be argued using archeological and historical evidence on the history of money, which indicates that money emerged as a form of debt.[1] This is a more well-supported history of money than the perhaps more common idea that debt emerged from money, which in turn was invented as a tool to reduce the cost of barter transactions. If we accept that money is a form of debt, then it is also implied that financial expansion is debt expansion. Brisk development of global finance must mean rapid growth in debt. Big finance can be a big problem (Bezemer 2013).

Second, in current research on the latest crisis there is mounting evidence on two as yet disparate issues: the 2007 crisis was due to overexpansion of the financial system, and the 2007 crisis was due to excessive growth in debt, especially household debt. Precisely the same peaking of debt and vigorous financial development characterized the previous big crisis, the crash of 1929. I have no reliable data further back, but this evidence is suggestive of debt as a cause of crisis.

Third, this in itself is not sufficient to explain the crisis which follows large debt growth. Precisely because debt is also credit, growth in debt may not be problematic as long as the credit that is its balance sheet counterpart is used productively and leads to income formation. In this benign scenario, debt growth begets income growth, from which the debt can be repaid. This is financially sustainable. What matters is the ratio of debt to income. If this rises, financial fragility rises.

Fourth, this calls for a categorization of debt transactions into those that stimulate income growth and those that do not. The only other way in which debt can be used, if it is not used for income formation, is to increase asset prices. And this is precisely what we observe prior to financial crisis: an increase in debt used to purchase existing assets, rather than to fund production and consumption of goods and services. In the years leading up to 1929, this was the increase in trade in corporate stock 'on margin'. In our day, the largest asset market has become the land and property markets. What we need in order to research the link between debt and crisis is a differentiation in the uses of debt: for income formation *versus* for asset market transactions. Let us label these two kinds of debt 'real-sector debt' and 'asset-market debt'. My hypothesis implies that the real-sector-debt-to-income ratio is stable while the rise in debt is mostly or entirely due to the rise in asset-market debt. I use data to show that this is indeed the case in the US, the Netherlands, and the UK. Debt issued to fund real-sector transactions does not increase the debt burden. Asset-market debt does.

Fifth, credit flowing to asset markets not only increases the debt-to-income ratio, but its growth is also self-accelerating. Recent years have seen an explosion of research into the mutual feedbacks between secured debt (such as mortgages) and the price of the collateral (such as property). This unhappy combination of growth in the debt *burden* – not just the debt level – and the positive feedback built into that growth, is the source of crisis.

This concludes my argument. In a nutshell, it starts form the historical datum that money and finance are forms of debt; that financial expansion is therefore debt expansion; that debt expansion increases the debt burden if it does not stimulate income growth commensurate with the debt growth; and that crisis-prone financial expansion is expansion of debt used for transactions in asset markets, because of the feedback between asset prices and the credit flows used to transact these assets.

The upshot is that the growth of unproductive debt should be our overriding concern with respect to crisis risks. In the conclusion of this chapter, I will consider some implications from and challenges to this claim.

Point of departure: The credit and state theories of money[2]

The theoretical background to this argument is the credit theory of money. Goodhart (1998) discusses two broad theories on how money historically emerged: the transactions-based account and the credit-based account. In the transactions-based view, money emerged as a means to economize on barter-transaction costs. In the credit-based view, money emerged as credit tokens came to be used as means of payments. In this latter view, all money is a form of credit. This will be important later on in my argument.

The proposition that money emerged when credit tokens came to be used as means of payments goes against a widely held belief, based on textbook economics, that money historically emerged when some commodity (e.g. shells or silver lumps) came to be used as a convenient unit of account to replace the cruder barter trade, and that the use of credit and debt was an optional extra, predicated on the prior existence of money. This convenient pedagogical narrative has been taught since times immemorial – at least since Aristotle, as

Ingham (2004) recounts. Nineteenth-century German textbooks made it part of the standard economics curriculum. But if assessed as actual financial history, it is found to be devoid of historical or ethnographic evidence to support it, to my knowledge.

There are good reasons (some of them reviewed by Wray 1998) why it is nonetheless a popular and persistent fable in economics. Money as a commodity fits hand-in-glove with a neoclassical view of the world, where everything is either input or output or price. Credit and debt is neither, and fits uneasily into general equilibrium models, the ultimate market-based view of how economies work. Not surprisingly, such models typically have no finance in them, which requires having balance sheets (Bezemer 2012). Neoclassical economics cannot deal with balance sheets, being exclusively formulated in flow terms, as Dennis Flynn in this volume explains (Chapter 2). This omission was arguably a major reason why the 2008 financial crisis was so unexpected and, conversely, why those who did 'see it coming' did not adhere to the neoclassical neglect of money (Bezemer 2010). Precisely because it was a credit crisis, and credit is absent from most models used by macroeconomists, central banks, and policymakers, the crisis was largely unforeseen. The reason is that the institution of credit-money is incompatible with multi-market equilibrium models – a problem nicely summarized in the title of Frank Hahn's paper 'On Some Problems of Proving the Existence of an Equilibrium in a Monetary Economy' (Hahn 1965). With actual money and finance included in the model, it cannot be solved and becomes quite useless. It is much more convenient to include a numéraire money – that is, no money. The latest crisis constituted a test for the money-less paradigm, which (as I argue in Bezemer, 2012) it failed. Post-crisis, the problem is still as relevant as ever, and it explains economists' continued obsession with commodity money, and their neglect, generally, of the historical facts.

Instead, consider evidence from the 'archeology of money' in favour of the credit origin of money. This comprises research in archeology, anthropology, and numismatics – see e.g. Wray (1998, 2004), Ingham (2004), and Hudson and Van de Mieroop (2002), building on early seminal contributions by Knapp ([1905] 1924) and Mitchell Innes (1913 and 1914). A major argument for this position is logical. It is that specialization of labour – which characterized societies as early as the Mesolithic age – must have implied credit relations. Specialization of labour and the attendant exchange of goods (e.g. between hunters, toolmakers, and gatherers) requires a social mechanism to bridge the time between delivery of the various goods. A hunter needs bow and arrow from the toolmaker before he can hunt and deliver meat in return. In the meantime, the hunter is a debtor, as he owes the toolmaker, who is a creditor. In societies also involving farmers, bakers, and so on, the web of debtor–creditor relations quickly becomes complex.[3] Such relations would therefore have been recorded in some way. This is not just another pedagogical narrative or speculation on how things might have been. Archeologists have found notched bones from Stone Age hunter–gatherer societies, where the notches have been interpreted by scholars as evidence of quite elaborate accounting systems (Gardiner 2004).

Also, highly developed ancient civilizations had credit-money. For instance, from Ancient Mesopotamia, i.e. from Sumer, Assyria, and Babylonia (from 3000 to 200 BC) there have been recovered thousands of clay tablets stating quantified obligations, most often of fungibles, owed by individuals to other individuals, temples, or the state. Many of these IOUs were sealed in cases inscribed with the same information. The oldest texts of this kind we know of, from the early third millennium BC, refer to obligations to institutions, most often temples. Like bills of exchange used in later times, these cased tablets were 'signed and sealed documents and passed from hand to hand' (Mitchell Innes 1913: 35; cf. Hudson 2004). When the debt described on the case was cleared, it was broken. Archaeologists have, however, recovered many such cases intact, indicating that, just like the outstanding stock of money in our economic system, their primary use had become to facilitate transactions, not to settle debt. They were tradable and functioned as means of payment, their value determined by the authorities setting tax levels. In short, these IOUs were money like there were other forms of money, such as silver ingots, and they existed long before states started to issue money in the form of coins.

So it was in Europe, where since the earliest times accounting tokens of creditor–debtor relations were used as money, i.e. to settle transactions of goods and services. In many medieval European societies, the form this took was the square wooden stick with notches, or tally (Wray 1998:41). It was created when a buyer became a debtor to a seller. Their names, with the date, were written on opposite sides of the stick. Then the stick was split down the middle but stopped about an inch from the base. Thus there were two smaller sticks with equal numbers of notches, one (called the 'stock' and retained by the creditor) longer than the other (the 'stub', held by the debtor). Stock and stub could always be matched to ensure they has not been tampered with, and to ascertain the debt to be paid. Again, it is obvious that tallies, like Sumerian IOUs, were a form of double-entry bookkeeping. And they likewise circulated as means of payment. Innes (1913) recounts how well-known medieval fairs, such as St. Giles in Winchester or Champagne and Brie in France, were primarily clearing houses, were merchants came to clear their tally stocks and stubs.

Tallies were used in ancient times, among other regions in the ancient Near East; they are mentioned in texts and a few have been preserved (Henkelman and Folmer 2016). Tallies in one form or another were also widespread throughout ancient and prehistoric Europe. For instance, copper pieces purposely broken like jigsaw puzzle pieces in analogy to stock and stub have been found in Italy, dating from between 2000 and 1000 BC (Wray 1998). Again, there is no evidence for the use of coins until centuries later: debt preceded money.

Graeber's (2012) fascinating history of debt shows how also in non-European societies, debts were central to social organization. Once African and Asian non-market societies came in contact with Europeans through trade, such traditional debt tokens often became means of payments, turning from debt into money. The conclusion is that credit cannot have evolved from token money, because credit chronologically preceded it. Historically, tax debts and trade debts were monetized as debt tokens became transferable and circulated as medium of payment, ultimately in the form of silver bullion, coins, notes, and electronic bits.[4] This suggests we should analyze debt structures, not their representations in clay tablets, wooden sticks, or coins (with or without silver).

In contemporary society, banks have replaced Babylonian temples and medieval European merchants as the institutions authorized to issue money. But banks still essentially do what was always done, and money is still a category of credit. As they grant loans, banks create new credit tokens (now electronic bits) in the form of bank deposits or 'liquid liabilities', which are transferable and widely accepted as means of payment. Just as debts are created at the point where a creditor–debtor relation starts (i.e. 'out of nothing'), so banks create money; 'out of nothing' – a fact which must appear mysterious when money is conceived as commodity. 'Banks actually create money when they lend it' (FRBD 2009). 'What they do when they make loans is to accept promissory notes in exchange for credits to the borrowers' transaction accounts. Loans (assets) and deposits (liabilities) both rise by the amount of the loan' (FRBC 1992: 3, 6). Earlier this year, the Bank of England issued a paper to explain that 'money today is a type of IOU'. The authors explain that '[t]he reality of how money is created today differs from the description found in some economics textbooks: rather than banks receiving deposits when households save and then lending them out, bank lending creates deposits' (McLeay *et al.* 2014).

This continuing reality of money emanating from the credit creation process is also borne out by modern theoretical and econometric research. Arestis and Sawyer (2006) discuss how credit money is endogenously created within the private sector, and how this in turn explains the effects of monetary policy better than other views of money which leave its credit nature out of account. Caporale and Howells (2001) use UK data to show with statistical causality tests in the context of a Vector Auto Regression framework that loans precede and 'cause' deposits. Banks extend loans, which give rise to bank deposits that are generally accepted as 'money'.

Why hammer away at this point – surely familiar to most of you – precisely at a 'silver' conference?[5] Because to say that money is a form of credit is to say that it emerges out of lending and borrowing relations. Two implications are that money relies on the level of trust and willingness to co-operate in those relations – which is widely acknowledged – but also that money is debt, and therefore financial expansion is debt expansion. Silver, or some commodity generally, cannot be the fundamental factor that influences money value or stability. Mayhew's point in this volume is precisely this. Silver may be one of many factors determining money values, among which interest rates, credit regulations, political stability, capital inflows, and asset prices may also be included. It is hard to see why silver or gold would merit a special place in this long list. Even in the classical Gold Standard era, from the 1870s to 1914, it was not the Gold Standard or gold supply and demand which ensured stability; it was trust and co-operation between central banks, as Eichengreen (1992) persuasively argues. When this co-operation failed in the interbellum Gold Standard, the Gold Standard failed.

To sum up, the Credit Theory of Money redirects our attention from the physical medium of credit, which is only the material token of the creditor–debtor relation, to that relation itself, the rules and laws that govern is, and the uses (interns of economic growth and stability) to which it is put. Especially, it stresses that money is debt[6].

Crises are caused by debt

Is it worrisome that money is issued as debt? Superficially, it does seem to be a dangerous thing.[7] Financial crises worth studying – that is, those that have a large impact on the real economy – are invariably debt crises. They result from the taking on of liabilities which turn out to be too large in relation to the income from which those liabilities must be served. For the latest crisis, there is abundant evidence that it was the growth in private debt which precipitated crisis. Lane and Milesi-Ferretti (2011) studied 50 countries over 1980–2012 and found that the cross-country incidence and severity of the 2008–2009 global recession is related to pre-crisis increases in the ratio of private credit to GDP. Giannone *et al.* (2011) find for 102 countries that policies that favor liberalization in credit markets reduce countries' resilience to the recent recession. Foos *et al.* (2010) study 16,000 banks across many countries over 1997–2005. They find that loan growth is significantly positively related to loan losses and negatively associated with bank profitability and solvency. And so on.

The run-up to a financial crisis is characterized by large amounts of money (often borrowed money) invested in assets which did not produce income, rather than investment in the productive, income-generating process which increases the GDP. This difference in the use of debt makes the difference between growth-sustaining debt growth and crisis-inducing debt growth. This distinction was made by Marx, Keynes, Schumpeter, and Minsky; I discuss this below and at length for Schumpeter in Bezemer (2014). In our time, Werner (e.g. 1997, 2005, 2012) has consistently made this distinction in his analysis.[8]

What is true for the 2007 crisis is true for other financial crises: they were preceded by, and arguably caused by, excessive growth in debt relative to income. The 2001 dot-com crisis was due to leveraged investments in tech stock. The 1997 Asian crisis was due to dollar lending in excess of domestic productive investment. So was the 1994 Tequila crisis, when after foreign lending had increased lending following Mexico's NAFTA entrance, and the 1980s Latin American debt crises precipitated by years of import-substitution program lending. The 1989 Japan land-market crisis was caused by excessive credit creation by Japan's banks, which ended up as mortgages inflating land prices. The 1987 Black Monday Crisis was a stock overinvestment bubble that burst. The 1986 US Savings and Loan crisis revolved around investment in loans which produced no income. The 1929 New York stock market crisis was triggered by trading stock 'on margin', i.e. leveraged. The Florida Real Estate Bubble of the 1920s was over-investment in land, not production. The British Railway Mania Bubble of the 1840s was a bubble in railway stocks, not in production. The South Sea Bubble in the 1710s was (1716–1720) due to investment in stocks thought to represent trade opportunities with South America, but which did not. The archetypal Dutch Tulip Mania of the 1630s was about investment in bulbs, not plant and machinery.

The list could easily be multiplied with many crises in smaller countries, such as Latvia in 2008, or Albania in 1997, or Sweden in 1992. I cannot possibly do justice to the differences in these crises; instead I want to draw attention to their common denominator. Money (which is debt), often leveraged again, is invested not to produce an income, but in the expectation of asset price gain, with the assets being American mortgages, tech stocks, Asian stocks, Mexican pesos, Japanese land, Wall Street stock, US thrift loans, Wall Street stock again, Florida land, Midlands and Northern England railway stock – anything, really. Often, the alleged 'real' productive asset (houses, land, railways, trade) was not even there. But even if it was, that is hardly the point. The point is that money is allocated, and debt created, to raise the prices of financial assets and property and to realize capital gains. Money is not created to increase and improve real-sector productive assets, producing more income. Debt rises, but income does not.

The disruptive impact of each of these crises can be traced to this essential feature. An asset is traded in the expectation of future price increase, i.e. it is speculated upon. This asset may be any good or ownership title. The difference between speculation and non-speculative trading is in the price elasticity of demand: negative for non-speculative goods, positive in speculative markets. Future transactions are pledged in the transaction; in other words, debt (future obligations) is taken on to buy the asset. This leverage determines the real-economy impact of speculation. Without it, the damage from a price collapse of the speculative good would be limited to lost past income. With it, the damage extends to future income.

Differentiating debt

If this was the whole story of debt, *Positive Money* and similar clubs would be justified in calling for a debt-free financial system. But there is another side. While all crises are caused by debt growth, not all debt growth leads to crisis. On the contrary, without debt and credit there would not even be an economy, or economic growth. Schumpeter wrote that 'the new combination of means of production and credit are the fundamental phenomena of economic development' (Schumpeter 1934: 74). For development to be realized, there must be additional liquidity advanced beyond the liquidity that circulates current output; in other words, there must be debt growth. Minsky (1963: 6) explained that '[i]t follows that over a period during which economic growth takes place, at least some sectors finance a part of their spending by emitting debt or selling assets'. Credit and debt, by creating new purchasing power, is indispensable for growth. But it may also cause crisis. So we must identify what sort of debt creates growth, and what debts tend to create crisis. Put bluntly, I will suggest that there is 'good debt' and 'bad debt'.

One way to do this is to return to the historical reality of money as debt. Once debt tokens are 'monetized' – that is, they circulate without direct link to a specific transaction between two parties – it is possible to create debt tokens without the accompanying transactions in goods and services. Since the growth of such liabilities is functionally separate from transactions of goods and services in the real economy, this debt may take on its own dynamic, growing out of proportion with the economy's ability to service debt.

Historically, the canonical example of this development is the second half of the seventeenth century when London's goldsmith-bankers formed a system of banking through mutual debt acceptance and inter-banker clearing, where promissory notes came to be used as paper money (e.g. Quinn 1997). But similar developments had also occurred in ancient societies, which already used monetized trade and tax debts as means of payments. Debt tended to grow faster than income. These economies therefore typically had in place social mechanisms to periodically clear the debt overhead, such as 'clean slate' or 'jubilee' debt cancellations in ancient Babylonian and Israelite societies respectively (for details, see Hudson and Van de Mieroop 2002).

Again, what was true in ancient societies for 'tally sticks' or IOUs or debt notes is in essence still true in ours. Only a minority share of newly created bank money is devoted to supporting transactions of goods and services. Most lending is in support of financial investment, that is, the creation of, and trade in, financial assets and instruments. Most of these assets are not generally accepted means of payment for goods and services, and so are not 'money'. Therefore all money is bank credit, but not all bank credit is money – most goes into financial and property investments.

This causes growth of debt relative to income. Each act of bank lending creates a liability to some customer (a debt payable to the bank) and the accompanying asset (the bank deposit, which is money). But the way in which credit is used determines whether, on a society-wide level, there will be growth of the debt-to-income ratio. If the loan is used for a self-amortizing investment in fixed capital formation, this creates value-added in the form of products and services that typically allows the debt to be paid off. If, on the contrary, the loan is 'invested' in the financial markets, this will push up the price of financial assets and create asset wealth for the owners. The assets may be traded many times by 'investors' who each took out a loan or drained liquidity from the real sector in order to finance the purchase, and each time the asset may increase in value – but the debt and/or drain from the real sector grows in parallel. It can only be repaid by withdrawing from the financial markets or from the real sector at least the liquidity equal to that created by the total of the loans.

This settles the debt, but also deflates the price of the financial assets to at most their original value.

This brief narrative in essence is the story of a crisis – an asset boom followed by a debt deflation. The two uses of credit broadly reflect, respectively, real-sector investment typical of commercial banking on one hand, and financial investment as done by, for instance, merchant banks and securities traders on the other. The important point is that in terms of liquidity growth, financial investment by itself is a zero-sum game. Financial markets can only grow sustainably by absorbing liquidity created in the real sector, which is based on self-amortizing loans. Alternatively, they can grow unsustainably by simultaneously diverting liquidity from the real sector and increasing indebtedness. This is unsustainable as it must, with axiomatic certainty, at some point end. Still, such (ultimately) unsustainable debt growth may be kept going over decades by expanding the stock of financial assets and instruments relative to the size of the economy. This has indeed been the general trend in industrialized countries, especially since the 1980s. We have shown that this increased financial fragility – that is, susceptibility to financial crisis (Grydaki and Bezemer 2013; Bezemer and Grydaki 2014).

The uses of credit

This helps to pin down what *sort* of debt helps growth, and what sort of debt causes crisis. Generically, the distinction is between debt that generates income and debt that generates capital gains. The difference may be difficult to observe in practice, but that should never be a reason to neglect its theoretical relevance. And fortunately, in our time the distinction has become particularly marked in practice, so that we can take this distinction to the statistics and construct empirical measures for it.

First, there is debt to nonfinancial business. An entrepreneur with a good idea but no money who borrows form a bank to build a factory increases the amount of debt in the economy. But he also increases the income generated in the economy. If the business plan is solid (and the bank should see to that), then the loan will generate income in the form of wages and profit and leave enough to repay the loan, as well as other costs. This is the good scenario: credit expands the economy. Debt rises, but so does income. The debt-to-income ratio need not rise. This is financially sustainable growth. This is real-sector, 'productive' debt.

The other scenario is where loans are taken out to be invested in existing assets, be they physical assets (such as already produced housing) or ownership titles or claims (such as stocks and bonds). In this case, the debt rises, but it is not paid to producers to produce, but to owners to part with whatever they own. Therefore, there is no income growth as a result of the debt. There may be collateral effects, such as new wallpaper in an existing house, but these effects are in the order of per cents of the debt growth. This is a far cry from the roughly one-on-one increase in debt and GDP which we observe for productive debt. This type of debt which is taken out to be invested in asset markets is 'unproductive' debt, in the Classical sense of not producing income.

This is not a new distinction. Marx, in Chapter 30 of *Capital* entitled 'Money-capital and real capital' already wrote of [real-sector] 'credit, whose volume grows with the growing volume of value of production', as different from 'the plethora of moneyed capital – a separate phenomenon alongside industrial production'. Likewise, Keynes wrote on the distinction between 'money in the financial circulations' as distinct from 'money in the industrial circulations' (1930: 217–218). James Tobin, in his 1984 Hirsch Memorial Lecture, said that 'we are throwing more and more of our resources, including the cream of our youth, into financial activities remote from the production of goods and services'. Minsky worried about how the 'money manager capitalism' that he saw emerging in the 1980s and 1990s undermined capitalism's viability by redirecting investment to financial, not real investments and capital formation (Minsky 2008 [1987]). Werner (1997) saw the principle at work in Japan and developed the same distinction for bank credit (Werner 2005, 2012). We must 'distinguish between different categories of credit, which perform different economic functions', as the LSE *The Future of Finance* report (LSE 2010: 16) urged. How to do that?

The functional differentiation of credit (Bezemer 2014) should distinguish between credit uses. If crises are caused by growth of debt in excess of income, then we should be looking for those types of debt which are not used for income generation – that is, not invested in productive capital goods (producer credit), or used to buy goods and services (consumer goods). What other types of debt are there? Werner (2005) argues that this should be any debt which is invested in assets other than capital goods, i.e. secured debt not extended to nonfinancial business. The two major categories into which this unproductive debt falls are mortgages to households and loans to financial firms. Both are invested in assets, while loans to non-bank financial business and consumer loans are invested in production and consumption. Can we observe this distinction in the statistical record? If we can, does it confirm that productive debt and income grow in tandem, while unproductive debt grows in excess of income? Yes and yes. In data for the last few decades, the ratio of productive debt to GDP (which is the sum of incomes) tends to be stable, while the ratio of asset-market debt to income tends to rise. Household mortgages are by far the largest part of asset-market debt.

Positive feedback: The link between debt for assets and crisis

Secured debt to financial business and to households not only increases the economy's debt-to-income levels, but it is also subject to a positive feedback between asset prices and debt levels – precisely because it is secured by collateral. This unhappy combination ensures that once debt-to-income levels and asset prices start rising in tandem, they will rise more. And yet more, to some point where debt levels relative to incomes are so high that lenders or borrowers, or both, start to doubt the sustainability of debts. Decreased appetite to take on debts will reduce debt growth, which in highly fragile asset markets is enough to send asset prices plunging. This invites a scramble for liquidity as borrowers try to pay down debt to below asset price levels. In the process, the real economy is sapped of spending power by saving and by debt service. A recession or depression results.

This scenario, which has once again become very familiar to us in recent years, implies that crisis and recession occur in those economies which have high levels of household mortgage debt. There is robust evidence that unproductive debt, above all mortgages, increases the risk of crisis and magnifies its real-sector recessionary impact. Büyükkarabacak and Valev (2010) study cross-country data for 1980–2005 and find that household credit expansion is a good predictor of banking crises, in contrast to enterprise credit. Jordà *et al.* (2014) study very long-run data, from 1870–2012, for 17 major economies. They find that mortgage-lending shares in all loans have increased sharply, as also shown in Figure 3.1, and that this increases the probability of banking crises as well as the output loss after a crisis. For similar findings, see IMF (2011, 2012).

In a recent working paper, we study credit booms in 37 economies over 1970–2012 (Bezemer and Zhang 2014). Credit booms are not all bad, but some lead to crisis. We ask which credit booms are going to lead to credit crisis, defined as a sharp contraction of the growth rate of credit. Figure 3.2 shows the one big difference between what we label 'good' booms, which may stimulate investment and innovation and unwind without damage, and 'bad' booms followed by credit contractions. This is that 'bad' booms are those booms in which the share of unproductive credit in GDP, above all mortgages, rises almost as much as much as does productive credit.

Conclusion

In this chapter, I have argued that money is a form of debt; that debt can be categorized as productive and unproductive debt; that the latter increases debt-to income ratios with positive feedback and therefore causes crisis; and that, while not the exclusive explanation for crisis, the rise of unproductive debt is always an element, and often *the* element, in understanding crisis. The current financial crisis did not start as a 'credit crisis'; it is a debt-to-income crisis, as I have argued since its start (Bezemer 2009).

One can think of a number of objections. Surely not all financial crises are debt crises. What about currency crises? Or maybe not all money is debt; consider bitcoins. Historically, it may be a bit hard to see that coins issued by kings and mints were forms of debt. What do we mean when we say that? And is this really new? Many have pointed to the dangers of debt before. Or perhaps bubbles can still be explained by fundamentals, not by debt growth, as Peter Garber (1990) argues. Again, does not the presence or absence of a gold standard, the capitalization of banks, perverse incentives implied in excessive bonuses, or for

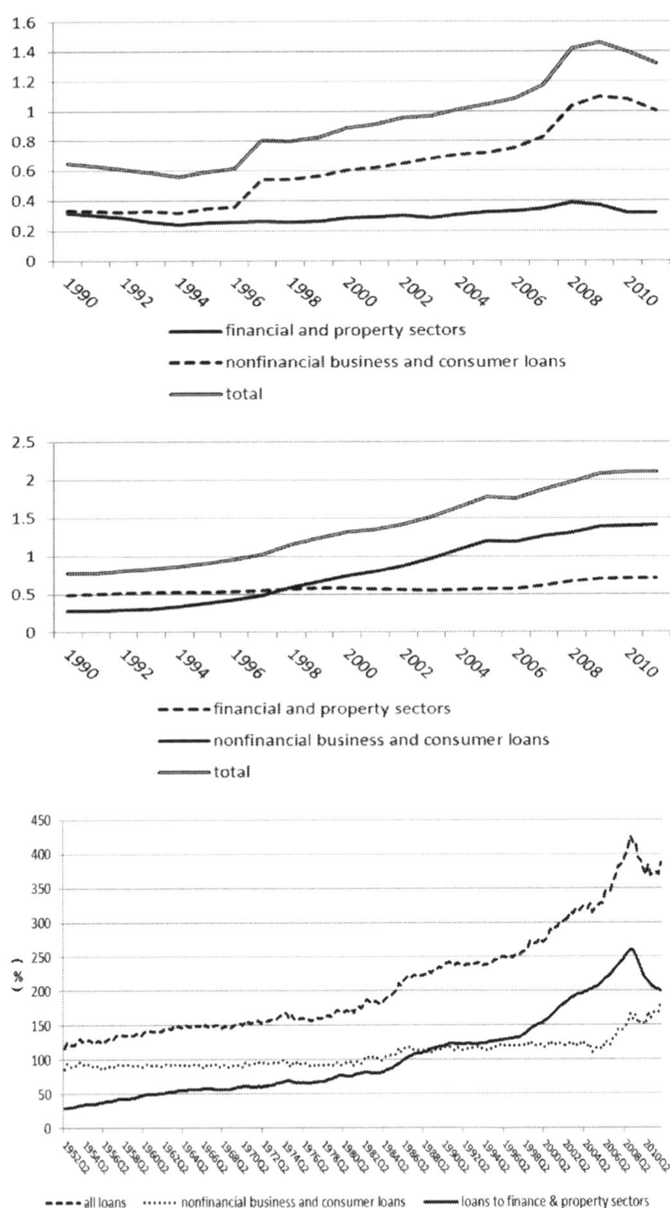

Figure 3.1 Bank loan stock by borrower category, as share of GDP for the UK (top panel) and the Netherlands (middle panel), 1990–2011. Loans by borrower category for the US, 1952–2012 (bottom panel).

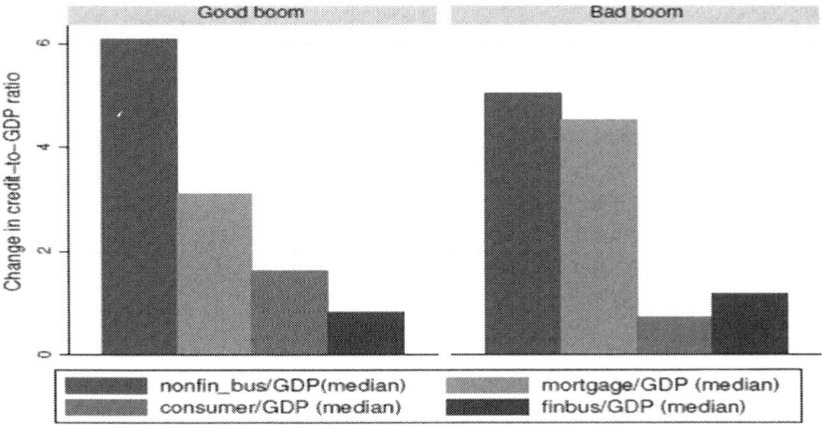

Figure 3.2 'Good' and 'bad' booms. In 'good' booms (not followed by credit growth contraction), asset-market debt rises moderately. Boom followed by busts ('bad' booms) see large increases in asset-market credit.

that matter the silver content of coins matter to financial crisis? Clearly, these and other issues must be addressed in future work.

Obviously, if this hypothesis is accepted, a policy implication is that the growth of unproductive debt should be restricted, though not eliminated. Mortgages, stocks, and derivatives have their uses, but when economies become over-leveraged to finance investment in assets and land, crisis risk increases. Research applications should also ask if the hypothesis is any good at explaining not just 'the' crisis, but past crises. I have briefly argued this above. But extending the hypothesis backwards in history in more solid fashion is work still waiting to be done.

Appendix 3.1

Some implications of the Credit Theory of Money for the study of money in history

The Credit Theory of Money raises questions with regard to the market study of money in history. Central to this approach is the idea that the study of financial and monetary history can be undertaken within a market paradigm, where money is viewed as a good with a price, subject to supply and demand pressures as all goods are. But if money is a form of debt, and debt used for goods and services transactions is subject to different dynamics than debt used for asset transactions, then how can 'money' be the subject of study, rather than different types of debt? A mortgage is not an entrepreneurial loan. The price and other attributes of each is governed by very different sets of factors; so is the impact on the economy of the quantity of each type of loan. This suggests that the idea of money demand is an overly aggregate concept: money is what money does. Goods-and-services shopping money (M2) is fungible with asset-market mortgage money, which have been made fungible with all kinds of derivatives. Lumping all this together was the cause of the breakdown of money demand functions in the 1980s, when money issued as unproductive debt started rising. To repeat that research program in financial and monetary history seems a bad idea.

There is a more fundamental problem which the debt nature of money poses for a market approach to money. If money is debt – that is, a claim on assets and goods and services, rather than a good itself – then how can it be sensibly studied as if it were a good? What are its supply and demand constraints? Surely the only reason for economists to want to study money as a good is because they can then apply demand-and-supply reasoning to it, with upward-sloping supply curves and downward-sloping demand curves and an equilibrium price. But how is this possible if the factors which motivate the slopes of demand and supply curves (saturation, rising production costs, elasticities) do not apply to money?

On the supply side, credit-money is 'produced' without inputs, and therefore its production is not limited by input scarcity. Money is created as a lender–borrower relation is forged; to call this 'production' is awkward at best. Relations appear, of course, 'out of nothing' and may vanish. It makes literally no sense to ask 'where they come from' as if they had to be produced from something that pre-exists. So it is with money. 'Where did all my money go?' was a common question a few years back. It was not a meaningful question. Money does not go anywhere and need not come from somewhere. Technically, banks can create money without limit. The 'production process' imposes no constraint, as is the case for goods. The only supply-side constraints are government regulations or bank balance sheets – quite a different situation from goods markets, which are supposed to work best without regulation and where balance sheets are thought to be irrelevant. Money supply is the growth of creditor–debtor relations. It is therefore, in principle, infinite as far as conventional demand and supply factors are concerned.

Money demand, as it turns out, also. Again, this is due to its credit nature. To supply credit is to supply purchasing power, and it is very hard to saturate the average person of purchasing power. Another way to see this is to note that all goods and services are settled in money, and therefore are subject to claims represented by money. But money itself is not subject to a claim by something else. Money is a claim on money. The receipt that savers used to receive for a bank deposit is itself a means of payment. In this, money is unique. One can pay with a claim on money, but one cannot ride on a claim to a horse, as Schumpeter (1954) wrote. Money 'fulfills its own function'. It is a claim on all present and future goods and services. People are not saturated of money as they are saturated from goods; they therefore want more rather than less money even if they already have a lot, which is not true for any good. The implication is that the demand for money is infinite. It follows that a supply-and-demand way of thinking about money is inappropriate, as it would be for the supply and demand of relations.

What goes for demand and supply, goes for price. Interest is supposedly the buying/selling price of money. (It is not; it is the rental price of money, as Gardiner, 2006 notes; cf. the critical remarks on the issue by Flynn, Chapter 2, this volume.) But if money is truly debt, and debt an institution with many attributes, only one of which is price, and used for many different purposes, then it is logically inconsistent that money quantities should respond precisely to interest rates. Indeed, they often do not. I do not know of empirical studies which show that lower interest rates cause larger money quantities to be demanded, as would be the case if money were a good. The reason must be that credit markets (that is, money supply/demand markets) are chronically rationed, as Stiglitz and Weiss (1981) have shown – and rationed markets are not price-clearing markets; indeed, one could question whether one can speak of markets at all, rather than some alternative allocation mechanism yet to be fully defined. Not every order is a market order, as Hayek (2014) pointed out.

With demand and supply infinite (as far as conventional demand and supply factors are concerned) and price disqualified as the equilibriating mechanism, it is hard to see how a market approach to the study of money can be salvaged. Of course, it is always possible to recast the actual determinants of debt growth and it uses – trust, regulations, institutions of many kinds – into the production-supply and demand-equilibrium framework. As *freakonomics*-type analysis demonstrates, anything can be made to fit that mould, if only one tries hard enough. And try we will. Although it is doubtful that this will produce new insights, the prize will be to have a framework where money can once again be studied as if it were a good, transacted on a (potentially competitive) market, with a market clearing price. Interest rates can then be correlated to quantities of debt tokens, be they in silver, clay, or wood. Perhaps some of these correlations will even be statistically significant.

In this respect, the market study of money is motivated by the same theoretical drive which supports the commodity money fable. The alternative is to study money as the institution it is, rather than as a good or even a commodity. Some of the chapters in this book show the potential of this approach.

Notes

1 Cf. Hudson (2004). For a discussion of money as commodity, see Chapter 2, Dennis O. Flynn, this volume, and Chapter 1, Introduction to this volume.

2 This section and the next draw heavily on my unpublished working paper 'Banks as social accountants: credit and crisis through an accounting lens', *Munich Personal RePEc Archive*, Paper no. 15766, June 2009, https://mpra.ub.uni-muenchen.de/15766/1/MPRA_paper_15766.pdf.

3 See the first of my 2013 four-part online lectures on 'Debt: The good, the bad and the ugly' entitled 'Debt, a great invention' at http://ineteconomics.org/institute-blog-0/dirk-bezemer-debt-good-bad-and-ugly. The Bank of England in 2014 adopted a variation on this explanation of the origin of money, in HYPERLINK "http://www.bankofengland.co.uk/publications/Documents/quarterlybulletin/2014/qb14q1prere-

leasemoneyintro.pdf" http://www.bankofengland.co.uk/publications/Documents/quarterlybulletin/2014/qb14q1prereleasemoneyintro.pdf.

4 An important dimension of debt-money is its dependence on authority. In pre-market societies, debt systems may have emerged from legal obligations of fines and punishment, and its value was upheld by authority rather than exchange (Wray 1998). This is the 'State Theory of Money', pioneered by Knapp (1924[1905]), which says that whatever the state determines to be legal tender and accepts in payment of taxes is therefore money. Theoretically, it is exceedingly implausible that individuals would have been able to coordinate on stable money values without central direction (Goodhart 1998). Political authorities did indeed uphold the value of debts and money in Europe, as Mayhew shows in Chapter 9, this volume.
5 There are important implications of the Credit Theory of Money for the study of money in history, particularly the market approach to studying money. They do not directly come into the argument I am making here, and I relegated them to Appendix 3.1.
6 Although not the thrust of my argument, another implication is that the study of silver in an attempt to better understand monetary systems is somewhat bemusing. The fact that silver and gold have been used as money in many cultures is no evidence at all of the special status of this material. In our part of the world, wood may have been just as prevalent, for all we know. But no one argues that people put special monetary trust in wood.
7 Which is why organizations such as Positive Money campaign for money with 100% cover by government reserves, or 'debt-free money'. In effect the proposal is to nationalize credit creation. If debt is what defines the nature of money, as I have argued, then debt-free money is akin to dry water. On the distinction between the credit theory of money and Positive Money proposals, see http://www.positivemoney.org/2013/04/dirk-bezemer-on-positive-money-a-response/.

References

Arestis, P. and Sawyer, M. (2008). 'A critical reconsideration of the foundations of monetary policy in the new consensus macroeconomics framework', *Cambridge Journal of Economics*, 32(5): 761–779.

Bezemer, D. (2009). 'This is not a credit crisis, it's a debt crisis', *Economic Affairs*, 29(3): 95–97.

Bezemer, D. (2011). 'The credit crisis and recession as a paradigm test', *Journal of Economic Issues*, 45(1): 1–18.

Bezemer, D. (2012). 'The economy as a complex system: The balance sheet dimension', *Advances in Complex Systems*, 15(5):1–22.

Bezemer, D. (2013). 'Big finance is a big problem', *Financial Times*, 2 November 2013.

Bezemer, D. (2014). 'Schumpeter might be right again: The functional differentiation of credit', *Journal of Evolutionary Economics*, 24(5): 935–950.

Bezemer, D. and Grydaki, M. (2014). 'Financial fragility in the great moderation', *Journal of Banking and Finance*, 49: 169–177.

Bezemer, D. and Zhang, L. (2014). 'From boom to bust in the credit cycle: The role of mortgage credit', *SOM Research Reports*, 14026-GEM.

Bezemer, D., Grydaki, M. and Zhang, L. (2014). 'Is financial development bad for growth?', *SOM Research Reports*, 14016-GEM.

Board (2009). *Guide to the Flow of Funds Accounts.* Washington DC: Board of Governors of the Federal Reserve System.

Büyükkarabacak, B. and Valev, N.T. 2010. 'The role of household and business credit in banking crises', *Journal of Banking & Finance*, 34(6): 1247–1256.

Domenico Giannone, D., Lenza, M. and Reichlin, L. (2011). 'Market freedom and the global recession', *IMF Economic Review*, 59(1): 111–135.

FRBC (1992). *Modern Money Mechanics*. Chicago, IL: Federal Reserve Bank of Chicago.

FRBD (2009). Federal Reserve Bank of Dallas website education section, at http://www.dallasfed.org/educate/everyday/ev9.html. Dallas, TX: Federal Reserve Bank of Dallas.

Garber, P. (1990). 'Famous first bubbles', *Journal of Economic Perspectives*, 4(2): 35–54.

Gardiner, G.W. (2004). 'The primacy of trade debts in the development of money', in Wray, L.R. (ed.) (2004): 128–72.

Gardiner, G.W. (2006). *The Evolution of Creditary Structures and Controls*. Houndmills, Basingstoke, Hampshire, UK: Palgrave McMillan.

Goodhart, C. (1998). 'The two concepts of money: Implications for the analysis of optimal currency areas', *European Journal of Political Economy*, 14(3): 407–432.

Graeber, D. (2011). *Debt: The first 5,000 Years*. New York: Melville House.

Grydaki, M. and Bezemer, D. (2013). 'The role of credit in the great moderation: A multivariate GARCH approach', *Journal of Banking and Finance*, 37(11): 4615–4626.

Hahn, F.H. (1965), 'On some problems of proving the existence of an equilibrium in a monetary economy', in Hahn, F.H. and Brechling, F.P.R. (eds.), *The Theory of Interest Rates*, London: Macmillan: 126–135.

Hayek, F. (2014 [1937–1975]). *The Market and Other Orders*. Series the Collected Works of F.A. Hayek, Bruce Caldwell (ed.). Chicago, IL: University of Chicago Press.

Henkelman, W.F.M. and Folmer, M.L. (2016). 'Your tally is full! On wooden credit records in and after the Achaemenid Empire', in Kleber, K. and Pirngruber, R. (eds.), *Silver, Money and Credit. A Tribute to Robartus J. van der Spek on the Occasion of his 65th Birthday on 18th September 2014*, Leiden, the Netherlands: Nederlands Instituut voor het Nabije Oosten: 133–239.

Hudson, M. (2004). 'The archeology of money: Debt versus barter theories of money's origin', in Wray, L.R. (2004): 99–127.

Hudson, M. and Van de Mieroop, M. (eds.) (2002). *Debt and Economic Renewal in the Ancient Near East*. Baltimore, MD: CDL Press.

IMF (2011). 'Global prospects and policies', *World Economic Outlook*. IMF (chapter 1): 1–69.

IMF (2012). 'Dealing with household debt', *World Economic Outlook*. IMF (Chapter 3): 89–124.

Ingham G.K. (2004). *The Nature of Money*. Cambridge, UK: Polity Press.

Jordà, Ò., Schularick, M. & Taylor, A.M. (2014). 'The great mortgaging: Housing finance, crises, and business cycles', *NBER Working Papers* 20501, National Bureau of Economic Research, Inc.

Keynes, J.M. (1930). *A Treatise on Money*. Reprinted as Keynes, J. (1978) in Johnson, E. and Moggridge, D. (eds.), *The Collected Writings of John Maynard Keynes*. London: Royal Economic Society.

Knapp, F. ([1924]1973). *The State Theory of Money*. Clifton, NY: Augustus M Kelley.

Lane, P.R. and Milesi-Ferretti, G.M. (2010). 'The cross-country incidence of the global crisis', *IMF Economic Review*, 59(1): 77–110

Marx, K. ([1887]1906). *The Capital* (first English-language edition). Chicago, IL: Charles H. Kerr and Co.

McLeay, M., Radia, A. and Thomas, R. (2014). 'Money creation in the modern economy', *Bank of England Quarterly Bulletin*, 2014(1): 1–14.

Minsky, H. (1963). 'Can "it" happen again?', in D. Carson (ed.), *Banking and Monetary Studies*, Homewood, IL: R.D. Irwin: 101–111.

Minsky, H. ([1986]2008). *Stabilizing an Unstable Economy*. New York: McGraw Hill.

Mitchell Innes, A. (1913). 'What is money?', *Banking Law Journal*, 30(5): 377–408, reprinted in Wray, L.R. (ed.). 2004: 14–49.

Mitchell Innes, A. (1914). 'The credit theory of money', *Banking Law Journal*, 31(2): 151–168, reprinted in Wray (ed.) (2004): 50–78.

Schumpeter, J. (1934). *The Theory of Economic Development*. Cambridge, MA: Harvard University Press.

Schumpeter, J. (1954). *History of Economic Analysis*. New York: Oxford University Press.

Stiglitz, J. and Weiss, A. (1981). 'Credit rationing in markets with imperfect information', *American Economic Review*, 71/3: 393–410.

Werner, R. (1997). 'Towards a new monetary paradigm: A quantity theorem of disaggregated credit, with evidence from Japan', *Kredit und Kapital*, 30(2): 276–309.

Werner, R. (2005). *New Paradigm in Macroeconomics: Solving the Riddle of Japanese Macroeconomic Performance*. Basingstoke, UK: Palgrave Macmillan.

Werner, R. (2012). 'Towards a new research programme on "banking and the economy" – implications of the quantity theory of credit for the prevention and resolution of banking and debt crises', *International Review of Financial Analysis*, 25: 94–105.

Wray, L.R. (1998). *Understanding Modern Money*. Cheltenham, UK: Edward Elgar.

Wray, L.R. (ed.) (2004). *Credit and State Theories of Money: The Contributions of Michael Innes*. Cheltenham, UK: Edward Elgar.

4 Deep monetization in Eurasia in the long run[1]

Jan Lucassen

Questions and concepts

This chapter introduces a comparative method to measure deep monetization levels (DMLs) across time and space. Originally based on a case study for the Netherlands (1200–1940), its results are tested here for several countries in Eurasia in roughly the same time span. Why study monetization, and in particular deep monetization? Monetization, i.e. the increase in the use of currencies as a means of exchange in a society may be regarded as the result of a demand for and supply of artefacts, such as coins and paper money. Monetary history is predominantly concerned with its supply side, and more especially with either the total sums involved (e.g. mass inflation) or with the big denominations: paper money, gold coins (the gold standard being one example), and large-denomination silver coins (with the flow of Spanish silver from the Americas).

Here I concentrate on the demand side, and more especially on the small denominations – fabricated, as a rule, from base metal. That is precisely the type of currency used by the common man, i.e. many more social actors are directly involved in the use of small change than in that of higher denominations. Therefore, this aspect of monetary history is interesting for scholars wishing to understand the role of social relations in determining demand, but also in understanding reactions to an inadequate supply of small change. As will be demonstrated, these social aspects of monetary history are particularly promising for the study of long-term trends in social and economic history across Eurasia. Similarities and differences across time and space point to converging and diverging overall trends.

A key role of currencies is to serve as a means of exchange, i.e. in return for goods or for services.[2] Means of exchange for goods are needed in different forms of trade; means of exchange for services are especially needed to pay labour. In this way, labour remuneration may be seen as the demand side and the production and distribution of currencies as the supply side. This function has a very long history: for over 2,500 years the remuneration of work and currencies – the means of exchange in which remuneration is often expressed – have been strongly interlinked in Eurasia. The relation between work and currencies therefore has a lot to tell us about both concepts.

The link between work, remuneration, and currencies is not straightforward. It is, however, important in a part of the world that saw markets develop long before our period, and in which tributary and self-sufficient reciprocal labour relations had already become insignificant early on.[3] In this world of 'commodified' labour, circulation of medium- and low-denomination currencies nearly always implies the remuneration of work, though remunerated work does not necessarily imply the circulation of currencies. The link between the two is weakest if currencies are primarily intended for large-scale or costly trade, or for the hoarding of large savings. In those cases, currencies consist of high-denomination coins – mostly gold or heavy silver pieces – and later on paper money, bills of exchange, and the like.[4]

There are three major situations in which work is not paid, or not paid in currencies.[5] First, we have the case of unfree and forced work. Of course, here, too, minimal remuneration is necessary in order to keep the worker alive, but it is done in kind, either provided directly by slave owners or grown by the slaves themselves on plots and in time slots allowed to them. This form of labour without wage is also encountered on estates worked by serfs, who grew their own food on small plots on the estate unless ordered to work without pay for their lord. Second, remuneration may be paid in kind instead of in currency. Live-in servants, who work in exchange for board and lodging (plus a token remuneration in money), are a well-known example. Soldiers and sailors also receive a substantial part of their remuneration in kind.[6] The Indian *jajmani* system should be mentioned here too. Here, craftsmen in the village community provide free services to local farmers in exchange for a share in the total harvest for their consumption. Third, and most common, unpaid work is found inside the household, in which notably women and children benefit from the income of its head, but perform all household chores for free.

To formulate it differently, apart from the relations mentioned – which pertain more to unfree than to free labour, and more to women and youngsters than to adult men – work in Eurasia was performed in exchange for currencies, directly in the case of independent producers (farmers, peasants, craftsmen, traders, peddlers, transporters, shopkeepers, and performers of services) or indirectly in the case of wage earners employed by them.

The debate on the social implications, especially on the advantages and disadvantages of a monetary economy for the common man in early modern Western Europe, has a long history. Some stress the negative effects of monetization for wage earners, others the more positive ones.[7] The optimists argue that increased 'dependency' on the market does not necessarily have only negative effects for the recipients of wages and other remuneration. As Samuel Johnson wrote to Boswell in 1777, money earnings had a liberating capacity, since those who lived off the land were also bound to it for lack of portable wealth. Wages paid in metal currencies, in contrast, supplied 'power of resistance and means of escape' from a feudal system.[8] This idea was fully developed by the German social scientist Georg Simmel (1858–1918) in his *Philosophie des*

Geldes, originally published in 1900.[9] At the same time, he realized very well that this freedom is relative:

> It is not the bond as such, but being bound to a particular individual master that represents the real antipode of freedom. [...] Only in most recent times has the scarcity of domestic servants in large cities occasionally provided the possibility of turning down a position for imponderable reasons. Both sides consider this a major step towards the independence of servants, even though the actual demands of the job are no less heavy than they previously were. [...] A formally similar development emerges for wage labourers in a money economy. In view of the harshness and coerced nature of labour, it seems as if the wage labourer is nothing but a disguised slave. [...] From the subjective aspect, however, the relationship to the individual employer has become much more loose compared with earlier forms of labour.[10]

Before this debate can be settled, we have to know more about actual monetization levels and the function of monetary exchange in daily life. If the remuneration of work is one side of the circulation of currencies, the spending of income is the other. Sums used in spending are smaller than sums received as remuneration for work. Farmers selling their seasonal harvests, who receive relatively large sums, will divide their spending over rent and the purchase of necessities to continue their businesses, as well as comestibles, clothing, and other goods that they do not produce themselves. All others – craftsmen and wage labourers – will spend most of their income on food and shelter and, if anything is left, on small luxuries.

We therefore should differentiate between sums received as remuneration for services (predominantly wages) and sums spent with these earnings. This brings us from medium-denomination coins most suitable for the payment of moderate sums at intervals of one, two, or a few weeks (the predominant frequency for the payment of wages, but also for advances that many craftsmen could not do without) to the coins used for weekly or daily purchases.[11] For these transactions, much smaller denominations are needed, both because of the amounts involved and because it is impossible for people always to pay with the exact money, thus creating a need for small change.

The degree of participation in a market economy is therefore reflected in the degree to which medium and small denominations are available for circulation. Because small denominations best reflect the frequency of exchanges in a society, they may be considered the most sensitive yardstick of commercialized human relations. To measure this across space and time, I recently proposed a formal definition of what scholars including Koen Verboven and Shailendra Bhandare have called 'deep monetization'. I take this to be 'a substantial stock of currencies per capita in circulation, consisting of denominations equalling the value of one hour or less of waged work'. The evidence presented in this and earlier articles suggests that 'substantial' may be roughly defined as 'a per capita stock equal to between five and ten times the prevailing hourly wage'.[12] In Figure 4.1, these definitions are recast in the style of a formula.

This approach provides a clear instrument to measure and compare monetization levels over time and space and to study the backgrounds to shifts. The application of this definition to different societies might provide an indication not only of levels of 'deep monetization', but also of shifts in labour relations at their root – shifts between remunerated and unremunerated work, between remuneration in kind and in currencies, and between frequencies of payment.[13]

The advantage of this approach is not only conceptual clarity as a precondition for historical comparisons, it also opens up methodological opportunities. Clearly, for societies with abundant records on mint output and circulation, links with social phenomena such as labour relations may be established immediately. For example, DMLs increase in tandem with proletarianization. However, for most parts of the world before, say, 1900, written data on output and circulation are lacking – even more so in the case of labour relations. On the other hand, archaeological evidence on coin circulation is much more universally available, because of the easy preservation of metals used for most types of currency. The academic discipline of numismatics is centuries old and has brought us not only catalogues of coins from all over the world, but also estimates of quantities produced and circulation patterns as mirrored in coin hoards and stray finds.[14] This enables us to formulate more specific questions about the demand side behind increasing or decreasing levels of deep monetization. Often we have only the DM approach to detect shifts in labour relations.

$$\mu = \frac{M^{SC}}{P} a \frac{T^{SC}}{V^{SC}}$$

Where

μ is the measure of monetization
M^{SC} is the total amount of available small change per capita
P is the price level of labour; we define this as the hourly wage
T^{SC} is a measure of the number of small-change transactions per capita
V^{SC} is a measure of the velocity of small change

Monetization is inversely proportional to the velocity of small change.

Here, small change is defined as all currency with a denomination equal to or less than an hourly wage.

Provisional definitions:
Low: $\mu < 1$
Medium: $1 \leq \mu < 5$
Deep: $5 \leq \mu < 10$
Extreme: $\mu \geq 10$ (indicating imbalances between small and insufficient medium-size denominations)

Note: I would like to thank Mathies Lucassen for his inspiration in designing this formula, which starts from Irving and Fisher's well-known formula MV=PT. See, more extensively, Lucassen 2014b: 78.

Figure 4.1 Deep monetization defined.

This chapter offers a provisional overview of the available evidence on the emergence of and fluctuations in deep monetization in some important parts of Eurasia. For practical reasons, the data presented here cover only the last millennium, even though the method could in principle be used from the very beginnings of coinage in Asia Minor, Northern India, and China some 2,500 years ago. After a brief discussion of historical theories about the demand for small change, we will move from the known to the unknown. An initial overview of DMLs at the end of the nineteenth century is possible for several countries in the North Atlantic. From this empirical basis it is possible to reconstruct long-term developments for a few Western-European countries and to find out when DM started there. The third step will be to apply these insights to long-term trends in India and China, which will enable us to conclude with some intra-Eurasian comparisons covering the last millennium.

Scholarly attempts to determine the demand for small change

The problem of how to match the demand and supply of specific denominations is as old as the phenomenon of coins itself. Strangely enough, guiding principles for small coin production appeared only very late and date back to the Enlightenment.[15] Possibly the earliest practical rule of thumb for the sufficient circulation of small change was formulated by Joseph von Sonnenfels (1732–1817), an Austrian member of the famous Illuminati. In the 1787 edition of his *Grundsätze der Polizey, Handlung und Finanzwissenschaft*, he remarked that mintmasters should not flood the market with small change, as this would drive up the price of large-denomination coins, thus endangering the collection of taxes. In a later edition[16] he defined what this implied in real terms: '*Scheidemünze*' (small change) should be produced 'so viel pro Kopf, wie die tägliche Consumtion der Arbeitenden Klasse beträgt' [in such quantities per capita as the amount of the daily consumption of the labouring class]. In a much-expanded edition in 1804, he formulated a fully fledged theory, which is important enough to warrant being quoted at length from the original (Figure 4.2).[17]

It is interesting to see that here Sonnenfels established the crucial link between monetization and wage payments that I derived from historical developments in the Low Countries (I was not aware of his study at that time). Since the mid-nineteenth century, comparative statistics of coin circulation in different countries have become increasingly available, in particular within the framework of monetary unions such as the Vienna Monetary Treaty of 1857 and the Latin Monetary Union of 1865, as well as of the 1873 German Coinage Act and international monetary conferences, a direct successor to the Latin Monetary Union, which first convened in Paris in 1867. Existing scholarly observations were now turned into official national legislation, stipulating how many coins of different metals and denominations were to be circulated.

'[...] die Münzkammern selbst müssen der Prägung der Scheidemünze Gränzen [...] in einem Verhältnisse gegen die allgemeine kreislaufende Masse zu erhalten wissen. Es ist schwer dieses Verhältniss eigentlich anzugeben. Gemeiniglich wird von der geldmasse eines States der zwanzigste Theil, oder 5% angenommen, welches zu unbestimmt scheint, da hier nicht vorzüglich das Verhältniss zu der allgemeinen Geldmasse, sondern das Bedürfniss der Ausgleichung, das ist, der kleinen Ausgaben in Anschlag kommen muss. Es ist wenigstens eine der Wahrscheinlichkeit am nächsten kommende Muthmassung, dass die Menge der Scheidemünze, auf das höchste angeschlagen, gleich seyn müsse, der Summe, wodurch die tägliche Verzehrung der arbeitenden Klasse bedeckt ist: da diese Klasse von dem täglichen Handlohne zu leben, mithin auch in Scheidemünze einzukaufen gewohnt ist.	'The mint authorities must themselves decide upon the fractions of small change in a proper proportion to the general coin production. It is, however, difficult to determine this proportion. Usually, one twentieth part or 5 per cent of the total sum of coins in circulation is taken. But this seems to be too vague as in this case not the relation to the total sum in circulation matters, but rather the demand, and in particular the demand for means of exchange needed for small expenses. It is at least rather plausible that the amount of small change, estimated at most, must be equal to the sum that covers the daily expense of the labouring class. Because this class is used to living on daily wages, it is consequently used to paying with small change.
In den vorigen Auflagen war das beyspiel dieser Berechnung auf folgende Art angegeben. Wenn bey einer Bevölkerung von 15 Millionen die Arbeitende Klasse 7 Millionen wären, und die tägliche Verzehrung eines Kopfes zu 4 Kreutzer, angeschlagen wird, sollte die umlaufende Scheidemünze 466,669 Gulden, ungefähreine halbe Million betragen. Eine genauere Vervolgung der täglichen Auslage hat mich überführet, dass diese Summe viel zu klein seyn würde. Es muss nämlich auf den Vorrath, den gleichwohl jede Familie, die wochenweise ihren Lohn erhält, durch einige Tagen liegen haben muss, auch auf die Zeit gedacht werden, durch welche die Scheidemünze umzulaufen hat, um wieder in die Hände der arbeitenden Klasse zu kehren: und nach diesem Anschlage scheint die Masse der Scheidemünze nicht zu stark angeschlagen: Dass sie seyn müsse gleich dem ganzen Wochenlohne der arbeitenden Volksklasse: das wäre bey 7 Millionen, die tägliche Erwerbung eines Kopfes in den andern zu 10 Kreuzer berechnet 7 Millionen.'	In the last edition I used the following example for this calculation. If in a total population of 15 million souls the labouring class amounts to 7 million, and if the daily spending per person is 4 *Kreuzer*, then the sum of all small change in circulation would have to be 466,669 *Gulden*. A more precise analysis of daily expenses has convinced me now that such a sum would be much too small. Therefore, the sum that remains for a few days with a family that receives its wages weekly should therefore also be taken into account, as well as the time this takes for the small change to circulate before it returns into the hands of the labouring class. And according to this consideration the amount of small change seems not to be assessed too high in the following way. It should be equal to the full weekly wages of the labouring class, which means for 7 million people with an average per capita daily income of 10 *Kreuzer* 7 million [*Gulden*].'

Figure 4.2 Sonnenfels's rule for estimating the actual demand for small change (1804).

An overall picture of monetization at the end of the nineteenth century

Enough data on deep monetization for the different parts of Europe, some adjacent countries, and the USA at about the same point in time are available only from the 1880s onwards. As a result of much trial and error by mintmasters over the preceding centuries and much thinking since the Enlightenment, the working of supply and demand in the case of small currencies had resulted in scholarly works and concomitant statistics. These earliest large-scale statistical overviews of coin circulation in different countries enable us to conduct comparative research into deep monetization.

A pioneer in this field was the Austrian monetary statistician Ottomar Haupt (1839–98).[18] He produced a comparative table of coin circulation, differentiating between *Monnaie d'appoint* (small change, including small silver coins) and *Monnaie de billon* (base metal).[19] Unfortunately, this distinction cannot be translated immediately into deep monetization, as in some countries hourly wages equal only base metal (copper, bronze, nickel, copper–nickel, billon) coins, whereas in other countries small silver coins also qualify. In the UK, for example, hourly wages of 7.2 pence in 1885 comprised the silver threepence and sixpence coins. However, starting from Haupt's detailed data, it is possible to reconstruct deep monetization levels (DMLs) for several dozen countries, including my original Dutch case (see Figure 4.3).

This overview is of course very preliminary and needs a lot of fine-tuning (including better wage data for the same categories of workers), but some observations can be made. Most Western-European countries show DMLs varying between 8 and 10. Portugal, Spain, Italy, and Austria-Hungary probably also belong to this group. For the Iberian Peninsula, figures have to be reassessed by deducting exports of coins to the colonies, for which I have been unable to find data. Austria-Hungary and Italy (as well as Serbia) are examples of countries in which recent coin reforms had temporarily caused the market (or at least the vaults of the mint houses) to be overstocked with small denominations. All other countries deviate from this 'main Western-European pattern'. They will be discussed in four clusters: Norway/Sweden, the Balkans with the Near East, the United Kingdom, and Russia with the USA.

Norway and Sweden contrast interestingly with the third Scandinavian country in this set, Denmark. Not only was Denmark much more prosperous than its northern neighbours, it had much higher rates of urbanization and concomitant occupational differentiation and agricultural specialization.[20] This situation apparently required many more transactions in Denmark than in Norway and Sweden. This is eloquently illustrated in the following description of Norway's rural population (85 per cent of the total population) by the British Consul–General Crow, written in Christiania (Oslo) and dated 9 November 1870.[21] He distinguishes three 'classes' among them: the seafaring peasantry along the coast, the 'Bonde', and the 'Field Bonde' or mountain peasant. The second group is the most important:

> The Bonde or real peasant is generally the owner of the land he farms. This class may be considered as the kernel of the nation. The property of the Bonde is not sufficiently large to exempt him from work, but large enough to afford him and his household establishment ample support. He farms in the majority of cases, *not so much to raise produce for sale* as to grow provisions and everything necessary for spinning wearing-apparel.

The equally low figures for the Balkans (Serbia's DML was temporarily so high because of oversupply) and the Middle East point to similarly low demand for small change as that in Norway and Sweden, even if other indicators of economic development (such as the high literacy rates in Scandinavia) differed substantially. It is, however, possible that this cross section shows a more primitive

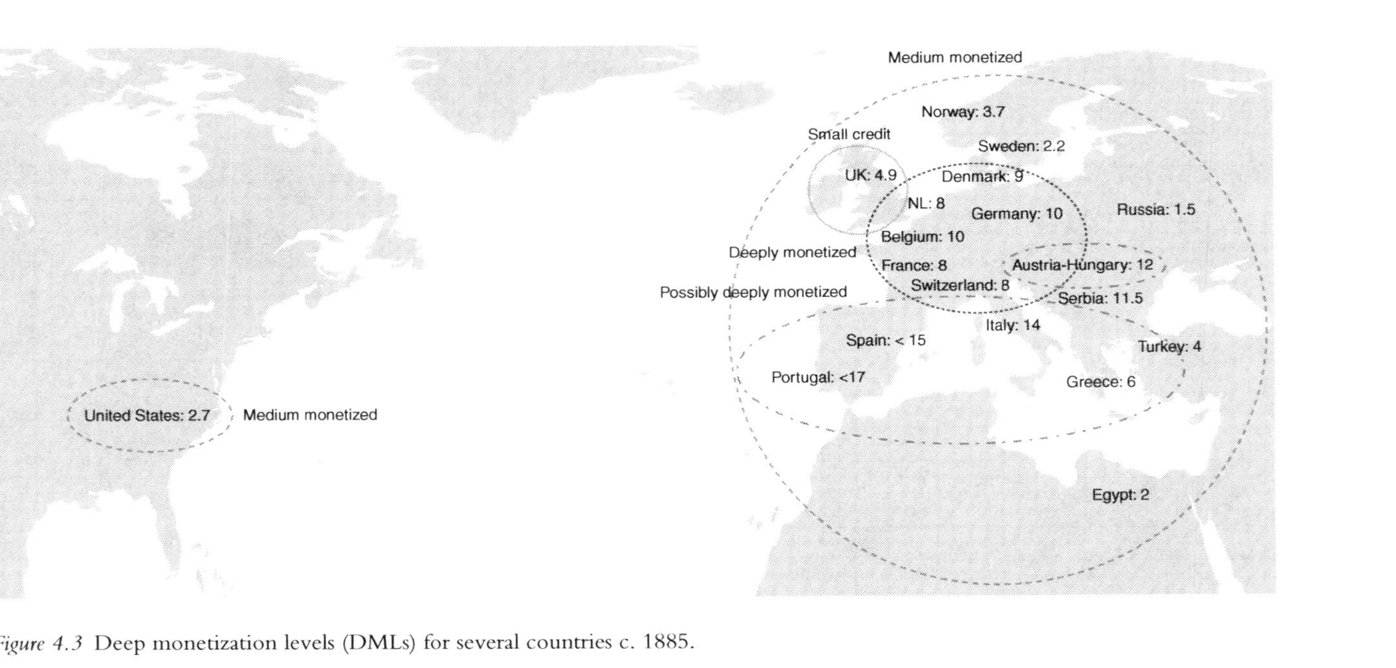

Figure 4.3 Deep monetization levels (DMLs) for several countries c. 1885.

situation than in the preceding decades. According to Michael Palairet, in the period 1878–1914 political freedom in the Balkans went hand in hand with economic decline.[22]

The comparatively low DML of Britain, midway between Greece and Turkey, cries out for an explanation (see the next section), one perhaps being the wide circulation of counterfeits and tokens.[23]

Finally, the low DMLs for the USA and especially for Russia seem to echo previous periods of widespread use of unfree labour, maintained without paying wages. These may be among the implications of what Kolchin has referred to as the commonalities of the post-emancipation USA and Russia: 'there was a common legacy of forced labor that Russia shared with the United States and with all other former slave societies as well. New forms of dependency that provided the ex-bondsman with at best semi-freedom became the rule.'[24]

As early as the eighteenth century, variations in unfree labour had an effect on the circulation of small change in Russia. Productive work by serfs was the norm, and only noblemen could own and employ them. The emerging non-noble industrialists who needed labourers were not allowed to own serfs. Legislation was therefore introduced to permit, under certain conditions, bourgeois entrepreneurs to hire serfs as paid labourers. Because of resistance by the nobility, the scope to actually do so fluctuated heavily and laws were as easily promulgated as repealed. These fluctuations in legislation were significant enough to influence markedly the demand for copper coins: the higher the number of serfs entering the paid labour market, the higher the production of copper coin, and vice versa. Furthermore, non-noble entrepreneurs are known to have asked the state authorities to provide more copper coin so that they could pay out wages.[25]

DMLs in Western Europe in the long run: England, the Low Countries, and France

How old are the DMLs demonstrated at the end of the nineteenth century? Because of the ready availability of sources, Western Europe is a good starting point for the study of long-term shifts in DMLs, particularly in England, the Low Countries, and France.

England[26]

With the exception of China, England has the longest and most detailed series of coinage statistics and estimates in the world, starting in the late eleventh century. Production figures (Table 4.1) suggest that sometime in the course of the twelfth century the value of pennies per capita increased four to five times, that between 1250 and 1280 it doubled again, and that the same might have happened in the first half of the fourteenth century, just before the Black Death, after which levels returned to those of 50 years before.

Table 4.1 Monetization and deep monetization levels (DMLs) in England, thirteenth to nineteenth centuries

Year	*Population (England and Wales unless otherwise stated), in millions*	*Coin: silver pennies per head*	*Volume of DM fractions in pounds sterling x 1000*	*Minted denominations below hourly wage*	*Money wage rate of building craftsman in Southern England, pence per hour*	*'Deep monetization' (DM)*		
						DM fractions		*DML*
						in pennies x million	*in pennies per head*	
1087	1.5–2.25	4–6						
1180	2.25–2.75	6.1–20.3						
1205	3–3.5	17.1–20						
1247	4–4.5	22.7–27.0						
1279	4.5–4.75	25.3–32.0			0.3			
1282	4.5–4.75	40.4–48.0	29	1/4d	0.3	7	1.5	5
1290	4.5–5.5	48	39	1/4d	0.3	9	1.8	6
1299	4.5–5.5	48.0–74.7	39	1/4d	0.3	9	1.8	6
1310	4.5–5.5	65.5–101.3	73	1/4d	0.4	17	3.4	8.5
			75	1/4d–1/2d		18	3.6	9
1319	4.5–5.5	82.9–122.6	93	1/4d	0.4	22	4.4	11
			95	1/4d–1/2d		23	4.6	11.5
1331	4.5–5.5	72.0–106.6	88	1/4d	0.4	21	4.2	10.5
			90	1/4d–1/2d		22	4.4	11
1351	3.5–4	56	40	1/4d	0.4	10	2.7	6.7
			100	1/4d–1/2d		24	6.4	16
1422		13	??	1/4d–1/2d	0.6	?	?	?
1470		29–33.6	??	1/4d–1/2d	0.6	?	?	?
1550–1575	3.5		??	1/4d–1d	1	?	?	?
1650–1700	4.9		??	1/4d–1/2d	1.8	?	?	?
1720	6 GB		162	1/4d–1/2d	2.2	39	6.5	3.0
1857	28 UK		1264	1/4d–4d	5.4	303	10.8	2
			2961	1/4d–6d		711	25.4	4.7
1885	36 UK		5282	1/4d–6d	7.2	1268	35.2	4.9

The question is what these three spectacular jumps mean in terms of deep monetization. This stage had certainly not yet been reached by the time of the Domesday Book, let alone before.[27] But what about the situation in *c.* 1200, 1250, or 1300, when, say, 20, 40, and 80 pennies in silver coin were available per capita? Bolton is clear:

> By the mid-thirteenth century the concentrated money supply in England had probably reached the critical point that would allow coins to be used as the normal medium or agent of exchange. They could be used to buy and sell goods, to pay wages and other dues that peasants owed to lords. They could be collected as taxes and offered or demanded in lieu of feudal military service, and kings could now pay their much larger armies with coins.[28]

To understand how England had reached the situation described by Bolton, I will try to reconstruct medieval levels of deep monetization (DML) more precisely, based on the composition of the volume of specific fractions of silver currency in relation to wage levels. I use two methods: first denominations minted, and second archaeological evidence of coin usage. The story of silver coins is simple up to 1279, when only pennies were minted. In that year Edward I also started to strike farthings (quarter pennies), halfpennies, and groats (four pence). The half-groat was added in 1351, the shilling around 1489, and larger-denomination silver pieces from Henry VIII onwards. At the lower end of the scale, apart from debasements, no innovations were made until the introduction of the sixpence in 1550, and the threepence, three-halfpence, and three-farthing coin in 1561. From Charles I onwards, the smallest denominations were no longer made of silver. With a few minor exceptions, denominations smaller than farthings have never been minted in England.[29]

For a long time the farthing was the only fraction meeting the DML criteria (i.e. coins equal to hourly wage or less). From *c.* 1350 onwards, halfpennies have to be included for our purpose, as the wage hike after the Black Death pushed carpenters' wages above four pence per day, nearly a halfpenny per hour. From the 1550s, pennies, too, have to be taken into account, when daily wages for builders exceeded eight pence.[30] Although wage levels kept rising, for the period *c.* 1650–1800 we need only consider the circulation of farthings and halfpennies if we are interested in DMLs, as, curiously enough, the coinage of all silver denominations less than the sixpence came to a complete halt under Charles II. It was not until 150 years later, under William IV, that threepences and groats (four pence) were once again minted.

With only very minor gaps, production figures for the halfpenny and farthing are available for the period 1279–1351. These enable us to follow in detail the deep monetization process in England. Actual circulation at certain dates has been reconstructed by Martin Allen. The two series differ because he takes into account both wastage and the production by mints for which no production figures are available, and foreign coins circulating in England.

His 'total currency' figures are therefore to be preferred, except for the last sub-period, for which his figures seem to be too low given previous output figures. For those years, total circulation of halfpennies and farthings should be raised to *c.* 100,000 pounds.[31] By applying the proportionate output figures, we can roughly reconstruct separately the circulation of farthings and halfpennies from the late-thirteenth to the mid-fourteenth century (Table 4.2).

Now we see that the initiative to start coining farthings in 1279 not only raised the total output of silver coins substantially, but also enabled circulation levels to reach five small coins per capita, in this case farthings – a denomination lower than an hourly wage of 0.3d.

English archaeology can help us be more precise about the growing usage of small fractions than is possible on the basis of available production statistics. This is crucial because it turns out that there was a widespread custom of cutting pennies into halves and quarters before actual halfpennies and farthings were produced by the mints. This happened on a massive scale, as Richard Kelleher has demonstrated. Based on national data, he has been able to estimate the proportions of the three fractions in daily use (Table 4.3).

Table 4.2 Mint output and small currency in circulation, England (in pounds sterling), 1279–1351

	Pounds sterling x 1000						
	Known cumulative output by English mints			*Total currency in circulation*			
	½d.	*farthings*	*Total*		*½d.*	*farthings*	*total*
1279-1281	5.106	13.815	18.921	1282	11	29	40
1279-1290	6.409	14.837	21.246	1290	16	39	55
1279-1299	7.361	20.205	27.566	1299	1	39	40
1279-1310	8.071	32.237	40.308	1310	2	73	75
1279-1319	8.636	36.131	44.767	1319	2	93	95
1279-1331	8.698	39.146	47.844	1331	2	88	90
1279-1351	70.979	47.996	118.975	1351	60	40	100

Note: Output after Allen 2012, Table C2; total currency after Allen 2001: 603 (adjusted for 1351).

Table 4.3 Full and fractional pennies, 1158–1279, as found in England

	Proportions of number of coins found		
	Pennies	*cut halves*	*cut quarters*
1158–1180	60	30	10
1180–1247	50	40	10
1247–1279	38	45	7

Source: Kelleher 2013: 104–8.

Applied to production figures (Table 4.1), this implies that, in the periods given, 4.2%, 5.0%, and 4.6% respectively of all pennies had been cut into farthings. What this means is that in 1180 a maximum of one farthing per capita was circulating; in 1205 between 3.5 and 4 farthings; in 1247 between 4 and 5.4; and in 1279 slightly more, between 4.5 and 5.9 farthings. In relation to a supposed hourly wage of 0.3 pennies, this yields DMLs of less than 1 in 1180, about 3 in 1205, between 3.3 and 4.5 in 1247, and between 3.7 and 5.8 in 1279.

Combining output and archaeological evidence, we may conclude that – in accordance with Bolton – England and Wales may be said to have reached the stage of deep monetization already by the mid-thirteenth century. And this level was to rise until the days of the Black Death. For the cross section 1351, taking into account the circulation of halfpennies and farthings together, the DML was actually 16. This is *stricto sensu* too favourable, as the hourly wages (4d. per day for a building craftsman in Southern England) were less than a halfpenny, but substantially higher than a farthing.[32]

More astonishing, however, is the subsequent fall in this level. Although we had to wait for centuries before new solid DML data became available, it is very likely that DMLs must have fallen soon after the disastrous mid-fourteenth century, as by the early fifteenth century the total silver output of the mint was just ten per cent of what it had been a hundred years before.[33] In the early eighteenth century, after the London Mint had been producing copper farthings and halfpennies for decades, the DML was three, the same level as three centuries earlier, and no substantial change was to occur until the end of the nineteenth century,[34] assuming we consider only those coins officially minted. Because of the scarcity of small change, a number of private initiatives were taken, sometimes with official sanction, sometimes not – in practice nonetheless condoned by the authorities, which made no effort to prosecute illegal producers and distributors.

Occasionally, the government allowed private individuals to provide small change, which helped cover the shortfall, at least between the early sixteenth and early nineteenth centuries. In 1613, James I authorized Lord Harrington to issue copper farthing tokens, and Harrington and his successors continued to do so until 1644, when issuance ceased by order of Parliament. As demand did not abate, in many towns this initiative was continued by private traders, who, between 1648 and 1672, produced enormous amounts of local farthings, halfpennies, and some pennies. In the mid-eighteenth century, counterfeit halfpennies performed the same role, doubling circulation in the process.[35] And between 1787 and 1813 local tradesmen, alongside large firms like Boulton, resumed the practice of issuing private tokens, predominantly halfpennies. To demonstrate the need for this private small change, it is enough to know that even these tokens were counterfeited, though less often so than the regal halfpennies.[36] For the general public, this did not matter.

All in all, between 1613 and 1813 and sometime later, England's DML may have been nearer five than three if we include small change of all sorts. When compared with the situation before the Black Death, that figure is still low for a well-developed country on the verge of becoming the first industrial nation, but it was less disastrous than official mint output figures suggest. During the nineteenth century this DML was maintained by the government at around five, apparently enough, according to general opinion, as no major complaints of a structural lack of small change were heard.[37] When the Chancellor of the Exchequer, William Gladstone, reported in Parliament on 4 August 1859 about the actual number of copper coins circulating (see Table 4.1) and their poor condition, proposing to introduce new bronze coins instead, the debate was very brief. Nobody complained about the numbers circulating. Instead, the few members participating in the debate were concerned that the new bronzes might be the first step on the path to the much-feared decimal system in use on the continent.[38]

Since the late Middle Ages, England (and later the United Kingdom, including Ireland after 1820), when it ceased to mint its own coins, had for many centuries apparently gotten accustomed to much lower DMLs than the continent. We can question the wage levels used by most historians, consider the effects of clipping in the seventeenth and eighteenth centuries (reducing the value of small silver coins by cutting their edges), and more detailed mint statistics for specific denominations might be published. However, it seems unlikely our conclusion will be affected substantially.[39] How did the British cope with this situation? Let us turn to the demand side, in particular to the development of wage labour.

Before the Black Death, production figures for low-denomination coins seem to reflect demand among wage labourers for precisely these means of exchange. This is demonstrated by the introduction of farthings and half-pennies in 1279, which obviated the need for the much-practised cutting of pennies, followed by halfpenny production outstripping that of the farthing in the 1330s. At that time, fields owned by the Westminster Abbey manor of Hardwicke in Gloucestershire could not be hoed because of a shortage of halfpennies to pay the labourers.[40] Chris Dyer tells us that in the fourteenth century,

> The proportion of people who obtained most of their living from wage work must have exceeded one third over the whole country, rising to two-thirds in parts of the east. There were concentrations of wage-earners in large towns; in York, for example, 32 per cent of the contributors to the poll tax were called servants.[41]

Pennies were needed to pay out the workers, who needed fractions to buy their necessaries at markets and shops. This social and geographical pattern is corroborated again by archaeology. Kelleher shows that the frequent use of cut farthings started at the London waterfront (the Vintry) as early as 1100, spreading first to other towns and especially to rural eastern England, then to the west-central region soon after 1200, and finally to the southwest and the northwest of the country.[42] The situation changed dramatically after 1350. By comparing the much larger small fraction output of Scotland in the late Middle Ages – which was more in step with general continental practice – with England, Nicholas Mayhew thinks England was exceptional:

> Mint tradition in England argued strongly against the production of copper, regardless of the needs of society, and the Scottish experience of black money was particularly negative. Mint contracts consistently failed to provide moneyers with an incentive to spend the extra time and effort necessary to produce adequate supplies of small change. Equally pressure on the mint to yield a royal profit may have pushed consideration of the needs of the economy into second place.[43]

This particular institutional set-up, leading to a serious under-supply of small change, was to last with minor ups and downs for more than four centuries. In 1696, the following complaint about the lack of coins was made from Ipswich:

> No trade is managed but by trust. Our tenants can pay no rent. Our corn factors can pay nothing for what they have had and will trade no more, so that all is at a stand. And the people are discontented to the utmost; many self murders happen in small families for want, and all things look very bleak, and should the least accident put the mob in motion no man can tell where it would end.[44]

In 1672, copper halfpennies and farthings were introduced by the Royal Mint, and the great silver recoinage of 1696–7 remedied some of these complaints. However, this did not change the situation much. This replacement of the smallest silver coins by copper did not take place until some 150–200 years after most of the continent, although the proportion of wage labourers in England was already high and had not diminished; indeed, it had actually risen. In 1688, Gregory King estimated that 47 per cent of the population depended on wages. This figure had risen to 60 per cent by the beginning of the nineteenth century.[45]

Many solutions were found for this lack of official and less-official coins, in particular the lack of small change. Group pay was one of these, although a very imperfect one.[46] Payments in kind were another alternative of course, but – contrary to what is sometimes believed – certainly not one preferred by employers. As the accounts of Robert Loder, a large farmer, around 1600 demonstrate, he paid his servants about 10 pounds 5 shillings a year in food and drink and only 3 pounds 15 shillings and 6 pence in cash. But, Muldrew explains, he 'constantly complained that it would be cheaper to keep fewer "unruly" servants and instead rely on wage labourers, and as a result in 1612 he hired his servants at board wages.'[47]

Craig Muldrew's most important contribution to the debate is his emphasis on the most common solution, i.e. the extension of small-scale local credit instead of cash payments. That was Britain's basic answer to an endemic lack of small change. This credit could take different forms: wages paid in arrears for weeks, months, or more (i.e. credit provided by wage labourers to their employers), or the concomitant shopkeepers who got their bills paid too late (i.e. credit provided by shopkeepers to wage labourers). This might lead to direct contact between the employer and shopkeeper, circumventing the labourer and leaving him totally dependent on third parties.[48]

To sum up, as early as the mid-thirteenth century England was a deeply monetized country, possibly the first in Europe. However, after the Black Death its DML fell quickly, recovering only several centuries later to the same level, though not higher. That was exceptional in the European context for two reasons. On the supply side because of the failure of the state to produce enough small change, allowing private initiative to fill the gap in the period between the early seventeenth and the early nineteenth century; on the demand side because this situation, combined with the growing proportion of wage labourers, led to new practices of extending credit to poor people. This practice was apparently so successful that Britain's DML continued to oscillate at around five while other developed neighbouring countries showed levels twice as high. If this is a basic difference between Britain and the continent, its implications for labour relations and social relations in general deserve more scholarly attention.

The Low Countries[49]

As in England, after the demise of the highly monetized Roman Empire, the feudal society of the early Middle Ages was typically redistributive, at a rather low level of intensity. Markets were non-existent or unimportant for the great majority of the population, few cities were left, and wage labour was inconsequential. A new round of monetization began with the emergence of towns in the southern Low Countries around 1100, followed by the north a century later. One single denomination was coined, the silver *denarius* or penny. Somewhat later than in England, around 1300 a multi-fractional system matured with the introduction of various silver denominations of two-and-a-half and eight *penningen*, greatly facilitating payments.[50] From the mid-fourteenth century, but not earlier, there appears to be a certain correlation between, on the one hand, the denomination coined most frequently over a longer period and, on the other, the level of the daily wage. This correlation suggests that the demand side preferred a currency equivalent to four times (*c.* 1350–1450) and later once or twice a wage earner's full daily wage. From the fifteenth century on, this comes down to once for the worst-paid and twice for the better-paid wage earner.[51] Although it is still difficult to reconstruct per capita circulation for the Burgundian Netherlands – we have production figures for certain provinces only, and population figures are very uncertain – this type of situation, in which production patterns follow wage levels, strongly suggests that a situation of medium monetization began to emerge in the Low Countries from about 1350. It also indicates an important shift to wage labour, as demonstrated by Bas van Bavel,[52] and to a custom of independent producers receiving advances from merchants or customers at the same rate as labourers received their wages.

Does it also represent a situation of deep monetization? This is still open to debate, but by 1550 the Low Countries were surely deeply monetized, as Table 4.4 suggests.

This might have applied to the more advanced parts of the Low Countries already at the end of the fifteenth century, as evidenced by the massive imports of Scottish black money into the woollen industry in parts of Flanders and the Zeeland Delta between 1484 and 1505, where they met the need for small change,[53] and by the production of tiny (the lowest denomination was 1/96 of an Utrecht *stuiver*) *holpenningen* by local authorities in Deventer, Nijmegen, Groningen, and some other parts of the east between 1460 and 1570.[54]

Yet the table demonstrates equally clearly that – as in England – once a high level of DM had been achieved, huge fluctuations could follow. Why did DMLs vary so much over time, and what kinds of solution were found for the regular lack of small change? Let us consider the fall in small-coin circulation in the second half of the seventeenth century. The country was prosperous, and overall coin production was impressive. However, the key merchants who required coins from the mint houses were much more interested in the (comparatively cheap and thus more profitable) minting of large denominations than in the production of the small, silver *dubbeltjes* or *stuivers*. And insofar

Table 4.4 Per capita circulation of small-denomination coins in the Netherlands, 1550–1940, in relation to wage levels (in guilders of account); N = the present-day Netherlands; B = present-day Belgium

Cross section	*Circulation per capita*	*Hourly wage*			*Circulation expressed in terms of hourly wages*	
		Antwerp	*Amsterdam*	*The Netherlands*	*Antwerp*	*Amsterdam/The Netherlands*
1550 N&B	0.33	0.045	0.027		> 7	< 12
1600 N&B	0.42	0.100	0.077		4	5
1650 N	0.89		0.125			7
1700 N	0.30		0.125			2
1750 N	1.37		0.125			11
1800 N	0.68		0.125			5
1840 N&B	0.49		0.125	0.108		> 4–5
1890 N	1.68		0.208	0.203		8
1940 N	4.18			0.479		9

Source: Lucassen 2014b, Table 3; for 1890 also Haupt 1894: 124–8 (per capita circulation 1893 *monnaie de bronze* fl 0.40 and *monnaie d'appoint* – which includes the *kwartje* – fl 1.70).

as they were interested in providing silver for coining small denominations, they sent most of the *stuivers* (0.05 guilders) and nearly all of the *dubbeltjes* (0.1 guilders) overseas.

After much hesitation, the response of the provincial governments to the high cost of small change was to increase the output of copper *duiten* ($^{1}/_{160}$ guilder) – and, for some decades, the tacit condoning of the circulation of (partially low-weight) *duiten* minted by small principalities and noblemen in border regions. When this proved insufficient after 1700, remedies were sought in improved machinery for striking *duiten* and government orders (instead of orders from merchants, which was the rule) for the minting of silver *pijlstuivers* after 1738. In the end, only the unitary state that emerged in the French period was capable of meeting public demand for small change.

This episode shows that supply and demand for specific fractions are not automatically in equilibrium. This is due not so much to technology as to which responsibilities governments are prepared to assume. Early on, the more unified Burgundian Netherlands and, later on, the Kingdom of the Netherlands were apparently more willing to act than the intermediate Dutch Republic, in spite of its very high *overall* level of monetization.

Echoing Volckart (and *pace* Sargent and Velde), this case study for the Low Countries shows that the problems of supply and demand in relation to small change had been mastered as early as the sixteenth century.[55] The occasional problems that arose in the Dutch Republic stem from its political structure and economic concepts, which determined who was responsible and which instruments were available. As a result, solutions were always inadequate, to the extent that in the second half of the seventeenth century unofficial coins had to be allowed into circulation – just as in mid-seventeenth and again in late eighteenth-century England.[56] Craig Muldrew has pointed to the extension of small credit in similar situations in England; this might also have played an important role in the Netherlands after *c.* 1750. At the same time, these institutional shortages of small change – as a result of failing governments in certain periods in Dutch and English history – caution against any automatic link between supply and demand.

Yet before we can speak of a (northern, northwest) European pattern, the evidence for England and the Low Countries should be supplemented by other case studies. This is currently impossible because research on what might be termed the social history of coin circulation has only just begun.[57] Here, I can discuss only briefly the implications of some estimates for the largest country in Western Europe, France.

France

For France, a good starting point is the revolutionary period, when a number of coin reforms took place, mainly for ideological reasons; they combined a desire for science-based politics with a demand for in-depth reports on the coins currently in circulation that had to be replaced. Contrary to the situation

Table 4.5 Estimates of coins in circulation in France (in *livres*)

	1789	*1801 (by Lambert)*	*1801 (by Desrousseaux)*	*c. 1806*	*1810*
Gold			986,000,000		746,231,976
Silver *écu* at 6 *livres*			1,700,000,000		1,863,014,796
Silver half *écu*			131,000,000		34,510,364
Silver 30 and 15 *sol*			23,000,000		25,278,019*
Silver 24, 12, and 6 *sol*			80,000,000		50,623,966**
Silver 5 franc			86,000,000		
Silver and gold (subtotal)	2,673,996,133	1,800,000,000	3,006,000,000		
Billon (1 and 2 *sol*)	12,398,786	12,000,000	12,000,000		9,601,414
Copper 'King's effigy'	22,758,547	20,000,000		5,000,000	
Copper *sous 'de cloche'*		20,000,000	18,000,000	15,000,000	31,302,897***
Copper 'Marianne'			20,000,000	15,000,000	
Subtotal billon and copper	35,157,333	52,000,000	50,000,000	35,000,000	40,904,3131
Grand Total	2,709,153,466	1,852,000,000	3,056,000,000		2,860,563,432
Billon/copper *livres* per capita****	1.26	1.73	1.67	1.17	1.08
Expressed in terms of hourly wage of 2 *sous* (DML)	12	17	17	12	11

Source: Desrousseaux 2012: 26–8, 88, 402–3; ibid.: 402–5, totals for 31 December 1813 (3,479,156,869 francs) and 1817, but without sufficient details for questions regarding deep monetization. See also Haupt 1894: 662–77.

Notes:

* I.e. 30 *sou* (17,811,193) and 15 *sou* (7,466,826).

** I.e. 24 *sou* (19,894,514), 12 *sou* (27,287,641), and 6 *sou* (3,441,811).

*** I.e. 2 *sou* (12,118,818), 1 *sou* (16,920,391), 6 *denier* (2,190,035), and 3 *denier* (73,653).

**** Assuming a population of 28 million in 1789, 30 million in 1800, and 38 million in 1810.

in contemporary England, the French state took full responsibility for the circulation of small change, resulting in high DMLs, varying between 11 and 17. For these years, deep monetization is reflected in coins equal to or lower than an hourly wage, which amounted to about two to three *sous*. Their circulation was particularly strong in the industrious northern departments. Also for France, output figures may be corroborated and detailed by archaeological evidence based on coin hoards and stray finds.[58]

How and when did these high levels come about? Was it not until 1789, when the Bastille fell, or earlier on? As the lowest silver fractions were six *sous*, the study of deep monetization of France between *c.* 1650 and 1810 may be restricted to billon and copper coins, all profusely brought into circulation, in particular since the end of the sixteenth century (see Table 4.6).

Table 4.6 Value equivalents of small change in France, *c.* 1600–1810

Denomination	*Deniers*	*Livre*	*Until 1793/4*	*1793/4–1815: decimal*
	30		Billon 1709–13	
				Bronze 2 *décime* An 4–5
2 *sou*	24	1/10	Billon 1738–64; bronze 1791–4	Bronze 1 *décime* An 2 [1793] 4–9 (1/10 franc); billon 10 *centime* 1807–10
	16		Billon 1696–1715	
	15		Billon 1641–1713	
Sou (sol) / douzain	12	1/20 (1/120 *écu*)	Billon *c.* 1450–1658; copper 1719–28; 1767–74; billon 1739–48; copper 1767–91; bronze 1791–3	Bronze 5 *centime* An 4–9; Copper 1808
½ *sou / sizain*	6		Billon 1628–58; copper 1710–12, 1719–24, 1767–91; bronze 1792–4	
	4		Copper 1696–1708	
Liard / ¼ sou	3	1/80	Billon 1575–1655; copper 1649–1721, 1767–91; bronze 1792	
		1/100		Bronze 1 *centime* An 6–8
Double (denier) tournois (1/6 sou)	2	1/120	Billon *c.* 1300–*c.* 1580; copper 1577–1708	
Denier tournois	1		Originally silver; billon *c.* 1300–1586; copper 1575–1649	

Source: Ciani 1926; Bruce 2004 and similar catalogues.

The introduction of the copper one and two *denier tournois* under Henri III was a particularly great success, apparently gratifying a huge demand,[59] even to such an extent that – more or less as in the Dutch Republic somewhat later – adjacent petty principalities such as Bouillon and Sedan, Chateau Renaud, Dombes, Nevers and Rethel, and Orange started producing similar petty coins on a huge scale. I am not aware of there being reliable production data for small change in France before the end of the eighteenth century. The data available for the end of that century clearly show that by then France was deeply monetized (see Table 4.5). Awaiting more detailed information for the preceding centuries, I venture to suggest that this level had been reached already by around 1600.

Based on these three case studies, however incomplete, a provisional conclusion for Western Europe may be formulated. Deep monetization as a response to the commodification of labour – first predominantly in the guise of independent producers, gradually shifting to paramount wage labour – may have started in England around 1250, in the most advanced parts of the Low Countries in the late Middle Ages, and spread to other maritime provinces in the sixteenth century and to France in the seventeenth century. Once achieved, deep monetization is not necessarily sustainable. Apart from shifts in labour relations leading to variations in demand for small change, the supply may vary along with the quality of state institutions. When governments fail, other suppliers from within or outside the polity might take over their role;[60] alternatively, credit relations may expand or contract accordingly.

India

Let us now turn to more easterly parts of Eurasia, and to relations between labour and coin circulation on the other side of the 'Great Divergence'. First India, which like Europe had been practising a multi-denominational and multi-metal currency system since the mid-first millennium BC.[61] The earliest reconstruction of the total money supply in India dates from around 1880 (see Table 4.7). Following the same procedure as above, this will be our starting point, from which we shall go back in time to periods for which data are scarcer and more difficult to interpret.

India c. 1880

Gold coins were used only for hoarding, for export, or in order to be melted down for ornaments. Silver coins were used for paying rents and taxes, and for petty trade transactions.[62] At the end of the nineteenth century, silver coins played a much greater role in India than in Europe. In the words of an old India hand in 1892:

> the whole trade of India [...] is now conducted by the actual transfer of coin from hand to hand, except in the Presidency towns, and some of the large up-country towns, and even there you will see at the present day men paying their debts, by bringing in bags of rupees, rupees in thousands.[63]

Table 4.7 Coin circulation in India, *c.* 1880

	Total circulation (in millions of rupees)	*Circulation per capita*	
		(in annas*)*	*Expressed in terms of hourly wage of ¼* annas *(DML)*
Gold coins	1,440.0		
Active silver rupee circulation	1,370.8		
Small silver coins	92.6		
Copper coins	48.1	3	12
Cowrie shells	insignificant		

Source: Lucassen (2007c: 366–7), supposing a wage level for agricultural labourers of two *annas* per day of eight hours *Report of the Committee* 1893: Minutes, 57, question 1432. For similar estimates (unfortunately not including copper coins) see *Report of the Committee* 1893: Report, 21, and Appendix III, 307–8. See also de Zwart and Lucassen 2015.

Throughout his entire life, however, the ordinary man would have seen only the lowest possible copper denominations.[64]

At first glance, the conclusion that India was already deeply monetized in the last quarter of the nineteenth century – much more so than the European periphery at that time – may be surprising and in need of two qualifications. First, wages outside agriculture might have been slightly higher and working days might have been longer than eight hours, but even so the result would have been a per capita copper circulation exceeding five times the hourly wage. Second, the actual copper circulation was probably higher, because the estimates might very well exclude both copper coins produced before 1862 – the first coinage under the British Crown – and 'native coins' that continued to circulate. Further, a small proportion of the coppers consisted of half *anna* pieces, which have to be deducted. Yet there are other reasons to suppose that the conclusion that India was already deeply monetized by 1880 might not be too wide off the mark. A recent reconstruction of labour relations for the subcontinent in 1900 showed levels of commodification (31.2% self-employed and 12.1% wage labourers) that are not very different from contemporaneous outcomes for European countries.[65]

India 1800–80

The next question is when would the threshold of deep monetization have been reached in India: just before 1880 or much earlier? And did India experience the same sort of fluctuations we saw in Europe? These questions cannot be easily answered. Attempts have been made to reconstruct the silver and gold stock of India on the basis of import figures for bullion (India has no silver mines), but copper coins, the currency of the common man, are completely absent from these stories.[66]

What would the situation have been like at the beginning of the nineteenth century? To answer this question, it is important to know that, by that time, India was not a country dominated by self-sufficient peasants outside the market and therefore not in need of coins. On the contrary, preliminary reconstructions of labour relations suggest similar levels of commodification at the start and at the end of the century.[67]

At the beginning of the century, most copper coinage was probably produced in mints under Indian control, but their output is largely unknown.[68] We know more about the English production of copper coins for India in the first half of the nineteenth century (see Table 4.8). It shows that this initial attempt to dominate Indian copper production (before the mass production of reduced-size coppers bearing Victoria's portrait, from 1862 onwards) already amounted to more than 31 million rupees, or more at a time when a number of native mints were still very active.[69] If we accept a total stock of coppers worth 40 million rupees and a population figure of roughly 200 million, the DML in the first half of the century would have been the same as around 1880.

These impressions find some corroboration in the more precise figures for the district of Benares.[70] In 1808, the amount of (copper) *pice* required for circulation in that district was estimated at 700,000 rupees.[71] Production figures for the preceding decades suggest that this was rather pessimistic.[72] The district, then still undivided, most likely coincided with the later Benares 'Division', with over five million inhabitants according to the census of 1901. Given an average population growth of 40 per cent in nineteenth-century India, the

Table 4.8 Copper coin production for India by the English (in millions of rupees)

	English mints per Presidency				*Native mints*
	Bengal	*Bombay*	*Madras*	*Total*	
1795–1796	0.03			?	?
1800–1808	0.22	[1802–8 unknown but large-scale production]	[1803–8 unknown but large-scale production]	?	?
1809–1812	1.29	0.28		1.57	?
1813–1825	1.52*	[1820–9 unknown]	0.25	>1.77	?
1826–1833	2.25			>2.25	?
1835–1848	20.21			20.21	?
1853	0.46			0.46	?
1857	0.73			0.73	?
1858	3.68			3.68	?

Source: Stevens 2012: 168, 263, 266, 269, 488 for the Bengal Presidency; Garg 2013: 164 (for Madras 1824–5), 172 (for Bombay 1809–19); Lucassen 2007c: 383 for 1835–48; Bruce 2004: 711 for later years.

Note: * Stevens 2012: 488. However, Benares copper coin production 1826–7 (here Rs 74,161 = 4,746,304 pice) is not consistent with ibid.: 379: total 94,322 *maunds* = 9,432,200 lbs. troy (ibid.: 557) = 54,329,472,000 grains = 543,294,720 *pice* (ibid.: 268) = 8,488,980 rupees (ibid.: 269). I have borrowed here the lower figure of 74,161 rupees.

number of inhabitants may have been some 3.7 million in 1808, ten per cent of whom lived in Benares city. The per capita copper coin circulation thus amounted to 0.2 rupees or 3 *annas* or 15 *pice*. The daily wage of a labourer being four *pice*,[73] this would imply that, with a DML of four, the district as a whole was on the verge of deep monetization. If we put aside questions of how representative Benares District was for India as a whole, the difference with 1880 is partly explained by the replacement of cowries by coppers, which took place on a massive scale in Bengal in the late eighteenth and early nineteenth centuries and causes figures for *c.* 1800 to be underestimated.[74]

India 1550–1800

Although we have almost no data on copper coin output before 1800, we are fortunate because the production of copper coin was largely dependent on Japanese and European imports, most of which went directly to the mint. Production figures for Indian and Nepalese copper mines are very scarce, but overseas trade statistics show on average constant figures for Japanese copper imported by the Dutch East India Company in Coromandel (200 tons per annum) and Bengal (100 tons), and rising figures for European (mainly Swedish) copper imported by the East India Company to Madras (from 100 tons in the 1750s to 200 tons in the 1760s) and Calcutta (from 100 tons in the 1730s to 300 tons in the 1770s).[75]

Before these growing copper imports in the later eighteenth century, confirmed by accepted impressionistic overviews of Indian numismatic history, output may have stagnated between, say, the first half of the seventeenth and the first half of the eighteenth centuries. This was in sharp contrast to the sixteenth century, when coinage activity increased threefold from 1525 to at least 1600.[76] Under the short-lived Suri Dynasty in Delhi (1538–54) and the first Mughal Emperor Akbar (1556–1605), mint output of gold, silver, and copper cannot be characterized other than as feverous. The previously common billon coins were replaced by copper *dams* of *c.* 20 grams (initially called *paisas*) and fractions down to one-tenth of a *dam/paisa*. This was an important step towards deep monetization, as these coppers were struck during many consecutive years and in great quantities. Furthermore, they met the needs of wage labourers, as the wages for an hour of an artisan's work equalled between one-quarter and one *dam*.[77]

This impression of deep monetization being under way may be confirmed by Akbar's probate inventory. According to Francisco Pelsaert, it recorded 230 million *Conincx peys* or *tacx*, making 766,666 *ropias* (30 *tacx* = 1 *ropia*). Supposing that this enormous quantity of *paisas* represents all the copper pieces minted during his lifetime, and that the massive Suri output still circulating more than balanced any wastage during Akbar's lifetime, this figure is equivalent to roughly 0.01 rupees or 3 *dams* per capita around 1600, when the population of the Mughal Empire is estimated at 100 million inhabitants. Divided by hourly wages of ½ to ¼ *dam*, this would yield a DML of between 6 and 12.[78] Too many uncertainties remain (for instance, the low output of small silver fractions might have been resolved by using more coppers), but it seems probable that deep monetization made much progress in the second half of the sixteenth century, although levels might have dropped subsequently before rising again after *c.* 1750.

India 1200–1550

As in Europe, however, the initial jump in Indian DMLs might well have occurred in the Middle Ages; quantifying this is very hard. Numismatic evidence for Northern and Central India from *c.* 1200 onwards[79] reveals an acceleration in the number of small-value coins (copper, billon, and silver of less than five grams) in India in the period 1275–1325/75, and a second acceleration between 1425–50 and 1525. Especially during the reign of Alauddin Muhammad Khalji, Delhi Sultan 1296–1316, in addition to gold and silver coins a huge number of two- and six-*gani* billon coins were put into circulation.[80]

Annual wages for unskilled workers (servants) were then 10 to 12 *tankas*, or $1^1/_3$ to $1^3/_5$ *jitals* per day, whereas for skilled workers like weavers and tailors they were 2 to3 *jitals*. Given that, according to the famous mintmaster Thakkura Pheru, the basis of the system was the one *gani-jital*, Alauddin's *dugani* (a 2-*gani* coin containing eight per cent silver) and a 6-*gani* coin with 25 per cent silver equalled more or less the wages for between one and three days' work. For our DM criteria, copper *paikas* of ¼ *jitals* and its fractions, which gradually replaced one-*jital* pieces, are therefore much more interesting. Unfortunately, they do not occur in such large numbers as the billon pieces.

Firoz Shah, Delhi Sultan 1351–88, made a new attempt to ensure enough small change by increasing copper coin output, in particular the number of half- and quarter-*jital* coins, being aware of the fact that 'if poor people bought something from the market and a balance in half or quarter *jitals* was left of the amount paid, the shopkeeper would not have the quarter change'.[81]

In sum, precise data are lacking for India, but trends are certainly visible. Clear steps towards deep monetization were set in the late Middle Ages, but it was only in the second half of the sixteenth century that India might have had DMLs of between 6 and 12. It is likely that these could not be sustained in the centuries afterwards, but a new increase might have led to DMLs of ten in the nineteenth century. We may speculate why these levels are so surprisingly high, given our understanding of India's economic performance. One reason might be, as already suggested, that proletarianization and commodification had become more widespread than expected. Another might be the underdevelopment of credit for the poorly paid.

China and Japan

China 'invented' coins at roughly the same time as – though most likely independently of – Northern India and the eastern basin of the Mediterranean. Nevertheless, it followed a different and very distinctive pattern.[82] The Qin state that eventually emerged victorious in 221 BC adopted the so-called 'cash' (*wén*) coins – cast round bronze, copper, or later brass coins with a square hole and a diameter of about two centimetres – as the only currency. This system was continued until 1900. It spread to Japan and Southeast Asia, and was used in Vietnam until at least 1933. In China, with a few exceptions, no other copper, silver, or gold fractions were coined for two millennia. Alongside these cash coins, only silver ingots were used in wholesale trade and for hoarding. For convenience, cash coins could be stringed in units of (ideally) one hundred or one thousand pieces. This mono-denominational currency system offers far fewer research problems than the multi-denominational and multi-metal systems prevailing in the western and southern parts of Eurasia. Moreover, plenty of data are available on the Chinese production of cash coins from the very inception of the system.[83]

The production statistics show varying degrees of intensity. As a rule of thumb, replacements necessary due to wear and tear amounted to a minimum of one per cent of total stock annually. Given a total per capita stock of 400 cash coins (see Table 4.9), we arrive at about four cash coins per capita for replacement.[84] Greater production in this case means an increase in the stock, lower production a decrease.

Table 4.9 Stock of cash coins in relation to wage levels in China, 9 CE–1750

Cross section in years CE	*Stock in billions*	*Population in millions*	*Stock per capita*	*Daily wage*	*Stock per wage sum*	
					daily	*hourly (=DML)*
9	20–30	60	300–500	<20	<15–25	<120–200
750	21.3–42.6		310–610			
1120	193.4–262	126	1530	145	11	88
1127	30 in private market and 98 in state treasuries	110	300 (1,200 if state treasuries included)			
1480				5–15 25–30		
1550	36–54	120–200	180–450	[25]	[7–18]	
1600	36–54	120–200	180–450	25–30		
1628–44				60		
1702			400		7–8	56–64
1750	122.8–146.8	300	400–80	50	8–9	64–72

Source: Lucassen 2005: 432, 439; Wang 2007: 67, 72 (wage of 600 coins per month for a captain, late Han); Von Glahn 1996: 85, 247; Scheidel 2009: 154; Moll-Murata 2005: 241; and Moll-Murata 2015, Appendix, for wages. Stock, population, and stock per capita 750, 1120, 1550, 1600, and 1750 after Liu 2015: 73, 123 for wages 1158 and 1480.

Apparently, monetization levels rose sharply in the eleventh century, when an imperial official underlined its significance as follows:[85]

> The utility of money derives from circulation and loan-making. A village of ten households may have 100,000 coins. If the cash is stored in the household of one individual, even after a century, the sum remains 100,000. If the coins are circulated through business transactions so that every individual of the ten households can enjoy the utility of the 100,000 coins, then the utility will amount to that of 1,000,000 cash. If circulation continues without stop, the utility of the cash will be beyond enumeration.

This was followed by a decrease between the twelfth and the sixteenth centuries, and an increase again in the eighteenth century. Although this periodization is important for the study of labour relations, it is not so easy to decide the question as to what per capita stock would represent 'deep monetization' as defined in the introduction to this chapter. At first sight, the requirements of 'a per capita stock equal to between five and ten times the prevailing hourly wage' are more than fulfilled (Table 4.9). However, we should not forget that a substantial proportion of the cash coins did not circulate as pieces, but as 'small' strings of (ideally) 100 pieces or 'large' strings of 1,000 pieces, which makes them comparable to medium and large silver coins in the southern and western parts of Eurasia.

The Japanese case can help us to distinguish between 'real small change' in the European and Indian sense and 'small change by default' in the Chinese sense. Until 1600 the Japanese imported Chinese cash coins and, with a few exceptions, did not produce their own coins. Tokugawa Japan, however, started to produce its own cast cash coins (called *mon*) alongside silver, gold, and paper currency.[86] That way it combined Chinese-like cash coins with a multi-metal and multi-denominational currency system. It is possible to reconstruct DMLs for *c.* 1640 and for the end of the nineteenth century. In 1640, only cash coins need to be counted according to our definition; in 1872, all copper coins qualify, including the highly devalued *tempo* pieces (cast 1835–68 and originally worth 96 *mon*); in 1879 we include all coppers plus the silver five-*sen* pieces; and in 1883 again only the coppers[87] (Table 4.10).

Table 4.10 Stock of DML coins in relation to wage levels in Japan, 1640–1886

	Stock DM coins (millions)	*Inhabitants (millions)*	*Stock per capita*	*Average wage of carpenter*		*DML*
				Per day	*Per hour*	
1640	3,300 cash	25.000	132 cash	200 *mon*	25 *mon*	5.3
1872	5.6 yen	33.111	0.17 yen	0.50 yen	0.075 yen	2.7
1879	12.7 yen	35.769	0.36 yen	0.41 yen	0.05 yen	7.0
1886	15.1 yen	37.869	0.40 yen	0.23 yen	0.03 yen	13.3

Source: 1640: Izawa 2013: 15; Van de Polder 1891; production 1872–86: Matsukata 2014; wages: Hanley and Yamamura 1977: 192; Van Leeuwen 2007: 239.

As, after 1600, Japanese DMLs appear to have been in a range similar to those of other parts of Eurasia with multi-denominational and multi-metal currencies, we can now compare the Chinese DML *c.* 1700 (Table 4.9) with the corresponding Japanese figure somewhat earlier (Table 4.11). Given similarities between the economies of Japan and eastern China at this point in time, this suggests that only *c.* ten per cent of the Chinese cash coins functioned as really small change, and that *c.* 90 per cent circulated in strung forms as a medium-monetization means of exchange.

Finally, we can use the long Chinese coin-production series to compare trends inside Eurasia. Interestingly, the chronology, which was rather similar between western and southern Eurasia, is different in China. There, monetization levels increased from the ninth century onwards, two or three centuries before India and Europe. The serious slump seen in China during the twelfth to the sixteenth centuries is not much visible in India and Europe, if we ignore the comparatively weak decrease seen during the Black Death. The increase in the eighteenth century can perhaps be seen in India as well, albeit slightly later. In the nineteenth century, China clearly lagged behind.

This distinctive Chinese DML pattern becomes understandable if we link it to shifting labour relations, in particular those described in detail by Christine Moll-Murata in the framework of the IISH Global Collaboratory on the History of Labour Relations 1500–2000.[88] It is significant that, around 1050, compulsory work for the Chinese state was converted into a tax, to be paid in cash. This suggests that self-employed peasants and craftsmen, as well as wage earners, became the new taxpayers. Kent Deng quotes the famous dictum by Eric Jones that Song China was just a 'hair's breadth' away from a genuine industrial revolution.[89]

Labour relations changed dramatically from the twelfth and thirteenth centuries onwards, and the rise of 'bond-servitude' in late Ming China implies a shift from free to unfree labour in these cash-ridden centuries.[90] This process is summarized by William Guanlin Liu as follows: "While depopulation and deurbanization after the Mongol conquest significantly weakened the structure of domestic markets, the demonetization of the Chinese economy was directly caused by the rise of a command economy after the establishment of the Ming dynasty. The early Ming had little use for monetary exchange as it was operated on the basis of a barter economy and 'corvée services'. In essence, early Ming farmers and artisans paid taxes in lieu of grains and other kinds of local products to the state and had little need for hard currencies".[91] In the fifteenth century, the rise of private coinage brought some relief.

In the eighteenth century, a clear shift to working for the market is visible in the CGLH data collected by Moll-Murata. Whether this was due to an increase in wage labour or an increase in the number of small, self-employed producers working for the market is not relevant. The former possibility is supported by the increase in wage labour in various industrial sectors such as printing, porcelain making, and shipbuilding.[92]

Conclusions

Building on earlier work on monetization intensities in India and on deep monetization levels (DMLs) in the Low Countries, this chapter demonstrates that the DML concept is appropriate for the analysis of long-term trends in major parts of Eurasia. A comparison of DMLs thus defined through space and time shows interesting constants, but also variations. Based mainly on traditional written sources, this chapter also draws on archaeological and other numismatic evidence. It has proven to be useful for the multi-metal and multi-fractional currency systems that prevailed in the west and the south, but also – with some caveats – for the mono-fractional Chinese system. In all cases, long-term shifts in levels of monetization are clearly visible.

The data available for different parts of Eurasia (the Low Countries, France, India, and China) show the following results: (1) similar levels in Western Europe and South Asia from *c.* 1100 to 1900; (2) similar periods of increasing and decreasing levels overall, but diverging in the seventeenth and eighteenth centuries (increase in Europe, decrease in India); (3) diverging developments between China and the rest (see Figure 4.4).

These results question to a certain extent accepted wisdom in historical debates on economic development. The similarity of the DMLs undermines the uniqueness of the processes of commodification and proletarianization in Western Europe. Here we see a strong link between monetary history and labour history. At the same time, similarities across Eurasia but also differences within Western Europe pose questions regarding the social function of credit. Why was Britain so different from the continent, while the continent showed more similarities with South Asia? Or, formulated differently, why the

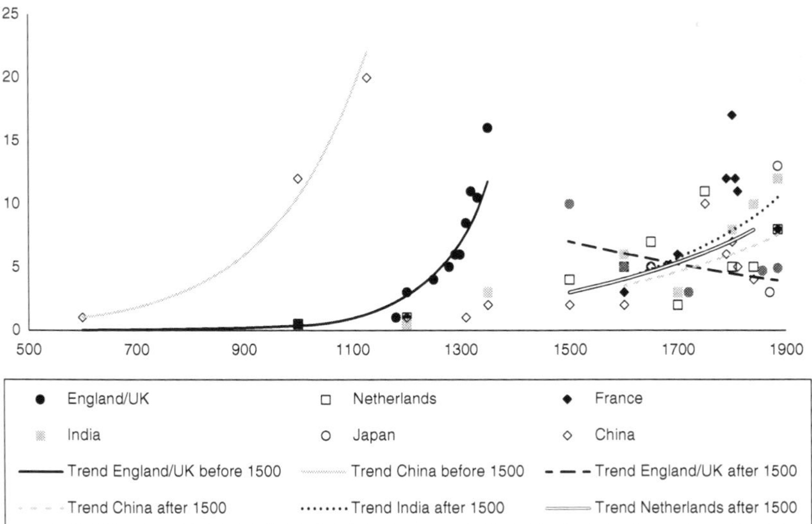

Figure 4.4 Deep monetization levels (DMLs) in Eurasia *c.* 600–1900.

promulgation of deferred payments in Britain in contrast with more immediate payments elsewhere?

Are we justified in linking this to Margariti's observations regarding differing credit relations among medieval merchants in Egypt and the Indian Ocean? There, she observed long-lasting credit and debt relations among merchants within small communities sharing family ties and the same religion, in contrast to the quick disbursement of credit and debt between strangers: 'Perhaps nothing served better than minted coins – with their power to assign value to complex assets, their portability, and their eminent transferability – to facilitate risky transactions between members of different faiths.'[93] My hypothesis would be that this applies not only to payment for goods, but also to payment for services, including wage payments.[94]

Appendix 4.1. Deep monetization levels in various countries in the 1870s–80s

By combining the data on small-coin circulation in particular countries collected by Ottomar Haupt with evidence on wage levels and working conditions in those same countries as published in British parliamentary papers, it is possible to reconstruct deep monetization levels for the period around the 1870s to the 1880s.[95] For now, this reconstruction is possible for a handful of countries.

For each country, the following will be addressed:

- the hourly wage for ordinary workers;
- the fractions equal to that sum or less;
- the circulation figures of these particular fractions;
- these circulation figures per capita;
- these per capita circulation figures divided by the hourly wage, i.e. the *deep monetization level.*

Country	*Hourly wage for ordinary workers*	*Fractions equal to that sum or less*	*Circulation figures of these particular fractions*	*Circulation figures per capita*	*Per capita circulation figures divided by the hourly wage, i.e. the deep monetization level*
Austria-Hungary	10 *Kreuzer* = $^1/_{10}$ *Florin* (assistant builder Vienna: *Further Reports* 1870: 554–9)	1858–91 all coppers ($^1/_2$, 1, and 4 *Kreuzer*) and billon coins of 5 and 10 *Kreuzer* qualify, from 1892 all coppers (1 and 2 *Heller*) and nickels (10 and 20 *Heller*) qualify, whereas 1 old *Kreuzer* = 2 new *Heller*	End June 1892, old billon coins 35.7 million *Florins*, old bronze 14.8 million, new bronze 0.2 million, new nickel 1.7 million, totalling 52.4 million *Florins* (Haupt 1894: 889–90)	1.22 *Florins* (Haupt 1894: 889–90)	12[96]
Belgium	0.25 Belgian francs or 25 *centimes* (a lot of data in *Further Reports* 1871: 21–66);	Bronze 1 and 2 *centime*, nickel 5, 10, and 20 *centime*	8.465 million francs in bronze and 6.6 million francs in nickel (Haupt 1894: 66, 227)	2.50 francs (Haupt 1894: 66,227)	10
Denmark	10 *skilling rigsmonts* (lower skilled workmen 6 *rigsdalers* per week = in 1854–74 96 *skilling rigsmonts* per day: *Further Reports* 1871: 141–3)	10 *skilling rigsmonts* (1854–74) ≈ 22 *øre* from 1874 onwards,[97] so that all bronze 1, 2, and 5 *øre* qualify as well as the (0.6) silver 10 and 25 *øre* pieces	700,000 krone coppers in 1885 and 880,000 coppers in 1893 (Haupt 1894: 339–40); silver 10 *øre* production 1874-84 = 1,234,000 kroner, and silver 25 *øre* production 1874 = 2,035,000 kroner; resulting in a total of 3,969,000 kroner in small change in 1885[98]	1.99 kroner	9

(*continued*)

Country	*Hourly wage for ordinary workers*	*Fractions equal to that sum or less*	*Circulation figures of these particular fractions*	*Circulation figures per capita*	*Per capita circulation figures divided by the hourly wage, i.e. the deep monetization level*
Egypt	2 *piastres* (men in cotton factories 1 shilling a day, quarrying 1 shilling 8 pence, good excavators 2 shillings 6 pence, workmen 2 shillings = 20 *piastres*: *Further Reports* 1871: 148–58)	Until 1885, 2 *piastres* (or *qirsh*) = 80 *paras* = $^{1}/_{100}$ pound; 1876-1909 2 *piastres* = 20 *ushr al qirsh* so that all coppers of 1 up to 40 *paras* struck in Cairo qualify; in addition, small silver pieces of 10 and 20 *paras* and 1 *qirsh*; from 1886–91 the Berlin mint provided nickels and bronzes	As production figures for small silver coinage are unknown before 1884, only coppers, valued at 152,734 Egyptian pounds, may be quantified (Haupt 1894: 71, 89–91)	Before 1884 0.022 Egyptian pounds in copper and an unknown but possibly equal sum in small silver, which would very roughly add up to 0.05 Egyptian pounds	2[99]
France	30 *centimes* (Charente: assistant artisans 3–5 francs per day, country labourer 2.50–3; Cherbourg town artisan 3, town labourer 2.25, country artisan 2.50, country labourer 2: *Further Reports* 1871, 171–85)	Bronze 1, 2, 5, 10 *centime*, silver 20 (hardly ever struck after 1869) and 25 *centime* (struck until 1848)	At the end of 1885 60 million francs in bronze coins (Haupt 1894: 674), plus silver 20 and 25 *centime*. Haupt does not distinguish between the different fractions of the silver *monnaie d'appoint* (all fractions between 20 *centimes* and 2 francs, totalling 250 million francs)	1.60 French francs in bronze and 6.50 francs in *monnaie d'appoint*, totalling for all denominations up to 25 *centimes c.* 2 French francs	8

Germany	1 *Silbergroschen* = 10 *Pfennigs* (Handarbeiter Silesia 1867–68 7 *Silbergroschen* in summer and 10 in winter: *Further Reports* 1871: 848–53)	As wages have risen since, all *Kaiserreich* copper fractions of 1 and 2 *Pfennig* and all nickels of 5, 10, and 20 *Pfennig* qualify	End 1885 45 million *Marks*; end 1892 61.5 million *Marks* (Haupt 1894: 66, 210–11)	100 *Pfennigs* or 1 *Reichsmark* (Haupt 1894: 66, 210–11)	10
Greece	40 *lepta* (*Further Reports* 1871: 194–201)	All coppers of 1, 2, 5, 10, 20 *lepta*, and silver 20 *lepta* (struck 1874–83) and 25 *lepta* (struck in very low numbers 1833–55)	October 1885 coppers circulating worth a total of 4.5 million drachmas (Haupt 1894: 135–7) plus silver *lepta* pieces, valued at *c.* 600,000 drachmas[100]	Copper 2.25 drachmas (Haupt 1894: 66), including small silver *c.* 2.50 drachmas	6
Italy	20 *centesimi* (*Further Reports* 1871: 210)	Copper 1, 2, 5, 10 *centesimi*, and silver *centesimi* (struck 1863–7)	Coppers struck 1862–86 at 76.2 million lire (Haupt 1894: 713–14[101]), plus 7 million lire in silver 20 *centesimi*[102]	2.75 lire	14
Norway	4 *skillings* (*Further Reports* 1871: 364–95)	4 *skillings* = $^1/_{15}$ of the new 2 krone pieces and its fractions as struck from 1875 onwards = 0.13 $^1/_3$ *øre*; therefore all bronze 1, 2, and 5 *øre* pieces qualify as well as the silver 10 *øre* pieces	In late 1885 400,000 kroner consisting of bronze pieces (Haupt 1894: 342–3), plus 681,000 kroner of silver 10 *øre* pieces struck 1875–83,[103] totalling 1,081,000 kroner	0.50 kroner	4

(*continued*)

Country	*Hourly wage for ordinary workers*	*Fractions equal to that sum or less*	*Circulation figures of these particular fractions*	*Circulation figures per capita*	*Per capita circulation figures divided by the hourly wage, i.e. the deep monetization level*
Portugal	30 *réis* (*Further Report* 1870: 152–7 rather vaguely suggests 300 *réis* per day)[104]	All copper and bronze fractions of 3, 5, 10, and 20 *réis* (silver only upwards of 50 *réis*)	1885 2 million *milréis* copper and bronze coins (Haupt 1894: 420–1)	0.50 *milréis* (Haupt: 1894: 421)	17[105]
Russia	10 kopeks (*Further Reports* 1871: 523–58)	Copper ¼, ½, 1, 2, 3, and 5 kopeks, silver 5 and 10 kopeks	10 million roubles in bronze coins (Haupt 1894: 766); plus[106] silver 5 kopeks 1867–85: 545,500 roubles and ditto silver 10 kopeks: 4,750,500 roubles, totalling 15,295,500 roubles	15.3 kopeks	1.5[107]
Serbia	20 *paras* (*Further Reports* 1871: 841)	All coppers of 1, 5, and 10 *paras*, all copper–nickel coins of 5, 10, and 20 *paras*	1,898,000 *dinars* in copper and 3,200,000 *dinars* in copper–nickel coins, totalling 5,098,000 *dinars* (Haupt 1894: 154)	Divided by 2.2 million inhabitants this yields 2.3 *dinars*	11.5[108]

Spain	0.8 *reales* (*Further Reports* 1871: 606–51)	0.8 *reales* = 8 *decimos* (1852–64) = 0.0304 oz. silver ≈ 23 *centimos*, according to the post-1869 system, which qualifies copper 1, 2, 5, and 10 *centimos* and silver 20 *centimos* (struck in insignificant numbers 1869–70) for inclusion	In 1892 57,199,652 pesetas in copper (Haupt 1894: 515-16)	3.50 pesetas (Haupt 1894: 515–16)	15[109]
Sweden	18 *öre* (*Further Reports* 1871: 656–7)	18 *öre* pre 1873 reform equals 20 *öre* afterwards. Therefore the following fractions in 1885 qualify: bronze 1, 2, and 5 *öre* and silver 10 *öre*	At the end of 1885 900,000 kronor in bronze coins (Haupt 1894: 341), plus[110] 1,079,100 kronor in silver 10 *öre* coins, totalling 2 million kronor	44 *öre*	2.2
Switzerland	19 *centimes* (*Further Reports* 1871: 669–87)	All bronze (of 1 and 2 *centimes* or *Rappen*) and nickel coins (of 5, 10, and 20 *Rappen*)	At the end of 1885 4,500,000 Swiss francs (Haupt 1894: 147; cf. 139ff, 360ff, 840ff, and 893ff)	1.50 Swiss francs	8
Turkey	30 *paras* (300 *paras* per day for a married day labourer: *Further Reports* 1871: 713–47, esp. 720 for Anatolia; see also information for Izmir, Kurdistan, etc., elsewhere in this report)	Coppers of 1, 5, 10, and 20 *paras* (excluding 44,170,000 copper pieces of 40 *paras*, and equalling 1 *piastre*), plus silver 20 *para* pieces	At the end of 1885 in copper 73 million *piastres* (113 million *piastres* in total minus 40 million coppers of 40 *paras*, struck AH 1255/ry 17–23), plus 5 million silver 20 *para* pieces, struck from AH 1255/ry 9 [1847] to AH 1293/ry 8 [1883] (Haupt 1894: 828–9),[111] totalling 78 million *piastres*	3 *piastres* or 120 *paras* (25 million inhabitants: Haupt 1894: 829)	4

(*continued*)

Country	*Hourly wage for ordinary workers*	*Fractions equal to that sum or less*	*Circulation figures of these particular fractions*	*Circulation figures per capita*	*Per capita circulation figures divided by the hourly wage, i.e. the deep monetization level*
United Kingdom	7.2 pennies per hour (Phelps Brown and Hopkins 1981: 11–12)	All bronze coins (mainly farthing, halfpenny, and penny) as well as small silver coins (3, 4, and 6 pence)	At the end of 1885 1.6 million pounds sterling in coppers (Haupt 1894: 491),[112] plus 3.682 million pounds in threepences, fourpences, and sixpences,[113] totalling 5.282 million pounds = 1,267.68 million pennies	Divided by 36 million inhabitants (England, Wales, Scotland, and Ireland) gives 35.2 pennies	4.9[114]
USA	15 cents (*Further Reports* 1871: 853–937)	Bronze 1 and 2 cents, nickel 3 cents, copper–nickel 5 cents, silver 10 cents or dimes	At the end of 1885 15 million dollars in billon coins plus 13,085,546 million dollars in silver dimes 1853–85, totalling 28 million dollars	50 dollar cents (cf. Haupt 1894: 562)	2.7

Notes

1 This chapter has grown out of a paper written for two different conferences. First, the workshop on 'Economic institutional change and global labour relations', at the IISH in Amsterdam (26–7 September 2014), and, second, the conference 'Coins, currency and crisis from c. 2000 BC to c. AD 2000. On Silver, paper and trust in historical perspective', at the Vrije Universiteit in Amsterdam (12–13 December 2014). I thank the participants at these conferences and other meetings at which I gave a presentation (Osaka, 3–4 March 2015, Utrecht, 29 June 2015, Valencia, 1 April 2016) for their input. In this new version, the monetary aspects have been elaborated upon more fully, while a chapter in a separate volume (here referred to as Lucassen 2017) concentrates on labour aspects. Both chapters refer to each other, so overlap is unavoidable. I am grateful to Chris Gordon for his stylistic and linguistic revisions.

2 Useful definitions can be found in Haselgrove and Krmnicek (2012); Maurer (2006); Feinman and Garraty (2010). In this article money is generally taken as 'general purpose money' (Maurer 2006: 20).

3 See https://collab.iisg.nl/web/labourrelations.

4 Spufford (2002, 2008); Margariti (2014).

5 Figure 1 in Lucassen (2017); cf. Feinman and Garraty (2010: 171): 'in all economies, ancient or modern, market exchange, when present, coexists with other modes of transfer and exchange'.

6 See, for example, Cardon and Lemaire (2014).

7 A good overview for England can be found in Valenze (2006). Reddy (1987) offers eloquent, well-researched pessimism.

8 Selgin (2008: 6).

9 Simmel (1908: 746–7, 1922: 314–21, 2009: 297–303); cf. Valenze (2006: 21, 69, 184–8).

10 Simmel (2009, 299–300) (original: Simmel 1922: 316–17); cf. Peebles (2010: 230).

11 There is a great need for more studies in this field, but see Biernacki (1995: 352–62). For the visualization of circulation patterns of medium and small denominations, see Lucassen (2007c: 242) and Welten (2015: 173).

12 Lucassen (2014b). Consequently, there are two possible definitions of 'medium monetization'. First, in a system where multiple denominations coexist (as has been the case worldwide since *c.* 1900 and was the case in many parts of Eurasia long before then), by replacing hour/hourly by day/daily, as I have done (without using the term 'medium monetization') in Lucassen (2007a and 2007b) and, second, in a mono-denominational system (in East Asia, as will be explained below), by lowering the definition of the per capita stock to be equal to between one and five pieces. In this chapter, I concentrate only on reconstructing 'deep monetization'.

13 Some colleagues have proposed using real instead of nominal wages. I consider this less appropriate and far less practical. In addition, an experiment by Pim de Zwart (International Institute for Social History, Amsterdam) regarding the Low Countries (see below) did not yield different trends. I am grateful to him for sharing these results.

14 Kelleher (2013).

15 Sargent and Velde (2002). My research in this respect is very preliminary.

16 Roscher (1881: 198-203, esp. 201, fn. 12) referring to Sonnenfels (1787: 287 [Part II, § 271]) and Friedrich Jakob Schmitthenner (1796–1850). For the historiography, see also Rössner (2016).

17 Sonnenfels (1804, Part II: 393–5 [§ 237]).

18 Haupt (1886; 1894); see also *Report of the Committee* (1893: Appendix II, 213: 273–5).

19 Haupt (1894: 66).

20 Cf. Grytten (2004).

21 *Further Report* (1871: 362); italics are mine.

22 Palairet (1997).

23 Selgin (2008: 266, 295, 297); Muldrew (2007: 409).

24 Kolchin (1987: 375). On the circulation of tokens in the American South after the Civil War, see Lurvink (2014).
25 Bacherikov (2013). Information kindly provided by Bacherikov's supervisor Gijs Kessler. See also Florén (1994) and Svirina (2014).
26 For this section, I learned much from discussions with Peter Spufford, Richard Kelleher, and Craig Muldrew. Only after the completion of this manuscript I was able to consult Allen (2015), which broadly confirms my conclusions.
27 Naismith (2012: esp. 284–90), where he discusses the problems of small change in Anglo-Saxon England.
28 Bolton (2012: 27, 132–5).
29 Fractions of farthings (half, third, and quarter) were struck occasionally between 1827 and 1913, partially for use in Ceylon and Malta. Compared with the larger coppers, their total value was insignificant.
30 Hourly wages of building craftsmen in Southern England according to Phelps Brown and Hopkins (1981: 11–12) (daily wages divided by ten); cf. Bolton (2012: 267–8).
31 This may be explained by the fact that – for reasons Allen does not mention – he seems to exclude 1319–44 (Allen 2001: 602). However, in this intermediate period the output of halfpennies and farthings (more than 36,000 pounds worth) was even higher than in the last sub-period, 1344–51 (see Allen 2012, Table C2).
32 For new evidence on wages and mobility of labourers after the Black Death, see Britnell (2015) and Dyer (2015).
33 See also Mayhew (2007: 217–18) and Allen (2012: 359–68).
34 Copper coinage in 1729–54, amounting to 818 tons or 175,000 pounds, will have improved the situation, but only slightly as it was also 'used as a means of filling the gap created by an attenuated silver circulation'. The next copper coinage, 1762–75, followed by a 24-year stop, amounted to only 234 tons (Dyer and Gaspar 1992: 434–8).
35 Dyer and Gaspar (1992: 436). Ibid. (446–8): between 1797 and 1800 some 275,000 pounds in new copper coins had been brought into circulation 'best adapted to the payment of the Laborious poor' as requested by Parliament. According to Dyer and Gaspar, this was 'not far short of the genuine coin' circulating in 1797, not including the numerous private tokens and counterfeits still used everywhere (Valenze 2006: 34–43).
36 Muldrew (2007); Selgin (2008); Valenze (2006: 264–70).
37 Besides, token coppers circulated at least until the 1880s (Selgin 2008: 266).
38 Selgin (2008: 289); *The Parliamentary Debates (Hansard). Official Report*, 4 August 1859, c. 978–9.
39 James Campbell and Julie Stevenson regard the figures published by Phelps Brown and Hopkins around 1700 as too high. Stevens prefers 18 d. per day instead of the 22 d. of Phelps Brown and Hopkins (personal communication from Craig Muldrew). Following Stevenson, the DML around 1720 would be 3.6.
40 Mayhew (2007: 213).
41 Quoted by Mayhew (2007: 213–14).
42 Kelleher (2013: 48, 70–73, 102); Kelleher and Leins (2008).
43 Mayhew (2007): 219; cf. Gemmill and Mayhew (1995, chapter 4); Spufford (2014).
44 Challis (1992: 387).
45 Muldrew (2007: 395); cf. Phelps Brown and Hopkins (1981: 70): 'If by a wage earner we mean one whose income in kind from any land he occupies is subsidiary, so that his material wellbeing depends mainly on his wages, then we believe it is generally reckoned that in the first half of the sixteenth century about a third of the occupied population in England were wage earners.'
46 Selgin (2008: 27–8); Lucassen (2017).
47 Muldrew (2007: 401, 404). On the relation between small credit and shortage of small change see recently also White (2016) for England and Smail (2016) for the Mediterranean. I would like to emphasize that this is not the same relation as between credit in general and the total money supply, which fluctuate much more in tandem, cf. Desan (2015: 191–230).

48 Cf. Selgin (2008: 208); Lucassen (2017).
49 For more detail see Lucassen (2007c); Welten (2010); Van Laere (2013); Martiny (2014); Vanhoudt (2015); Welten (2015, chapter 8).
50 For a general overview of circulation patterns in Europe, see Spufford (1988, 2002, 2008).
51 Lucassen (2007c: 260–1).
52 Van Bavel (2006).
53 Spufford (2014): most frequent were fractions of 3d. Scottish = 4 mite = $^1/_{12}$ *stuiver* = 0.0042 guilders of account.
54 Pannekeet and Cruysheer (2013).
55 Volckart (2008); Sargent and Velde (2002).
56 Muldrew (2007); Selgin (2008).
57 Lucassen and Zuijderduijn (2014).
58 See Desrousseaux (2012): 147 (Haute-Garonne/Toulouse 1811: 'les manouvriers, qui gagnent 15 à 20 sous par jour sont payés en cuivre et en billon'); cf. Prunaux (2013); Touitou-Michon and Michon (2013); Cardon and Lemaire (2014).
59 In the late sixteenth and seventeenth centuries, hourly wages were more like one *sou* than two *sous*. See, for example, Goubert (1968: 333–40), and Le Roy-Ladurie (1969: 123). This coincides well with the end of the *denier tournois* after 1650 and of the *double tournois* after 1700; for wage labour in France see Béaur *et al.* (2010).
60 Cardon (2012); Cardon and Lemaire (2014).
61 Ray (2006).
62 *Report of the Committee* (1893: Appendix I, 148–9).
63 Ibid. (minutes, 81, question 1913). According to another interviewee it was only recently that paper money had begun to play a role (ibid.: 118, question 2634).
64 Ibid. (117, question 2629); Stevens (2012, 362).
65 Lucassen and Stapel (2014, table 23).
66 The earliest attempt I know of is by Francis Capel Harrison (1863–1938), who estimated India's silver stock in 1493 at 290 million rupees, net imports 1493–1800 at 1,510.6 million rupees, 1800–35 at 611.9 million, and 1835–92 at 3,428.5 million. See *Report of the Committee* (1893: appendix 3, 307–8). For modern estimates of imports since 1493, see Subrahmanyam (1994) and Prakash (2004).
67 Lucassen and Stapel (2014). Data for neighbouring Goa since the late 1830s (ongoing work within the framework of a collaborative project with Paulo Mattos, Lisbon) have since confirmed this impression.
68 Lucassen (2007c), Lingen and Lucassen (2007, 2010–11, 2012–13).
69 Stevens (2012: 491–2); 66Lucassen (2007b).
70 Stevens (2012: 264–5, 319–23, 336–42, 355–67, 378–9, 488); *Imperial Gazetteer of India* (1908) for information on Benares Division, District and City.
71 Stevens (2012: 264–5) in fact gives a figure of 700,000 *lakhs* or 70,000,000,000 units (1 *lakh* = 100,000). Supposing these units stand for coins, this would result in 20,000 *pice* coins per capita, which is impossible. The data for the districts of Burdwan, Jessore, and Purneah also clearly show that the units meant must be rupees.
72 Stevens (2012: 322) (annual *pice* production 1775–86 of about 6 million pieces as compared with a stock of 44.8 million pieces in 1808; 1782–1805 annual production in *maunds*, although incomplete, points in the same direction); ibid. (341) (*pice*, valued at 110,000 rupees or *c.* 7 million (*pice*) pieces, was supposed to be necessary for Benares in 1806–7, according to the Calcutta Mint Committee); ibid. (488).
73 Stevens (2012: 321) (in a report from 1786).
74 Stevens (2012), *passim*; Lucassen (2007a: 31–2); Hogendorn and Johnson (1986).
75 Shimada (2006: 107–28). For the ratio between Indian and foreign copper, see Prinsep, who in 1780 contrasted average annual copper imports (for four years) of 11,106.20 *maunds* with Rotas mines' production of only 2,000 *maunds* per annum (Stevens 2012: 112); for Indian copper mines see also Lingen and Lucassen (2007).

76 Lucassen (2014a, 34).
77 Lucassen (2014a); cf. Deyell (1987), Habib (1987), Martin (1987); for wages Habib (1987: 154), and Prakash (1987; 2007); Haider (2007; 2015); De Zwart and Lucassen (2015).
78 Kolff and Van Santen (1979: 117). Although Pelsaert here equates *paisa* and *taka*, for 1565 he equates one *taka* to $^1/_{20}$ rupee (ibid.: 84), suggesting 1 *tanka* = 2 *paisa/dams* which is correct (Haider 2007: 307–8). On fluctuating *dam*: rupee rates: ibid. (318–21); Habib (1987: 145–50); Prakash (2007: 340–3); inhabitants: Haider (2007: 293).
79 Deyell (1990) has termed the preceding centuries as India 'living without silver'. For Central and Northern India see Lucassen (2014a), for Southern India – still less researched – see Stein (1989: 41–2), and Palat (2015: 122–30, 161, 171–5).
80 Lucassen (2014a); Habib (1994); Haider (2011; 2015).
81 Haider (2015: 90).
82 Lucassen (2005; 2007a) (based on the work of Richard von Glahn, Hans Ulrich Vogel, and others); Wang (2004); Scheidel (2009).
83 Lucassen (2005: 431–2); Weirong (2005: 95–7); Burger (2008); Scheidel (2009: 154, 194, 199); Liu (2015: 68–76, 218–21).
84 Lucassen (2005: 432).
85 Shen Kua, quoted in Palat (2015: 145).
86 Shikano (2007); Kovalchuk and Depeyrot (2012). I would like to thank Christine Moll-Murata for her information.
87 Apart from the works quoted in the other footnotes, see also Gramlich-Oka (2008), Izawa (2013), and Noriko (2016).
88 Moll-Murata (2012); since elaborately confirmed by Liu (2015).
89 Deng (2015: 326).
90 Chevaleyre (2012).
91 Liu (2015: 74); cf. Von Glahn (2010: 83ff).
92 Moll-Murata (2008; 2015: 275–6).
93 Margariti (2014: 196); cf. Peebles (2010).
94 To push this speculative argument somewhat further: mixed religious populations as in parts of post-Reformation Europe and India after the introduction of Islam, but also in relation to caste distinctions, might have a bearing on conventions regarding small-scale credit and DMLs.
95 Haupt (1894) and *Further Reports* (1870, 1871).
96 Haupt (1894, 890), commenting on the release of the new coins and notes, which appears to have been excessive given the existing stock.
97 Until 1874, 1 *rigsdaler* (0.4064 oz. silver) = 96 *skilling rigsmonts*; 1 *krone* (0.1929 oz. silver) = 100 *øre* from 1874 onwards. Therefore 1 *skilling* equals 0.0042 $^1/_3$ oz. silver, while 1 *øre* equals 0.001929 oz. silver, or 1 *skilling* ≈ 2.2 *øre*. Cf. Märcher (2013), who suggests that in Denmark deep monetization started in the late eighteenth century.
98 My calculation of total production for 1874–85 based on Bruce (2004).
99 Even after the new small coins had arrived from Berlin (126,217 Egyptian pounds in nickels and 5,317 Egyptian pounds in bronzes), Haupt (1894, 91) comments: 'On voit que l'émission de la petite monnaie se tient dans les limites très étroitement tracés.'
100 My calculation based on Bruce (2004).
101 There are reasons to believe that there was an extreme oversupply of coppers as none were struck in the 28 years between 1867 and 1895; nickel 20 *centesimi* pieces did not appear until 1894. Compare this with neighbouring France.
102 My calculation based on Bruce (2004).
103 My calculation based on Bruce (2004).
104 For similar wages on the Azores, see *Further Reports* (1871: 430–7); for Madeira *Further Reports* (1871: 438–41).
105 Probably partially circulating in the colonies, such as Angola. See Haupt (1894, 423–4), and Crib, Cook, and Carradice (1990, 238, 248, 253, 256–7, 262).
106 My calculation based on Bruce (2004).

107 A figure that subsequently rose. For instance, at the end of 1891 the small-change stock had risen to nearly 20 million roubles, giving a DML of nearly 2.

108 Note that all coppers were struck solely in 1868 and 1879 and all copper nickels only in 1883 and 1884, whereas coining these small denominations was resumed only from 1904 onwards. It is likely that at the end of 1885 most small coins were still in stock in Belgrade, to be released into circulation only piecemeal in the years to come.

109 As in the Portuguese case, a substantial portion was sent to the colonies, especially Cuba, but also to Puerto Rico and the Philippines. See Haupt (1894, 314, 517, 691); Crib, Cook, and Carradice (1990, 288, 290).

110 My calculation based on Bruce (2004).

111 Plus my calculation based on Bruce (2004).

112 Cf. 1.3 million pounds in bronze coins in circulation in 1877 and more than twice that sum around 1900. This increase was due also to automatic machines operated by pennies and to the fares of the new electric trams (Dyer and Gaspar 1992, 546).

113 Total production of threepence, fourpence, and sixpence coins 1817–85 was 5.231 million pounds (calculated based on Bruce 2004), less about 12 per cent for exports to colonies (Haupt 1894, 491) makes 4.603 million pounds, less 20 per cent withdrawn (the percentage estimated by Haupt 1894: 490 for all silver coins) gives a figure of 3.682 million pounds. The small amount of bronze exported to the colonies has been ignored here. For the circulation of English copper coins, valued at 35,000 pounds, in New South Wales (Australia), see Haupt (1894: 797). See also Dyer and Gaspar (1992, 546), who report for 1877 that only 8.5 per cent of the bronzes had been shipped overseas.

114 On similar lines the DML for 1857 may be calculated as 2 by excluding the sixpence and as 4.7 by including it (copper coin circulation valued at 800 million pounds; see Dyer and Gaspar (1992, 509) and Selgin (2008, 299).

References

Allen, M. (2001). 'The volume of the English currency, 1158–1470', *Economic History Review*, 54 (4): 595–611.

Allen, M. (2012). *Mints and Money in Medieval England*, Cambridge, UK: Cambridge University Press.

Allen, M. (2015). 'Coin finds and the English money supply, c. 973–1544', in Allen, M. and Coffman, D. (eds.), *Money, Prices and Wages. Essays in Honour of Professor Nicholas Mayhew*, Basingstoke, UK: Palgrave Macmillan: 7–23.

Bacherikov, P. (2013). 'Monety i zarplaty: vypusk monetykh denominatsii kak indikator rasprostranenii naemnogo truda v Rossii v XVII veke', unpublished course paper Higher School of Economics and New Economic School.

Béaur, G., Jessenne, J.P., Menant, F., and Vivier, N. (2010). 'Northern France, 1000–1750', in Van Bavel, B. and Hoyle, R. (eds.), *Social Relations: Property and Power*, Turnhout, Belgium: Brepols, 111–48.

Biernacki, R. (1995). *The Fabrication of Labor: Germany and Britain, 1640–1914*. Berkeley, CA: University of California Press.

Bolton, J. (2012). *Money in the Medieval English Economy, 973–1489*. Manchester: Manchester University Press.

Britnell, R. (2015). 'Labour turnover and wage rates on the demesnes of Durham priority', in Allen, M. and Coffman, D. (eds.), *Money, Prices and Wages. Essays in Honour of Professor Nicholas Mayhew*, Basingstoke, UK: Palgrave Macmillan: 158–179.

Bruce, C. (2004). *Standard Catalog of World Coins: 1801–1900*, Iola, WI: KP Books.

Burger, W. (2008). 'Coin production during the Qianlong and Jiaqing reigns (1736–1820): Issues in cash and silver supply', in Hirzel and Kim (eds.) (2008): 171–89.

Cardon, Th. (2012). 'Les petites monnaies étrangères en Normandie au XIVe–XVe siècles: provenances, modalités d'introduction et circulation', in Chameroy, J. and Guihard, P.-M. (eds.), *Circulations monétaires et réseaux d'échanges en Normandie et dans le Nord-Ouest européen (Antiquité – Moyen Âge)*, Caen, France: CRAHM: 207–28.

Cardon, Th. and Lemaire, F. (2014). 'Les sous des soldats de Napoléon au camp de Boulogne (1803-1805). Étude des monnaies issues des fouilles des camps napoléoniens d'Étaples-sur-Mer et Camiers (Pas-de-Calais, France)', *The Journal of Archaeological Numismatics*, 4: 67–176.

Challis, C. (ed.) (1992). *A New History of the Royal Mint*, Cambridge, UK: Cambridge University Press.

Chevaleyre, C. (2012). 'Acting as master and bondservant: Considerations on status, identities and the nature of "bond-servitude" in late Ming China', in Stanziani, A. (ed.), *Labour, Coercion, and Economic Growth in Eurasia, 17th–20th Centuries*, Leiden, the Netherlands and Boston, MA: Brill: 237–72.

Ciani, L. (1926). *Les monnaies royales françaises de Hugues Capet à Louis XVI*, Paris: s.n.

Cribb, J., Cook, B. and Carradice, I. (1990). *The Coin Atlas: The World of Coinage from Its Origins to the Present Day*. London and Sydney: Macdonald.

Deng, K. (2015). 'Imperial China under the Song and late Qing', in Monson, A. and Scheidel, W. (eds.), *Fiscal Regimes and the Political Economy of Premodern States*, Cambridge, UK: Cambridge University Press: 308–42.

Depeyrot, G. (ed.) (2013). *Three Conferences on International Monetary History*. Wetteren, Belgium: Moneta.

Desan, Ch. (2015). *Making Money. Coin, Currency, and the Coming of Capitalism*. Oxford: Oxford University Press.

Desrousseaux, S. (2012). *La monnaie en circulation en France sous Napoléon*. Paris: Éditions les Cheveau-Léger.

Deyell, J. (1987). 'The development of Akbar's currency system and monetary integration of the conquered kingdoms', in Richards (1987): 13–67.

Deyell, J. (1990). *Living without Silver: The Monetary History of Early Medieval North India*. New Delhi: Oxford University Press.

De Zwart, P. and Lucassen, J. (2015). 'Poverty or prosperity in Bengal c. 1700–1785? New evidence, methods and perspectives', unpublished paper, WEHC Kyoto, August 2015.

Dyer, Ch. (2015). 'A golden age rediscovered: Labourers' wages in the fifteenth century', in Allen, M. and Coffman, D. (eds.), *Money, Prices and Wages. Essays in Honour of Professor Nicholas Mayhew*, Basingstoke, UK: Palgrave Macmillan: 180–195.

Dyer, G. and Gaspar, P. (1992). 'Reform, the new technology and Tower Hill, 1700–1966', in Challis, C. (ed.), *A New History of the Royal Mint*, Cambridge, UK: Cambridge University Press: 398–606.

Feinman, G. and Garraty, Ch. (2010), 'Preindustrial markets and marketing: Archaeological perspectives', *Annual Review of Anthropology*, 39:167–91.

Florén, A. (1994). 'Social organization of work and labour conflicts in proto-industrial iron production in Sweden, Belgium and Russia', *International Review of Social History*, 39 [Supplement]: 83–113.

Further Reports from Her Majesty's Diplomatic and Consular Agents Abroad Respecting the Condition of the Industrial Classes and the Purchase Power of Money in Foreign Countries (1870). House of Commons Parliamentary Papers 1870. London: Harrison.

Further Reports from Her Majesty's Diplomatic and Consular Agents Abroad Respecting the Condition of the Industrial Classes and the Purchase Power of Money in Foreign Countries (1871). House of Commons Parliamentary Papers 1871. London: Harrison.

Garg, S. (2013). *The Sikka and the Raj: A History of Currency Legislations of the East India Company, 1772–1835*, New Delhi: Manohar.

Gemmill, E. and Mayhew, N. (1995). *Changing Values in Medieval Scotland: A Study of Prices, Money, and Weights and Measures*, Cambridge, UK: Cambridge University Press.

Goubert, P. (1968). *Cent mille provinciaux au XVIIe siècle. Beauvais et le Beauvaisis de 1600 à 1730*, Paris: Flammarion.

Gramlich-Oka, B. (2008). 'Shogunal administration of copper in the mid-Tokugawa period (1670–1720)', in Hirzel and Kim (eds.) (2008): 65–105.

Grytten, O. (2004). 'Economic growth and purchasing power parities in the Nordic countries, 1830–1910', in Heikkinen, S. and Van Zanden, J.L. (eds.), *Exploring Economic Growth: Essays in Measurement and Analysis. A Festschrift for Riitta Hjerppe on her 60th Birthday*, Amsterdam: Aksant: 89–104.

Habib, I. (1987). 'A system of trimetallism in the age of the "price revolution": Effects of the silver influx on the Mughal monetary system', in Richards (ed.) (1987): 137–70.

Habib, I. (1994). 'The price regulations of 'Ala'uddin Khalji – a defence of Zia' Barani', in Subrahmanyam, S. (ed.), *Money and the Market in India 1100–1700*, Delhi: Oxford University Press: 85–111.

Haider, N. (2007). 'Structure and movement of wages in the Mughal Empire, 1500–1700', in Lucassen, J. (ed.) (2007): 293–321.

Haider, N. (2011). 'Coinage and the silver crisis', in Habib, I. (ed.), *Economic History of Medieval India, 1200–1500*, New Delhi: Longman: 149–62.

Haider, N. (2015). 'Fractional pieces and non-metallic monies in medieval India (1200–1750)', in Leonard and Theobald (eds.) (2015): 86–107.

Hanley, S. and Yamamura, K. (1977). *Economic and Demographic Change in Preindustrial Japan, 1600–1868*, Princeton, NJ: Princeton University Press.

Haselgrove, C. and Krmnicek, S. (2012). 'The archaeology of money', *Annual Review of Anthropology*, 41: 235–50.

Haupt, O. (1886). *L'histoire monetaire de notre temps*, Paris: Truchy.

Haupt, O. (1894). *Arbitrages et parités: traité des opérations de banque: contenant les usages commerciaux, la théorie des changes et monnaies, les dettes publiques et la statistique monétaire de tous les pays du globe*. Paris: Truchy.

Hirzel, Th. and Kim, N. (eds.) (2008). *Metals, Monies, and Markets in Early Modern Societies: East Asian and Global Perspectives*. Berlin: LIT Verlag.

Hogendorn, J. and Johnson, M. (1986). *The Shell Money of the Slave Trade*. Cambridge, UK: Cambridge University Press.

Imperial Gazetteer of India, Vol. VII (1908). Oxford: Clarendon Press.

Izawa, E. (2013). 'Developments in Japanese copper metallurgy for coinage and foreign trade in the early Edo period', in Kim, N. and Nagase-Reimer, K. (eds.), *Mining, Monies, and Culture in Early Modern Societies*, Leiden, the Netherlands and Boston, MA: Brill: 11–24.

Kelleher, R. (2013). 'Coins, monetisation and re-use in medieval England and Wales: New interpretations made possible by the Portable Antiquities Scheme', unpublished Ph.D. thesis, University of Durham. Online. Available HTTP: http://etheses.dur.ac.uk/7314.

Kelleher, R. and Leins, I. (2008). 'Roman, medieval and later coins from the Vintry, City of London', *The Numismatic Chronicle*, 168: 167–233.

Kolchin, P. (1987). *Unfree Labor: American Slavery and Russian Serfdom*. Cambridge, MA: Harvard University Press.

Kolff, D. and Van Santen, H. (eds.) (1979). *De Geschriften van Francisco Pelsaert over Mughal Indië, 1627. Kroniek en Remonstrantie.* The Hague, the Netherlands: Nijhoff.

Kovalchuk, M. and Depeyrot, G. (eds.) (2012). *Documents and Studies on 19th c. Monetary History. Japan. Selection of British and US Documents (1857-1898).* Wetteren, Belgium: Moneta.

Leonard, J. and Theobald, U. (eds.) (2015). *Money in Asia (1200–1900): Small Currencies in Social and Political Contexts.* Leiden, the Netherlands and Boston, MA: Brill.

Le Roy-Ladurie, E. (1969). *Les paysans de Languedoc.* Paris: Flammarion.

Lingen, J. and Lucassen, J. (2007). 'The "mansuri" or "munsooree paisa" and its use: combining numismatic and social history of India, c. 1830–1900', *Numismatic Digest,* 31: 187–220.

Lingen, J. and Lucassen, J. (2010–1). 'Copper circulation in Northern India in 1830', *Numismatic Digest,* 34–35: 148–83.

Lingen, J. and Lucassen, J. (2012–13). 'Warfare and coin circulation. Two lacs of Bharatpur and Bindrabund rupees and 15 bags of copper pyce, captured at Dig on Christmas' Eve 1804', *Numismatic Digest,* 36–37: 157–81.

Liu, W. (2015). *The Chinese Market Economy 1000–1500,* Albany, NY: SUNY Press.

Lucassen, J. (2005). 'Coin production, coin circulation, and the payment of wages in Europe and China 1200–1900', in Moll-Murata, Ch., Jianze, S. and Vogel, H. (eds.), *Chinese Handicraft Regulations of the Qing Dynasty: Theory and Application,* Munich, Germany: Iudicium: 423–46.

Lucassen, J. (2007a). 'Introduction: wages and currency, 500 BCE–2000 CE', in Lucassen, J. (ed.) (2007): 9–58.

Lucassen, J. (2007b). 'The logistics of wage payments: Changing patterns in Northern India in the 1840s', in Lucassen, J. (ed.) (2007): 349–90.

Lucassen, J. (2007c). 'Wage payments and currency circulation in the Netherlands from 1200 to 2000', in Lucassen, J. (ed.) (2007): 221–63.

Lucassen, J. (2014a). 'Deep monetization, commercialization and proletarianization: Possible links, India 1200–1900', in Bhattacharya, S. (ed.), *Towards a New History of Work,* New Delhi: Tulika: 17–55.

Lucassen, J. (2014b). 'Deep monetisation: The case of the Netherlands 1200–1940', *Tijdschrift voor Sociale en Economische Geschiedenis,* 11: 73–121.

Lucassen, J. (2017). 'Labour and deep monetization in Eurasia', paper to be published in Hofmeester, K. and De Zwart, P. (eds.), *Colonialism, Institutional Change and Shifts in Global Labour Relations,* Amsterdam, the Netherlands: Amsterdam University Press.

Lucassen, J. (ed.) (2007). *Wages and Currency: Global Comparisons from Antiquity to the Twentieth Century.* Bern, Switzerland: Lang.

Lucassen, J. and Stapel, R. (2014). 'Shifts in labour relations in India 1800–2000', paper for the X International Conference on Labour History, Noida (India), 22–24 March 2014.

Lucassen, J. and Zuijderduijn, J. (2014). 'Coins, currencies, and credit instruments: Media of exchange in economic and social history', *Tijdschrift voor Sociale en Economische Geschiedenis,* 11: 1–13.

Lurvink, K. (2014). 'Strapped for cash: Non-cash payments on Louisiana cotton plantations, 1865–1908', *Tijdschrift voor Sociale en Economische Geschiedenis,* 11: 123–51.

Märcher, M. (2013). 'Bronze and copper coins in 19th century Denmark – and found at Koldekilde on Bornholm', in Depeyrot (ed.) (2013): 103–22.

Margariti, R. (2014). 'Coins and commerce. Monetization and cross-cultural collaboration in the Western Indian Ocean (eleventh to thirteenth centuries)', in Trivellato, F., Halevi,

L. and Antunes, C. (eds.), *Religion and Trade: Cross-Cultural Exchanges in World History 1000–1900*, Oxford: Oxford University Press: 192–215.

Martin, M. (1987). 'The reforms of the sixteenth century and Akbar's administration: Metrological and monetary considerations', in Richards (1987): 68–99.

Martiny, J.-C. (2014). *Het Munthuis in Gent van de Karolingers tot de Calvinistische Republiek 768–1584*. 3 Vols. Ghent, Belgium: Snoecks.

Matsukata, M. (2014). 'Report on the adoption of the gold standard in Japan (1899)', republished by Depeyrot, G. and Kovalchuk, M. in *Documents and Studies on 19th c. Monetary History*. Wetteren, Belgium: Moneta.

Maurer, B. (2006). 'The anthropology of money', *Annual Review of Anthropology*, 35: 15–36.

Mayhew, N. (2007). 'Wages and currency: The case in Britain up to c. 1600', in Lucassen, (ed.) (2007): 211–20.

Moll-Murata, Ch. (2005). 'Maintenance and renovation of the Metropolitan City God Temple and the Peking City Wall during the Qing dynasty', in Moll-Murata, Ch., Jianze, S., and Vogel, H. (eds.), *Chinese Handicraft Regulations of the Qing Dynasty: Theory and Application*, Munich: Iudicium: 233–62.

Moll-Murata, Ch. (2008). *State and Crafts in the Qing Dynasty (1644–1911)*, Tübingen, Germany: Habilitationsschrift.

Moll-Murata, Ch. (2012). 'China, Taiwan, Japan 1500–2000', paper for the May 2012 conference of the IISH Global Collaboratory on the History of Labour Relations 1500–2000.

Moll-Murata, Ch. (2015). 'Legal conflicts concerning wage payments in eighteenth- and nineteenth-century China. The Baxian cases', in Leonard, J. and Theobald, U. (eds.) (2015): Brill: 265–308.

Muldrew, C. (2007). 'Wages and the problem of monetary scarcity in early modern England', in Lucassen (ed.) (2007): 391–410.

Naismith, R. (2012). *Money and Power in Anglo-Saxon England: The Southern English Kingdoms, 757–865*, Cambridge, UK: Cambridge University Press.

Noriko, I. (2016). 'Copper in Edo-period Japan', in Nagase-Reimer, K. (ed.), *Copper in Early Modern Sino-Japanese Trade*, Leiden, the Netherlands and Boston, MA: Brill: 10–31.

Palairet, M. (1997). *The Balkan Economies c. 1800–1914: Evolution without Development*. Cambridge, UK: Cambridge University Press.

Palat, R. (2015). *The Making of an Indian Ocean World-Economy, 1250–1650. Princes, Paddy fields, and Bazaars*. Basingstoke, UK: Palgrave Macmillan.

Pannekeet, K. and Cruysheer, A. (2013). 'Holpenningen in Nederland (ca. 1460–1570)', *Jaarboek voor Munt- en Penningkunde*, 100: 59–127.

Peebles, G. (2010). 'The anthropology of credit and debt', *Annual Review of Anthropology*, 39: 225–40.

Phelps Brown, H., and Hopkins, S. (1981). *A Perspective of Wages and Prices*, London and New York: Methuen.

Prakash, O. (1987). 'Foreign merchants and Indian mints in the seventeenth and early eighteenth century', in Richards (ed.) (1987): 171–92.

Prakash, O. (2004). *Bullion for Goods: European and Indian Merchants in the Indian Ocean Trade 1500–1800*, New Delhi: Manohar.

Prakash, O. (2007). 'Long distance trade, coinage and wages in India, 1600–1960', in Lucassen (ed.) (2007): 323–48.

Prunaux, E. (2013). 'La question du cuivre-papier au début du 19ème siècle. Les banques de sols et la loi du 24 germinal an XI', in Depeyrot (ed.) (2013): 147–70.

Ray, H. (ed.) (2006). *Coins in India: Power and Communication*, Mumbay: Marq.

Reddy, W. (1987). *Money and Liberty in Modern Europe: A Critique of Historical Understanding*, Cambridge: Cambridge University Press.

*Report of the Committee Appointed to Inquire into the Indian Currency (with Minutes of Evidence, Correspondence, Index, Further Papers(London, 1893) (*2011*), republication as* Kovalchuk, M. *and* Depeyrot, G. *(eds.), Documents and Studies on Monetary History India.*. Wetteren, Belgium: Moneta.

Richards, J. (ed.) (1987). *The Imperial Monetary System of Mughal India*, Oxford: Oxford University Press.

Roscher, W. (1881). *System der Volkswirtschaft. Ein Hand- und Lesebuch für Geschäftsmänner und Studierende.* Dritter Band: *die Nationalökonomik des Handels und Gewerbefleisses.* Stuttgart, Germany: Cotta.

Rössner, P. (2016). 'Velocity! The speed of monetary circulation as a historical protagonist in European economic thought and practice, c. 1350–1800', unpublished paper XLVIII Settimana di Studi Fondazione 'F. Datini', Prato, 8–11 May 2016.

Sargent, Th. and Velde, F. (2002). *The Big Problem of Small Change.* Princeton, NJ: Princeton University Press.

Scheidel, W. (2009). *Rome and China: Comparative Perspectives on Ancient World Empire.* Oxford: Oxford University Press.

Selgin, G. (2008). *Good Money: Birmingham Button Makers, the Royal Mint, and the Beginnings of Modern Coinage, 1775–1821.* Ann Arbor, MI: The University of Michigan Press.

Shikano, Y. (2007). 'Currency, wage payments, and large funds settlement in Japan, 1600–1868', in Lucassen (ed.) (2007): 113–37.

Shimada, R. (2006). *The Intra-Asian Trade in Japanese Copper by the Dutch East India Company during the Eighteenth Century*, Leiden, the Netherlands and Boston, MA: Brill.

Simmel, G. (1908). *Soziologie. Untersuchungen über die Formen der Vergesellschaftung.* Leipzig, Germany: Duncker & Humblot.

Simmel, G. (1922). *Philosophie des Geldes.* Munich and Leipzig, Germany: Duncker und Humblot.

Simmel, G. (2009). *The Philosophy of Money* (3rd edition, edited by David Frisby). London and New York: Routledge.

Smail, D. (2016). *Legal Plunder. Households and Debt Collection in Medieval Europe*, Cambridge, MA and London: Harvard University Press.

Spufford, P. (1988). *Money and Its Use in Medieval Europe.* Cambridge, UK: Cambridge University Press.

Spufford, P. (2002). *Power and Profit: The Merchant in Medieval Europe.* London: Thames and Hudson.

Spufford, P. (2008). *How Rarely Did Medieval Merchants Use Coin: Vijfde Van Gelder-lezing Gehouden Voor Geldmuseum en Stichting Nederlandse Penningkabinetten Te Leiden Op 16 November 2006.* Utrecht, the Netherlands: Geldmuseum.

Spufford, P. (2014). 'Scottish black money in the Low Countries c. 1484–1506', *The British Numismatic Journal*, 84: 125–39.

Stein, B. (1989). *The New Cambridge History of India*, Vol. 1.2: *Vijayanagara.* Cambridge, UK: Cambridge University Press.

Stevens, P. (2012). *The Coins of the Bengal Presidency.* London: Baldwin.

Subrahmanyam, S. (ed.) (1994). *Money and the Market in India 1100–1700.* Delhi, UK: Oxford University Press.

Svirina, E. (2014). 'Money circulation in the Siberian region of the Russian Empire', in Depeyrot, G. (ed.), *Documents and Studies on 19th c. Monetary History. When Orient and Occident Meet*, Wetteren, Belgium: Moneta: 319–22.

Touitou-Michon, B. and Michon, S. (2013). 'Mémoire de Léonard de Martin Nadaud ou De l'usage de sou au XIXe siècle en France', in Depeyrot (ed.) (2013): 171–78.

Valenze, D. (2006). *The Social Life of Money in the English Past*, Cambridge, UK: Cambridge University Press.

Van Bavel, B. (2006). 'Rural wage labour in the sixteenth-century Low Countries: An assessment of the importance and nature of wage labour in the countryside of Holland, Guelders and Flanders', *Continuity and Change*, 21: 37–72.

Van de Polder, L. (1891). 'Abridged history of the copper coins of Japan', *Transactions of the Asiatic Society of Japan*, 19: 419–500, illustrations 1–123 plus appendix.

Vanhoudt, H. (2015). *De munten van de Bourgondische, Spaanse en Oostenrijkse Nederlanden en van de Franse en Hollandse periode 1434–1830*. Heverlee, Belgium: Vanhoudt.

Van Laere, R. (2013). 'The Nieuwerkerken hoard and the circulation of copper coins in the Prince-Bishopric of Liege during the late 18th century', in Depeyrot (ed.) (2013): 179–229.

Van Leeuwen, B. (2007). *Human Capital and Economic Growth in India, Indonesia and Japan: A Quantitative Analysis, 1890–2000*, s.l.: Box Press Shop.

Volckart, O. (2008). '"The big problem of the petty coins", and how it could be solved in the late Middle Ages', working papers no. 107/08, London School of Economics.

Von Glahn, R. (1996). *Fountain of Fortune: Money and Monetary Policy in China, 1000–1700*. Berkeley, CA: University of California Press.

Von Glahn, R. (2010). 'Monies of account and monetary transition in China, twelfth to fourteenth centuries', *Journal of the Economic and Social History of the Orient*, 53: 463–505.

Von Sonnenfels, J. (1787). *Grundsätze der Polizey, Handlung, und Finanzwissenschaft*. Munich, Germany: Strobel.

Von Sonnenfels, J. (1804). *Grundsätze der Polizey, Handlung, und Finanz*, 2 Volumes. Vienna, Austria: Camesina.

Wang, H. (2004). *Money on the Silk Road: The Evidence from Eastern Central Asia to c.* ad *800. With a Catalogue of the Coins Collected by Sir Aurel Stein*. London: British Museum.

Wang, H. (2007). 'Official salaries and local wages at Juyan, North-West China, first century BCE to first century CE', in Lucassen (ed.) (2007): 59–76.

Weirong, Z. (2005). 'Chinese coins: Alloy composition and metallurgical research', in Wang, H., Cowell, M., Cribb, J., and Bowman, S. (eds.), *Metallurgical Analysis of Chinese Coins at the British Museum*, London: British Museum: 95–7.

Welten, J. (2010). *Met klinkende munt betaald. Muntcirculatie in de beide Limburgen 1770–1839*, Utrecht, the Netherlands: Geldmuseum.

Welten, J. (2015). *Antihelden. Bijzondere levens van gewone mensen uit de tijd van Napoleon*, Leuven, Belgium: Davidsfonds.

White, J. (2016). *Mansions of Misery. A Biography of the Marshallsea Debtor's Prison*, London: The Bodley Head.

5 Money, silver and trust in Mesopotamia

R.J. van der Spek, J.G. Dercksen, K. Kleber and M. Jursa

A man who owns silver counts it every day.[1]

Introduction: The magic of silver – Bert van der Spek

Karl Marx has for long framed the discussion of the economy of the ancient Near East by his concept of the 'Asiatic Mode of Production' (*Asiatische Produktionsweise*). This model (first of all developed for India and China) is characterized by an autocratic state in which the king owns all the land, while the people live in villages, live off their ancestral plots and have to pay taxes in kind to the palace, which in turn redistributes it among the elite of favourites (civil servants, soldiers, temples). Hence, there was no market and no real trade. The villagers got the products that they did not produce themselves by reciprocity and barter in the village. This model was taken up by various later scholars, such as Karl Wittfogel (1957), Karl Polanyi (1957) and Johannes Renger (1994; 1995; 2005). In such a model there is hardly room for free trade and thus hardly a demand for the use of a means of exchange, a means of account and store of value, functions which come together in the phenomenon 'money'.

This model has some value indeed, as it is clear that great institutional households of the palace and the temple did have a great impact on the economy. Organizations of this size did not exist in the Graeco-Roman world. Redistribution by the great institutions played a role in providing food and clothing to many people, but it is also true that this model may blur a clear understanding of the ancient Near Eastern economy. It has been established in many studies that it is not true that the king owned all the land, that private property existed in Mesopotamia in the third millennium already, that trade was important for the exchange of goods and obtaining necessities of life. There was always interplay of demand and supply and thus the establishment of the value of goods by means of prices. Hence, there was a market in all periods of the Mesopotamian history. That does not mean, however, that the market functioned at all times in the same way. At the beginning of the third millennium, the temples of the early Sumerian city-states dominated economic life;

later, the palace asserted a prominent place in the economy. But private property existed at all times and over time occupied an increasing role, especially in the first millennium BC.[2]

When there is trade, a means of exchange is required for facilitating trade. In Mesopotamia, several materials functioned as money: barley, lead, copper or bronze, tin, silver and gold.[3] In addition (or perhaps even earlier) debt documents could be used as money (cf. Bezemer, Chapter 3, this volume). There has been a lively debate on the role of (coined and uncoined) silver as money in antiquity (Powell 1996; Von Reden 1995, 2007; Le Rider 2001; Jursa 2010: 469–753). Prices were sometimes expressed as a combination of these moneys (so much silver and so much copper; cf. Radner 1999: 128–9). Silver was already a means of payment in the third millennium BC (cf. Krispijn 2016; Powell 1996) and this remained so during the entire history of ancient Mesopotamia. The standard unit of measuring silver was the shekel (*šiqlu* from *šaqālu*, 'to weigh', but also 'to pay', cf. e.g. Dercksen 2016; many examples in the Chicago Assyrian Dictionary [CAD] s.v. *šaqālu*) weighing 8.33 gr. Especially in the Neo-Babylonian period fractions of the shekel were in use (up to 1/24 [*girû*, 'carob-seed'] and 1/40 [*hallūru*, 'chick-pea']) and were indeed used in daily transactions.

Silver was thus the main money material. Possession of silver was very important as an indication of wealth. Trust in silver and protection of the value of silver was a main concern. Assyrian and Babylonian kings boasted that they collected huge amounts of booty and tribute, among which silver and gold were ubiquitous. We read the same boasts as regards King Solomon of Israel.[4] We see the interest in the (relative) value of metals in the claims made by king Sargon II of Assyria (722–705 BC) in one of his royal inscriptions. In this period, copper, bronze and silver were used as money in Assyria, but before 712 BC copper was preponderant. In 712, Sargon II conquered Carchemish and brought home a huge amount of silver. After that campaign, silver replaced copper as the main currency, and silver is measured in the mina of Carchemish (Postgate 1979: 18; Müller 1997: 120; Radner 1999: 129). We observe this in Assyrian letters to king Sargon:

> To the king, my lord: Your servant Adda-hati. Good health to the king, my lord! [4] The silver dues of the prefects and village managers imposed on the local population have been handed over: two talents and 18 minas of silver according to the standard of Carchemish (*ina ma-né-*⌜*e*⌝ *š*[*a* uru *gar-g*]*a-mis*). In addition I have sent to the king, my lord, half a shekel of gold, two [tog]as and three tunics with my messenger.
>
> (Parpola 1987: 138 = SAA I, no. 176: 1–9)

Sargon II plundered so much booty in that campaign that he boasted that from that time on the exchange value (*mahīru*) of silver was to equal that of bronze (Annals from Khorsabad 232–4 = Fuchs 1994: 130 ff.). Actually, he boasts here a reversal of Gresham's Law that good money drives out bad money. Modern economists would perhaps doubt if a sudden devaluation of the silver is really so good.

Many Mesopotamian texts give testimony of concern for the purchasing power of silver. Prices of bulk goods in the Near East were expressed as the purchasing power of silver rather than as prices of products, as we also observe in the Biblical story on the siege of Samaria by Ben-Hadad (II Kings 7:1–2). Concern for it is expressed in royal propaganda texts. From Assurbanipal's Coronation Hymn, we can deduce how desirable a good exchange value of the shekel was:

> 5-7 Just as grain and silver, oil, [the catt]le of Šakkan and the salt of Bariku are good, so may Assurbanipal, king of Assyria, be agreeable to the gods [of his] land! … 9–11 May the people of Assur buy 30 kor (= 5400 litres) of grain for one shekel of silver! May [the people] of Assur buy 3 seah (18 litres) of oil for one shekel of silver! May [the peopl]e of Assur buy 30 minas (15 kg.) of wool for one shekel of silver!
>
> (Livingstone 1989: 26–7 = SAA III, no. 11)

These are pious, wishful thoughts with no relation to reality. Closer to real life is the Neo-Babylonian king Nabonidus (556–539 BC). He boasts in his so-called Tariff Stela from Babylon that favourable exchange values were realized during his reign:

> At the command of Sîn (moon god, supreme deity for Nabonidus), king of the gods, Adad (weather god) released the rain for me and Ea (god of sweet water under the earth) opened for me lavishly his sources; wealth, fertility and plenty he established in my country. 234 litres of barley for one shekel, 270 litres of dates for one shekel, 66 litres of sesame for one shekel, [x+^{5}]18 litres of oil for one shekel, 5 pounds of wool for one shekel, 1 pound of tin$^{?}$ for one shekel, wine, the beer of the mountains, that does not exist in my country: 18 litres of wine for one shekel of silver was the exchange value in my country.
>
> (Schaudig 2001: 530–2, No. 3.4:2'–12')

Now this is a propaganda text, but actually not far off the mark. The ideal exchange value was 1 *kurru* (= 180 litres in this period) for both barley and dates for 1 shekel, and these equivalencies occurred, but prices fluctuated. In Nabonidus' reign, the rate of barley fluctuated between 90 to 257.1 litres (Jursa 2010: 445), and the rate of dates up to 259.5 litres of dates per shekel is attested (cf. Jursa 2010: 585: n. 3179 and 593–4). The Tariff Stela shows the real concern of the king as regards the purchasing power of the shekel.

The same concern for the purchasing power of silver we find in the work of Babylonian scholars, versed in the art of divination, i.e. futurology by the interpretation of omens. The study of the abundant corpus of Mesopotamian omen texts is an extremely valuable tool in understanding the concerns of ancient

Mesopotamian man. Many omens mention the purchasing power of the shekel, which means that the volatility of prices was a major concern indeed. However, it is often misunderstood by Assyriologists. It is good to note that the word *mahīru*, written epigraphically KI.LAM, is often incorrectly translated in the dictionaries, especially the Chicago Assyrian Dictionary. The word refers to 'receiving' = 'what is received' in exchange for something else and in particular for silver.[6] The basic meaning, correctly observed in the *Akkadisches Handwörterbuch* of Wolfram von Soden, is thus 'exchange value' (AHw II: 583, s.v. *mahīru(m)*: 'Gegenwert, Kurs'). As a derivative, the term may mean: 'Market, market place; business' (to do business is 'to give and receive', *nadānu u mahāru*). The CAD, however, starts with this interpretation and applies it to circumstances that do not fit, as e.g. in the omen texts. The omens are concerned with 'good exchange rates' = people receive much grain for one shekel, referring to low prices, and with 'bad exchange rates' = people receiving little grain for a shekel = high prices. I discuss a few omen apodoses, discussed by the CAD[7]: KI.LAM *ina* KUR ŠUB *kaspu ul ibašši*, 'the exchange value (of the shekel) will be annihilated, (because) there will be no silver' (KAR427: 4). In the above quoted passage, the CAD translates as 'business will collapse', which is not the issue. It stresses the role of silver: when there is no silver, there can be no exchange. *Māt šarri ša sunqa īmuru* KI.LAM *napša mātu ikkal* (BRM 4 13: 58) does not mean 'the king's country that has experienced hard times will enjoy good business', but 'the country will enjoy (lit. 'eat' (!)) abundant exchange value (= receive abundant grain for a shekel)'. Hence, trust in the purchasing power is seen as the foundation of welfare.

The interest of the scholars is nicely exemplified by the so-called Astronomical Diaries. These diaries, called *naṣār ša ginê*, 'regular observations', contain daily records of regular phenomena, first of all, movements of celestial bodies, but also omens, historical events, the level of the Euphrates and last but not least prices, that is: records of the purchasing power of silver, 'the exchange rate of so-and-so much grain, dates, mustard, sesame and wool that was given in the land for one shekel of silver' (Van der Spek 2016b). These scholars also made datasets of historical events alone ('chronicles') and so-called 'price lists'. These price lists have a similar name: *naṣār ša nadān*, 'observation of the exchange rates' (Slotsky and Wallenfels 2009, text 2: 1; cf. Van der Spek 2016b). All this shows that these scholars were fascinated by a scientific inductive method of the study and prediction of the purchasing power of silver.

In this chapter, we discuss the development of silver as money in the second and first millenniums BC up to the time of Alexander the Great. For the Hellenistic period, see Chapters 6 and 7. Dercksen discusses the abundant evidence from the Assyrian traders' colony at Kanesh in southeast Anatolia; Michael Jursa compares the use of silver in daily exchange in the Old Babylonian period and the Neo-Babylonian period, while Kristin Kleber pays attention to an exceptional stage in the development in between, the Kassite period, when gold replaced silver as the standard currency.

The Old Assyrian period (2000–1700 BC) – Jan Gerrit Dercksen

Introduction

The use of various forms of money is documented in texts written on behalf of the Assyrian city-state (the king, other institutions) and its trading colonies in Anatolia (*kārum*, 'colony', *wabartum*, 'trading station') and, by far the majority of the evidence, in texts written by merchants from Assur and their families. In addition, a small number of texts stems from members of the Anatolian urban elite (priests, merchants). As a consequence, all direct evidence concerns only a small part of society. With few exceptions, all textual evidence has been excavated at the site of Kültepe (north-east of modern Kayseri), ancient Kanesh.[8]

The aim of the Old Assyrian trade was to obtain silver and gold by selling tin and woollen textiles (and smaller quantities of carnelian, lapis lazuli and iron) imported via Assur into Central Anatolia.[9] The merchants often received payment in copper, but since it was uneconomic to ship that to Assur in view of considerable costs of transportation and other copper sources closer to Assur, such copper had to be shipped to and sold in an Anatolian town. The same applied to wool and woollen fleeces that might be obtained. The silver and gold acquired as proceeds were sent to the central colony at Kanesh and from there were shipped to Assur.

Money

The metals copper and silver were commonly used as means of payment, tin and bronze on a limited scale and gold rarely. Silver was widely used as a unit of account, gold only within the context of *naruqqum*-investments and tin only within the *awītum*-system (see below, 'Role of the state'). The value of these metals depended on their purity and market value and important price differences are documented.[10] However, for practical purposes, Assyrian merchants seem to have used the relative value of 60:6:1 for copper, tin and silver, respectively, in Anatolia.

The different contexts for the use of money in Old Assyrian society can be listed thus:

- to purchase merchandise and services in Assur: silver, copper; gold was first converted into silver;
- to pay export tax in Assur: expressed in silver and partly paid in silver.
- hoarding by the city-state: gold;
- votive offerings: silver, gold;
- to pay Assyrian taxation in the *awītum*-system: tin (on Kanesh-bound shipments), silver (on Assur-bound shipments);
- to pay tolls to authorities in North Syria: tin (Kanesh-bound) and silver (Assur-bound shipments);

- to pay tolls and taxes to Anatolian authorities: copper; exceptional: silver; means of payment prescribed in treaty;
- to pay dues to Assyrian authorities in Anatolia: copper, silver, but also in kind (textiles);
- to purchase goods and services in Anatolia: copper, silver; exceptional: tin, gold;
- to express financial punishment when breaking a contract in Anatolia: silver.

Metals

Metal was used as money because of its intrinsic value. Silver circulated in the shape of rings and coils, ingots of various sizes and shape, pieces of scrap and lumps of native silver. Copper (and tin) changed hands as ingots or fragments thereof. Refined copper and a quality called *šikkum* (about one-third of the price of refined copper) were used in Anatolia; impure 'black' copper was rarely accepted.[11] Silver circulated in Anatolia in different qualities.[12] Although the Assyrians aimed at obtaining good-quality silver (*dammuqum*, 'fine'), they sometimes received pieces of impure metal. Such impure pieces were exchanged for another material or given to a smith for remelting; any losses had to be accepted by the owner. Amounts of silver mentioned in loan documents are usually qualified as refined (*ṣarrupum*), which represented the best quality and apparently was comparable to checked (*ammurum*) silver.[13] It is unknown whether and how 'fine' or 'refined' silver differed from 'checked' silver. One may perhaps compare the checked silver to Old Babylonian 'sealed silver', denoting pieces of silver carefully weighed and packed by an official institution, without, however, indicating any quality.[14]

Silver was remelted in Kanesh before being sent to Assur; impure elements were removed and the metal could be cast in standardized forms (bars, round ingots).[15] The loss of metal during refining at Kanesh (on average 4.3%) was substantially higher than in the secondary (or tertiary) refining that could be undertaken in Assur (0.8%).[16] Note that according to a recent study of silver metallurgy in the Old Babylonian city of Mari (ca. 1770 BC),[17] refining of silver led on average to losses of 4%; however, a case of undoubtedly secondary refining led to a loss of 0.8%. This situation must have resulted from the refining of (impure) silver coming from different sources in the first instance (similar to the situation in Kanesh), and, in the second instance, re-refining of good-quality silver at the palace.

The intrinsic value of bronze and copper vessels and tools made these objects valuable;[18] kitchen inventories could be used as pledge or even be confiscated, and some caravans paid with copper or bronze scrap metal (e.g. old sickles) in North Syria.

Copper circulated widely in Anatolia and often served as means of payment for the costs of living.[19] A perhaps not uncommon procedure was to sell good-quality copper for silver to a smith; this is described in a letter according to which the silver was to be used to purchase barley.[20] Silver occasionally was in short supply on the market place (*mahīrum*) or elsewhere, leading to a temporary halt in trading.[21] Prices of slaves, foodstuff, firewood and similar items are frequently expressed in silver,[22] but may sometimes represent calculations of amounts actually paid in copper, in particular where small amounts of silver are concerned.[23] In other instances, a debt in silver could be repaid in barley. Still, the evidence suggests that silver was accepted as payment even by sellers of goods such as bread, meat (whole animals or cuts of meat), beer, onions, firewood and footwear. It follows that silver, next to copper, played an important role in the economy of an urban centre such as Kanesh, and in this respect resembled the situation in the city of Assur.

Gold

Gold only sporadically functioned as a means of payment.[24] The merchants tried to obtain gold in Anatolia by buying it with copper or silver, sometimes by selling merchandise. Gold was sometimes qualified as 'of the road to the city (Assur)' (*ša harrān ālim*), possibly denoting destination or quality.[25] When gold arrived in Assur, it had to be sold for silver (presumably to the House of the city) before any purchases could be made with it. This would also have been the procedure for gold sent to women in Assur in order to buy grain.[26] The gold that was sent to Assur in the shape of sun disks, earrings, etc., was meant for votive offerings and personal jewellery. The city-state chose gold as standard for long-term joint-stock partnerships (*naruqqum*), although silver was the standard measure of value and means of payment for trade-related purchases in Assur.

Gold, often in the shape of worked objects, was important as a material for diplomatic gifts. The Old Assyrian evidence is limited to occasional references to the use of gold as a gift to Anatolian kings, and the treaty with the town of Hahhum contains a clause stipulating that several members of the town's ruling elite are entitled to purchase gold at a discounted price from Assyrian merchants travelling to Assur.[27] Information on possible payments made by Assur to other states as part of the trade is lacking, but evidence from the palace of king Zimrilim at the city of Mari may shed some light on this. Several texts found there document how gold and silver were sent as gifts to the ruler of Elam, a state which held a key position in the supply of tin to Mesopotamia. Moreover, gold was used on several occasions to purchase tin in Elam.[28]

Credit

Credit in Old Assyrian trade[29] meant the advancement of money (usually silver, sometimes copper) that had to be paid back. It also applied to the sale of merchandise on credit. Money could be borrowed at interest from the office ('house') of specialized merchants (*bēt tamkārim*); the 'house of the Anatolian' (*bēt nuāim*) formed a local equivalent in Kanesh. The rates of interest charged on borrowed money or on defaulting traders range from the standard rate of 30% p.a. to lower rates for trusted debtors or higher rates for debtors deemed unreliable.[30]

Credit could also be provided in the form of a partnership (*tappā'ūtum*) or other form of financial cooperation, such as the *naruqqum* (see below).[31]

Repayment of debts could be problematic. Apart from cases of a temporary lack of money, traders were highly mobile, and many travelled between towns in Anatolia or even between Assur and Kanesh. This gave rise to the creation of debt-notes on which the creditor was simply identified as 'the merchant' instead of by name. This type of debt-note has been compared to bearer's cheques.[32]

The role of the state

The city-state of Assur did not issue coined metal, but it had an assayer's office to assess the quality of gold and silver.[33] Moreover, one of its institutions possessed the standard weight stones that served as point of reference for the stones used by the traders. It was not unusual for the city-state to have claims on merchants as a result of backlogs in the payment of taxes or merchandise. The city-state's central economic institution was the 'House of the City' or 'of the Year-Eponym' (*bēt ālim/līmim*), the office where the eponym official resided.[34] This office possessed the standard weight stones and measures of capacity, sold certain commodities, levied taxes and sold confiscated property. Any claims by the House of the City were expressed as claims to the eponym during whose term of office the debt had originated. An extreme measure to collect payment was to confiscate a merchant's house in Assur and ultimately put that up for sale. Several letters sent by female relatives of merchants contain details of the pressure put on them by the eponym's servants and of the personal jewellery or bronze kitchenware that had to be used as partial payment. The confiscation of houses at one time became politically hazardous, and the city assembly had to reschedule the outstanding debts.[35] The impact of economic measures, called *addurārum* by kings Ilušumma and Erišum, remains unclear.[36] This term usually refers to the royal cancellation of non-commercial debts and sales, and the word is, apart from Assur, attested for in the early second millennium in Syria[37] and Anatolia (Kanesh)[38] and under the term *mīšarum* in the Old Babylonian period.[39] However, we do not know whether the 'reversion to a previous situation' declared in Assur consisted of similar measures.[40] King Ilušumma declared the 'reversion' of Akkadians, possibly in an attempt to increase Assur's attractiveness as a trading centre. The mention that he 'washed their (i.e. the Akkadians') copper' remains enigmatic. His successor, Erišum, wrote in an inscription that he declared an *addurārum* in his city Assur concerning, among other commodities, silver, gold, copper, tin, barley and wool. This measure may have been aimed at the remission of debts in these commodities to the city.

The city-state actively supported the trade by developing rules and mechanisms to facilitate it. It concluded treaties with all rulers affected by the trade, of which documents only few have been excavated.[41] It is likely that the city-state also supervised the creation of the long term joint-stock partnerships (*naruqqum*), in which assets were generally expressed in gold and which existed during part of the nineteenth c. BC.[42] The state prohibited the use of gold in commercial dealings with non-Assyrians.[43] In order to facilitate the computation and payment of taxes by caravans travelling between Assur and Kanesh, the value of a caravan was expressed in a single metal. This value was called the *awītum* or 'declared value', and expressed in tin on shipments travelling to Kanesh (textiles and donkeys received a value in tin), and in silver on those heading for Assur (gold was expressed in silver).[44] Payment was made in the commodity that formed the bulk of the transport and amounts of tin and silver were provided to the caravan leader for this purpose.

The checking of the quality of silver and gold also occurred in the 'House of the Market' (*bēt mahīrim*) of the Anatolian state of Kanesh.[45]

The creation of 'money'

Money was generated by the sale of imported commodities in Anatolia, allowing for a net profit of about 50%.[46] Some merchants spent part of the profit on the purchase of expensive property in Assur.[47] Another way in which money was created consisted of the addition of interest (*ṣibtum*) to claims originating from loans or from defaulting traders who had received goods on credit.[48] The rate of interest established by the colony of Kanesh was equivalent to 30% per year; this rate was commonly used among merchants, but a creditor was at liberty to charge a different percentage.

Investments in a *naruqqum*-contract were usually made in silver, for which a share was booked expressed in gold at a rate of 4:1; for example, an investment of 8 pounds of silver resulted in a share of 2 pounds of gold. According to a passage in one of the *naruqqum*-contracts, any investor who withdraws his (or her) share before the end of the contract can do so and receive the investment back at the rate of 4:1. At a market rate for gold of about 8:1, this has been taken as meaning that under normal circumstances an investor would realize a 100% profit at the end of the contract.[49] This requires a (state) guarantee that such a higher exchange rate will apply, or the physical presence of gold.

The destruction of money

The commonest form of removing money from circulation was to present an object of silver or gold as a votive offering to the gods, or to use gold for jewellery.[50] Gold and silver were also used for apotropaic purposes in a funerary context, and individuals were buried together with some of their gold jewellery.[51] Money was further destroyed as a result of irrecoverable claims.

The Old Babylonian period (nineteenth to seventeenth centuries BC) – Michael Jursa

The state of the question

Some scholars investigating the Old Babylonian data for silver use argued for a silver-poor economy in which the precious metal served principally as a money of account and a measure of value, while others saw much evidence for the circulation of physical silver. Stol (2004: 860ff.; 900ff.) presented a survey of the discussion and the evidence which brought him to side, tendentially, with the latter position. Silver circulated in the form of 'ring silver', one ring often weighing (around) 5 shekels. In palace archives, references to precious items made of silver abound; there was a distinction between the value of an object's raw material and its actual, higher value (*nību*, literally 'quote') that resulted from the added value of the material's artisanal elaboration. Silver in small, weighed and standardized quantities (between 15 ŠE, 0.7 grams, and 1 shekel, 8.3 grams) was kept, and allowed to circulate, in small leather bags (*kin-kum*); the fiduciary value of the sealing and the bulla which states the weight was often referred to, and was contrasted with the lesser value of 'open' (*piṭru*) silver. Quantified references to different degrees of the silver's purity, however, are absent. For Stol, silver was a ubiquitous means of exchange in the Old Babylonian period (Stol 2004: 909); and, indeed, a survey of randomly chosen test corpora confirms, or seems to confirm, this picture. For instance, the hundreds of real-estate sale contracts from Northern Babylonia published by Dekiere (1994–7) state the purchase price as a rule in terms of a quantity of silver.[52] Turning to private archives, taking archives of Old Babylonian priests as a test case, we find a wide range of silver use attested.[53] Silver is used for the purchase of real estate (e.g. UET 5, 140); there are silver debt notes (e.g. YOS 12, 67); house rentals are paid in silver (BIN 2, 83); temple offices are bought for silver (e.g. YOS 12, 297), as are slaves (e.g. YOS 8, 86). Silver also appears explicitly as a money of account, as in a long, itemized list of expenses for a marriage ceremony stating the silver value of numerous items such as oil, garment, sesame, barley, garments, et cetera.[54]

There is no lack of references to silver in contexts for which there can be no doubt that physical silver is intended. This is in particular true for letters, in particular private letters, a text type abundantly attested in the Old Babylonian period – the following remarks are based on a corpus of roughly 800 of these texts, which have been selected at random from among the full corpus of several thousands.[55] These texts are useful in the present context because their format and phraseology is not as highly standardized as is the case, for instance, with real estate sale documents. In the latter texts, a reference to 'silver' may or may not have been intended to refer to physical silver (see note 52). The terseness of the sale contracts' formulary may conceivably have caused practical details of the transaction, such as the actual nature of the purchase price, rather than just its value (customarily expressed in silver) to remain unexpressed. In letters no such restrictions apply, and it is possible – at least in a majority of cases – to distinguish references to silver as money of account and standard of value from references to physical silver.[56]

In the Old Babylonian letters, silver is mentioned frequently, but silver is clearly not the only money medium in use. In some contexts, scrap metal and copper appear as means of payment,[57] but the real competitor of silver is barley. Wages, for instance, are much more often quantified (and paid) in barley than in silver.[58] In actual practice, the two money media were clearly mutually exchangeable, but they were not encountered with equal frequency. Especially in the context of trade, silver was a preferred medium of payment owing to its easy portability, but its availability could by no means be taken for granted. Barley was the less convenient, but generally available, alternative.[59] In one letter there is the revealing statement: 'open the sealed storeroom and set apart ten *kurru* of barley for seed and fodder and ten *kurru* of barley for silver for the palaces (*ana* é.g[al]-*a-ni*)' (*AbB* 11, 187); apparently, demands made by the state were phrased in silver, but they were met in barley.

Overall, the importance of silver for the Old Babylonian economy can be evaluated best by drawing on two types of document which necessarily reflect property patterns very closely and are unlikely to refer to 'silver' as a money of account only: inheritance divisions and dowries. Sweet noticed the rarity of silver in inheritance divisions, a 'troubling' observation, according to Stol, who in general argues in favour of an important role played by silver and duly notes that some inheritance divisions indeed do mention silver.[60] The data are as follows: in the corpus of 154 inheritance documents analysed in Weszeli (1991), only ten documents (from Sippar, Nippur, Kutalla, Larsa and Ur) mention silver shares: silver is therefore absent in the vast majority of inheritance divisions. Leaving aside one exceptionally rich inheritance from Ur (YOS 8, 98), none of the single inheritance shares consisting of silver (19) is higher than 25 shekels. The mean and median are around 8 shekels (disregarding the outlier YOS 8, 98). In marriage documents,[61] cash silver given to the groom as a dowry is practically unknown,[62] and only occasionally silver rings weighing a few shekels and other types of jewellery are listed.[63] The *terḫatu* ('bride-wealth') payment made by the groom to the bride's family, on the other hand, is quantified in silver. It ranges from one to 40 shekels, but most often lies between five to ten shekels. These are sums that lie far below the corresponding payments in the sixth century.[64] In the present context, the main point to be made is that the rarity of silver in these texts cannot be disregarded: the dowry and inheritance documents necessarily reflect the composition of patrimonies quite closely. In line with the impression given by our survey of the letter corpus, with Sweet and *pace* Stol, cash silver was infrequently part of estates in significant quantities. This absence must reflect a genuine silver scarcity within the economy (but by no means a near-complete absence of physical silver). The sale contracts for high-value purchases, which, as we have seen, ubiquitously speak of (significant amounts of) silver, therefore refer to silver as money of account only. For the actual payment, other types of money (barley, dates, wool or a combination thereof, possibly including also physical silver) were used.

Conclusion

The Old Babylonian economy depended on a variety of monies, barley being the most important. Silver was crucial especially for long-distance trade and was by no means absent from everyday circulation. But overall it was scarce, and many of its appearances in private archives have to be considered examples of its use as a money of account only.

The Middle Babylonian Period (c. 1500–1155 BC) – Kristin Kleber

Silver had been used in Babylonia as the standard of value since the earliest phases of its history until the end of Mesopotamian civilization. There was only one exception, namely the Kassite period (c. 1500–1155 BC), when a gold standard was suddenly introduced. This rare and economically nonsensical step has puzzled scholars for a long time. The following contribution is a summary of a study that re-evaluates the Kassite gold and Post-Kassite silver standards in Babylonia in the period between the fifteenth and tenth centuries BC.[65]

Historical Background

The Middle Babylonian period is sandwiched between two 'dark ages'. In the sixteenth century, the Old Babylonian kingdom declined; its capital, Babylon, was sacked during a Hittite raid. Sometime thereafter (the length of the leaderless phase is unknown), the Kassites, originally a people from outside Babylonia, established a dynasty that lasted until the end of the thirteenth century. We have very little written sources from the early phase of Kassite rule from Babylonia itself, but we do have a few letters by Babylonian kings to the pharaoh in Egypt (Amarna correspondence). Babylonian texts became more numerous not before the reign of Burna-buriaš (c. 1359–1333). With the turn to a drier climate, the Late Bronze Age civilization in the western parts of the Near East collapsed around 1200. The aridity led to famines and large-scale migrations. The decline began and ended later in Mesopotamia but was no less severe. Settlement surveys demonstrate a sharp decrease in the number and size of large cities, a trend that had started during the Kassite phase but culminated in the Post-Kassite period (twelfth through tenth centuries). The dwindling population lived in villages and hamlets or took up nomadic lifestyles.[66] Post-Kassite Babylonia returned to a general silver standard.

Previous approaches

The first discussion of the introduction of gold as standard of value in Babylonia is presented by Edzard (1960). He concluded that the Kassite kings must have had a predilection for the yellow metal. He and other scholars also attributed the change to a shortage of silver in the mid-second millennium, possibly because the traditional silver mines in Anatolia did not yield any more, or because access was blocked for political reasons.[67] This explanation sometimes goes hand in hand with the idea that plenty of Egyptian gold was available through trade contacts.[68]

We can indeed observe that silver in Babylonia virtually disappeared as a means of payment in the latter half of the second millennium. Due to the absence of pertinent sources, we do not know whether this had external political or internal economic reasons. The latter is more likely, because silver continued to be used as a means of payment and as a standard of value in Northern Mesopotamia, Syria and the Levant. It is also true that New Kingdom Egypt was able to procure more gold than before because it dominated Nubia and intensified the exploitations of the gold mines in the Eastern Desert, in addition to applying technical innovations. Nevertheless, the total gold output was low,[69] certainly not high enough to cause deep economic changes, not in Egypt and certainly not in the economy of a distant state like Babylonia. Moreover, the gold boost was short-lived: during the Amarna period, Egypt had lost its control over Nubia, and by the thirteenth century the production of gold in the Eastern Desert had ceased completely.

Gold as an artificial currency in the Kassite Period

The sources from Kassite Babylonia date mostly from the middle of the fourteenth to the middle of the twelfth century. Gold appears as the standard of value, but physical gold is rare in commercial transactions. Even high- and middle-range sales were normally conducted without precious metals; the purchase price was paid by convenience goods and items such as garments, wool, animals, barley, shoes, daggers or tables.[70] The use of money in Kassite and Post-Kassite Babylonia may have been more common among businessmen involved in international trade, but the rest of the population – even in urban centres – engaged in a moneyless exchange. The texts distinguish two types of gold:

1 'White' gold or gold without colour specification with a gold-silver ratio of 1:4. It was used as the index of value.
2 'Red' gold with a gold–silver ratio of 1:8. 'Red' designates the deep golden hue of gold of a high fineness, not gold with a copper alloy. 'Red' gold appears rarely in our texts, and only in very small quantities, but it was a commodity used for payments.

Fire assay was known in Kassite Babylonia, but only experts (e.g. goldsmiths) had the technical means to carry out tests of fineness. 'Red' gold was purified gold,[71] and its colour (deep golden) and its softness were indicators of its high value. By contrast, gold that did not have the intensive golden hue was unpractical as a means of payment because its value was uncertain and extremely variable. I have argued that the Kassite (generic) *Gold* (with its variant '*White*

Gold') was an artificial standard of value and normally not used as a commodity.[72] White gold or gold without colour specification is rarely mentioned as a commodity (e.g. in the form of jewellery or ingots), but was not normally used for payments.[73] We do have a small number of texts in which the price is not recorded as having been paid in the form of convenience goods; they only give a price in gold. However, this does not necessarily mean that gold had indeed been paid. The legal form of the sale contracts often hides purchases on credit. Some of the transactions even contain hints that this had been the case.[74]

Inspiration for the gold standard

But why did *Gold* replace the traditional silver standard at all? In order to give a tentative answer, we must consider the following facts. First, silver was extremely scarce – we do not have a single transaction in which silver was used as money in the Kassite period. Second, Egypt in the fifteenth century – at the peak of its power – enjoyed the highest prestige among the great powers of the Late Bronze Age international scene. It showed off by sending lavish gifts of golden objects to other royal courts. Gold became *the* status symbol; it played a prominent role in the conspicuous consumption of the international elite in that period.[75]

The gold–silver ratio 1:8 for gold of high fineness ('red') may have been real in fifteenth-century Babylonia when Egypt started to procure more gold. But red gold was too expensive to be practical as a monetary standard. Cheaper gold of lesser purity (with a whitish hue) may have inspired the introduction of the artificial Babylonian *Gold* standard with a ratio of 1:4 (gold–silver).[76] It was low enough to be used as an index of value for those transactions that needed recording (non-fungible goods, normally of higher value).[77] In practice, the everyday economy functioned without the involvement of precious metal. In fact, the introduction of an index of value four times higher than silver worked only because the economy was oriented towards moneyless exchange. This economic pattern stands in contrast to the preceding Old Babylonian period where silver was available to the urban population, not only to administrators and merchants, and in sharp contrast to the Babylonian economy from the sixth century onwards, which was monetized to a relatively large extent.

The silver standard of the Post-Kassite Period

From the middle of the thirteenth down to the twelfth century (hence, towards the end of the Kassite period), the *Gold* standard was not ubiquitous anymore. Silver and copper appear alone or alongside gold as indices of value. In the Post-Kassite period, a period characterized by recurring dry spells and very scarce textual documentation, items continued to be paid for by convenience goods. However, something new appeared: from 1100 BC on, the silver standard became exclusive. Simultaneously, a new scribal practice was introduced that 'counted' silver instead of giving the amount in weight.[78] That means that the mina-boundary was ignored by the scribes. Values of more than 60 or 100 (shekels) appear, and the unit shekel – indicating a weight – is skipped in writing. This is a reflex of an artificial standard of value, now called *Silver*. Physical silver did not normally change hands; therefore, we cannot establish the value of silver as a commodity.[79]

This unusual scribal practice ended in the mid-ninth century.[80] From then on, (physical) silver appeared as a commodity and was used as a means of payment. Consequently, prices were again given in the weight-based system of minas and shekels. The overall economy improved: international trade was revived, and the agricultural performance improved, resulting in population growth. More people began to live in larger settlements again, thereby reversing the rural settlement trend of the Kassite and Post-Kassite periods. This upward trend culminated in the monetized Babylonian society in the second half of the first millennium.[81]

The first millennium BC – Michael Jursa

The eighth and seventh centuries BC: A period of transition

Physical silver circulated in the country in not indifferent quantities; it was the principal means of payment in the context of important land transactions and in the realm of the merchant. Merchants appear also in their traditional role as money lenders, owing to their access to ready silver. For everyday, low-value transactions, silver was at best one of several means of exchange, staples such as wool or dates or barley having a higher utility, owing to their lesser purchasing power. In institutional households, the traditional redistributive system based on salaries in kind was fully intact. Diachronically speaking, the eighth and seventh centuries then represented an intermediate stage in Babylonia's transition from the nearly silver-free economy of the Kassite and post-Kassite period to the strongly monetized economy of the sixth century (and later centuries).[82]

Monetization in the 'long sixth century'

The 'long sixth century' (from the fall of Assyria 626/612 BC to the Babylonian rebellions against Xerxes, 484 BC) was characterized by a high degree of monetization of exchange and by a near ubiquity of silver.[83] Throughout this period, silver was weighed, not coined. Much attention was given to its physical characteristics and to its fineness. The wide range of silver qualifications that appeared early in the sixth century attests to the need to distinguish silver forms and qualities, as well as to standardize the fineness of silver that was in circulation and/or convey an institutional guarantee of a certain fineness.

Quantified references to the fineness of silver appeared for the first time around 600 BC and were common only from about 565 onwards. The most common type was silver of 87.5 % fineness, probably the standard fineness until at least the 480s. Silver of 83.33% fineness appears at the beginning of the sixth century; at least, in Uruk its use was discontinued suddenly around 565, certainly as a result of official intervention. Other degrees of fineness occurred rarely (91.66% at the beginning of the sixth century, 80% in the last decade of Nebuchadnezzar's reign, 95.83% and 90% occasionally in the Achaemenid period, after 539 BC). Institutional interference with the physical form in which money circulated is also found in the case of the *ginnu* characteristic from the mid-sixth century onwards. This is a distinctive mark on, or form of, silver (but it does not refer to any known type of coinage). It conveyed information about the silver's purity and/or the institution guaranteeing this purity. From 530 to the 480s, silver designated as 'income of the treasury' (*erbu ša aranni*) was attested occasionally. This type of silver came with a quality guarantee of the royal treasury, but we do not know how the guarantee was conveyed.[84]

Silver used to be seen as 'high-range money', owing to its high purchasing power, and hence as unsuitable for everyday exchange involving low-value goods (e.g. Bongenaar 1999). However, silver quantities as small as 1/40 of a shekel (one *hallūru*,[85] the equivalent of roughly three litres of barley around the middle of the century) demonstrably changed hands: silver did not function as high-range money only in our period. It circulated much more widely in the economy than the proponents of the high-range money thesis would allow. There is little information on the acquisition of everyday commodities through payment in kind. Such transactions may not have been uncommon, of course, but they were certainly not the predominant method of exchange for everyday items.

In the economy of the large temple institutions, silver was the near-exclusive means of payment for all transactions reaching beyond the confines of the temple households. For their engagement in cash-crop agriculture (the principal source of the temple's money income) and for hiring labour, the temples depended on monetized exchange. Furthermore, a significant number of temple-internal payments were in fact made in cash. Salaries (or 'rations') of temple dependants and payments for priestly service, both of which traditionally were payable in kind, were frequently substituted by silver payments. The social range represented by the individuals who appear in the temple archives as recipients of temple silver is very wide: clearly, for most sections of the population, it was a fairly common occurrence to conduct low-value transactions with silver.

The importance of silver-based transactions for the non-institutional sector of the economy emerges also from the private archives of city dwellers (Jursa 2010: 624ff.). For propertied urbanites, silver was a common means of hoarding wealth. Silver appears frequently in dowry lists and estate divisions, but staples do not. Valuable items – land as well as movable goods such as animals or slaves – were practically always bought and sold for silver. But also low-value commodities changed hands for silver; 'cheap' monies (barley, wool, base metals) were not the only means of acquiring items of everyday consumption; for goods whose money values range between one and four shekels of silver (which is 40–160% percent of the median monthly wage, 2.5 shekels, in the mid-sixth century), silver was by far the predominant means of payment, and for goods of lesser value it was frequently used.

The work of free hirelings, including hired mass labour working on state-sponsored, large-scale building projects (of which there were many in this period), was nearly always paid with silver money. Wages in kind were only common in the case of slaves and for part-time employment or very low wages, but even in these cases silver wages were not unusual.

Silver money was used for many rental payments in the fifth century (including field rents), and in the realm of taxation (including indirect taxes such as harbour dues, gate tolls and so forth) and labour services. A few types of taxes called for payment in kind, but silver was used for the large majority of payments made in connection with state-imposed obligations. Heads of land-owning households that were subject to royal demands for labour service hired substitute labourers or soldiers who had to be paid in cash. They therefore had to have access to silver; this forced them into the market for staples. Also indirect taxes (harbour taxes etc.) and occasionally genuine direct taxes extracted on the basis of land-for-service schemes were payable in silver.

What kind of monetization in the sixth century?

The expansion of the role of silver in the economy from the late seventh century onwards can be placed into a historical context (Jursa 2014a): it must be connected with the political circumstances of the late seventh and the sixth century when Babylonia was at the centre of an empire which attracted, by compulsion or through trade, large amounts of wealth from the entire Near East. The purchasing power of silver fell as a result. The spending policy of the Babylonian kings contributed substantially to this development by bringing large amounts of money into circulation. The need to hire numerous workers for the building projects of the crown allowed a wide-ranging circulation of silver. Both the increasing specialization of agriculture in the institutional sphere (and generally the imbalance of the institutional household economy) and the intensive horticultural regime typical of urban landowners were dependent on, and increased the importance of, money-based exchange: cash crops had to be sold and surpluses marketed, and recipients of money salaries had to be able to buy their daily needs. In addition, the tax and service obligations imposed on urban landholders, labour specialization in the city and probably a rise of consumption above the level of subsistence needs all contributed to the increased importance of money-based exchange.

Can we take the argument for 'monetization' in the sixth century any further, in terms useful both for general comparative economic history? Lucassen (Chapter 4, pp. 57–8) states that 'deep monetization' requires a substantial (per capita equal to between five and ten times the prevailing hourly wage) stock of currencies in circulation, consisting of denominations equalling the value of one hour or less of waged work. Does this apply to the sixth century? In the absence of coined money, hoards, die studies et cetera, Babylonian material remains, and textual data do not allow giving a straightforward answer to this question. However, it is possible to build a model based on comparative evidence that allows integrating extant information and leads to a hypothetical answer. We will use, as a test case, the economy of the well-known city of Borsippa. This site has left numerous archives of priestly families. Their property portfolios and business activities suggest that in general these families could dispose of an income of about four to six times subsistence requirements (Jursa 2010: 304). In terms of the model proposed for income distribution in the Roman empire by Scheidel and Friesen, this would put these families on income 'levels' 2 and 3 (3.3–6.7 times subsistence) (Scheidel and Friesen 2009: 84). According to the 'optimistic' scenario proposed by Scheidel and Friesen, which we will adopt,[86] these income bands correspond to 4.5% of the population. For Borsippa, this is plausible. Assuming 400 households of priestly families and families of similar wealth lived in Borsippa (Jursa 2010: 441 with note 2465),[87] we would arrive at a total of 8,890 nuclear households or an urban population of 35,560 – roughly 150 per hectare for this 240-hectare site (Kaniuth 2007: 15), a credible figure for a large and hence not necessarily very densely occupied city.[88]

There are no data that would allow establishing directly the size of any other income group. Scheidel and Friesen based their model on Pareto's discovery that 'the distribution of income tends to fall into a predictable pattern governed by power laws' (Scheidel and Friesen 2009: 79). In our simulation for Borsippa, we will continue to use the distribution of income levels proposed by Scheidel and Friesen for the Roman empire,[89] and thus arrive at the figures in Table 5.1.

The remaining 3% of the population, according to the model used, belong to an 'elite' group whose income,[90] in Scheidel and Friesen's model, amounts to 17–26% of the total of all incomes: 17% in the optimistic scenario, in which middling incomes (defined as incomes between 2.4 and 10 times subsistence) of up to 12% of the population amount to 27% of the total gross income. Gross income beyond gross subsistence is as follows (see Table 5.2, taken from Scheidel and Friesen's Table 11, the optimistic scenario only).

Through dowry lists, we can gain an insight into the quantity of disposable cash that circulated in priestly families (see Jursa 2010: 807ff.). The median

Table 5.1 Hypothetical income distribution in Borsippa

'Level'	*Number of households (rounded figures)*	*Characteristics*
5	71 (0.8%)	8.4–10 times subsistence
4	107 (1.2%)	6.7–8.4 times subsistence
2 and 3	400 (4.5%)	3.3–6.7 times subsistence
1	578 (6.5%)	1.7–3.3 times subsistence
0.75–0.99	1689 (19%)	1.25–1.69 times subsistence
0.50–0.74	4889 (55%)	At or close to subsistence
< 0.49	889 (10%)	Below subsistence
Total	8623 (97 %)	

Table 5.2 A model for the distribution of 'disposable income'

Elite	38%
Middling incomes (c. levels 1–5)	47%
Others	16%

Table 5.3 Disposable cash in 'middling' income ranges in Borsippa

'Level'	*Number of households*	*Cash silver (shekels)*
5	71 (0.8%)	10,430
4	107 (1.2%)	12,800
2 and 3	400 (4.5%)	32,000
1	578 (6.5%)	23,110
Total	1156 (13%)	78,340

dowry in our priestly families was around 40–60 shekels (332–500 grams) of silver.[91] On the – improvable – assumption that such a dowry amounted to half the disposable cash available in a household,[92] this means that families in income bands 2 and 3 could dispose, as a minimum, of 80 shekels of physical silver.[93] On the further assumption that the quantity of cash silver follows the general income distribution, this allows us to calculate as following the hypothetical total of silver held in Borsippa (Table 5.3).

In a final step, we can extrapolate the hoarded/disposable[94] silver for elite and low-income levels[95] on the basis of the figures given in Table 5.2: the small elite should have 81% (38/47) of the middling groups' silver, the lower income ranges, 34% (16/47): 78,340 + 64,455 + 26,636 = 169,431 shekels = c. 1,412 kilograms of silver. Per capita, assuming a population of 35,560, this amounts to 4.76 shekels, well above a month's wage (2–3 shekels in the mid-sixth century). It should be emphasized that silver was a means of storing wealth, obviously, but dowry silver, just as silver in private hands in general, was just as likely, or even more likely, to be brought into circulation at some point. On the basis of this hypothetical reasoning, therefore, the first condition for 'deep monetization' would be met. And it would be met rather easily, with a wide margin of error and potential inaccuracy.

Lucassen's second condition for 'deep monetization' states that money should be in circulation 'consisting of denominations equalling the value of one hour or less of waged work'. As said above, silver of as little as 1/40 of a shekel (0.207 grams) actually changed hands. If we assume that the work-day was divided into six 'hours', one hour of the average wage (of 2.5 shekels per month under Nabonidus) corresponds to 0.115 grams (2.5 'barleycorns' of silver, in Babylonian terminology): the 1/40 of a shekel is not that far off. Again, the point of the foregoing speculations is not to prove conclusively that the Babylonian economy in the sixth century was characterized by what has been defined as 'deep monetization' – the available data do not bear the weight of such an argument. What they do allow is an arguably plausible modellization of silver use and income structure that would fit a 'deeply monetized' economy. If we wanted to construe the data to speak for 'shallow monetization', our priestly families, about whose property structure we are well informed, would have to be a tiny elite. This runs counter to what we know about their social position and their income structure in general. Furthermore, these families are too numerous for placing them in a position on the very top of the income scale: we would arrive at implausibly high overall population figures for the known surface area of the city of Borsippa.

Conclusion

In the sixth century BC, the Babylonian economy was largely silver-based, and monetization had reached an unprecedented level – a level which on the basis of comparative data may well have met the requirements for being labelled as 'deep monetization'. The findings for the sixth century are thrown into sharp relief by a survey of corresponding data from the Old Babylonian period. The Old Babylonian economy depended on a variety of monies, barley being the most important. Silver was crucial especially for long distance trade and was by no means absent from everyday circulation. But overall it was scarce, and many of its appearances in private archives have to be considered examples of its use as a money of account only. The argument made here turns against the assumption of a 'millennial' continuity in the Babylonian economy. Similarities in the typology of the abundant documentation on occasion hide deep structural differences in the economy the documentation reflects.

Concluding remarks – Bert van der Spek

The economy of Ancient Mesopotamia (as well as other parts of the Middle East) functioned with money from the third millennium on. The predominant money material was silver, though other means of payments existed, such as barley, copper, bronze, gold and tin. The problem with money material is that it is 'money' and a commodity at the same time. Possession of it thus created intrinsic pleasure for two reasons. It is a complicating factor in nearly all economies of the past, as is exemplified in Chapter 2 by Dennis Flynn. The fact that silver was used as money does not mean that the economies in three millennia did not change. In the Old Assyrian period, silver was first of all a commodity that was sought for by the Assyrian merchants in southeast Anatolia, who lived there in the city of Kanesh with certain extraterritorial rights. Nevertheless, it served as all-purpose money, but not for all purposes to the same extent. This holds true for Babylonia as well in all periods. We must be cautious, however, in making general statements on the role of money over the course of three millennia. Silver started to be used as means of payment and unit of account in the third millennium already, and it gained a prominent place in the Old Babylonia period, though in many respects next to other types of money, such as barley and other valuables. Fairly suddenly, however, the role of silver as currency disappeared in the Middle Babylonian period, when the Kassites ruled Babylonia. Gold became the standard, though it was used for great transactions only and served mainly as 'ghost money', that is, as unit of account. Physical silver had become scarce, and the transition to the gold standard marked a period of extreme contraction. A comparison may be made here with the end of the Roman empire in the West, when (trustworthy) silver (coins) retreated while the main coin and standard of reference became the golden *solidus*, introduced by Diocletian in AD 301 and issued on a grand scale by Constantine the Great after 312; it remained the main unit of account in East and West until the tenth century. Just as in Kassite Babylonia, it was a period of contraction in which taxes and payments increasingly were made in kind and cities declined. Gold was an anchor in difficult times. After the retraction of the Middle Babylonian period and the crisis of the twelfth through ninth centuries, Mesopotamia began to recover, and silver regained its primary importance in economic exchange. In Assyria, the role of silver got an extra stimulus thanks to the Assyrian conquests, in particular the conquest of Carchemish in 714 BC. The Neo-Babylonian Empire was also successful in extracting silver from its conquered territories. In the 'long sixth century' BC, silver became all-purpose money in all respects, and it is argued here that the economy became 'deeply monetized'. Silver became the one and only means of account, the predominant means of payment in daily transaction and the preferred store of wealth, as is exemplified by the author of a letter mentioned at the head of this article. But even in this period, silver was hardly coined. There were marks of fineness, as e.g. when packed in a sealed bag. Coins were introduced in the Persian Empire, but they played a marginal role and were mainly used by mercenaries in the western parts of the empire. The introduction and victory of coinage in the Greek world and the Near East is discussed in Chapter 6, this volume. It was Alexander the Great who, after his conquest of Mesopotamia in 331, introduced coinage as the only acceptable currency. But even then, weight and purity of the silver remained a prime concern. The measure of monetization and circulation in the Seleucid empire (in comparison with the Euro in the European Union) will be treated in Chapter 7.

Physical silver did not always change hands in economic transactions. Cheques and promissory notes (payable to bearer) functioned as money in the Old Assyrian period already, but also in later periods in Babylonia, though it is hard to evaluate the economic importance of this. Credit thus played its role, but the interest rates were fairly high (30%, often 20%), and they were in some respects more considered penalty costs and determined by tradition rather than by market forces, though these were not absent.[96]

The role of the state in the creation of money was different from the modern world. Silver was a commodity, and as such it circulated freely – there was no state monopoly on the issue of money. There was an important role for the state and other institutions, though. It seems that temples and the king guaranteed the quality of the silver by sealing and branding. Another point is that the state by its imperial policy was always concerned with imports of silver. The prosperity of the Neo-Assyrian and Neo-Babylonian empires was founded on these imports. The silver could be used for salary payments for workers who built cities, made roads and dug canals. The influx of silver is reflected in the rising prices, but due to the scarcity of labour wages rose as well. The growing availability of silver was thus an impetus for growth. In the Persian period, the situation changed in that the core of the empire now lay outside Mesopotamia, in what is now southwest Iran. It meant that a lot of silver and other products went to the capitals Susa and Persepolis. High taxation and disregard for the Babylonian elite led to unrest in Babylonia. Revolts under Darius I (522) and Xerxes (482) testify to this. In particular, the crushing of the revolts under Xerxes was a blow for the local elites, and it started the marginal position of the province of Babylonia.

Money was created, but also lost. As we have seen, there were periods of scarcity of silver. Silver was constantly robbed, remelted, used for other purposes than money (and vice versa). Credit and negotiable credit notes functioned as money, and failed redemption of debts caused extinction of money. Money played a major role in the economy of Ancient Mesopotamia, silver was the main money material and trust in silver was a main concern.

Notes

1 Statement in a Babylonian letter from the sixth century BC (Hackl *et al.* 2014: No. 114).
2 See Van der Spek *et al.* (2015) for a discussion of the functioning of the market over time.
3 Powell (1996: 227).
4 1 Kings 10:21: = 2 Chronicles 9:20; 1 Kings 10:27 = 2 Chronicles 1:15.
5 Probably nothing is in the gap; hence, simply 18 litres (information K. Kleber).
6 It is interesting to note that in the late period, at least in the Hellenistic period, the word *nadānu* ('what is given; gift') was used, which is actually the opposite of *mahīru*. Cf Van der Spek, (2016a and b).
7 See CAD M[I] s.v. *mahīru* 2 c.
8 For a recent overview of the Old Assyrian period, see Veenhof (2008).
9 For details, see Dercksen 2014. Estimates of the volume of the trade can be found in Veenhof (2008: 90) and Barjamovic (2011: 11–13).
10 Dercksen 2005; for prices of copper, see Dercksen (1996: 227).
11 Dercksen (1996).
12 For silver, see Dercksen (2005); Veenhof (2014).
13 For checked silver, see Sturm (1995); Veenhof (2014: 394–95).
14 See the labels from Larsa in Arnaud, Calvet, Huot (1979: 17–20); see also below.
15 On refining, see Dercksen (2005: 23–4); Veenhof (2014: 404–13); for ingots, see Müller-Karpe (1994: 139). For an example of a hoard of scrap silver, excavated at Acemhöyük, see Öztan (1997).
16 Dercksen (2005: 24); Dercksen (2013: 355).
17 Arkhipov (2012).
18 Dercksen (1996: 76–80).
19 Dercksen (2005: 25; 2014: 98).
20 Text AKT 2, 26, see Dercksen (1996: 72; 2005: 30).
21 Dercksen (2014: 73).
22 Some examples have been collected in Ulshöfer (1995: 467).

23 Payments of 15 barleycorns (= 0.7 gr) of silver occur in Kültepe text Kt 88/k 71, lines 43, 44, 58, 60, discussed in Dercksen (2008: 97). This equals 10 shekels of copper at a rate of 1:120. But note that amounts of 15 barleycorns could be weighed according to Powell (1989–90: 510).
24 For gold, see Dercksen (2005: 25–7, 2014: 88–91). Gold was used to obtain the even more precious meteoric iron, according to Kültepe text Kt n/k 1686; see Sturm (2001: 496).
25 Veenhof (1995: 1734, 2008: 89); Dercksen (2004: 82–3).
26 Dercksen (2014: 91).
27 Günbattı (2004: 260).
28 Joannès (1991: 73).
29 Veenhof (1999a).
30 Garelli (1963: 259–60); Veenhof (1978, 2001).
31 Larsen (1977, 1999); Veenhof (2008: 90–1); Larsen (2015: 27).
32 Veenhof (1997: 351–64).
33 Dercksen (2004: 37–9).
34 Dercksen (2004).
35 Veenhof (1999b).
36 See the edition in Grayson (1987: 15, 18, 22–3).
37 Charpin (1990a, 2014).
38 Balkan (1974); Veenhof (2008: 193–217).
39 Kraus (1984); Charpin (1987, 1990b, 2000).
40 Veenhof (2008: 126–9).
41 Eidem (1991, 2011, 417–26); Çeçen and Hecker (1995); Günbattı (2004); discussion in Veenhof (2008: 183–218).
42 Larsen (1999).
43 Veenhof (1995: 1733).
44 Veenhof (1972: 229–33); Dercksen (2004: 151–7); Dercksen (2014: 85).
45 Dercksen (2004: 32).
46 Dercksen (2014: 84–7).
47 Veenhof (2011: 225–8).
48 Dercksen (2004: 47, 2014: 94–6).
49 Larsen (1999: 183).
50 Dercksen (2015: 39–40).
51 Diadems and pieces of gold foil that once covered eyes and mouth were found on several skulls, see Kulakoglu and Kangal (2011: nos. 319–28); Dercksen (2015: 42).
52 Supporters of the silverless economy would take these texts to refer to silver as a money of account only, but by and of themselves the texts give no clear indication that this should be the case. We will return to this point in the discussion below.
53 Our test corpus comes from Ur (Charpin 1986).
54 UET 5, 607 (Charpin 1986: 65). The overall value of the goods is 2.67 minas of silver – most of which consists of expenses in kind; cash expenses, which are also included, amount to less than a third of a mina.
55 The corpus is made up of the volumes 10, 11, 12 and 14 of the series *AbB* (*Altbabylonische Briefe*) (Leiden 1985ff).
56 To clarify by means of an example: a sale contract for a slave might state that the slave was bought for 20 shekels of silver. This may or may not refer to physical silver. A letter might state that a slave was to be bought for 20 shekels of silver – and then ask for the said silver to be sent. In this case, the text assuredly speaks of physical silver.
57 *AbB* 14, 109; see also *AbB* 11, 95, 153, 181.
58 E.g. *AbB* 14, 23, 54, 110, 146, 204; silver: *AbB* 54.
59 See e.g. *AbB* 12, 95; 10, 145; 12, 38.
60 Stol (2004: 909), where also Sweet's contribution (from an unpublished dissertation) is cited. See also Kalla (1998: 42).
61 The corpus can be found in Westbrook 1988 (c. 100 texts).

62 Exception: 'PNF has brought in 19 shekels of silver for PN her husband', BE 6/2, 40 = Westbrook 1988: 114.
63 E.g. 'half a shekel of silver about her neck, a silver ring of 2 shekels, a silver ring of 1 shekel', CT 8, 2a = Westbrook (1988: 118).
64 See Jursa (2010: 810f.) for pertinent comparisons.
65 Kleber (2016) for the references. Post-Kassite is understood as the latter part of the Middle Babylonian period, namely the time between the end of the twelfth and the end of the tenth century.
66 See Brinkman (1984) and Jursa (2010: 40f.) for an evaluation of this survey. The total settled area had been 1,791 hectares during the Old Babylonian period and 1,308 hectares during the Kassite period. It dropped to only 616 hectares in the Post-Kassite period (a table displaying the numbers can also be found in Kleber 2016: 45).
67 Edzard (1960: 45f. and 54); Renger (1995: 298) (in Assyria the silver standard had been replaced by copper and tin). Müller (1982: 270) attributed the change to political and economic changes and shifts in international trade but does not elucidate on that.
68 Paulus (2014b: 87).
69 Klemm *et al.* (2001: 658).
70 Edzard (1960: 39 and 43); Müller (1982: 270); Del Monte (2009, 104); Paulus (2014a, 140); Kleber (2016: 39).
71 For the ability to purify gold, see Kleber (forthcoming).
72 Kleber 2016: 40–2.
73 With one exception, namely Gurney (1983, no. 41). The text records a payment of one shekel (8.3 grams) of gold (without further qualification) in addition to two shekels of red gold. The gold (without colour specification) was gold of a lower but uncertain fineness. Because of the small quantity, the uncertainty about its real value had been accepted by the buyer.
74 Gold may have been paid in some cases, but probably after a goldsmith had certified its fineness. See Kleber (2016: 40 with n. 17) for the evidence.
75 We know from the Amarna letters that all the other important players on the international scene were keen on receiving gold artefacts as diplomatic 'gifts', usually in return for other merchandise, or as bride-wealth in return for a princess sent to the Egyptian court. Letters by the Babylonian king report on how he intended to use the gold, namely for the decoration of palaces and temples. See Moran (1987, 7–23) (EA 3, 5, 7, 9, 10, 11).
76 Naturally, gold with a whitish hue can have (but by no means must have) half the value of red gold.
77 Sale contracts were not issued for fungible goods (e.g. barley, wool, sheep).
78 Equivalents were traditionally recorded as silver weight, even if silver did not change hands. The basic unit was the shekel (8.33 grams) and 60 shekels were one mina. Hence, sums of and above 60 shekels were given in minas (and shekels).
79 Only once in our corpus a silver ring was used as a means of payment. It is striking that the value of the ring in *silver* units was three times higher than the weight of the ring. Because it is a single example, we do not know whether this is indeed significant or whether we are dealing with a scribal error. See the discussion in Kleber 2016: 46f. The scarcity of silver prevailed; silver was certainly not available in larger quantities before the ninth century.
80 The first transaction using the new scribal practice dates from the reign of Enlil-nādin-apli (1103–1100 BC), the last one from the reign of Nabû-mukīn-apli (979–944). The first text with the traditional weight-based notation of silver comes from the reign of Marduk-zākir-šumi (854–819). It is likely that the return to a weight-based notation did not occur before the ninth century (Kleber 2016: 48f. with n. 58).
81 See Jursa (2010).
82 See more detailed discussions in Jursa (2010: 500ff., 2016).
83 Detailed references can be found in Jursa (2010, chapter 5).

84 The term may refer to a local form of coinage or to leather bags bearing the seal of the treasury and containing silver of a standardised fineness.
85 0.208 grams, which is still heavier than some of the early Lydian coins (Jursa 2010: 631, n. 3340; Duyrat 2015: 371f. for tiny coins from Phoenicia and Philistia, down to 0.15–0.04 grams).
86 It should be remembered that sixth-century Babylonia experienced a period of unprecedented economic expansion and prosperity (Jursa 2010: 811–6.).
87 This assumption is based on the data itself and on the comparison of Borsippa with the – demographically speaking – better known city of Uruk, whose priestly elite was studied by Kessler (2005).
88 See the observations in Van de Mieroop (1999: 95–7) and the bibliography cited there.
89 But note that we have merged their levels 2 and 3 – which correspond to our priests, whose income, in terms of multiples of the subsistence requirements of a household, forms the 'Archimedean point' (such as it is) of the present exercise. Scheidel and Friesen's model falls into the middle range in terms of division of property, and inequality attested for several historical societies and thus imposes itself as a useful point of departure also from this point of view.
90 The sociological identity of this group is immaterial in this scenario; it can be postulated on the strength of the Pareto model alone. In Assyriological terms, here is the niche in the model for the temple households and high-ranking royal officials and their establishments.
91 The mean is significantly higher (Roth 1989/90; numerous unpublished texts from Borsippa).
92 It may well have been less, much less likely more.
93 It is in fact likely to have been a smaller share in most cases, which increases the quantity of silver available in the priestly households.
94 It should be remembered that silver was by far the most common means of hoarding wealth.
95 I.e. the 19% of the population whose income is above mere subsistence but below that of level 1.
96 Jursa (2014b).

References

[Note: Abbreviations not mentioned in this list can be found in the CAD, vol. 20.]

Arkhipov, I. (2012). *Le vocabulaire de la métallurgie et la nomenclature des objets en métal dans les textes de Mari*. Matériaux pour le Dictionnaire de Babylonien de Paris. Tome 3. Leuven, Belgium: Peeters Publishers.

Arnaud, D., Calvet, Y. and Huot, J.-L. (1979). 'Ilšu-ibnišu, orfèvre de l'*E.babbar* de Larsa. La jarre L.76.77 et son contenu', *Syria*, 56: 1–64.

Balkan, K. (1974). 'Cancellation of debts in Cappadocian tablets from Kültepe', in Bittel, K., Houwink ten Cate, Ph.H.J. and Reiner, E. (eds.), *Anatolian Studies Presented to Hans Gustav Güterbock on the Occasion of his 65th Birthday*, Istanbul: Nederlands Historisch-Archaeologisch Instituut: 29–41.

Barjamovic, G. (2011). *A Historical Geography of Anatolia in the Old Assyrian Colony Period*. Copenhagen: Museum Tusculanum Press.

Bongenaar, A.C.V.M. (1999). 'Money in the Neo-Babylonian institutions,' in Dercksen (ed.) (1999): 159–74.

Brinkman, J.A. (1984). 'Settlement surveys and documentary evidence: Regional variation and secular trend in Mesopotamian demography', *Journal of Near Eastern Studies*, 43: 169–80.

CAD = *The Assyrian Dictionary of the Oriental Institute of the University of Chicago*. 21 Volumes. Chicago: The Oriental Institute, 1956–2010 (also freely accessible online: http://oi.uchicago.edu/research/publications/assyrian-dictionary-oriental-institute-university-chicago-cad.

Çeçen, S. and Hecker, K. (1995). '*Ina mātīka eblum.* Zu einem neuen Text zum Wegerecht in der Kültepe-Zeit', in Dietrich, M. and Loretz, O. (eds.), *Vom Alten Orient zum Alten Testament. Festschrift für Wolfram Freiherrn von Soden zum 85. Geburtstag am 19. Juni 1993,* AOAT 240, Münster, Germany: Ugarit-Verlag: 31–41.

Charpin, D. (1986). *Le clergé d'Ur au siècle d'Hammurabi (XIXe-XVIIIe siècles av. J.C.).* Geneva: Librairie Droz.

Charpin, D. (1987). 'Les décrets royaux à l'époque paléo-babylonienne, à propos d'un ouvrage récent', *Archiv für Orientforschung,* 34: 36–44.

Charpin, D. (1990a). 'L'*andurârum* à Mari', *Mari, annales de recherches interdisciplinaires,* 6: 253–70.

Charpin, D. (1990b). 'Les édits de « restauration » des rois babyloniens et leur application', in Nicolet, C. (ed.), *Du pouvoir dans l'antiquité: mots et réalité,* Geneva, Switzerland: Librairie Droz: 13–24.

Charpin, D. (2000). 'Les prêteurs et le palais: les édits de *mîšarum* des rois de Babylone et leurs traces dans les archivesprivées', in Bongenaar, A.C.V.M. (ed.), *Interdependency of Institutions and Private Entrepreneurs.* Proceedings of the Second MOS Symposium (Leiden 1998), Leiden, the Netherlands: Nederlands Instituut voor het Nabije Oosten: 185–211.

Charpin, D. (2014). 'Si quelqu'un fait appel à toi, sois présent!» Les interventions royales dans la vie économique et juridique à Mari', *Syria,* supplément 2: 407–20.

Dekiere, L. (1994-1997). *Old Babylonian Real Estate Documents from Sippar in the British Museum.* Ghent, Belgium: University of Ghent.

Del Monte, G. (2009). 'La formazione dei prezzi delle derrate in età cassita', *Revista di Storia Economica,* 25: 103–42.

Dercksen, J.G. (1996). *The Old Assyrian Copper Trade in Anatolia.* Istanbul: Nederlands Historisch-Archaeologsich Instituut.

Dercksen, J.G. (ed.) (1999). *Trade and Finance in Ancient Mesopotamia.* Istanbul: Nederlands Historisch-Archaeologisch Instituut.

Dercksen, J.G. (2004). *Old Assyrian Institutions.* Leiden, the Netherlands: Nederlands Instituut voor het Nabije Oosten.

Dercksen, J.G. (2005). 'Metals according to documents from Kültepe-Kanish dating to the Old Assyrian Colony Period', in Yalçın, Ü. (ed.), *Anatolian Metal III.* Der Anschnitt - Beiheft 18, Bochum, Germany: Deutsches Bergbau Museum: 17–34.

Dercksen, J.G. (2008). 'Subsistence, surplus and the market for grain and meat at ancient Kanesh', *Altorientalische Forschungen,* 35: 86–192.

Dercksen, J.G. (2013). 'Review of Arkhipov 2012', *Babel und Bibel,* 7: 353–69.

Dercksen, J.G. (2014). 'The Old Assyrian trade and its participants', in Baker, H.D. and Jursa, M. (eds.), *Documentary Sources in Ancient Near Eastern and Greco-Roman Economic History,* Oxford: Oxbow Books: 59–112.

Dercksen, J.G. (2015). 'The goddess who was robbed of her jewellery. Ishtar and her priest in an Assyrian colony', *Anatolica,* 41: 37–59.

Dercksen, J.G. (2016). '*Kaspam lašqul.* "Let me weigh out the silver". Mesopotamian and Anatolian Weights during the Old Assyrian Period', in Kleber and Pirngruber (eds.) (2016): 13–25.

Duyrat, F. 2015. 'The circulation of coins in Syria and Mesopotamia in the sixth to first centuries BC', in Van der Spek, R.J., Van Leeuwen, B. and Van Zanden, J.L. (eds.) (2015): 363–95.

Edzard, D.O. (1960). 'Die Beziehungen Babyloniens und Ägyptens in der Mittelbabylonischen Zeit und das Gold', *Journal of the Economic and Social History of the Orient,* 3: 38–55.

Eidem, J. (1991). 'An Old Assyrian treaty from Tell Leilan', in D. Charpin and J. Joannès (eds.), *Marchands, diplomates et empereurs. Etudes sur la civilisation mésopotamienne offertes à Paul Garelli*, Paris: ERC: 185–207.

Eidem, J. (2011). *The Royal Archives from Tell Leilan. Old Babylonian Letters and Treaties from the Lower Town Palace East.* Leiden, the Netherlands: Nederlands Instituut voor het Nabije Oosten.

Fuchs, A. (1994). *Die Inschriften Sargons II. aus Khorsabad.* Göttingen, Germany: Cuvillier.

Garelli, P. (1963). *Les Assyriens en Cappadoce.* Paris: Adrien Maisonneuve.

Grayson, A.K. (1987). *Assyrian Rulers of the Third and Second Millennia* BC *(to 1115* BC*).* The Royal Inscriptions of Mesopotamia. Assyrian Periods. Volume 1. Toronto, ON: University of Toronto Press.

Gurney, O.R. (1983). *The Middle Babylonian Legal and Economic Texts from Ur.* London: British School of Archaeology in Iraq.

Günbattı, C. (2004). 'Two treaty texts found at Kültepe', in J.G. Dercksen (ed.), *Assyria and Beyond. Studies Presented to Mogens Trolle Larsen*, Leiden, the Netherlands: Nederlands Instituut voor het Nabije Oosten: 249–68.

Hackl, J., Jursa, M. and Schmidl, M. (2014). *Spätbabylonische Privatbriefe.* Münster, Germany: Ugarit Verlag.

Joannès, F. (1991). 'L'étain, de l'Elam à Mari', in L. De Meyer and H. Gasche (eds.), *Mésopotamie et Elam*, Actes de la XXXVIème Rencontre assyriologique internationale, Gand, 10–14 juillet 1989, Ghent, Belgium: University of Ghent: 67–76.

Jursa, M. (2010). *Aspects of the Economic History of Babylonia in the First Millennium* BC*: economic geography, economic mentalities, agriculture, the use of money and the problem of economic growth* (with contributions by J. Hackl, B. Janković, K. Kleber, E.E. Payne, C. Waerzeggers and M. Weszeli). Münster, Germany: Ugarit Verlag.

Jursa, M. (2014a). 'Babylonia in the first millennium BCE – economic growth in times of empire', in L. Neal and J.G. Williamson (eds.), *The Cambridge History of Capitalism.* Volume I. *The Rise of Capitalism: From Ancient Origins to 1848*, Cambridge: Cambridge University Press: 24–42.

Jursa, M. (2014b). 'Factor Markets from the late seventh to the third century BCE', *Journal of the Economic and Social History of the Orient*, 57: 173–202.

Jursa, M. (2016). 'Silver and other forms of elite wealth in seventh century BC Babylonia', in Kleber and Pirngruber (eds.) (2016): 61–71.

Kalla, G. (1998). 'Nachlass. B. Altbabylonisch', in: *Reallexikon der Assyriologie*, 9: 36–42.

Kaniuth, K. (2007). 'Some remarks on the Mesopotamian travels of Robert Ker Porter', in D. Fortenberry (ed.), *He Who Travels Sees More. Artists, Architects and Archaeologists Discover Egypt and the Near East*, Oxford: Oxbow Books: 1–16.

Kessler, K. (2005). 'Zu den ökonomischen Verhältnissen von Uruk in neu- und spätbabylonischer Zeit', in Baker, H.D. and Jursa, M. (eds.), *Approaching the Babylonian Economy*, Münster, Germany: Ugarit-Verlag: 269–87.

Kleber, K. (2016). 'The Kassite Gold and the Post-Kassite Silver Standards Revisited', in Kleber and Pirngruber (eds.) (2016): 37–56.

Kleber, K. (forthcoming). 'As skilful as Croesus. Evidence for the parting of gold and silver by cementation from second and first millennium Mesopotamia', in Van Alfen, P. and Wartenberg, U. (eds.), *White Gold: Studies in Early Electrum Coinage*, New York: American Numismatic Society.

Kleber, K. and Pirngruber, R. (eds.) (2016). *Silver, Money and Credit. A Tribute to Robartus J. van der Spek on Occasion of his 65th Birthday on 18th September 2014.* Leiden, the Netherlands: Nederlands Instituut voor het Nabije Oosten.

Klemm, D., Klemm, R. and Murr, A. (2001). 'Gold of the Pharaohs – 6000 years of gold mining in Egypt and Nubia', *Journal of African Earth Sciences*, 33: 643–59.

Kraus, F.R. (1984). *Königliche Verfügungen in altbabylonischer Zeit*. Leiden, the Netherlands: Brill.

Krispijn, Th.J.H. (2016). 'Early silver: Thoughts about the sign KU_3 in the earliest documents from Uruk', in Kleber and Pirngruber (eds.) (2016): 1–10.

Kulakoglu, F. and Kangal, S. (2011). *Anatolia's Prologue, Kültepe Kanesh Karum, Assyrians in Istanbul*. Kayseri, Turkey: Kayseri Metropolitan Municipality.

Larsen, M.T. (1977). 'Partnerships in the Old Assyrian trade', *Iraq*, 39: 119–45.

Larsen, M.T. (1999). 'Naruqqu-Verträge (*naruqqu*-contracts)', *Reallexikon der Assyriologie*, 9: 181–84.

Larsen, M.T. (2015). 'The relative chronology of the Old Assyrian Period and its consequences', in Kulakoglu, F. and Michel, C. (eds.), *Proceedings of the First Kültepe International Meeting*, Turnhout, Belgium: Brepols: 23–8.

Le Rider, G. (2001). *La Naissance de la monnaie. Pratiques monétaires de l'Orient ancien*. Paris: Presses Universitaires de France.

Livingstone, A. (1989). *Court Poetry and Literary Miscellanea*. State Archives of Assyria III. Helsinki, Finland: Helsinki University Press.

Moran, W.L. (1987). *The Amarna Letters*. Baltimore, MD: Johns Hopkins University Press.

Müller, G. (1997). 'Gedanken zur neuassyrischen Geldwirtschaft', in Waetzoldt, H. and Hauptmann, H. (eds.), *Assyrien im Wandel der Zeiten*, Heidelberg, Germany: Heidelberger Orientverlag: 115–21.

Müller, M. (1982). 'Gold, Silber und Blei als Wertmesser in Mesopotamien während der zweiten Hälfte des 2. Jahrtausends v.u.Z.', in Dandamaev, M.A., Gershevitch, I., Klengel, H., Komoróczy, G., Larsen, M.T. and Postgate, J.N. (eds.), *Societies and Languages of the Ancient Near East, Studies in Honor of I.M. Diakonoff*, Warminster, UK: Aris and Phillips: 270-287.

Müller-Karpe, A. (1994). *Altanatolisches Metallhandwerk*. Neumünster, Germany: Wachholtz Verlag.

Öztan, A. (1997). 'Acemhöyük gümüş hazinesi', *Belleten*, 61/231: 233–72.

Parpola, S. (1987). *The Correspondence of Sargon II*, Part I, *Letters from Assyria and the West*. State Archives of Assyria I. Helsinki, Finland: Helsinki University Press.

Paulus, S. (2014a). *Die Babylonischen Kudurru-Inschriften von der kassitischen bis zur frühneubabylonischen Zeit*. Münster, Germany: Ugarit-Verlag.

Paulus, S. (2014b). 'Babylonien in der 2. Hälfte des 2. Jts. v.Chr. – (K)ein Imperium? Ein Überblick über Geschichte und Struktur des mittelbabylonischen Reiches (ca. 1500–1000 B.C.)', in Geller, M. and Rollinger, R. (eds.), *Imperien und Reiche in der Weltgeschichte. Epochenübergreifende und globalhistorische Vergleiche*, Teil 1, Wiesbaden: Harrassowitz Verlag: 65–100.

Polanyi, K. (1957). 'Marketless trading in Hammurabi's time', in Polanyi, K., Arensberg, C.M. and Pearson, H.W. (eds.), *Trade and Market in Early Empires. Economies in History and Theory*, Glencoe, Ill.: The Free Press: 12–26.

Postgate, J.N. (1979). 'The economic structure of the Assyrian Empire', in Larsen, M.T. (ed.), *Power and Propaganda. A Symposium on Ancient Empires*, Copenhagen, Denmark: Akademisk Forlag: 193–221.

Powell, M.A. (1989-1990). 'Masse und Gewichte' [Measures and Weights; article in English], in *Reallexikon der Assyriologie*, 7: 457–517

Powell, M.A. (1996). 'Money in Mesopotamia', *Journal of the Economic and Social History of the Orient*, 39: 224–42.

Radner, K. (1999). 'Money in the Neo-Assyrian Empire', in Dercksen (ed.) (1999): 127–57.

Renger, J. (1994). 'On economic structures in Ancient Mesopotamia', *Orientalia*, 63: 157–208.

Renger, J. (1995). 'Subsistenzproduktion und redistributive Palastwirtschaft: Wo bleibt die Nische für das Geld?', in Schelkle, W. and Nitsch, M. (eds.), *Rätsel Geld. Annäherungen aus ökonomischer, soziologischer und historischer Sicht*, Marburg, Germany: Metropolis Verlag: 271–324.

Renger, J. (2005). 'K. Polanyi and the Economy of Ancient Mesopotamia', in Clancier, Ph., Joannès, F., Rouillard, P. and Tenu, A. (eds.), *Autour de Polanyi. Vocabulaires, théories et modalités des échanges*, Paris: De Boccard: 45–65

Roth, M.T. (1989/90). 'The material composition of the Neo-Babylonian dowry', *Archiv für Orientforschung*, 36/37: 1–55.

Schaudig, H. (2001). *Die Inschriften Nabonids von Babylon und Kyros' des Großen samt den in ihrem Umfeld entstandenen Tendenzschriften. Textausgabe und Grammatik*. Münster, Germany: Ugarit Verlag.

Scheidel, W. and Friesen, S.J. (2009). 'The size of the economy and the distribution of income in the Roman Empire', *Journal of Roman Studies*, 99: 61–91.

Slotsky, A.L. and Wallenfels, R. (2009). *Tallies and Trends. The Late Babylonian Commodity Price Lists*. Bethesda, MD: CDL Press.

Stol, M. (2004). 'Wirtschaft und Gesellschaft in altbabylonischer Zeit', in Charpin, D., Edzard, D.O. and Stol, M., *Mesopotamien. Die altbabylonische Zeit*, Fribourg, Germany: Academic Press / Göttingen, Germany: Vandenhoeck & Ruprecht: 641–975.

Sturm, Th. (1995). '*Kaspum ammurum*, ein Begriff der Silbermetallurgie in den Kültepe-Texten', *Ugarit-Forschungen*, 27: 487–503.

Sturm, Th. (2001). 'Puzur-Annā - ein Schmied des Kārum Kaniš', in Van Soldt, W.H. (ed.), *Veenhof Anniversary Volume*, Leiden, the Netherlands: Nederlands Instituut voor het Nabije Oosten: 475–501.

Ulshöfer, A.M. (1995). *Die altassyrischen Privaturkunden*. Stuttgart, Germany: Franz Steiner.

Van de Mieroop, M. (1999). *The Ancient Mesopotamian City*. Oxford: Oxford University Press.

Van der Spek, R.J. (2016a). 'KI.LAM = *nadānu* in Late Babylonian', *Nouvelles Assyriologiques Brèves et Utilitaires* 2016/1: 53 (no. 28).

Van der Spek, R.J. (2016b). 'KI.LAM = *nadānu*, "exchange rate": More evidence from the price lists', *Nouvelles Assyriologiques Brèves et Utilitaires* 2016/3 : 139–41 (no. 83).

Van der Spek, R.J., Van Leeuwen, B. and Van Zanden, J.L. (eds.) (2015). *A History of Market Performance from Ancient Babylonia to the Modern World*. London, New York: Routledge.

Veenhof, K.R. (1972). *Aspects of Old Assyrian Trade and its Terminology*. Leiden, the Netherlands: Brill.

Veenhof, K.R. (1978). 'An ancient Anatolian money-lender. His loans, securities and debt-slaves', in Hruška, B. and Komoróczy, G. (eds.), *Festschrift Lubor Matouš*, Budapest: Eötvös Loránd Tudományegyetem, Ókori Történeti Tanszekek: 279–311.

Veenhof, K.R. (1995). '"In accordance with the words of the stele": Evidence for Old Assyrian legislation', *Chicago-Kent Law Review*, 70: 1717–44.

Veenhof, K.R. (1997). '"Modern" features in Old Assyrian trade', *Journal of the Economic and Social History of the Orient*, 40: 336–66.

Veenhof, K.R. (1999a). 'Silver and credit in Old Assyrian trade', in Dercksen (ed.) (1999): 55–83.

Veenhof, K.R. (1999b). 'Redemption of houses in Assur and Sippar', in Böck, B., Cancik-Kirschbaum, E. Richter, T. (eds.), *Munuscula Mesopotamica. Festschrift für Johannes Renger*, Münster, Germany: Ugarit-Verlag: 599–616.

Veenhof, K.R. (2001). 'The Old Assyrian period', in Westbrook, R. and Jasnow, R. (eds.), *Security for Debt in Ancient Near Eastern Law*, Leiden, the Netherlands: Brill: 93–159.

Veenhof, K.R. (2008). 'The Old Assyrian period', in Veenhof, K.R. and Eidem, J., *Mesopotamia. The Old Assyrian Period*, Fribourg, Germany: Academic Press / Göttingen, Germany: Vandenhoeck & Ruprecht: 13–264.

Veenhof, K.R. (2011). 'Houses in the ancient city of Assur', in Düring, B.S., Wossink, A. and Akkermans, P.M.M.G. (eds.), *Correlates of Complexity*, Leiden, the Netherlands: Nederlands Instituut voor het Nabije Oosten: 211–31.

Veenhof, K.R. (2014). 'Silver in Old Assyrian trade. Shapes, qualities and purification', in Csabai, Z. (ed.), *Studies in Economic and Social History of the Ancient Near East in Memory of Péter Vargyas*, Budapest, Hungary: L'Harmattan: 393–422.

Von Reden, S. (1995). *Exchange in Ancient Greece*. London: Duckworth.

Von Reden, S. (2007). *Money in Ptolemaic Egypt. From the Macedonian Conquest to the End of the Third Century BC*. Cambridge: Cambridge University Press.

Westbrook, R. (1988). *Old Babylonian Marriage Law*. Horn, Austria: Berger 1988.

Weszeli, M. (1991). Untersuchungen zu den altbabylonischen Erbteilungsurkunden. MA thesis, University of Vienna.

Wittfogel, K.A. (1957). *Oriental Despotism. A Comparative Study of Total Power*. New Haven, CT: Yale University Press.

6 Introducing coinage

Comparing the Greek world, the Near East and China

J.A. Mooring, Bas van Leeuwen and R.J. van der Spek

Introduction

The invention of money is often confused with the invention of coinage. Rather, some other form of money, fulfilling (some of) the function(s) of money, preceded the introduction of coins. The invention of coinage is nevertheless an important step in the history of money. With coins we mean usually round, flat pieces of metal with a mark, used as means of exchange, unit of account, and/or store of wealth. Although the weight and the content of a coin are of great importance, the step to coinage means that, increasingly, payments were made by tale rather than by weighing coins. The first coins we come across in ancient Lydia (seventh or sixth century BC)[1], although we believe these coins hardly functioned as money there. That step was taken in the Greek world, and very hesitatingly in the Persian empire. It was Alexander the Great who introduced coinage in the Near East on a grand scale. The very first coins were made of electrum, a natural alloy of gold and silver. In the Greek world, silver and to a much lesser extent gold were the main coinage specie. Around the middle of the fifth century, bronze coins entered the scene. In China, basically skipping the step of precious-metal coinage, copper and bronze appeared at the scene at around the same time as in the Greek world, i.e. around 350 BC, arguably being an independent invention. Silver money remained uncoined in China and paper money preceded the use of silver as a means of payment in China, a really surprising development (see also Von Glahn, Chapter 12, this volume). In this chapter we shall not extensively discuss the emergence of coinage; this has been done in several articles and books.[2] Rather, it is our intention to look at the phenomenon of coinage from a broad perspective, from Greece via the Near East to China, and use this comparison to tentatively distil some factors explaining the introduction of coinage.

The introduction of coinage in Asia Minor and the Greek World

We first consider the introduction of silver and gold coinage, which occurred in the Greek city states and the Near East as opposed to China. It is well known from historical and archaeological sources that the first coins appeared in Lydia, in present-day Turkey, in the seventh or sixth century BC. In the Lydian kingdom, natural electrum was found in the river Pactolus (Kroll 2012: 38). These natural resources were, among other applications, used by the Lydian kings to 'finance' their expansion. To achieve this expansion, they needed not only support from the Lydian elite, but also from mercenaries to fight for them. To reward the elite for its support and the mercenaries for their services, precious gifts were given, just like it was done for centuries and how it came to be reflected in the ancient stories sung by Homer. However, in Lydia this was done in a more regular, structural way, so the Lydian court found a controlled way to support its expansion. The natural electrum riches[3] were made into small pieces with the symbol of the Lydian king: a fierce, roaring lion. This perfect gift from the king would certainly buy him the support of those who received it (cf. Le Rider 2001: 74; Konuk 2012: 47). In terms of the function of money, this implies that, from a simple gift, it soon developed the function of 'store of wealth'. As soon as these 'coins' got a monetary function, this also led to the temptation for the kings to make a profit by lowering the precious metal contents in the coin. Indeed, according to Le Rider, the kings made a profit by issuing the coins, as the nominal value exceeded the intrinsic value of the bullion by 15–20%, and in classical Athens the nominal value of the coins exceeded the intrinsic value by 5% (Le Rider 2001: 80 and 95). One should take into account, however, that the production of coins incurs costs (cf. Flynn, Chapter 2, this volume). Hence, as soon as the coins started to be used as money, they ran the risk of not being accepted anymore due to the uncertain content (see below).

This habit of making small gifts was soon also known by the Greeks on the Ionian shores, who were in close contact with the Lydian court, either on friendly terms or, at times, also as the opponents to the Lydian king. Looking at the Lydian coins, there are some remarkable observations to make:

- They were made of electrum, although it was possible to separate the gold and silver.
- The gold content of these coins varied considerably. The natural alloy was 73% gold and 23% silver; this was reduced in the coins to 54% gold, 27% silver, and 1–2 % copper (Le Rider 2001: 95; Kroll 2012: 38–9).
- There were many different images on the coins.

From these observations, several conclusions can be drawn. The technical knowledge was available to make coins in small denominations with great precision. However, we tend to believe that these coins were not used as means of payment, nor as means of account, as the gold content varied. Therefore, the intrinsic value varied accordingly, so it was hard to calculate the value of these pieces. In addition, there were many different images on the coins. This indicates that the pieces of electrum were more pieces of art than means of payment; after all, 'devices' used for payments must be recognized and trusted instantaneously, and changing appearances would not stimulate its acceptance. Even though it may have had 'store of wealth' as its monetary function, one might question whether these electrum pieces may be called coins, as coins are defined as 'a piece of metal (or, rarely, of some other material) certified by a mark or marks upon it to be of a definite exchange value, and issued by governmental authority to be used as money'.[4] Electrum coins obviously lacked a definite exchange value.

Yet, in the second half of the sixth century BC, something remarkable happened: in Lydia, King Croesus (r. 560–547) started with the separation of the gold and silver content of electrum and thus created a bimetallic system with fixed rates for the exchange between gold and silver (Le Rider 2001: 101–21; Kroll 2012: 38–9). This was possibly done because there was a demand for a stable store of wealth and, to a lesser extent, money of account and means of exchange. Electrum coins could not fulfil these roles, as they varied in value as the gold–silver ratio fluctuated and the store of wealth functions first suffered from loss of trust. In addition, they were devaluated, that is, the share of gold in electrum coins was on average lower than that found in mined electrum (Kroll 2012: 38–9; see Van Leeuwen, Iossif and Foldvari, Chapter 6, this volume). So, Croesus had to create gold and silver coins to assure their use in society and by fixing a ratio between silver and gold. He was the first to create a bimetallic currency (Konuk 2012: 50). And, even though a bimetallic system was created in Lydia, coins in the Greek world outside Asia Minor were made largely of silver, replacing the electrum coins almost completely by the end of the sixth century. This focus on silver outside of Lydia can be explained by the simple fact that electrum and gold resources were outside the territory of the minting Greek poleis, but silver was available and, relatedly, that silver was the most current money specie in the Near East (Kroll 2012: 36–7).

One could say that, with the choice to use silver (and to a much lesser extent gold) for coins, it had now become possible to add the means of account functionality to coinage simply because the value of the coins could be measured and calculated. In this way, the means of storing wealth was connected to the rather abstract means of account and, through that combination, it provided an excellent means of payment, creating ready-to-go, all-purpose money. It is not very helpful to discuss whether this increasing functionality of silver coins first occurred in Lydia or in the Greek poleis of Ionia. The fact is that this became rapidly popular throughout the Greek world. Coinage was used in several Greek city-states to facilitate state payments. In times of war or extensive building projects, coinage made it easier to budget for such expenses, but also to pay them. However, there was similar governmental spending in the Ancient Near East, which was paid in uncoined silver. There the use of bullion for payments was common practice for ages, and is well-attested in sources. Obviously, this way of paying sufficed, and the advantages of coinage were not acknowledged. Indeed, some Greek coins found in the Near East bear chisel marks, a sign that they were treated as bullion. It should be noted that also in Greece the use of uncoined silver preceded the use of coins (Kroll 2012: 37).

The introduction of coinage in the Near East was a slow process at first. Although coinage was invented in Lydia in Asia Minor, the actual use of coins as money started in Greece, as observed above. Lydia was conquered by the Persians in 547 BC, and the Persians started to imitate the Lydian coins by striking 'Croeseids' and later Darius I created the gold darics and the silver *sigloi* (Le Rider 2001: 101–205. Cf. the thesis of Nicolas Corfù, that these coins were not Persian but the coins of the local mint in Sardes; Corfù (2010)). The gold darics had the *weight* of a Babylonian shekel (c. 8.3 grams – see below) and it was equivalent to 20 silver *sigloi*, weighing 5.4, later 5.6 grams (Le Rider 2001: 156). As such, it was bimetallic system. These coins, however, never reached the status of standard means of payment. It was especially used in the western part of the empire to pay mainly Greek mercenaries. It seems as though the Persians in this respect accommodated to Greek taste. But in the core of the empire, in Persia and Babylonia, uncoined silver bullion remained the norm.

Though other types of money existed – such as IOUs (clay documents), gold, bronze, and grain – silver, i.e. bullion silver, had been the major unit of account, store of value, and means of payment. The silver had the form of silver ingots, objects, rings, scraps of silver, but it could also function as a sort of ghost money, as gauge of value and unit of account alone. It was only in the sixth century BC that silver started to play its role as means of payment in the streets of Babylon, so that one might tentatively speak of 'deep monetization'. The crucial point in this type of bullion silver money is weight and quality. So, paying is weighing. Trust in this type of money is ascertained first by the weight and the quality of the metal. Silver is, like any other product, valued by the forces of demand and supply. Yet, there is another aspect, by which its value rises on top of the normal market forces: that is the role of the state. The state did not issue money, like later states issued coins, but it ordained a certain weight system. Key measures in Mesopotamia were the mina (*manû*), weighing c. 1 metric pound, which consisted of 60 shekels (*šiqlu*) of c. 8.33 grams. More importantly, the state accepted silver as payment of debts and taxes and used it as unit of account. As soon as silver was accepted as payment, the value of silver accrued due to the increased demand. Hence, confidence in money was based on a combination of market value and support by the state. In Chapter 5, this volume, the history of money in Mesopotamia before Alexander the Great is discussed in more detail.

Greek city-states issued each their own coins with their own denominations, but all systems reckoned in a subdivision that was based on the weight system of Mesopotamia, with as crucial weight measure the *mnâ*, derived from the Mesopotamian *manû* (mina), and the *statēr*, lit. 'weight', a translation of the Akkadian word *šiqlu*, Hebrew *šeqel*, shekel, 'weight'. The silver stater consisted in many places of two drachmas, but in Athens it was four drachmas (though the gold stater there was two drachmas). The weights were defined differently in different city-states, but due to the economic and political predominance of Athens in the fifth century, the Athenian coins according to the Athenian subdivisions gained widespread acceptance in the eastern Mediterranean.

The Athenian, or 'Attic', weight system had a mina of c. 430 grams, which consisted of 100 drachmas of c. 4.3 grams. The stater or tetradrachm thus weighed 17.2 grams.

The interesting point in coinage is that, as before, weight and quality played a part in the appreciation of the money specie, but that the state issued standard lumps of silver (and gold and bronze) with a stamp on it indicating a guarantee of weight and content by the state. Accordingly, apart from 'paying by weighing', now also payment by tale was introduced. That made money even more complicated. The value of a coin was determined by the guarantee of the state *and* by its content and weight. It seems, however, that gradually the guarantee of the state was accepted as the main factor, so that payment by tale became the standard. It must be added that this acceptance was not only based on the stamp only, but also by the fact that the state accepted coins as payment of debts and taxes. The process of introducing coins can be illustrated nicely by the hoard found in the city of Colophon (Kim and Kroll 2008).

Colophon was a Greek polis situated in Ionia (Asia Minor), which was conquered by the Lydian king Gyges in approximately 660 BC. The city came under Persian rule from the 540s. As of the 520s, Colophon minted silver coins, but there are no indications from the Archaic Period as to why Colophon minted coins. Maybe this was due to the fact that the city was well known for its prosperity, and therefore coinage as an economic institution was required. Although the reason for the authorities in Colophon to introduce coinage is unclear, we can gain more insight into the process of introduction. A large hoard (CH I.3), now in the Ashmolean Museum, contained 903 silver coins and 77 pieces of unminted silver. The coins were all small fractions from Colophon: 1 twelfth stater, 353 twenty-fourths staters, and 552 forty-eighths staters, weighing approximately 0.92, 0.43 and 0.21 grams each and minted in the last third or quarter of the sixth century. The unminted pieces were unusually small in size, and two thirds were flat, hammered disks. The hoard leaves the impression that coined and uncoined silver was used simultaneously: the coins to supplement the uncoined pieces to exactly match the required weight. This is noticeable, as it was presumed for long that large denominations appeared first, to be complemented with small change later on. Also, the scale of minting is noteworthy: die analysis revealed that the production of the mint must have been in the order of hundreds of thousands to millions of pieces.

From this hoard several conclusions can be drawn. The first one is that in the early stage of coinage coins and unminted silver were used next to each other. Second, the monetization in this early stage was quite deep as such a large production of small change (at least more than ten coins per inhabitant) was struck. Third, the government in Colophon apparently saw good reasons to invest time and money in striking small coins to regulate the payment processes in the polis. The costs to produce such tiny coins, which show a strong adherence to the weight standard, must have been relatively high. To further facilitate the use of these tiny coins, monograms indicating the denomination of the coins were added towards the end of the sixth century: HM for *hēmiobolon* ('a half obol') and TE for *tetartēmorion* ('a quarter'). To conclude, the exact occasion why Colophon started to mint coins is unknown, but part of the purpose was clearly to facilitate the payments made in the polis. It cannot be the only reason, though.

Jack Kroll assumed that the success of coinage was simply due to its sheer practicality (Kroll 2012: 40). We might perhaps not overstate the practicality. The striking of coins required production costs. The difference in weight standards hampered international trade, and the state could easily manipulate content and weight of the coins. And if the coins were so practical (and in historical perspective, they appeared to be very successful), why was this practicality not recognized in the Near East, in which coins were only introduced by Alexander?

Many explanations have been proposed for the fact that coinage did not root in the Near East before Alexander the Great. The reason is most often sought in the character of the Near Eastern economy. This is, in particular by students of the classical world, usually described as a so-called redistribution economy. To put it in the words of Robin Seaford (2004: 69): 'redistribution has become the enforced collection of goods and services at a central building (notably temple or palace), where they are used for the upkeep of the central institution, for redistribution among the population, and for communal functions such as storage against famine, the administration of justice and irrigation'. In such a system, it is argued, trade in the true sense of the word was impossible, and so no exchange on the market took place and thus no need for coins existed. We see the same view expressed in the recent book by Alain Bresson (2016: 103–8; 264–70).[5]

This approach does not satisfy, however. In recent years, the concept of the redistribution system has come under various attacks, as is recognized by Seaford. But, to his defense, he quotes studies that underscore the idea of a redistribution system in the third and second millennia. It is true indeed that palace and temple were important land owners, and that kings collected many taxes in kind, but trade and private property existed from the beginning of the historical records. And even if the concept of redistribution may have had some value in the third and second millennia, coinage was a phenomenon of the first millennium BC and it is in the first millennium that the model of the redistribution economy loses force. We see in sixth century Babylonia the emergence of trading companies, complex financial instruments and wage labour in the building projects of the kings, where labourers were increasingly paid in silver. Private entrepreneurs went on joint ventures for trading purposes; private land-owners produced new crops for the urban market. Temples still owned large tracts of land, but these temples chose to produce for the market, and thus specialized in such cash crops as grain, wool, or dates (Jursa *et al.* 2010: 209, 217, 468, 754–804 *et passim*). As pointed out by Michael Jursa (Chapter 5, this volume), silver was not only a unit of account, but was used for actual payments on the market in very tiny fractions, and Babylonia was deeply monetized. Under Persian rule, there was a flow of silver cash out of Babylonia to Persia (Susa and Persepolis), but the system was set up in order to assure that a substantial part of this silver eventually ended up in local circulation again (Jursa *et al.* 2010: 779).[6] 'Royal spending for ambitious public building projects brought money into circulation, and the structure of the labour force, i.e. the importance of hired labour for building and for military and corvée service (rather than compelled labour), assured that money circulated quite widely, even among the less affluent strata of the urban population and in the countryside' (Jursa *et al.* 2010: 782).[7] And still the Near East did not go for coins.

In our view, the option for coinage in the Greek world was a combination of contingency (the idea of making 'coins' as gifts in Lydia by kings, but probably also by local warlords), political and social use by individuals in the Greek world (tyrants, aristocrats, wealthy citizens for generating support), combined with local city-pride and solidarity (see below), thus mainly for non-economic reasons. All these reasons fit better with a Greek city-state than with an empire. Soon, however, the coins were accepted as means of payment in the city-state. Trust was a local phenomenon in this city-state. We shall discuss this in the final section.

The introduction of coinage in the Near East by Alexander the Great

Even though initially coinage did not find solid ground in the Near East, this changed with the arrival of Alexander the Great. Indeed, Alexander the Great ushered in an important new stage in the history of money in the Ancient Near East. Nearly overnight he introduced Greek coins as standard means of payment. Alexander, used to coinage as expression of national pride in the Greek world, apparently appreciated the enormous value of coinage for propagandistic purposes. In a world without means of mass communication, such as newspapers, radio, television, and internet, coins are a ready instrument to convey messages all over the empire. In addition, by choosing for the Attic standard, he could make a connection with the Athenian monetary network. Either because of national pride or because of economic insight, he did not build on the Persian coinage. There was another advantage of coinage, perhaps not valued already by Alexander.

Since it was the state that issued coins, the state could manipulate the coins by lowering the weight or reducing the content of the silver. By debasements, the king could increase the money stock. That might induce direct inflation, but at first this only happened on a limited scale. The content of the coins in the Seleucid empire remained stable until the reign of Antiochus IV (175–164), when debasements started (Mørkholm 1991: 8). But even these debasements need not be very detrimental as long as the state accepted the debased coins at face value, i.e. by creating a de facto further separation between the intrinsic and nominal value. This aspect is well treated by Butcher for the Roman Empire (Chapter 8) and Mayhew for England (Chapter 9).

As said, Alexander adhered (with some minor exceptions) to the Attic standard, taking the tetradrachm of 17.2 grams as standard coin (*statēr*). There were some lighter tetradrachms in the beginning, though. In Babylon, satrap Mazaeus issued tetradrachms which had on the obverse a seated Ba'al of Tarsus (with Aramaic legend), and on the reverse a walking lion. These weighed 17.2 grams, indeed, but the weights of these coins, also called lion staters, that were issued after his death in 328 BC until 280 BC became irregular, with some pieces in good condition weighing below 16.00 grams. In many cases, now the Seleucid anchor was added. Another remarkable issue concerned the elephant staters, commemorating Alexander's victories in India. Also, Seleucus issued 'elephant staters' of irregular but mostly lower weight, probably related to his deal with King Chandragupta, the founder of the Mauryan Empire (r. 321–298 BC), from whom he received 500 elephants. Julien Monerie assumes that these lion and elephant staters were designed for the local market, but were nevertheless exchangeable with 'imperial' tetradrachms. Even some coins on the daric standard were issued.[8] In general, however, the coinage of Alexander and of the Seleucids followed the Attic standard. His successors in the Near East, the Seleucids, adopted these practices (with variations; Houghton and Lorber 2002, vol. 1.2, 1–4) and they were the first to introduce the bronze coinage in Mesopotamia and the Upper Satrapies.

One might well ponder about the way the Babylonians and other Orientals perceived this new coined money. Did they treat it just as before, as bullion, of which the only innovation was that they were *marked* lumps of silver? In other words: did they weigh the coins or did they count them when they wanted to pay?

There are several arguments for the view that the Babylonians continued to weigh the coins. In the first place, they were used to weighing; their trust had always been based on weight, so why change it? Furthermore, some coins had deviant weights, as we have seen above. In the third place, the formulary of the cuneiform documents suggests so. All Babylonian documents continue to reckon in the Babylonian weight system, the shekel. Administrative documents that mention prices use the formula 'x shekels of silver in staters of Alexander' – under later kings, normally the reigning king (cf. Várgyas 2004). Sometimes specific coins are mentioned in the description of the price, such as the 'elephant staters' and the 'lion staters'. Therefore, it seemed that the coins were weighed according to the Babylonian weight system. There is an enigmatic expression in some price formulas which might support this idea: *manûtu ša Bābili*, lit. 'the counting of Babylon', as if a certain conversion rate existed between Babylonian shekels and Greek coins (more on this below). And it is in fact not a bad procedure; especially when a huge number of coins are at issue, it is easier to weigh, and manipulation of the weight of the coin can be detected at the same time. It has been an argument of the view, and Van der Spek long adhered to the view that content and weight of the coin was considered more important than number (e.g. Van der Spek 2007: 417).

Recently, however, the insight has grown that behind this Babylonian formula a simple truth was hidden, viz. that one Babylonian shekel (8.33 grams) equalled two drachmas (8.6 grams). There is evidence for it in non-Babylonian sources, viz. Aramaic papyri from Achaemenid Elephantine (Egypt) and the Greek translation of the Hebrew Bible, the Septuagint, where the Hebrew shekel is translated as *didrachmon* = a two-drachma piece (evidence in Van der Spek 2017). And there is one exceptional cuneiform tablet from Babylonia that records the wages of five labourers who remove the debris of the Esagila temple, where the wage is specified as '1/3 mina (= 20 shekels) of silver, the weight (KI.LÁ = *šuqultu*) of 10 staters, the wages of five wage labourers who remove the debris'.[9] This means that the stater exactly equalled 2 shekels, so that the shekel was a *didrachmon* indeed.

This was the case in Babylonia from then on. In earlier publications, Van der Spek suggested that this was not more than a rule of thumb that emerged over time (1998: 211; 246–7; 2014: 205), but Monerie in his recently published dissertation[10] argued that it was a rule from the beginning, and that the expression *manûtu ša Bābili* exactly means that. He translated the term as 'taux de Babylone', 'rate of Babylon', and the rate was simply: one shekel is two drachmas, *irrespective* of the weight of the drachma or didrachm or tetradrachm. The coins had to be accepted at face value even if the lighter lion staters were at issue. Reinhard Pirngruber adhered to this view (Pirngruber 2017: 43). It means that payments were made by tale!

Van der Spek (2017) agrees now to this view, but with a minor qualification. The meaning of *manûtu ša Bābili* does not mean 'the conversion rate of Babylon', but the 'subdivision of the Babylonian mina'. The expression only occurs in price quotations where the mina is mentioned. Since the Babylonian mina consisted of 60 shekels (= 120 drachmas) and the Greek mina consisted of 100 drachmas, it was necessary to make sure that the Babylonian mina was intended, equalling 30 staters, not the Greek mina, consisting of 25 staters. But this observation supports Monerie's opinion that the coins were counted now rather than weighed. Nevertheless, weight became not pointless. The state might ordain that coins should be taken at face value, but that does not mean that it always happened in the market streets. Not without reason the coins are described as 'Lion stater', 'Elephant stater', or 'Stater of king so and so'. Trust is always a combination of intrinsic value and guarantee by the state. That was so in ancient Babylonia, and it was so later. This subtle balance is well discussed in the chapters by Butcher (Chapter 8) and Mayhew (Chapter 9) in this volume.

The introduction of coinage in China

In many ways, the rise of coinage in China in the eighth through tenth centuries BC resembles that of other regions, with various artefacts functioning as money. On the one hand, money was devised in the form of a cowry shell while metal payment was done in the form of various tools and knives. One might guess that the round copper/bronze coin that came into existence in China in the fourth century BC found its origin in the cowry shell, but this is pure speculation. Other hypotheses concern contacts with the Greek world, or any other reason. Yet the fact that these coins all ended up being round, even though initially, just as in the Greek World, round coins circulated together with other types of money, suggest that there must at least have been a common factor in China, the Near East, and the Greek World.

Yet the remarkable thing in this development of coinage is the lack of silver coins, which did exist in other parts of the world. Certainly, just as in seventh-century Lydia, silver in China was used as government gifts to vassals and other states, and partly because of the rise in high value trade by e.g. merchants, gold and silver bullion became increasingly used in monetary exchange. In other words, just like in the Near East and the Greek world, it had the function of 'store of wealth', and to a lesser extent 'means of exchange'. However, contrary to the Near Eastern empires and the Greek city–states, where gold and especially silver eventually got a 'money of account' function, this did not occur in China. Indeed, as pointed out in the *Han shu* ('History of the Han'), '[w]hen Qin [c. 221 BC] united the world, it made two sorts of currency: that of yellow gold, which was called *yi* and was the currency of the higher class; and that of bronze, which was similar in quality to the coins of Zhou, but bore an inscription saying Half Ounce, and was equal in weight to its inscription' (see e.g. Swann 1950). Even though gold was used in high-level monetary exchange, it did not function as unit of account, since the low-value *banliang* coin was measured, indeed, even named, after its weight in copper rather than in silver or gold.

As to why China in the first centuries BC did not develop a money of account function in gold and/or silver, various reasons are mentioned in the literature. First, there was a large-scale trade between China and the West, and much gold ended outside the empire as the profit of brokers. Second, in order to maintain a good relationship with western and neighbouring countries, emperors of the Han dynasty sent large amounts of gold to those countries, thus reducing the amount of gold within China even further. Third, even though the vast majority of gold belonged to the state, it was used for decoration of large palaces and temples (Zhang 2009). Fourth, contrary to the Greek states, China was relatively homogenous. Hence, there was no need to stamp silver to distinguish mints from different (city-)states, as was arguably necessary in the Greek world. Indeed, for most Chinese silver pieces (there are no silver coins), or even copper coins, it is unknown where they were minted. Fifth, China lacked gold deposits and, to some extent, also silver deposits. However, copper was plentifully available, thus making it attractive for the government to create a currency based on copper (Horesh 2014).

Most likely, various other reasons for the introduction of copper coins and the lack of silver ones must exist. Yet the fact remains that, for either cultural or economic reasons, it was necessary that another metal than gold or silver started to function as a monetary standard. This function was placed on the copper coin (*wen/qian*), which is pointed out above as well by the quote from the *Han shu*. Even though in theory based on silver, in practice the silver/*wen* ratio could be set by the government, while payments in silver hardly occurred.

In other words, as argued by Xu and Van Leeuwen (Chapter 13, this volume), such a system based on precious metal, in which there is no actual convertibility in specie, is a fiat money in disguise. Only in the fifteenth century AD, after many centuries and monetary crises, China would follow the same route as the Near East and the Greek city-states and make silver also the unit of account, even though it remained unminted, like in the Near East before Alexander (Peng 1958).

The role of trust

So we have seen that some Greek poleis started to mint for political reasons. It started with the Lydian kings who struck coins as precious gifts for his followers and soldiers. The same may have been true for other warlords in the region.[11] A relation of trust between leader and followers was thus created. That aspect was used in the Greek world by aristocrats and tyrants, and finally by city-states as community. Thomas Martin has pointed at the need for aristocrats to find followers in the city-state, which eventually led to the liturgical system, where rich people funded important civic duties, 'liturgies', such as the equipment of warships or the organization of festivals. Martin coins this early stage as a 'proto-liturgical tradition' (Martin 1996: 270). This was certainly not the case in Han China. Even today it has been argued that civil society in China is marginalized, but that was certainly true for the Han dynasty. In that period, the main incentive of the government was to take power away from the local elite (and potential warlords). Examples include the famous granary system: if a private individual had a granary, he/she could only open it to the public in case of famine after approval by the government (Swann 1950).

The reason for the Chinese dislike of this type of coinage is exactly the reason why it was liked in the Greek World: coinage was also a ready instrument for tyrants seeking support, exemplified by Pisistratus in Athens. Coinage supported this process of seeking support among the mass of the population; a relation between patron and clients on a grand scale emerged, so that the relation became impersonal; in such a situation, the coins were a ready-marked instrument (Martin 1996: 271). The coinage also fitted in with the wish of the tyrants to create a polis community. This finds expression in the organization of national festivals, such as the Panathenaic games by Pisistratus. By that means, the coins become an expression of the emerging city-state as such. It stimulated local pride, and at the same time stimulated competition between city-states.[12] Obviously, this is a positive development in a system consisting of city-states, but poses a great risk for unified empires like China.

The consequence of this development is that the competition helped to spread coinage over the Mediterranean, first in the Greek city-states and then also in others, while in the case of China no silver coins emerged. This 'peer-polity interaction' between city-states was the cultural background of this spread, like so many other phenomena, such as military techniques, political structures, crafts, and tastes (Howgego 1995: 15). The adoption in the third century BC of silver coinage (*denarii*) by the Romans, who were used to bronze lumps and coins, fits in this process.

This observation does not contradict another observation, viz. that the coins soon were used in economic transactions; they soon were used as an all-purpose money in many city-states and also in China. It may indeed explain the ready acceptance in all these diverse areas. The acceptance would have helped people take the nuisance of money-changing for granted, as well as accept that weighing coins is not necessary in daily transactions. Copper and bronze coinage in China was done by counting strings of up to thousand coins, rather than weighing. We should, however, not attach too much value to this argument. First, many coins were still weighed. And even in the case of China, where coins were counted, strings could vary in the actual number of coins, from as low as 400 to over 1,000, thus generating a de facto weighing system. Second, in certain regions, such as the Roman colonies, coins were still struck, even though they could easily have used Roman or other coinage, thus implying that in those cases it was not solely an economic motive to start minting a local coin (Termeer 2015).

But what was really introduced by the minting of coins? The new element was that coins were pre-weighed pieces of metal, which was obvious in the case of China, where coins were even named after their weight. In the case of the coins found in the Colophon hoard, these were probably used to speed up the weighing process. But when the whole payment could be done with coins, it was not necessary to weigh the silver at all. This did not seem to be a big step, and the added value was considered scant to the peoples in the Near East, judging from the lack of coinage there. There were indeed some drawbacks to the use of coins. As there were several local standards of weights and measures in Archaic Greece, it was important to know on which standard the coin was struck. With that knowledge, the size indicated the denomination and thus the value. It will be obvious that these coins were only used locally, as it required much knowledge and experience to identify the mint, the weight standard, and the denomination before the value of the coin was known. The first few instances someone received a coin as a payment, it would certainly be weighted and inspected, just like a payment in bullion. But after some positive experiences with coinage, confidence in the correct weight would have grown. To reinforce this process, the designs on the coins seem to have stabilized in the second half of the sixth century BC. Just like the bullion in China, electrum coins are often hard to attribute to a specific mint, and even if the subject of a design was stable, this was depicted in several ways. When silver coins appeared, the coins started to look very similar. Maybe the best illustration of this stabilizing phenomenon is the introduction of the famous 'owls' in Athens at the end of the sixth century BC to replace the *Wappenmünze*, which bore different images; the Athenian silver 'owls' stayed the same until the middle of the first century BC, when the Romans replaced the drachma with the Roman *denarius*. Bronze coins with owls were coined until c. AD 267.

The main innovation of coinage was the addition of a different kind of trust, viz. not on the basis of content and weight, but of a mark stamped on it by the state. After all, when the amount of silver to be paid in a transaction was not weighted on a balance, but just counted in coins, there had to be trust that the coins matched exactly the denominational weight. That guarantee was provided by the minting authority, but as Greek society was divided into countless poleis, each using different kinds of weighing standards, coins were only used on the domestic market.[13]

It is difficult to measure trust in modern society, let alone in antiquity. How can we compare trust levels in the ancient Near East and Archaic Greece? Steven Johnstone wrote *A History of Trust in Ancient Greece*[14], which was basically an inventory of institutions that reflected the implicit agreements on various topics in ancient Greece. These institutions contributed to the confidence of people, but were not unique to Greek culture. Besides, these institutions were more the results of the trust embedded in society than the cause of it. The roots of trust must be sought in human interaction. Repetitive experiences cause future behaviour of people to become predictable. This creates trust, or distrust, in specific persons but also in fellow human beings in general. Due to the limited number of inhabitants, in small communities the social interaction between members is larger than in big communities; therefore, the trust level is higher. The same is true for network relations, where a bad reputation rapidly spreads to all network members, and the chances increase that no one within the network will want to have any dealings with someone who has failed to meet their obligations.[15] A third stimulus of trust is a shared set of norms, so the behaviour of the counterparty is likely to be as expected based upon the shared norms. On all these three indicators the Greek poleis scored higher, as the communities were smaller than in the Near East (let alone China), had extensive network contacts, and shared the same culture in contrast to the mixed culture of the Near East.

Conclusion

Between c. 600 and 300 BC, coined money emerged in the Near East, Greece, and China as a new institution for governments that wanted to regulate the cash flows in their state. We have seen that the development of coinage in Greek culture was taken step by step from gift exchange, through means of payment to finally fiduciary money, and was introduced by government order in the Near East under Alexander the Great. This was very different in China, though, where precious metals like silver and gold never made that step. Only in the fifteenth century AD would China introduce silver as the money of account, albeit still unminted.

The introduction of silver coinage in the Greek world was based on political division and local pride. For that reason, it did not occur in China, where the government tried to limit the power of civil society. However, in China, bronze coinage was mostly introduced for economic motives, even though still tightly controlled by the government. Indeed, this difference between the Greek world and China largely depended on trust in the society. As the level of trust was high, the Greeks could make the switch from weighing silver to counting coins. Even though this also in theory occurred in China by introducing strings of coins, in practice these strings varied strongly by region in number of coins, thus de facto leading to a weighing system rather than payment by tale.

In the Near East, in many ways a form in between China and the Greek world developed. On the one hand, just like China, it was a world of empires (Assyrian, Babylonian, Persian) used to bullion silver as money specie in connection with payments in kind (though, in China, silver functioned only as store of value, while at least from the sixth century on silver was used as all-purpose money in Babylonia), which might have reduced the need to switch to coins. On the other hand, it was much more fragmented. Hence, its control over the local elite on the fringes of the empire was much more limited than in China. This explains why coinage was first accepted in the western part of the Persian empire, in the Greek and Carian cities on the shores of Asia Minor, and in the interior of Asia Minor and the Phoenician cities.

The broader introduction of coinage in the Near East must in part be attributed to historical contingency, i.e. the arrival of Alexander the Great who introduced coinage on a much wider scale. Yet, contrary to China, at the time of his conquests, coinage had already reached a mature state, and the trust between inhabitants (horizontal trust) that existed in the Greek poleis could be replaced by trust in the government and its institutions (vertical trust), something the Chinese government was still unable to do for gold and silver.

Notes

1 The date of the first coins is controversial. Price (1983) and Le Rider (2001) dated the coins to 560 BC; Konuk (2012: 48–9) dated the strata where the first coins were found to 640–630 BC placing the introduction of the coinage in the second half of the seventh century BC.

2 To mention a few: Price (1979, 1983); Carradice and Price (1988); Howgego (1995); Le Rider (2001); Seaford (2004); Harris (ed.) (2008); Von Reden (2010); Metcalf (ed.) 2012); Psoma (2001); Sargent and Velde (2003); Schaps (2004); for the Near East: see Chapter 5, this volume; for China, see Chapter 12, this volume.

3 Recently, the general opinion has shifted, and it is now believed that coins were not made from naturally mined electrum, but from a man-made alloy. This will be reflected in the proceeding of the congress 'White Gold', published by the American Numismatic Society and edited by Peter van Alfen, Ute Wartenberg, and Haim Gitler.

4 Webster's Dictionary, second edition, (= Neilson *et al.* 1934), quoted by Metcalf (2012: 3), adding that the definition omits the element of weight. The most recent definition in Webster's online is simpler: 'a usually flat piece of metal issued by governmental authority as money'; https://www.merriam-webster.com/dictionary/coin.

5 "[T]here was a radical difference between the Achaemenid world and that of the Greek city states [...] the world of the Greek city states was a world whose centre was the agora. This public square was a place of exchange among equals in which, in operation of exchange itself (of course not in society at large), inequalities of birth or fortune were

of little or no importance. […] In Persian society, which was stratified with the king at its summit, a hierarchical circulation of wealth (the levying of tributes or the distribution of rations) left little room for exchange among equals, because social relationships were fundamentally asymmetrical" (Bresson 2016: 268).

6 Jursa *et al.* (2010: 775–80, Section 6.1.5.2), 'The range of monetised exchange'.

7 Jursa *et al.* (2010: 780–3, Section 6.1.5.3), 'Money, prices and markets'.

8 More information and analysis: Mørkholm (1991: 48–9); Houghton and Lorber (2002: 44); Duyrat (2015: 375–85); Monerie (2017: 101 *ad* n. 342).

9 Jursa (2002: 120, text no. 8, a document dated to 7 January 321 B.C.) See Van der Spek (2017: 35, n. 6) for the option that in this case (321 BC) we might think that the wage was established at 10 stater, but that it was paid out in bullion silver from the temple cashboxes. If so, this would be a habit that died out soon.

10 Monerie (2017, section 2.1.4., esp. pp. 336; 339–40).

11 This might be reflected in the names of some unknown people written on the coins; cf. Konuk (2012: 47).

12 This aspect was already brought forward by Moses Finley (1985: 166–7), stressing the nuisance of the different standards in the different city-states, for the benefit only of the money-changers. It is strange that Martin rejects so vehemently Finley's thesis, as it fits in so well with his own ideas of political use of coinage by the elite in the early city-states. It is a small step towards taking coinage as a political statement by the city-states as such. 'Thus coinage functioned as an essential mechanism in the evolving political structures of the Greek *polis* at this early stage of development' (Martin 1996: 267).

13 There are only a few exceptions to this rule. These were coins that had such a good reputation that they were also used in international trade and abroad. Examples are Athenian *owls*, Corinthian *pegasi*, Aeginetan *turtles* and the *Kroiseioi*. See Von Reden's (2010: 65–91) Chapter 3 on international monetary networks.

14 Johnstone (2011).

15 Mosch and Prast (2008 : 24).

References

Bresson, A. (2016). *The Making of the Ancient Greek Economy. Institutions, Markets, and Growth in the City-states.* Princeton, NJ: Princeton University Press.

Carradice, I. and Price, M. (1988). *Coinage of the Greek World.* London: Spink & Son Ltd.

Chen Chunsheng (2010). 'Contribution, market and material life. A study on the relationship between the input of American silver and the changes of Chinese society', *Journal of Tsinghua University (Philosophy and Social Sciences)*, 2010(5) = 陈春生，贡赋、市场与物质生活——试论十八世纪美洲白银输入与中国社会变迁之关系，2010(05): 65–81.

Chen Zhiqiang (2004). 'Some misunderstandings in the study of Byzantine coins', *Nankai Journal (Philosophy and Social Sciences)*, 2004(5): 57–65 = 陈志强,拜占庭铸币研究中的某些误区，南开学报哲学社科版，2004(5): 57–65.

Corfù, N.A. (2010). 'Die sogenannten achaimenidischen Bogenschützenmünzen – Die Herkunft von Dareikoi und Sigloi', *Archäologische Mitteilungen aus Iran und Turan*, 42: 165–206.

Duyrat, F. (2015). 'The circulation of coins in Syria and Mesopotamia in the sixth to first centuries', in Van der Spek *et al.* (eds.) (2015): 363–95.

Finley, M.I. (1985). *The Ancient Economy. Second Edition.* London: The Hogarth Press.

Harris, W.V. (ed.) (2008). *The Monetary Systems of the Greeks and Romans.* Oxford: Oxford University Press.

Horesh, N. (2014). *Chinese Money in Global Context: Historic Junctures between 600 BCE and 2012.* Stanford, CA: Stanford University Press.

Houghton, A. and Lorber, C. (2002). *Seleucid Coins. A Comprehensive Catalogue*. Vol. I. *Seleucus I through Antiochus III*, New York: American Numismatic Society.

Howgego, C. (1995). *Ancient History from Coins*. London: Routledge.

Jiatengfan (1962). *A Textual Research on Chinese Economic History* = 加藤繁,中国经济史考证,商务印书馆中译本. Beijing: The Commercial Press.

Johnstone, S. (2011). *A History of Trust in Ancient Greece*. Chicago, IL: University of Chicago Press.

Jursa, M. (2002). 'Florilegium babyloniacum: Neue Texte aus hellenistischer und spätachämenidischer Zeit', in Cornelia Wunsch (ed.), *Mining the Archives. Festschrift for Christopher Walker on the Occasion of His 60th Birthday*, Dresden, Germany: ISLET Verlag: 107–30.

Jursa, M. (2010) with contributions by Hackl, J., Janković, B., Kleber, K., Payne, E.E., Waerzeggers, C., and Weszeli, M., *Aspects of the Economic History of Babylonia in the First Millennium B.C. Economic Geography, Economic Mentalities, Agriculture, the Use of Money and the Problem of Economic Growth*. Münster, Germany: Ugarit-Verlag.

Kerschner, M. and Konuk, K. (forthcoming). 'Electrum coins and their archaeological context: The case of the Artemision at Ephesus', in Gitler, H. (ed.), *White Gold Symposium, June 2012*. Jerusalem.

Kim, H.S. and Kroll, J.H. (2008). 'A hoard of archaic coins of Colophon and unminted silver (CH I.3)', *American Journal of Numismatics*, 20: 53–103.

Konuk, K. (2012). 'Asia Minor to the Ionian Revolt', in Metcalf (ed.) (2012): 43–60.

Kroll, J.H. (2008). 'The monetary use of weighed bullion in archaic Greece', in Harris (ed.) (2008): 13–37.

Kroll, J.H. (2012). 'The monetary background of early coinage', in Metcalf (ed.) 2012: 33–42.

Le Rider, G. (2001). *La naissance de la monnaie. Pratiques monétaires de l'Orient ancien*. Paris: Presses Universitaires de France.

Martin, Th. (1996). 'Why did the Greek *polis* originally need coins?', *Historia*, 45: 257–83.

Metcalf, W.E. (ed.) (2012). *The Oxford Handbook of Greek and Roman Coinage*. Oxford: Oxford University Press.

Monerie, J. (2017). *L'économie de la Babylonie à l'époque hellénistique (IVème – IIème siècle avant J.C.)*. Berlin: De Gruyter.

Mosch, R.H.J. and Prast, H.M. (2008). *Confidence and trust: empirical investigations for the Netherlands and the financial sector*. DNB Occasional Studies 6/2. Amsterdam: De Nederlandsche Bank. https://www.dnb.nl/en/binaries/OS_Vol6_2_08_tcm47-175279.pdf (accessed 2017-10-02).

Mørkholm, O. (1991). *Early Hellenistic Coinage from the Accession of Alexander to the Peace of Apamea (336–186 B.C.)*. Cambridge, UK: Cambridge University Press.

Neilson, W.A., Knott, T.A., and Carhart, P.W. (eds.) (1934). *Webster's New International Dictionary* (*Second Edition*). Springfield, MA: G. & C. Merriam Company.

Peng Xinwei (1958). *The History of Chinese Currency* = 彭信威，中国货币史，上海人民出版社. Shanghai: Renmin Publishing House.

Pirngruber, R. (2017). *The Economy of Late Achaemenid and Seleucid Babylonia*. Cambridge, UK: Cambridge University Press.

Price, M.J. (1979). 'The function of Greek bronze coinage', *Atti del Istituto Italiano de Numismatica*, 25: 351–58.

Price, M.J. (1983). 'Thoughts on the beginnings of coinage', in Brooke, C.N.L.,Stewart, B.H.I., Pollard, J.G., and Volk, T.R. (eds.), *Studies in Numismatic Method Presented to Philip Grierson*, Cambridge: Cambridge University Press: 1–10.

Psoma, S. (2001). *Olynthe et les Chalcidiens de Thrace*. Stuttgart, Germany: Steiner Verlag.

Sargent, Th.J. and Velde, F.R. (2003). *The Big Problem of Small Change*. Princeton, NJ: Princeton University Press.

Schaps, D.M. (2004). *The Invention of Coinage and the Monetization of Ancient Greece*. Ann Arbor, MI: University of Michigan Press.

Seaford, R. (2004). *Money and the Early Greek Mind*. Cambridge, UK: Cambridge University Press.

Swann, N. (1950). *Food & Money in Ancient China: The Earliest Economic History of China to* ad *25. Han Shu 24 with Related Texts, Han Shu 91 and Shih-Chi 129*. Princeton, NJ: Princeton University Press.

Termeer, M.K. (2015). Latin colonization in Italy before the end of the Second Punic War: Colonial communities and cultural change. Groningen, the Netherlands: PhD dissertation, University of Groningen.

Van der Spek, R.J. (1998). 'Cuneiform documents on Parthian history: The Raḫimesu Archive. Materials for the study of the standard of living', in Wiesehöfer, J. (ed.), *Das Partherreich und seine Zeugnisse. The Arsacid Empire: Sources and Documentation. Beiträge des internationalen Colloquiums, Eutin (27–30. Juni 1996)*. Stuttgart, Germany: Steiner: 205–58.

Van der Spek, R.J. (2007). 'The Hellenistic Near East', in Scheidel, W., Morris, I., and Saller, R. (eds.), *The Cambridge Economic History of the Greco-Roman World*, Cambridge, UK: Cambridge University Press: 409–33.

Van der Spek, R.J. (2014). 'Factor markets in Hellenistic and Parthian Babylonia (331 BCE–224 CE)', *Journal of the Social and Economic History of the Orient*, 57: 203–30.

Van der Spek, R.J. (2017). '*Manûtu ša Bābili* = the Babylonian subdivision of the mina', *Nouvelles Assyriologiques Brèves et Utilitaires*, 33–7 (no. 20).

Van der Spek, R.J., Van Leeuwen, B., and Van Zanden, J.L. (eds.) (2015). *A History of Market Performance – From Ancient Babylonia to the Modern World*. London: Routledge.

Várgyas, P. (2004). 'Le libéralisme séleucide et l'essor économique de la Babylonie: un rapport de cause à effet?', in Chankowski, V. and Duyrat, F. (eds.), *Le roi et l'économie. Autonomies locales et structures royales dans l'économie de l'empire séleucide*, Paris: De Boccard: 333–47.

Von Reden, S. (2010). *Money in Classical Antiquity*. Cambridge, UK: Cambridge University Press.

Xiezhou (2014). 'The characteristics of the traditional Chinese currency system', *Heilongjiang Chronicles*, 2014(17): 201–3= 谢舟,论传统中国货币制度之特征，黑龙江史志，2014(17): 201–3

Zhangjie (2009). 'The dilemma of China's monetary standard: historical origin and evolution mechanism = 张杰,中国的货币本位困境——历史根源与演进机理,东岳论丛，*DongYue Tribune*, 2009(08): 5–25

Zhang Yalan (2009), 'The European silver shortage and China's currency substitution' = 张亚兰,欧洲银荒与中国的货币替代, 中国金融, *China Finance*, 2009(10): 66–7.

7 The introduction of coinage in the Seleucid Empire and the Euro in the European Union

A comparison of stock and velocity

Bas van Leeuwen, Panagiotis P. Iossif and Peter Foldvari

Introduction

Since 2002, the new Euro currency in its physical form was introduced in the countries of the Eurozone (see Appendix 1 on the introduction of Euro coins). This introduction occurred in an already completely monetized region by replacing the existing currencies with a new one. Looking at the long and difficult process in establishing such a monetary union, we sometimes forget that this development within the EU was by no means unique. Not only the EU but many empires in the history, deliberately or not, attempted to achieve a monetary integration. For long stretches of time, large parts of the world used a widely exchangeable currency. One of the earliest examples of monetary integration is the Seleucid Empire, which existed in the Middle East from the time that Alexander the Great defeated the Persian Empire in 331 BC and got its name from the Seleucid dynasty that succeeded Alexander in the Middle East.

Any comparison between economies divided by two and a half millennia is a difficult task, due to fundamental differences in technology, consumption, and institutions. Yet it is not impossible, as attested by a wide range of studies that adopt the modernist view on ancient economies. All patterns we observe at the level of the economy are fundamentally aggregates of individual behaviour, and in this sense our ancestors were more like us than some influential twentieth-century historians (especially Karl Polanyi and Moses Finley) were willing to believe.[1] Such a specialization necessitated the exchange of goods and, hence, gave rise to coinage and the flow of coins. Indeed, the Seleucid Empire moved from predominantly bullion and barter to one in which coins were dominant (see also Chapter 6 by Mooring *et al.*, this volume). More specifically, the core area of what become the Seleucid Empire, i.e. Babylonia, had already achieved a high level of monetization by the sixth century BC, as argued by Jursa (2015: 85–9 and Chapter 5, this volume).[2]

Besides the level of monetization, both regions were also regionally diverse. Whereas the EU is a union of sovereign states, the Seleucid Empire was, in theory, a unified state. Nevertheless, both entities exhibit some common features. Although in Europe sovereign states are at issue, it was a common decision to introduce the Euro in the first place. In addition, the Seleucid Empire was far from a unified empire. Although it was the successor state to the Persian Empire, it was an amalgam of regions with different histories and traditions of autonomy. We see this in the various Greek and Phoenician city–states, but also in ancient regions that were once territorial states, such as Babylonia, Persia, and Judea. So, in both cases, in the Hellenistic Near East and in the European Union we can compare the introduction of new currency over a large geographical area with different political and economic backgrounds. In addition, in the Seleucid Empire there were mints with their own characteristics all over the empire, while in the European Union coins are struck in all participating countries with clear marks of the place of origin. In both cases it is thus possible to study the circulation of the coins, as we will discuss in the following sections.

In view of the differences between the European Union and the Seleucid Empire, we restrict our comparison to two of the above mentioned main indicators of monetization that can be relatively objectively measured, that is, the stock of money and the velocity of money in circulation.

We subdivided the paper into five sections. Given that the EU simply replaced existing currencies with another modern-type currency within an already highly monetized economy, while in the Seleucid case large parts of the economy were still dealing with barter and bullion silver, in the next section we briefly discuss the rise of currency within the less developed economy of the Seleucid Empire. In the third section, we estimate the level of monetization within the EU and the Seleucid realm. We find that, as expected, the level of monetization, and more specifically deep monetization, was about four times higher in the Euro Zone compared to the Seleucid Empire. Yet, this still says little about the actual use of coins, since we still lack information on how fast money changes hands. Unfortunately, we do not have direct observations on this part of the economy. But using some indirect proxy, we nevertheless find in the fourth section that the velocity (in terms of bronze coins) was c. four times slower in the Seleucid Empire than in the EU. The final section concludes with the finding that, using the Fisher equation, the difference in the Seleucid and EU GDP per capita (c. 25 times) is roughly equal, with the difference in deep monetization times the difference in the velocity of money (c. 24 times), thus lending credence to our estimates.

Introduction of silver and bronze coinage in the Middle East

For the European Union, understanding the introduction of the common currency is relatively straightforward. No matter whether we think the main reason is an increasing integration of the capital market, or the increased possibility to conduct a monetary policy, in all cases existing currencies were replaced with another one in a highly monetized economy. This, however, was not the case in the Seleucid Empire. Therefore, to understand the use of coins in the Seleucid Empire, a few words on the introduction of coinage in human history are necessary.

Following the latest analyses in numismatics, the first coins (i.e. the round-shaped objects which are counted and not weighted) were introduced around 640–630 BC, as can be deduced from the lumps of electrum found in a stratum of the Temple of Artemis at Ephesos.[3] The Lydian kings were responsible to the issuing of this coinage, but the phenomenon is generally considered to be of Greek origin, since it was extensively adopted by the Greek states (Howgego 1995: 1–2).

The reasons coinage was introduced are not clear; Le Rider (2001) offers one possible analysis of the phenomenon (for a further discussion, see Mooring *et al.*, Chapter 6, this volume). He proposes an interesting hypothesis to explain the birth of electrum coinage by the Lydian kings: profit made by the kings based on the low percentage of gold in the electrum alliance for the fabrication of these coins (there was over 70% of gold in the natural electrum alliance *contra* 54% in the coins). The electrum coins, possibly because they lost trust by the population, were replaced by gold and silver coins already under the reign of King Croesus: the famous Croeseids (Le Rider 2001: 41–100; 101–122). This coinage was adopted by King Cyrus of Persia after the conquest of the Lydian kingdom in 547. The Greek cities adopted the precious metal coinage, especially silver, around the same period, and its use was extended almost everywhere in the Greek world.[4]

The bronze coinage, the fiduciary coinage *par excellence* in antiquity, was a later phenomenon and appeared as an innovation of the Greek city–states of Magna Graecia and Sicily around the last quarter of the fifth century BC (Price 1979; Psoma 2001). Earlier bronze 'monetary objects' already appeared in the Greek cities of the Black Sea, but they did not have the round metallic shape that characterizes later coins (i.e. dolphins, arrow tips, etc.). From there, this coinage spread to the rest of the Greek world. Both coinages (silver and bronze) were already well established in the Greek world when Alexander conquered the Achaemenid Empire. His successors in the Middle and Near East, the Seleucids, adopted these practices (with variations; Houghton and Lorber 2002, vol. 1.2: 1–4), and they were the first to introduce the bronze coinage in Mesopotamia and the Upper Satrapies. Therefore, the Seleucid Empire is, from a monetary point of view, an optimal case for comparison with the EU, since it was relatively highly monetized, covered an extended area from the shores of the Aegean Sea to modern Afghanistan, and was an open economy, i.e. allowed the use and circulation of all coins based on the Attic-standard (of a drachma or a theoretic weight of 4.3 grams).

The discussion on the reasons coins in gold, silver, and bronze were introduced into the Greek city–states' economy is long and complicated; furthermore, no consensus is reached among numismatists on that point (as mentioned, Le Rider (2001) offers one hypothesis). Leaving the reasons for the introduction of coinage aside (since this is not the purpose of this chapter and is furthermore discussed by Mooring *et al.*, Chapter 6, this volume), it is more interesting to point out the purposes of these coinages. In general, fiscal authorities ordered the minting of coins to make state payments, especially for paying the soldiers,[5] even though various other, more commercial purposes have also been suggested. Bronze coins, on the other hand, had a low economic value and were mostly destined to pay values smaller than those of the lower silver fractions (Le Rider and de Callataÿ 2006: 28; Duyrat 2015; Iossif 2016). These small coinages were almost certainly used as provision money for soldiers, and perhaps also for labourers on the state payroll.

Monetization in the Seleucid Empire and the Euro Zone

As argued above, facing a developing monetary system in the Seleucid Empire and a more advanced system in the Euro Zone, in order to quantify their monetary systems, as a first step we need to calculate the level of monetization. Whereas for the Eurozone these data are relatively easily available, as we will see later, for the Seleucid Empire it is less straightforward. Therefore, recently, Iossif (2015, 2016, 2017a, 2017b, and forthcoming) proposed a new method for approaching the original size of the precious metal issues produced by the Seleucids. He did this by constructing two databases. In the first database, he gathered all available and published hoards containing at least a single Seleucid coin. This dataset, called the 'Seleucid Hoard Database' (SHD), consists of 253 hoards with a total of 12,615 coins (10,230 tetradrachms; 826 drachms and silver fractions; 1,559 bronze coins). These hoards are coming from all regions that once constituted the Seleucid realm, offering thus a relatively satisfactory geographic coverage.[6] Obviously, this database will over represent the more expensive (silver) coins, as they are more likely to be hoarded. For that reason, Iossif (2016 and forthcoming) also composed a database, called the 'Seleucid Excavation Database' (SED). This database records more than 8,300 coins from c. 70 different sites in the Near and Middle East (Iossif forthcoming).

Both datasets can aid us in calculating the level of monetization within the Seleucid Empire. For silver coinage, recently Iossif (2015, 2017a, 2017b, and forthcoming) matched the SHD database (with 1.5% annual coin loss) to the years reported in the studies of Antioch and Ecbatana. This allows the calculation of the ratio between the number of coins found in the hoards and the number of coins minted. Assuming that, within the SHD, the ratio with the other mints holds, this means we can aggregate both Antioch and Ecbatana mints into annual coin production in the Seleucid period (240–235 BC) of 180 talents of silver. Obviously, this number excludes non-Seleucid coins which may have been in circulation. The SHD shows that, in the long-run, one in five silver coins found in the early Seleucid period was minted by the Seleucids, i.e. a total coinage of 5*180=900 silver talents annually.

A similar analysis can also be done for the period 204–75 BC where we arrive at 185 talents per annum. Combined with a ratio of Seleucid to non-Seleucid coins of c. 50%, we arrive at 185*2 = 370 talents minted annually. Assuming a 1.5% coin loss per annum, we can arrive for the early period at around 23,000 talents coins in circulation and for the later period, which excludes large stretches of territory, 13,000.

Obviously, we still have to deal with bronze coins. As mentioned before, in both the SHD and the SED we can find bronze denominations. However, the percentage of bronzes in the SED is c. 99%, obviously much higher than the 16.5% of the SHD. Whereas the SHD may have a strong underestimate of the amount of bronze, since most people will hoard silver, the SED have underestimated the share of silver, since any coins lost will more likely occur to bronze compared to silver. Since many financial instruments have a log-linear distribution, we take the log average of the inverse between both numbers and arrive at a share of bronze in the actual coins in circulation of 98.9%. Applying the same method to the 2nd century BC, we arrive at a share of bronze coins of 98.3%.

We can combine our estimates of silver and bronze in circulation in Table 7.1. As can be seen, the money in circulation was relatively limited. But we can compare it in two ways. First, the Ptolemies minted an annual amount of c. 430 talents for the earlier period. resulting, under the same assumptions of coins loss, in c. 15,000 talents in circulation. Given the different population sizes, this implies that, as is also indicated in the literature, the Seleucid economy was slightly behind in terms of money in circulation. A second way to cross-check is by looking at the number of coins per head of the population. Assuming a population of 30 million in the first century and 5 million, on a much-reduced territory, in the second/first century on average, we arrive at Table 7.2. Since one tetradrachm is c. 17 grams, this implies that per head there was about 20.4 grams of silver available, not much different from the estimate of Xu and Van Leeuwen (Chapter 13, this volume) for seventeenth-century China. The same may, in fact, be observed for bronze coins. Where in seventeenth-century China a stock of c. 400 copper *wen* per capita was available, this amounted to c. 222 *chalkoi* in the second-century BC Seleucid Empire. Considering that one *chalkous* is roughly 0.034 grams of silver (Doyen 2014: 275),[7] while a *wen* is 0.033, this suggests

Table 7.1 Currency in circulation in the Seleucid Empire

In no. coins in talent of silver					
	tetradrachm	*Bronze*	*silver*	*bronze*	*sum*
3th century BC	34,895,066	3,183,415,517	23,000	4,196	27,196
2nd century BC	19,723,298	1,111,412,685	13,000	1,465	14,465

Table 7.2 Coins per capita in the Seleucid Empire

	Tetradrachm	*bronze*
3th century BC	1.2	106.1
2nd century BC	3.9	222.3

that monetization in the Seleucid Empire is perhaps slightly less compared to seventeenth-century China, even though the difference is relatively small.

Another way of assessing the same data is to look at deep monetization as defined by Lucassen (Chapter 4, this volume) as 'a substantial stock of currencies per capita in circulation, consisting of denominations equalling the value of one hour or less of waged work', in which substantial is defined as 'a per capita stock equal to between five and ten times the prevailing hourly wage'. For the Seleucid Empire, the level of deep monetization may be calculated using wages of 3.1 shekels per month for the third, and 2.5 shekels per month for the second century BC (Pirngruber 2016), which means 6.2 and 5 drachmas per month respectively for Babylonia. In the West of the Empire, however, wages were probably higher. A mercenary soldier earned 1 drachma per day, i.e. 30 a month. Yet, soldiers must have earned more than ordinary labourers. Indeed, an agricultural labourer in Egypt earned 2 obols a day (Préaux 1978: 364), i.e. 6 drachmas per month if they worked every day for 20 days (for the 20-days standard, see e.g. Allen 2001; Scheidel 2010).[8] Even though we thus think that a margin of c. 5–6 drachmas a month should be about the average wage, we do not know for sure whether there was no side income. Thus, we might set a maximum of c. 15 drachma per month (about half a soldier's pay, for both the third and second century BC). Again, following Allen (2001) and Scheidel (2010), using c. 20 working days a month, with 8 hours a day, we are able to obtain the hourly wages, which results in monetization levels for the third century of 26 and the second century of 67, i.e. between 26 and 67 times the hourly wage is available in per capita coins with a value less than 1-hour wage).[9] These figures change into 11 for the third and 22 for the second century, when taking the hypothetical maximum of 15 drachma a month.

We should make two reservations here. First, the results also depend on our assumptions regarding the *chalkous*. We converted all bronze coins into a *chalkous* of a standard weight, even though it is shown that there were classes of bronze coins with various weights, with what we call *chalkous* being the most frequent. However, a small percentage of bronze coins were substantially larger than the *chalkous*, and they may, in fact, have exceeded the hourly wage. Second, we may notice a very large increase in deep monetization from the third to the second century. This may have various reasons. Of course, since in the third century bronze coins were first introduced, this increase may be real. However, we should realize that from the third to the second century, the Seleucid Empire also lost large stretches of territory. Hence, deep monetization levels on the second century are also dependent on our assumptions on population size and on the situation that it were mainly the peripheral regions, with presumably lower deep monetization levels, that were lost.

To place this level of deep monetization in perspective, we can make a similar estimate for the Euro area. Within the Euro Zone, in 2002 a total number of notes and coins were introduced that were, at least in theory, required given the size of the economy. In 2002, Euro notes of c. 220 billion in value were issued, followed by an increase to over 1,000 billion in 2015. Likewise, for coins the total value issued was 18 billion euro, increasing to 28 billion euros in 2012. Obviously, these amounts only cover part of the actual money in circulation, as a large share is in digital form. Indeed, M1 (cash plus short-term deposits) amounts to no less than 6,500 billion Euro (c. 2,000 billion in 2002). Hence, c. 50–80% of M1 was in the form of deposits. Given that short-term deposits by definition are below one hour of waged labour, the only thing we need to do is subtract the banknotes with value of more than one hour of wage. According to the ILO report, this boils down on average to c. 20 euro in 2002. Hence, we assume that only banknotes of 50 Euro and higher fall outside of this definition. As pointed out, in 2002 the total amount of money in circulation (M1) in the Euro area was c. 2,000 billion. Subtracting the value of all 50-Euro and higher bills in circulation (c. 150 billion euro), we arrive at a total in circulation of 1,850 billion. With a population of c. 300 million, the level of deep monetization becomes 1,850 billion Euro/300 million/20 euro per hour = c. 300, i.e. c. 4–6 times the level of the Seleucid Empire.

Velocity of money: A speed of diffusion approach

Above estimates of money in circulation (or M1) are only part of the story, as the use of money in a society also depends on how they circulate among persons, i.e. $Mv = GDP$. In a less monetized economy, this becomes $Mv/\delta = GDP$, where M, v, and δ denote the amount and the velocity of money, and the degree of monetization, i.e., the share of transactions that is done with the use of money respectively. Yet, a direct estimation of the velocity of money is difficult, if not impossible. Therefore, we follow the literature (e.g. Hek *et al.* 2002) on the Euro diffusion and calculate the speed of diffusion from region A to region B.

We must stress two things here. First, the speed of diffusion is not a measure of the velocity, but rather should be considered as its proxy. Second, this method is sensitive to the size of the chosen regions. For example, if a geographical unit consists of two regions, one with 99.9% of all coins and the other one with a 0.1% share, obviously a relatively small amount of coins will cross the border of the big region, while a relatively big amount will cross the borders of the small region. For that reason, a few words on the territorial units in this paper are in order.

Within the Seleucid Empire, we distinguish the regions of coin production into Mesopotamia and Media, the Levant and Syria, Bactria, Armenia, Asia Minor, the Upper Satrapies, and, formally outside the Empire, Greece. Especially Mesopotamia and Media, and the Levant and Syria, had a high coin production (and circulation).[10] Since we want our European data to be comparable, we choose to focus on Germany within the Euro Zone, which has a comparable share within the Euro Zone as the most important regions within the Seleucid Empire (for the spread of coins in a small country see Appendix at the end of the book).

Calculating the speed of diffusion of EU coinage to and from Germany is straightforward, since we have direct monthly observations about the share of domestic coins in Germany between January 2002 and the present. Because the data are very detailed, we had to make an additional restriction, which is also common in the literature. First, we do not distinguish among different denominations. This assumption is the same as for the Seleucid Empire. Even though in the Seleucid data we do distinguish between silver and bronze coins, we do not make any further distinction in different types of bronze or silver.

The general trend is as expected (Figure 7.1). The share of domestic coins in Germany (i.e. Euro coins issued by the five German mints bearing the types of the Federal Republic of Germany) started out at 100% when the Euro coins were introduced in circulation but dropped quickly to 92% in January, implying a considerable coin exchange among EMU countries during the first weeks. The diffusion process seems to follow an exponential trend, with the share of domestic coins decreasing by 0.24% per month, (2.8% after the first year, and 25% by the end of the tenth year). Hence, the 2.8 out of 100 coins gives a fair indication of the speed of diffusion. For the latter years, the speed of diffusion estimate is affected by the fact that the chance that a German coin crosses the border decreases with the outflow of German coins. Hence, it is safer to assume that the estimate for the first year, 2.8%, is the best estimate for the annual speed of diffusion.

The question is how to compare this dataset to the Seleucid Empire, since we have only hoard (SHD) and excavation data (SED) with varying minting and burial dates (see Maps 7.1 and 7.2). An obvious way to reconstruct the diffusion process of the coins is to use their ratio as an estimator of the share of domestic coins in circulation. First, we divide the data into classes by the time differential between minting–burial and observe the number of foreign and

Figure 7.1 Share of German coins in Germany.

Source: http://www.eurodiffusie.nl/

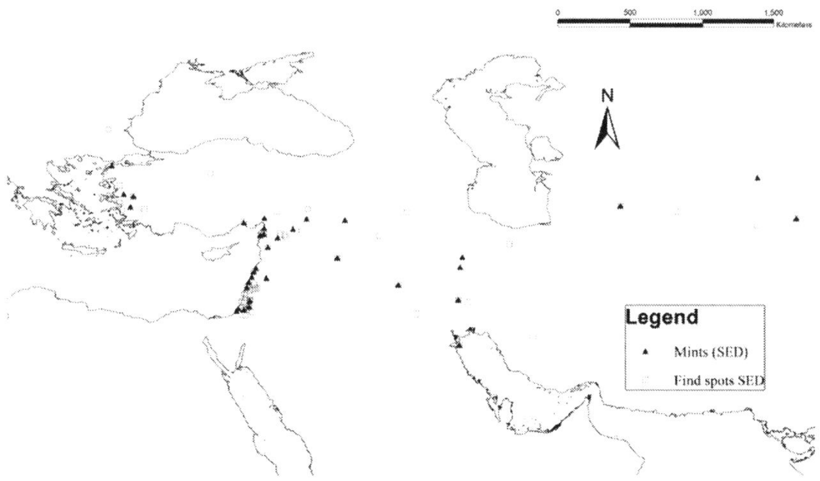

Map 7.1 Places of find and minting (SED).

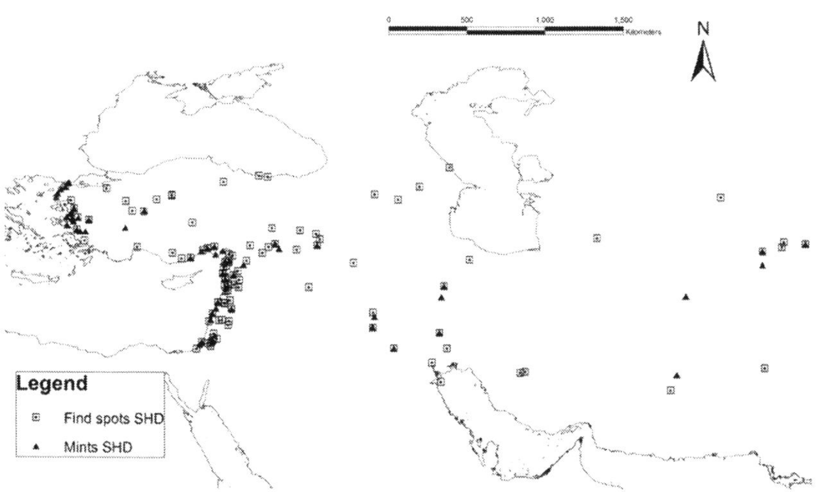

Map 7.2 Places of mint and find (SHD).

domestic coins per class (n_k^f and n_k^d respectively, where k denotes the kth class, *f* and *d* are for foreign and domestic). The share of domestic coins in circulation is hence:

$$g_k^d = \frac{n_k^d}{n_k^d + n_k^f} \tag{3}$$

Equation 3 can be rewritten as:

$$g_k^d = \frac{1}{1 + \frac{n_k^f}{n_k^d}} \tag{4}$$

That is, we can use the observed ratio of 'foreign' to 'domestic' coins as an estimator of the coin diffusion.

To estimate diffusion for silver coins, we can use the SHD database as described in the previous section. However, as already indicated, this dataset consists of coins buried together on purpose (and lost for different reasons), which may not be indicative of bronze coinage. Therefore, Iossif (2016 and forthcoming) has created the SED database in which stray, often unrelated finds are reported coming either from organized excavations (with archaeological context considered) or from excavations and stray finds combined (where, in most of the cases, it is impossible to reconstitute the original context of the finds).[11] Therefore, we are left with two samples: on bronze coins from the SED and for silver from the SHD dataset. The results are reported in Table 7.3. As one can see in Column 3, we have in total 2,131 observations where information on both the region of minting and burial are available. Of these 2,131, 845 cases are for bronze coins in excavations, and the remaining 1,286 cases are available for silver coins (i.e. drachms and tetradrachms alike, but with a strong predominance of the latter, higher denomination)[12] in hoards.[13]

Tables 7.4–7.5 contain our estimates for the share of domestic coins for the two types of coins (bronze excavations and silver in hoards) (see Equation 2). The patterns are visualized in Figures 7.2 and 7.3. In both cases, we find a strong indication that the time difference between minting and burial (Column 1) is underestimated, since none of the estimates start out near 100% share for domestic coins, which is the expected value. For this reason, it is better to treat Figures 7.2–7.3 as if they were shifted to the left, and even the first class reflects the state of coin diffusion with a delay of a few years.

In case of bronze excavation data (Table 7.4, Figure 7.2) the overall pattern indicates a gradual but limited diffusion process. The results for the silver hoard coins (Table 7.5, Figure 7.3) suggest a quicker diffusion in the first years followed by a gradual and slower reduction afterwards, converging to between 20% and 30%. This is much lower than we found for bronze coins, which end up with c. 50% share of domestic coins.

Table 7.3 Summary statistics: Number of coins in the Seleucid Empire

Coin	*Number of coins in database*	*Cases*	*Total used in our sample*	*Mean (per case)*	*St. dev.*	*Min*	*Max*
Bronze (SED)	8,273	845	7,778	9.2	73.1	1	1936
Silver (SHD)	11,056	1,286	7,174	5.58	34.2	1	1160

Table 7.4 Distribution of bronze coins by time difference between burial and minting (SED)

Time difference (year)	*Mean time difference (year)*	*No. domestic cases*	*No. foreign cases*	*Share domestic cases (%)*	*No. domestic coins*	*No. foreign coins*	*Est. share of domestic coins*
0	0	72	30	70.6%	240	61	79.7%
1–10	6.8	15	4	78.9%	49	12	80.3%
11–20	15.9	35	29	54.7%	734	129	85.1%
21–30	25	29	22	56.9%	103	228	31.1%
31–40	34.6	36	24	60.0%	113	139	44.8%
41–50	46.8	39	31	55.7%	2223	227	90.7%
51–60	56.1	39	10	79.6%	479	31	93.9%
61–70	64.9	21	11	65.6%	68	78	46.6%
71–	124.9	162	234	40.9%	1502	1362	52.4%

Table 7.5 Distribution of silver coins (tetradrachms) by time difference between burial and minting (SHD)

Time difference (year)	*Mean time difference (year)*	*No. domestic cases*	*No. foreign cases*	*Share domestic cases (%)*	*No. domestic coins*	*No. foreign coins*	*Est. share of domestic coins*
0	0	6	11	35.3%	54	28	65.9%
1–10	5	171	190	47.4%	2833	871	76.5%
11–20	15.3	86	196	30.5%	443	916	32.6%
21–30	26	59	100	37.1%	312	317	49.6%
31–40	33.1	28	93	23.1%	150	404	27.1%
41–50	44.9	52	88	37.1%	96	289	24.9%
51–60	54.5	7	33	17.5%	9	67	11.8%
61–70	65	5	65	7.1%	7	140	4.8%
71–	104.6	18	78	18.8%	36	202	15.1%

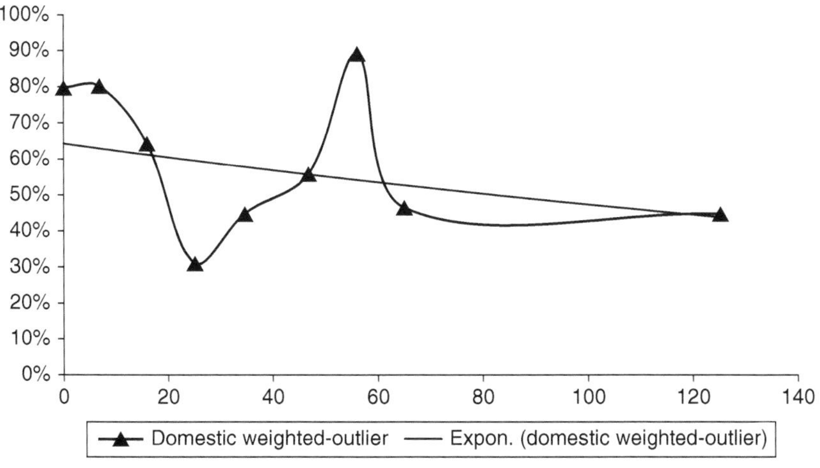

Figure 7.2 Estimated share of domestic bronze coins in circulation (%) as function of time difference between minting and burial (SED).

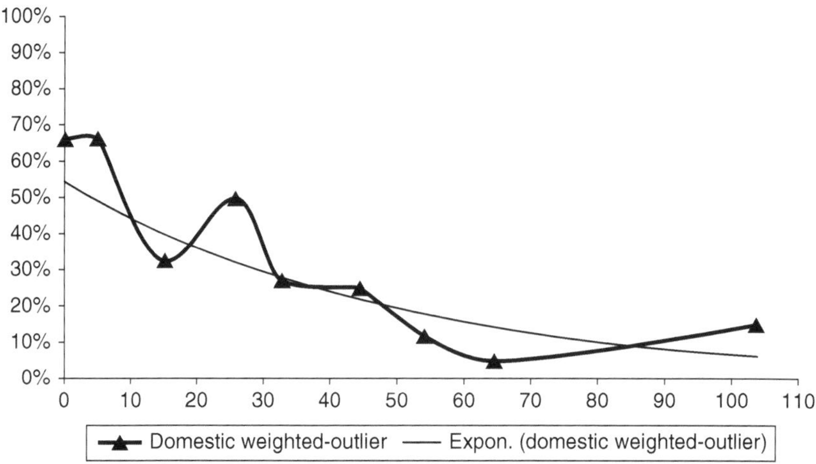

Figure 7.3 Estimated share of domestic tetradrachms in circulation (%) as function of time difference between minting and burial (SHD).

But how fast was the diffusion in the two periods and regions? We can make a rough estimate by plotting the exponential function in a similar way as we did for the EU, suggesting that silver tetradrachms circulated by 2% per annum versus c. 0.5% per annum for bronze coins. We can calculate that after ten years, the share of domestic bronze coins would reduce by only 6% while the share of domestic silver coins declined by 22%. This result is about equal to the spread of coin diffusion in Germany, which was, after one year, 2.8% with a decline of 25% after ten years.

Hence, silver coins within the Seleucid Empire diffused at about the same speed as Euro coins, while copper travelled much slower. However, the use of the two coins was very different. For silver, there are several reasons for a quicker diffusion of these more valuable coins. The first way is by official payments, which is even today the standard way to release a new series of coins into the circulation: the government paid the wages of soldiers and officials, or other labourers working on state projects with the new coins. In the same way Crawford explained the purpose of Roman coinage, in his traditional view: 'it [coinage] was used to pay the state's debts to its servants and to collect taxes' (Crawford 1970: 40–8). Such payments obviously were not limited to the same region where the coins were minted.[14] Another way is trade, when coins left the region with negative trade balance toward regions with positive trade balance (this was mostly the way Le Rider explained long-distance money transfers in his rich bibliography, and this is what Bresson does too).[15] Carrying bronze coins must have been cumbersome; hence, silver coins were most likely the preferred coins for long-distance money transfers. Within the EU, however, the Euro functions more in everyday fringe payments. We may calculate that the bronze *chalkous* in value may be roughly identical to 1 Euro.

Hence, when we compare bronze coin circulation with the diffusion of the Euro it turns out to be four to five times slower.

Conclusion

Motivated by the introduction of the Euro in the common market in 2002, in this paper we have tried to place it in perspective by comparing it with the levels of monetization and the velocity of money in circulation of the Seleucid Empire c. 2,000 years earlier. Based on this analysis, we find that basic principles of economic development, even with large differences in welfare and complexity, applied equally to both the Euro Zone today and the Seleucid Empire 2,000 years ago. Indeed, we find that in terms of the stock of money in circulation per capita, the Seleucid Empire was at a level slightly below seventeenth-century China, but, when expressed in deep monetization, about four to six times lower than present day EU.

Of course, this is only part of the story, since the velocity of money can also affect monetization of the economy. Therefore, as a proxy, we calculated the speed of coin diffusion both within the EU in the first two decades of the twenty-first century and within the Seleucid Empire during the fourth through first centuries BC. Despite the two-and-a-half-millennia time difference, we find that the speed of coin diffusion was comparable between silver Seleucid coins and Euro coins, i.e. c. 2% per annum and 25% over ten years. Only Seleucid bronze coins have a very slow rate of diffusion (c. 6% in ten years) due to their nature and limited role in Seleucid economy. One has to be aware, though, that in value, bronze coins were of about the same value as Euro coins today, i.e. the velocity of money proxied by the speed of diffusion was four to six times lower within the Seleucid Empire.[16]

Combining this evidence with the earlier mentioned equation $Mv/\delta = GDP$, we only require evidence on GDP to complete the equation. For Mesopotamia, Foldvari and Van Leeuwen (2012) calculated GDP per capita of 618 GK dollars. Yet, since Mesopotamia is richer than the Seleucid Empire, we assume for the whole of the Empire GDP per capita is 10% lower, i.e. 556 GK dollars. For the Euro Zone, we take a GDP per capita of c. 15,000 GK dollars in 2002 (Bolt and Van Zanden 2014), i.e. the Euro Zone is c. 20 times richer. Adding that into the equation, we arrive at $6 * 6/\delta = 25$, i.e. the increase in the share of monetization, δ, is c. 1.5. Given that monetization in the EU is close (but not equal) to 100% – say, 90% – monetization in the late Seleucid Empire is estimated to have been 90%/1.5 = 60%.

Notes

1 Obviously, coins were only partially the means of payment within the Seleucid Empire (e.g. de Callataÿ 2006). For an alternative point of view, see Aperghis (2004), who argues for a highly (contested) monetized Seleucid economy, let alone within the EU where digital money took over the vast share of money transfers. Also, the role played by coins then and now is different; nevertheless, they are good markers of the movement of goods and individuals, even today.

2 See Iossif (2015) for a relatively low estimation of monetization (in gold and silver) for the Seleucid and Ptolemaic economies.
3 Price (1983) and Le Rider (2001), having access to earlier archaeological data, dated the coins to 560 BC; Michael Kerschner and Koray Konuk (forthcoming), based on the study of the ceramic material, dated the stratum to 640–630 BC, placing the introduction of the coinage in the second half of the seventh century BC.
4 The ratio gold:silver varied from 1:15 to 1:10, as it was fixed around the time of Philip II; see Le Rider (1996: 71; 2001: 159–60); Le Rider and de Callataÿ (2006: 25).
5 De Callataÿ (1997) shows the relationship between issues and effort of war during the Mithridatic wars; see also Le Rider and de Callataÿ (2006: 174); Iossif (2015; 2017a; 2017b).
6 Some biases are to be observed with some regions (e.g. Syria and the Levant) being overrepresented due to more intense excavations activities and better recording of the data.
7 Doyen (2014: 275): 'Dès lors, le chalque se définit désormais comme le 1/128e de la drachme en argent plutôt que comme une fraction de l'obole'; therefore, 4.3 grams divided by 128 gives 0.034 grams. The *chalkous* was thus not a fraction of the obol.
8 In Classical Athens, workers earned 1 drachma per day. Yet, this must have been substantially higher than in the Seleucid Empire on average.
9 There is consensus that the *chalkous* represented the smallest (and earliest) bronze denomination. On that question, an essential one for any study converting bronze coins into silver values, cf. now Psoma (2012) (based on conclusions in Gatzolis 2010).
10 For possible biases due to a better archaeological investigation of these areas, cf. Iossif (2015).
11 For excavation coins versus hoard coins as better indicators of economic life and circulation patterns, cf. Butcher (2004: 149–51).
12 cf. Iossif (forthcoming).
13 The Seleucid data, however, have two main problems. First, the distribution of coins is by no means representative of the composition of the money stock. In case of hoarding, high-value coins are preferred, as they are easier to carry and hide, and because silver represented a higher monetary value as compared to the largely fiduciary bronze denominations. This may also explain the relatively low number of silver coins found in the excavations database. Furthermore, bronze coinages were mostly confined to an area around the mint of production (e.g. Meadows 2014). Yet, even though it is thus difficult to compare silver and bronze coinage, we can make the less restrictive assumption that the number and geographical distribution of either silver or bronze coins in our sample is representative of the population distribution. We can identify whether a coin was buried in the same province where it was minted (labelled as 'domestic' coin) or if it arrived from a different province (called 'foreign' coin). Second, the observed number of coins in the Seleucid data have extreme ranges due to two dominant observations (1,936 and 1,160 coins in a single find, respectively), which results in high standard deviations in Table 7.2. This can be solved by either taking the unweighted average of all hoards (i.e., meaning that large finds have a similar weight as small finds), or weighted (i.e., the big finds have a much higher weight). Since both methods have their advantages and disadvantages, we will provide both methods in the analyses below.
14 For coinage used as payment for the army, there is a very rich bibliography; cf. for the Hellenistic world, esp. de Callataÿ (1997, 2000); Psoma (2009) for bronze as means of payments; for the Roman army, see, among others: Casey (1986: 82); Reece (1987: 125–26); Duncan-Jones (1990: 30–47); Butcher (2004: 143, 245–51).
15 Bresson (2016: *passim*) and Bresson (forthcoming). We would like to thank Alain Bresson for sending us the manuscript of his paper before publication.
16 Of course, the speed of diffusion also varied among different denominations of Euro coins.

References

Allen, R. (2001). 'The great divergence in European wages and prices from the Middle Ages to the First World War', *Explorations in Economic History*, 38: 411–47.

Aperghis, G.G. (2004). *The Seleukid Royal Economy: The Finances and Financial TAdministration of the Seleukid Empire.* Cambridge, UK: Cambridge University Press.

Bolt, J. and Van Zanden, J.L. (2014). 'The Maddison Project: Collaborative research on historical national accounts', *The Economic History Review*, 67: 627–51.

Bresson, A. (2016). *The Making of the Ancient Economy: Institutions, Markets, and Growth in the City–States.* Princeton, NJ: Princeton University Press.

Bresson, A. (forthcoming). 'Coins and trade in Hellenistic Asia Minor: he Pamphylian hub', in Woytek, B. (ed.), *Infrastructure and Distribution in Ancient Economies*, Vienna: Österreichische Akademie der Wissenschaften.

Butcher, K. (2004). *Coinage in Roman Syria.* London: Royal Numismatic Society.

Callataÿ, F. de (1997). *L'histoire des guerres mithridatiques vue par les monnaies.* Louvain-la-Neuve, Belgium: Département d'archéologie et d'histoire de l'art, séminaire de numismatique Marcel Hoc.

Callataÿ, F. de (2000). 'Guerre et monnayage à l'époque hellénistique. Essai de mise en perspective suivi d'une annexe sur le monnayage de Mithridate VI Eupator', in Andreau, J., Briant, P., and Descat, R. (eds.), *Économie antique. La guerre dans les économies antiques*, Saint-Bertrand-de-Comminges, France: Musée archéologique départemental: 337–64.

Callataÿ, F. de (2006). 'Réflexions quantitatives sur l'or et l'argent non monnayés à l'époque hellénistique (pompes, triomphes, réquisitions, fortunes des temples, orfèvrerie et masses métalliques disponibles', in Descat, R. (ed.), *Approches de l'économie hellénistique*, Saint-Bertrand-de-Comminges, France: Musée archéologique de Saint-Bertrand-de-Comminges; Paris: De Boccard: 37–84.

Casey, J. (1986). *Understanding Ancient Coins. An Introduction for Archaeologists and Historians.* London: B.T. Batsfort.

Crawford, M. (1970). 'Money and exchange in the Roman World', *Journal of Roman Studies*, 60: 40–8.

Doyen, C. (2014). 'Le système monétaire et pondéral d'Antiochos IV', in Feyel, C. and Graslin-Thomé, L. (eds.), *Le projet politique d'Antiochos IV*, Nancy: A.D.R.A.: 261–99.

Duncan-Jones, R.P. (1990). *Structure and Scale in the Roman Economy.* Cambridge, UK: Cambridge University Press.

Duyrat, F. (2015). 'The circulation of coins in Syria and Mesopotamia in the sixth to first centuries', in: Van der Spek, *et al.* (2015): 363–95.

Földvári, P. and Van Leeuwen, B. (2012). 'Comparing per capita income in the Hellenistic world: The case of Mesopotamia,' *Review of Income and Wealth*, 58(3): 550–68.

Gatzolis, C. (2010). *Η κυκλοφορία του χάλκινου νομίσματος στη Μακεδονία, 5ος-1ος αι. π.Χ.*. Unpublished PhD thesis, University of Thessaloniki.

Hek, G. M., Nuyens, M., Van der Ploeg, H., Planque, B., and Vermeulen, E. (2002). 'Het grote internationale eurodiffusie-experiment', *Natuur & Techniek*, 11: 56–62.

Houghton, A. and Lorber, C. (2002). *Seleucid Coins. A Comprehensive Catalogue.* I. *Seleucus I through Antiochus III.* New York: American Numismatic Society.

Howgego, C. (1995). *Ancient History from Coins.* London: Routledge.

Iossif, P.P. (2015). 'Who's wealthier? An estimation of the annual production of the Seleucids and the Ptolemies', *Revue belge de Numismatique*, 161: 233–72.

Iossif, P.P. (2016). 'Using site finds for statistical analyses of the Seleucid numismatic production and circulation. An introduction to the method', in Duyrat, F. and

Grandjean, C. (eds.), *Les monnaies de fouille du monde grec (VIe –Ier s. a.C.). Apports, approches et méthodes*, Bordeaux, France: Ausonius Éditions: 263–96.

Iossif, P.P. (2017a). 'Antiochos' III precious metal numismatic production seen through hoard data. A quantitative perspective', in Graslin, L. and Feyel, C. (eds.), *Antiochos III et l'Orient*, Nancy: A.D.R.A.: 37–76.

Iossif, P.P. (2017b). 'The numismatic production of Antiochos IV: Tool of diplomacy or legitimacy? A quantifying approach of hoard evidence', *Electrum*, 24: 61–94.

Iossif, P.P. (forthcoming), *Analyse quantitative et statistique des données numismatiques séleucides. Approche économique, religieuse et iconographique*, Liège, Belgium.

Jursa, M. (2015), 'Market performance and market integration in Babylonia in the 'long sixth century BC', in Van der Spek, R.J. *et al.* (eds.) (2015): 83–106.

Kerschner, M. and Konuk, K. (forthcoming). 'Electrum coins and their archaeological context: The case of the Artemision at Ephesus', in Gitler, H. (ed.), *White Gold Symposium, June 2012*. Jerusalem.

Le Rider, G. (1996). *Monnayage et finances de Philippe II. Un état de la question*. Paris: De Boccard.

Le Rider, G. (2001). *La naissance de la monnaie. Pratiques monétaires de l'Orient ancient*. Paris: Presses Universitiares de France.

Le Rider, G. and De Callataÿ, F. (2006). *Les Séleucides et les Ptolémées. L'héritage monétaire et financier d'Alexandre le Grand, Collection Champollion*. Paris: Éditions du Rocher.

Meadows, A. (2014). 'The spread of coins in the Hellenistic world', in Bernholz, P. and Vaubel, R. (eds.), *Explaining Monetary and Financial Innovation. A Historical Analysis*, Cham, Switzerland: Springer: 169–194.

Pirngruber, R. (2016), 'The value of silver: Wages as guides to the standard of living in 1st millennium BC Babylonia', in Kleber, K. and Pirngruber, R. (eds.), *Silver, Money and Credit. A Tribute to Robartus J. van der Spek on the Occasion of His 65th Birthday on 18th September 2014*, Leiden, the Netherlands: Nederlands Instituut voor het Nabije Oosten: 107–18.

Préaux, C. (1978). *Le monde hellénistique. La Grèce et l'Orient (323–146 av. J.-C.)*. 2 volumes. Paris: Presses Universitaires de France.

Price, M.J. (1979). 'The function of Greek bronze coinage', *Atti del Istituto Italiano de Numismatica*, 25: 351–58.

Price, M.J. (1983). 'Thoughts on the beginnings of coinage', in Brooke, C.N.L., Stewart, B.H.I., Pollard, J. G., and Volk, T.R. (eds.), *Studies in Numismatic Method presented to Philip Grierson*, Cambridge, UK: Cambridge University Press: 1–10.

Psoma, S. (2001). *Olynthe et les Chalciidiens de Thrace*. Stuttgart, Germany: Steiner Verlag.

Psoma, S. (2009). '*Τάς σιταρχίας και τους μισθούς* ([Arist.], *Oec.* 1351b). Bronze currencies and cash allowances in mainland Greece, Thrace and the Kingdom of Macedonia', *Revue belge de Numismatique*, 155: 3–38.

Psoma, S. (2012), 'Obols, drachms, and staters of bronze during the Hellenistic Period', *American Journal of Numismatics*, 24: 11–19.

Reece, R. (1987). *The Coinage of Roman Britain*. London: Seaby.

Scheidel, W. (2010). 'Real wages in early economies: Evidence for living standards from 1800 BCE to 1300 CE', *Journal of the Economic and Social History of the Orient*, 53: 425–62.

Van der Spek, R.J., Van Leeuwen, B. and Van Zanden, J.L. (eds.) (2015). *A History of Market Performance. From Ancient Babylonia to the Modern World*. London and New York: Routledge.

8 Monetary policy in the Roman Empire

Kevin Butcher

Introduction

In writing about Roman money, one faces many fundamental problems. First, a monetary history of the Roman empire cannot yet be written. This might seem an extravagant generalization given that there are many accounts of the development of Roman coinage, but careful study of these accounts often reveals the uncertainties that underlie their apparent confidence, particularly on basic matters of production, distribution and use.[1] Roman numismatists are no different from other scholars in wishing that they could be more certain of their material. Unfortunately, the scarcity and ambiguity of hard evidence for Roman monetary history has sometimes led to a habit of treating as fact what is in reality quite insecure.

This is in part a consequence of the way in which scholarship on the subject has developed. At the risk of caricature, I will attempt to outline the key features of relevance here. At its heart is the matter of whether the Romans mismanaged their currency to the extent that it caused an economic crisis, and whether they had any monetary policy beyond debasing their silver coinage to overcome fiscal difficulties.[2] That such fundamentals can still be debated shows how far we are from a proper understanding of the material.

Renaissance and Enlightenment scholars who studied Roman coinage were not much interested in its evolution, or in any evidence of monetary instability.[3] Instead, they sought to define what they viewed as a relatively static system, which some held up as an ideal. Their identification of many of the denominations that made up the Roman currency was a major achievement of the sixteenth and seventeenth centuries. Working from obscure metrological texts and asides in classical sources, they managed to identify the *aureus*, *denarius* and *sestertius*, the three main denominations that had formed the core of the imperial monetary system until the third century AD. While it was recognized that the silver *denarius* had become debased in the third century, few felt it necessary to elaborate on the reasons for this. It seems to have been assumed that the causes were the same as many debasements in their own time: that Roman rulers had needed to cover the costs of their wars. The study of

Roman coinage as money, however, remained very much subsidiary to its study as a source for history and art.

A key figure in the history of scholarship on Roman monetary history is Theodor Mommsen (1817–1903). Mommsen was attuned to the possibility that the changes he could observe in the coinage could have been the consequence of monetary or fiscal problems, and his interpretations still deserve study to this day. Though most of his monumental *Münzwesen* (1860) concentrates on the coinage of the Roman Republic, he also provided a comprehensive account of the development of imperial coinage, backed up by data in the form of both ancient texts and archaeological finds.[4] He also argued from comparative historical cases in more recent times. His account was the first serious attempt to create monetary history from Roman coins. It charted the gradual decline of the Republican and early imperial monetary system and the 'crisis' of the third century, which in turn led to the monetary systems of late antiquity. These late antique systems were much less well-understood than the earlier one, and to this day most of the denominations from the late third century onwards remain obscure in both name and their relationship to one another.

One mystery that Mommsen attempted to solve concerned the face value of a silver coin that was introduced by the emperor Caracalla in AD 215. This coin was important, because it became the main denomination to be issued for most of the third century. Previous scholars had viewed the coin as just another sort of *denarius*, heavier than the normal one. Some had suggested that because it weighed 1.5 times the weight of the normal *denarius*, this 'heavy *denarius*' had been worth 1.5 times more than the normal one. Mommsen dubbed the coin the '*antoninianus*' and proposed that it had been created by Caracalla to serve as a double *denarius*. Effectively, its introduction represented a debasement. Observing that his *antoninianus* became increasingly debased during the third century until it was little more than a copper coin, and noting that these heavily debased coins appeared in large numbers in hoards, Mommsen proposed that the new denomination had been responsible for high inflation that resulted in the 'collapse' of the old monetary system. He drew a parallel with modern paper currency, and in the French translation of the *Münzwesen* (1873) the parallel was made even more explicit: the *antoniniani* were like the French *assignats* that had caused extraordinary hyperinflation at the end of the eighteenth century.[5] The reader could scarcely doubt that the *antoninianus* was a hyperinflationary coin. As such, it occupied the liminal space between the monetary system of the Republic and early empire on the one hand and that of late antiquity on the other.

Though it provided an explanation for the apparent collapse of the early imperial monetary system, many students of Roman coinage in the nineteenth and early twentieth centuries remained unconvinced that the *antoninianus* was an overvalued double *denarius*.[6] Only Mommsen's name for the coin was preserved, though he was rarely acknowledged as the original authority. During the 1920s, however, the notion of the double *denarius* gained influential converts, none more so than Harold Mattingly, one of the authors of the standard catalogues of Roman coins, *The Roman Imperial Coinage* and *A Catalogue of the Roman Coins in the British Museum*. His accounts of the ensuing hyperinflation were clearly coloured by the European hyperinflations of the 1920s, and those events may have been decisive in helping him to change his opinion – previously he had espoused the idea that the *antoninianus* was a 1.5 *denarius* coin.[7] Modern hyperinflation, particularly that experienced in the Weimar Republic in 1923, was seen by many scholars working in the 1930s and 1940s as the model for what had happened in the third century.[8] By introducing the *antoninianus*, the Romans had destroyed their admirable currency in gold, silver, brass and copper.

The period from the 1950s to the 1980s saw the consolidation of what might be termed the 'substantivist' or 'primitivist' view of Roman coinage, which dominated thoughts about Roman currency up to the beginning of the present century.[9] While the *antoninianus* had already gained widespread scholarly acceptance as an inflationary double *denarius* and a leading cause of an economic crisis in the third century, it was noted that debasement of the silver coinage had occurred much earlier, beginning in the reign of Nero (r. AD 54–68). If such earlier debasements were not monetary adjustments (now deemed too subtle for the ancient mind to conceive), what had caused them? It was argued that the Romans had no notion that an increase in the money supply or a debasement of the coinage might cause inflation. Indeed, anything that seemed like an economic or monetary explanation for changes to the coinage was dismissed as incredible.[10] Some allowances were made for Rome's first emperor, Augustus, who was considered to be the architect of the imperial coinage and was credited with some financial acumen. But proof that Rome was otherwise ruled by the 'economically illiterate' seemed to come in the person of the emperor Diocletian (r. AD 284–305), who had tried to regulate prices to prevent inflation.[11] The manifest truth of market forces was considered beyond the reasoning of such characters, and any policy that granted emperors or their administration the slightest economic wisdom was deemed false.

Instead, all change in Roman coinage tended to be treated as the result of fiscal difficulties. Monetary explanations, such as an increase in the supply of coinage in one metal affecting its value relative to coins in other metals, were normally dismissed, although the possibility of such monetary adjustments was admitted for the Republican period (in times sufficiently remote from the age of imperial decadence). The financial difficulties of the empire, however, were of a different order: change, and particularly change to the silver coinage, was regarded solely as a consequence of fiscal shortcomings. If one follows this reasoning, the *antoninianus had* to be a double *denarius* rather than a 1.5 *denarius* piece, because its introduction had to represent an attempt to save money.[12] Otherwise the denomination would not have existed.

In this model, the price of metals had no influence on the quality of the coinage. It was argued that metal prices did not change significantly (though there was little to support this assertion). The only real pressures on the coinage of the Roman state were fiscal: the tax system was inefficient and there was resistance to increased taxation, so the only alternative was to debauch the currency to cover increasing shortfalls as the costs of maintaining an empire mounted (there was, and still is, no clear evidence for state borrowing).[13] All money was coined money, and therefore the supply of currency was restricted by the supply of metals used to make it.[14] The only way to stretch the supply of money was to stretch the existing metal across an increased number of coins – hence the debasements. Evidence for occasional improvements in fineness (such as that under Domitian; see the 'Nero to Trajan' section of this chapter) made no sense and were dismissed as impractical, doomed experiments.

Most importantly, it was argued that Roman coinage was not really money as we understand it. The state made coins only in order to cover its debts, usually in the form of salaries to its employees (notably the military). It had no interest in coinage as a medium of exchange (despite the fact that ancient sources explicitly said that coinage was designed for that purpose); instead, exchange emerged naturally and incidentally when the population found it useful for the purpose.[15] Coinage was merely a means of payment for the state. However, it was questionable whether this sort of credit relationship between the state and its employees could really be considered a full monetary one,[16] and proponents of the model needed to find a way of ensuring that the state payments could be transferable to a third party. Taxation provided a solution. The state could kickstart the system of exchange by insisting on precious metal coins as taxes, requiring the population to acquire coins at the very least for this purpose. Base metal coin could be exchanged for tax coins, which helped explain the existence of an array of low-value denominations (their existence being one of the chief objections to the model of coins as state payment).[17]

The model was thus relatively coherent and overcame a big problem in the study of Roman money: how did the state distribute its coinage without a banking system? The answer was that it gave the coinage to those to whom it owed money, and no one else. Taxation would enable a certain degree of coin circulation; otherwise, circulation was incidental. Thus, there had to be an intimate link between state finances and the production of coinage, and even low-value bronzes produced in limited quantities by small Mediterranean cities were regarded as evidence of the state's financial requirements. The distribution of coinage was also a political rather than an economic activity. Coins went to pay soldiers and state employees, and to finance wars and other state projects. Free minting was absolutely out of the question, and all coinage was produced on government account.[18] This meant that the state's ability to access metals influenced the coinage and its ability to finance its expenditure. It was argued that Rome relied heavily on gold and silver mined in Spain, and when this supply was interrupted and went into decline in the later second century AD, the Roman monetary system and state finances ran into trouble.[19]

Roman conceptions of money and coinage

The purpose of this rather long description of scholarly perspectives is to explain why the account of Roman coinage has assumed the shape that it has today: a rather moralizing tale of financial incompetence and monetary mismanagement leading to currency collapse and economic crisis. While Renaissance and Enlightenment scholars might have seen in Roman coinage something worthy of emulation, the prevailing modern narrative would appear to treat the Romans as less than a model of financial probity. There also seems to be a contrast between the comparative stability of coinage under the Republic and Augustus and its instability under the empire.

However, in recent years there has been something of a move away from the substantivist model, at least for the period up to AD 200. This is no doubt partly due to the waning influence of substantivism on other aspects of the study of the economy in antiquity. The substantivist image of a Roman Mediterranean dominated by cellular, self-sufficient micro-economies simply does not tally with the growing body of evidence for long-distance movement of commodities and large-scale specialist production geared specifically for export, or with the evidence for a degree of economic growth in the Roman empire. In tandem with this, our understanding of Roman money has also experienced something of a mutation. It has been pointed out that the modern insistence that coinage was produced solely to enable state payments contradicts just about every statement from antiquity about its function, which was to enable exchange.[20] The importance of credit money has been recognized, and some allowances for reforms as monetary adjustments have also been considered.[21] Yet it remains challenging to make a case that the Romans were thinking seriously about monetary issues.

The few statements we have from the Roman perspective suggests that their understanding of money was far from 'primitive'. A judicial view of coinage is provided by the jurist Paulus in Justinian's *Digest*.[22] Like most of the few statements about Roman coinage that survive from antiquity, it has received extensive study. It presumably supplies the state's view of its own coinage, and it is interesting to us because it claims that coinage was a *pretium* (a price) and not a *merx* (a commodity). The feature that enabled this transformation of commodity metal was the fact that a coin was *forma publica percussa* ('struck with the state's design'). This seems to suggest that the state recognized that the value of coinage was symbolic and not based on 'intrinsic' value. A statement by the jurist Gaius makes it clear that coinage was valued by tale and not by weight.[23] Such statements would appear to throw into question the focus of many studies on presumed relationship between the fineness and weight of the coinage, and in particular the silver coinage.[24] Proponents of the notion of a coinage of 'intrinsic' value have sometimes suggested that the third century was the period in which the Romans moved from an intrinsic to a fully fiduciary currency, but this seems an unnecessary qualification. Coins were always intended to be more valuable than bullion, even in periods when they were made of carefully refined, unalloyed bullion.[25]

However, it is important not to lose sight of what the archaeological evidence tells us. Hoards of the period show us that people valued gold and silver coinage as a store of wealth and were prepared to withdraw it from circulation to act as savings. Presumably they favoured these metals because it was believed that their high commodity value would help sustain their face value over longer periods; or, if they failed to maintain their face value, the commodity would ensure they did not become worthless. The rarity of gold and silver coins as single finds on archaeological sites contrasts with the ubiquity of base metal coin in the single finds record. Base metal would appear to have been valued for use in small-scale transactions but not for savings, since it is less commonly encountered in hoards. The hoards also show us that people were aware of differences in fineness and weight, and were capable of preferentially selecting heavier or finer coins when assembling hoards.[26] Thus, the quality of coin mattered, and public opinion about it could have an impact, potentially constraining the state's ability or willingness to implement drastic changes. The state's awareness of public interest in coin quality may explain a number of the strategies that we observe.

Inflation

Another problem for the claim that there was a direct relationship between debasement and inflation comes from the evidence for prices. Price data for the Roman empire are very poor, and the only region for which we have any sets (if 'set' is not too grand a word to describe random survivals) is Egypt.[27] The problem with this evidence is that Egypt had its own coinage and seems to have operated a closed currency system. The changes to Egyptian coinage do not always coincide with changes to imperial coinage, so any effect that these changes had on Egyptian prices may not apply to the whole empire. There appears to have been a doubling of prices in Egypt during the 160s to 190s, which coincides with a halving of the silver content of the Egyptian tetradrachm in the 160s; but which was cause and which was effect?[28] There was another inflationary episode about a century later, in the 270s, when prices rose by about ten times. Finally, we have a set of price ceilings from outside Egypt in the form of Diocletian's Edict on Maximum Prices of AD 301, which indicate further price rises, though it is not certain whether this period of inflation had been prolonged or whether it was recent; as Rathbone has pointed out, the tone of the preamble to the Edict would seem to suggest the latter.[29] At any rate, it would be hard to find in the evidence anything that would qualify as sustained 'hyperinflation' – a monthly rate of 50% or above, equivalent to an annual rate of 600% or above – continuing through the third century, despite frequent use of this term to describe the third-century price rises.[30] Compared to modern times, the Roman empire would appear to have experienced very low inflation, at least until the later third century AD. Is there any evidence to indicate that this low inflation was related to the fact that Rome had a currency made of gold and silver up to about AD 260, and that the period(s) of inflation were provoked by the advent of a largely fiat money?

The character of the coinage

Before proceeding with an account of the main changes to Roman coinage in the first three centuries AD, it is necessary to outline the form of the coinage, which is more complicated than suggested by the term 'Roman coinage'. The main mint for most of the period was at Rome. Exactly how this mint operated, and how it was controlled, is unclear. Ultimate authority no doubt rested with the emperor. His financial secretary must have been charged with general decisions about production.[31] The senate continued to provide three junior members as overseers of gold, silver and base metal coinage, as it had done under the Republic, but it is unclear what role they had. The coinage itself reveals little. Gold and silver bear no marks of authority apart from the portraits, names and titles of the emperor or members of his family. Usually the names and titles are in the nominative case, giving no clear indication of ownership. However, under Trajan (r. AD 98–117) they are in the dative, with the formula 'The Senate and the People of Rome, to the Best Prince'.[32] Whether this sort of dedicatory formula is relevant to the question of minting is uncertain. A group of epigraphic dedications on stone by mint personnel under Trajan shows them to have been imperial freedmen and slaves, suggesting that the mint was firmly under the emperor's control.[33] The brass and copper coinage of Rome almost invariably bears the abbreviation *S(enatus) C(onsulto)*, 'by decree of the senate', but, given the close connection between the base metal coinages and their gold and silver counterparts, it is unclear what role (if any) the senate had in coin production, and the meaning of the abbreviation in the context of the coinage remains disputed.[34]

Gold coinage was produced almost entirely – with hardly any exceptions – by the state mint(s). It seems to have circulated widely, and was also exported. Silver was produced in a variety of forms. The state mint mainly produced *denarii*, but in the eastern provinces silver coinage of a local or regional type was produced. These eastern silver coinages were usually based on Hellenistic antecedents: cistophoric tetradrachms of the Attalids; Attic tetradrachms of the Seleucids; or Egyptian tetradrachms of the Ptolemies, to name some of the best-known examples. Who controlled their production is not clear, and it is possible that no single mode applied to the variety of provincial silver. It is fairly clear, however, that the procurement of metal for these coinages was episodic, as was their production.[35] In this respect they differ from the silver coinages minted at Rome. However, sometimes *denarii* and gold coins were issued at certain provincial mints, as if these centres had become branch mints of Rome. These arrangements were often temporary, but from the middle of the third century AD, Antioch began to operate as a branch of the mint of Rome on a regular basis, while still continuing to issue provincial silver tetradrachms.[36]

The provincial silver coinages had relatively restricted circulation. The Egyptian tetradrachms are not found in any significant quantities outside Egypt; Syrian tetradrachms are confined to Syria; and cistophoric tetradrachms to western Asia Minor, and so on. *Denarii*, on the other hand, are found more widely, although there is little evidence for their circulation in Egypt, so it cannot be claimed that they were conceived of as an empire-wide coinage, although their distribution comes close. The pure silver *denarii* of the early imperial period were exported to India; later, baser silver *denarii* of the second century are found beyond the empire in northern Europe; but provincial silver does not generally seem to have been exported.

At Rome, Augustus introduced a set of base-metal denominations in brass and copper, chief among which were the brass *sestertius* and the copper *as*. By the middle of the first century AD, this coinage had replaced local and older Republican coinages in the west, but in the eastern provinces the Greek tradition of cities minting their own currencies continued, and in many places the base metal coinage of Rome did not circulate to any appreciable degree.[37] It is debatable what sort of supervision of this local minting existed. Some city coinages record imperial permission, but most do not. As a result, it is not certain whether there was any central control of the supply of these coinages. Since they generally circulated only within a restricted area around the issuing city or region, oversupply need not have caused more widespread inflation. Cities were not the only entities issuing coins: we also find coinages issued by *koina* (associations of cities organized around provincial imperial cults) and by the rulers of kingdoms allied to Rome.

Conventionally, numismatists have distinguished the coinage of Rome (*aureus*, *denarius*, *sestertius* and *as*, etc.) as 'imperial', and other coinages as 'provincial'. Given the more restricted circulation of provincial coins, scholars have tended to focus more on the imperial coinages as evidence for the condition of state finances and for economic performance, and it is on this imperial coinage that we will concentrate.

Debasements and stability

Two features of Roman coinage during the first three centuries of the empire seem to stand out: the stability in the relationship between the denominations; and the stability of the weights of the denominations. This does not mean that the weights remained entirely stable over long periods, and there was a tendency in some periods for slight reductions to be made, perhaps to compensate for declining weight of the monetary stock already in circulation and/or changes in the price of one of the metals, although after certain denominations like the silver *denarius* began to be alloyed with copper, this weight decline seems to have slowed. Another feature of the coinage was that the purity of the gold coinage remained very high, while silver coinage began to be alloyed with copper to a greater or lesser degree.

To maintain this kind of stability in a coinage composed of various denominations in a variety of different metals is surely worthy of note. While modern narratives stress decline and instability, the fact that the system of denominations remained remarkably stable over a period of several centuries hints that the modern fixation on decline may be only a part of the story, particularly given that prices appear to have remained fairly stable over the same period. This apparent monetary stability is all the more remarkable given that the coinage of the early empire was very complex for a pre-modern society. As noted above, it made use of four different metals: gold, silver, brass and copper. During the first two centuries AD, coinage in all four metals was produced regularly and often on a large scale. This so-called 'Roman imperial' coinage contrasts with Republican coinage, which was composed mainly of silver *denarii* (and sometimes a half denomination, the *quinarius*) and copper alloy coins, mainly composed of *asses* (originally valued at a tenth of a *denarius*, but later revalued at a sixteenth). From the middle of the second century BC, the *denarius* had been produced on a massive scale. The copper alloy coinage had been produced in considerable quantities down to the mid-second century BC (almost to the exclusion of silver coinage between about 170 and 150 BC[38]), but thereafter production was intermittent. Between 78 and 49 BC, the state struck no base metal coinage at all. Older base metal coins continued to circulate, however, and may not have been completely eliminated from circulation until the first century AD.

Republican period

The very simplicity of the Roman Republican coinage compared to the imperial coinage may be one of the reasons why it appears to have been stable. Under the Republic, the state did not have to manage a coinage composed of multiple denominations in four different metals. Even so, there were monetary and financial problems under the Republic. Something must have caused the revaluation of the *as* relative to the *denarius* in the 140s BC. One possibility that has gained widespread credibility is the proposal that oversupply of *asses* in the first half of the second century led to a rise in the value of silver relative to base metal – a clear monetary explanation of the sort that would be less well-favoured if it were applied to the imperial period.[39] In the 80s BC, the *denarius* was slightly debased, which may be the reason why we find references to testing coins and fluctuating values in this period.[40] Two decades later, in 63 BC, there seems to have been a liquidity crisis with widespread hoarding following a contraction in *denarius* output.[41]

Julius Caesar and Augustus

Towards the end of the Republic some major changes occurred.[42] Julius Caesar in 46 BC began striking gold coinage on a massive scale. Previously there had only been small issues of gold. We know from later sources that the main gold denomination, the *denarius aureus*, was worth 25 silver *denarii*, producing a gold-to-silver ratio of 1:12. Both the gold and silver in this period were made from carefully refined metal of a high purity. If one takes the weight of Caesar's *aureus* and assumes it was worth 25 *denarii*, the ratio of his gold to silver is indeed 1:12, with a *denarius* struck at 84 to the pound and an *aureus* at 42. When we take into account later developments, the system looks like an attempt to establish a bimetallic system.

Numismatists have tended to regard the coinage of the Roman empire as the creation of Augustus, and it is not uncommon to find it referred to as the 'Augustan' coinage. The coinage of Augustus is treated in modern scholarship as the original standard for imperial coinage, and later developments are regarded as adulterations of this standard. Yet the system of gold and silver appears to be an arrangement created by Julius Caesar, not Augustus. The significance of Augustus in Roman monetary history seems to me to have been exaggerated, to the extent that it has obscured or even trivialized the significance of changes under his successors. While there were developments under Augustus, who made some modifications to Caesar's system and introduced major coinages in both brass and copper, more significant and far-reaching changes were introduced by later emperors.

That the gold and silver component of the Roman imperial monetary system was not the creation of Augustus is apparent from the fact that under Augustus the weight standards declined slightly from those of Julius Caesar. Further weight reductions took place under Augustus' successors, and production of silver coinage faltered. In contrast, production of gold seems to have remained high. This does raise the question of whether the changes we observe are the consequence of a gradual rise in the price of silver relative to gold, with the result that the silver *denarius* became increasingly unprofitable to produce at the existing standard. Such a change in price could explain what happened next.

Nero to Trajan

In about AD 64 the emperor Nero (r. 54–68) reduced the standards of the gold and silver coinage. The importance of this reform can scarcely be exaggerated. Nero's standards remained in use for more than a century, and later emperors like Diocletian went back to them after the monetary changes of the third century. The coinage of the High Roman Empire was Neronian, not Augustan. It is this reform, or rather series of reforms, and their consequences that I want to concentrate on, because I think they demonstrate that the Romans were thinking quite carefully about the management of their coinage.

That said, no ancient source mentions the reform. Consequently, its purpose is disputed, with most scholars pointing to Nero's alleged financial difficulties as the reason for the change. Attention has focused on the silver coinage. For the first time, this was alloyed with a substantial portion of copper – 20%. This is normally seen as evidence that Nero was running out of money, but few have ventured to explain why the standards were chosen. In my view, they were not arbitrary. The *denarius* was reduced in weight to about 3.45 grams

(96 to the pound), which was a weight standard used in the Greek East for the drachma. It is possible, therefore, that one of the aims of the reform was to bring the *denarius* and drachma into equivalence. There is some evidence that the discrepancy between the local silver coinages of the provinces and the *denarius* had caused complications when assessing tax, and simplification may have been the main purpose of the harmonization of the standards of imperial and provincial silver coinages.[43]

The reforms were also accompanied by a change in the location of the mint for gold and silver. Under Augustus and his successors, the *aureus* and *denarius* had been produced not at Rome, but at Lugdunum in Gaul; now Nero stopped production of gold and silver at Lugdunum and opened a mint for coinage in these metals at Rome.

The reduction in the fineness of the *denarius* may have proceeded in stages, since the earliest *denarius* issues after the reform seem to be comparatively fine – over 90% – but employ the new weight standard.[44] Soon, however, the mint switched to a *denarius* at 80% fine. This was the first time the mint of Rome had produced such a base *denarius*. Silver–copper alloys were common in the Greek East, and a standard of 80% was in use for some provincial coinages, suggesting yet another link between the new Neronian *denarius* and its provincial counterpart. The source of metal was also different. Lugdunum had relied on western sources – initially products of the mines in Spain, but, latterly, in Gaul – whereas Rome seems to have specialized in recycling old *denarii*. This recycling was to become a key component of monetary strategy as the first century progressed.

The gold coinage was also reduced in weight. It remained pure gold, but was now struck at 45 to the pound. The reason for this reduction seems to have been in order to maintain a notional 1:12 ratio – the ratio that would have existed had the *denarius* still been made of pure silver. In reality, the ratio was about 1:9.5. We cannot be certain how much the *denarius* was overvalued in relation to gold, but some degree of overvaluation is implied by the fact that in AD 68, at the end of his reign, Nero raised the fineness to 90%, and during the civil wars following his death, the various contenders for the throne issued pure or nearly pure *denarii* on the Neronian weight standard at mints in Spain and Gaul.

It would appear, then, that under Nero the *denarius* was understood to be a token coin, worth much more as a coin than as a piece of silver. If we are to consider the system 'bimetallic', by which I mean it was a system in which gold and silver coins were legal tender in a common unit of account,[45] it was merely a 'limping' bimetallism, with gold as the standard and silver as a token. This token *denarius* would seem to vindicate the jurists' conception of coinage as symbolic of value. However, public reaction to the changes reveals that other conceptions of the value of coinage existed.

First, the evidence of coin hoards. There are now a number of coin hoards containing *denarii* from Republican times through to the eve of Nero's reforms. In contrast, there are no known hoards closing with Nero's post-reform *denarii*.

Clearly, some people regarded the post-reform coins as different, and preferentially selected the pre-reform coins when hoarding. The Lugdunum issues were also exported to India, presumably for their bullion value. This process of export may well have begun under Nero's predecessors, when (as surmised above) the *denarius* was becoming increasingly undervalued at its old weight and fineness, but its continuation after Nero is assured because one coin from India bears a countermark of Nero's successor Vespasian (r. AD 69–79).

However, not everyone chose to separate pre- and post-reform *denarii*, even after the emperor Otho (r. AD 69) and his successors reverted to the 80% standard of fineness. Evidently, reactions to the reform varied. We assume that pre- and post-reform *denarii* were meant to circulate at par, but that is merely an assumption. The changes that took place in the later first century AD may have been attempts to combat the development of an unofficial discounting of the new *denarius* against the old. First, in AD 82, Domitian (r. 81–96) restored the *denarius* to a pure silver coin, but did not restore pre-Neronian weight standards (his coin may have been slightly heavier than a Neronian-reformed *denarius*, at about 3.55 grams).[46] He also increased the weight of the gold coinage, this time to pre-Neronian standards. This produced a gold to silver ratio of 1:11.5, close to the pre-reform ratio. But the reform does not appear to have been a success, to judge from the evidence of mint output.[47] As had happened in the period before Nero's reform, gold production was high and silver production declined precipitously. Three years after the reform, Domitian returned to Nero's weight for the *denarius*, using the revised standard of fineness of 90% that Nero had employed at the end of his reign. It looks as if Domitian was a convinced metallist who wanted to break with Nero's coinage, but was forced to concede that the traditional ratio of 1:12 was no longer cost effective. Even after he had reduced the fineness in AD 85, he still sought to maintain the *denarius* at the higher 90% standard of fineness, and he continued to mint *aurei* at a standard above Nero's, ensuring a ratio of about 1:10.

We have no useful price data from the period, and no way to evaluate what effect any of this had on prices – whether, for example, Domitian's improvements were deflationary. In any case, a substantial proportion of the circulating medium continued to consist of Republican and pre-Neronian *denarii*, if hoards are any guide, so much of what was available for exchange was equivalent in silver content to, if not better than, Domitian's new coinage. However, what happened next strongly suggests that the continued presence of pre-Neronian reform *denarii* in circulation was perceived to be a problem. Over the next few decades, this older coinage was removed from circulation. What is remarkable is how comprehensive this removal was. Republican and pre-Neronian reform *denarii* disappear from hoards between the reigns of Trajan (r. AD 98–117) and Hadrian (r. AD 117–138) and never reappear. As mentioned above, the mint of Rome specialized in recycling old coin, and continued to do so until the reign of Trajan, when we can see a dramatic change in the trace element profile of its silver supply. The mint gradually switched from recycled material to something that possibly represents a freshly mined source.[48] This roughly coincides with a remark by the third-century historian Cassius Dio that Trajan called in obsolete coinage.[49]

Trajan

Trajan also returned the *denarius* to its Neronian standard of 80% fine, and the *aureus* to its Neronian weight (older *aurei* at heavier weight standards rapidly disappeared). His reign therefore witnessed the successful implementation of Nero's coinage standards, by doing away with the pre-Neronian reform coinage. Given that the volume of Republican coinage still in circulation in early imperial times was probably enormous, it is possible that Trajan was merely completing a long-term Neronian scheme to replace old with new, a scheme that had been interrupted by Domitian's attempt to restore a full-bodied coinage.

The switch from recycled silver to a new source in the reign of Trajan is striking. The traditional model has stressed that supplies of silver were running out and that the financial system was under strain. Yet if so, we might have expected to see signs of intensive recycling as the state attempted to acquire whatever silver was available. Instead, we see the opposite: the *denarius* coinage of the entire Roman world was renewed through recycling between Nero and Trajan, after which the state seems to have moved to a single source of supply. What that source was we cannot yet say. However, another source comes on line during the course of the second century alongside the first, which may be Dacian in origin (Trajan having annexed Dacia in AD 106). Study of this material is still in progress.

Septimius Severus

The rest of the second century witnessed some minor fluctuations in fineness, and possibly a slight reduction in the weight of the *denarius* (and perhaps the *aureus*), but no major deviations from the Neronian standards.[50] However, in AD 194, Septimius Severus (r. 193–211) reduced the silver content of the *denarius* to just under 50% fine. No changes were made to the weights of either *aureus* or *denarius*. As with the Neronian reforms, we have no useful price data, but hoards once again show a certain amount of preferential hoarding of pre-194 *denarii*, and their export – not to India this time, but to northern Europe instead. As before, we assume that old and new *denarii* were meant to circulate at par. While some hoards show a preference for pre-Severan reform denarii, others show that pre- and post-194 *denarii* were hoarded together, just as pre- and post-64 *denarii* had been hoarded together down to the time of Trajan and Hadrian. The Neronian reforms thus supply a partial parallel for the one under Severus.

Whether this Severan debasement tells us anything about the changing price of silver relative to gold is hard to determine. It may simply be the case that Severus decided to increase the rate of overvaluation of silver to gold. Even so, strange things happened to the gold coinage during the third century. While there is evidence for continued production at high levels, gold coinage was rarely hoarded, either within or without the empire.[51] What became of it is unclear. What is more, by the reign of Severus Alexander (r. AD 222–235) the *aureus* no longer appears to have been issued at a fixed weight standard, which suggests that it no longer bore a fixed relationship to the rest of the coinage.[52] It looks as if gold had effectively become demonetized.

Caracalla and the antoninianus

There is much else that is mysterious about the coinage of the third century, the period of supposed hyperinflation. Most serious of all these mysteries is the face value of the silver coin introduced by Caracalla (r. 198–217) in AD 215, conventionally called an *antoninianus* or 'radiate' because its real name is unknown. We have seen how Mommsen proposed that it was an overvalued double *denarius*, and perhaps this is correct, but numismatists and historians have been remarkably cavalier in pronouncing it so. Caution is necessary when one's understanding of an entire currency system depends on it. The substantivist historian A.H.M. Jones stated that there would have been no point in issuing the *antoninianus* unless it had represented a debasement, and many Romanists concur (see above). Yet there remains another possibility: that history was effectively repeating itself, and the public were discounting post-194 *denarii* compared to pre-194 ones, and hoarding or exporting pre-194 *denarii*, forcing the state to take action. Caracalla's solution was the same as Domitian's: to restore the pre-reform *denarius*; but he chose to restore it alongside the post-reform one by introducing a new coin. Rather than being innovative, the introduction of the new coin was conservative: it restored the Neronian *denarius* or drachm, but in a new form.

Later developments

Making full sense of the coinage in the decades that followed is not currently possible. Too little is known about either the weight or fineness of the silver coinage, and the erratic weights of the gold coins do little to convince one that any consistent standard lay behind it. It would appear that by about AD 270 the former complexity of Roman imperial coinage had been reduced to a single denomination: the *antoninianus*, which by now had a nominal silver content of about 2% and was otherwise made of copper (and perhaps some tin). Most provincial coinages, whether of silver or base metal, had ceased (except for Egypt); gold is strangely absent from the archaeological record, although the number of dies employed to strike gold coins implies that it was apparently still produced in some quantity; the *denarius* was no longer produced in any substantial numbers, but continued to function as a unit of account (assuming that the accounting term '*denarius*' refers to the smaller coin and not to the larger, radiate *antoninianus*); and imperial base metal denominations had likewise all but ceased. It looks as if a proper fiduciary currency had been established (though of course even that is debatable). Freed from the constraints imposed by a coinage made from valuable commodities, and with a gold coinage of floating value against a notional *denarius* of account,[53] it seems that later emperors of the fourth century could revalue this billon coinage by fiat. In AD 301, Diocletian was able to double the value of a denomination (or maybe several denominations).[54] 20 years later, in about 321, the emperor Licinius halved the value of his main base metal unit, the *nummus*, from 25 to 12.5 *denarii*.[55] Such options had not been available to rulers of the first and second centuries. If this characterization of the differences between the coinage of the early and late empires is correct, then the ways in which the Roman state managed its coinage must have differed, too: removing the fixed relationships between coinages of different metals freed late Roman emperors from the constraints of the earlier, rigid system, but seems to have ushered in a period where the billon and base-metal denominations were subject to successive devaluations, giving us the impression of continued monetary instability from the third century onwards.

This change from a regime of low inflation to one characterized by periods (perhaps short and intermittent) of high inflation seems to be accompanied by a change from a complex coinage with denominations standing in fixed relationships to one another, and made of valuable commodities, to a simpler coinage consisting of billon coins with a largely nominal value and gold coins with a floating value. This would seem to argue in favour of a currency backed by metallic value as the more stable model, but we cannot be certain whether the lack of flexibility posed by the earlier system was not a hindrance that the changes of the third century were intended to solve. The changing prices of metals could have placed a strain on the earlier, more rigid system, resulting in falling production levels of certain denominations and threats to the level of liquidity, and the need to remove large populations of older coins. Corrections or restorations of fineness and weight could have had unintended deflationary consequences. After a debasement, the hoarding of precious metal coins deemed more valuable could also have impacted on liquidity. Without good data on wages and prices, it is difficult to say what were the wider consequences on society of the changes we observe. Some studies have argued for increasing demand for coin and increasing monetization as the coinage became more debased, suggesting that, if coinage was intended to serve as a medium of exchange, the late antique system was a successful one, and that increased supply and debasement did not necessarily result in persistent inflation.[56]

Without clearer information about output, fineness and even the face values of the coins after the beginning of the third century, it is often very hard to be decisive about either the rationale for changes or the outcomes of those changes. Recovering the monetary history of the Roman empire is essentially an exercise in prehistoric archaeology, in that there is plenty of material evidence but almost no helpful documentary data. Modelling and the use of comparative material seems the most fruitful way forward. A current research project aims to outline the fineness of Roman silver coinage, and at the same time characterize the metal supplied to the mints, whether freshly mined or recycled. This has revealed some of the complexities alluded to above. Even so, there remains some resistance on the part of many Roman numismatists to thinking about coinage in economic terms, which is no doubt the legacy of substantivism. Despite mounting evidence to the contrary, the preferred interpretation of hoarding patterns, such as those terminating with Nero or Septimius Severus' reform, is that they are evidence for wars or barbarian invasions and payments or transfers of money to soldiers or barbarians, not evidence for public reactions to coinage reforms or flows of undervalued coins to places where their bullion value would be realized. The movement of coinage is almost always treated as evidence for state payments or troop movements rather than exchange. While there is a tendency nowadays to rebrand the third century 'crisis' as a 'transformation', the currency of that period is still said to have suffered a 'collapse'. Here too, however, 'transition' might be a better description, since it could be argued that, in spite of some key changes that may have occurred, the third-century coinage presents us with a continuum rather than a complete monetary rupture.

Conclusion

I fear that much of the above will seem unduly pessimistic. However, there are reasons for optimism. Happily, we are living in an age where the monetary history of the Roman world is becoming a major research area. There are important projects underway that seek to understand the composition of the coinage and the supply of metals, and the patterns of hoarding both within and without the empire. In a few years, we may be able to revisit the topic of Roman monetary policy with more confidence in our certainties.

Notes

1 E.g. Harl (1996).
2 Crawford (1978).
3 Butcher and Ponting (2014: 53–62).
4 Mommsen (1860).
5 Mommsen (1860: 830; 1873: 147).
6 On the history of thought about this denomination, see Butcher (2015).
7 For Mattingly's view prior to the Weimar inflation, see Sydenham (1919: 134), and Mattingly and Sydenham (1923: 29); for his later position, see Mattingly (1927: 126).
8 E.g. Giesecke (1938: 161); Hammond (1946: 78–9).
9 Jones (1974, especially 189–227); Crawford (1970).
10 Jones (1974: 74).
11 The quote is from Silver (2011: 19). Diocletian's lack of economic knowledge is commonly stressed, e.g. Jones (1970: 308).
12 Jones (1974: 194n); Crawford (1975: 565).
13 Jones (1974: 189–190).
14 Jones (1974: 188): 'The currency was strictly cash.'
15 Crawford (1970).
16 De Cecco (1985).

17 Reece (1987: 125).
18 The general acceptance of this model of the Roman monetary system meant that there was a major difference between the rationale for ancient coinage and many medieval coinages, with the result that there has been very little dialogue between medievalists and students of the ancient monetary economy.
19 See Jones (1980) on the proposed link between Spanish mines and imperial coinage.
20 Howgego (1990).
21 Harris (2008); but see also Rüfner (2016).
22 *Digest* 18.1.1.
23 Gaius, *Institutes*, 1.123.
24 Walker (1976, 1977, 1978).
25 On the transition, see Strobel (2002). The observation that the maximum price for gold in Diocletian's Prices Edict is the same whether in bars or in coin (Graser 1940: 413, 30.1a; Hendy 1985: 450), seems to me to be irrelevant here. If the maximum price for bullion exceeded that of coin, gold coinage would be rendered unprofitable to produce.
26 A good example of this kind of discrimination is demonstrated by the Beau Street hoard, discovered in the city of Bath in 2007 (Ghey 2014). It consisted of over 17,000 coins separated into eight leather bags. One bag contained almost exclusively silver *denarii*, four more contained almost exclusively finer radiates down to the joint reigns of Valerian and Gallienus (AD 253–260) and three bags contained mainly base radiates of the period of the sole reign of Gallienus (AD 260–268) onwards. The latest coins in the hoard (and in many of the bags) were of Tetricus (AD 270–274).
27 Corbier (2005: 425); Rathbone (1996). See for a recent overview and discussion of the grain prices: Rathbone and Von Reden (2015).
28 Rathbone (1996: 334); on the tetradrachm's fineness, see Howgego, Butcher and Ponting (forthcoming). The prices of wheat and barley in Roman Egypt are collected by Dominic Rathbone in Rathbone and Von Reden (2015: 210–225, tables A8.12–A8.16).
29 Rathbone (1996: 321).
30 Cagan (1956: 25) (making allowances for variations in the rate over successive months both below and above the 50% rate during a hyperinflationary period). Third-century inflation characterized as hyperinflation: Silver (2011: 14).
31 Statius, *Silvae* 3.3 85–105. The fact that this key information about the financial secretary's role in the coinage is to be found within a highly metaphorical piece of poetry tells us much about the nature and quality of the evidence with which students of the ancient economy have to work.
32 SPQR OPTIMO PRINCIPI. This formula is presumably a continuation of the obverse inscription giving Trajan's names and titles in the dative: IMP CAES NERVAE TRAIANO AVG GER DAC P M TR P COS V P P: 'The Senate and the People of Rome, to the best *princeps*, imperator Caesar Nerva Trajanus Augustus Germanicus, Dacicus, Pontifex Maximus, holder of the tribunician power, consul for the fifth time, father of the fatherland'.
33 Woytek (2010: 46).
34 Bay (1972).
35 Butcher and Ponting (2014).
36 Butcher (2004: 118–127).
37 Howgego (1985); Butcher (1988); Burnett, Amandry and Ripollès (1992).
38 Woytek (2012: 330).
39 Buttrey (1957).
40 See the discussion in Crawford (1985: 187–193).
41 Crawford (1985: 240–241).
42 What follows is based on Butcher and Ponting (2014, 2011, 2012).
43 Rathbone (2008: 266).
44 For this and what follows, see Butcher and Ponting (2014: 201–288).
45 Redish (2000: 4).

46 Walker (1976: 115); Butcher and Ponting (2014: 377–389).
47 Carradice (1983: 160).
48 Butcher and Ponting (2012; 2015).
49 Cassius Dio (68.15).
50 Butcher and Ponting (2012).
51 Bland (2013).
52 Bland (1996).
53 The gold *solidus*, a coin introduced by Constantine (AD 306–337), remained remarkably stable in both weight and fineness throughout late antiquity, and over a much longer period than the earlier gold *aureus*. This stability may have been aided by the fact that it had become divorced from a fixed system in relation to billon and base metal coins. See Abdy (2012: 591–592).
54 Opinions vary: Harl (1996: 153) (all denominations); Estiot (2012: 548–549) (some denominations); Abdy (2012: 585) (one denomination).
55 Hendy (1985: 463–465).
56 Rathbone (1996).

References

Abdy, R. (2012). 'Tetrarchy and the House of Constantine', in W.E. Metcalf (ed.), *The Oxford Handbook of Greek and Roman Coinage*, Oxford: Oxford University press: 584–600.

Bay, A. (1972). 'The letters SC on Augustan Aes Coinage', *Journal of Roman Studies*, 62: 111–122.

Bland, R. (1996). 'The development of gold and silver coin denominations, AD 193–253', in King, C.E. and Wigg, D. (eds.), *Coin Finds and Coin Use in the Roman World. The Thirteenth Oxford Symposium on Coinage and Monetary History, 25–27.3.1993*, Berlin: Gebr. Mann Verlag: 63–100.

Bland, R. (2013). 'What happened to gold coinage in the 3rd c. A.D.?', *Journal of Roman Archaeology*, 26: 263–280.

Burnett, A., Amandry, M. and Ripollès, P.P. (1992). *Roman Provincial Coinage, Volume I. From the Death of Caesar to the Death of Vitellius*. London: British Museum Press.

Butcher, K. (1988). *Roman Provincial Coins. An Introduction to the Greek Imperials*. London: Seaby.

Butcher, K. (2004). *Coinage in Roman Syria. Northern Syria, 64 BC–AD 253*. London: Royal Numismatic Society.

Butcher, K. (2015). 'Debasement and the decline of Rome', in Bland, R. and Calomino, D. (eds.), *Studies in Ancient Coinage in Honour of Andrew Burnett*, London: Spink & Son Ltd: 181–205.

Butcher, K. and Ponting, M. (2011). 'The *denarius* in the first century', in Holmes, N. (ed.), *Proceedings of the XIV International Numismatic Congress, Glasgow 2009*, Glasgow: University of Glasgow: 557–568.

Butcher, K. and Ponting, M. (2012). 'The beginning of the end? The *denarius* in the second century', *Numismatic Chronicle*, 172: 63–83.

Butcher, K. and Ponting, M. (2014), *The Metallurgy of Roman Silver Coinage. From the Reform of Nero to the Reform of Trajan*, Cambridge, UK: Cambridge University Press.

Butcher, K. and Ponting, M. (2015), 'The reforms of Trajan and the end of the pre-Neronian denarius', *Annali dell'Istituto Italiano di Numismatica* 61: 21–42.

Buttrey, T.V. (1957). 'On the retariffing of the Roman *denarius*', *American Numismatic Society Museum Notes*, 7: 57–65.

Cagan, P. (1956). 'The monetary dynamics of hyperinflation', in Friedman, M. (ed.), *Studies in the Quantity Theory of Money*, Chicago, IL: University of Chicago Press: 25–43.

Carradice, I. (1983). *Coinage and Finances in the Reign of Domitian*. Oxford: B.A.R.

Corbier, M. (2005). 'Coinage, society and economy', in Bowman, A.K., Garnsey, P. and Cameron, A. (eds.), *The Cambridge Ancient History. Vol. 12: The Crisis of Empire,* ad *193–337*, Cambridge, UK: Cambridge University Press: 393–439.

Crawford, M.H. (1970). 'Money and exchange in the Roman world', *Journal of Roman Studies*, 60: 40–48.

Crawford, M.H. (1975). 'Finance, coinage and money from the Severans to Constantine', in Temporini, H. and Haase, W. (eds.), *Aufstieg und Niedergang der Römischen Welt*, II.2, Berlin: Walter de Gruyter: 560–593.

Crawford, M.H. (1978). 'Ancient devaluations: A general theory', in Mrozek, S. (ed.), *Les dévaluations à Rome*, I, Rome: EFR: 147–158.

De Cecco, M. (1985). 'Monetary theory and Roman history', *Journal of Economic History*, 45: 809–822.

Estiot, S. (2012). 'The later third century', in Metcalf, W.E. (ed.), *The Oxford Handbook of Greek and Roman Coinage*, Oxford: Oxford University Press: 538–560.

Ghey, E. (2014). *The Beau Street Hoard*. London: The British Museum.

Giesecke, W. (1938). *Antikes Geldwesen*, Leipzig, Germany: Verlag K.W. Hiersemann.

Graser, E. R. (1940). 'Appendix: Diocletian's edict on maximum prices', in Frank, T. (ed.), *An Economic Survey of Ancient Rome*, Vol. V. *Rome and Italy of the Empire*, Baltimore, MD: Johns Hopkins Press: 307–421.

Hammond, M. (1946). 'Economic stagnation in the early Roman empire', *Journal of Economic History*, Supplement 6: 63–90.

Harl, K. (1996). *Coinage in the Roman Economy, 300* BC–AD *700*, Baltimore, MD: Johns Hopkins Press.

Harris, V.W. (2008). 'The nature of Roman money', in Harris, V.W. (ed.), *The Monetary Systems of the Greeks and Romans*, Oxford: Oxford University Press: 174–207.

Hendy, M.F. (1985). *Studies in the Byzantine Monetary Economy, c. 300–1450*, Cambridge, UK: Cambridge University Press.

Howgego, C.J. (1985). *Greek Imperial Countermarks*. London: Royal Numismatic Society.

Howgego, C.J. (1990). 'Why did ancient states strike coins?', *Numismatic Chronicle*, 150: 1–25.

Howgego, C.J., Butcher, K. and Ponting, M. (forthcoming). 'Coinage and the Roman economy in the Antonine period: The view from Egypt', in Bowman, A. and Wilson, A. (eds.), *Mining, Metal Supply and Coinage in the Roman Empire*, Oxford: Oxford University Press.

Jones, A.H.M. (1970). *A History of Rome through the Fifth Century*. Volume II: *The Empire*. New York: Walker & Company.

Jones, A.H.M. (1974). *The Roman Economy*. Oxford: Blackwell.

Jones, G.D.B. (1980). 'The Roman mines of Rio Tinto', *Journal of Roman Studies*, 70: 146–165.

Mattingly, H. (1927). *Roman Coins from the Earliest Times to the Fall of the Western Empire*. London: Methuen.

Mattingly, H. and Sydenham, E.A. (1923). *The Roman Imperial Coinage*, Volume I. *Augustus to Vitellius*. London: Spink & Son.

Mommsen, Th. (1860). *Geschichte des römischen Münzwesens*. Berlin: Weidmannsche Buchhandlung.

Mommsen, Th. (1873). *Histoire de la monnaie romaine, traduit de l'Allemand par le Duc de Blacas, et publiée par J. De Witte, membre de l'Institut, tome troisième*. Paris : Librairie A. Franck.

Rathbone, D. (1996). 'Monetisation, not price-inflation, in third-century AD Egypt?', in King, C.E. and Wigg, D. (eds.), *Coin Finds and Coin Use in the Roman World. The Thirteenth Oxford Symposium on Coinage and Monetary History, 25–27.3.1993*, Berlin: Gebr. Mann Verlag: 321–339.

Rathbone, D. (2008). 'Nero's reforms of *vectigalia* and the inscription of the *lex portorii Asiae*', in Cottier, M., Crawford, M.H., Crowther, C.V., Ferrary, J-L., Levick, B.M., Salomies, O. and Wörrle, M. (eds.), *The Customs Law of Asia*, Oxford: Oxford University Press: 251–278.

Rathbone, D. and Von Reden, S. (2015). 'Mediterranean grain prices in classical Antiquity', in Van der Spek, R.J., Van Leeuwen, B. and Van Zanden J.L. (eds.), *A History of Market Performance from Ancient Babylonia to the Modern World*, London, New York: Routledge: 149–235.

Redish, A. (2000). *Bimetallism. An Economic and Historical Analysis*, Cambridge, UK: Cambridge University Press.

Reece, R. (1987). *Coinage in Roman Britain*. London: Seaby.

Rüfner, T. (2016). 'Money in the Roman law texts', in Fox, D. and Ernst, W. (eds.), *Money in the Western Legal Tradition. Middle Ages to Bretton Woods*, Oxford: Oxford University Press: 93–109.

Silver, M. (2011). 'Finding the Roman empire's disappeared deposit bankers', *Historia* 60.10: 1–27.

Strobel, K. (2002). 'Geldwesen und Währungsgeschichte des Imperium Romanum im Spiegel der Entwicklung des 3. Jahrhunderts n. Chr. – Wirtschaftsgeschichte im Widerstreit von Metallismus und Nominalismus', in Strobel, K. (ed.), *Die Ökonomie des Imperium Romanum: Strukturen, Modelle und Wertungen im Spannungsfeld von Modernismus und Neoprimitivismus*, St Katharinen, Germany: Scripta Mercaturae Verlag: 86–168.

Sydenham, E.A. (1919). 'The Roman monetary system', *Numismatic Chronicle*, 19: 114–171.

Walker, D.R. (1976). *The Metrology of the Roman Silver Coinage*. Part I. *From Augustus to Domitian*, Oxford: B.A.R.

Walker, D.R. (1977). *The Metrology of the Roman Silver Coinage*. Part II. *From Nerva to Commodus*, Oxford: B.A.R.

Walker, D.R. (1978). *The Metrology of the Roman Silver Coinage*. Part III. *From Pertinax to Uranius Antoninus*, Oxford: B.A.R.

Woytek, B. (2010). *Die Reichsprägung des Kaisers Traianus (98-117)*. Vienna, Austria: Österreichische Akademie der Wissenschaften.

Woytek, B. (2012). 'The *denarius* coinage of the Roman Republic', in Metcalf W.E. (ed.), *The Oxford Handbook of Greek and Roman Coinage*, Oxford: Oxford University Press: 313–334.

9 Money in England from the Middle Ages to the nineteenth century

Nick Mayhew

Introduction

This book deals with fundamental questions about the nature of money, and our answers may have implications both for contemporary economics and for the way we study the past.

In this chapter, I will argue that the contrast between 'commodity' and 'fiat' money has been exaggerated. Precious metal coins are a liquid means of exchange, making them significantly different from bullion. Coins have more in common with other forms of money, including fiat moneys, than with bullion or other commodities. The essential money-ness of money lies in government action creating money and supporting it by law.[1]

Accordingly, there is clear a distinction between coined money and bullion, illustrated by the fact that coins typically command a face value greater than their intrinsic value. For gold and silver coins, that premium – usually about 5 or 10% over their intrinsic content – reflected the cost of making the coins plus a seignorage charge, which people paid for the convenience of coin. Governments reinforced the desirability of coin by accepting – indeed, requiring – it in payment of tax.

Ultimately, with government support, anything – with or without commodity value – can serve as money,[2] although obviously such government support could only float a currency as far as its own writ can. Beyond the boundaries of the coin-issuing state, any currency only has value in line with its intrinsic content, or for the purposes of buying goods or services within that coin-issuing state. In short, a distinction needs to be drawn between the domestic and the international functioning of any currency. Historians have tended to focus on exchange rates – the international value of currencies – perhaps neglecting the importance of the domestic circulating means of exchange. The domestic economy and price structure were determined by the government valuation of money.

Evidence in support of these propositions will be drawn from the history of the English currency. I hope to show that bullion-based money was no more immune to monetary problems than fiat money. Concentrating too much on the physical form which money takes can divert attention from how money actually behaves. It also has implications for modern historical practice. Converting nominal prices to their silver-weight equivalent may facilitate international price comparison, and an understanding of intrinsic content does inform our understanding of currencies. But this paper seeks to demonstrate that the widespread practice of converting prices or wages to equivalent weight of silver in order to compare standards of living is both philosophically and historically unsound.

Much comparative work on international price and wage history has involved the conversion of different currencies to their silver weight,[3] and this process is also thought to simplify comparison over time when intrinsic content may have varied.[4] However, this methodology extracts the raw historical data from its context, distances historians from the usual practice of the time, and can lead to a fundamental misunderstanding of the nature of money.

Moreover, while an appreciation of the intrinsic content of historical currencies can be useful, the conversion of nominal prices and wages to their silver-weight equivalents has no bearing whatever on the international comparison of standards of living, which are based on the *ratio* of prices to wages. That ratio is entirely independent of the currencies involved, so conversion to silver weight is completely unnecessary. The time and energy expended on such calculations would be better spent improving our nominal price and wage data, which may not always be adequate to support the conclusions based upon it.[5]

Finally, it needs to be firmly understood that the mint prices for silver, on which conversions are based, are not the same as market prices, from which they can often diverge very significantly.[6]

Nominalism

In the first place, it should be noted that coin in medieval and early modern England (and much of Europe) ordinarily passed within the kingdom at its nominal face value (by tale) as defined by government, rather than by weight. The model in Sargent and Velde's influential work *The Big Problem of Small Change* (2002) is founded on the assumption that coins of a given denomination circulate by tale.[7] They trace the evolution of medieval law from Roman and canon law origins, which gradually came to treat intrinsic content as paramount,[8] through to the later Middle Ages when the importance of the face value of money of account began to be recognized, to a marked shift in the sixteenth century and thereafter when they found the value of money to be legally determined by government.

Sargent and Velde's principal interest lies in the development of small denominations with a face value set above their intrinsic content, and their focus is largely on continental Europe. In England, however, the right of government to determine the value of money is apparent from before the Conquest. In ninth-century Northumbria, base *stycas* circulated by government fiat until the Viking invasions rendered them worthless, while in southern

England Anglo-Saxon kings asserted their right to vary the intrinsic content of their pennies without a change in face value.[9] Of course Anglo-Norman kings exploited concerns about the intrinsic value of coin in order to justify the exaction of supplementary payments by the Exchequer, though many, perhaps most, payments were made by tale.[10] On rare occasions, Plantagenet government permitted and even encouraged the weighing of coins by the public.[11] After the introduction of gold coinage in England, the greater value of individual pieces made them more likely to be weighed,[12] but the value of the sterling currency was still set by government; refusing the king's coin at the value he set on it was a punishable offence.[13]

Christine Desan's study of the English law and practice pertaining to monetary payments and obligations[14] distinguishes between the Justinian Code, which affirmed the right of government to set the value of money, and later glosses which tried to deal with the realities of debased coin. It is these glosses and the arguments of canon lawyers which Sargent and Velde find in the theory and practice of continental Europe. England, however, was different, as Desan shows: there money remained strong as governments generally funded their activities through taxation rather than debasement, and English kings retained a strong hold on the coinage, including the right to determine the value of the coinage and of the money of account, irrespective of its intrinsic value. Because English kings generally maintained the intrinsic content of the coinage, respecting the prevailing open-market value of metals, there was less occasion to challenge their right to manage the currency. The courts repeatedly confirmed that the nature and value of money was determined by the crown rather than by its intrinsic content.[15]

The situation in later medieval Scotland was more complex as king, Parliament, and the courts tried to balance the legitimate case for debasement to provide small change and to reflect the changing price of precious metals against the hardship and injustice inflicted by sudden alterations in the nominal values of money. Fifteenth-century Scottish kings asserted their right to alter the currency while parliament fretted about the need to respect the interests of debtors and creditors. The early Stewart kings generally acknowledged parliament's concerns while consistently ignoring them in practice. It required a baronial coup d'etat in 1482 to halt the over-issue of inflationary base small change. The burgh court in Aberdeen generally followed the law as established by central government: payment was valid if the coins tendered were current at the stated value on the day in question, and such coin could not be refused, but money could be altered and even demonetized altogether overnight.[16]

For England, Desan's full-length review of this question affirms the practice of nominalism. The courts were particularly likely to rule on this question at times of recoinage, when earlier issues were demonetized. Common law required that coin be taken at its nominal or face value: the writ of debt identified the count of money, not the weight of silver, as the medium that settled obligations. Desan cites a series of judgments beginning with Pavely v. Basset in 1250. The early thirteenth-century *On the Laws and Customs of England*, attributed to Henry of Bracton, distinguished between coined money, which went by count, and other items, which went by weight or by measure.[17] Cases resolving the difficulties caused by crockards and pollards around 1300 confirm the right of the crown to determine the face value of coin, independently of its intrinsic content.

From the 1340s, English money was gradually devalued in a series of steps which cut the silver weight of the currency in line with the rising international value of silver. This process prompted parliamentary comment and some legal disputes, but the courts consistently upheld the rights of the crown to determine the value and content of the money, even when that right was abused by Henry VIII. The most celebrated judgement, handed down by the Privy Council in 1605, affirmed the right of Elizabeth to debase the Irish currency.[18] Despite all these reductions in the intrinsic value of the coinage, prices and debts were still set and met in money of account. Desan writes, 'The vocabulary thus identified the substantive obligation of debt with an abstract monetary value [e.g. *solidus* or *libra*], not a weight.'[19] Though the weight of the English penny fell from about 22 grains of sterling silver in the early fourteenth century to about 7.7 grains in the early seventeenth century, the penny remained a penny regardless of its weight.[20]

Accordingly, within the kingdom money generally passed at its nominal, face value (by tale), rather than by weight. Apart from the implied challenge to the royal prerogative, regular weighing and/or assaying of payments by the public would have been enormously time-consuming and inconvenient, and would have destroyed much of the utility of coin. If payments had been consistently weighed, neither debasement nor clipping would have occurred, since both processes depend for their profit on the acceptance of the debased or clipped coin at face value. Yet we know the weight of the medieval English currency was officially reduced on four principle occasions,[21] while illegal clipping certainly occurred, shaving silver from individual coins which were then passed in payment at their face value.

England thus maintained the established principle of nominalism, prioritizing the role of government in fixing the nominal face value of the currency. Elsewhere in Europe, repeated bouts of severe debasements gave the courts, and particularly the Church, a real interest in protecting the value of rents and other debts.[22] Yet, as Sargent and Velde show, from the sixteenth century onwards the use of moneys of account, and the legitimate need of government to be able to issue small change with a face value in excess of its intrinsic content, was increasingly recognized in the continental courts.

In fact, the questions raised by moneys of account and the problems of small change were apparent in Europe long before the sixteenth century. The case of medieval Florence provides a particularly illuminating example. In the fourteenth century, Florence maintained an internationally admired gold currency of unchanging weight and fineness, alongside a silver currency which included a number of denominations struck at differing standards. Cipolla has shown that the silver contents of the *grosso*, *quattrino*, and *denaro piccolo* varied somewhat disproportionately but continued to pass domestically at the face value set on them by the Florentine government. Moreover, government did not hesitate to alter fine content and/or face value of these denominations as and when international fluctuations made it necessary. The Florentine case thus illustrates a number of themes: the distinction between the behaviour of currencies domestically and internationally; the ability of government to set variable values on coins based on different pricing of silver between different denominations circulating together at the same time; and the need for occasional devaluations by government fiat.[23]

So despite occasional exceptions, money passed in its own territories by tale at the face value set on it by government. That valuation was by no means necessarily accepted abroad. Sovereigns regularly scrutinized the intrinsic content of foreign coin within their kingdoms and set a value for such coin accordingly. Thus, exchange rates between currencies were closely based on intrinsic content, but domestic prices and wages were necessarily expressed in terms of the local currency at values set by the local government.[24]

Actual and theoretical intrinsic content of currency

This principle of nominalism, long established in England and certainly adopted elsewhere from the later middle ages, should remind us that coins commonly passed domestically at a face value only loosely connected to their intrinsic content. Indeed, historians seem to have been more preoccupied with the intrinsic content of the currency than were the domestic users of that currency. The English coinage in the late-seventeenth and eighteenth centuries demonstrates how far the silver currency might drift from its theoretical intrinsic value while remaining in circulation at its face value.[25] Since this means that the theoretical weights on which historians base their estimates of intrinsic content were often invalid, it is worth exploring how this occurred in a little more detail.

From the restoration of Charles II until the Napoleonic Wars, the theoretical English mint valuation of silver fell well below that which prevailed internationally. The debasements of Henry VIII and Edward VI had left England with a horror of any kind of alteration of the currency. Accordingly, whenever enhancing the value of silver was again considered in England, it was rejected.[26] This mentality prevented the English mint from responding to the rising world price of silver in the later seventeenth century, when rising demand for silver exceeded rising supply. Consequently, silver output from the London mint dwindled, while such full-weight silver coin as could be found was increasingly likely to be carried abroad to the Continent and beyond, where silver was more highly prized.[27] In the absence of new English silver coin, the domestic currency consisted of old, worn silver of increasingly light weight.

This state of affairs was fully recognized at the time, and led to the famous Lowndes–Locke debate about possible solutions. It was universally recognized by the 1690s that reform and recoinage were required; the argument hinged on whether England should recognize the internationally rising price of silver by reducing the weight of its own silver coinage.[28] This was the course proposed by Lowndes, who pointed out that similar reductions in the weight of sterling had successfully been carried out repeatedly in the later Middle Ages. Locke, however, energetically opposed such a policy, and his argument won the day. Accordingly, the great recoinage of 1696 replaced the worn silver currency with new silver, at the full, old weight, which more or less immediately left the country. Not only was full-weight English silver coin likely to be carried abroad to regions where it enjoyed a higher price; in the eighteenth century, the uncompetitive English mint price offered for silver bullion ensured that pitifully small quantities of silver were brought in for sale to the Mint.[29] In short, silver coin became extremely scarce and worn in eighteenth-century England. This demonstrates that currencies can be too strong – having too high an intrinsic content – as well as too weak. While much attention is rightly paid to the evils of debasement, over-valuing the currency or under-valuing silver can also create severe difficulties. Tying the currency to bullion does not allow governments to escape the difficult task of setting the value of their currency.

The fact that the actual silver content of eighteenth-century English currency was below its theoretical content means that converting English prices and wages to their theoretical legal weight of silver perpetrates an historical fiction. Payments were increasingly likely to be made in gold, copper, or by credit of one sort or another, and such silver as was to be found was accepted at face value despite very significant loss of weight. For most of the eighteenth century, the actual silver weight of the circulating coinage was well below the weight at which the Mint struck it, but the problem was already evident before the Great Recoinage of 1696. The weight of silver coin then brought for recoinage was found to be almost 50% below its theoretical weight.[30] As we have already noted, the Recoinage solved nothing. By 1754, *The Gentleman's Magazine* observed that crowns and half-crowns were rarely to be seen, since most were thought to have been melted or exported, while many shillings and sixpences were of low weight.[31] A series of more quantitative contemporary estimates of the state of the silver currency over the century has been assembled by Clancy, including authoritative examinations by the Mint in 1786, 1787, 1798, 1807, and 1816.[32] These confirm that shillings and sixpences became particularly worn: shillings were 23% light by 1786, sixpences 36% light. By 1816, shillings were 30% light, sixpences 40%. In 1817, the £2.6 million in old silver withdrawn for recoinage was found to have lost an aggregate 26% of its theoretical legal weight.[33]

Government had recognized this state of affairs in 1774, ruling that silver should only be taken by weight in payments over £25, but this meant that for payments of less than £25 worn coin was acceptable at face value regardless of weight.[34] Clancy has characterized this as 'a tacit devaluation'.[35] Moreover, employers seeking silver to pay wages found themselves obliged to pay one half or 1% over the face value of the silver, despite knowing full well that its intrinsic value was perhaps 40% light.[36]

Thus, it is simply not now possible to speak with confidence about the weight of coin involved in any specific payment unless it was weighed and recorded at the time. On top of this uncertainty, it needs to be recognized that a widespread shortage of silver coin meant that payments were often not made in silver at all.[37] Clancy has estimated that by 1790 the Mint had issued some 170 million copper coins, while counterfeit copper halfpennies and farthings exceeded that number. On top of that, from 1787, millions of privately produced copper tokens were struck, tolerated by the authorities since they appeared to be supplying a real need.[38]

Tokens of one kind or another were also struck in silver in an attempt to liberate the currency from the uneconomic mint price to which Locke had committed it a century before. The Bank of England issued tokens, as did numerous British towns and cities. The Mint also countermarked Spanish dollars for issue by the Bank, giving them currency at face values more closely aligned to the prevailing open market price for silver than the Mint was permitted to recognize for its own official issues. These silver issues illustrate clearly the predicament in which the Mint found itself: the uncompetitive mint price set by Parliament left the Mint unable to strike the official British silver coinage, so it had recourse to unofficial alternative issues not shackled to an outdated mint price.[39]

In short, payments were either not made in silver at all, or if they were made in silver the weight of circulating coin was likely to be well below the legal standard. Consequently, from the restoration of Charles II until after Waterloo, the legal weight of the sterling silver coinage is no guide to the weight of circulating currency. So converting face-value prices and wages to a silver equivalent based on the theoretical weight of the silver coinage is a mistake.

Of course, other countries experienced worn currency too, but this problem was particularly acute in Britain between 1660 and 1817,[40] because the mint price for silver offered there was further from the prevailing international level than elsewhere. This means that converting prices and wages to their theoretical legal weight would overestimate silver contents generally, but to a greater extent in Britain than elsewhere. Converting nominal sums to silver weight not only creates inaccuracies, but it does so inconsistently.[41] Comparisons based on silver weight conversion can only be regarded as a very approximate guide.

The variable value of silver

Silver weight conversion is unhistorical because the theoretical weight significantly exceeded the reality, but the idea of calculating in terms of silver weight is also philosophically flawed, in so far as it assumes (as Locke did) that silver provides some kind of constant yardstick which can be applied over centuries and continents. In fact, the value of silver varied markedly over time and place. This truth can most simply be illustrated by observing the behaviour of gold:silver ratios. As long ago as 1967, Andrew Watson drew attention to the disparity of gold:silver ratios between the early medieval West and the Middle East.[42] Fourteenth- and fifteenth-century gold:silver rates in China stood as low as 1:5, rising to about 1:10 in the seventeenth century, when European rates were around 1:15.[43] Whether between neighbouring countries or trading continents, bullion flows wherever it is more highly prized. Even if the relative differences were not great, merchants were quick to recognize the advantage in buying abroad with whatever metal enjoyed a higher price. The resulting bimetallic bullion flows have often been noted within Europe, but they also characterize inter-continental trade. Most clearly, while early modern England (and to a lesser extent Europe as a whole) valued gold at around 12 to 15 times the value of silver, in China gold:silver ratios commonly stood at around 1:9 to 1:11, though Chinese–European gold:silver ratios tended to converge from the second half of the eighteenth century.[44] Fluctuating gold:silver ratios of this sort demonstrate clearly that the value of silver was not constant historically or geographically.[45]

Conversion to silver weight unnecessary

However, I confess it came as a surprise to me to realize that the results derived from converting nominal face-value prices and wages to silver weight, and those reached by directly comparing nominal price:wage ratios, are in fact identical. So long as both sides of the price:wage ratio are treated the same, we could as well multiply by any number as by the imagined weight of the silver currency; neither affects the *ratio*. This demonstrates the pointlessness of converting to silver weight; it fails to reflect the historical reality of practice at the time, and it promotes the fallacy that silver is or has ever been a constant measure. Yet it does not alter the fundamental ratio between wages (or preferably earnings) and the cost of living.

So beyond the problems of conversion to silver-weight equivalents, such conversions are not even necessary. In any case, the original data on prices and wages have first to be collected in nominal face-value prices. The cost of living can then be calculated relative to the wages of craftsmen or labourers, yielding a simple ratio, free of currency complications, which can still be compared internationally or over time. Converting the raw prices and wages to silver weight does not alter the ratio derived from nominal face-value prices and wages, but is an unnecessary additional calculation, which may introduce error.[46]

Primacy of the underlying data

What remains important for all international comparisons, however conducted, is that the underlying raw data and their interpretation are sound. Put bluntly, we must re-emphasize the history in economic history. Allen, for example, has made several caveats, recognizing that more research is needed in order to determine the appropriate allowance for housing costs within his estimate of the cost of living.[47] Phelps Brown and Hopkins also lamented the lack of data on rent, but additionally emphasized uncertainty about the number of days actually worked, which might vary because of holidays and still more because of the unavailability of work during 'hard times'.[48] Further concerns have been raised by Jane Humphries, who recently questioned some of Allen's calculations, challenging his concept of Britain as a high-wage economy.[49] In reply, Allen has accepted that he underestimated the family's calorific requirements, but stands by his central contention that English wages compare favourably with those elsewhere.[50] In short, far more work needs to concentrate on improving the basic price and earnings data, rather than unnecessarily, and misleadingly, converting it to silver weight.

Nominal price and wage data in Strasbourg and China

For example, even a cursory re-examination of the price and wage data from Strasbourg and China suggests there is room for improvement.

The Strasbourg series of prices and wages forms the reference point for Allen's pioneering paper, 'The great divergence in European wages and prices from the Middle Ages to the First World War' (2001).[51] Allen's Strasbourg wages are drawn from Hanauer's *Etudes économiques sur l'Alsace ancienne et moderne* (1878), but are in fact Alsatian wages, including much material from towns such as Mulhouse and Colmar, as well as Strasbourg itself.

Before 1600, the Hanauer series is composed mostly of Strasbourg wages, together with some from Haguenau (30 km south of Strasbourg) and Eschau (8 km south of Strasbourg), so in this early period this series does constitute a reasonable guide to Strasbourg wages. However, in the seventeenth century the series is dominated by wages from Mulhouse (117 km from Strasbourg) and Colmar (79.5 km from Strasbourg). Such explicitly Strasbourg prices which are noted are consistently higher than the averages presented by Allen.

Thus, Hanauer records a Strasbourg wage of 10.5 grams of silver for 1631. This is included in Allen's average of around 6 grams, but Allen's figure is actually driven mostly by Colmar and Mulhouse wages. From 1633 to 1694, a single average figure of 6.1 grams is suggested, but the rare Strasbourg wages recorded were 7.9 grams (1646), and 7.6 grams (1670). Eschau and Haguenau wages from close to Strasbourg were similarly higher than those from further south.[52] In the eighteenth century, genuine Strasbourg wages are even scarcer. From 1702 to 1764, the Mulhouse and Colmar averages stood at 4.32 grams, while the sole Strasbourg wage in this period recorded by Hanauer was for a worker's wage set by the town in 1753 at 12 *sous*, or 144 *deniers tournois*.[53] Subsequently, Mulhouse wages rise gently from 4.5 grams (1765–72), to 5.4 grams (1773–9), to 6.75 grams (1780–1800), but the Strasbourg-based average for 1801 to 1815 of 11.25 grams confirms the impression that wages in Strasbourg stood significantly above those from southern Alsace. In a nutshell, the seventeenth- and eighteenth-century Alsatian wage series is not a reliable guide to Strasbourg wages.

Hanauer's data for Strasbourg prices, especially the price of grain, are much stronger, though he is at pains to point out, as Allen also confirms, that the price of bread is what really matters for the urban cost of living.[54] Nevertheless, bread prices are far from straightforward. Obviously, the price of wheaten bread differed from that of rye bread, but wheat loaves cost nearly twice as much in Strasbourg as in Colmar, because the quality of wheat flour also varied greatly between wholemeal and the finest bolted flour. Local custom and regulation varied enormously from place to place and over time. The yield of flour from the grain might also vary according to whether the grain was milled dry or wet. Regulations and taxes varied from place to place and over time, while bakers selling their own bread operated with different rules from those baking householders' own flour or dough (the *hussfürer* or *hussbrotbecher*.)[55] The complexity of the matter is such that it may be difficult to be sure of the comparability of bread tariffs from town to town. Grain prices, though standing at one remove from the retail price of bread, may actually be more comparable.

Comparing prices and wages between China and Britain is made all the more difficult since silver was not used in ordinary payments for goods or wages in China, which were actually acquitted in copper 'cash' (*wén*).[56] Moreover, the value of cash in terms of silver was also highly variable.[57] Fluctuations in the value of cash explain why conversion to silver weight might seem desirable, but they also show how unreliable silver as a yardstick must be. Allen and his co-authors calculate the wage rate in ounces (*tael*) of uncoined silver ingots (*sycee*),[58] yet conclude, 'The wage rate thus derived seems extraordinarily low', which they attribute to an unspecified additional wage in food.[59] This is no doubt an important factor, as is confirmed by O'Brien and Deng, and by Kaixiang Peng,[60] though one also wonders about the accuracy of the cash–silver conversion, which was highly variable over time and from place to place.

The variable relationship between uncoined silver, in which government operated, and the copper cash, which served the daily needs of the common people, must raise doubts about international comparisons based on silver. Peng Xinwei and Von Glahn offer tables presenting cash–silver equivalents which demonstrate this variability, rather than providing a usable exchange rate for conversions.[61]

Qing government attempted to fix the silver–copper ratio at 1 ounce (tael) of silver to 1000 cash, but market prices were more variable, with light and heavy cash in circulation together, with different purchasing power; heavy coins were often melted and turned into privately issued lighter cash. Thus, in 1702 heavy cash of restored weight were rated at 1000 to the ounce of silver, but new light cash were also officially issued at 1000 to 0.7ounce silver, to try to meet the need served by privately issued cash. Nevertheless, heavy cash continued to rise in price, buying an ounce of silver for well below 1000 cash. By 1722, an ounce of silver exchanged at 780 'capital large coins', though different rates applied to small coins or privately issued imitations. The attempt to fix the price of an ounce of silver at 1000 cash was renewed in an edict of 1730, but in 1732 capital large standard coins were still at 800 per ounce silver.

Despite the government's wish to stabilize the exchange price of an ounce of silver at 1000 cash, the market price was generally significantly lower. Huang Ang's contemporary account of 1752 noted: 'After 1740–41, the use of silver declined and the circulation of coin increased, to the point where today coin is employed almost exclusively. Even in transactions of ten or a hundred taels coin is used rather than silver. … Previously the silver:coin exchange ratio was 1 ounce to 840 cash (at the beginning of the dynasty it had been 1:900). Later it declined to 1:800, and now it has fallen to 1:700. Coin is much more abundant than before. Yet in the past when coin was scarce its value was stable, but now the value of coin has risen sharply even though there is an abundant supply.'[62]

However, the nineteenth century brought a turning point in the silver and copper cash exchange rate. Earlier copper cash had been expensive, and silver relatively cheap. Thereafter, silver became expensive and coins cheap. Private minting of small coins and an influx of light foreign coins increased the supply of cash, while silver became more expensive as it had started flowing abroad. In the eighteenth century, an ounce of silver had exchanged for 700 to 800 cash, rising during the Jiaqing period [1796–1821] to over 1000 cash. By the middle of the nineteenth century, the price was rising to 2000 cash.[63] Peng X. argues that the opium trade reduced the quantity of silver sent to China after the end of the eighteenth century, and in the nineteenth century, English merchants began to export silver from China.[64]

However, Irigoin introduces a further element into the story, distinguishing between the silver ingots and the Spanish-American silver coins imported into China. The variable and uncertified weight and fineness of ingots made coined silver particularly attractive.[65] The absence of an officially issued Chinese silver coin before 1899 allowed foreign merchants to exchange dollars, especially the old Carolus dollar, in China for ingots (*sycee*) at a profit. In short, while the quality, weight, and availability of the copper coinage varied, so too did that of uncoined silver.[66]

Pitfalls in the path of the historian of Chinese prices and wages thus include the fluctuating international and Chinese values of silver bullion, silver coin, and copper, and the widespread circulation of both heavy and light official cash and of privately issued light-weight cash. The manufacture of silver ingots was also decentralized.[67] Regional variations in a country the size of China were obviously highly significant, both between north and south and between town and country.[68]

As if these difficulties were not formidable enough, information on wages, and especially actual earnings, is hard to find.[69] Comparison between England and China in silver weight thus involves converting English prices and wages to silver weights which did not reflect reality, and converting Chinese cash prices and scanty wage data to uncoined silver weight according to formulae founded on patchy, and sometimes contradictory, surviving evidence.

Given such reservations about the quality of the international data with which the English evidence is to be compared, it seems we should focus effort on a fuller appreciation of the detailed prices and wage data as recorded originally in nominal face-value terms. Silver conversion is an unnecessary diversion, since the *ratio* between prices and wages is unaltered by conversion to silver weight.

Monetary policy

Moreover, conversion of the original data to silver-weight equivalent also obscures the role of national monetary policies, and the fact that currencies can hold different values domestically and internationally. And there are in fact other ways to make international price-wage comparisons. Broadberry chooses to approach living standards by comparing estimated GDP per capita. This method does not engage with actual wages at all, but it has the merit of using nominal prices in local currencies adjusted for purchasing power parity.[70] Purchasing power parity (PPP) is a concept which recognizes that currencies enjoy a different value domestically in terms of goods and services from that indicated by foreign exchange rates. Since labour was not internationally tradable, the analysis of wages needs to focus on the domestic value of currency. PPP focuses on domestic price and wage structures, rather than foreign exchange rates, just as prices and wages expressed in domestic face-value money of account are a better guide than converted silver weight prices.

Nevertheless, the fact of price divergence from place to place is not to be disputed. Price differentials and divergence between more and less prosperous regions are normal and recur throughout history. Then, as now, price differentials are the fundamental basis of trade, moving goods from regions readily supplied to those of greater demand. The cheaper grain from Poland commanded a higher price if shipped to the Low Countries; livestock farmed in Scotland and the north of England was sent to supply demand from southern towns and agricultural regions growing grain. In this way, a region's natural advantages promoted local production and dietary habits of a particular character, and coloured trading patterns with its neighbours. Trading relations across continents performed in the same way, as Spanish-American silver was shipped to Europe and to Asian suppliers of textiles, dye stuffs, tea, and spices.[71] Nor is it disputed that international trade made some regions more prosperous than others. A healthy, long-term balance of payments founded chiefly on wool and cloth allowed England to establish a strong currency of high intrinsic content, which is well attested from the early Middle Ages until modern times.[72] The importance of divergence lies above all in the rise and fall of regions' prosperity and the measures taken to achieve or retain advantage.

Strong currencies are the hallmark of prosperous trading nations, which typically enjoyed a higher standard and cost of living necessarily accompanied by higher wages. Germany or Japan supply similar contemporary examples of the same phenomenon, though it may be noted that the recent strength of the mark and yen was built on much weaker post-war exchange rates which facilitated reconstruction. While prosperous trading nations were characterized by hard or strong currencies, less fortunate regions tended to devalue, that is to say in a historical context, to debase. Debasement and devaluation could of course generate ruinous inflation, destroying any confidence in the currency, but a well-judged devaluation could promote exports, stimulate the economy as a whole, and provide a much-needed boost to the domestic money stock. Conversely, the attempt to maintain a currency which was too strong could restrain nominal prices but also deny the domestic economy an adequate circulating means of exchange, depressing economic activity. In short, establishing the appropriate strength for the currency had important implications for the performance of the economy as a whole. While these truisms appear trite and commonplace for economists and modern economic historians, it needs to be fully appreciated that the same mechanisms were at work in an age of bullion-backed currencies. Though foreign exchange values depended on the balance of payments and the intrinsic content of currencies, the domestic economy – including the internal price and wage structure – was determined by the national government's valuation of its own currency. Yet considerations of this sort are completely masked by the conversion of prices and wages to silver weight.

Preoccupation with intrinsic content is an obstacle to a proper understanding of how currency operates. It obscures the essential continuity between currencies composed of, or backed by, precious metal and modern currencies without such backing. Silver weight conversions are essentially 'a barbarous relic'.

Additional note

The useful databases made available by the University of California, Davis,[73] take their evidence for the silver content of the English currency from Jastram's *Silver: The Restless Metal,* when Challis' *New History of the Royal Mint* would have provided a sounder guide.[74] Consequently, Clark's calculated silver weights for the English currency during the sixteenth-century debasement period completely miss the significance of the Great Debasement.[75]

Such mishaps can only become more likely with every additional calculation which distances the data from its evidential base. Even where the calculations are sound, they may obscure as much as they reveal. For example, concentrating on silver weight prioritizes the currency adjustment of 1351, when the big story here is the seismic shift in population and the supply of and demand for labour. In the same way, the falling silver weight of wages resulting from currency adjustments in 1412, 1464, and 1526 mask the fact that the value of that silver had risen.

Notes

1 I owe this insight to Christine Desan (2014).

2 The sixteenth-century English author of *A Discourse of the commonweal of this realm of England* speaks of coin 'since it is stricken with the King's seal to be current', asking

rhetorically, 'what makes it the matter what metal it be of, yea, though it were but leather or paper?' The author has been variously identified as Thomas Smith, William Strafford, or John Hales. Cf. Dewar (1969; xviii–xxvi), arguing convincingly for Sir Thomas Smith as the author. I owe this quotation to Kevin Clancy.

3 For recent examples of conversions to silver weight, see, for example, Robert C. Allen (2001 and 2015, esp. p. 9–10), and Rogoff, Froot, and Kim (2001). [Note of the editors: conversion of shekels into grams of silver was practised in Van der Spek *et al.* (2015), but with the simple rule that the shekel represented 8.33 grams of silver at all times. Before Alexander the Great, when silver bullion was the norm, debasements in weight could not occur (and in content hardly, as the state did not issue bullion as money). After Alexander the Great, coined silver became the norm, and the rule was fixed that the shekel, still mentioned in the cuneiform documents, represented two drachmas; thus, payments by tale, rather than by weight became the rule. So after that time, the shekel did in fact not represent exactly 8.33 grams anymore. Cf. Chapter 6, this volume].

4 The conversion of currencies to their silver weight equivalent can usefully measure the extent of debasements, though it is important to recognize that silver is not itself a measure of unchanging value. In periods of heavy debasement, contemporaries and historians do need to measure the degree of mutation. The French debasements of the fourteenth and fifteenth centuries gave rise to the *pied de monnaie*, which indicated the intrinsic content of each issue, but such arrangements were not required unless money lost touch with the open-market price of bullion. Harry Miskimin (1996), an authority on French mutations, makes the case for silver weight calculations, while I put an alternative view in Mayhew (1996).

5 It may be noted that the term 'nominal price' has sometimes been used to include silver equivalent conversions. In this paper, I distinguish between nominal prices and silver conversions based on them. For the avoidance of doubt, I generally refer to nominal or face value or money of account prices and wages.

6 This is one of a number of problems besetting general equilibrium theory in which a 'numeraire good' allows the market prices of all goods to be expressed relative to one good, which might be silver, gold, wheat, etc. Determining the fluctuating market price of the numeraire good may be highly problematic.

7 Sargent and Velde (2002: 17, 24 [citing Adam Smith in support] and 37).

8 However, it may be that such legal opinion merely railed against governments' continuing assertion of their right to set the content and value of their money.

9 On stycas, 'the first substantial base-metal coinage in the post-Roman West', see, for example, Naismith (2012: 247). On weight variations, see Petersson (1969), though the interpretation of these variations remains a matter of debate.

10 Johnson (ed.) (1950: xxxviii–xli). Johnson's introduction describes the various methods of payment and receipt employed at the Exchequer, and he concludes from the Domesday Book that payments were normally made by tale, with exceptions only on royal manors. Payment by weight was not very common, and payments in assayed coin were very rare. However, a reorganization c. 1129–30 may have introduced blanch payment for the farms of the counties.

11 King John issued coin weights to allow the people to verify the weight of circulating coin in order to combat clipping and justify the recoinage of worn coin Mayhew (1992: 97–8). On coin weights generally, see Biggs (1990).

12 In 1421, Henry V's government made weights and scales available at a price, to enable the weight of gold coins, afflicted by an epidemic of clipping, to be checked. See Martin Allen (2012: 151–2 and 285–6).

13 Perhaps the earliest explicit statement of an obligation to accept the king's coin is to be found in Edgar's tenth-century law code, II/III Edgar, Chapter 8, Liebermann (ed.) (1903: 204); transl. Whitelock (ed.) 1979: 433): 'One coinage should be current throughout the king's dominion, and no man is to reject it.' See Naismith (2014: 56). See also

Davis (2015: 145), temp. Edward I and Henry VII. Also, Mayhew (1999: 49–50) for the royal enforcement of its currency values during and after the Tudor debasements.

14 Desan (2014).

15 As early as the twelfth century, John of Salisbury argued that even the intrinsic value of money depended on the nominal value conferred by public opinion; cf. James Davis (2015: 147).

16 Gemmill and Mayhew (1995, chapter 4). It might of course be argued that the prosecution of those refusing the king's money merely proves that some were refusing it. It may also be that sellers inflated prices if they were paid in debased money.

17 Desan 2014: 86–9. See also the medieval treatise on the common law of England *Fleta* (Richardson and Sayles 1953: 206) and Plucknett (1956). Law Year Books for 1310 and 1321 confirm the distinction between things, like money, which are numbered, as distinct from other commodities which are weighed or measured.

18 See also Fox (2011).

19 Desan (2014: 87). The pound of 240 pennies had long parted company with the pound weight.

20 In 1504, for example, Parliament explicitly confirmed the legitimacy of all silver pennies with the king's stamp. Throughout the middle ages, clipped money could exceptionally be legally refused, though in practice much passed unchallenged. Governments attempted to enforce a distinction between worn coin, which they needed to remain in circulation by tale until they chose to recall it for a recoinage, and clipped coin, which could be rejected on sight.

21 In this paper, the term 'debasement' is used to refer to any downward alteration in the intrinsic content of coin, whether achieved by reduced weight, reduced fineness of metal, or both. The weight of English coin was significantly reduced in 1351, 1412, 1464, and 1526, but these reductions reflected the rising international price of precious metals and did not result in rising prices. By contrast, the debasements of 1542–51 imposed highly inflated face values on coins of increasingly reduced intrinsic content.

22 The debasements of fourteenth- and fifteenth-century France were intended to generate royal profits to finance war, and they sharply reduced the intrinsic content of the currency. There is an important distinction to be made between monetary changes which merely followed the international bullion price and those which very severely overvalued the silver content in the currency. The French *mutations* provoked the indignant complaints of Nicolas Oresme, *De Moneta* (c. 1355; cf. Johnson 1956).

23 Cipolla (1982: 32–3).

24 In Scotland and on the continent foreign coins were given a face value in terms of the local currency at which their circulation was permitted. Such tolerance was only exceptionally offered to foreign coin in England, though the mutual toleration of groats and double patards in England and the Burgundian Netherlands in the second half of the fifteenth century provides an interesting example.

25 Feavearyear (1963: 121): 'Nothing could have shown more clearly that the value of the unit of account did not depend primarily upon the quantity of silver in the coins.'

26 In 1625–6, Sir Robert Cotton persuaded the Privy Council to abort a plan for recoinage just as it began to be implemented. See W.A. Shaw (1896). For a contemporary discussion of the Irish debasement of 1603, which did take place, see 'Sir Roger Wilbraham's diary' (ed. H.S. Scott 1902). I am most grateful to Simon Healy for these references. It is interesting that Charles I did not debase in order to escape from his financial and political difficulties. Ireland, however, was a different matter: see above, at n. 18.

27 Mayhew (2012) shows how silver in England was shared between the Mint, the goldsmiths, and the East India Company. If the Mint failed to match the price for silver offered elsewhere in London, it came to strike only gold and copper.

28 The rising international price of silver meant that coins representing a given face value could contain less silver. The high silver content of the English currency was effectively undervaluing silver.

29 Clancy (1999: 23) estimates than some 84% of the eighteenth-century silver circulation was struck before 1700. Much of what follows is drawn from Clancy's unpublished doctoral thesis. However, very similar conclusions were drawn independently by Gary Oddie (2001).
30 Clancy (1999: 3, citing Challis 1992: 380–2); Feavearyear (1963: 129–31).
31 Clancy (1999: 19).
32 Clancy (1999: 231–2, table 2). A similar table was independently compiled by Oddie (2001).
33 Clancy (1999: 145).
34 However, gold was treated differently. Worn gold was recoined in the 1770s, and gold coins were liable to be weighed; balances for this purpose survive from the period.
35 Clancy (1999: 12–13). Coin hoards show that silver was often worn so smooth that coins could no longer be read. Clancy (1999: 210).
36 Clancy (1999: 35–6).
37 Challis (1992: 435): 'It was said in 1754, for example, that poor people were paid almost wholly in copper.'
38 Clancy (1999: 33–4).
39 Kelly (1976).
40 From 1817, Britain formally established a gold standard, leaving the silver as a token coinage of restricted currency for sums up to two guineas. The weight of the silver was reduced to allow 66s to be struck from the pound weight, though the Mint no longer struck in response to the demands of silver bullion holders, but only when the government judged the striking of new silver desirable. See Challis (1992: 481, 484).
41 We cannot even be certain that the poor weight of the silver currency affected prices and wages equally. Social as well as economic factors may have allowed the more powerful party to any transaction to secure a better deal.
42 Watson (1967: 21–31).
43 Peng (1993: 764–8); Flynn and Giraldez (2002). In the sixteenth century the price of silver in terms of gold in China was twice the price in Spain.
44 Flynn and Giraldez (2002: 395) cite Newton's 1717 opinion that 'in China … the ratio is 9 or 10 to 1 and in India 12 to 1, and this carries away silver from all Europe' Peng (1993). Von Glahn (2003: 200) also notes convergence of gold:silver ratios between China and Europe in the 1640s, but confirms the later seventeenth century divergence and then renewed convergence in the later eighteenth century.
45 See also, Najaf Haider (1996: 349–55) for fluctuating gold:silver:copper ratios in India.
46 Appendix 1 details mistakes arising from converting to silver weight at the time of the sixteenth-century English debasements.
47 Allen (2001: 422, 426) set housing costs at 5% of labourer and craftsman expenditure, citing Horrell 1996. However, it may be noted that Horrell's figures range from 5.8% to 10.5%, being notably higher in the nineteenth century and varying from one group of workers to another. Allen allows more spent on candles and lamp oil than on housing costs, which seems odd. Elizabeth Gilboy (1936: 135–6) suggests that 15% of the average labourer's expenditure was devoted to rent and fuel, citing studies by Eden and by Davies. Arthur Young found that rent tended to equal about one-sixth of the labourer's annual wage (Gilboy 1936: 139). Dorothy George (1951: 90–6) provides evidence suggesting rents consuming as much as 12.5% of income, while noting that her source might have been keen to demonstrate the inadequacy of wages. In any case, the assumption of a constant proportion of expenditure devoted to housing costs across the world may also require re-examination.
48 Phelps Brown and Hopkins (1956: 179).
49 Humphries (2013).
50 Robert C. Allen (2015). Allen continues to convert English and French price and wage data to silver weight. For the latest contribution to this debate now see also, Jane Humphries and Jacob Weisdorf (2015), who wisely use nominal wages and costs.

51 Allen, R.C. (2001). The values of all the compared cities are presented in terms of their ratio to the Strasbourg values.

52 Eschau (1672 and 1681: 8.8); Hagenau (1694: 7.8). Hanauer presents his prices both in the original local money of account and in its equivalent in mid-nineteenth-century francs. I have converted these franc wages to their silver weight equivalent (at 22 centimes per gram, after Hanauer 1876: 9), for ease of comparison with Allen's wages given in silver weight.

53 Hanauer (1878: 416) converts this 12 sous to 2.40 francs, implying a silver weight of 10.9 grams. This is in any case a labourer's rather than a craftsman's wage, though the regulations for summer and winter work, with or without food and wine, with additional special payments for those not taking half-hour breaks for lunch and tea, are of some interest.

54 Hanauer (1878: 92–103) for the price of grains, p. 106 for the importance of bread prices,

55 See Hanauer (1878: 104–62).

56 Chinese cash (*wén*) are variously described as copper cash (Peng) or bronze cash (Von Glahn). Chinese cash are known from different periods in both brass (copper-zinc) and bronze (copper-tin), so 'copper alloy' describes them best; see Cowell and Wang (1998) and Cowell, Cribb, Bowman, and Shashoua (1993).

57 Allen, R.C., Bassino, Ma, Moll-Murata, and Van Zanden (2011). Deng and O'Brien (2015). Alejandra Irigoin (2013) illustrates the variable fineness of silver coin and bullion in China. Also, Kuroda Akinobu (2013) for the variability of ingots.

58 Peng X. (1994, volume 1; xl) defines the Qing Treasury ounce (*tael*) as 37 grams. For refined ingots see Cribb 1992.

59 Allen, R.C. *et al.* (2011: 35). The authors recognize the limitations of their calculated wage rate, using only the resultant trend, not the wage level.

60 Deng and O'Brien (2015) point out that money wages were still exceptional in China, and those we do know of would probably have been supplemented by payments in kind; they were certainly insufficient to support a worker and his family. Uncertainties remain about the numbers of days worked per year, and about the role of supplementary income earned by other family members. Deng and O'Brien conclude, 'almost all the data ... remains sparse, insecure and difficult to interpret'. Peng Kaixiang's impressive recent study (Peng 2015) fully illustrates the complexity of the situation, for example, distinguishing three separate elements in wages – labour costs, food costs, and a commission.

61 For the following passage on silver-copper cash values, see Peng X. (1994: 732–3; 736 fn. and table 1; 739–40, including table 2; and 759). Although Peng offers tables indicating the price of silver in standard cash, together with tables indicating the price of rice in both cash and uncoined silver, he warns frankly: 'Naturally changes in the silver-cash coin exchange price influenced prices in general, but the nature of that influence depended on what money was used to express a price or what money was used to pay for something' (Peng X. 1994: 740–1). Again, according to Peng X. (1994: 744), 'prices varied according to the type of coins people offered in exchange'. Von Glahn also offers a table of highly variable silver/cash exchange rates, together with rice prices in silver and in cash from 1600 to 1800, indexed on 1691–1700 (Von Glahn 2003: 191, table 9.1).

62 Quoted by Von Glahn (2003: 193), who also notes that the use of cash rather than uncoined silver became standard in the grain trade by the 1740s and dominant in wage contracts in the 1760s. Von Glahn found that cash also became normal in sales of arable land spreading from Shandong in the 1760s to the Yangzi Delta in the 1770s, and to Beijing in the 1790s. Peng Xinwei's Table (Peng X. 1994: 736) also illustrates regional variations.

63 Peng X. (1994: 740).

64 For prices and wages in the Beijing area in the nineteenth century, see most recently Peng Kaixiang (2015). He successfully constructs an exchange ratio between Jing Cash money of account and silver tael, which appears to have been reasonably constant in

the first half of the century until this stability was shattered by the Taiping Rebellion. Thereafter, Jing Cash-silver ratios fluctuated between 10,000 and 15,000 before rising in the first two decades of the twentieth century towards 20,000 and 30,000 in the 1920s. This pattern is broadly reflected in Peng Kaixiang's consolidated price and wage indices, though his real wage index reveals a good deal of variation.

65 Sycee tested in the British Museum ranged from 99.6% to 93.2% silver, while their weight and size varied from 2098 grams to 26 grams; see Cribb 1992: 316. The fineness of dollars (*pesos*) also varied somewhat between different issues, but such changes were controlled, allowing users to distinguish between issues on sight. Distinguishing the fineness of ingots (*sycee*) required testing by shroffs, or pawnbrokers, since although ingots were stamped with makers' marks there was no government control of their manufacture.

66 Irigoin (2013) also suggests that it was the scarcity of Carolus dollars which led merchants to send opium to China in exchange for silver ingots (*sycee*).

67 Cribb (1992: 15): 'Both central and local government chose to pass the responsibility for making the ingots and setting the standards for their use to local bankers.'

68 For further detail on the complexity and variability of Chinese currency, see also John E. Sandrock (1995).

69 Peng X. (1994: 738) is clear that Qing wages were very low, though his evidence is fragmented. Allen, R.C. *et al.* (2011) rely on Gamble's series, which seems to be the best we have, though it is very hard to know how far it is representative of wages for other types of work, or other regions. However, see now Ma and Yuan (2014), who draw attention to an important new source, which holds out the prospect of a very significant addition to the available data on Chinese prices and silver:cash ratios. For the nineteenth-century, see Peng K. 2015.

70 Stephen Broadberry (2013). Comparisons are made on the basis of 1990 international dollars. Since these international dollars are based on purchasing power parity exchange rates, they have the merit of reflecting the domestic value of currencies rather than their foreign exchange rate. It should be noted, however, that working in 'international dollars' has its own problems.

71 Broadberry notes the special role of long-distance trade in developing divergence, citing Acemoglu, D., Johnson, S., and Robinson, J. (2005).

72 Indeed, the strength of sterling, and the high wages and cost of living which are associated with it, are a constant feature of English economic history before the twentieth century.

73 Arroyo Abad and Lindert (eds) (n.d.) at gpih.ucdavis.edu/Datafilelist.htm (accessed on 2014-02-10).

74 Jastram (1981: 164–88; C.E. Challis 1992). For a detailed tabulation of English mint prices, finenesses, and pence struck per pound, see Antony Hotson (2017: appendix, 189–208). For the London market's gold and silver prices including weekly quotations, see Hotson (2017: 64–87).

75 A table illustrating this discrepancy appears in Mayhew (2015: 434, Table A16.1).

References

Acemoglu, D., Johnson, S., and Robinson, J. (2005). 'The rise of Europe: Atlantic trade, institutional change, and economic growth', *American Economic Review*, 95: 546–79.

Akinobu, K. (2013). 'Anonymous currencies or named debts, local credits and units of account', *Socio Economic Review*, 11: 57–80.

Allen, M. (2012). *Mints and Money in Medieval England*, Cambridge, UK: Cambridge University Press.

Allen, R.C. (2001). 'The Great Divergence in European wages and prices from the Middle Ages to the First World War', *Explorations in Economic History*, 38: 411–47.

Allen, R.C. (2015). 'The high wage economy and the industrial revolution: A restatement', *Economic History Review*, 68: 1–22.

Allen, R.C., Bassino, J.-P., Ma, D., Moll-Murata, Chr., and Van Zanden, J.L. (2011). 'Wages, prices, and living standards in China, 1738–1925: In comparison with Europe, Japan, and India', *Economic History Review*, 64, Series 1: 8–38.

Arroyo Abad, L. and Lindert, P.H. (eds.) (n.d.). *Global Price and Income History Group*. Institute of Governmental Affairs, UC Davis. http://gpih.ucdavis.edu/ (accessed 2017-07-12).

Biggs, N. (1990), 'Coin-weights in England – up to 1588', *British Numismatic Journal*, 60: 65–79.

Broadberry, S. (2013). 'Accounting for the Great Divergence', (26 January 2013). Circulated paper. https://pdfs.semanticscholar.org/2d9e/fa4bad2c3639561d13d009f2a733999a6736.pdf (accessed 2017-07-12).

Challis, C.E. (1992). *A New History of the Royal Mint*. Cambridge, UK: Cambridge University Press.

Cipolla, C.M. (1982). *The Monetary Policy of Fourteenth-Century Florence*. Berkeley, CA, Los Angeles, and London: University of California Press.

Clancy, K. (1999). *The recoinage and exchange of 1816–17*. University of Leeds PhD Thesis.

Cowell, M. and Wang, H. (1998). 'Metal Supply for the Metropolitan Coinage of the Kangxi Period (1662-1721)', *Numismatic Chronicle*, 158: 185-96.

Cowell, M.R., Cribb, J., Bowman, S.G.E., and Shashoua, Y. (1993). 'The Chinese cash: Composition and production', in Archibald, M.M. and Cowell, M.R. (eds.), *Metallurgy in Numismatics* 3, London: Royal Numismatic Society: 185–98.

Cribb, J. (1992). *A Catalogue of Sycee in the British Museum: Chinese Silver Currency Ingots*. London: British Museum.

Davis, J. (2015). 'The morality of money in late medieval England', in Allen, M. and Coffman, D. (eds.), *Money, Prices and Wages: Essays in Honour of Professor Nicholas Mayhew*, Basingstoke, UK: Palgrave-MacMillan: 143–57.

Deng, K. and O'Brien, P. (2015). 'Locating a chronology for the Great Divergence: A critical survey of published data deployed for the measurement of nominal wages for Ming and Qing China', *Economic History working paper series*, 213/2015. London: The London School of Economics and Political Science. http://eprints.lse.ac.uk/60798/ (accessed 2017-07-11).

Desan, C. (2014). *Making Money: Coin, Currency and the Coming of Capitalism*. Oxford: Oxford University Press.

Dewar, M. (ed.) (1969). *A discourse of the commonweal of this realm of England*. Charlottesville, VA: University of Virginia Press.

Feavearyear, A.E. (1963). *The Pound Sterling: A History of English Money*. Oxford: Clarendon Press.

Flynn, D.O. and Giraldez, A. (2002). 'Global economic unity through the mid-eighteenth century', *Journal of World History*, 13: 391–27.

Fox, D. (2011). 'The *Case of Mixt Monies*: Confirming nominalism in the common law of monetary obligations', *Cambridge Law Journal*, 70: 144–74.

Gemmill, E. and Mayhew, N. (1995). *Changing Values in Medieval Scotland*, Cambridge, UK: Cambridge University Press: 1995.

George, M.D. (1951). *London Life in the Eighteenth Century*, 3rd ed. London: London School of Economics and Political Science.

Gilboy, E.W. (1936). 'The cost of living and real wages in eighteenth century England', *The Review of Economics and Statistics*, 18/3: 134–42.

Haider, N. (1996). 'Precious metal flows and currency circulation in the Mughal Empire', *Journal of the Social and Economic History of the Orient*, 39: 298–64.

Hanauer, A. (1876). *Études économiques sur l'Alsace ancienne et moderne*, I. *Les monnaies*. Paris: A. Durand & Pédone-Lauriel; Strasbourg: Simon Librairie.

Hanauer, A. (1878). *Études économiques sur l'Alsace ancienne et moderne*, II. *Denrée et salaires*. Paris: A. Durand & Pédone-Lauriel; Strasbourg: Hagemann Librairie.

Horrell, S. (1996). 'Home demand and British industrialization', *Journal of Economic History*, 56: 561–604.

Hotson, A. (2017). *Respectable Banking: The Search for Stability in London's Money and Credit Markets since 1695*. Cambridge, UK: Cambridge University Press.

Humphries, J. (2013). 'The lure of aggregates and the pitfalls of the patriarchal perspective: A critique of the high wage economy interpretation of the British industrial revolution', *Economic History Review*, 66: 693–714.

Humphries, J. and Weisdorf, J. (2015). 'The wages of women in England, 1260–1850', *Journal of Economic History*, 75: 405–47.

Irigoin, A. (2013). 'A Trojan Horse in Daoguang China? Explaining the flows of silver in and out of China', LSE Working Paper No. 173/13. http://www.lse.ac.uk/economicHistory/workingPapers/2013/WP173.pdf (accessed 2017-07-11).

Jastram, R.W. (1981). *Silver: The Restless Metal*. New York: John Wiley.

Johnson, C. (ed.) (1950). *The Course of the Exchequer*. London: Thomas Nelson and Sons.

Johnson, C. (ed.) (1956). *The* De Moneta *of N. Oresme, and English Mint Documents*. London: Thomas Nelson and Sons.

Kelly, E.M. (1976). *Spanish Dollars and Silver Tokens. An Account of the Issues of the Bank of England 1797–1816*. London: Spink & Son.

Liebermann, F. (ed.) (1903). *Die Gesetze der Angelsachsen*. I. *Text und Übersetzung*. Halle, Germany: Max Niemeyer.

Ma, D. and Yuan W. (2014). 'Discovering economic history in footnotes: The story of Tŏng Tàishēng merchant archive (1790–1850) and the historiography of modern China', *Economic History Working*, Paper Series, 201/2014. The London School of Economics and Political Science, London, UK. http://eprints.lse.ac.uk/56332/ (accessed 2017-07-12).

Mayhew, N. (1992). 'From regional to central minting, 1158–1464', in Challis, C.E. (ed.), *A New History of the Royal Mint*, Cambridge, UK: Cambridge University Press: 83–178.

Mayhew, N. (1996). 'Sterling, not silver: A reply to Prof. Miskimin', *Economic History Review*, 49: 361.

Mayhew, N. (1999). *Sterling. The History of a Currency*. London: Penguin.

Mayhew, N. (2012). 'Silver in England 1600–1800: Coinage outputs and bullion exports from the records of the London Tower Mint and the London Company of Goldsmiths', in Munro, J.H. (ed.), *Money in the Pre-Industrial World: Bullion, Debasements and Coin Substitutes*, London: Pickering & Chatto: 97–110.

Mayhew, N. (2015). 'The circulation of money and the behaviour of prices in medieval and early modern England', in Van der Spek *et al.* (eds.) (2015): 412–41.

Miskimin, H. (1996). 'Silver, not sterling: a comment on Mayhew's velocity', *Economic History Review*, 49: 358–60.

Naismith, R. (2012). *Money and Power in Anglo-Saxon England*. Cambridge, UK: Cambridge University Press.

Naismith, R. (2014). 'Prelude to reform: Tenth-century English coinage in perspective', in Naismith, R., Allen, A., and Screen, E. (eds.), *Early Medieval Monetary History: Studies in Memory of Mark Blackburn*, Farnham, UK: Ashgate: 39–84.

Oddie, G. (2001). 'The circulation of silver 1697–1817', *Token Corresponding Society Bulletin*, 7: 5–36.

Peng K. (2015). 'Money supply and the price mechanism: The interaction of money, prices and wages in Beijing in the long nineteenth century', in Van der Spek, R.J. *et al.* (eds.) (2015): 442–69.

Peng X. (1994). *A Monetary History of China*, Shanghai: Qunlian Publishing: 1954, translated by E.H. Kaplan. 2 volumes. Bellingham, WA: Center for East Asian Studies, University of Western Washington.

Petersson, H.B.A. (1969). *Anglo-Saxon Currency*. Lund, Sweden: Gleerup.

Phelps Brown, E.H. and Hopkins, S.V. (1956). 'Seven centuries of the prices of consumables, compared with builders' wage-rates', *Economica* 1956: 296–314, reprinted in Carus-Wilson, E.M. (ed.), *Essays in Economic History*, II, London: Edward Arnold: 1962: 168–96

Plucknett, Th.F.Th. (1956). *A Concise History of the Common Law*. Indianapolis, IN: Liberty Fund.

Richardson, H.G. and Sayles, G.O. (1953). *Fleta*. Vol. 2. In Publications of the Selden Society, vol. 72. London: Bernard Quaritch.

Rogoff, K., Froot, K.A. and Kim, M. (2001). 'The law of one price over seven hundred years', IMF Working paper WP/01/174. https://www.imf.org/external/pubs/ft/wp/2001/wp01174.pdf (accessed 2017-07-10).

Sandrock, J.E. (1995). *Copper Cash and Silver Taels. The Money of Manchu China*. Baltimore, MD: Gateway Press.

Sargent, Th.J. and Velde, F.R. (2002). *The Big Problem of Small Change*. Princeton, NJ: Princeton University Press.

Scott, H.S. (1902). *The Journal of Sir Roger Wilbraham (1593–1616)*. Camden Miscellany X, Camden Society, 3rd series IV. London: Royal Historical Society.

Shaw, W.A. (1896). *Select Tracts and Documents Illustrative of English Monetary History, 1626–1730*. London: Wilsons & Milne; reprinted Ithaca, NY: Cornell University Library: 2009.

Van der Spek, R.J., Van Leeuwen, B., and Van Zanden, J.L. (eds.) (2015). *A History of Market Performance from Ancient Babylonia to the Modern World*, London and New York: Routledge.

Von Glahn, R. (2003). 'Money use in China and changing patterns of global trade in monetary metals, 1500–1800', in Flynn, D.O., Giraldez, A., and Von Glahn, R. (eds.), *Global Connections and Monetary History, 1470–1800*, Aldershot, UK: Ashgate: 187–205.

Watson, A.M. (1967). 'Back to gold – and silver', *Economic History Review*, 2nd ser., 20: 1–34.

Whitelock, D. (ed.) (1979). *English Historical Documents*. I. *c*. 550–1042. London: Eyre Methuen.

10 Incentives and interests

Monetary policy, public debt, and default in Holland, c. 1466–1489[1]

Jaco Zuijderduijn

Introduction

In 1504, a few government agents of Philips the Handsome (r. 1482–1506) reported on the finances of the town of Leiden, in the province of Holland. At the time, the town had already been in dire straits for many years, struggling with a towering public debt that the town had not managed to shrug off. Convinced that the town's finances should have improved by 1504, the government agents wrote a devastating report, in which they accused local magistrates of self-enrichment, and spoke of 'defunct government'.[2]

Leiden was not the only town in Holland experiencing severe financial problems, causing both contemporaries and historians to wonder how the situation could have gotten out of hand. Why did so many towns create debts they eventually failed to service?[3] To answer this centuries-old question, this chapter formulates the hypothesis that town magistrates decided to shape their public debt in such a way that it contained a speculative element. They used a financial construction that initially reduced the interest payments the towns were due in an artificial way. The town magistrates speculated on the continuing depreciation of coins: as long as the ruler continued to decrease the silver content of silver coins, as he did in the 1470s and 1480s,[4] the towns' interest payments decreased as well. This construction, which will be explained in detail in the following Section, allowed the towns to let their public debt rise to unprecedented levels.

Of course, this was bound to go wrong. The towns of Holland created substantial public debts over the 1470s and 1480s, but they faced an enormous problem when Maximilian of Habsburg (regent 1482–1493; regent 1506–1515) decided to increase the silver content of silver coins at the end of 1489. Now the towns all of a sudden faced far larger interest payments, causing them to renege on their obligations.[5] In 1492, Maximilian was forced to allow the town of Haarlem a moratorium, protecting them from claims.[6] Since this town could no longer pay interest on its public debt, the town government feared angered creditors would seek compensation with citizens of Haarlem – something creditors were legally entitled to do. Shortly after, Dordrecht, Leiden,

Amsterdam, and Gouda also received moratoriums – apparently Delft was the only of Holland's large towns that could do without.

Elsewhere in the Low Countries, towns such as Antwerp, Bois-le-Duc, and Lier struggled with similar problems.[7] Historians have therefore linked the towns' financial problems to the rulers Charles the Bold (r. 1467–1477) and Maximilian and their increasing demand for funds. To meet such demands, towns had to turn to financial markets, where they contracted long-term loans, usually at very reasonable interest rates ranging from c. 5–10%. In this way, the rulers' demand for funding contributed to the towering public debts the towns of Holland struggled with.[8] Usually the towns borrowed individually, but in 1482–1483 several of them had also teamed up to borrow an enormous amount of money. In this case, several towns shared the obligation for timely interest payments; as soon as one of them reneged, all were in trouble.[9] Such problems became even more likely due to war, partisan strife, and a slumping economy that caused urban revenues to decrease during the final decades of the fifteenth century.

The idea that towns constructed their public debt in such a way as to profit from the depreciation of silver coins contributes to the historiography in several ways. First, it links up with literature on the reorganization of public finance in Holland in the sixteenth century, described by James Tracy as a financial revolution. In this process, the organization of public debt moved from individual towns to the Estates of Holland, the representative body that quickly gained importance and became Holland's governing body during the Dutch Revolt (1572–1648). According to Tracy, this centralization of public debt paved the way for the public finance of the Dutch Republic.[10] Elsewhere, we have argued that this centralization must be regarded as a reaction to the financial problems of the 1480s and 1490s.[11] The idea that towering public debt and the increase of the silver content of silver coins in 1489 contributed to the collapse of town finances is well known. The idea that this towering public debt was the result of speculation is new, however, and may help explain why towns continued to increase their public debt – even 'to an absurd extent', to speak with the historian Jan Marsilje.[12] Surely the town magistrates involved – coming from the ranks of merchants and entrepreneurs – were clever enough to come up with a shrewd technique to keep interest payments low in the short term. However, it seems they lost sight of the long term, and especially of the possibility for the ruler to change his policy of continuing coin depreciation, and the risks this posed to urban finances.[13]

Second, the hypothesis we put forward in this chapter can help explain the disastrous depreciation of silver coins in the 1470s and 1480s. In this respect, the historian Wim Blockmans pointed out that the mighty towns of Flanders did not appear to have opposed this development: during meetings of the Estates of Flanders, coin depreciation was hardly ever discussed. Blockmans concluded:

> The towns reacted quite indifferently to the ruler's autocratic and opportunistic behaviour, perhaps out of respect for his seignorage, and surely also because there were few ways to check coin circulation.[14]

It is indeed puzzling to see that the towns, commercial centres dependent on a solid monetary system, apparently did not react to coin depreciation. Opposition came not from townsmen, but from nobles and ecclesiastics: the historian Peter Spufford noticed these groups protested against rulers' monetary policies because they were often dependent on income from rents and annuities. Due to coin depreciation, they faced a reduction in their incomes. According to the chronicler Jean Molinet (1433?–1507), the abbot and knight of the order of the *Toison d'or*, Jean of Lannoy (1410–1493), was a major spokesman for *qui avoyent rentes*.[15]

This chapter tests the hypothesis that town magistrates constructed public debt in such a way that it consisted a speculative element. They expressed debts in silver coins, and thus profited from the ruler's depreciation policy: in this way, they managed to keep urban public debt manageable. They did not do the obvious thing: to express debts in the far more stable gold coins, which was a much-used method to safeguard transactions from losses due to depreciation.[16] I focus on developments in Holland, where public debt caused a severe financial crisis, which also must be connected to the aforementioned sixteenth-century developments in the field of public finance. However, the speculative mechanism we present in this chapter may also be instructive for other areas: many medieval rulers used coin depreciation as a source of income,[17] and the creation of public debt by selling annuities in financial markets was also very common in large parts of the Northwest of Europe.[18]

This chapter starts with a short introduction to monetary policy in the fifteenth century. Next, in the third section, we explain how towns, under specific circumstances, could reduce interest payments by expressing debts in silver coin. A fourth section presents evidence for speculation: towns do not appear to have opposed the ruler's policy of coin depreciation. Furthermore, towns appear to have switched from expressing debts in gold coin to silver coin in the 1470s, so right when coin depreciation gained momentum. Due to this switch, urban public debt was no longer protected against fluctuations of the exchange rate between gold and silver coins, but rather exposed to this. We end with the conclusion.

An introduction to monetary policy in the fifteenth century

In the late middle ages, coinage was an important source of income for rulers: rulers levied a tax over coinage (in Holland this tax was called *sleischat*), they could temporarily alienate coinage[19], and they could profit from coin manipulation.

For the counts of Holland, taxation of coinage was an important source of income dating back to the fourteenth century.[20] However, for them to tax coinage, the counts had to make sure coins were produced in the mint. They therefore tried to ensure a steady supply of precious metals going to the mint, but since other rulers tried to achieve the same thing, competition for precious metals was fierce, especially between the dukes of Burgundy (who were counts of Holland since 1433) and the kings of England. The arena was mainly the important wool staple of Calais: since the fourteenth century, the dukes came with regulations aimed at preventing precious metals flowing to England via Calais. The English king, Edward IV (r. 1461–1483), in his turn tried to foster this flow of precious metals, as he could use these to finance the Wars of the Roses (1455–1485) and to protect the wool staple of Calais. Edward ordered that in Calais, buyers of English wool had to pay at least half of the purchase price in good English coin or precious metals – and not use financial instruments such as bills of exchange. His goal was to make sure at least half of the levies on imports could be received in precious metals, which would go to the royal mint of Calais for re-melting – allowing Edward to profit.[21]

Edward's monetary policy would go at the expense of Duke Philip the Good of Burgundy (r. 1433–1467): 'good coin' and precious metals would flow to the mint of Calais, ultimately contributing to Edward's revenues, while 'bad coin' with a low alloy would circulate in Philip's territories. Philip therefore reacted with a ban on imports of English cloth.[22] English cloth traders were forced to leave the important trading towns of Antwerp and Bergen-op-Zoom and relocate to Utrecht, which was not yet under Burgundian rule. Only after Philip's death in 1467 did this situation end: Charles the Bold (r. 1467–1477) improved the ties with Edward and the latter abandoned his monetary policy in 1473, ending the period of 'bullionism' in Anglo-Burgundian relations.[23]

In spite of this 'bullionism', Philip's reign was characterized by monetary stability as the duke abstained from coin manipulation. Perhaps this was in part due to the influence on monetary affairs the towns of Holland had acquired since the mid-fourteenth century.[24] Since Philip had succeeded Countess Jacqueline of Bavaria in 1433, Holland experienced a period of coin stability,[25] which ended under his successor Charles the Bold: he ordered his mint masters to gradually decrease the alloy of silver coins. This monetary policy was continued by Maximilian of Habsburg, who used coin manipulation to finance rising military expenses due to war with France, the revolt of the Flemish towns (1482–1485), and other revolts in the Low Countries (1488–1492).[26]

Mint manipulation affected the alloy of the Flemish groat, the most important silver coin of the Low Countries, whose silver content was gradually decreased between 1466 and 1489 (Figure 10.1). This only came to an end in 1489, when the silver content of the Flemish groat was brought back to its 1466 level. Of course, the gradual decline of the silver content before did not go unnoticed: merchants and money changers were quick to find out. As a result, the dukes of Burgundy had to adjust exchange rates between weakened silver coins and stable gold coins: the exchange rates of gold coins mounted, especially in the 1480s.

Reducing debt by specifying interest payments to be in silver coin

In the late Middle Ages, the towns of Holland created public debt through annuity sales: these financial instruments allowed them to attract large sums

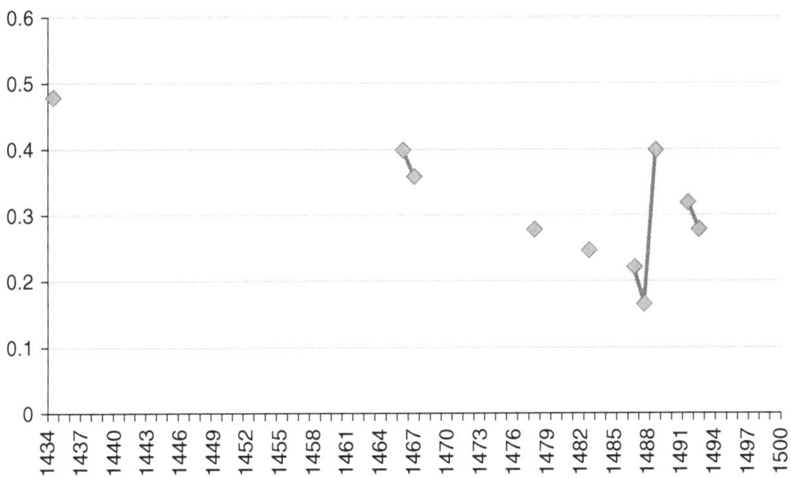

Figure 10.1 Silver content of Flemish groat 1434–1494.

Source: Van Gelder and Hoc 1960: 14, 20, 27, 38, 44, 49, 53, 54.

of money. The towns sold life annuities (*lijfrenten*) to the purchaser, who paid a principal to receive an annuity for the rest of his or her life. The annuity usually was c. 10% of the principal. A second financial instrument the towns sold, redeemable annuities (*losrenten*), were hereditary: annuities were paid to the purchaser, or his or her heirs, until the town redeemed the principal. The annuity usually was 6.25% of the principal.[27]

Life annuities and redeemable annuities could be expressed in gold or silver coin. Gold coin offered the advantage of hardly ever being tampered with,[28] which is why many creditors and debtors decided to express transactions involving postponed payment in gold coin.[29] Stable gold coin thus helped participants in exchange to reduce the 'fundamental problem of exchange'.[30] However, during the period of coin debasement in the 1470s and 1480s, the towns of Holland decided to express their annuities in unstable silver coin. In doing so, they used moneys of account (*rekenmunten*): fictitious currencies used for accounting purposes, and to make dealing with silver coins less elaborate. Moneys of account were used within financial administrations and did not exist as real currencies.[31]

There were two types of moneys of account: the first was a currency based on the Carolingian division 1 pound = 20 shillings = 240 pennies. Multiples of the *basismunt*, such as the *Vlaamse groot* (Flemish groat), were expressed in shillings and pounds. Thus, 12 *Vlaamse groten* were one shilling, 240 *Vlaamse groten* one pound. The second type was based on an existing coin. For our period, the *Rijnse gulden* (Rhenish guilder) of 20 *stuivers* (stivers) provides a good example: this money of account also existed as a real coin.[32] Initially, the money of account *Rijnse gulden* and real coin *Rijnse gulden* had the same value

(20 *stuivers*), but this changed due to depreciation of the silver coin. As a result, in 1489 there was a money of account *Rijnse gulden* of 20 *stuivers* and a real coin worth 45 *stuivers* of Utrecht.[33]

The annuities the towns of Holland sold in the second half of the fifteenth century were usually expressed in *ponden Vlaamse groten*, a money of account that connected the annuities to the silver Flemish groat. However, when these annuities were purchased or paid out by the towns, gold coins were used: annuities and annuity payments involved large sums that could not be paid out in hundreds of silver coins. This construction, whereby the principal was paid in gold coin and the annuity was paid out in gold coin, but the contract was expressed in silver coin, exposed the participants in exchange to depreciation risk. This construction can best be compared to a present-day contract where the creditor pays the principal in euros, the debtor pays interest in euros, but the contract is expressed in dollars. The result is both creditor and debtor being exposed to fluctuations in the exchange rate of euros/dollars.

In the fifteenth century, the same applied to the exchange rate between gold and silver coins: since annuity payments were expressed in silver coin but made in gold coin, in the event of debasement of silver coin, towns could do with decreasing payments in gold coin. Two examples may help clarify this: in the first, someone purchases an annuity with the town of Haarlem in 1477. He pays a principal of 160 Rhenish guilders and acquires an annuity of 10 Rhenish guilders. The parties agree to express the annuity in the Rhenish guilder, a stable gold coin. In this case, the debasement of silver coin does not affect the annuity payment: every year, the town of Haarlem pays 10 Rhenish guilders.

In the second example, someone purchases an annuity with the town of Haarlem in 1477. He pays a principal of 160 Rhenish guilders and acquires an annuity of 10 Rhenish guilders. However, now both parties agree to express the annuity in a money of account that is linked to the Flemish groat – the contract mentions an annuity of 1.67 *ponden Vlaamse groten*. As long as the silver content of the Flemish groat declined, the town of Haarlem could suffice with paying the annuity with fewer gold coins. In 1489, shortly before the revaluation of silver coins, Haarlem could suffice with paying c. 7.5 Rhenish guilders – which means the creditor lost 2.5 Rhenish guilders per annum.

The consequences this had for Haarlem's public debt between 1466 and 1500 are depicted in Figure 10.2. The town 'borrowed' money by selling life annuities and redeemable annuities: these were the financial instruments used most often to attract large funds. Life annuities were purchased by a creditor, who paid for an annuity that was paid for the remainder of his or her lifetime. The annuity was usually c. 10% of the principal. Redeemable annuities were hereditary and had to be paid until the debtor had repaid the principal. The annuity was usually 6.25% of the principal.[34]

Figure 10.2 shows three elements: first, the estimated total public debt of the town of Haarlem. This consisted of life annuities and redeemable annuities the town was due to pay every year. We should point out, however, that

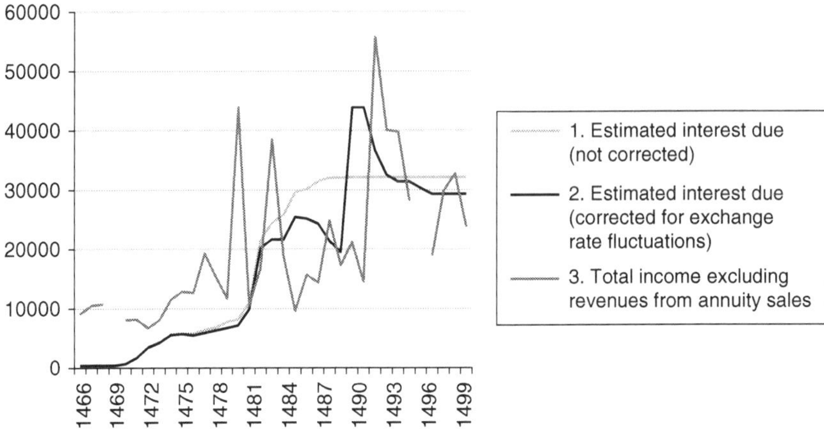

Figure 10.2 Scenario's development annuities Haarlem was due 1466–1500 (lb. Hollands).

Source: J.C. van Loenen, 'De rente-last van Haarlem in de vijftiende eeuw' (unpublished manuscript, available in Noordhollands archief Haarlem).

Note: The figure shows two scenarios, based on annuity sales by the town of Haarlem between 1466–1500. The scenarios show annual annuity payments based on the following assumptions: a) The life annuities and redeemable annuities sold in this period were not terminated or redeemed. b) All annuities sold in this period were linked to silver coin. The objective of the figure is not to give a precise reconstruction of the annuities Haarlem was due (we lack the evidence to do such a thing) but to show broadly the effects of the mechanism we discuss in this chapter.

Figure 10.2 presents a scenario based on the data of Haarlem's annuity sales between 1466 and 1500. A few elements were not taken into account: annuities sold before 1466,[35] annuities sold after 1466 but terminated before 1500, life annuities due to the passing away of creditors, redeemable annuities due to the town repaying the principal (which did not happen very often). The line is therefore tentative.

Following this scenario, a first line expresses what would have happened if all annuities were expressed in gold coin. A second line expresses what would have happened if all annuities were expressed in silver coin and subject to debasement. Both scenarios do not differ much until 1482. Between 1483 and 1489, this changes: in case Haarlem had linked its public debt to silver coin, the town profited from the ruler's monetary policy. The maximum difference between the gold and silver coin scenario was 12,000 lb. Hollands in 1489 – as also becomes evident from Figure 10.3, which shows the development of the difference between both scenarios. Using a silver coin scenario, Haarlem could reduce its expenses, as becomes clear from line three in Figure 10.2, which gives the total revenues of Haarlem, excluding 'borrowing' by selling new annuities. Those of Haarlem could thus reduce annuity payments by expressing life annuities and redeemable annuities in silver coin and moreover: in the

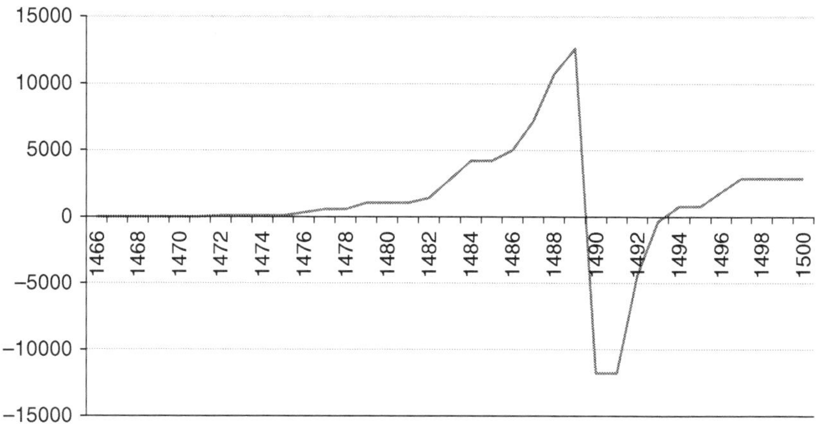

Figure 10.3 'Reductions' gained by Haarlem according to scenarios in Figure 10.2 (lb. Hollands).

Source: J.C. van Loenen, 'De rente-last van Haarlem in de vijftiendeeeuw' (unpublished manuscript, available in Noordhollands archief Haarlem).

silver coin scenario, annual payments even declined after 1485, even though the town continued to sell annuities for several years.

As soon as Maximilian decided to increase the content of silver coin in 1489 to the level of 1466,[36] those of Haarlem no longer profited from favourable exchange rates. In 1490, the town paid 44,000 lb. Hollands for annuities, while this had been less than 22,000 lb. Hollands a year before. Since at that point the town had already lost half of its revenues on annuity payments, a doubling of these expenses amounted to a disaster.[37] Not only towns were confronted with an unpleasant surprise: others that had made transactions involving postponed payments – rents, loans, down payments, et cetera – suffered as well. Debtors who had made transactions for an amount expressed in silver coin had to pay more after the mint ordinance of 1489; creditors, on the other hand, profited.

This may raise questions about financial expertise, first among town magistrates. They caused the towns of Holland to enter a demolition course, creating a large public debt that would become unsustainable in the event of a revaluation, such as that of 1489. It is difficult to imagine that experienced town magistrates, usually themselves active in trade and industries, did not see this risk. And with repect to annuity buyers, were they tricked by the towns? This may be true for some of the annuity buyers, but the majority of them came from the political and economic elite – surely they too would have known a thing or two about finance?[38] It may have simply been the case that annuity buyers took the risk of fluctuations in the exchange rate: in practice, coins were repeatedly revalued and devalued, which meant during some periods they received less than anticipated, and during others more.[39]

Speculation of towns

Jan Marsilje, an expert of late-medieval urban finance, characterized the growth of public debt in the second half of the fifteenth century as absurd. The mechanism described earlier may help us understand this absurdity: it reduced annuity payments, causing urban finance to remain in order – albeit using a financial trick. Towns could continue paying annuities for a relatively long time and maintain their creditworthiness, allowing them to continue selling annuities for a relatively long time as well.

Was this a strategy used by town magistrates to extend the urban budget? Or, to put it another way, did town magistrates use the ruler's monetary policy by speculating on ongoing debasement? Two elements may illuminate this issue: attempts by towns to stop debasements, and the linking of annuity contracts to gold and silver coin.

Let us first of all take a look at the towns' reactions to the rulers' monetary policy: what did town magistrates think of this? Did they discuss the issue during meetings of the representative council, the *Staten van Holland*? Unfortunately, little is known about how often 'monetary policy' was on the agenda. The data of the historian Henk Kokken, who studied the representative council in this period, do not allow for singling out coinage as a fiercely debated topic among the towns of Holland.[40]

A look at the situation in Flanders may be instructive, though. Earlier we mentioned Wim Blockmans' conclusion that, during the debasements, the towns of Flanders did not really show much of an interest in monetary policy. This is remarkable, because towns usually favoured good economic institutions, such as stable coinage.[41] For example, in the first half of the fifteenth century, we see the towns frequently, and succesfully, interfering in monetary affairs. For this influence they paid a price: the towns 'paid' the ruler to abstain from debasement, for instance, by agreeing to the latter's requests for taxation. Back then, urban influence on monetary affairs was so strong that declaration of new mint ordinances often depended on the fiat of the towns in the Estates General and Provincial Estates.[42]

In the second half of the fifteenth century, towns no longer managed to exert much influence on monetary affairs, enabling the debasement. It is possible to single out a few reasons for this. The first is straightforward: it was not always possible to influence the rulers' monetary policy. Sometimes the latter decided on monetary affairs without allowing the towns a say, such as happened in 1474.[43] But on the other hand we see few urban attempts to put a stop to debasement.[44] Monetary affairs hardly featured on the agenda of the Estates between 1477 and 1488 – only 20 times, or on average 1.7 times per year. Figure 10.4 shows that monetary affairs were much more often discussed before and after – over the period of 1385–1506, on average five times per year. Also, when we look at 'monetary policy' compared to other issues, such as internal and external affairs, finance, defence, trade, industries, justice, the period 1477–1488 is a low: 'monetary policy' amounted to 4.95% of all topics discussed, while over the period of 1385–1506, this was 10%. After 1488, we witness an increase to 4.8 meetings per year between 1488 and 1492. This increase was probably caused by the enormous problems that followed after the revaluation of the silver coin in 1489; this did not have anything to do with the prior devaluation.

To be sure, the moderate interest the towns of Flanders displayed was not caused by the Revolt of the towns of Flanders (1482–1485): between 1477 and 1488, Blockmans still counted 294 meetings of the Estates of Flanders, on average 26.7 per year (to compare: between 1385 and 1506 there were 4,055 meetings, on average 36 per year).[45] We interpret the limited interest in putting a stop to debasement as the result of the 'incentives' coming from the large public debt the towns of Flanders, such as Ghent, had created since 1453.[46] Surely, the towns did not want to further their own demise by opposing the debasement policy that allowed them some much-needed breathing space. This must be why they kept silent time and again, not protesting the continuous debasements of silver coin Figure 10.4)

The political actions of the towns of Flanders are in line with the hypothesis of town magistrates speculating on ongoing debasement of silver coin. However, speculation implies a conscious choice: in this case, a choice linking public debt to silver coin, thus exposing annuity payments to fluctuations in the exchange rate and refraining from linking public debt to stable gold coin. The latter was a well-known technique that was frequently used in the late Middle Ages, as becomes evident from data collected in the appendix.

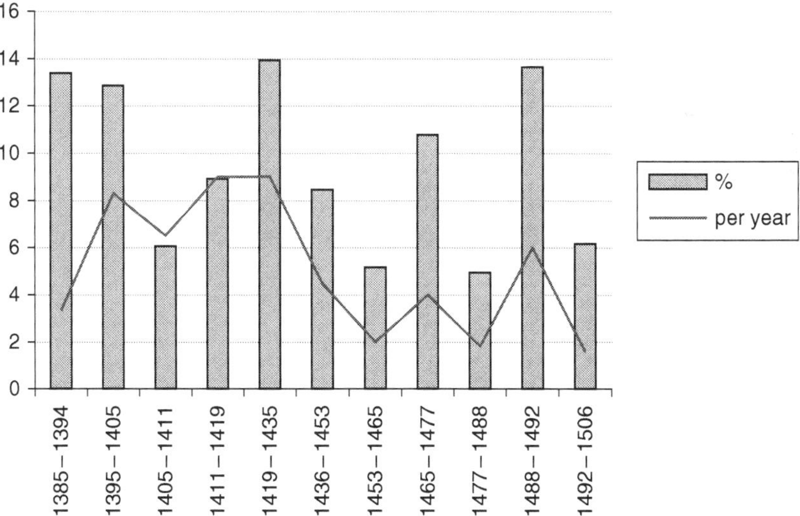

Figure 10.4 Meetings about monetary policy of the Estates of Flanders, 1385–1506.

Source: Blockmans 1978: 545.

Note: The line indicates the average number of meetings where monetary policy was discussed, during eleven periods. The columns give the share of the topics related to monetary policy out of the total number of topics. The periods are based on the typology Blockmans used.

These data are based on the sample of fifteenth-century annuity contracts sold by towns in the Northern Low Countries, and edited by J.H. Kernkamp.[47] Until the 1470s, towns expressed annuities in gold coin, thus safeguarding these transactions against fluctuations in the exchange rate. After this, we see a gradual shift: the towns of Leiden, Amsterdam, and Schiedam began issuing annuities expressed in silver coin. The same is true for Dordrecht, examined by Verloren van Themaat *et al.* (1985). In the 1470s, we observe a shift to silver coin.[48] Jan Marsilje saw the same development in Leiden, concluding that in the second half of the fifteenth century the town switched from gold to silver coin in the annuity contracts.[49]

Why do we observe this shift at the time of ongoing debasement of silver coin? The most straightforward explanation is to think that towns anticipated on their rulers' monetary policy. Such speculation would also explain why we do not see a linear development in the use of either silver or gold coin over time: it rather seems that towns decided for either one based on circumstances. To give some examples, in the fourteenth century, annuity contracts were linked to silver coin.[50] From the beginning of the fifteenth century, they were expressed in gold coin.[51] Next, we again observe a return to silver, as is indicated in the appendix. Finally, after 1489, Schiedam and Dordrecht continued to issue annuities linked to silver coin:[52] did they speculate that after the revaluation of 1489 they had entered a new era of continuous debasement?

Finally, it is useful to look at the coin revaluation of 1489: the ruler, Maximilian, did lend his towns a helping hand. The decree ordering the revaluation did contain a transitional arrangement for annuities and other obligations contracted since 1487, because the ruler recognized the revaluation would cause enormous problems.[53] However, as soon as it turned out this arrangement did not suffice, Maximilian granted many towns a moratorium. As a result, the people that had invested in annuities ultimately paid the price: they had to wait for their annuities, or had to agree with reduced annuity payments. The construction ruler and towns agreed to may therefore be considered as strategic default: well-timed reneging with limited consequences.[54] Usually rulers opted for strategic default, but it is imaginable that towns followed suit as soon as they became important intermediaries between ruler and financial market.

Conclusion

In this paper, we formulated the hypothesis that the towns of Holland speculated on ongoing debasement of silver coin. We have demonstrated how towns could profit from this, by expressing their public debt in silver coin, thus reducing their annuity payments. This technique allowed towns some much-needed breathing space in a financially difficult period, and even allowed towns to prolong 'borrowing' in financial markets – perhaps it even invited town magistrates to do so. The towering – and absurd – public debts the towns created must in part be understood as the result of this mechanism.

The towns hardly resisted against coin debasement: during meetings of the Estates of Flanders, coinage was hardly discussed – not even in the 1470s and 1480s, when debasement soared. It seems what we observe is a 'lock-in effect', where the public interest gained the upper hand, and town magistrates realized that continuation of the rulers' monetary policy was beneficial for the town's treasure chest. Putting a halt to debasement would increase pressure on urban finances; revaluation would amount to a disaster. As a result, town magistrates could no longer support the private interest: a stable coin, to be obtained by opposing the rulers' monetary policy. In the late fifteenth century, such opposition therefore did not come from town magistrates, but from nobility and clergy.

Considering this lack of opposition, town magistrates apparently knew very well what was at stake. As long as the towns did not oppose the rulers' monetary policy, they stood a good chance of continuing debasement, allowing them to profit from expressing annuities in silver coin. As we have seen, towns did not decide to reorganize their public debt by expressing newly issued annuities in gold coin, thus preventing future problems. This suggests that town magistrates, spurred on by financial demands of the rulers, preferred short-term policies, speculating on ongoing coin debasement. Perhaps they even anticipated a transitional arrangement in the event of a revaluation – after all, the towns were too important as financial intermediaries for the rulers to allow them to collapse.

When we look at this from a modern perspective, it is worth noting that the initial developments amounted to a debasement policy that resulted in the lowering of public debt. This technique was not unheard of in this period.[55] However, the highly idiosyncratic public debt structure of the later Middle Ages – towns acting as intermediaries in financial markets on behalf of the ruler – created a coordination problem. In Holland and elsewhere in the late-medieval Low Countries, the sovereign was responsible for coinage and the towns were responsible for the largest part of sovereign debt. This division did not entirely prevent the towns from fabricating an inflatory policy – we have seen how they managed to reduce public debt payments for more than a decade, albeit in an indirect way. However, since they did not command coinage, the towns were not in control of financial policy, as they painfully found out. Had Maximilian been responsible for the debts that had been incurred to support the dukes of Burgundy, he might have thought twice before revaluating the groat in 1489.

To dwell a little more on the topic of recent crises, even today unexpected changes in the value of currencies can result in losses. This 'depreciation risk' entails 'the risk of losses arising from unfavourable movement of foreign exchange rates', for instance, in the event a party earns revenues in a local currency, but pays expenses in another currency.[56] Such risk is believed to have contributed to several recent financial crises, such as the Asia crisis of 1997, but also the Mexican (1994), Argentinian (1995), and Russian (1998) crises, to name but a few.[57] The late-medieval example we have discussed in this article stands out because here a crisis was not caused by exchange-rate fluctuations among various international currencies, but by those between the currency of the sovereign – the Duke of Burgundy – and the ghost money the towns used to express their public debt. To put it another way, here we see how strictly *domestic* depreciation risk could trigger a crisis, without any role played by *foreign* exchange rates. The crisis the towns of Holland, and other towns in the realms of Burgundy, experienced was therefore a typical exponent of the late-medieval absence of a notion of a national economy. Lacking this, two currencies could coexist: a real currency commanded by the duke, and a ghost money commanded by his subjects. The latter's underestimation of depreciation risk caused a severe crisis, and may raise the question whether the real currency minted by the Duke of Burgundy was – from the perspective of many of his subjects – not really a foreign currency after all.

Appendix 10.1 Payment techniques, annuities fifteenth century

Year	*Town*	*Payment*	*Gold/silver*
1402	Haarlem	40 gouden Gentsche nobel	Gold
1408	Leiden	7 ½ Engelse nobelen	Gold
1435	Utrecht	3 lb. 6 s. 8 p. 'alse enen Wilhelmus Hollantse schilt laetst tot Dordrecht geslegen voir vier pont gerekent'	Gold
1458	Utrecht	100 pont gelts 'alse enen overlansche Rijnschen gulden voir deser tijt gemunt ende geslagen voir vijff pont gerekent'	Gold
1464	Amsterdam	'20 guede goudene Gwilhelmus Hollantse schilden lest Dordrecht geslagen, joff payment dat also guet is'	Gold
1472	Amsterdam	33 guede goudene overlantse coirvorste Rhijnsche guldene of payment also guet	Gold
1472	Leiden	7 gouden Rijnse guldens 'voir datum des briefs geslegen'	Gold
1476	Amsterdam	1 lb. gr. Vl.	Silver
1479	Amsterdam	1 lb. gr. Vl.	Silver
1480	Utrecht	30 lb. … alse enen Rijnsche gulden current, viertich groeten Vlaemsch voer elcken Rijnsche gulden, in elcker tijt der betalinge voer vijf pont gerekent'	Silver
1485	Leiden	4 lb. gr. Vl.	Silver
1486	Amsterdam	5 s. 10 p. gr. Vl.	Silver
1486	Schiedam	1 lb. gr. en 10 s. gr. Vl.	Silver
1493	Schiedam	8 lb. Hollants 2026 'mit alsulcke paymenten als in buersen gaen zullen'	Silver

Source: Kernkamp (1961).

Notes

1 This paper is a reworked version of Zuijderduijn (2012: 27–46).
2 ...*sobren ende crancken regemente*... Hamaker 1898: 181–207, 184. Cf. corruption: Damen (2005: 68–94); Blockmans (1985: 231–247).
3 There is a rather large literature on the financial problems of the towns of Holland. See e.g. Prins (1922); Dijkhof (1985: 20–29); Sewalt (2001: 18–23); Dokkum and Dijkhof (1985: 87–88); Downer *s.a.*; Bangs (1983: 75–82).
4 Van Gelder (1951).
5 Although we should point out that the ruler, in the 1489 decree that called for increasing the silver content of silver coins, was aware of the problems this could cause for towns and tried to limit the effects of this as far as possible. However, such attempts were of no avail (Groustra-Werdekker 2001: 72–73; Stuurman 1984: 3–4).
6 The date of this first moratorium is derived from Sewalt (1994: 127–130).
7 Hanus (2007); Blondé (1990); Van der Wee (1963: 106–107).
8 Except for the literature mentioned above, the development of the rulers' demand for funding is described in Ryckbosch (2007); Van Cauwenberghe (1982); Van der Wee (1963: 105–109).
9 Zuijderduijn (2010a: 3–24; 2010b).
10 Tracy (1985).
11 Zuijderduijn (2010a).
12 Marsilje (1985: 316).
13 On the reliability of town magistrates in the aforementioned articles, see Damen (2005), Blockmans (1985), and Van der Heijden (1999: 133).
14 'Zij betoonden zich vrij lankmoedig tegenover autokratisch en opportunistisch optreden [van de landsheer], misschien uit respekt voor het heerlijk muntrecht, en beslist ook omdat de kontrolemiddelen op de muntcirkulatie weinig efficiënt waren' (Blockmans 1978: 508).
15 Spufford (1989: 318; 1986).
16 Van der Wee (1963, II: 108).
17 Spufford (1989).
18 Zuijderduijn (2009).
19 Spufford (1970: 144–145).
20 Zuijderduijn (2009: 55); Bos-Rops (1993: 34).
21 Munro (1965: 158–160).
22 Ibid.: 163–164.
23 Ibid.: 178.
24 Bos-Rops (1993: 182–183).
25 Spufford (1989: 312–313).
26 Spufford (1970: 141–142); Van Gelder (2002: 59–60); Van Cauwenberghe (1982: 328–342).
27 Cf. surveys: Van der Heijden (2006); Verloren van Themaat (1985); Kernkamp (1961).
28 Van Gelder indicates that the gold guilder of Burgundy 'contained a constant quantity of gold' (Van Gelder 1951: 49); Van Gelder and Hoc (1960: 19, 36, 47). Cf. the stability of gold coins in the late Middle Ages: Fantacci (2008: 58–59).
29 Marsilje (1985: 154, 239) writes: 'thus payments were [by expressing them in gold coin] safeguarded against debasement of silver coin, which soared during the reign of the house of Bavaria' [1354–1433]'. Cf. Van der Wee (1963, II: 108); Stuurman (1984: 22).
30 Greif (2000).
31 Van Gelder (1986–2002: R31–R32).
32 For the rise of the Rhenish guilder as unit of account, see Spufford (1970: 18–19).
33 Van Gelder (1986–2002).
34 A more elaborate survey in Van der Heijden (2006: 24–26); Hanus (2007: 14–16); Verloren van Themaat (1985: 7–15).

35 The public debt that existed before 1466 was probably quite modest: between c. 1435 and c. 1466, the towns of Holland were hardly active in financial markets, and they gradually managed to reduce the number of annuities they owed (Zuijderduijn 2009: 152–168).
36 According to Van Gelder (1951: 48–49), Maximilian's main motive was this: after suppressing the revolt of the towns of Flanders, and the end of the war with France, in 1489, the ruler's financial situation improved, so he could abandon his debasement policy.
37 Zuijderduijn (2009: 152–168).
38 Boone (1990; Tracy 1985).
39 Drelichman and Voth (2011) recently suggested that the creditors of Philip II agreed to temporary defaults, because they knew that their investments would be profitable in the long run.
40 Kokken (1991: 257–261). Kokken classified negotiations about coinage, together with numerous other topics, as 'trade'.
41 Spufford (1970: 151); Marsilje (1985: 155–156).
42 The influence of the estates general and provincial estates on monetary issues has been discussed in Spufford (1966).
43 Kokken (1991: 258).
44 One of the scarce attempts is visible in the *Groot Privilege* of 1477, when the towns tried to gain a say in monetary policy (Kokken 1991: 258–260).
45 Blockmans (1978: 545).
46 Cf. the increasing public debt of Ghent after the *Vrede van Gavere* (1453): Ryckbosch (2007: 19–24 and especially figure 2).
47 Kernkamp (1961).
48 Verloren van Themaat (1985: 123–127).
49 Marsilje (1985: 247) blames 'a gradual growth of the practice of relating financial obligations directly or indirectly to silver'.
50 Cf. various examples such as Vangassen (1964: 12–17).
51 For example, Vangassen (1964).
52 Schiedam: appendix; Dordrecht: Verloren van Themaat (1985: 125–126).
53 Groustra-Werdekker (2001: 72–73); Stuurman (1984: 3–4).
54 Cf. *strategic default*: Barzel (1992); Veitch (1986: 31–36).
55 Kusman and Demeulemeester (2015).
56 Matsukawa and Habeck (2007: 7).
57 Corbett and Vines (1999: 168); Mendoza and Uribe (2000: 239).

Bibliography

Bangs, J. (1983). 'Hollands civic lijfrente loans (XVth century): Some recurrent problems', *Publication du centre europeen d'études Burgondo-Médianes*, 23: 75–82.

Barzel, Y. (1992). 'Confiscation by the ruler: The rise and fall of Jewish lending in the Middle Ages', *The Journal of Law and Economics*, 35: 1–14.

Blockmans, W. (1978). *De volksvertegenwoordiging in Vlaanderen in de overgang van middeleeuwen naar nieuwe tijden (1384–1506)*. Brussels, Belgium: Koninklijke Academie voor Wetenschappen, Letteren en Schone Kunsten van België.

Blockmans, W. (1985). 'Corruptie, patronage, makelaardij en venaliteit als symptomen van een ontluikende staatsvorming in de Bourgondisch-Habsburgse Nederlanden', *Tijdschrift voor Sociale Geschiedenis*, 11: 231–247.

Blondé, B. (1990). 'De saneringspogingen van de Bossche stadsfinanciën in de eerste helft van de zestiende eeuw: spiegel van een politieke, sociale en economische realiteit?', *Driemaandelijks Tijdschrift van het Gemeentekrediet in België*, 172: 63-–75.

Boone, M. (1990). *Geld en macht. De Gentse stadsfinanciën en de Bourgondische staatsvorming (1384–1453)*. Gent, Belgium: Maatschappij voor Geschiedenis en Oudheidkunde te Gent.

Bos-Rops, J. (1993). *Graven op zoek naar geld. De inkomsten van de graven van Holland en Zeeland, 1389-1433*. Hilversum, the Netherlands: Verloren.

Corbett, J. and Vines, D. (1999). 'Asian currency and financial crises: Lessons from vulnerability, crisis, and collapse, *The World Economy*, 22: 155–177.

Damen, M. (2005). 'Corrupt of hoofs gedrag? Geschenken en het politiek netwerk van een laatmiddeleeuwse Hollandse stad', *Tijdschrift voor Sociale en Economische Geschiedenis*, 2: 68–94.

Dijkhof, E. (1985). '"Omme de meeste schade metter mynstere te verhuedene." Lijf- en erfrenten in Gouda', *Skript*, 7: 20–29.

Dokkum, H. and Dijkhof, E. (1985). 'Oude Dordtse lijfrenten', in VerLoren van Themaat *et al.* (eds.) (1985): 37–90.

Downer, W. (*s.a.*). 'De financiële toestand van de stad Leiden omstreeks 1500' (unpublished manuscript, available in the *Regionaal Archief Leiden*).

Drelichman, M. and Voth, H.-J. (2011). 'Serial defaults, serial profits: Returns to sovereign lending in Habsburg Spain, 1566–1600', *Explorations in Economic History*, 48: 1–19.

Fantacci, L. (2008). 'The dual currency system of Renaissance Europe', *Financial History Review*, 15: 55–72.

Greif, A. (2000). 'The fundamental problem of exchange: A research agenda in historical institutional analysis', *European Review of Economic History*, 4: 251–284.

Groustra-Werdekker, A. (2001). *De muntordonnantie van 11 december 1489*. Utrecht, the Netherlands: Het Nederlands Muntmuseum.

Hamaker, H. (1898). 'De stad Leiden in staat van faillissement', *Verslagen en Mededeelingen van de Vereeniging tot Uitgaaf der Bronnen van het Oud-vaderlandsch Recht*, 3: 181–207.

Hanus, J. (2007). *Tussen stad en eigen gewin. Stadsfinanciën, renteniers en kredietmarkten in 's-Hertogenbosch (begin zestiende eeuw)*. Amsterdam: Aksant.

Kernkamp, J. (ed.) (1961). *Vijftiende-eeuwse rentebrieven van Noordnederlandse steden*. Groningen, the Netherlands: Wolters.

Kokken, H. (1991). *Steden en staten. Dagvaarten van steden en Staten van Holland onder Maria van Bourgondië en het eerste regentschap van Maximiliaan van Oostenrijk (1477–1494)*. The Hague, the Netherlands: Stichting Hollandse Historische reeks.

Kusman, D. and Demeulemeester, J.-L. (2015). 'From near-default to debt-restructuring: the inventive methods of the duke of Brabant and its council around 1313–1320 for the salvation of public finances', in Fondazione Istituto Internazionale di Storia Economica "F. Datini", Prato, (ed.), *Le crisi finanziarie: gestione, implicazioni sociali e consequenze nell'età preindustriale / The Financial Crises: Their Management, Their Social Implications and Their Consequences In Pre-Industrial Times*, Florence, Italy: Firenze University Press: 263–282.

Marsilje, J. (1985). *Het financiële beleid van Leiden in de laat-Beierse en Bourgondische periode +/- 1390–1477*. Hilversum, the Netherlands : Verloren.

Matsukawa, T., and Habeck, O. (2007). 'Review of risk mitigation instruments for infrastructure financing and recent trends and developments', *Trends and Policy Options*, 4. Washington, D.C.: World Bank.

Mendoza, E. and Uribe, M. (2000). 'Devaluation risk and the business-cycle implementations of exchange-rate management', *Carnegie-Rochester Conference series on public policy*, 53: 239–296.

Munro, J. (1965). *Wool, Cloth and Gold: Bullionism in Anglo-Burgundian Commercial Relations, 1384–1478*. Toronto, ON: University of Toronto Press.

Prins, I. (1922). *Het faillissement der Hollandsche steden: Amsterdam, Dordrecht, Leiden en Haarlem in het jaar 1494, uit de wordingsgeschiedenis van den Nederlandschen Staat.* Amsterdam: Van Looy.

Ryckbosch, W. (2007). 'Stedelijk initiatief of hertogelijke repressie? Financiële hervormingen en kredietbeleid te Gent (1453–1495)', *Tijdschrift voor Sociale en Economische Geschiedenis*, 4: 3–28.

Sewalt, E. (1994). 'Atterminatie ende staet. De rol van het landsheerlijk gezag bij de ondercuratelestelling van de stad Haarlem in de late middeleeuwen' (MA thesis Haarlem 1994, available in the Noordhollands Archief, Haarlem).

Sewalt, E. (2001). '1501: Haarlem onder curatele', *De Klopkei: Mededelingenblad van de heemkundekring "De Erstelinghe"*, 25(4): 18–23.

Spufford, P. (1966). 'Coinage, taxation and the Estates-General of the Burgundian Netherlands', *Anciencs pays et assemblées d'états. Standen en landen*, 40: 61–88.

Spufford, P. (1970). *Monetary Problems and Policies in the Burgundian Netherlands 1433–1496.* Leiden, the Netherlands: Brill.

Spufford, P. (1989). *Money and Its Use in Medieval Europe.* Cambridge, UK: Cambridge University Press.

Stuurman, J. (1984). 'Met gelijke munt betalen eind XVe eeuw: het volle pond', in De Schepper, H. (ed.), *Miscellanea consilii magni. Bijdragen over rechtspraak van de Grote Raad van Mechelen* II, Amsterdam: University of Amsterdam: 3–69.

Tracy, J. (1985). *A Financial Revolution in the Habsburgh Netherlands. 'Renten' and 'Renteniers' in the County of Holland (1515–1565).* Berkeley, CA, Los Angeles, London: University of California Press.

Van Cauwenberghe, E. (1982). *Het vorstelijk domein en de overheidsfinanciën in de Nederlanden (15de–16de eeuw). Een kwantitatieve analyse van de Vlaamse en Brabantse domeinrekeningen.* Brussels, Belgium: Gemeentekrediet van België.

Van der Heijden, M. (1999). 'Stadsrekeningen, stedelijke financiën en historisch onderzoek', *NEHA bulletin voor de economische geschiedenis in Nederland*, 13: 129–166.

Van der Heijden, M. (2006). *Geldschieters van de stad. Financiële relaties tussen stad, burgers en overheden 1550–1650.* Amsterdam: Bert Bakker.

Van der Wee, H. (1963). *The Growth of the Antwerp Money Market and the European Economy (Fourteenth–Sixteenth Centuries).* II. *Interpretation.* Leuven, Belgium: Nijhoff.

Vangassen, H. (1964). *Bouwstoffen tot de historische taalgeografie van het Nederlands. Noordhollandse charters.* Brussels, Belgium: Belgisch Interuniversitair Centrum voor Neerlandistiek.

Van Gelder, H. (1951). 'De muntpolitiek van Philips de Schone, 1482–1496', *Jaarboek voor Munt-en Penningkunde*, 38: 42–54.

Van Gelder, H. (1986–2002). 'Rekenmunt', in Van Beek E., (ed.), *Encyclopedie van munten en bankbiljetten*, Alphen aan den Rijn: Samsom: R31–R32.

Van Gelder, H. (2002). *De Nederlandse munten: het complete overzicht tot en met de komst van de euro.* Utrecht, the Netherlands: Spectrum.

Van Gelder, H. and Hoc, M. (1960). *Les Monnaies des Pays-Bas Bourguignons et Espagnols 1434–1713.* Amsterdam: J. Schulman.

Veitch, J. (1986). 'Repudiations and confiscations by the medieval state', *Journal of Economic History*, 46: 31–36.

Verloren van Themaat, L. (1985). 'Geschiedenis van de lijfrente', in Verloren van Themaat *et al.* (eds.) (1985): 7–15.

Verloren van Themaat L., *et al.* (eds.) (1985), *Oude Dordtse lijfrenten. Stedelijke financiering in de vijftiende eeuw* Amsterdam: Verloren.

Zuijderduijn, J. (2009). *Medieval Capital Markets. Markets for 'Renten', State Formation and Private Investment in Holland (1300–1550).* Leiden, the Netherlands; Boston, MA: Brill.

Zuijderduijn, J. (2010a). 'De laatmiddeleeuwse crisis van de overheidsfinanciën en de financiële revolutie in Holland', *Bijdragen en Mededelingen betreffende de Geschiedenis der Nederlanden*, 125(4): 3–24.

Zuijderduijn, J. (2010b). 'The emergence of provincial debt in the county of Holland (thirteenth–sixteenth centuries)', *European Review of Economic History*, 14: 335–359.

Zuijderduijn, J. (2012). 'De schuldvraag. Monetaire politiek, publieke schuld en wanbetaling in Holland, ca. 1466–1489', *Low Countries Journal of Social and Economic History – Tijdschrift voor Sociale en Economische Geschiedenis*, 9(3): 27–46

11 Enter the ghost

Cashless payments in the early modern Low Countries, 1500–1800[1]

Oscar Gelderblom and Joost Jonker

Introduction

In 1974, the distinguished French economic historian Michel Morineau found himself in a quandary. He had drawn together available data on coins produced in France, Britain and the Low Countries during the seventeenth and eighteenth centuries for a tentative estimate of the money circulating in those countries (Morineau 1974). To his surprise, he found that the period's most dynamic economy, the Dutch Republic, had by far the lowest per capita money in circulation, even with the Amsterdam Wisselbank's deposits taken into account. From this, Morineau concluded that businessmen in the Dutch Golden Age must have known ways to economize on the use of coin, but he remained at a loss to explain how.

In this paper, we argue that merchants chiefly economized on coin by using money of account or ghost money, a well-known but underrated phenomenon that facilitated payments to a much higher degree than hitherto appreciated. Just as the plot of Hamlet hinges on a ghost, early modern payment systems cannot be understood without ghost money. In the Low Countries and probably elsewhere in Europe, too, ghost money eliminated many problems associated with paying cash by enabling people to settle transactions in a widely accepted fictional currency. Tied to new administrative practices such as double-entry bookkeeping and bilateral current accounts, ghost money also gave merchants a means to create money in the form of book debts, which must have rendered M1 far more elastic than hitherto suspected.

This last aspect links our argument to two wider academic debates concerning money and credit in the early modern age. A considerable body of literature suggests that poor coinage and coin scarcity probably hampered economic exchange and, by extension, growth (Day 1978; Munro 1983, 1988; see however Sussman 1998). This looks plausible. We know the circulation to have been deficient. Recurrent debasements and devaluations made good large coins scarce, while a fear of counterfeits supposedly reduced small coin production to a trickle (Munro 1988; Sargent and Velde 2002). Some historians link those currency deficiencies to the widespread use of credit and conclude that the scarcity of cash forced people to rely on credit (Muldrew 1998;

Willems 2009). That particular type of credit is thought to have been mostly a function of the social relations between creditor and debtor, as often as not a consequence of economic dependency (Lambrecht 2003; Fontaine 2008; Matthews 2009; Vickers 2010; Rykbosch and Decraene 2014; see however Ogilvie, Küpker and Maegraith 2012).

By taking cash payments as a sign of economic modernity and, conversely, their paucity for backwardness, this last strand of literature echoes the old idea of economies evolving from a *Naturalwirtschaft* via a *Geldwirtschaft* into a *Kreditwirtschaft*. Societies would have moved from subsistence production and barter, via a first stage of market-oriented production in which coins facilitate the exchange of goods and services, to a second stage in which credit provided by banks and other financial institutions replaces coin. In its essence, this stage theory rests on a specific, debatable, conception of how money evolved. One main function of money, means of settlement, would have preceded the two others, gauge of value and store of wealth, and penetrated societies by way of increased market-oriented production. Further echoes of the stage theory of money can be found everywhere in the literature, usually in the form of normative judgements about individual actors, households, or even whole sectors of production being advanced or backward, depending on their apparent level of financial sophistication as evident from the way in which they use money. Cash settlements are then taken as a sign of market-oriented production and an advanced economy, cashless exchange as backward barter.

The view that currency deficiencies handicapped exchange and the stage theory of money share a number of defects. First, the underlying assumption of both is that people prefer to use cash if they can. However, this is not true even in societies today. Many people regard the simplest form of payment, cash in the form of perfect coins or notes, as a chore, so they tend to avoid it and use alternatives like credit cards or Paypal instead. Second, there is no reason to assume the settlement function to have preceded the other two (see e.g. Bezemer, ch. 3, this volume). Indeed, the fact that early currency systems started by issuing large silver or gold coins renders it likely for the gauge of value function to have spread first, because these coins were impractical for transactions below a certain, fairly high, value. Third, the numismatic literature has started to doubt whether cash was the preferred option in the past by questioning the nexus between cash payments and economic modernity (Bolton 2012; Munro 2012; Spufford 1988, 2008; Lucassen and Zuijderduijn 2014). Fourth, Kuroda's insight about currency systems as consisting of complementary forms of money used differently by different social groups (Kuroda 2008a, b) was taken a step further by Vickers. He shows how various forms of money, modes of payment and types of credit did not function as discrete categories, but as a seamless continuum of closely related options from which people picked whatever suited them best at a given moment in time (Vickers 2010). Such a continuum has also been demonstrated for groups of poor people in developing countries today, who use it to maximize scarce resources (Collins 2010).

An absence of cash payments may thus signify the existence of cashless payment networks, in which cash and credit could both substitute and complement each other, or perform entirely different functions, depending on circumstances. We need to see credit as one amongst a number of options to conclude a transaction, and the choice for a particular option as inspired by a much wider variety of reasons than currency vicissitudes or asymmetric social relations. That means we must know whether people did have a choice to settle a transaction, for instance, in the absence of good coin. We explore this question for the Low Countries, where ghost money spread throughout the entire area from the fourteenth century onwards. As a result, two functions of money, standard of value and means of settlement, functioned smoothly, leaving the third one, store of wealth, to whatever gold and silver coins were available. Since most transactions could be settled in money of account, the poor coin circulation is unlikely to have affected whether or not people took credit. Moreover, money of account gave people a means to price the credit which formed part of so many transactions, so if they did not do so this must have been choice rather than force of circumstances.

Cash

Throughout the early modern period, people needed some determination if they wanted to pay or receive cash because that was highly inconvenient. When in 1577, for example, a Limburg bailiff put up the 300 guilders caution required for his function, he did that with a total of more than 210 coins of 19 different types from all over the Low Countries and abroad.[2] In 1583, a Leiden merchant's household possessed cash worth almost 670 guilders made up of 28 different coin types from the northern and southern Netherlands, France, Italy, Spain, and even Portugal.[3] Some sixty years later, a Holland house buyer wanted to pay the purchase price of 448 guilders and one stiver (*stuiver*) in cash. At the time, the most common type of silver guilder coin weighed about 20 grams, so he would have to amass upwards of 450 coins weighing roughly 9 kilos of silver. To reduce the tedium of collecting, sorting, and counting that lot our buyer decided to use gold coin, which was scarce at the time and thus not only expensive relative to silver, but difficult to get hold of. As a result, he had to scrape together more than fifty coins of seven different types, including some foreign ones.[4]

This profusion of coin types stretched all the way down to the smallest copper ones. A Brabant monk listing coin types current at the end of the sixteenth century identified no fewer than seven coins below the stiver, one-twentieth of a guilder and the smallest silver coin, valuing six of them but giving up on the value of the seventh.[5] Consequently even simple acts like buying daily provisions or paying rent required juggling with figures and fractions by everyone handling money, which means that the coin confusion must have promoted basic numeracy skills in the entire population. Moreover, people needed to carefully assess the weight and quality of individual coins exchanged. When a tenant of Mariënweerd Abbey near Utrecht paid 10 Philip guilders in rent in 1533, he did so in six different coin types, one of which had two different values, presumably because the coins were worn or clipped.[6]

These examples neatly illustrate one key obstacle of paying cash: the huge variety of local and foreign coins in circulation, a chaos to modern eyes (Polak 1998). To make matters worse, the value of those coins, even ostensibly similar ones, could vary considerably. Minting was, and remains, a sovereign right. Nowadays economic motives dominate currency issuing policy, but in the early modern period sovereigns managed currencies for their own benefit, manipulating weight and precious metal content of coins to suit their financial needs. As a result, successive issues of one type of coin, say the guilder, often varied in weight and fineness, and therefore in value. Sometimes changes in value were openly advertised by a different coin design, sometimes the changes were made surreptitiously. Such manipulations affected a coin's absolute value, but its relative value, its value as expressed in another coin, also fluctuated. Relative values depended on factors such as gold and silver prices, a shortage or abundance of particular coins, or a general degradation of the quality of a particular range of coins. Thus, the gold St Andrew guilder introduced by Philip the Good in 1466 initially valued 21 silver stivers, but as the quality of stiver issues declined this rose by 30 per cent to 28 stivers in 1496. In that year, the St Andrew guilder was replaced by a lighter St Philip guilder worth 24 stivers, which in turn made way for the yet lighter Carolus or Charles guilder issued from 1521 with a value of 20 stivers. During the second half of the sixteenth century exchange rates between coins spiralled upwards; the value of the heavy silver *rijksdaalder* (rixdollar) expressed in stivers rose from 28 in 1548 to 48 in 1616, the gold ducat doubled from two to four silver guilders.[7]

Anyone handling guilders therefore needed to know not only the specific type of coin, but also its actual value in stivers at that moment. In addition, transacting parties, notably in the wholesale trade which often handled coins by the sackful, had to agree on what constituted proper payment: coins counted by weight or by tale, that is to say by their face value. The latter practice could easily lead to disputes if a counterparty tried to pass off worn, torn, or clipped coins as full weight currency. Smaller denomination coins were often rolled together to substitute for other, larger denominations, rendering it difficult for receivers to check what they got.[8] Even the chambers of the Dutch East India Company VOC tried to cheat each other with underweight coins, prompting the central board to ban such behaviour in 1608.[9]

Then again, the handling of coins in loads was not always possible because the available supply rose and fell. Coins could disappear from circulation through massive hoarding if a depreciation was imminent, or else because international merchants exported them to settle trade deficits. Conversely, trade surpluses produced an inward flow of coins, as did the issuing abroad of light coins mimicking heavier local ones, fostered now by the political rivalry between princes, now by the economic competition between autonomous mints. The dukedom of Gelre, for instance, pestered surrounding provinces of the Habsburg

Netherlands with substandard coin issues until Charles V finally took possession of it in 1543. However, this failed to bring about a uniform coinage in the realm because during the 1550s mints in formally independent enclaves resumed the production of various foreign coin types. That flow increased sharply from the late 1560s when, following the Dutch Revolt, breakaway provinces asserted their autonomy by starting to mint all kinds of coins. Philip II's government in Brussels succeeded in re-imposing a centralized currency policy for the southern Netherlands, but it took the Estates General of the Dutch Republic more than a century to wrest control over minting in the north from the autonomous provincial mints.[10] This continuing currency fragmentation failed to have an impact on the north's rapid economic expansion, because ghost money provided a common denominator for handling every kind of coin.

Money of account

Governments tried to combat the reigning confusion by regularly issuing lists with official exchange rates between local and foreign coins in circulation. Cashiers and money changers were legally obliged to observe the official rates, but in the absence of means to enforce them, the lists only served as a guide to what government offices would accept in payment (Van Gelder 1990, 1995). Market prices could differ considerably, depending on the balance between supply and demand for particular coins or for gold and silver.[11]

A more effective remedy against confusion was the convention of a fictive currency, money of account, or ghost money.[12] These units had their origins either in the Medieval convention of a pound of silver from which to mint 20 shillings, groats or other standard coin, or in a gold or silver standard coin which, having disappeared from circulation, continued as an accounting convention which presumably spread from government administration into society.[13] Thus Flanders had its Flemish pound, Brabant the Brabantine pound, the different local pound weights accounting for their different value. Neither had been minted as a coin and they were really reference units of silver against which all coins in circulation could be properly valued according to their weight and fineness. By contrast, during the fourteenth and fifteenth centuries, the city of Deventer had several fictive units, ghosts remaining from gold coins long gone but, similarly to the pounds of silver, really serving as set weights of bullion against which to value circulating coins (De Meyer and Van den Elzen 1980). The life of these ghosts was perpetuated because the public administration continued to use them as reference values for transactions and for setting exchange rates, thereby providing a practical gauge for commercial transactions as well. Coupled with the gradual penetration of bookkeeping standards and mutual current accounts between merchants, these ghosts facilitated cashless settlements of transactions and equally served as standard gauges to value whatever coin was available if settling in cash.[14] Thus, contrary to Cipolla's interpretation of ghost money as an odd relic confined to the public administration and the higher reaches of commerce, it was really a widely used convention (Cipolla 1967). International bills of exchange were as a rule made out in one form of ghost money or another.[15]

Originally every city possessed its own money of account, and within some cities dedicated cloth halls even had their own money of account for doing business on the premises.[16] Over time regional ones emerged and the commercial power of the Flemish cities combined with Philip the Good's unifying policy to propel the Flemish pound into a supra-regional currency. By 1498 even commercial rival Brabant had adopted it.[17] As a consequence, the demand for money changers' services dropped, causing this profession to almost disappear from Flanders and Brabant during the second half of the fifteenth century.[18] The handful of money changers which managed to hold on, did so by taking on other business, such as buying bullion for the official mints, keeping cash for other businesses, and attracting public finance transactions. In effect, money of account provided people with a very simple and safe expedient for switching between currencies without the need for intermediation.

In 1526, Charles V attempted to harmonize the ghost moneys current in his Low Countries' possessions by ordering the adoption of the guilder of 20 stivers each subdivided in 12 *deniers* as such.[19] Known as the Carolus guilder, this coin did become a widely used money of account, though habits die hard in a society wedded to conventions.[20] The Flemish pound remained in widespread commercial use. Bankers and international wholesalers in the southern Netherlands often stuck to it, though the retail end of the supply chain switched to guilders.[21] Rural Flanders still used the pound during the second half of the eighteenth century.[22] Flemish pounds also continued to be used in the provinces that broke away following the Dutch Revolt. The Amsterdam securities trade, for instance, adopted 500 Flemish pounds as the standard amount for dealing in VOC shares following the company's launch in 1602.[23] The Middelburg *Wisselbank* kept its accounts in the same currency, as did the local chamber of the VOC. Moreover, as late as the 1760s, city officials of that bank guilder bastion, Amsterdam, regularly expressed amounts of money in Flemish pounds rather than guilders.[24] In doing so, the city fathers rather trailed commercial custom, which had long since converted to guilders.

Money of account offered a low-cost solution to the four handicaps of cash: its weight, the profusion of circulating coins, the uncertain values of those, and their fluctuating availability. Coin was a commodity whose price and availability fluctuated, whereas money of account was always available and could perform two monetary functions, standard of value and means of settlement, cheaper than cash, which retained an advantage only in effecting the third one, store of value. Consequently, there is no reason to suppose, as the literature sometimes does, that a shortage of coin generally or particular deficiencies in the circulation of coins hampered economic growth (Cf. Sussman 1998). The supposition that it did usually rests on taking M in Fisher's famous equation of exchange MV = PT to mean cash alone instead of total money, and taking velocity V as a constant, in which case a drop in available coin necessarily puts pressure on prices P and/or economic activity T.

We will not discuss here the suitability or otherwise of applying Fisher's equation to the early modern period or the likelihood of V remaining ever constant.[25] For our present purpose we only want to underline the common mistake of taking M as cash alone, because of the many ways in which money was created. Bankers, cashiers, and money changers did so by opening book credits and extending formal loans, and the spread of bookkeeping standards enabled more and more merchants to follow suit. Bills of exchange circulated in rising numbers and their use widened to include a growing number of cities and merchants. Assignments, a form of cheques, and bills obligatory already were a central feature of the Antwerp market of the mid-sixteenth century, their use boosted by a system of clearing run by cashiers and by a better negotiability following the introduction of formal rules governing endorsement.[26]

The nub of the matter is that the many handicaps of cash discussed above put a premium on using alternatives, with the effect of widening M. Sudden shortages of cash caused by a rush for liquidity did, of course, continue to happen quite regularly, but in normal circumstances the alternatives provided sufficient stretch to remedy currency deficiencies.[27] Having ghost money as a common denominator greatly facilitated this stretch, even more so when coupled with the use of basic administrative skills. Such skills were not vital for adopting ghost money as a gauge of value. At Hondschoote, the leading Flemish cloth production centre from the early fifteenth century, money of account was commonly used long before the habit of formal bookkeeping spread throughout the business community.[28] By 1530, people like the small Mariënweerd tenant mentioned earlier were familiar with the concept.[29] Presumably supply chains functioned as conduits, money of account trickling down from wholesalers, for whom the premium for using it was highest, to the retail trade. Retailers must have kept track of store credit in money of account unless they dealt with a floating customer base. Stallholders at food markets, innkeepers, and the ubiquitous itinerant peddlers must have dealt in coin with their customers, but in early eighteenth-century Holland shopkeepers and professional service providers like barber-surgeons appear to have been paid only once or twice a year, so they and their customers must have reckoned in ghost money.[30] People needed to be familiar with ghost money since both their work and occasional transactions required it. This was true for women as much as for men, at least at the top of society. When Magdalena Thijs, for instance, started her own financial administration on being widowed in 1616, she used money of account, which she must have learned as a girl or otherwise from her late husband or from her father, prominent merchants both (Maarschalkerweerd 2012).

Creating money

But in combination with basic administrative skills ghost money acquired an entirely new dimension. Bilateral current accounts gave merchants the opportunity to create money by opening book debts in ghost money.[31] We can observe this functionality at work by looking at the surviving business records of two wholesale merchants active either side of 1600, Jaspar van Bell and Arend Kenkhuis. Styled as a memorial, an aide mémoire, the documents look remarkably alike, listing details of individual transactions, from initiation to completion, one after the other in no apparent order. The character of the respective entries, however, reveals significant differences between the two businesses concerned. The Bois-le-Duc merchant Jasper van Bell conducted an intraregional trade in fabrics and ironmongery products, with occasional consignments to Spain (Pirenne and Formsma 1962). Judging from his 1560s memorial he funded his operations to a considerable degree with debt in the form of IOUs, issued to cover either postponed payment for deliveries received, or for round sums of money raised at interest. As a rule, the IOUs were not directly secured on Van Bell's real estate, so creditors probably had only his reputation as surety, that is to say, his person and goods, a formula customary for IOUs.

Whatever the collateral, by entering book debts Van Bell in effect created money. Doing this was part and parcel of the Low Countries' early modern economy. Merchants practised it on a wide scale, and in financial centres like Bruges, Antwerp, and later Amsterdam money changers, cashiers, and bankers did so, too, as a matter of course, another reason to doubt whether a shortage of good coin did hamper exchange. Since ghost money was a widely recognized and used money equivalent easily convertible in cash, we should see it in modern terms as belonging to narrow money M1. Tied as it normally was to supplies of goods or services, the money or M created by book debts tended to rise more or less in tandem with transactions T and not lead to inflation because neither velocity nor prices would have to rise in order to keep MV equal to PT. Moreover, the character of commercial exchange provided safeguards for the prudent use of ghost money created. Entering into a current account relationship required a considerable degree of mutual trust between merchants. Once established, they maintained it by a regular exchange of account statements and a prompt settlement of balances outstanding. Prompt settlement counted as the hallmark of a merchant's probity, which served as a check on taking too much credit. Merchants could thus monitor both the volume of money created and on the link between M and T, while in the normal course of business the money they created was also periodically destroyed again by clearing or settlement. In short, the social embeddedness which ensured a regular flow of commerce by the monitoring and enforcement of contracts also regulated the volume of ghost money created. Conversely, this embeddedness also explains what puzzled Morineau, i.e. how the Dutch economy could expand with so little coin per capita: in closely knit commercial networks, M1 could rapidly expand or contract according to economic need.

Returning to Van Bell, he usually wrote the figures concerning his many and varied deals in ghost money, Carolus guilders of 20 stivers, occasionally switching to Flemish pounds and more rarely to Philippus guilders of 25 stivers.

Recalculating his receipts of local coins into money of account must have been second nature to him, but he also received Spanish coins. These obviously presented a difficulty to him, so Van Bell did those sums in ducats, reals, and maravedis. Some twenty years later, another wholesaler, the Delft merchant Claes Adriaensz van Adrichem, also translated his local receipts and expenses into guilders of account, but tabulated the expenses incurred in the Sound or in Danzig in the local money of account and recalculated the total into guilders.[32] A 1583 list of a Leiden wholesaler's possessions, already mentioned, is unique in revealing the complexity of day-to-day commercial reality normally hidden behind the screen of accounting conventions.[33] Such lists were usually drawn up in ghost money, but this one shows the composition of a sum of 670 guilders in cash found, which was made up of more than 470 coins of over 27 different types from all over the Low Countries, Spain, Portugal, France, and Italy. All coins except four were recalculated into money of account according to the latest official exchange rates published in 1579, so the clerk drafting the list clearly knew the market rates. One wonders, though, why he made the error of counting one stiver as a guilder, that is, a factor of twenty difference.

Complexities of a very different kind dominate the ledger of Arend Kenkhuis, from the 1620s into the 1640s, who was active in the north-eastern Almelo region, part of the more farming-oriented provinces bordering on the German lands (Hesselink-Van der Riet 2008). We do not know the size of his business, which was as varied as Van Bell's, without his exports to Spain but Kenkhuis did import overseas timber, at least once.[34] In keeping with custom, Kenkhuis recalculated all his transactions into money of account. Actual coins appear only occasionally in the book, for instance to specify a sum of cash lent. What sets the Kenkhuis ledger apart from Van Bell's administration is the character of the transactions recorded. The entries usually summarize the settlement of multiple transactions between Kenkhuis and his counterparties, as often as not covering a considerable time, months or even years.[35] The individual transactions were only partly monetized, in two senses. First, the parties concerned valued the goods and services exchanged in money, but very rarely used cash to settle the balance, which was either carried over to a next meeting or offset by a specified future supply of goods or services. Money thus performed one function, gauge of value, because the transactions recorded were not barter but always pivoted around money. But ghost money served as the means of exchange, not cash.

The second sense in which Kenkhuis's transactions were only partly monetized concerns their credit side. Like most merchants Kenkhuis created money as a matter of course, but as often as not in an undifferentiated way. Whereas Van Bell, for instance, wrote down the terms and conditions of all credit received and extended, Kenkhuis's credit remained largely unmonetized and even undetermined as to its term. His notebook shows three different kinds of credit: time lapses between delivery and payment, balances carried forward, and formal loans. In the first two credit always remained implicit, without an apparent set term, and unpriced. We cannot make out his overall balance, but the entries give a strong impression of it always being overwhelmingly positive. Moreover, the sequence of entries appears to suggest that Kenkhuis practised a rudimentary form of fractional reserve banking by careful scheduling of his settlements, which may have been geared to his travelling around the country in set patterns. As for the third type of credit, formal loans, Kenkhuis did charge interest on some of them, but the summary nature of his jottings prevents us from understanding why he did so for some but not others, nor why some were covered with a formal bond, others not.[36]

Thus, whereas the terms and conditions of goods and services exchanged were monetized in the sense of being clearly defined and expressed, those for credit often were not. In such cases Kenkhuis could have used money of account for its definition, yet he did not, so both sides must have preferred to leave the credit undefined. That is to say, they either failed to perceive the hidden costs of credit, for instance if a counterparty's unfamiliarity with money of account forced Kenkhuis to barter, or else they ignored them. If they ignored them, that means they accepted them in return for social or economic benefits which we can no longer observe. In any case, we should be wrong to interpret the swapping of goods and services as a sign of an underdeveloped economy, of backwardness, in terms of the older literature the persistence of a *Naturalwirtschaft* before the onset of the modern *Geldwirtschaft*. First, because Kenkhuis clearly knew how to price and collateralize credit and he understood the advantages of doing so, but chose not to for reasons unknown.

Second, this type of cashless transaction remained very common throughout the early modern Low Countries regardless of commercialization levels. They occurred regularly until well into the seventeenth century in Hondschoote, which by then had been a leading textile production centre for more than two hundred years.[37] At Markegem in inland Flanders, a big farmer performed a similar ghost money-based intermediary function to Kenkhuis's during the third quarter of the eighteenth century and a big farm in the Walloon part of Brabant did the same around 1800.[38] In the Salland region of Overijssel during the 1740s, the manager of the Rechteren manor ran a cashless settlement system with all his tenant farmers which benefitted notably the small ones since it enabled them to draw on credit in hard times and repay with labour (Kooijmans and Jonker 2015).

Mutual settlement systems avoiding cash payment appear to have been ubiquitous elsewhere, too. They have been found from seventeenth-century Cheshire to Württemberg, across the early modern French countryside, and in colonial New England (Hoffman 1996, Matthews 2009, Vickers 2010, Ogilvie *et al.* 2012). Perhaps cultural values such as attitudes to money determined whether or not people made the credit component of a transaction explicit; perhaps social relations, and more specifically asymmetric or mutual dependency, did (Muldrew 1998, Fontaine 2008, Howell 2010). Kinship does not appear to have entered into the equation (Sabean 1990, 1998, Mathieu, Sabean, and Teuscher 2007, Krausman Ben-Amos 2000). What matters here is that, whether in Twente, Salland, Hondschoote, or Markegem, money of account gave people the option to define and price credit, but at times they still preferred not to do so for reasons unknown to us.

Let's rephrase what we have just observed. The character of payments changed over time, from a periodic settlement of numerous transactions to the conclusion of a single one following more or less immediately after an exchange of goods or services. During this process, the Siamese twin money and credit separated into two distinct economic transactions serving different purposes and priced accordingly. The tempo of the process varied widely, over time, from area to area, and from one social group to another. Money of account was an important driver. It had been available across the entire area by the late Middle Ages, so we must explain any lags in monetization from factors other than the availability of money: the scale of transactions, cultural attitudes, convenience, education, the nature of relationships. Thus, we conclude that cash shortages did not necessarily force people into debt. Credit conditions may have been opaque and credit's invisible price high, but people familiar with ghost money always possessed a means of payment if they wanted to avoid it. But did that also hold for people unfamiliar with that convention?

Cash and credit

As we have surmised, money of account probably did not reach people with subsistence incomes whose use of money remained limited to small-scale selling of cheap goods or services and to purchasing daily necessities. We thus need to know whether or not they had to take credit because small coin was in short supply. According to Sargent and Velde (2002) it was. Early modern governments restricted the minting of small coins because the available technology did not permit a production of sufficient quality to deter the counterfeiting of what was in effect fiat money. If true, the consequent shortage of small coin might have forced retail customers to take credit. However, in the Low Countries the supply of small coin appears to have been sufficient overall.[39] The government of Charles V initiated the production of small copper coins to replace medieval billon coins, also called black money because of the colour which the inferior silver alloy assumed over time.

Following the Revolt, mints in the north started producing copper coins by the million, the south following suit a few years later. Both regions continued minting copper coin at an apparently high level.[40] When, during the War of the Spanish Succession, the Brussels government had lost power over some of the southern Netherlands provinces, various mint entrepreneurs started competing with each other in producing floods of copper coin (De Witte 1909). The authorities did limit the minting of small coppers, not for fear of counterfeits, but because producing them was so profitable that, without limitations, copper would drive the smallest silver coins out of circulation.[41] The desirability of providing small coin to facilitate exchange was not lost on the VOC, which during the entire eighteenth century minted large amounts of copper *duiten* or doits for export to Java, where they proved to be very popular (Feenstra 2014).

We can observe the phenomenon of coppers closely at the retail level. Shopkeepers, pub landlords, tax collectors, and public charity collections received small copper coins in such abundance that they stuck them together into paper covered rolls to form silver coin equivalents.[42] Called *worp*, *cahot*, *packjes*, or *knapper*, such rolls appear to have circulated unhindered by the fact that receivers could not check their exact value, a problem all the more pressing because poor quality coppers circulated in great numbers. In 1643, for instance, a Delft charity sold an estimated 37,600 copper coins for just over half their face value.[43] The Meertens Institute Boedelbank database of probate inventories shows rolls of copper to have been present in the northern Netherlands as early as 1628 and ubiquitous in its western provinces by the beginning of the eighteenth century. They do not show up in the probates from the eastern provinces, but at least by the 1740s they were common enough in the southern Netherlands. Limburg shopkeepers sent rolls to suppliers in areas with shortages, so presumably the more highly commercialized provinces drew copper coins from the less commercially oriented ones.[44]

Copper money also flowed in from abroad, channelled by specialized coin traders.[45] Changing economic circumstances drove a more or less constant ebb and flow of copper, like there was in silver and gold, resulting in occasional or even recurrent shortages (Hoc 1934).[46] For instance, the high bullion prices which drove silver coins out of circulation during the first decades of the eighteenth century must have driven up demand for rolls of coppers to substitute for small silver coins. This appears to have drained the copper coin circulation, leading to an influx of inferior coppers from elsewhere.[47] By 1738, the circulation had deteriorated to such a degree that Amsterdam shopkeepers refused to accept any copper at all. The resulting inconvenience drove citizens to vent their anger by occupying city hall, prompting the authorities to start minting new coppers.[48] The incident highlights at the same time the occurrence of occasional coin shortages and the fact that the public considered them a nuisance, while the official response shows the authorities aware of the need for an effective remedy. We may thus confidently assume that structural shortages of small coin did not really occur.[49] As an aside we want to point to the retailers' role in sparking the incident. The money of account convention enabled supply chains to pass down the cost of coinage deficiencies, that is to say the foreign, underweight, clipped, or defaced coins, or the need for credit during occasional shortages, to the interface with consumers. In effect that cost will have been borne by retailers serving customers unable to run up debts large enough to settle in full money, and by those customers. And, as noted above, large amounts of poor coin ended up in charity collection boxes.

Thus, at both the wholesale and retail level the means were generally available to separate credit and payment, so currency reforms are unlikely to have caused the apparent decline of credit in eighteenth-century Antwerp noted by Willems.[50] Clearly the availability of coin was a necessary but not a sufficient condition for reducing the amount of credit people took: if they did so, it was because low and irregular incomes or long intervals between wage payments reduced the amount of ready money they had available, or because they found cash a chore.[51]

Cash, credit, and debt in probate records

Finally, we examine probate inventory data for a link between coin availability and credit in the Dutch Republic. Before we turn to the data, first a word about the pitfalls of probate data in general.[52] Probate inventories do not provide a good cross section of society, because some social groups are underrepresented in them, or indeed entirely absent. Such documents were drawn up for specific reasons, in the case of our sample mostly to provide the inheritors with a clear overview of the deceased's estate so as to either facilitate its division, or protect the interests of surviving minors. Given the cost of drafting them, inheritors will therefore only have commissioned probate inventories if the estate was worth it, that is to say, if the assets outweighed liabilities. Consequently, our data set excludes a very large social group, people whose net worth fell below a certain threshold.[53] A different issue concerns the representation of social elites in the set. Having one's possessions counted was not to everyone's taste; in particular the nobility and people aspiring to it appear to have eschewed commissioning probate inventories. Such norms will have differed from place to place and from period to period without us knowing to what extent this affects our set. Finally, real property was usually included but often not valued, rendering it impossible to calculate net wealth.

Moreover, the information in probates from the northern Netherlands varies from place to place. In Flanders and probably Brabant as well probates mostly served to meet legal requirements, assessing a household's possessions with a view to securing a sound financial base for the proper care for any minors left behind, so the local orphan trustees would see to a correct and complete inventory.[54] By contrast, the northern Netherlands probates in the Meertens set were mostly drawn up without the supervision of officials, so it depended on the diligence of the notaries and clerks concerned whether or not all possessions were listed and properly valued. In addition, probate inventories were drawn up following a specific occasion, a person's death, but not at a specific moment in time after that had happened. Days or even weeks could pass before the clerks had done their counting and drafting, a process which itself could take days in some households. During that period, some household costs might have been paid, anxious creditors might have presented their claim, and been paid or not, needy inheritors might have helped themselves from the available cash, reducing the amount registered.

Therefore, the amount of cash listed in probates probably tended towards the lower side of what would on average have been present in the household concerned. Moreover, we must also assume that the peculiarities of the coin circulation impacted variously on cash levels. They probably dropped and rose with the ebb and flow of coins noted earlier unless, as seems possible, variations in the velocity of circulation buffered such fluctuations. In addition, the cash level of some probates will have been influenced by chance events, death occurring the day after large payments or receipts for instance. Again, we have no way of ascertaining to what extent these factors affect our data. Since at present we want to do no more than identify broad trends over time, however, we may take the aggregate per time period and region as more important than the details of individual estates.

The Meertens data set reflects all of these problems. It consists of 2,586 inventories collected from seven smaller towns, where all inventories from the seventeenth and eighteenth centuries were photocopied, then entered into a database.[55] For the purpose of finding out whether the phenomenon noted by Willems, i.e. the gradual supplanting of debt by cash, occurred in the northern Netherlands as well, we first split the data into two subsets, one for the western and one for the eastern provinces, to see if the known economic differences between these two parts of the country shaped patterns of debt and cash holdings differently. We then grouped the data for each region into four 50-year periods and ranked them by the amount of debt and/or cash which they held (Tables 11.1 and 11.2). When looking at the data, the first thing to notice is the scarcity of probates in our set for the period 1600–1649, a total of 14 for the north and 22 for the south, so those data are not very firm. Fortunately, for the later periods our set has enough probates for both parts of the country so we can identify the broad trends we are looking for. The disparity between western and eastern provinces stands out. In the west, a large majority of estates held on average very substantial sums of cash, whereas a minority of eastern estates averages much smaller amounts of cash. However, both sets show a trend towards greater indebtedness, much more marked in the west than in the east. And neither set shows signs of cash supplanting debt as found by Bart Willems for Antwerp. A considerable number of estates (107 in the western provinces, 427 in the eastern ones) held neither cash nor debt. A further 188 probates had only cash and no debt (142 western versus 46 eastern), whereas 226 probates had only debt and no cash (74 western, 152 eastern). The remaining 437 probate inventories, printed in bold type, held both cash and debt. With this group of probates, we can examine whether cash did supplant debt, but this appears not to have been the case. In all four time periods and in both regions, the amounts of cash and debt rose in tandem. Moreover, higher amounts of cash are typically associated with higher amounts of debt, not lower ones. Thus, based on the Meertens Boedels, the two asset types would seem to have been complements, they did not substitute for one another.

Conclusion

In the early modern Low Countries, paying cash was a chore, so people, and not only merchants (Spufford 2008), avoided it whenever possible. We show that ghost money provided a ready alternative to coin by facilitating cashless payments in a fictive, stable, unit of account. Moreover, in tandem with bilateral current accounts, ghost money facilitated the creation of money in the

Table 11.1 Meertens probate set, cash and debts in Western Region probates in four time periods, 1600–1799

1600–1649	*Debts outstanding*						
Cash holdings	*0*	*0–10*	*10–100*	*100–1000*	*1000–10000*	*≥ 10000*	*n =*
0	1	0	1	0	1	0	3
0–10	0	0	0	0	0	0	0
10–100	1	0	0	**1**	**1**	0	3
100–1000	0	0	0	**3**	**3**	0	6
1000–10000	0	0	0	**1**	**1**	0	2
≥ 10000	0	0	0	0	0	0	0
n =	2	0	1	5	6	0	14

1650–1699	*Debts outstanding*						
Cash holdings	*0*	*0–10*	*10–100*	*100–1000*	*1000–10000*	*≥ 10000*	*n =*
0	44	1	4	10	12	0	71
0–10	3	0	0	0	0	**1**	4
10–100	14	0	**2**	**3**	**7**	0	26
100–1000	8	0	**4**	**6**	**14**	**4**	36
1000–10000	1	0	0	**4**	**9**	**3**	17
≥ 10000	0	0	0	0	0	0	0
n =	70	1	10	23	42	8	154

1700–1749	*Debts outstanding*						
Cash holdings	*0*	*0–10*	*10–100*	*100–1000*	*1000–10000*	*≥ 10000*	*n =*
0	30	2	7	9	4	0	52
0–10	4	0	0	**4**	**2**	0	10
10–100	13	0	**3**	**14**	**8**	0	38
100–1000	18	0	**6**	**29**	**19**	**2**	74
1000–10000	9	0	**1**	**6**	**22**	**6**	44
≥ 10000	0	0	0	**1**	**1**	**1**	3
n =	74	2	17	63	56	9	221

1750–1799	*Debts outstanding*						
Cash holdings	*0*	*0–10*	*10–100*	*100–1000*	*1000–10000*	*≥ 10000*	*n =*
0	22	0	3	11	9	0	45
0–10	4	0	**2**	**7**	**3**	**0**	16
10–100	23	4	**11**	**29**	**8**	**1**	76
100–1000	31	0	**8**	**48**	**45**	**5**	137
1000–10000	12	0	**1**	**18**	**40**	**13**	84
≥ 10000	1	0	0	**3**	**6**	**4**	14
n =	93	4	25	116	111	23	372

Table 11.2 Meertens probate set, cash and debts in Eastern Region probates in four time periods, 1600–1799

1600–1649	*Debts outstanding*						
Cash holdings	*0*	*0–10*	*10–100*	*100–1000*	*1000–10000*	*≥ 10000*	*n =*
0	12	0	0	1	0	0	13
0–10	0	0	**1**	0	**1**	0	2
10–100	1	0	0	**2**	0	0	3
100–1000	0	0	**1**	**2**	**1**	0	4
1000–10000	0	0	0	0	0	0	0
≥ 10000	0	0	0	0	0	0	0
n =	13	0	2	5	2	0	22
1650–1699	*Debts outstanding*						
Cash holdings	*0*	*0–10*	*10–100*	*100–1000*	*1000–10000*	*≥ 10000*	*n =*
0	70	0	5	5	2	0	82
0–10	2	0	0	**1**	0	0	3
10–100	7	0	**1**	**4**	**1**	0	13
100–1000	4	0	0	**2**	**3**	**1**	10
1000–10000	1	0	0	0	0	**0**	1
≥ 10000	0	0	0	0	0	0	0
n =	84	0	6	12	6	1	109
1700–1749	*Debts outstanding*						
Cash holdings	*0*	*0–10*	*10–100*	*100–1000*	*1000–10000*	*≥10000*	*n =*
0	119	2	15	15	5	0	156
0–10	1	0	**1**	**1**	0	0	3
10–100	2	**1**	**2**	**2**	**1**	0	8
100–1000	3	0	**1**	**4**	**1**	**1**	10
1000–10000	0	0	0	0	0	0	0
≥ 10000	0	0	0	0	0	0	0
n =	125	3	19	22	7	1	177
1750–1799	*Debts outstanding*						
Cash holdings	*0*	*0–10*	*10–100*	*100–1000*	*1000–10000*	*≥10000*	*n =*
0	226	12	43	38	9	0	328
0–10	3	0	**2**	**2**	0	0	7
10–100	12	**2**	**7**	**13**	**5**	0	39
100–1000	10	**1**	**1**	**11**	**5**	**1**	29
1000–10000	0	0	0	**1**	**1**	**1**	3
≥ 10000	0	0	0	0	0	0	0
n =	251	15	53	65	20	2	406

form of book debts, rendering the volume of M1 in circulation very elastic. The fact that any expansion of M1 in this way was closely tied to the sale of goods and services minimized the danger of inflation, while the system's social embeddedness limited the potential for abuse. Ghost money thus solves the puzzle posed by Morineau, i.e. the Dutch Republic's rapid economic growth with a low coin circulation.

Our findings have several implications for the way in which we think about the evolution of money and credit in general. First, the gauge of value function of money was probably far more important than the settlement or store of value functions were. For barter transactions to work, they must revolve around some common standard, or else people will not be able to agree. That means we need to abandon the stage theory of monetization progressing from barter via cash to credit because it simply does not work. Instead, we need to rethink what we mean by commercialization and monetization, because what looks like barter was probably already monetized in the sense of using some form of standard. In other words, deep monetization in the sense of Lucassen (2014) must have been preceded by money as a gauge of value.

Second, we should expect a poor currency system to put a premium on people devising alternative means of settlement, rather than reducing their transactions. Ghost money was only one way of doing this, arguably far more practical than the cigarettes serving as currency in Germany following the collapse of the Nazi regime.

Third, if people always possessed a way to settle transactions, credit relations were shaped by choice, not by the necessity of having to take credit in the absence of means of payment. Of course, credit could still be a sign of social or economic dependency, as it was in Markegem, Flanders, but not necessarily so: stewards and tenants on the Rechteren estate in Salland used cashless payments and credit simply because it was more practical. That is to say, we need to push the arguments of Muldrew, Vickers, and Kuroda further and start appreciating the social dimension of payments. How Van Bell, Kenkhuis, or the New Englanders studied by Vickers settled debts and claims depended heavily on their relationship with the counterparty in question, so examining patterns of settlement tells us more about how their society worked. Even today, similar telling social differences in ways of paying persist, in the composition of what people carry in their wallets, in the various classes of credit cards and loyalty schemes, or in the penetration rate of paying by smartphone.

From this third point it follows that, in most places and most of the time, cash and credit functioned seamlessly together as slightly different forms of obligations to pay or rights to receive, rather than distinct and differently priced economic categories, let alone stage posts in a hypothetical evolution from barter via money to credit. That means we ought to focus more on what makes people separate cash from credit by putting terms and price on payments due. In the Low Countries, for instance, rebates (*rabatten*) for early payment were common in commercial centres like Antwerp and Amsterdam at least by 1600, if not before. Perhaps cultural attitudes determined their spreading outwards from there, for instance capitalism rendering people more sensitive to the value of money (Howell 2010, Muldrew 1998). Perhaps commercial pressures did, or both working in tandem. For now, all we can say is that the availability of cash money did not matter, since other kinds of money were always readily available.

Notes

1 The research for this paper was made possible by generous fellowships at the Netherlands Institute for Advanced Studies (NIAS) in Wassenaar. The Meertens Institute and Hester Dibbits kindly allowed us to use their probate inventory database, which Heidi Deneweth's incomparable efforts reorganized so we could analyze the data. We thank participants at seminars in Utrecht and at the Federal Reserve Bank of Atlanta, and at the Silver in World History conference, VU Amsterdam, December 2014, for their valuable suggestions.
2 Nijssen and Van Laere (2001: 270–271).
3 Van Gelder (1972–1973, Vol. I: 436–437).
4 Van Deursen (1994: 148).
5 Nijssen and Van Laere (2001: 280–281).
6 Van Bavel (1993: 361–362). In 1539 another tenant paid with a Spanish ducat, a coin rarely seen, so the monk who accepted made a mistake in valuing it (ibid.).
7 Van Gelder (2002: 115).
8 Welten (2010: 25–33); Teeuwen (2014b: 152–153); Scheffers (2013: 151).
9 National Archives, The Hague (henceforth NA) 1.04.02 VOC inv. no. 221, index resolutions 1602–1736, fol. 340–341, 4 August 1608.
10 Van Gelder (2002: 45, 80, 94, 105, 140).
11 An example from the 1630s in Van Deursen (1994: 148). The fledgling Amsterdam *Wisselbank* did not stick too closely to official exchange rates during its first two decades in existence, but weighed coins instead; see Van Dillen (1929: 29; 1933: 880–883); Van der Wal (1940: 73–74, 76).
12 See Cipolla (1956: 38–51). The issue of ghost money well summarized by Chown (1994: 17–19 and 39–40). A modern interpretation given by Bordo and Schwartz (1987). We are indebted to Michael Bordo for this reference. Cf. Aerts (1976: 184–193, 196–197); Lemmens (1998: 12); De Meyer and Van den Elzen (1980); Peeters (*s.a.*); Pierson (1906); Spufford (1970: 13–28); Van Uytven (1961: 56–70); Van Werveke (1934); Spufford (2016); Aerts and Van Der Wee (2016); ghost money is something entirely different from coins of account, see Zuijderduijn (2010); Tas (2009).
13 Van Werveke (1934: 123–124) distinguishes three different types of ghost money. Since these distinctions do not matter for the functionality of ghost money we want to describe, we have omitted to discuss them. Cf. the excellent summary by Wolters (2008: 37–54), of the debate between Van Werveke and Luigi Einaudi about the true nature of moneys of account.
14 About the penetration of bookkeeping conventions see Gelderblom (2013: 94–100).
15 Boyer-Xambeu, Deleplace and Gillard (1994: 28–29, 70, 106–109, 134).
16 Vercouteren (1985: 10–11); Aerts (2011: 97–98).
17 However, business in the Flemish town of Hondschoote, an important textile production, largely stuck to the rival Paris pound (Coornaert 1930: 326).
18 Vercouteren (1985: 16–23); Van der Wee and Materné (1987: 69–72); Aerts (2011: 97–98, 100). Despite hosting important regional fairs Deventer could make do with a single money changer during the fifteenth century. His main occupation was taking poor coins out of circulation and sending them to the local mint for recoinage (Sneller 1934: 491–492, 496).
19 Van Gelder (1952: 37).

20 Cf. Van Deursen (1994: 95–96) for the surprising longevity of Catholic conventions concerning dates among Protestants.
21 Janssens (1957: 5–6).
22 Lambrecht (2003: 242).
23 Van Dillen (1958: 33).
24 Van Dillen (1933: 1103, 1104, 1108, 1110, 1111, 1146, 1281 ff).
25 See for that discussion Aerts (1994: 51–57).
26 Van der Wee (1963, II: 29, 334, 1993: 50–152); Aerts (2011); De Smedt (1940–1941).
27 Cf. for such shortages or *stretezzas* for instance Van der Wee (1963, II: 29, 57, 141, 148, 149, 200, 203, 205, 240, 243, 260, 263, 264, 266, 267, 282, 359).
28 Coornaert (1930: 325–326).
29 Van Bavel (1993: 361–362).
30 Van Deursen (1994: 111, 126–127); Faber (1980: 152, 155); De Muinck (1965: 241).
31 Cf. Boyer-Xambeu, Deleplace and Gillard (1994: 149–152): merchants could also create money with bills of exchange.
32 Winkelman (1981, III: 534–569).
33 Van Gelder (1972–1973, I: 436–437).
34 Hesselink-Van der Riet *et al.* (2008: 287, no. 742).
35 Cf. for instance Kenkhuis's transactions with Lambert Hagedoorn over a period of 20 years, Hesselink-Van der Riet *et al.* (2008, no. 89; 437–438, nos. 1233 and 1234).
36 For instance, Hesselink-Van der Riet *et al.* (2008: 70, no. 145).
37 Coornaert (1930: 327–328).
38 Lambrecht (2003). Cf. Hoffman (1996) and Meuvret (1971) on France, and Vickers (2010) on colonial New England.
39 Polak (1998) omits small coin from his data for the northern Netherlands, but the Van Cauwenberghe and Verachten data set about southern Netherlands minting does give them: http://www.geldmuseum.nl/museum/content/dataset-monetaire-geschiedenis-van-de-zuidelijke-nederlanden-1493-1789. Cf. also Munro (1989); Van Gelder (2002); Hoc (1934); Baerten *s.a.*; Janssens (1957); Scheffers (2013), the latter drawing together scattered production data for eighteenth-century Holland to give a convincing impression of the general availability of copper coin. See also Volckart (2008) for more general objections to the Sargent and Velde thesis.
40 A large part of Scheffers (2013) is devoted to the production of small coin in the Republic. On the penetration of money in the Low Countries in general see Lucassen (2007, 2014). For the southern Netherlands see Peeters (*s.a.*: 86, 94–95, 98–100); Janssens (1957: 8, 21, 23–25).
41 Van Gelder (2002: 164–167); Janssens (1957: 52–53); for an earlier period, Munro (1989: 26, 36–37).
42 Welten (2010: 25–33); Teeuwen (2014b: 152–153); Scheffers (2013: 151).
43 Teeuwen (2014b: 163–165), Teeuwen (2014a: 30–33).
44 Welten (2010: 29–30); Janssens (1957: 178–179).
45 Scheffers (2013: 229), referring to a complaint voiced by the Holland mintmasters in 1753.
46 Janssens (1957: 21) mentions one extreme case during the War of the Spanish Succession, when an imminent devaluation of large coins caused a flight from gold and silver into copper and an acute shortage of small coin.
47 Van der Wal (1940: 116–117).
48 Scheffers (2013: 142, 204–220).
49 Janssens (1957: 22–25).
50 Willems (2009: 91–127).
51 Cf. Lambrecht (2003: 244, 253); on the long wage intervals Lucassen (2007).
52 On the intricacies of Low Countries probate data see Wijsenbeek-Olthuis (1995) and Rykbosch (2012).
53 This was the sensible policy of the Amsterdam orphan trustees: see McCants (2007).

54 Rykbosch (2012: 40).
55 For the set's construction, see http://www.meertens.knaw.nl/boedelbank/index.php?actie=info, consulted on 1 April 2015. The towns are: Weesp, Medemblik and Twisk, Doesburg, Lichtenvoorde and Groenlo, Maasland, Maassluis, Oirschot.

Bibliography

Aerts, E. (1976). 'De inhoud der rekeningen van de Brabantse algemeen-ontvangerij (1430-1440). Moeilijkheden en mogelijkheden voor het historisch onderzoek', *Bijdragen tot de Geschiedenis*, 59: 165–199.

Aerts, E. (1994). 'De economische geschiedenis van het geld tijdens het Ancien Régime, kennismaking met een discipline', *Belgisch Tijdschrift voor Numismatiek en Zegelkunde*, 140: 43–69.

Aerts, E. (2011). 'The absence of public exchange banks in medieval and early modern Flanders and Brabant (1400–1800): a historical anomaly to be explained', *Financial History Review*, 18: 91–117.

Aerts, E. and Van Der Wee, H. (2016). 'Les Pays-Bas espagnols et autrichiens', in Van Heesch, J., Yante, J.-M. and Owagie, H. (eds.), *Monnaies de compte et monnaies réelles, Pays-Bas méridionaux et principauté de Liège au Moyen Age et aux Temps modernes*, Louvain la Neuve: Association Professeur Marcel Hoc: 163–200.

Bolton, J.L. (2012). *Money in the Medieval English Economy, 973–1489*. Manchester: Manchester University Press, 2012.

Bordo, M. D. and Schwartz, A. J. (1987). 'The ECU, an imaginary or embryonic form of money: What can we learn from history?', NBER Working Paper No. 2345. Cambridge, MA: National Bureau of Economic Research. http://www.nber.org/papers/w2345. Accessed 2017-07-17.

Boyer-Xambeu, M. T., Deleplace, G. and Gillard, L. (1994). *Private Money and Public Currencies, the 16th Century Challenge*. Armonk, NY: M.E. Sharpe.

Chown, J. F. (1994). *A History of Money from* ad *800*. London: Routledge.

Cipolla, C. M. (1956). *Money, Prices, and Civilisation in the Mediterranean World, Fifth to Seventeenth Centuries*. Princeton, NJ: Princeton University Press.

Cipolla, C.M. (1967). *Money, Prices, and Civilisation in the Mediterranean World, Fifth to Seventeenth Centuries*. Gordian Press: New York.

Collins, D., Morduch, J., Rutherford, S. and Ruthven, O. (2010). *Portfolios of the Poor: How the World's Poor Live on $2 a Day*. Princeton, NJ: Princeton University Press.

Coornaert, E. (1930). *La draperie-sayetterie d'Hondschoote (XIVe–XVIIIe siècles), un centre industriel d'autrefois*. Rennes: Imprimeries réunies.

Day, J. (1978). 'The great bullion famine of the fifteenth century', *Past and Present*, 79: 3–54.

De Meyer, G. and Van den Elzen, E. (1980). 'Van geschenk tot getal, geschiedenis van een hoofse rekenmunt', *Revue belge de philologie et d'histoire*, 58: 317–336.

De Muinck, B. (1965). *Een regentenhuishouding omstreeks 1700, gegevens uit de privéboekhouding van mr. Cornelis de Jonge van Ellemeet, ontvanger-generaal der Vereenigde Nederlanden (1646–1721)*. Den Haag: Nijhoff.

De Smedt, O. (1940-1941). 'De keizerlijke verordeningen van 1537 en 1539 op de obligaties en wisselbrieven, eenige kanttekeningen', *Nederlandsche Historiebladen*, 3: 15–35.

De Witte, A. (1909). 'Fabrication illicite de liards', *Revue Belge de Numismatique et de Sigillographie*, 65: 174–181.

Faber, J. A. (1980). 'Inhabitants of Amsterdam and their possessions, 170–1710', *AAG Bijdragen*, 23: 149–155.

Feenstra, H. A. (2014). 'Dutch coins for Asian growth, VOC-duiten to assess Java's deep monetization and economic growth, 1724-1800', *Tijdschrift voor Sociale en Economische Geschiedenis*, 11: 153–183.

Fontaine, L. (2008). *L'économie morale, pauvreté, crédit et confiance dans l'Europe préindustrielle.* Paris: Gallimard.

Gelderblom, O. (2013). *Cities of Commerce, the Institutional Foundations of International Trade in the Low Countries, 1250–1650.* Princeton, NJ: Princeton University Press.

Hesselink-Van der Riet, T., Kuiper W. and Trompetter, C. (eds.) (2008). *Het schuldboek van Arend Kenkhuis.* Amsterdam: Aksant.

Hoc, M. (1934). 'La circulation des menues monnaies étrangères dans la province de Namur au XVIIIe siècle', *Revue belge de numismatique et de sigillographie*, 90: 43–53.

Hoffman, P. (1996). *Growth in a Traditional Society, the French Countryside, 1450–1815.* Princeton, NJ: Princeton University Press.

Howell, M. (2010). *Commerce before Capitalism in Europe, 1300–1600.* Cambridge: Cambridge University Press.

Janssens, V. (1957). *Het geldwezen der Oostenrijkse Nederlanden.* Brussels: Koninklijke Vlaamsche Academie.

Kooijmans, T. and Jonker, J. (2015). 'Chained to the Manor? Payment patterns and landlord-tenant relations in the Salland region of the Netherlands around 1750', *Tijdschrift voor Sociale en Economische Geschiedenis*, 12: 89–116.

Krausman Ben-Amos, I. (2000). 'Reciprocal bonding: Parents and their offspring in early modern England', *Journal of Family History, Studies in Family, Kinship and Demography*, 25: 291–312.

Kuroda, A. (2008a). 'What is the complementarity among monies? An introductory note', *Financial History Review*, 15: 7–16.

Kuroda, A. (2008b). 'Concurrent but non-integrable currency circuits, complementary relationships among monies in modern China and other regions', *Financial History Review*, 15: 17–36.

Lambrecht, T. (2003). 'Reciprocal exchange, credit and cash: agricultural labour markets and local economies in the southern Low Countries during the eighteenth century', *Continuity and Change*, 18: 237–261.

Lemmens, K. (1998). 'Rekenmunt en courant geld', *Jaarboek van het Europees Genootschap voor Munt- en Penningkunde*, 1998: 19–52.

Lucassen, J. (2007). 'Wages, payments and currency circulation in the Netherlands from 1200 to 2000', in: Lucassen, J. (ed.), *Wages and Currency, Global Comparisons from Antiquity to the Twentieth Century*, Bern: Peter Lang: 221–263.

Lucassen, J. and Zuijderduijn, C. (2014). 'Coins, currencies, and credit instruments, media of exchange in economic and social history', *Tijdschrift voor Economische en Sociale Geschiedenis*, 11: 1–14.

Lucassen, J. (2014). 'Deep monetization: The case of the Netherlands', *Tijdschrift voor Economische en Sociale Geschiedenis*, 11: 73–122.

Maarschalkerweerd, D. (2012). *Magdalena Thijs en haar memoriaal.* MA Thesis, Utrecht University.

McCants, A. (2007). 'Goods at pawn, the overlapping worlds of material possessions and family finance in early modern Amsterdam', *Social Science History*, 31: 213–238.

Mathieu, J., Sabean, D. and Teuscher, D. (eds.) (2007). *Kinship in Europe, Approaches to Long-Term Development (1300-1900).* New York, NY: Berghahn.

Matthews, S. (2009). 'Money supply and credit in rural Cheshire, c. 1600-1680', *Continuity and Change*, 24: 245–274.

Meuvret, J. (1971). 'Circuits d'échanges et travail rural dans la France du XVIIe siècle', in Meuvret, J. (ed.), *Études d'histoire économique, receuil d'études*, Paris: A. Colin:184–200.

Morineau, M. (1974). 'Quelques remarques sur l'abondance monétaire aus Provinces Unies', *Annales ESC*, 29: 767–776.

Muldrew, C. (1998). *The Economy of Obligation, the Culture of Credit and Social Relations in Early Modern England*. Basingstoke: Macmillan.

Munro, J. (1983). 'Bullion flows and monetary contraction in late-Medieval England and the Low Countries', in: Richards, J. (ed.), *Precious Metals in the Later Medieval and Early Modern world*, Durham NC: Carolina Academic Press: 97–158.

Munro, J. (1988). 'Deflation and the petty coinage problem in the late-medieval economy: the case of Flanders, 1334-1484', *Explorations in Economic History* 25: 387–423.

Munro, J. (1989). 'Petty coinage in the economy of late-Medieval Flanders: Some social considerations of public minting', in: Van Cauwenberghe, E. (ed.), *Precious Metals, Coinage and the Changes of Monetary Structures in Latin-America, Europe and Asia (Late Middle Ages–Early Modern Times)*, Leuven: Leuven University Press: 25–56.

Munro, J.H. (2012). *Money in the Pre-Industrial World, Bullion, Debasements and Coin Substitutes*. London: Pickering & Chatto, 2012.

Nijssen, R. and Van Laere, R. (2001). 'Muntcirculatie in de zestiende en zeventiende eeuw: drie Limburgse teksten', *Het Oude Land van Loon*, 80: 267–282.

Ogilvie, S., Küpker, M. and Maegraith, J. (2012). 'Household debt in early modern Germany: Evidence from personal inventories', *Journal of Economic History*, 72: 134–167.

Peeters, J.-P. (s.a.). 'De Middeleeuwse rekenmunt in de Nederlanden, een status quaestionis', in: Baerten, J. (ed.), *Muntslag en muntcirculatier in de Nederlanden, Noord en Zuid op de weegschaal*, Brussels: Vrije Universiteit, Centrum Strukturen en Economische Conjunctuur.

Pierson, N. (1906). 'Bijdrage tot de verklaring van middeleeuwsche rekenmunten', *De Economist*, 55: 263–296.

Pirenne, L. and Formsma, W. (eds.) (1962). *Koopmansgeest te 's Hertogenbosch in de vijftiende en zestiende eeuw, het kasboek van Jaspar van Bell 1564-1568*. Nijmegen: Centrale Drukkerij.

Polak, M. (1998). *Historiografie en economie van de 'muntchaos', de muntproductie van de Republiek (1606–1795)*, 2 vols. Amsterdam: NEHA.

Rykbosch, W. (2012). *A Consumer Revolution under Strain, Consumption, Wealth, and Status in Eighteenth-Century Aalst (Southern Netherlands)*. PhD Thesis Antwerp and Ghent.

Rykbosch, W. and Decraene, E. (2014). 'Household credit, social relations, and devotion in the early modern economy, a case study of confraternities and credit relations in the Southern Netherlands', *Tijdschrift voor Sociale en Economische Geschiedenis*, 11: 1–28.

Sabean, D. (1990). *Property, Production, and Family in Neckarhausen, 1700–1870*. Cambridge: Cambridge University Press.

Sabean, D. (1998). *Kinship in Neckarhausen, 1700–1870*. Cambridge: Cambridge University Press.

Sargent, Th. and Velde, F. (2002). *The Big Problem of Small Change*. Princeton, NJ: Princeton University Press.

Scheffers, A. (2013). *'Om de kwaliteit van het geld', het toezicht op de muntproductie in de Republiek en de voorziening van kleingeld in Holland en West-Friesland in de achttiende eeuw*. PhD thesis Leiden. Voorburg: Clinckaert.

Sneller, Z. (1934). 'Het wisselaarsbedrijf in Nederland vóór de oprichting der stedelijke wisselbanken', *Tijdschrift voor Geschiedenis*, 49: 486–502.

Spufford, P. (1970). *Monetary Problems and Policies in the Burgundian Netherlands, 1433-1496*. Leiden, the Netherlands: Brill.

Spufford, P. (1988). *Money and Its Use in Medieval Europe*, Cambridge: Cambridge University Press.

Spufford, P. (2008). *How Rarely Did Medieval Merchants Use Coin?* Utrecht: Geldmuseum.

Spufford, P. (2016). 'Moneys of account in the Burgundian Netherlands', in: Van Heesch, J., Yante, J.-M., and Owagie, H. (eds.), *Monnaies de compte et monnaies réelles, Pays-Bas méridionaux et principauté de Liège au Moyen Age et aux Temps modernes*, Louvain la Neuve: Association Professeur Marcel Hoc: 137–161.

Sussman, N. (1998). 'The late Medieval bullion famine reconsidered', *Journal of Economic History*, 58: 126–154.

Sussman, N. (2003). 'Commodity money inflation: theory and evidence from France in 1350–1436', *Journal of Monetary Economics*, 50: 1769–1793.

Tas, M. (2009). *Rekenpenningen, 540 rekenpenningen van de zestiende en eerste helft van de zeventiende eeuw*, s.l.

Teeuwen, D. (2014a). 'A penny for the poor, the widespread practice of monetary charitable donations in Dutch towns, 17th–18th century', *Tijdschrift voor Sociale en Economische Geschiedenis*, 11: 15–38.

Teeuwen, D. (2014b). *Generating Generosity, Financing Poor Relief through Charitable Collections in Dutch Towns, c. 1600–1800.* PhD Thesis Utrecht University.

Van Bavel, B. J. P. (1993). *Goederenverwerving en goederenbeheer van de abdij Mariënweerd (1129–1592).* Hilversum: Verloren.

Van der Wal, G. (1940). *Rekeneenheid en Ruilmiddel.* Den Helder: De Boer.

Van der Wee, H. (1963). *The Growth of the Antwerp Market and the European Economy*, 3 vols. The Hague: Nijhoff.

Van der Wee, H. (1993). 'Antwerp and the new financial methods of the 16th and 17th centuries', in: Van der Wee, H. (ed.), *The Low Countries in the Early Modern World*, Aldershot: Ashgate: 145–166.

Van der Wee, H. and Materné, J. (1987). 'Het kredietsysteem in Brabant tijdens de late Middeleeuwen en in het begin van de Nieuwe Tijd', in Van den Eerenbeemt H., (ed.),*Bankieren in Brabant in de loop der eeuwen*, Tilburg: Stichting Zuidelijk Historisch Contact: 59–78.

Van Deursen, A. Th. (1994). *Een dorp in de polder: Graft in de zeventiende eeuw.* Amsterdam: Bert Bakker.

Van Dillen, J. G. (1929). *Bronnen tot de geschiedenis van het bedrijfsleven en het gildewezen van Amsterdam.* Volume 1 (1512–1611). The Hague: Martinus Nijhoff.

Van Dillen, J. G. (1933). *Bronnen tot de geschiedenis van het bedrijfsleven en het gildewezen van Amsterdam*, Volume 2 (1612–1632). The Hague: Martinus Nijhoff.

Van Dillen, J. G. (1958). *Het oudste aandeelhoudersregister van de Kamer Amsterdam der Oost-Indische Compagnie.* The Hague: Martinus Nijhoff.

Van Gelder, H. E. (1972–1973). *Gegevens betreffende roerend en onroerend bezit in de Nederlanden in de 16e eeuw.* 2 vols. The Hague: Nijhoff.

Van Gelder, H. E. (1952). 'Geschiedenis van de gulden', in *Muntverslag over het jaar 1951*, Den Haag: Staatsdrukkerij en uitgeverijbedrijf: 35–42.

Van Gelder, H. E. (2002). *De Nederlandse munten, het complete overzicht tot en met de komst van de euro.* Utrecht: Het Spectrum.

Van Gelder, H. E. (1990). 'Gedrukte muntplakkaten in de Nederlanden (1485-ca. 1800)', *Jaarboek Munt- en Penningkunde*, 77: 26–90.

Van Gelder, H.E. (1995). *Gedrukte Muntplakkaten, Catalogus van Gedrukte Muntplakkaten vóór 1815 in de Collecties van Rijksmuseum Het Koninklijk Penningkabinet te Leiden en Het Nederlands Muntmuseum te Utrecht.* Leiden, the Netherlands: Koninklijke Penningkabinet.

Van Uytven, R. (1961). *Stadsfinanciën en stadsekonomie te Leuven van de XIIe tot het einde der XVIe eeuw*. Brussels: Paleis der Academiën.

Van Werveke, H. (1934). 'Monnaie de compte et monnaie réelle', *Revue Belge de Philologie et d'Histoire*, 13: 123–152.

Vercouteren, E. (1985). 'De geldwisselaars in Brabant (1430-1506), een bijdrage tot de economische geschiedenis van de Zuidelijke Nederlanden', *Bijdragen en Mededelingen betreffende de Geschiedenis der Nederlanden*, 100: 3–25.

Vickers, D. (2010). 'Errors expected: the culture of credit in rural New England, 1750–1800', *Economic History Review*, 63: 1032–1057.

Volckart, O. (2008). '"The Big Problem of the Petty Coins", and how it could be solved in the late Middle Ages', LSE working paper 107/08. London: London School of Economics. http://www.lse.ac.uk/economicHistory/pdf/WP107.pdf.

Welten, J. (2010). *Met Klinkende munt Betaald, Muntcirculatie in de Beide Limburgen 1770–1839*. Utrecht: Geldmuseum.

Wijsenbeek-Olthuis, T. (1995). *Boedelinventarissen*. The Hague: Instituut voor Nederlandse Geschiedenis.

Willems, B. (2009). *Leven Op de Pof: Krediet Bij de Antwerpse Middenstand in de Achttiende Eeuw*. Amsterdam: Aksant.

Winkelman, P. (ed.) (1981), *Bronnen voor de geschiedenis van de Nederlandse Oostzeehandel in de zeventiende eeuw*. Vol. 3. *Acten uit de notariële archieven van Amsterdam en het noorderkwartier van Holland 1585–1600. Het koopmansarchief van Claes van Adrichem*. The Hague: Martinus Nijhoff.

Wolters, W. (2008). 'Heavy and light money in the Netherlands Indies and the Dutch Republic, dilemmas of monetary management with unit of account systems', *Financial History Review*, 15: 37–54.

Zuijderduijn, C. (2010). 'Schuiven, schenken, strooien of sparen? Het gebruik van rekenpenningen in de 16[de] eeuw', *Historisch Tijdschrift Holland*, 43: 24–36.

12 Paper money in Song-Yuan China

Richard von Glahn

Introduction

The precocious development of paper money during the Song dynasty (960–1276) was an integral part of a medieval 'commercial revolution' marking the definitive emergence of a money economy in China. The invention of paper money coincided with prodigious growth in mint output (the highest levels in Chinese history) of low-value bronze coin, whose use permeated most regions of China down to the level of ordinary farming families. The multiple currency monetary system of the Song dynasty—which encompassed uncoined silver specie, iron coins, and other negotiable paper instruments in addition to paper money and bronze coins—was divided into a number of distinct monetary regions. But the pervasive impact of 'fiscal circulation'—the monetization of taxation, interregional transfers of revenues, and state procurement and expenditure—facilitated the integration of these diverse currencies into a coherent monetary order. The crucial importance of fiscal circulation—on a scale far greater than what we witness in Europe and the Islamic world at that time—explains why the Song government (and its Mongol successor, the Yuan dynasty [1271–1368]) succeeded in maintaining a viable paper currency. The diminished importance of fiscal circulation—in addition to monetary and fiscal mismanagement—also explains the demise of paper money in the early decades of the Ming dynasty (1368–1644).

Basic characteristics of the Chinese monetary system

From the founding of the first unified empire of Qin in 221 BC, 'money' in China invariably referred to a state-issued, low-value bronze coin. The Qin state and its long-lived successor, Han, issued coins in a single denomination designated by weight. Although the early Han rulers repeatedly adjusted the weight of its coins, from 112 BC the government established a uniform weight (*wuzhu*, or 3.35 g) that remained the official standard for the Han and its successor regimes down to the seventh century. Before the Qin unification, from the sixth to the third centuries BC, a great variety of bronze currencies (mostly in the shape of knives and two-pronged spades rather than round coins) had proliferated; many of these currencies were issued by royal governments, but many more were issued by local cities and clearly intended to serve as a means of market exchange. Under the empires the coin became a principal instrument of revenue collection. The Han government collected capitation taxes as well as a variety of commercial and consumption taxes in coin, which constituted nearly half of total state revenues (the rest mostly paid in grain and fodder) in the first century BC. Although it remains unclear whether the Qin imposed taxes in coin, it assessed legal fines to be paid in coin and also made loans in coin to its subjects (private lending was forbidden under Qin law). During its brief existence, the Qin Empire was unable to establish a uniform currency standard. Despite its reputation for severe laws, the Qin state tolerated deviations from its monetary standard and instructed its officials to accept substandard coins in payment. A wide variety of coins remained in circulation in the early Han before the creation of the *wuzhu* standard.

Ample evidence exists for the use of coin in market transactions before and after the establishment of the unified empire. Still, according to Walter Scheidel, the Han economy remained considerably less monetized than the Roman Empire. The per capita money supply of Han China in the first century BC was roughly half the level of the Roman Empire in its heyday. Money figured more significantly as a means of state payment in Han China, whereas a larger portion of the money stock remained available for trade and private savings in the Roman world. State payments consumed 30 percent or more of the total amount of coin in circulation in Han China, in contrast to probably less than 10 percent in the case of Rome.[1] Of course, the composition of the Han money supply wholly differed from that of Rome. Coin in circulation in the Roman Empire circa AD 160 consisted (in value) of approximately 60 percent gold coins, 30–35 percent silver coins, and 5–10 percent bronze coins, while the Han money supply was comprised almost entirely of low-value bronze coins.[2]

In contrast to Rome, where only the oligarchic senatorial elite and affluent citizens could afford to accumulate gold coins, the circulation of money penetrated more deeply into the lower strata of Han society.[3] Prices, wages, and debts all were calculated in coin, and it was routine practice to describe great family fortunes in terms of millions (or hundreds of millions) of coins. But already in the later Han empire (first to second centuries AD) the mounting costs of manufacturing bronze coin sharply curtailed mint output. The state increasingly substituted silk cloth in lieu of coin in tax collection and disbursements. After the fall of the Han Empire in AD 220 coin largely ceased to circulate in the heartland of North China. The revenue systems devised by northern rulers—the *hudiao* system created by Cao Cao and its successors—assessed taxes in grain, cloth, and labor service, entirely omitting coin. The principal features of this tax system were retained (under the rubric *zu-yong-diao*) by the Tang dynasty (618–907) as well, but the Tang reunification of the empire encouraged the growth of the market economy. Although the Tang supplanted the *wuzhu* coinage with a new standard currency (the Kaiyuan coin, first issued in 621), demand for coin greatly exceeded the limited supply Tang mints could provide. Silk continued to prevail over coin in the Tang fiscal system.

The subsequent Song dynasty witnessed dramatic growth in the market economy that often has been described as a 'medieval economic revolution'.

Rapid expansion of wet-rice farming and the development of commercial agriculture (tea, fibers, oil seeds, sugar, and timber), key technological developments in iron metallurgy, porcelain manufacture, shipbuilding, and silk-weaving, and the growth of maritime foreign trade spurred the formation of local, regional, and international market networks. During the tenth century, when China was divided into a half-dozen or more regional kingdoms, rulers waged monetary warfare by issuing debased currencies (using iron and lead coins as well as bronze alloy coins) to discourage the export of coin. After restoring a unified empire, the Song government made prodigious efforts to restore a unified monetary system and increase the money supply. Total mint output during the Northern Song era (960–1127) has been estimated at 260–300 billion coins. Yet demand continued to outstrip supply, and the Song was repeatedly plagued by 'coin famines' (*qianhuang*). Nor was the Song able to fully reunify its monetary system. The Song retained the iron currency system established in the tenth century by a regional regime in the western region of Sichuan, and often resorted to issuing iron coin currencies in the northern frontier provinces, which bordered the hostile steppe kingdoms of Liao and Xia. At the same time, the Song exacerbated the strain on the money supply by steadily increasing the proportion of revenues collected in coin, which rose from 48 percent in 977 to a peak level of 81 percent in 1077. The state's difficulty in supplying sufficient coin to satisfy the growing demand intensified in the twelfth century, when the main copper mines became exhausted and mint output fell to only a small fraction of the levels achieved in the eleventh century.[4] Demand for media of exchange as well as means of state payment compelled the state to experiment with alternative currencies, and led to the creation of paper money.

The origins of negotiable paper instruments in China

The invention of paper currency, it goes without saying, depended first of all on the technologies of paper-making (which became widespread in China by the second century AD) and printing (first developed in China in the eighth century). Beyond these basic technological requirements, the viability of any fiat currency depended on the willingness of the public to accept paper bills as tokens of real value in place of metallic currency. The faith in the value of paper money was conditioned by a range of variables including the credibility of the issuing agent (whether a government or a private entity), the range of its utility within the marketplace, the extent to which it was convertible with hard currency, and its acceptability in payments to the state. Just as the value of metallic money was conditioned by its physical properties (size, weight, fineness, and the insignia inscribed on it), so too the tangible features of paper money—the quality of the paper and the designs imprinted on it—were part of the calculus that determined its worth. In Song China paper money was manufactured using multiple printing plates (six to ten plates, depending on the issue) and three colors (red, black, and blue). The designs were changed with each issue (i.e. every two to three years), and serial numbers also were inscribed by hand on the notes.[5]

One of the significant drawbacks of base currencies such as bronze coin was their considerable weight relative to their value, a handicap that was even more pronounced in the case of iron coins. Song coins were commonly strung together in units of 100 (*mo*) or 1,000 (*guan*) coins; a string of 1,000 Song bronze coins would weigh between 3.0 and 3.4 kilograms.[6] Iron coins were even more cumbersome; for example, it would require 1½ kilograms of iron coins to purchase one kilogram of salt in the iron coin-using region of Sichuan.[7] Not surprisingly, it was in Sichuan—a nationally prominent commercial center for silk, tea, printing, and medicines—that paper money first evolved, as a substitute for iron coin, at the turn of the eleventh century.

Paper bills were already in use as financial instruments by this time. Evidence for written loan contracts dates back to pre-imperial times, and the oldest surviving loan contracts written on paper date from the seventh century.[8] By the Song period, written contracts were routinely used in a wide range of commercial and civil matters such as marriage, adoption, inheritance, employment, debts, property transfers, and business transactions. The crucial importance of contracts in business dealings in turn created a demand for intermediation. Brokers (*yaren, shikuai, zangkuai*)—some licensed by the state, others working in the shadows of legality—offered a wide range of intermediation services such as negotiating sales of goods and real property, notarizing contracts, registering deeds, acting as guarantors, hiring laborers and servants, making tax payments, handling consignments of goods, and operating inns and warehouses. Farmers often marketed their crops through brokers. In addition, brokers negotiated advance sale contracts (known as *she*) whereby merchants would make payments to farmers and weavers in exchange for future purchases at pre-arranged prices.

Major commercial centers boasted a broad array of specialists in financial and credit services, including goldsmiths and silversmiths, moneychangers, pawnbrokers, and dealers in bills of exchange and commercial paper such as salt and tea certificates. By the late eleventh century, merchants commonly settled accounts through assignment transfers on bank deposits. Merchants often negotiated consignment contracts (also known as *she*) to obtain goods on credit. In 1092 the prefect of Hangzhou asserted that 'as a rule cash is scarcely used in private trade in recent times. Instead retail shops rely on guarantees provided by trustworthy and wealthy individuals to make purchases on consignment from traveling merchants. Year after year they redeem the old debts and make new purchases.'[9]

The inconvenience of bulky, low-value coins prompted the Tang government in the early ninth century to create depositories at the capital of Chang'an where merchants could submit coin in return for bills of exchange known as *feiqian* ('flying cash') that could be redeemed for cash at major provincial cities. The Song dynasty continued this practice under the rubric of 'convenient cash' (*bianqian*), accepting payments of gold, silver, coin, or silk in return for notes (referred to as *quan* 券, a term commonly used to denote a debt instrument) denominated in bronze coin, for which the government charged a fee of 2 percent of the value of the note. By 997, the volume of 'convenient cash' notes, which were payable on sight (and thus could be transferred to third parties), had reached 1.7 million *guan*, a figure that rose to 2.83 million *guan* by 1021.[10] Private deposit banks (*jifupu*) also issued coin-denominated certificates in return for deposits of gold, silver, coin, and other valuables, but the government prohibited—with limited success—the circulation of such notes beyond the city in which they were issued.[11]

In addition, the Song began to use similar paper instruments to mitigate the logistical burden of supplying the large standing armies that defended its northern frontiers. In the 980s, the Song government began to offer tea licenses known as 'exchange certificates' (*jiaoyin*) to merchants who delivered grain, fodder, cloth, and other provisions to the frontier armies. The tea licenses authorized the bearer to purchase a certain quantity of tea from government agents in the Huainan region of central China, where the sale of tea was restricted by government monopoly.[12] Shortly afterwards this practice, known as *ruzhong*, was extended to highly lucrative salt licenses as well, prompting a surge in demand. The *ruzhong* merchants who delivered supplies to the frontier camps often sold the licenses to third parties rather than engage directly in the salt and tea trades. Over time, however, the costs claimed by *ruzhong* merchants rose substantially, eroding the state's fiscal savings from this system, and the state began to resume direct management of military logistics. In 1048, the government decoupled the salt licenses from frontier provisioning. Instead, salt merchants purchased salt licenses (*yanchao*) directly from the state monopoly bureau at the capital of Kaifeng by making payments in coin or silver, and the government delivered the funds to frontier commissariats to provision the armies. The market demand for salt certificates hovered around 2.1 million *guan* per year, although when pressed for funds the government issued considerably more certificates, as much as 5.2 million *guan* in one year. The salt certificates were negotiable instruments that could be transferred to third parties, and several dozen 'exchange certificate dealers' (*jiaoyinpu*) sprang up in Kaifeng to trade in these bills.

By the early Song period, then, paper instruments for transmitting sums of money over time and distance were well-established commercial practices. The key difference from the development of the bill of exchange in the Mediterranean world, of course, was the prominent role of the state in issuing 'convenient cash' notes and exchange certificates and the integration of these paper instruments into the government's fiscal operations. By the same token, trust in such bills was supported by public confidence in the state's commitment and ability to honor them, which undoubtedly reduced financial risk and the transaction costs of dispute resolution. The main drawback of the exchange certificates was the state's tendency to issue bills in greater quantities than the available stocks of monopoly commodities, whether tea or salt, which could result in steep discounting. In most years, however, the state maintained a reasonable balance between the volume of exchange certificates and the stocks of monopoly commodities.

The invention of paper currency

Despite the central role of the state in the creation of exchange certificates, the development of paper money originated in private initiative rather than state action.[13] In the mid-990s, following a damaging rebellion in Sichuan that forced the closure of local mints, private merchants in the regional capital of Chengdu began to issue paper bills known as 'exchange bills' (*jiaozi*) to help compensate for shortages in the local iron currency. *Jiaozi* had no standard denomination; at the time the bill was drawn the issuer inscribed the value of the bill in ink. Initially these bills were backed by deposits of coin, silver, and silk. But unscrupulous merchants also issued bills without hard currency reserves that proved irredeemable, throwing the local economy into turmoil. In 1005, the prefect of Chengdu reopened the local mint to issue iron coins in two denominations (1-cash and 10-cash coins) and at the same time introduced government regulation and oversight to the issuance of *jiaozi* bills. The privilege of issuing *jiaozi* was restricted to a consortium of sixteen reputable merchant houses chosen by the authorities. The size, color, and format of *jiaozi* were standardized, but the bills also were marked with distinguishing insignia to identify the issuer. The bearer of the bill could redeem it for hard currency by paying a 3 percent service charge.

The overvalued 10-cash iron coins quickly disappeared from circulation, and in 1014 they were replaced by a 2-cash coin that quickly became the standard circulating coin in Sichuan. But the issuers of *jiaozi* bills encountered financial difficulties and often failed to redeem their bills. Although the local authorities favored abolishing the bills altogether, in 1023 a proposal by a newly appointed Chengdu prefect for a state takeover of the privilege to issue *jiaozi* won the endorsement of the central government. The format of the government-issued *jiaozi* largely copied earlier private issues. The value of *jiaozi* was restricted to a range between 1 and 10 *guan*, which as in the past was inscribed on the note.[14] The key innovation introduced by the government was a two-year term of expiry, after which the notes had to be redeemed either for cash or for new notes. The fixed term of expiry ensured that worn bills would be retired (discouraging counterfeiting) and also limited the quantity of bills in circulation. The quota for each two-year issue of *jiaozi* was set at 1.26 million *guan*.[15] Thus was born the world's first viable paper currency.

Although the circulation of the *jiaozi* paper money was confined to the iron-coin region of Sichuan, the new medium soon became an indispensable part of public finance. Merchants who obtained *jiaoyin* exchange certificates for delivering provisions to the frontier armies in the northwest had the option of cashing in the *jiaoyin* bills for *jiaozi* in Sichuan, where many of these merchants were based. In 1072, amid escalating military expenses resulting from renewed war with the Tanguts on the northwestern frontier, the state doubled the amount of *jiaozi* in circulation to 2.5 million *guan* by emitting two issues simultaneously. The value of *jiaozi* began to falter; in 1077, the notes were circulating at a 4 percent discount, which rose to 10 percent by 1086. In the first decade of the twelfth century, with the dynasty reeling from escalating military spending, the central government abandoned all restraint in monetary management and put 24 million *guan* of *jiaozi* into circulation. This ten-fold increase in the quantity of *jiaozi* caused the notes' worth to plummet to a mere 10 percent of face value by 1107. In an effort to arrest this stark depreciation of paper money the government replaced the *jiaozi* with a new paper currency designated *qianyin* ('cash draft'). Holders of *jiaozi* could exchange the old notes for the new at a ratio of 4:1, or a discount of 75 percent. Apparently, few were willing to accept this rate, and the introduction of the *qianyin* note did little to revive the value of paper currency. Finally, in 1111, the government voided all outstanding paper bills, declaring that only the new issue of *qianyin* (no. 44, since the numbering of *qianyin* issues simply succeeded those of the old *jiaozi*) would be accepted as legal tender. The quota for *qianyin* was reduced to 1.25 million *guan*, while the term of expiry was raised from two to three years.

These measures succeeded in restoring some measure of monetary stability, but the Jurchen invasion of 1126 inaugurated a 15-year war in which the Song court lost the North China heartland and was forced to seek refuge in the southeast, establishing its provisional capital at Hangzhou (the period 1127–1276 is thus designated the Southern Song). Once again, the issue of *qianyin* in Sichuan swelled to 25 million *guan* by 1136, and their market value fell to roughly 30–40 percent of their face value. With the cessation of hostilities in 1141, fiscal exigencies diminished and the value of *qianyin* stabilized. Although the volume of *qianyin* rose again with the renewal of war with the Jurchen in the 1150s (reaching 40 million *guan* by 1160 and rising to 45 million *guan* in 1178), depreciation remained modest. Iron coin (exclusively minted in 2-cash denomination) comprised only 1–2 percent of the region's total money supply. *Qianyin* notes had largely eclipsed coin in both private commerce and state payments in Sichuan, and their general acceptability as a means of payment curbed the inflationary effects of increases of the volume of currency in circulation.

Before the mid-twelfth century, the use of paper money in Song China was confined to the iron-coin region of Sichuan. But as the vast output of bronze coin by state mints slowed to a trickle in the early Southern Song period, shortages of currency began to cause acute distress across the empire. In 1160, the prefect of Hangzhou—now the imperial capital—began to issue paper bills known as *huizi* (in imitation of privately issued bills already in circulation in the city) as legal tender. In the following year the prefect persuaded the central government—once again ensnared in war with the Jurchen—to take over the issue of *huizi* on a large scale as a means of deficit financing. In the first year the government issued 4 million *guan* of *huizi* in denominations of 1, 2, and 3 *guan*. (Smaller denominations of 200, 300, and 500 *wen* were issued beginning in 1164.) By 1167, the total amount of *huizi* in circulation had swelled to 28 million *guan*. Although in principle the notes were convertible with coin, the state had set aside only nominal reserves to back them, and the inability of note holders to redeem them for hard currency caused steep depreciation. Emperor Xiaozong (r. 1162–89), a man of scrupulous caution in fiscal affairs, had been skeptical about the new paper currency from the outset and ordered his officials to withdraw *huizi* from circulation. In 1166–67 his government disbursed 3 million *liang* (112,500 kg) of silver to redeem and retire the *huizi* notes. By redeeming the notes with silver, however, the state inadvertently boosted popular confidence in their value. The market value of *huizi* surged, and in response to this positive reaction in the marketplace the court reversed course and instituted *huizi* on a permanent basis in 1170. Like the *qianyin*, the *huizi* was a regional currency; the circulation of *huizi* was confined to the southeastern provinces where bronze coin had been the standard currency. Subsequently the Southern Song introduced two additional regional currencies in the iron coin-using regions of Huainan and Hubei, along the Jurchen borders. By 1200, the Southern Song territory had been divided into four separate currency regions, each with its own distinctive form of paper money in combination with bronze or iron coins.

Regulations adopted in 1170 governing the issue of *huizi* notes established a three-year term of expiry, with each issue limited to a total of 10 million *guan*. But one year later, in 1171, the government decided to allow two issues of *huizi* to circulate concurrently, raising the total amount of paper currency to 20 million *guan*. Although denominated in bronze coin, the notes were inconvertible to hard currency. Nonetheless, the state routinely intervened to purchase excess notes using its stocks of precious metals whenever their market value faltered. In 1175, for example, the ministry of revenue disbursed 4 million *guan* in silver and gold to buy up *huizi*. In addition, the government incorporated *huizi* into its fiscal system by establishing multiple currency quotas for payments and disbursements. In 1170, local officials were instructed to accept up to 50 percent of payment of money taxes in *huizi*. In 1172, the formula for soldiers' pay was set at 20 percent bronze coin, 30 percent silver, and 50 percent *huizi*. State grain purchases on the open market were made using a ratio of 22 percent bronze coin, 22 percent silver, and 56 percent *huizi*. Merchants seeking to purchase salt monopoly licenses were required to provide a minimum of 24 percent of the price in silver, with most of the rest paid in *huizi*. Although silver remained uncoined, in effect the state had created a tripartite monetary system. The government's periodic practice of buying up excess *huizi* notes with payments in silver established an integral relationship between silver and paper money, although bronze coin remained the unit of account in both public and private transactions throughout the Southern Song period.[16]

Beginning in the 1190s, rising deficits compelled the Song government to increase the quantity of *huizi* notes in circulation. With the simultaneous outbreak of civil war in Sichuan and renewed warfare with the Jurchen in 1206, military expenditures soared and the state resorted to prolific printing of both *huizi* and *qianyin*. In 1207, the court simultaneously emitted three issues of *huizi* (nos. 11–13), raising the total quantity of *huizi* in circulation to nearly 140 million *guan*. Not surprisingly, the value of *huizi* (and other regional paper monies) plummeted. After peace was restored in 1211 the government tried to reduce the excess supply of paper money by introducing two new issues of *huizi* (nos. 14–15) to replace the issues (nos. 11–13) already in circulation. But the old issues could be redeemed only at a 50 percent discount. This official discounting proved unwise. The market value of the discredited bills collapsed and the creditworthiness of the new bills remained dubious. Despite efforts to prevent the appreciation of bronze coin by imposing an official 'short-string' exchange rate for *huizi* (770 *wen*) and strictly enforcing laws forbidding hoarding of coin or carrying coin away from the capital, the market valuation of *huizi* fell to only about 50–60 percent of their nominal value.[17] In addition, the Song government abandoned the principle of fixed terms of expiry; the new *huizi* issues (nos. 14–15) were expected to circulate indefinitely. Although this change enhanced the utility of paper money as a store of value, at the same time it invited counterfeiting on a greater scale.

Consequently, public confidence in paper money evaporated. Wu Yong, a Sichuan native who had recently received appointment to the state armaments bureau in Hangzhou, described the impact of the devaluation of the old paper notes in these terms: 'When the new order was issued, public opinion expressed shock and dismay. Sounds of bitter wailing filled the streets. The august lineages and great families went as far as piling their paper money in the streets and setting them ablaze. Such was the extent to which the currency had lost the people's trust.' Wu's comments indicate that paper money, despite its lack of intrinsic value, had come to serve as a significant form of savings for wealthy households. Other contemporaries confirm this point. In 1217, the Fuzhou prefect Wei Jing observed that since 1170 the value of *huizi* had been tied to silver, and thus government monetary policy had aimed, with a reasonable degree of success, at maintaining a balance in the exchange values of *huizi* and silver. But the uncontrolled issue of paper currency since 1207 had upset this balance. Both the rich and households of middling property saw the value of savings held in the form of *huizi* evaporate.[18]

Despite the steep depreciation of *huizi* relative to bronze coin, it appears that this monetary crisis actually discouraged savings in coin. Although bronze coin remained the lifeblood of everyday retail trade, it had lost much of its utility as a means of commercial exchange and as a store of value to paper currency and silver. Instead of seeing stocks of coin as a hedge against the depreciation of paper money, it is more likely that the wealthy feared that monetary distress would further erode the official value (pegged to paper money) of the bronze coin they held as savings. The most expedient response would have been to dispose of their stocks of coin in favor of holding precious metals, whose value was not subject to state regulation. The sharp rise in the value of Chinese coin in overseas markets provided a profitable outlet for doing so. Although maritime commerce boomed in East Asia at this time, no state other than Song issued coin, and thus Song coin became the region's *de facto* international currency, most notably in Japan, but also in Vietnam and Java. Beginning in the 1170s, shortly after the introduction of *huizi*, exports of bronze coin abroad surged, despite long-standing prohibitions against the export of coin. During the thirteenth century, the flow of Song coin to Japan became a flood. Song coin was recognized as legal tender by the Kamakura shogunate in 1226, and subsequently served as virtually the only form of currency in Japan down to the sixteenth century.[19]

Despite the sharp depreciation of paper monies during the 1206–08 military crises, the value of paper money stabilized by 1215. The exchange value of paper money had fallen sharply relative to its face value in bronze coin, yet the impact on prices, which remained steady in the 1210s–1230s, was modest. During this period paper money largely displaced bronze coin in commercial and real estate transactions; contracts and legal cases involving land sales from the 1220s onward invariably specify the price of land in *huizi*. From the mid-1230s, the fiscal distress of the Song court invited increasingly ill-advised monetary policies, further eroding the value of paper money. In 1240, the government introduced issue number 18 *huizi* to retire the issue number 16 notes, but at the same time devalued the still-circulating number 17 notes (first issued in 1234) by 80 percent, sending the market value of number 17 notes skidding to a mere 5 percent of face value. Still, the monetary system staved off collapse until the Mongol invasions began in earnest in 1257. The final chapter of Song monetary history began in 1264, when the government abruptly replaced the *huizi* and other regional currencies with a new, empire-wide paper money issue entitled 'Gold/Silver/Ready Coin Sureties' (*jinyin xianqian guanzi*). Despite its name the new paper money was inconvertible with precious metals or coin, and the sudden abandonment of the steeply depreciated but familiar *huizi* set off a panic in the marketplace. The much-maligned new currency appears to have been an abject failure; the few documents on monetary circulation—such as loan contracts—from the decade prior to the Mongol conquest of the Southern Song in 1276 suggest that the number 18 *huizi* remained the principal commercial currency.

During the Southern Song, then, paper money became an integral component of a tripartite monetary system in which it was linked to both bronze coin and uncoined silver. Bronze coin remained the universal measure of value (and paper money was denominated in bronze coin units), but its former predominance as a means of exchange and of state payments diminished considerably. Bronze coin remained the common currency of petty commerce, since the smallest *huizi* denomination was 200 *wen*, and most *huizi* were issued in 1-*guan* denominations, while daily wages ranged from 30 to 300 bronze cash.[20] Despite the new prominence of silver as a means of state payments, as a store of value, and as the *de facto* reserve currency for paper money, silver did not function as a means of exchange at this time. Surviving specimens of silver ingots are based on a full-*ding* ('ingot') weight (1950–2000g) equivalent to 50 ounces (*liang*) of 39–40 g. Most specimens are distributed among three weight classes: full-*ding*, half-*ding*, and 'small-*ding*' (one-quarter *ding*), although there are some 1/8 and 1/16 *ding* ingots as well. These silver ingot units corresponded neither to bronze coin denominations nor even to the standard weight measure (*liang*) for silver.[21] Clearly these ingots were intended solely as stores of value, or perhaps large lump-sum payments.[22] Nonetheless, the linkages between silver and paper money established in the Southern Song would deepen during the Mongol epoch (1280–1368), when silver emerged as the measure of value for paper currency.

Paper currency under Mongol rule

It was Marco Polo who, having resided in China during the final two decades of Khubilai Khan's (r. 1260–94) reign, first reported to an incredulous European audience that the subjects of the great khan conducted trade exclusively using paper money as a means of exchange. Indeed, Polo's testimony about the ubiquity of paper money in the Mongol Empire was one of the main reasons why many contemporary European readers dismissed Polo as an outlandish fabulist:

> This paper money is circulated in every part of the Great Khan's dominions; nor dares any person, at the peril of his life, refuse to accept it in payment. All of his subjects receive it without hesitation, because, wherever their business may call them, they can dispose of it again in the purchase of merchandise they may require; such as pearls, jewels, gold, or silver. With it, in short, every article may be procured.... All of his Majesty's armies are paid with this currency, which is to them of the same value as if it were gold or silver. Upon these grounds, it may certainly be affirmed that the Great Khan has a more extensive command of treasure than any other sovereign in the universe.[23]

We now have ample evidence to support Polo's assertions. In contrast to Song policymakers, for whom paper money was one component of a multiple currency system, the Mongols sought to eliminate bronze coin and silver specie entirely. Apart from a couple of short-lived, abortive trials, the Mongol rulers of China did not issue any coin, but rather relied entirely on paper currency for public and private transactions alike.

The Jurchen-ruled Jin dynasty, which seized North China from the Song in 1127, also tried to establish paper currencies within its newly conquered domains, since it lacked the resources to sustain the minting of bronze coins (which it ceased altogether in 1189). The Jin's successive experiments with paper currency failed, however, while bronze coin virtually disappeared from the Jin realm, bringing commercial life to a standstill. After subjugating the Jin territories—partially in 1215 and completely in 1234—the Mongol rulers principally collected revenues from their North China subjects in silver. In the 1250s–60s in particular the Mongols extracted enormous quantities of silver from the former Jin territories, most of which was carried off to West Asia by the *ortoq* merchants (Central Asians, including many Muslims, of diverse origins) who acted as financial agents for the Mongol nobility.[24] The silver ingot that became the standard money of account of the far-flung Mongol empire (known as *yastuq* in Mongolian and *balish* in Persian) was derived from the Chinese *ding*.[25] Despite these sizable silver revenues, evidence for the use of silver in exchange in Mongol-ruled parts of China at this time is sparse. Individual Mongol rulers (including Khubilai Khan's mother) introduced paper currencies modelled on the Jin precedents (but denominated in silver or silk) within their personal appanages.

Upon his election as great khan in 1260, Khubilai undertook a broad array of measures to re-center the Mongol Empire on China and to complete the conquest of the Southern Song. Khubilai immediately conducted a sweeping consolidation of monetary media within his realm, issuing a new paper currency (the *Zhongtong chao* [which I will abbreviate as ZTC]), denominated in bronze coin units, and barring the use of coin, gold, or silver in exchange.[26] Khubilai made a concerted effort to replace bronze coin altogether with paper currency, and largely succeeded in doing so. In contrast to the Song paper currencies, the ZTC was issued in small denominations (11 altogether, from 10 *wen* to 2 *guan*). To be sure, the incorporation of the Southern Song territories (far more populous than North China) into the Yuan Empire (1271–1368; the dynastic name adopted by Khubilai in 1271) posed formidable fiscal and monetary problems. In response, the Yuan increased the output of ZTC more than ten-fold. Lacking sufficient silver stocks, the government also rendered the ZTC inconvertible with hard currency.

The ZTC notes, and later Yuan paper currencies as well, continued to bear images of strings of coin that provided visual illustration of the notes' value. But Yuan officials at both the local and imperial levels kept fiscal accounts using silver units (*ding* [= 50 *liang*], *liang*, and decimal fractions of *liang*). These units did not refer to silver specie, however, but rather to ZTC notes. Khubilai had established an official exchange rate for ZTC (2 *guan* of paper currency = 1 *liang* of silver specie). In 1282, the Yuan created a new unit, the fiscal *liang*, to replace the *guan* as the accounting unit for paper currency. In accordance with the prevailing exchange rate, 2 fiscal *liang* of paper currency were equivalent to 1 *liang* of silver specie. But the actual silver value of the ZTC in the marketplace fell sharply, and in 1287 the government devalued the ZTC by 80 percent by issuing a new paper currency, the *Zhiyuan chao* (ZYC), at an official exchange rate of 5 ZTC = 1 ZYC. In the marketplace, though, the two paper currencies traded at roughly equal value. The actual silver value of the ZTC (which persisted as the unit of account for the state's fiscal administration, even though after 1287 the government mostly issued ZYC notes) held steady throughout the 1290s, but fell sharply in the first decade of the fourteenth century. After 1320, though, the value of paper currency rebounded and then stabilized until the collapse of effective Mongol rule in the 1340s.

The Yuan thus established a dual paper currency system in which ZTC served as the unit of account in both public finance and private trade, while the great majority of the circulating currency consisted of ZYC notes. Popular nomenclature referred to paper currencies by their equivalent in silver units. For example, the bill conventionally known as 'one-and-a-half *liang*' actually was a ZYC bill with a face value of 300 *wen*. 'One-and-a-half *liang*' referred to its value in ZTC (at the official rate of 5 ZTC = 1 ZYC), the standard unit of account. Similarly, bills bearing the inscribed value of 'one *mo*' (i.e. 100 coins) were popularly referred to as 'one *qian*' notes, which designated their nominal equivalent in silver (*qian* was one-tenth of a *liang*).[27] The available evidence, meagre as it is, suggests that this dual paper currency system functioned effectively for as long as the Mongols maintained political control over their Chinese territories. Although there is some evidence for the persistence of bronze coin in the hinterland regions of the former Southern Song territories, in the more commercially advanced regions both trade and public finance employed the common medium of paper currency.

Strikingly, by the middle of the Yuan era, the practice of expressing the value of paper currency in silver units of account had become widely diffused. It appears that the linkage between paper currency and silver forged by the Southern Song state prepared the way for the emergence of a new money of account based on silver. The Yuan paper currency system was a synthesis of earlier Jin and Song precedents as well as the silver unit of account widely adopted by Mongol rulers in the initial stages of imperial conquest. The establishment of a stable dual paper currency system fostered the widespread popular adoption of this silver unit of account in denominating paper currency. In contrast to the usual progression in monetary history, in which monies of account typically are the vestiges of a defunct circulating currency ('ghost monies,' in Luigi Einaudi's memorable phrase), in the Chinese case the use of silver units of account to denominate paper currency actually preceded the widespread adoption of silver specie as the major form of market money from the fifteenth century onward.

By the 1350s, however, with the empire wracked by insurrection and Mongol rule crumbling, Yuan paper money quickly became worthless. Old Song bronze coins resurfaced, but supplies remained short, and the practice of using short strings (with as few as 40–100 coins rated as equivalent to the 1,000 coin *guan* unit) proliferated in the commercial heartland of Jiangnan. Silver, too, came into use as a means of exchange, and the value of silver relative to both gold and coin reached its historical peak. The founder of the Ming dynasty, the Hongwu Emperor (r. 1368–1398), held profoundly anti-mercantile views and sought to curb what he regarded as the pernicious influences of the market on the people's welfare. Hongwu reverted to an emphasis on in-kind taxation and labor services in place of money taxes, prohibited private maritime commerce, and expropriated the lands and possessions of the wealthiest landowning elite. Like his Yuan predecessors, Hongwu also sought to create a purely fiat paper currency. But the Ming *baochao* currency, first issued in 1375, was thoroughly rejected in the private market. In 1394, when the value of the *baochao* in coin had fallen to 16 percent of its face value, Hongwu took the extraordinary step of banning the use of even his own coin as well as silver in trade, but such measures failed miserably. In the 1430s, the Ming government effectively repudiated Hongwu's monetary policies and accepted the use of silver in trade and tax payments. Ming paper money quickly became defunct. The Ming did not mint any bronze coin for the remainder of the fifteenth century, and silver already was fully established as the principal currency of the Chinese world before the massive influx of foreign silver, first from Japan and later from Spain's American colonies, began in the 1540s.[28] The Chinese experiments with paper money came to an end, and not until 1935 would a Chinese government again make a concerted effort to replace silver currency with paper money.

Paper money and Chinese monetary theory

The prevailing view within Chinese economic thought subscribed to the cartalist tenet that money is a creature of the state, the invention of the sage-kings of yore intended to provide for the popular welfare by enabling the circulation of goods in times of distress.[29] In contrast to Greek and medieval philosophy, Chinese monetary thought devoted little attention to the problem of 'just price.' In contrast, too, to Aristotle's postulation that the value of money derives from its innate worth as a commodity, Chinese monetary theory—enshrined in the *Guanzi*, an eclectic body of writings on political economy compiled in the third–second centuries BC—rested on the principle that monetary substances lacked intrinsic value. Instead, the ruler, through his monetary and fiscal policies, manipulates the supply of money in circulation and thereby controls the value of money and the prices of commodities. The cartalist views of the *Guanzi* gave birth to the fundamental axiom of Chinese monetary theory: 'the purchasing power of the medium of exchange was solely a result of its quantity, in the form of money, in relationship to the supply of all other commodities.'[30] Gold and silver (and jade and pearls) were deemed too scarce for the ruler to be able to wield effective control over their supply. Copper, in contrast, was believed to be sufficiently abundant for the ruler to increase or decrease the quantity of bronze currency in circulation—and by extension lower or raise the prices of goods—at will.[31] Thus, Chinese monetary thought was favorably disposed to the idea that bronze coin essentially was fiat currency.

In practice, however, Chinese policymakers adopted strategies that blended theoretical cartalism with practical metallism. Fully aware that debasement of the monetary standard would invite counterfeiting, fiscal ministers staunchly defended the necessity of maintaining full-bodied coin.[32] This principle meant that rather than extracting seigniorage profit from minting currency, the Chinese state generally incurred losses, since the costs of manufacturing bronze coin exceeded its market value. Moreover, despite confident assertions that the ruler could increase or decrease the supply of bronze coin at will, the harsh reality was that the Chinese economy suffered from perpetual shortages of coin. Debasement at times became a practical necessity in order to maintain the liquidity of the money supply. One consequence of this situation was that the value of currency was determined less by its intrinsic value, or its quantity in relationship to the supply of commodities, than by its relative abundance compared to other means of exchange. Chinese monetary history is replete with cases where substantial increases in the emission of bronze coin resulted in an enhancement rather than a diminution of its value relative to silver.[33] For the same reason, private coin, despite its substandard quality, was widely tolerated in the marketplace when full-bodied, state-issued coin was in short supply. For ordinary consumers, variations in the intrinsic worth of low-value bronze currency were insignificant.

Paper money provided the most severe test of the cartalists' faith in the power of the ruler to determine the value of money by fiat. The theory of paper money drew on a corollary to the axiom of exchange values enunciated earlier, according to which the values of money and commodities were determined by their relative quantities. This same principle was believed to apply to the relative values of different types of currency. Chinese theorists viewed bronze coin as the primary currency (the 'mother,' in their argot); other forms of money (cloth, iron and lead coins, and paper money) were deemed to be subsidiary ('child') currencies. The monetary authority could achieve monetary stability by maintaining a stable ratio in the emission of subsidiary currencies relative to bronze coin. It was also recognized that in order to sustain popular confidence in its paper money the state had to be willing to redeem its paper notes in hard currency. The twin principles of specie convertibility and stability in the relative quantities of paper money and bronze coin were universally acknowledged as the fundamental requirements of a sound fiat currency system. But the success of *huizi* and *qianyin* notes in the second half of the twelfth century propelled an important shift in monetary philosophy among Song statesmen, who began to emphasize the acceptance of paper money in state payments rather than specie convertibility as the key to maintaining the value of fiat currencies.

Although military exigencies provoked Song policymakers to abandon prudent monetary policies, most commentators on monetary matters defended the principle of fiat currency. In the thirteenth century, with vast quantities of paper money now in circulation, policymakers largely focused their attention on the problem of maintaining a stable ratio between the quantities of coin and paper currency in circulation (what contemporaries referred to as *chengti*, or 'adjusting the balance scales'). In their view, if too much paper money was issued and its value began to decline, the state could correct the imbalance by issuing more coin. Thus, most observers blamed the depreciation of paper notes on shortfalls in the minting of coin, rather than a surfeit of money. They rarely considered the problem of exchange value from the angle of the total quantity of money. One of the few analysts to perceive that inflation was caused by an excess in the total stock of money rather than simply an imbalance in the quantities of coin and paper currency was an obscure scholar named Dai Zhi (fl. after 1233). Dai condemned the Southern Song government's wanton abuse of paper money, but he concluded that paper money was no different in kind than coin. Both, Dai insisted, were 'useless' substances employed as tokens to facilitate the exchange of useful commodities. The value of paper money, like that of coin, was simply a function of its quantity relative to the quantity of goods in the marketplaces. Dai dismissed the prevalent view that increasing the quantity of coin would enhance the exchange value of paper money, and instead contended that inflation could be curbed only by reducing the total quantity of money to a level commensurate with the supply of commodities.[34]

As the Southern Song state increasingly relied on the expediency of printing enormous quantities of paper currency in order to cope with mounting fiscal deficits, many statesmen abandoned cartalist beliefs and embraced some form of metallism instead. The retreat from cartalism also reflected diminished faith in the power of the state to manage the economy. This reorientation in monetary thought can be seen in the writings of the Southern Song statesman Ye Shi (1150–1223). Deviating from the trend that had long prevailed in Chinese monetary analysis, Ye articulated a catallactic conception of money that underscored the primacy of the medium of exchange function: 'Currency arose from merchants and tradesmen who travelled and traded widely throughout the four corners of the world. Since goods themselves could not be transported over such long distances, gold and coin were carried instead.' Ye envisioned the society of high antiquity as simple and contented, a time when the people themselves produced all the goods needed for their subsistence. With the progress of time, increasing complexity of social organization engendered a division of labor and hence a need for exchange. Money thus established itself as a measure of value as well as a means of exchange. Other commodities were reduced to quantifiable sums of exchange value: cloth began to be measured in feet and inches, and grain in pecks and bushels. Coin, because of its convenience, gradually supplanted all other media of exchange. By the Han dynasty, jade, pearls, and even gold had been reduced to merely ornamental uses.[35]

Ye Shi's recapitulation of the history of money deviated sharply from the predominant cartalist tradition. Ye believed the failures of the paper currencies of his day amply confirmed his metallist analysis. Both the state and wealthy individuals hoarded coin because of its intrinsic value. The more paper money was put into circulation, the more coin was withdrawn. At the same time, the rampant inflation ignited by the imprudent issue of paper currency eroded incomes and hampered production. Only by abolishing the use of this 'empty money' could the court re-establish a reliable currency (i.e. coin) and regain some leverage over the ratios of exchange.

But Ye's disaffection was a fairly isolated case. Many of his contemporaries concurred that paper money failed to fulfil one of the basic functions of money, that of serving as a store of value, a role that only hard currencies could perform. Yet it was generally accepted that paper currency provided a viable means of exchange as long as the state regulated its quantity. The crucial role of the state in managing the money supply in order to balance the exchange ratios between money and commodities and thus satisfy the needs of both producers and consumers remained beyond dispute. During the Yuan dynasty, even amid bouts of paper currency depreciation in the 1280s and 1310s, restoration of bronze currency was staunchly repudiated. Erosion in the value of paper currency was attributed to abandonment of specie convertibility.

But, in the wake of the collapse of the Yuan monetary system in the 1340s, scholars and statesmen swiftly abandoned cartalist principles to affirm practical metallism. 'Paper currency is nothing but empty script, while coin is a tangible object' wrote Wang Yi in the mid-1350s, in a policy proposal advocating coinage of silver and gold as well as bronze currency.[36] The ignominious demise of Ming paper money provided, in the eyes of Chinese statesmen, irrefutable confirmation of Wang's statement.

Conclusion

Fiat currency is fundamentally fiduciary currency, money whose value rests on the confidence its users have in the issuer—whether a state agency or a private bank—to guarantee its acceptability in monetary transactions. The private bankers who initiated the *jiaozi* currency in Sichuan in the late tenth century ultimately failed this test of trust. But the Song state, after taking over the issue of *jiaozi* bills, succeeded. Public trust in the Song state's paper currencies owed primarily to their acceptability in state payments and the substantial role of fiscal circulation in the Song economy. Specie convertibility did not figure importantly in establishing the viability of Song paper money, but the crucial use of silver as a reserve currency at times when popular confidence in paper money began to falter certainly did. Although paper monies were not the authors of economic crisis in Song-Yuan times, economic crises inflicted severe strains on fiat currencies. Song statesmen discovered that the most effective response to evaporating popular confidence in paper money was to utilize silver as a reserve currency to buy back excessive notes. Even though successive military crises forced the Southern Song state to issue paper currencies in ever more inflated quantities that engendered severe depreciation, paper currency remained the staple commercial money down to the final demise of the dynasty.

Despite the ultimate abandonment of paper currency in the early Ming, the Song-Yuan experiments with paper money had lasting consequences for the Chinese monetary system. Bronze coin—long the monetary standard, and still in late imperial times the only currency officially emitted by the imperial state—was reduced to a subsidiary currency largely relegated to retail trade. Silver was not yet in common use as a means of exchange in the Song period, but its growing employment in state payments, as a reserve currency for paper money, and as a store of value heralded the emergence of (uncoined) silver as the new monetary standard (both public and private) and the principal currency of commerce in the fifteenth century. Silver specie had the virtue of remaining immune to manipulation by the state, although at the expense of higher transaction costs that hindered monetary integration. Yet the advent of the silver standard itself was inseparable from its integral relationship to the Song and Yuan paper currencies.

Notes

1 Scheidel (2009: 204).
2 For the Roman data, see Scheidel (2009: 177–78).
3 Gold coins remained almost entirely in the hands of the wealthy elites of the Roman Empire. Silver coins achieved wide distribution (geographic and social) through trade and army payments, but the production and circulation of bronze currencies were highly localized. See Katsari (2011: 167–78, 207–8); Von Reden (2010: 86–91).
4 To stretch its limited copper resources, the Southern Song primarily minted 2-cash coins known as *zhe'er* rather than the standard single cash coins (*xiaoping*).
5 Unfortunately, no actual Song paper money specimens survive, and the authenticity of extant printing plates has been a subject of dispute. For an analysis of Song paper money

printing plates and the documentary evidence regarding the physical features of Song paper currency, see Von Glahn (2006).

6 Often the *mo* and *guan* units contained fewer than the full number of coins. The exact number of coins in 'short-string' units varied by region, and even within a single town different trades applied different short-string standards.

7 A string of 1,000 iron coins weighed 3.87 kilograms, and the value of iron coins was substantially lower than that of bronze coins.

8 On the use of contracts in China in this era, see Hansen (1995).

9 Cited in Katō (1952: 224).

10 To put these values into perspective, at this time 1 *guan* purchased 230–320 liters of rice, sufficient to feed a family of four for 1½–2 months.

11 Hino (1983: 177).

12 The tea certificate system was abrogated in 1059, when the government ended the monopoly on tea sales in the southeastern provinces.

13 For a more detailed examination of the development of paper money in Song China, see Von Glahn (2005).

14 In 1039 the government mandated that *jiaozi* be issued in two standard denominations of 5 and 10 *guan*. From 1068, in an effort to make *jiaozi* more generally useful to the public rather than only to merchants, the government issued *jiaozi* in two denominations of 500 *wen* (0.5 *guan*) and 1 *guan*.

15 Annual mint output of iron coin in Sichuan at this time was 210,000 *guan*. See Gao (1999: 246).

16 Von Glahn (2013).

17 Wang (2003, 2: 706–9).

18 Wu Yong and Wei Jing statements are taken from Von Glahn (2013: 29). The evisceration in the value of savings held in the form of *huizi* after the 1211 monetary reform also was noted in a memorial of 1217 by Yuan Xie, also cited in ibid.

19 Von Glahn (2014).

20 For the regrettably exiguous data on wages at this time, see Gao (1999: 28–30).

21 The five standard silver ingot weights were equivalent to 50, 25, 12.5, 6.25, and 3.125 *liang*.

22 On Song silver ingots see Von Glahn (2010: 476–78).

23 Polo (1926: 160–61).

24 On the possible impact of this outflow of silver from China in the expansion of the minting of silver coins in Europe, see Kuroda (2009).

25 The *yastuq/balish* weighed 2000g, equivalent to the *ding*. Both terms mean 'pillow,' referring to the shape of the *ding* ingot, which resembled a Chinese ceramic pillow.

26 This digest of the Yuan monetary system is based on Von Glahn (2010).

27 Von Glahn (2010: 491–93).

28 On Ming monetary policies, the emergence of silver as the monetary standard, and the impact of foreign silver imports, see Von Glahn (1996).

29 Although mainstream monetary thought emphasized the essential role of the ruler in the creation of money, an alternative interpretation that ascribed the origins of that money to the need for a medium to facilitate exchange among farmers, artisans, and rulers remained an undercurrent in Chinese monetary philosophy. For a more extended discussion of classical monetary theory in China, see Von Glahn (1996: 23–47).

30 Hartwell (1967: 71).

31 Chinese monetary theory also differentiated the utility of different forms of money in terms of their physical properties. Thus, gold and silver, because their value was determined by their scarcity rather than imperial fiat, were well-suited to be the standards of value; bronze currencies, because of their abundance, fungibility, and divisibility, best served as media of exchange; while silk cloth was eminently suitable as a store of value. See Von Glahn (1996: 39).

32 In addition, since state-issued coin embodied the sovereign authority of the ruler, any debasement of the currency represented a symbolic diminution of imperial authority.
33 The most notable instances occurred during the eleventh and eighteenth centuries.
34 Von Glahn (1996: 45).
35 Von Glahn (1996: 45–6).
36 Cited in Von Glahn (1996: 69).

References

Gao, C. (1999). *Songdai huobi yu huobi liutong yanjiu (Studies in Money and Monetary Circulation in Song Dynasty China)* (in Chinese). Baoding: Hebei daxue chubanshe.

Hansen, V. (1995). *Negotiating Daily Life in Traditional China: How Ordinary People Used Contracts, 600–1400*. New Haven, CT: Yale University Press.

Hartwell, R. (1967). 'The Evolution of the Early Northern Sung Monetary System, A.D. 960–1025', *Journal of the American Oriental Society*, 87: 280–89.

Hino, K. (1983). 'Nan Sō Rinanfu no shika kaishi ni tsuite (Private *Huizi* Notes in Southern Song Hangzhou)', in Hino, K. (ed.), *Hino Kaisaburō Tōyō shigaku ronshū (Selected Essays on Oriental History by Hino Kaisaburō)*, vol. 7, *Nan Sō no kahei to kin'yū (Money and Finance in Southern Song)* (in Japanese). Tokyo: Sanichi shobō: 177–211.

Katō, S. (1952). 'Sōdai no shōshūkan 'sha' ni tsuite (On the Commercial Practice of '*She*' in the Song Dynasty)', in Katō, S. (ed.), *Shina keizai shi kōshō (Studies in Chinese Economic History)*, vol. 2, (in Japanese), Tokyo: Tōyō bunko: 222–34.

Katsari, C. (2011). *The Roman Monetary System: The Eastern Provinces from the First to the Third Century* AD. Cambridge: Cambridge University Press.

Kuroda, A. (2009). 'The Eurasian Silver Century (1276–1359): Commensurability and Multiplicity', *Journal of Global History*, 4: 245–69.

Polo, M. (1926). *The Travels of Marco Polo [The Venetian]*. New York, NY: Liveright Publishing Co.

Scheidel, W. (2009). 'The Monetary Systems of the Han and Roman Empires', in Scheidel, W. (ed.), *Rome and China: Comparative Perspectives on Ancient Empires*, New York, NY: Oxford University Press: 137–207.

Von Glahn, R. (1996). *Fountain of Fortune: Money and Monetary Policy in China, 1000–1700*. Berkeley, CA: University of California Press.

Von Glahn, R. (2005). 'Origins of Paper Money in China', in Rouwenhorst, K.G. and Goetzmann, W.N. (eds.), *Origins of Value: The Financial Innovations that Created Modern Capital Markets*, New York, NY: Oxford University Press: 65–89.

Von Glahn, R. (2006). 'Re-examining the Authenticity of Song Paper Money Specimens', *Journal of Song-Yuan Studies*, 36: 79–106.

Von Glahn, R. (2010). 'Monies of account and monetary transition in China, twelfth to fourteenth centuries', *Journal of the Economic and Social History of the Orient*, 53: 463–505.

Von Glahn, R. (2013). 'Cycles of Silver in Chinese Monetary History', in So, B. (ed.), *The Economy of Lower Yangzi Delta in Late Imperial China: Connecting Money, Markets, & Institutions*, London: Routledge: 17–71.

Von Glahn, R. (2014). 'The Ningbo-Hakata Merchant Network and the Reorientation of East Asian Maritime Trade, 1150–1300', *Harvard Journal of Asiatic Studies*, 74: 251–81.

Von Reden, S. (2010). *Money in Classical Antiquity*. Cambridge: Cambridge University Press.

Wang, S. (2003). *Liang Song huobi shi (Monetary History of Song China)* (in Chinese). Beijing: Zhonghua shuju.

13 Stagnation is silver, but growth is gold

China's silver period, circa 1430–1935[1]

Yi Xu and Bas van Leeuwen

Introduction

According to standard theory, metal currencies such as copper, silver and gold may fulfil three functions in a society: they may function as a monetary standard (to which all money in a society can be related), as a coin to be circulated (means of exchange), and as a base for hoarding (i.e. store of wealth). Obviously, these three functions are strongly intertwined and can be fulfilled either by the government or private parties. Indeed, Chinese monetary policy from Han times (206 BC–AD 220) onwards has been based on conflicting thoughts of metallism (i.e. money in circulation has the value of the metal it is made of) and cartalism (i.e. money has the value the state or any other party attaches to it). In the case of metallism, money could function well for hoarding as, in adverse circumstances, the coin kept its value. In the case of cartalism, however, it depended on trust; either in the government itself, or in the monetary standard. After all, if a party, often the government, lowers the intrinsic value of the coin and, at the same time does not have enough precious metal to back up the monetary standard, we face a *de facto* situation of fiat money in which lost of trust can generate massive inflation. Of course, there is a natural tendency to move towards the cartalist system to generate extra income for the government or private person issuing this money. Indeed, in China, from the fifth century AD onwards, the cartalist view became dominant, implying that the state got entrusted with the task of keeping the balance between increasing production and maintaining the purchasing power of the people.

The fifth-century currency system can be traced back to the Western Han Dynasty (202 BC–AD 8), from which period onwards the successive Chinese empires witnessed a multiple metal currency system, in which copper or iron coins, the *wen,* functioned as the basic currency in day-to-day transactions while long-term business and government finance were paid in either gold or silver. However, the hoarding and the monetary standard were mainly performed in the strongest metal, being gold.

This situation lasted until, due to lack of metal currency in circulation, the late Northern Song government (AD 960–1127) had to tentatively introduce the paper money backed by copper. The shift towards uncoined silver as a money of account took place during the Jin Dynasty (1115–1234) which slowly replaced the Song Dynasty in Northern China. This Dynasty issued paper notes backed by silver. Yet, it was only during the Mongol Yuan Dynasty (1271–1368) that several attempts were made to create fiat paper money, that is, even though silver was still money of account, the paper currency was not convertible anymore in silver (Von Glahn 2010 and Chapter 12, this volume). The bad economic and political situation combined with shortages of copper and silver induced strong inflation in this period. After the fall of the Yuan Dynasty, the Ming rulers (1368–1644) initially tried to re-establish a system based on paper money as money of account backed by copper. Since the Ming rulers encountered the same inflation issue as the Yuan did, the Ming rulers in the 1430s changed the paper money system back to bimetal currency system, in which copper coins were the basic currency for day-to-day transactions and uncoined silver was used both for large transactions and money of account. Even though at times there were attempts to increase the money stock (for example, by printing paper money), this situation of an essentially bimetallic currency system with uncoined silver and minted copper coins remained in place from the 1430s up to the start of the twentieth century.

The period between the 1430s, when silver was finally formally accepted as a monetary standard by the government, and the start of the twentieth century when the silver standard was abolished, is the topic of this chapter. During this period, silver can be argued to be the anchor in the Chinese monetary system. This does not imply that it was fully accepted by the government. Indeed, except for the final decades in this period, the government did not mint any silver. At the same time, private coins existed and various discussions and attempts to reduce the role of silver occurred, but ultimately failed.

The main question in this chapter is therefore why silver acted for a period of well over half a millennium as an *anchor* for the Chinese monetary system notwithstanding all forces trying to change this. We have to stress that we look in this case at only one *aspect* of one the three monetary functions, i.e. money of account. After all, to stabilize a monetary system, one might link, in case of a multimetallic system to a precious metal, most often silver or gold, without counting in that metal (another aspect of the money of account function), or even having access to it. For example, in the Bretton Woods system, the link was only to other fiat currencies which, in turn, were linked to a gold dollar. That is, without necessarily having (access to) gold, many currencies were still based on gold.

Obviously, multimetallic systems can exist in various metals both precious (e.g. silver and gold) or non-precious (like copper) metals. Yet, in most instances in world history the precious metals are preferred simply because they provide more stability to the monetary system. This was also the case in China. In various dynasties, there were gold interludes when gold was also used as an export product and found in hoards. Yet, silver dominated in the long run.

The prime reason for this domination of silver in a bimetallic system is, as argued by Friedman (1990), based on the situation that the gold to silver ratio set by the government diverges from that in the market. If the market price is higher, i.e. gold is more expensive, people will keep using silver and hoard the gold, which is exactly what happened in China since 1430. Vice versa, silver will be extracted from the economy.

The question thus becomes what causes a change in the gold to silver ratio. Various, mainly monetary, arguments have been brought forward, mostly related to the availability of silver, e.g. the existence of extensive silver deposits (and lack of gold), government preference for silver, cultural preferences for silver, etc. (e.g. Scheidel 2009; Horesh 2014). Indeed, it is well known that during the period under study, these factors contributed to a gold to silver ratio which was well below that in the Western world thus leading to an outflow of gold and, hence, a de facto silver standard (see following sections).

Yet, contrary to the mainly monetary arguments, in this chapter we would like to draw attention to the development in the real economy. Recent studies seem to indicate that Chinese per capita growth was negative in most of the Ming and Qing dynasties. Following Fisher's Equation, this must imply an excess of coins in circulation and thus decrease their price. Following Gresham's Law, which states that bad money drives out good money if the exchange rates remain constant (i.e. if there are no monetary changes; see e.g. Mundell 1998), this causes outflow, or hoarding, of the highest valued metal, i.e. gold. This will eventually cause the replacement of gold by silver as the monetary standard, at least as long as there is less trust in the cheaper currency (Sullivan 2005).

Again, we have to stress that this real economy effect is additional to monetary shocks rather than being mutually exclusive. We also do not claim that in all cases in which per capita growth declines, we witness a silver standard. Whether or not that will happen depends on the interplay of a great many monetary and real economy factors.

Hence, in order to deal with the question, we start in the following sections by looking at monetary arguments brought forth in the literature. In the next section, we deal with the claim about the (lack of) silver famines. If silver famines existed, we would expect declining (rather than rising) gold to silver ratios. Yet, we find no evidence for such famines. In the following section, we look at the assumption that, even with a massive influx of silver in the economy, the price of silver nevertheless increased. Given Fisher's Equation, which essentially says that the real economy must be equal to the amount of money in circulation, this rising amount of silver combined with price increases of silver, suggest that there was real economic growth. Yet, we point out that neither is there a rise in the price of silver, nor is there economic growth per capita. After having dealt with, and rejected, the two earlier mentioned main monetary arguments for the existence of a silver standard, in the second to last section we argue that, *ceteris paribus*, a silver anchor is advanced in societies that experience economic stagnation and decline (i.e. when the money in circulation is too high given the level of economic development such as in China). Again, this does not mean that in all societies that experience economic decline a silver standard dominated as there are many other reasons why countries move from one standard or another. Yet we argue that, just as in China, real economic decline per capita might be one factor that plays a role.

The (lack of) silver famines and the stock of money in circulation

As pointed out in the introduction, one of the monetary arguments as to why silver persisted for such a long period of time, is its sheer availability, which depressed the price of silver and, hence, increased the gold to silver ratio. This seems to contradict the argument brought forth by various authors about shortages of silver during the Ming-Qing transition (around 1644) as well as during the late Qing (last decades before 1912). To assess this question of the so-called silver famines, we will look at how these assumed reductions in supply affected the stock of money in circulation. Indeed, the availability of money (or the stock of money, i.e. both silver and other types of money) in a society is long considered an important indicator of economic development.[2] The problem with the stock, however, is that it can be defined in various ways. Perhaps the easiest way to define it is the monetary base (M0), i.e. the amount of coins and specie, which is also the most common in pre-modern economies such as for our study.[3] Since the stock of money is based on a precious metal (i.e. silver) with copper being ancillary, it is in principle based on what Tlaga (2002) called an 'honest' monetary system, i.e. where the money of account (i.e. silver) and the actual coins (i.e. copper) are related via their intrinsic value. In such a system, any increase or decrease of the stock of money carries with it the risk of debasements and other money generating, silver saving, activities that may undermine the system. Hence, it is important to look at whether such 'silver famines' indeed existed and assess why they did not lead to a change in the system.

Indeed, in the 500 years under study, according to some authors several of such 'silver famines' occurred. For example, the 'seventeenth century crisis thesis' argues that the collapse of the silver inflow, due to smaller imports from the Spanish Americas and the contraction of Japanese silver, caused rising prices and economic hardship leading to a breakdown in commercialization. This has been argued to have ultimately led to the fall of the Ming Dynasty in 1644 and its replacement by the Qing Dynasty (1644–1912). Likewise, the Kangxi (1662–1722) and Daoguang (1821–1850) depressions (e.g. Lin 2006) have been attributed to reductions in silver inflow. So why was the silver-based system able to sustain irrespective of these supply-side shocks?

As argued by Von Glahn (1996a and b), it may be questioned if the silver famines were as serious as is sometimes claimed. Perhaps the most contested is the silver famine in the mid-seventeenth century, which allegedly caused the fall of the Ming dynasty and where various authors have suggested a large drop in silver inflows. Looking at the actual inflow of silver in this period, we follow e.g. Flynn and Giraldez (1995; 1997) and subdivide it into four main sources. There was a domestic production, but most of the silver supply originated from Japan or from South America (the latter flowing into China either via Manila or Europe, both of which ultimately drew their silver from the Latin American mines [TePaske 1983]). Domestic production was indeed relatively modest even though the annual silver production significantly increased from 30,000 to 220,000 *tael* at the end of the fourteenth and start of the fifteenth century. Due to severe corruption, however, official silver production declined from 1453 onwards so that annual silver production dropped to 49,000 *tael*. From 1520 to 1644, the Ming government even abandoned silver mining altogether. Even though, after the rise of the Qing dynasty in 1644,domestic silver production resumed, it remained, with an annual production of 12,000 *tael*, at a low level (see Table 13.1, Figure 13.1), only to increase during the mid-Qing.

This relatively low level of domestic production was expanded by imports of silver from Japan, Manila and Europe. The main import of silver from Japan took place between 1550 until this started to decline in the 1640s. This silver import has been quantified by many scholars (see Table 13.2). Most seem to agree on an annual import of circa 1 million *tael*, which declined after 1650.

A third main source of silver is the trade with Manila, which took off after its founding in 1571. Table 13.3 shows current estimates of the imports of silver from Manila. These estimates are to a certain extent controversial since a large amount of smuggling occurred (e.g. Flynn and Giraldez 1995). Hence, calculations vary widely (see Table 13.3). However, as argued by Wu (2001), for the period between 1550 and 1649, Von Glahn (1996a), Liang (1989), Wang (1964) and Peng (1958) ignored parts of import of silver from Manila to China. On the contrary, Wan's (2004) estimate was based on double counting of part of the silver that was imported into China. Therefore, we follow the estimates from Wu (2001) and Zhuang (1995) the average of which we will use further in this chapter.

Finally, from 1550 onwards, European merchants shipped some silver to China in exchange for Chinese products. As Table 13.4 shows, most scholars seem to agree on annual imports in the order of circa 400,000 *tael*. Indeed, as

Table 13.1 Official annual production of silver in China between 1380 and 1880

Year	*Annual production (tael)*
1380–1400	30,000
1401–1434	230,000
1435–1520	49,000
1662–1700	12,000
1700–1750	377,197
1750–1800	439,631
1800–1850	172,742
1800–1880	70,795

Source: Wu (2001); Qing archive of mining industry.

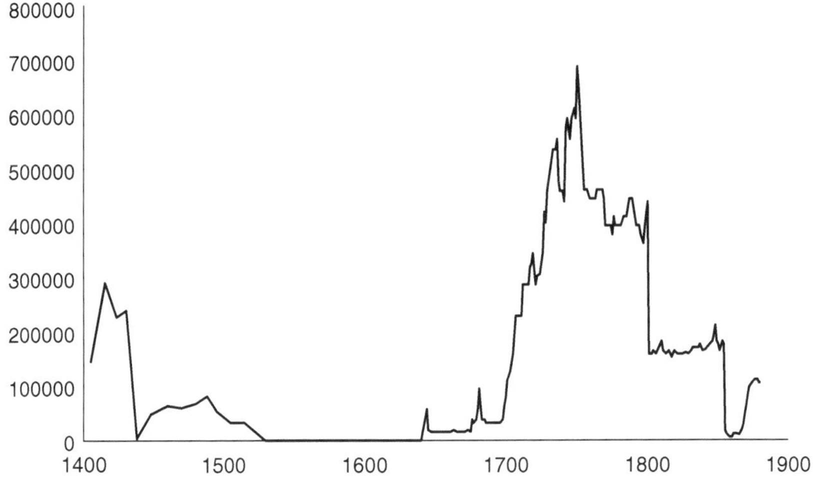

Figure 13.1 Official annual production of silver between 1380 and 1880 (tael).

Source: Wu (2001); Qing archive of mining industry.

Table 13.2 Comparison of different estimates of silver imports from Japan Between 1530 and 1708 (tael)

year	*Total amount of import*	*Annual import*	*source*
1530–1644	175,000,000	1,535,088	Zhuang (1995)
1585–1640	14,900,000	270,909	Boxer (1988)
1550–1645	98,990,000	1,042,000	Von Glahn (1996a)
1540–1647	79,581,250	743,750	Wu (2001)
1550–1645	224,000,000	2,357,895	Yamamura and Kamiki (1983)
1648–1700	27,733,333	533,333	Wu (2001)

Table 13.3 Comparison of different estimates of the import of silver from Manila to China (tael)

Year	*Total amount of imports*	*Annual import*	*Source*
1550–1645	61,570,000	648,105	Von Glahn (1996a)
1550–1645	35,200,000	370,526	Yamamura and Kamiki (1983)
1573–1644	20,450,000	288,028	Liang (1989)
1571–1644	38,160,000	522,740	Wang (1964)
1567–1644	43,200,000	561,039	Peng (1958)
1570–1644	203,200,000	2,745,946	Wan (2004)
1570–1649	68,552,250	867,750	Wu (2001)
1567–1643	75,000,000	986,842	Zhuang (1995)
1650–1699	14,837,000	302,796	Wu (2001)

Liu (2009) argued, Wan's (2004) estimate suffers from severe double counting. Therefore, we take average from the, very similar, estimates of Von Glahn (1996a) and Zhuang (1995).

Combing the information on silver from domestic production, Japan, Manila and Europe (Tables 13.1–13.4) we can get some information on the total silver inflows into China around the Ming-Qing transition in the mid-seventeenth century (see Table 13.5). Yet, in order to arrive at the total stock of money (M0) in circulation, we need to make an additional step of adding up these values before 1650 and subtracting roughly 50% (10% for wear and tear and 40% for hoarding) (Wu 2001: 228). Doing so results in roughly 130 million *taels* of silver in circulation in 1650 (see Table 13.6). This value corresponds to estimates from Liu (2005) who estimated the amount of silver in circulation to increase from 20 million *taels* in 1550 to around 130 million in 1650. It is clear from Table 13.6 that, even though there may have been a drop in imports of silver during the Ming-Qing transition in 1644, this is very unlikely to have had a serious impact on the total stock of silver in circulation. At best, it would have diminished the stock in circulation by 5%, which implies a per capita availably of silver of 38 instead of 40 grams.

But if there is little evidence of a significant silver famine in the mid-seventeenth century, perhaps there were more significant 'famines' during the Kangxi (c. 1700) and Daogang (c. 1830) depressions. Even though also in these years silver imports dropped, Table 13.6 does not show much evidence of any significant effect on the money in circulation. Nevertheless, two observations need to be made. First Irigoin (2013) stresses that the Daoguang crisis was not

Table 13.4 Comparison of different estimates of the Chinese imports of silver from Europe (tael)

Year	*Total amount of imports*	*Annual imports*	*Scholars*
1550–1645	32,800,000	345,263	Von Glahn (1996)
1570–1644	133,340,000	1,801,892	Wan (2004)
1569–1636	27,000,000	402,985	Zhuang (1995)
1700–1751	49,010,000	960,980	Yu (1940)

Table 13.5 Annual increase in silver in China via imports and home production (tael)

	Imports from Japan	*Imports from Philippines*	*Imports from Europe*	*Domestic production*	*Export to Europe*	*Net inflow*
1540–1644	1,200,000	928,000	374,000	——		2,502,000
1645–1700	570,000	303,000	——	12,000		885,000
1701–1759	95,624		416,667	404,331		1,436,755
1760–1799			5,532,650	414,915	3,135,275	2,812,290
1800–1834			7,377,400	170,690	9,750,057	–2,201,967
1834–1856						-8,050,000

Source: Tables 13.1–13.4; Irigoin (2009).

Table 13.6 Narrow money (M0) in circulation in benchmark years in China (tael)

	Silver	*Copper*	*Notes*	*Total*
1550	20,000,000	47,000,000	-	67,000,000
1650	130,000,000	47,000,000	-	177,000,000
1750	317,000,000	133,000,000	-	450,000,000
1855	1,169,000,000			*1,169,000,000*
ca. 1900	907,900,000	365,400,000	194,600,000	1,467,900,000
ca. 1930	648,000,000	72,000,000	814,320,000	1,534,320,000

Sources: This text; Liu (2009); Lin (2006: 5); Yan (2011).

a supply, but a demand-driven crisis where the demand for high quality coins induced imports of the peso. When the peso declined in quality due to Latin American independence, this led to deflation in China, which is also visible in the rising number of copper coins that needed to be paid for silver. Yet, even if this argument is true, the share of foreign silver was small. Unfortunately, we do not have early nineteenth century information but, as shown by Dai (2003), in circa 1930 the share of foreign coins in the total Chinese silver circulation only made up 4.5%. In addition, as shown in the next section, most of the inflationary effects occurred during the Taiping rebellion (1850–1864), which, as shown by Shi and Xu (2008), were mostly caused by the government minting of low quality copper coins as well as the introduction of copper-based paper notes. Likewise, as shown by Ni (2012) customs accounts show little, if any, sign of depression in this period. Hence, little evidence exists that the influx of low quality silver nor the demand for high quality silver coins affected the Chinese monetary economy.

Here we should make a second observation about the expansion of the money stock. From the mid-nineteenth century onwards, other ways to increase the money stock became available. For example, the government increasingly tried to engage in paper currency, basically enhancing its capability to extract wealth. As pointed out by Lin (2006: 166), in various studies, Wang Maoyin suggested 10 million, Bao Sichen 60 million, Huashana 100 million, and Wang Liu 900 million *tael* of paper notes be introduced. Even though initially rejected, in the second half of the nineteenth century they were introduced anyway with increasing success. Huashana was the closest with his initial observation that circa 12% of the money supply could be in paper money, as well as his suggestion that these initial notes should be convertible. But not only the increase in the money base (M0) with paper money is important. Another indirect increase follows from the introduction of new financial instruments. As pointed out by Dai (2003), 768 million *tael* was stored at credit accounts circa 1930 and could therefore be attributed to M1 money stock, increasing M0 by about 50%. All these changes do show that the increase of the stock of money was substantial: whereas between 1650 and 1850 the population increased about three times, the stock of money increased about eight times, a number which would have been even larger if we had calculated it for 1930.

Hence, there is little evidence of a lack of money in circulation compared to the real economy and, therefore, as argued in the introduction, no pressure on the silver standard existed.

Monetization and the demand for silver

A second monetary argument was that there was a shortage of silver due to fast growth of the economy leading to a higher demand for silver (e.g. Frank 1998; Atwell 2005: 476). This argument poses two problems for our argumentation. First, it runs counter to the existence of a rising gold to silver ratio necessary to switch to a silver standard (see the following section). Second, it runs counter to our argument of declining per capita growth leading, via Gresham's Law, to a switch towards a silver standard.

The simplest way to deal with this hypothesis of economic growth is to refer to direct estimates of per capita output. Indeed, Xu *et al.* (2016) and Broadberry *et al.* (2012), show that the Chinese economy had embarked on a downward per capita path (and a very minor increase in total size) during this silver period. More complex is explaining how the apparent influx of silver, combined with an equally apparent rise in the value of silver, is not caused by economic growth (Figure 13.2).

A first step is to look at inflation. Looking at the silver prices of rice by Peng Xinwei (1958), we find very little evidence of inflation between the fourteenth and seventeenth centuries. For the eighteenth and start of the nineteenth century, we do see a strong rise in rice prices, but this is mainly caused by a rise in the price of food, rather than a decline in the price of silver (e.g. Deng 2015). Another way of looking at this is by assessing the copper (coin) to silver ratio. This ratio was stable until the mid-eighteenth century after which it rose, but much less than the price level, thus suggesting that silver increased in value versus copper (i.e. there was too little silver).

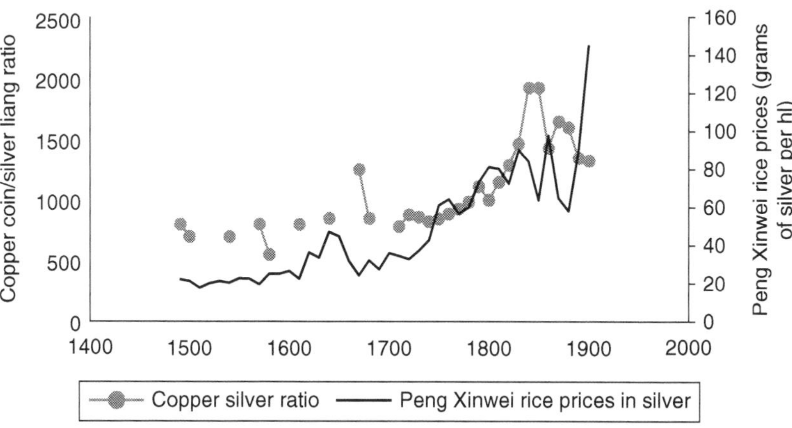

Figure 13.2 Copper coin/silver ratio and silver rice prices.

This apparently confirmed the argument that economic growth occurred. However, this assessment is incorrect for two reasons. First, as shown by Table 13.7, even though the coin/silver ratio undoubtedly increased in the eighteenth and nineteenth centuries (with more coins given for the same amount of silver), once corrected for purity and weight, the intrinsic copper to silver ratio remained roughly stable (with perhaps even a minor decrease in the seventeenth century) suggesting that there was no real abundance or shortage of silver and, hence, there is no evidence of real economic growth either.

Second, much of the silver flowing into the country did not actually increase the amount of coins and specie to match economic growth. Rather, increasingly different currencies and barter trade were replaced by silver. Indeed, the often quoted, 'Single Whip' reform in which a part of Chinese taxes was bundled into one silver tax may be seen as evidence for this move from a country based on barter to one based on silver. This reform introduced by the Ming government in order to convert tax into silver, had started in certain provinces already in the 1530s, and lasted about 100 years before being complete. As Table 13.8 shows, the percentage tax expressed in silver went from close to zero percent in 1450 to over 20% in 1620. This changed even further after 1651 since, after its rise to power, the Qing dynasty started a serious reform by on the one hand increasing taxes paid in silver as much as possible and, on the other hand, by abolishing non-silver taxes which, at that time, still accounted for 1~2% of total revenue. As Table 13.8 shows, non-currency taxes in textiles had been completely abolished, mainly because the government did not control textile production anymore, but the main difference was that the government had aborted many of its non-currency-based activities. These reforms caused government finances to be 64% in silver. Hence, it follows that there is little evidence of an undersupply of silver when looking at the silver to copper ratio. Neither do we find evidence, based on tax data, that the silver that came into the country was used for increasing the stock of money to cover economic development. Rather, it increased the stock to replace existing other means of payments such as produce or textiles.

In sum, even though the use of silver as a means of payment only increased slowly, it is clear that the majority of silver that came into China became used

Table 13.7 Copper coin/silver liang ratio corrected for share copper in coins

Copper coin/silver		*Percentage copper in copper coin*	*Copper coin weight (grams)*	
1505	700	90%	3.72	630
1550	700	90%	3.72	630
1575	800	94%	3.72	750
1625	1000	50%	3.72	500
1740	830	50%	4.46	498
1800	1070	52%	3.72	556
1890	1530	54%	2.23	496

Source: Peng (1958); Yang (1962); Qian and Guo (1985); Liu (2003).

Table 13.8 Chinese government income by category (expressed in tael of silver)

Tax in produce	*Tax in textiles*	*Tax in copper*	*Tax in paper cash*	*Tax in silver*	*Total tax*
1450	25,880,000	255,500	4,737	-	26,140,237
1500	30,900,000	766,000	3,247	32,000	31,701,247
1552	26,590,000	386,500	2,414	2,433,000	29,411,914
1602	28,370,000	345,500	0	4,582,000	33,297,500
1620	27,800,000	270,500	8	7,552,000	35,622,508
1651	10,482,525	2,430,722	64	23,065,302	35,978,614

Source: Wu (2001); *shizu zhanghuangdi shilu*, vol. 60.

Note: 5 benchmarks from 1450 to 1620 were annual government revenue in the Ming dynasty. The taxation levied by the Ming government was comprised of non-currencies, which were levied in wheat, rice, cotton clothing, and silk textile, as well as currencies, which were levied in both paper and silver cash. Based on the official price of both non-currencies and paper cash in silver, we convert both non-currencies and paper cash to silver. According to government policies, 1 shi in rice or wheat costs 1 tael in silver; 1 pi in cotton clothing costs 0.5 tael in silver; 1 pi in silk textile costs 1 tael in silver; 100 guan in paper cash = 1 tael in silver in 1430; 1000 guan in paper cash = 1 tael in silver between 1440 and 1470; 2000 guan in paper cash = 1 tael in silver between 1480 and 1620.

The benchmark in 1651 was government revenue in Qing dynasty. The taxation levied by the Qing government still consisted of both non-currencies, which were levied in wheat, rice and hay, as well as currencies parts, which were levied in copper coin, paper and silver cashes. The official price of non-currencies, copper coin and paper in silver are following: 1 shi in rice or wheat costs 1 tael in silver; 1shu in hay costs 1 tael in silver; 1000 wen in copper coin costs 1 tael in silver; 2000 guan in paper cash = 1 tael, which is taken from Ming price.

to finance the transition from a barter economy to one based on precious metal payments. This is also confirmed by a constant silver to copper ratio, suggesting that not only was there no silver shortage, but also that per capita economic development was stagnant or even declining.

In silver we trust?

In the previous sections, we argued that the main monetary factors suggested in the literature, although at times important, do not seem to have been influencing the existence of the silver standard to a large extent over this 500-year period. We find rather that the inflow of silver was mainly directed at replacing the old produce used for exchange. But even after subtracting this effect, the remaining net silver influx was an oversupply causing declining silver to copper ratios.

So, the monetary factors discussed earlier did not upset the silver period over a period of over 500 years. This does not mean there was no effect, but these effects were often short-lived. A similar situation we can find in other countries facing a period dominated by an (implicit or explicit) silver standard like England in the seventeenth century, or ancient Babylonia,[4] neither of which had immediate access to large silver deposits and which faced, at times, a shortage in silver. Nevertheless, both regions maintained their focus on silver.

But obviously, other monetary factors such as culture or government intervention might have had an effect as well. For example, Scheidel (2009) argues that the government wanted to maintain silver because it was able to debase copper and, hence, make a profit. Indeed, some debasement occurred as the share of copper in the coins diminished over time (see Table 13.7). However, as Lin (2006) already argued, in many cases the costs of minting coins were in fact higher than their value. Indeed, some suggestions of arbitrage for profit making within the government were in fact rejected. The argument was that the Chinese government had a socio-economic duty to maintain balance between the monetary situation and the purchasing power of the people as we already noted in the introduction. This essentially socio-cultural argument (see also Scheidel 2009) may thus also be enhancing the stability.

All we can thus conclude is that the main monetary factors (silver shortage) suggested in the literature had only a limited effect. By implication, other factors such as the role of the government and culture, including the effect of real economic development (GDP per capita growth), also must have had an effect, even though we cannot determine exactly to what extent. Yet, because of its absence in the literature, in this section we will focus on the effect of the real economy on the choice of monetary standard.

Hence, we do not argue that monetary factors such as the flows of silver (e.g. Horesh 2014), stable anchor (Bordo *et al.* 2003), culture (Scheidel 2009) and government (Scheidel 2009) did not play a role, but rather that we have to add real economic development as an additional explanatory factor. Indeed, following Mundell (1998) and Butler (2002), we argue that this is caused by Fisher's Equation. According to Fisher's Equation, the amount of money in circulation has a relation to the real economy. During periods of stagnation, *ceteris paribus* the real economy declines, implying that too much money is in circulation. According to Gresham's Law, when filtering out the effects of monetary factors (i.e. assuming a constant gold to silver ratio) the high quality, strongest coins (i.e. gold) will be hoarded or transported abroad thus creating a de facto silver standard. Vice versa, if economic development occurs, expansion of the monetary base is necessary. This can be done by importing or dishoarding valuable metals like gold, or even by losing other types of money, for example through exports, that have a fixed relation with gold. In this way, a de facto gold standard comes into existence.[5]

Butler (2002) tested this hypothesis by looking at the historical experience of various countries switching back and forth from the silver (and gold) standard. For that purpose, Butler (2002) divides history into four periods of thousand years of economic advance, i.e. the Early Bronze Age (3200–2300 BC), the Middle and Late Bronze Age (2000–1200 BC), the Roman period (700 BC–AD 337) and the modern period (1000–present). All periods are followed by an interlude of economic contraction. The end of these periods is marked by an increased devaluation of the silver and a growth of the importance of gold, which actually heralds the interlude of decline. After the interlude, silver returns to its role as the primary monetary metal. After the Bronze Age, the 'Dark Ages' witness a severe breakdown of the market economy; the same is true for the period at the end of the Roman Empire and the Early Middle

Ages. As we are now at the end of the fourth wave, with a gold standard in the nineteenth and early twentieth centuries, Marion Butler predicts a new contraction coming soon.

Yet, as pointed out, switching between gold and silver standards depends in addition to real economic development, also on a dazzling number of monetary factors. Disentangling these factors is close to impossible thus making it impossible to use actual historical outcomes as proof of the importance of the real economy for the stability of the Chinese silver system. All we can say is that, as Maddison (1998) showed, Chinese long-term growth from the Western Han Dynasty around AD 1 to the Qing Dynasty in 1912 could be divided into two phases. In the first phase, which lasted until the Song Dynasty around AD 1000, the economy showed some small growth in per capita terms, even though countrywide turmoil and disasters sometimes interrupted the general pattern of growth. This phase experienced multiple metal currency systems with copper coin as money of account. It knew a gold interlude in which gold had a role, small as it might have been, in the monetary system, just before the collapse, in the three richest dynasties, i.e. the Western Han Dynasty (206 BC–AD 9), Tang Dynasty (618–907) and Northern Song Dynasty (960–1127). As Peng (1958) and Fang (2015) point out, gold was a standard currency in Western Han Dynasty, and played an important role of money of account in both the Tang Dynasty and Northern Song Dynasties.

A second way to look at the hypothesis is to look at the hoarding and export of gold. Indeed, looking at the dynasties from Han to Song, all had their, admittedly limited, number of gold coins in circulation after which they disappeared almost completely. The main reason must have been the well-recorded exports of gold, as well as a widespread hoarding of this metal over the post-Yuan dynasties. Indeed, hoarding was extensive as gold ingots were found in hoards in Ming and Qing China (Peng 1958). Obviously, this implies that, since gold was valued more than silver, not only the more expensive metal (gold) was rapidly taken out of circulation, but also the value of gold increased versus the value of silver during these 'silver periods'. This can be directly observed by looking at the data. As shown by Peng (1958), the gold to silver ratio varied in the order of magnitude of 5–6 (i.e. gold is valued at 5–6 times as much as silver) up to circa AD 1000, roughly the start of the Song dynasty. After some fluctuations in the turbulent period of the Northern and Southern Song and Yuan dynasties, we can witness a rise in the gold to silver ratio from circa 5–6 at the start of the Ming dynasty, to 15 in the Qing dynasty, and rising even further in the Republican period.

So, the real economy might indeed have, besides monetary factors, also had an impact on the stability of the silver system in China between the fifteenth and twentieth centuries. But what does this tell us about the fall of the silver standard in China in 1935, even though that period still witnessed on average rising gold to silver ratios? Of course, it is important to first look at the short-run dynamics. As shown by Xu *et al.* (2016), per capita GDP remained roughly similar, even though there was a small growth in total GDP. This was accompanied by an almost constant gold to silver ratio (Kong 1988, 481–83). This relation breaks down, however, from 1929 onwards when the value of gold strongly increased against that of silver.

No doubt wartime sentiments played a role in this increase, as did international relations. Yet they were mostly monetary factors that played a decisive role in the fall of the silver standard. As the financial department in the Republican Chinese Government claimed (1958), the silver purchase act of 1934 in the USA created a drain of silver from China and, hence, caused a strong deflation pushing China off the silver standard, and into real economy decline. But the severe economic and political turmoil caused also a further drain of all precious metals, among which was gold, causing strong deflation as can be clearly seen from the decline in prices in Jiangsu between 1928 and 1934. The silver drain, combined with the rise on gold to silver ratio, caused by a drain of silver, required the Republican government to replace silver with paper money, named *fabi*, as fiat money (Zhao and Sui 2011) causing initially a modest inflation, followed by very strong deflation in the late 1930s and 1940s.

Conclusion

China witnessed a history of money that deviates from that of the Middle East and Europe. In China, the first money consisted of copper coins, followed by paper money and finally a long period of silver money. In the West, we see a development of silver to a combination of silver and copper, to paper money and other money instruments such as cheques. At all times, gold played some role in the background. Silver appears to have functioned well over very long periods of time. This is also true for China from the 1430s to the middle of the twentieth century. This means that the history of China on the one hand and Mesopotamia, Classical antiquity and Europe on the other hand before the 1430s can hardly be compared as to the role of silver and gold. Yet, after the 1430s, there are many parallels. Silver appeared to be a stable anchor in the economy.

The reason for this stability is found in the gold to silver ratio. If this ratio in the market is higher than that set by the government, as was the case in China, we witness a withdrawal of gold from the monetary system. This is exactly what occurred in China between the 1430s and the twentieth century. But what was driving this? Various monetary and real factors may be the cause. In this chapter, we rejected two of the main monetary arguments both related to a shortage of silver.

Obviously, other factors such as higher gold to silver ratios abroad (thus leading to gold exports), culture and the role of the government each play their role. Yet, in this paper we added, besides the abundance of silver, as an additional argument that we should also take account of the real economic development since a combination of Fisher's Equation and Gresham's Law suggest that, in cases of economic decline, the chance of obtaining a silver standard increases.

Notes

1 The research leading to these results received funding from the European Research Council under the European Union's Horizon 2020 Programme/ERC-StG 637695 – HinDI, as part of the project 'The historical dynamics of industrialization in Northwestern Europe and China ca. 1800–2010: a regional interpretation.' Part of Section 2 is based on a previous paper published in Van Leeuwen and Xu (2016: 119–132).

2 It has been argued to affect the real economy via prices, foreign exchange and real business cycles. Hence, the money stock may explain a boom or depression in the real economy but it will not affect long-run growth patterns. It remains the question, however, whether this is true given that many empirical analyses in this field have taken too little notice of the underlying structure of the economy when trying to measure the effect of monetary shocks on the real economy (e.g. Rasche 1998: 89). Indeed, monetary shocks may not only affect the financial system, but also changes the income distribution as well as the relative prices in a country thus placing it on a different trajectory of growth (e.g. Bordo 1998; Van der Spek *et al.* 2015). In more complicated monetary systems also demand deposits are added to the stock (M1) or even saving deposits (M2). Obviously, in historical settings M0 will be the largest and easiest to calculate. However, with the rise of the financial sector, also demand and saving deposits gain in importance hence causing the various M-indicators to diverge.

3 In more complicated monetary systems also demand deposits are added to the stock (M1) or even saving deposits (M2). Obviously, in historical settings M0 will be the largest and easiest to calculate. However, with the rise of the financial sector, also demand and saving deposits gain in importance hence causing the various M-indicators to diverge.

4 Babylonia had a silver-based economy for nearly 2,000 years, apart from a few exceptions such as the Kassite period and Assyria in the eighth century.

5 At a first look, it appears that such a system is gold based but in fact it is a fiat system as, for example, 10 grams of gold is expressed in 10 token coins rather than in actual gold coins and these token coins or notes often are not convertible in gold.

References

Atwell, W. S. (2005). 'Another look at silver imports into China, ca. 1635–1644', *Journal of World History*, 16 (4): 467–489.

Bordo, M. D., Dittmar, R. D. and Gavin, W. T. (2003). 'Gold, fiat money and price stability', *Working Paper Series*. Research Division – Federal Reserve Bank of St. Louis.

Bordo, M. (1998). 'Monetary regimes and economic performance: lessons from history', in Wood, G. (ed.), *Money, Prices and the Real Economy*, Cheltenham: Edward Elgar: 42–57.

Boxer, C. R. (1988). *The Great Ship from Amacon*, Macao: Instituto Cultural de Macau.

Broadberry, S. N., Guan, H. and Li, D. (2012). 'China, Europe and the great divergence: a study in historical national accounting', Paper presented at the Asian Historical Economics Conference, Hitotsubashi University Tokyo.

Butler, M. (2002). 'When gold is king', Gold-Eagle.com (http://www.gold-eagle.com/article/when-gold-king).

Dai, J. (2003). *Silver and Chinese modern economic 1890–1935*. Phd Thesis of Fudan University, April 23, 2003. (戴建兵，白银与中国近代经济1890–1935，复旦大学博士学位论文2003年4月23日)

Deng, K. (2015). 'China's population expansion and its causes during the Qing period, 1644–1911', London School of Economics, Economic History Working Papers 219.

Fang, T. (2015) 'Prediction and fall of a shining golden dynasty', http://mp.weixin.qq.com/s/dn1oUk0eGIC6TE4qq8zR-Q (方天戟：《一个金光闪闪的王朝的谶语和灭亡》，微信公众号《文博山西》2015年11月20日。)

Flynn, D. O. and Giraldez, A. (1995). 'Born with a "silver spoon": The origin of world trade in 1571', *Journal of World History*, 6 (2): 201–21.

Flynn, D. O. and Giráldez, A. (eds.) (1997). *Metals and Monies in an Emerging Global Economy.* Aldershot: Ashgate/Variorum Press.

Frank, A. G. (1998). *ReOrient: Global Economy in the Asian Age*, Berkeley: University of California Press.

Friedman, M. (1990), 'Bimetallism revisited', *Journal of Economic Perspectives*, 4: 85–104.

Horesh, N. (2014). *Chinese Money in Global Context: Historic Junctures between 600 BCE and 2012.* Stanford, CA: Stanford University Press.

Irigoin, A. (2009). 'The end of a silver era: The consequences of the breakdown of the Spanish peso standard in China and the United States, 1780s–1850s', *Journal of World History*, 20 (2): 207–243.

Irigoin, A. (2013). 'A "Trojan Horse" in Daoguang China?: Explaining the flows of silver (and opium) in and out of China', MPRA Paper 43987, University Library of Munich, Germany.

Kong, M. (1988). *Material Collection of Nankai Economic Index.* Bejing: Chinese social Science Press.

Liang, F. (1989). *Liang fangzhong's symposium on economic history.* Beijing: Zhonghua book company. (梁方仲:《梁方仲经济史论文集》，北京：中华书局1989年版。)

Lin, M.-H. (2006). *China Upside Down: Currency, Society, and Ideologies, 1808–1856.* Harvard: Cambridge University Press.

Liu, Jun (2009). 'Analysis of the volume of import of silver to China during Ming and Qing dynasties', *Journal of Dongbei Finance and Economics University*, 15 (6): 3–6. (刘军:明清时期白银流入量分析《东北财经大学学报》2009年第6期).

Liu, G.W. (2005) *Wrestling for Power: The State and the Economy in Later Imperial China*, Doctoral dissertation, Harvard University.

Liu, L. (2003). 'Ratio between silver and copper in Ming and Qing dynasties', *Journal of Zhaoqing University* 24 (3): 34–38. (刘利平, 明清时期银钱比价初探, 肇庆学院学报第24卷第3期 2003年6月).

Maddison, A. (1998). *Chinese Economic Performance in the Long Run.* Paris: OECD Development Centre.

Mundell, R. (1998). 'Uses and abuses of Gresham's Law in the history of money', *Zagreb Journal of Economics*, 2 (2): 57–72.

Ni, Y. (2012), 'A re-study of the "Daoguang Depression"', *The Harvard-Yenching Institute talk.*

Peng, X. (1958). *Currency History in China*, Shanghai: Shanghai People's Publishing House (彭信威:《中国货币史》，上海：上海人民出版社1958版。).

Qian, J. and Guo, Y. (1985). *China Monetary History Outline*, Shanghai: Shanghai People's Publishing House (中国货币史纲要, 上海人民出版社 1985年6月).

Qing archive of the mining industry, First Historical Archives of China and library of Institute of Economics in CASS (Chinese Academy of Social Sciences).

Rasche, R. (1998). 'Money and real output', in Wood, G. (ed.), *Money, Prices and the Real Economy*, Cheltenham, UK: Edward Elgar: 82–93.

Scheidel, W. (2009). 'The monetary systems of the Han and Roman empires,' in Scheidel, W. (ed.), *Rome and China: Comparative Perspectives on Ancient World Empires*, New York: Oxford University Press: 137–207.

Shi, Z., and Xu, Y. (2008). *Fiscal History in Late Qing, ca.1851~1894*. Shanghai: Shanghai Finance and Economic University Press.

Shizu zhanghuangdi shilu (1985) *vol.60*. Beijing: Zhonghua Book Company Beijing. (《世祖章皇帝实录》，中华书局*1985*年影印，北京。)

Sullivan, N. (2005). 'Gresham's law, fact or falsehood?', *Student Economic Review*, 19: 17–25.

TePaske, J. J. (1983). 'New world silver, Castile and the Philippines, 1590–1800', in Richards, J. F. (ed.), *Precious Metals in the Later Medieval and Early Modern World*, Durham, NC: Carolina Academic Press.

Tlaga, J. N. (2002). 'Gold standard = fiat in disguise', Gold-Eagle.com (http://www.gold-eagle.com/article/gold-standard-fiat-disguise)

Van der Spek, R. J., Foldvari, P. and Van Leeuwen, B. (2015). 'Growing silver and changing prices: the development of the money stock in ancient Babylonia and medieval England', in Van der Spek, R. J., Van Leeuwen, B. and Van Zanden, J. L. (eds.), *A History of Market Performance from Ancient Babylonia to the Modern World*, London and New York: Routledge: 489–505.

Van Leeuwen, B., and Xu, Y. (2016). 'Silverization of China during the Ming-Qing transition (ca. 1550–1700) and the consequences for research into the Babylonian economy', in Kleber, K. and Pirngruber, R. (eds.), *Silver, Money and Credit. A Tribute to Robartus J. van der Spek on the Occasion of His 65th Birthday on 18th September* 2014, Leiden, the Netherlands: Nederlands Instituut voor het Nabije Oosten: 119–132.

Von Glahn, R. (1996a). *Fountain of Fortune. Money and Monetary Policy in China, 1000–1700*. Berkeley: University of California Press.

Von Glahn, R. (1996b). 'Myth and reality of China's seventeenth-century monetary crisis', *Journal of Economic History*, 56 (2): 429–454.

Von Glahn, R. (2010). 'Monies of account and monetary transition in China, twelfth to fourteenth centuries', *Journal of the Economic and Social History of the Orient*, 53: 463–505.

Wan, M. (2004). 'Economy silverization in Ming dynasty and relationship between China and world', *Academic Journal of Hebei Province*, 24 (3): 145–154 (万明:《明代白银货币化：中国与世界连接的新视角》，《河北学刊》2004年第3期。)

Wang, S. (1964). 'International trade development among China, Manila and Mexico in late Ming period', *Journal of Geography*, 7: 31–59. (王士鹤:《明代后期中国—马尼拉—墨西哥贸易的发展》，《地理集刊》1964年第7号。)

Wu, C. (2001). *Modernization in China: Market and Society*. Beijing: Shanlian Bookshop. (吴承明.中国的现代化：市场与社会[M].北京：三联书店，2001.)

Xu, Y., Shi, Z., Van Leeuwen, B., Ni, Y., Zhang, Z. and Ma, Y. (2016). 'Chinese national income, ca. 1661–1933', *Australian Economic History Review*, doi:10.1111/aehr.12127.

Yamamura, K. and Kamiki, T. (1983). 'Silver mines and Sung coins: a monetary history of medieval and modern Japan in international perspective', in Richards, J. F. (ed.), *Precious Metals in the Late Medieval and Early Modern World*, Durham, NC: Carolina Academic Press: 329–62.

Yan, H. (2011). 'Currency supply, currency structure and trend of China's economy from 1650 to 1936', *Journal of Financial Research*, 7: 57–69. (燕红忠, 货币供给量、货币结构与中国经济趋势：1650—1936, 《金融研究》（京）)

Yang, D. (1962). *A Monetary History of the Qing Dynasty*. Beijing: SDX Publishing Company (杨端六, 清代货币金融史稿, 三联书店1962).

Yu, J. (1940). *An Estimate of Silver Import and Products Export in China: ca.1700~1937*. Beijing: Commercial Press. (余捷琼.1700-1937年中国银货输出入的一个估计,北京：商务印书馆1940版。)

Zhao, L. and Sand Sui, F. (2011). 'American silver policy and Chinese economy during Great Depression', *Research of Chinese Economic History*, 4: 31–43.（赵留彦、隋福民：《美国白银政策与大萧条时期的中国经济》，《中国经济史研究》2011年第4期。）

Zhuang, G. (1995). 'An estimate of amount of silver inflow to China from 16th to 18th centuries', *Journal of China Currency*, 3: 3–10. (庄国土:《16—18世纪白银流入中国数量估算》，《中国钱币》1995年第3期。)

14 Confronting financial crises under different monetary regimes

Spain in the Great Depression years[1]

Juan Castañeda and Pedro Schwartz

Introduction

A number of historians have suggested that the Great Contraction of the US economy from 1929 to 1933 and the banking failures and subsequent financial upheaval in Europe after 1931 played a large role in the breakdown of the Second Spanish Republic, founded in 1931, and in the final nemesis of the Civil War (1936–39).[2] Yet, in this chapter, we underline the fact that Spain fared much better than other countries during the crucial years of 1929–1933. Taking 1929 as the base year for all countries, as shown in Figure 14.1, Spain's GDP certainly did not fall as much as in France, the United States or Germany.

First, we attribute the relatively mild character of the recession of those years mainly to domestic factors. And secondly, we discount a faltering private sector investment or a supposedly deflationary monetary policy of the Bank of Spain as the main causes of that mild recession. We attribute it to a sudden attempt to rebalance the budget in 1930 with a drastic retrenchment of public investment. This change of policy was felt to be necessary because the Spanish Government found it impossible to go on sustaining the growth model of the mid-1920s. In any case, the change in budgetary policy did not affect the greater part of the private sector, especially agriculture and consumer industries; and the relative downturn did not originate with the Bank of Spain, whose quick reaction when depositors took fright at the sudden fall of the monarchy, avoided a catastrophic bank run in 1931.[3] To evidence this, we estimate the Bank of Spain *reaction function* in those years and thus show that the Bank acted as a successful lender of last resort in 1931.

Apart from looking at the structure of the Spanish economy, we give another reason for our view that there was nothing more than a short-lived domestic downturn from 1929 to 1933: the downturn looked artificially large by comparison with the boom of the late twenties brought about by an unsustainable expansion of Government investment. This can be seen by looking at the secular growth trend (see Figure 14.3).

Data for unemployment, company returns and international trade (Tables 14.4 to 14.6) show that the mild Spanish recession of the thirties left

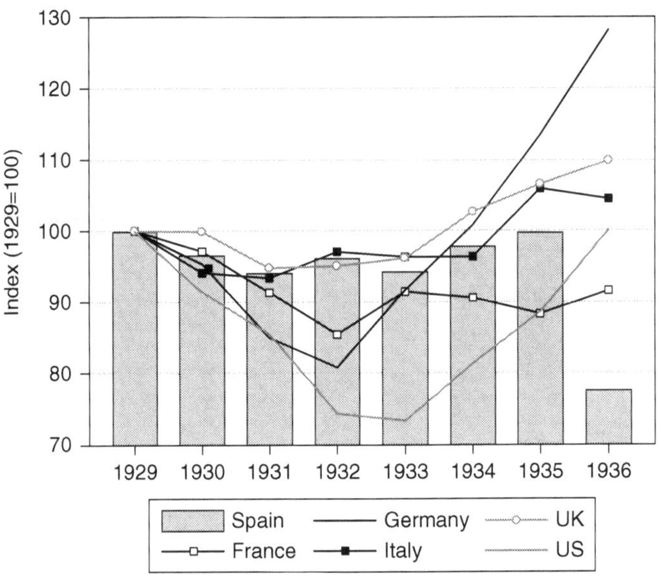

Figure 14.1 Real GDP growth in selected European countries and the United States.

Source: GDP data for Germany and France from Mitchell (2003), UK GDP from Feinstein (1972), as quoted by Cole and Ohanian (2007). US GDP from the US Bureau of Economic Analysis Statistics. Spain GDP from Prados (2003).

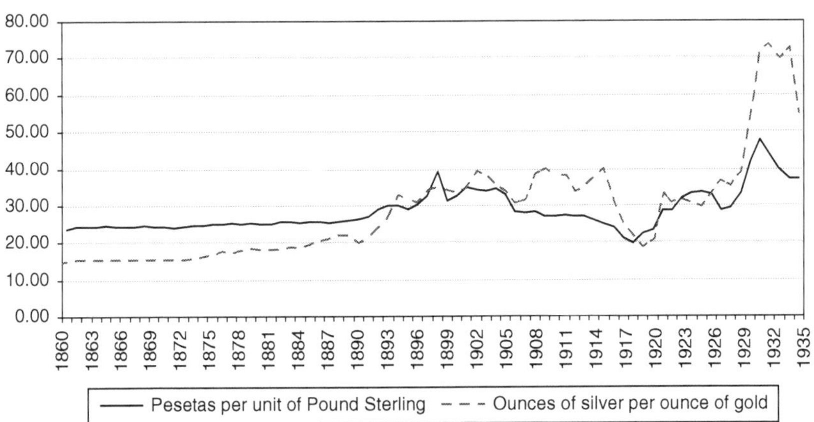

Figure 14.2 Exchange rate of silver versus gold and of the peseta versus the pound sterling (1860–1935).

Source: Data on the exchange rate of silver versus gold from Officer and Williamson 2014. The exchange rate of the peseta versus sterling from Fernández Baños (1930), as quoted by Tena (2005).

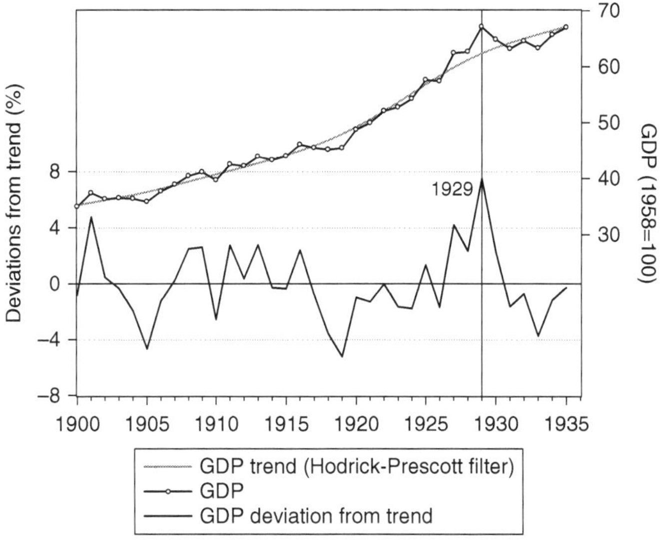

Figure 14.3 Spanish GDP (1900–35), deviations from trend.

Source: GDP data from Prados (2003).

Table 14.1 Spain: Primary sector and the GDP

	(1) Wheat		*(2) GDP*			
	Harvest (thousands of tons)	*Rate of growth (%)*	*Value added by primary sector (growth, %)*	*GDP (Total, %)*	*GDP (Index, 1958 =100)*	*GDP (deviations from H-P trend, %)*
1920	3772	7.22	5.12	7.22	48.75	−1.00
1921	3950	4.71	−1.96	2.47	49.95	−1.32
1922	3415	−13.54	3.01	4.26	52.08	−0.03
1923	4276	25.21	−6.27	1.29	52.76	−1.67
1924	3314	−22.49	−0.1	2.82	54.25	−1.80
1925	4425	33.52	10.32	6.18	57.61	1.35
1926	3990	−9.83	−9.1	−0.37	57.39	−1.71
1927	3942	−1.2	16.39	8.66	62.37	4.19
1928	3338	−15.32	−13.87	0.39	62.61	2.33
1929	**4198**	**25.76**	**20.6**	**7.07**	**67.04**	**7.51**
1930	3993	−4.88	−13.58	−3.35	64.78	2.27
1931	3659	−8.36	6.97	−2.54	63.14	−1.67
1932	**5013**	**37**	**10.87**	**2.15**	**64.50**	−0.74
1933	3762	−24.95	−10.57	−1.95	63.24	−3.76
1934	**5085**	**35.16**	**11.84**	**3.77**	**65.62**	−1.20
1935	4300	−15.43	−0.89	2.01	66.94	−0.29

Source: (1) Data from GEHR (1991) as quoted by Barciela *et al.* (2005). (2) GDP calculations based on data from Prados 2003. In bold years of extraordinary wheat harvests.

Table 14.2 Expansion of the industries connected with construction and public works

	Quarries, bricks, cement & glass	*Annual rate of growth (%)*	*Basic metal*	*Annual rate of growth (%)*	*Metal industries*	*Annual rate of growth (%)*	*Transport goods*	*Annual rate of growth (%)*
1920	7.99		25.95		15.00		41.50	
1921	7.33	–8.30	32.27	24.36	18.96	26.37	43.81	5.57
1922	14.40	96.46	25.09	–22.24	16.77	–11.56	46.57	6.29
1923	18.06	25.42	42.50	69.39	26.42	57.60	25.77	–44.65
1924	20.38	12.82	44.34	4.33	27.40	3.68	42.39	64.48
1925	26.95	32.25	49.89	12.51	31.44	14.75	38.46	–9.28
1926	25.75	–4.44	50.60	1.41	32.00	1.78	75.04	95.12
1927	41.35	**60.54**	57.65	**13.93**	36.09	**12.79**	105.32	**40.36**
1928	46.78	**13.14**	58.33	**1.18**	38.76	**7.38**	89.07	**–15.43**
1929	51.65	**10.41**	68.60	**17.60**	43.69	**12.74**	96.45	**8.29**
1930	45.41	–12.07	61.18	–10.81	40.03	–8.38	52.22	–45.86
1931	43.87	–3.41	48.42	–20.85	31.94	–20.22	38.01	–27.21
1932	40.60	–7.45	38.08	–21.37	26.03	–18.50	14.66	–61.42
1933	36.76	–9.46	37.63	–1.17	26.51	1.85	11.40	–22.25
1934	25.62	–30.29	40.91	8.71	29.73	12.13	9.60	–15.79
1935	24.81	–3.16	37.94	–7.26	32.00	7.66	9.40	–2.07

Source: Data from Prados (2003).

Table 14.3 Monetary base and money supply (% annual growth)

	Monetary base	*Money supply*
1928	3.40	6.68
1929	1.72	7.13
1930	2.84	6.45
1931	**10.47**	**–2.53**
1932	–4.30	0.88
1933	–0.65	2.15
1934	–3.43	3.10
1935	5.63	3.80

Source: Data from Aceña and Pons (2005).

Table 14.4 Industry and banks. Return on Equity Ratio (ROE)

	Average across sectors	*Consumption goods*	*Capital goods*	*Banks*
1920	11.6	15.2	7.8	11.4
1921	9.5	11.1	8.6	10.6
1922	9.8	12.5	8.3	11.1
1923	9.7	12.7	6.4	10.6
1924	10.4	15.5	6.9	10.6
1925	9.8	10.6	7.0	10.4
1926	9.9	9.0	8.2	9.7
1927	9.0	9.3	9.9	10.7
1928	9.9	10.2	10.6	11.6
1929	10.4	10.6	9.4	10.6
1930	9.4	11.1	9.4	9.8
1931	7.0	11.0	5.5	7.0
1932	6.6	8.9	2.6	7.0
1933	5.9	8.6	–0.7	6.8
1934	6.0	8.9	–0.9	7.0
1935	6.0	13.3	5.1	7.9

Source: Return on equity data from Tafunell (2000) as quoted by Tafunell (2005).

some sectors practically unscathed, given the weight of agriculture in the Spanish economy and the relative isolation of Spain from the world. The *de facto* flotation of the peseta also helped – but then made for a weaker recovery in the thirties compared to other countries. The Republic in 1931 brought acute social conflict, which finally led to the 1936–39 civil war. This is what deviated Spain from its secular growth path – not world depression.

In sum, the thesis of the present chapter is that the recession was much lighter in Spain than in the United States, Italy, Germany or France (see Figure 14.1); that the causes of the contraction were domestic rather than epidemic; and that the relative shallowness of the contraction in Spain, and of the United Kingdom after abandoning gold, may have been due in some measure to similarly flexible monetary arrangements.

Table 14.5 Unemployment rate: International comparison

	United Kingdom	*Germany*	*US*	*Spain*
1927	6.8	8.8	4.1	–
1928	7.5	8.4	4.4	–
1929	7.3	13.1	3.2	–
1930	11.2	15.3	8.7	–
1931	15.1	23.3	15.8	–
1932	15.6	30.1	23.6	5.15*
1933	14.1	26.3	24.9	7.14
1934	11.9	14.9	26.7	7.70
1935	11.0	11.6	20.01	7.77
1936	9.4	8.3	16.9	9.24*

Source: US data from Historical Statistics of the US (as quoted by Hernandez Andreu 1986: 181, table 7.1; page 181). Germany and UK unemployment rates from Mitchell (2003). Own calculations of Spain unemployment rate, based on the working population data for 1930 from Nicolau (2003) and registered unemployment from Balcells (1971: 53).

Note: * Data available up to the end of June.

Table 14.6 Evolution of the rate of growth of exports (%, year on year): international comparison

	Spain	*US*	*Germany*	*UK*	*France*	*Italy*
1928	23.02	5.72	13.66	1.97	–5.60	–4.18
1929	–10.25	2.52	9.83	0.83	–3.77	1.58
1930	7.99	–26.68	–10.73	–21.81	–14.57	–20.46
1931	–15.98	–37.11	–20.26	–31.58	–28.95	–15.75
1932	–7.22	–33.73	–40.21	–6.41	–35.26	–33.29
1933	–3.23	4.51	–15.12	0.55	–6.25	–12.05
1934	3.43	27.50	–14.47	7.90	–3.38	–12.79
1935	–3.32	6.81	2.47	7.32	–13.19	0.27
1936	–	96.88	11.69	3.53	–0.40	4.20

Source: Spanish data from Tena (1992) as quoted by Tena (2005). Exports growth for the other countries are own calculations based on the League of Nations Statistical Yearbook Information (1936–37).

Spain on silver

For centuries, the Spanish currency had had a special link with silver. The discovery in the sixteenth century of a cheap method of separating the metal from sulphur without toasting the mineral allowed Spain to inundate the world with silver discovered in American mines. The loss of the greater part of the Empire at the beginning of the nineteenth century plunged the monetary arrangements of Spain into disarray. In 1868, a Revolutionary Government tried to mend matters by joining the Latin Monetary Union. To that end the new peseta was made the standard of the country, coined with the same silver weight and fineness as the French, Swiss and Belgian francs. Spain however did not follow suit when the continent of Europe joined the United Kingdom in adopting gold as the anchor. Though Spain was officially bimetallic and for a short period gold coins were minted, in effect the peseta was purely on silver. This was made official in 1883 when the reference to gold and gold coinage and convertibility of notes was officially abandoned. As silver slowly lost value up to World War I and after 1920 (see Figure 14.2), the peseta coins did not change their face value. The result was that the Spanish currency functioned as a nominal currency. This slow loss of value except for the years of the Spanish-American war and during World War I did not lead to inflation: the reason was that the Bank of Spain note issue was limited by law. This monetary arrangement lasted up to the Civil War in 1936 and served Spain well during the Great Depression.[4]

Two institutional constraints

Apart from the silver anchor, two further institutional constraints must be noted for the period leading to the Depression. The first is protection and relatively little foreign trade. Fifty years of protectionism had led to industry being mainly concentrated in two regions, the Basque Country and Catalonia. The industrialists in both regions were able to argue that a return to free trade (attempted from 1868 to 1891) would create unemployment and inflame passions:[5] hence the relentless march towards greater protection, starting with the Tariff law of 1891 and culminating with the virtually prohibitive Cambó tariff of 1921.

Another institutional constraint was the creation of a legal banking cartel with the pretext of a reordering of the banking sector in 1922. This was also at the hand of the Catalan minister Francesc Cambó, who was trying to protect the Spanish financial sector from events such as that of the bankruptcy of the Banco de Barcelona. According to the new dispensation banks registered with the Superior Banking Council (in Spanish, 'Consejo Superior Bancario') enjoyed the guarantee of a Deposit Insurance scheme. Banking licenses were frozen. Territorial limits to banking competition were drawn up. The Bank of Spain, the monopoly note issuer, became subject to intervention by the Government, which henceforth appointed the Governor. The Bank was also required to discount Government debt whenever presented to it by the banks on the official register. The positive side of the new regime was that the Bank of Spain was expected to act as lender of last resort for the financial establishments in its 'club'. In sum, competition was restricted both in foreign trade and in finance.

A second institutional element, which turned out to be decisive when the recession struck, was, as mentioned before, that after the demise of the silver Latin Monetary Union in 1883, the peseta stayed on a silver standard, while sterling, dollar, franc and mark went over to gold. In the years that followed silver slowly lost value but the five peseta silver coins did not change their face value and neither did the bank notes. The peseta thus became a fiduciary currency in fact if not in name.

The Spanish economy in the twenties and thirties

The Spanish gross domestic product (GDP) in the twenties followed an expansive path similar to that of the United States and other European countries. In the case of Spain, the 1925 to 1929 expansion was mainly due to the direct and indirect effects of a large increase in public works during the Primo de Rivera dictatorship (1923–1930), which was helped by an excellent 1929 harvest. However, the spectacular trend of Spanish growth in the first 35 years of the century hides a number of weaknesses. One is the lingering dependence on agriculture, and extensive agriculture at that time. Another is the skewed development of industry behind a tariff wall, enhanced by an oligopolistic banking sector. And the third one is the politically driven role of public works financed by ballooning debt. In the years of the Great Recession the Spanish GDP fell but not by as much as in other industrial countries (see Figure 14.1). It seems however that the downturn of 1930–31 had little to do with the Wall Street crash and the world depression. It was rather due, first, to an attempt to rebalance the budget after the profligate governments of General Primo de Rivera; and secondly to the financial panic caused by the fall of the monarchy. The rest of the GDP series reflects the bumper 1932 and 1934 harvests and the pick-up in public works in 1932–34: there was however no strong recovery as in the United States and the United Kingdom (or in Germany for other reasons). And in the middle of 1936, civil war started.

The GDP deviations from its long-term trend (see Figure 14.3) clearly show the two crises of 1905 and 1917, and the unsustainable above-trend growth in the last three years of the expansionary fiscal policy under general Primo de Rivera. The 'output gap' reached a 7% above trend in 1929; it ended with a return to orthodox policies in the early thirties (see Table 14.1). Public investment had increased markedly and this policy resulted in an economy artificially driven by the over-expansion of industries associated with construction and public works.

Agriculture

During the first thirty years of the twentieth century, the productive structure of Spain had slowly evolved from that of a mainly agricultural country to one where industry progressively gained weight. A good or a bad harvest, however, still made a great deal of difference to national production; and domestic agricultural prices, modified by the ups and downs of food exports, told markedly on the economy.

Spain still had quite a significant primary sector in the 1920s and 1930s with large agricultural employment. In 1900, the people employed in agriculture and fisheries amounted to 63.3% of the total working population; by 1930 that proportion had fallen to 45.5%. Mining, industry and construction, on the other hand, went from 16% to 26.5%. Services only grew 7 percentage points compared with the ten and a half percentage points of the secondary sector. As regards output, agriculture accounted for around 30% of the GDP in 1920 and 26% in 1929. Cereals (in particular wheat) and beans took up more than 75% of the total arable land. Agricultural growth rates, both positive and negative, were not governed by the macroeconomic situation or even by foreign markets but by rainfall. Spain had enjoyed bumper wheat harvests in 1929 (a 25% growth on the previous year) and in 1932 (a 37% increase on 1931) (see Table 14.1). In each case harvests reverted to trend.

Increasing protectionism

The 1921 'Cambó tariff' increased the isolation of the Spanish economy under the 1883 tariff. The effect of protection was to turn Spain into a relatively isolated economy, with low exposure to international trade (18% in 1929, nearly half that of the rest of the European countries in the twenties, see Figure 14.4). Hence, the driving elements of the Spanish economy in the twenties were: domestic demand and, as regards output, the primary sector, public works with their inputs, and low value-added industry, especially in textiles.

Also, as already noted, the peseta was tied to silver and floated mostly downwards in a gold standard world. Its depreciation from the mid-twenties onwards (which continued in the early thirties), reduced the effects of world trade contraction on the export oriented sectors and made Spanish goods and services – at least in some degree – more competitive.

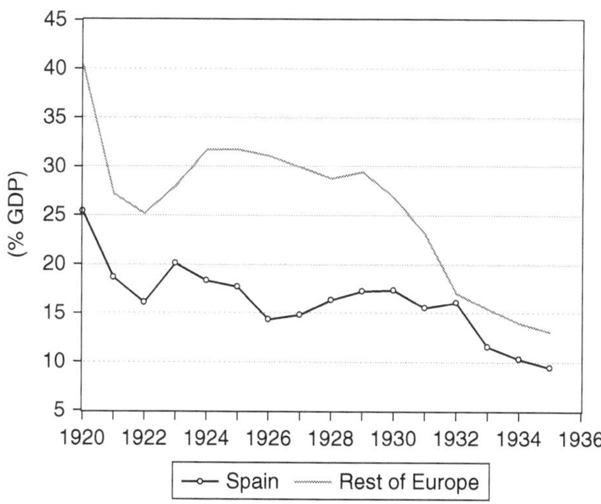

Figure 14.4 Spain's degree of openness (exports + imports)/GDP.

Source: Data for Spain and Europe (average of Germany, France and Italy) from Tena (1992), as quoted by Tena 2005, Appended CD, chart 8.3.

The banking oligopoly and its ties to big industry

The banking sector was highly concentrated and strongly tied to heavy industry (Tortella and Palafox 1983). The so-called 'six large banks' (Banco Hispano Americano, Banco de Bilbao, Banco de Vizcaya, Banco Urquijo, Banco Central and Banco Español de Crédito) accounted for more than 40% of the total capital of the banking sector, and more than 50% of deposits. At the behest of Government these banks took a major interest in the larger industrial companies (mining, railways, iron and steel and electric power). Conversely, this conglomerate of big banks and industry, especially up to 1931, captured Government economic policy. These mutual links were particularly strong during Primo de Rivera's dictatorship. In those years, the Government set in train an ambitious public works plan, mostly concentrated on creating and improving basic infrastructures (roads, railways and dams for hydroelectric power), with some positive effects on construction and related industrial sectors. This policy was financed with 'extraordinary budgets' and their corresponding public debt, side by side with 'ordinary budgets' financed with taxes. This active fiscal policy fostered domestic industrial expansion and hence domestic demand.

Thus, at the end of the Directorate in 1929 the amount of public investment had more than tripled that of 1923 (see Figure 14.5). In 1926, public investment was still under 10% of total investment in the economy: from 1927 to 1929 public investment on average almost reached 20% of total investment. Even though private investment did not grow as fast as public investment, it also experienced an average 10% rate of growth in those six years. This was the consequence of a deliberate plan to foster domestic investment, though

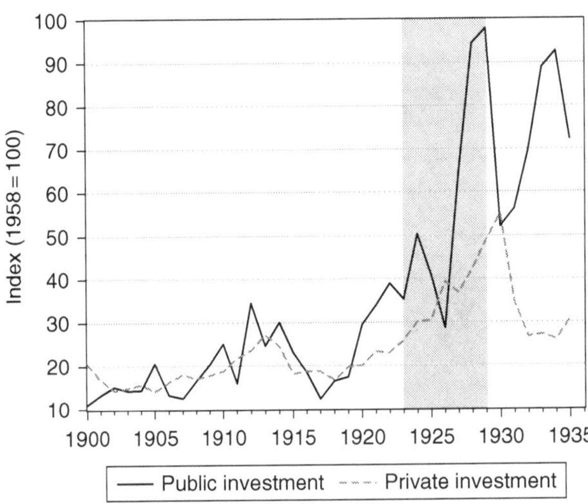

Figure 14.5 Public investment vs. Private.

Source: Data from Prados (2003). Shaded area corresponds to the Primo de Rivera Directorate.

the public sector stimulus had a more moderate spill-over effect on the private sector. Even though the size of the public sector was quite modest at that time (10–15% GDP) it is difficult to deny that the expansionary fiscal policy of the late twenties had a direct effect on the economy and also led to an increase of private investment in industry and construction. As shown in Table 14.2, the exceptional increase in public works led to an expansion of metal goods industries (basic and transformed), transport goods and construction inputs (quarries, bricks, cement and glass), especially after 1927.

The result, as shown in Figure 14.6, was that manufacture and construction showed a sustained positive trend between 1923 and 1929, with a yearly average growth rate close to 5% for manufacture and to 6% for construction. However, the consumption goods industry followed quite a different path from that of heavy industry and construction. The significant increase of public works from 1923 to 1929 mostly benefited heavy industry, much more than small and medium industries concentrated on the production of consumption goods, such as textiles, leather goods and processed foods (see Table 14.4).

Clearly, the highly protected and oligopolistic character of the industrial sector reduced the trickling down effect of public investment. However, the general opinion at that time was that the only way to promote sustainable growth was to protect and privilege national industry (Palafox 1980a). Keynes in his *General Theory*[6] clearly saw that autarky was a condition for state expenditure having its full effect on domestic activity and employment. Experience has shown, however, that this kind of policy is in the end not sustainable. Those extraordinary investment plans resulted in successive and substantial public deficits that imposed a heavy financial burden on the Government, as they had

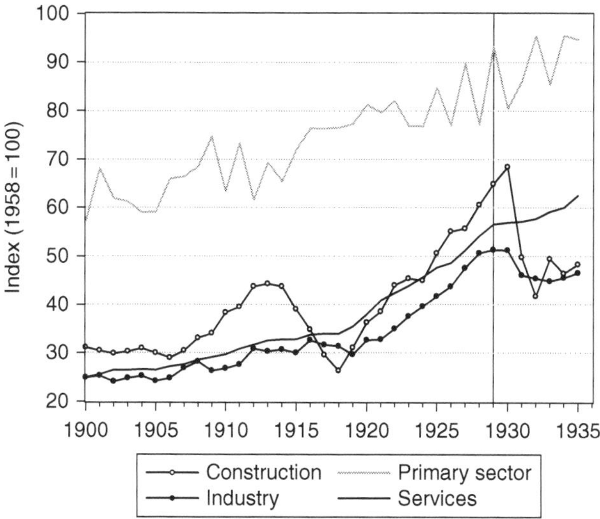

Figure 14.6 Value added by industry.

Source: GDP estimates from Prados (2003).

to be financed by a massive issue of public bonds. By 1930, the debt service had come to represent around 25% of total public expenditure. Retrenchment seemed inevitable and came in 1929 and 1930 with the fall of Primo de Rivera. This retrenchment may have contributed to the public unrest that helped bring the fall of the monarchy in 1931.

Exports and imports

As to the balance of payments, Spain's neutrality during World War I boosted Spanish exports and the industries associated with them. This led to massive surpluses in the balance of trade during the war years and to a significant increase of international reserves of the Bank of Spain.[7] However, the underlying lack of competitiveness of the Spanish economy led to consecutive and considerable trade deficits from 1920 to 1935 (see Figure 14.7).

From the end of the World War I to the proclamation of the Second Republic in 1931, the silver peseta depreciated by more than 100% in relation to gold standard currencies, with the only exception of 1925 and 1926 (see Figure 14.7). The very active expansionary fiscal policy conducted must be one of the factors explaining that depreciation. Within a relatively closed

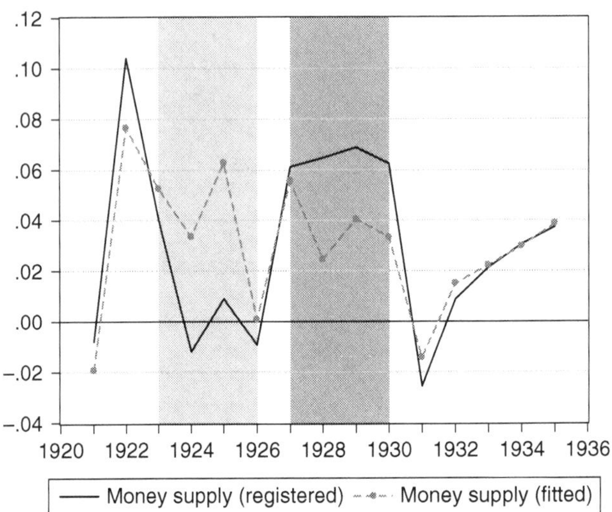

Figure 14.7 Registered vs. fitted money supply growth. Estimated equation: (DL) Money Supply (t) = C + (DL) Money Supply (t–1)+ (DL) Public borrowing (t) + (DL) Reserves (t).

Source: Money supply data from Aceña and Pons 2005.

Notes: All variables in first differences of the logarithm (see Table A14.3 in Appendix). Dark shaded area corresponds to the years (1928–1930) of excessive money growth in relation to the prescription of our estimated rule. And light shaded years (1923–26) correspond to a lesser money growth in relation to its prescriptions. DL above reads for the first difference of the logarithm of the series.

and very rigid economy, where administered prices and price-setting oligopolies were still the norm, the fiscal and trade imbalances of the Spanish growth model of the twenties had to lead to a larger depreciation of the peseta than in a more flexible economy.[8]

Monetary developments in the twenties: A conservative Bank of Spain

The role of the *Banco de España* as the Government banker was reinforced by the 1922 Cambó banking law. The Bank was obliged to discount any amount of treasury bonds presented by establishment banks and thus, indirectly to finance the treasury. Hence from 1921 on, the Bank of Spain started to provide regular funds to registered banks with public bonds as collateral. Crucially, those banks, as long as they had bonds in their portfolios, could borrow unlimited amounts from the Bank of Spain. This new financial facility provided the banks with a parallel channel to borrow at a lower rate than at the discount window (see Tortella and Palafox 1983). Given that registered banks and industrial and construction companies were highly concentrated and interconnected, the new financial facility allowed the Government to favour large corporations by injecting bonds that the banks could easily discount and then invest in and lend to client corporations. Thus, the new financial regulations strengthened the links of an interventionist government with large industry and big banks, and multiplied the effects of an active economic policy.

Since the law limited the amount of notes the Bank of Spain could issue at any given moment, periods of public profligacy were always followed by sharp corrections. The loose monetary and fiscal policy brought about by special

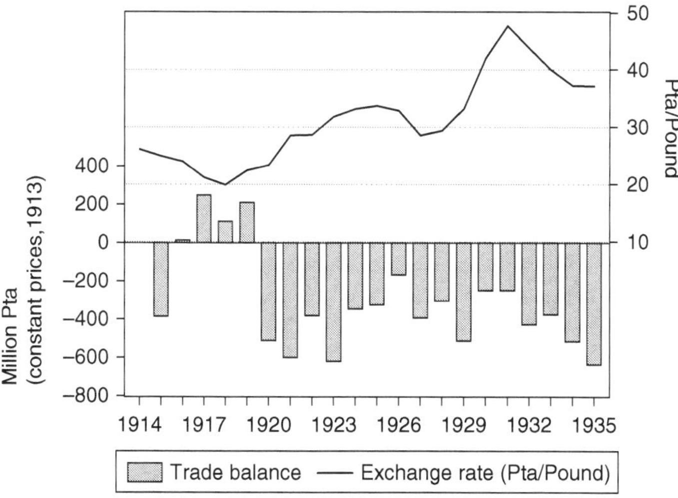

Figure 14.8 The floating peseta and the trade balance.

Source: Peseta/sterling exchange rate data from Fernández Baños (1930) as quoted by Tena (2005) and Spain's trade balance data from Tena (2005).

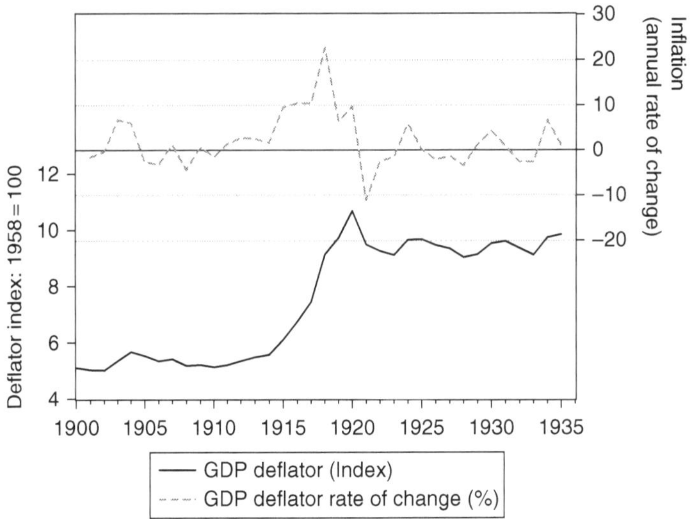

Figure 14.9 Prices and inflation.

Source: Deflator figures estimation from Prados (2003).

circumstances were soon reined back. So the Spanish-American War was followed by the 1902–03 stabilization of minister Villaverde; World War I inflation of neutral Spain was checked by the 1921 recession; and the deficits of dictator Primo de Rivera by an orthodox effort to balance the budget. The result was that despite a *de facto* fiduciary currency inflation never got totally out of hand.

The 'reaction function' of the Bank of Spain

The financial policy of the government reinforced its traditional links with the Bank of Spain and the credit needs of the government in the end had an effect on money supply. This is confirmed by regressing money supply growth[9] on changes in government borrowing from the Bank of Spain, on changes in the volume of gold and silver reserves kept at the Bank of Spain and changes on money supply growth in the previous years. With conventional regression analysis, we have identified the following determinants of money supply growth from 1920 to 1935: (1) the inertia component revealed by the correlation of money supply growth with that of the previous year; (2) changes in government borrowing; and (3) changes in Bank of Spain reserves. All three are statistically significant (see Tables A14.3 and A14.4, Appendix). Regarding demand for credit by the treasury, an increase in Bank of Spain loans to the government is followed by an increase in money supply, though less than proportional.[10] As to variations in reserves, the weight of the coefficient reveals its major importance as a determinant of money growth. As a result, we have identified the following *reaction function* for the Bank of Spain from 1920 to 1935:

Money Supply (t) – Money Supply (t–1) = 0.47 [Money Supply (t–1) – Money Supply (t–2)] + 0.10 [Public Borrowing (t) – Public Borrowing (t–1)] + 0.46 [Reserves (t) – Reserves (t–1)] (eq. 1)

As shown in Figure 14.10, with the exception of the World War I years, money supply grew only modestly, and remained quite stable up to 1926 (and even below real GDP growth in 1925 and 1926). However, from 1928 to 1930 money supply grew above real GDP. This, combined with the considerable depreciation of the peseta in the same period, resulted in a more expansionary monetary policy than before: the effectiveness of the fiscal stimulus increased but the policy in the end proved unsustainable in a weak and artificially protected economy.

It may be surprising that the depreciation of the peseta did not fuel inflation. True, the massive inflow of reserves in the World War I years led to a large and temporary money supply growth, which resulted in two digit inflation from 1915 to 1918 (see Figure 14.9). But after the end of the war monetary policy went back to aiming at stability:[11] and between 1920 and 1935 money base and broad money supply grew at moderate annual rates (on average, 2% and 3.8%, respectively). Rather than inflation, what the depreciation of the currency did do was to keep the price level steady when other countries saw prices tumble into deflation.

In sum, even though open to accommodating the financial needs of the treasury, the Bank of Spain conducted monetary policy on sound financial principles. It is as if it was obeying a *sustainable monetary rule*, since money

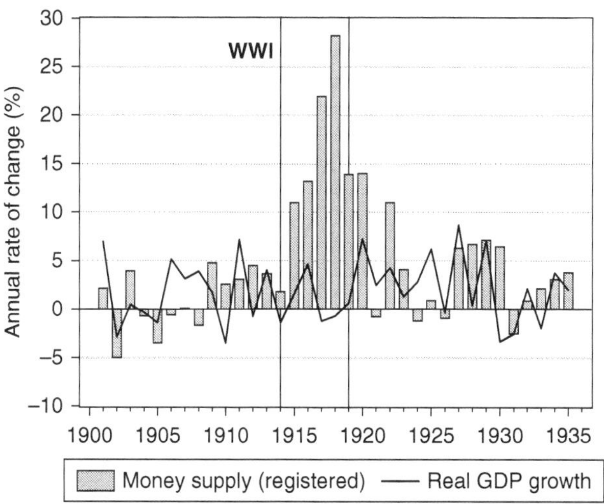

Figure 14.10 Broad money growth and real GDP growth.

Source: Money supply data from Aceña and Pons (2005). And GDP growth calculations based on Prados' (2003) figures of Spanish GDP.

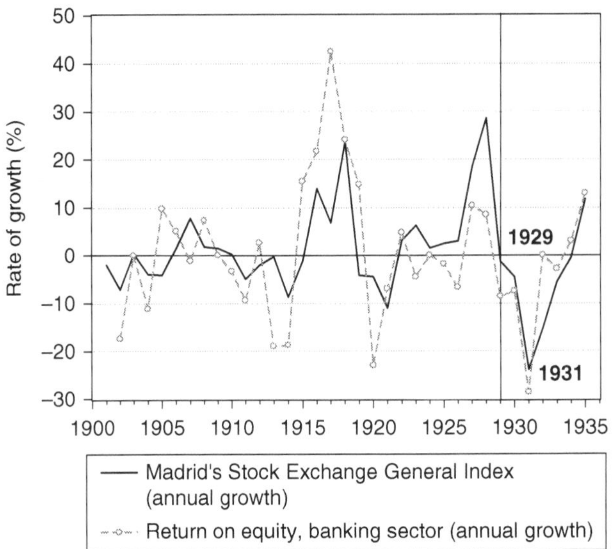

Figure 14.11 The financial sector.

Source: Return on equity data from Tafunell (2000) as quoted by Tafunell (2005). Madrid's index data from Hoyo (2001) as quoted by Tafunell (2005).

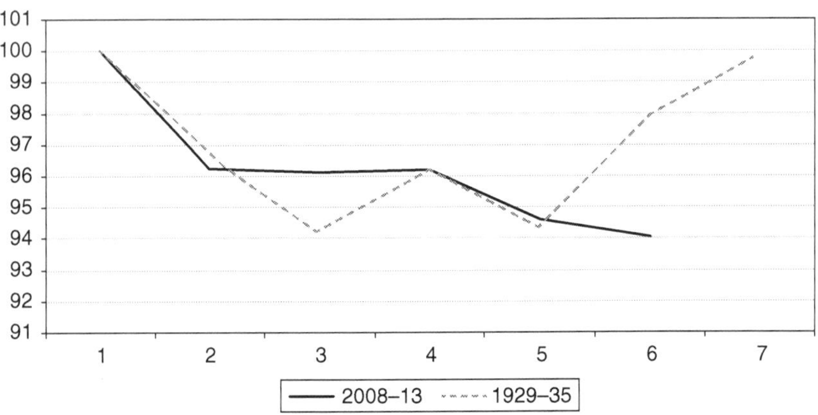

Figure 14.12 GDP levels in Spain (1929 = 100, 2008 = 100).

Source: Own calculations from estimates of the GDP (value added) in 1930s from Prados (2003). GDP volumes at market prices 2007–2013 from Eurostat (accessed online).

growth was made to offset any changes in the reserves kept at the Bank. Given a variable exchange rate, this policy resulted in price stability on average, as mild inflations were offset by subsequent deflations. In fact, the GDP deflator index in 1922 was almost at the same level as in 1935, which shows a contained domestic inflation trend during this period.

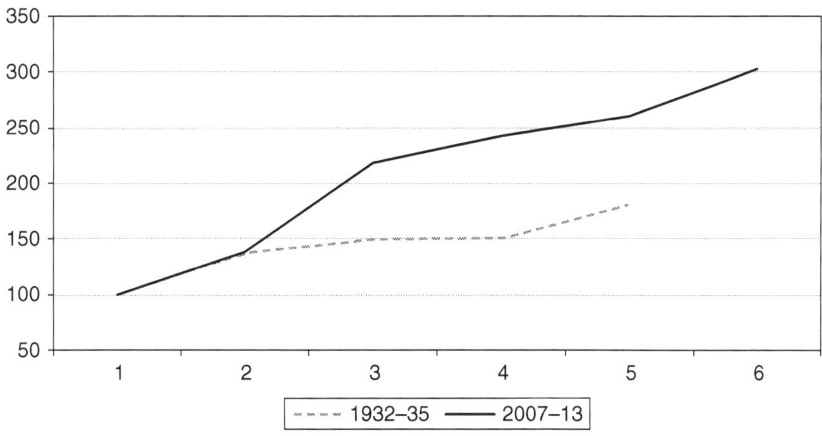

Figure 14.13 Unemployment rate in Spain (1932 = 100, 2007 = 100).

Source: No estimate of the unemployment rate prior to 1933 (see Table 14.5 notes and sources). Rate of unemployment (2007–2013) from Eurostat (accessed online).

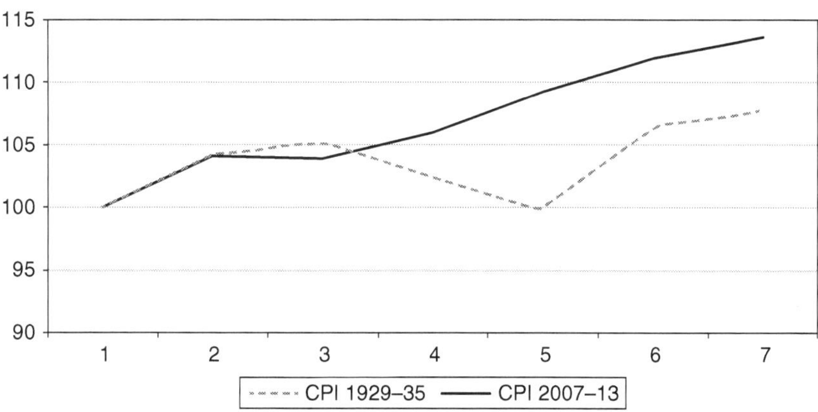

Figure 14.14 CPI in Spain (1929 = 100, 2008 = 100).

Source: Harmonised Index of Consumer Prices – HICP (2007–13) from Eurostat (accessed online). GDP deflator data (1929–1935) from Prados (2003).

As for the financial sector, while the number of commercial banks increased in the 1920s there was only one large bankruptcy in 1920 (Banco de Barcelona) and another one in 1931 (Banco de Cataluña). This is in sharp contrast with the large number of bank failures in the United States and in other European countries. In terms of capital, credit or deposits, the operations of the commercial banks expanded significantly: from 1920 to 1930 bank balance sheets nearly doubled. The positive evolution of Madrid's stock index also confirms this upward pattern in the financial markets (see Figure 14.10). The return on equity in the banking sector, however, was unspectacular except during World

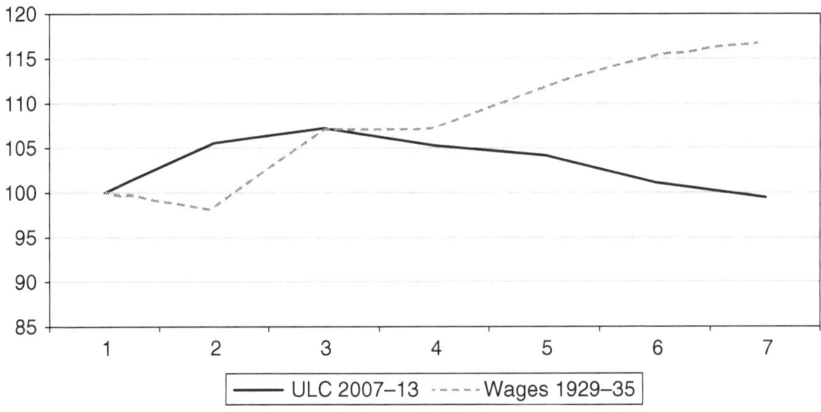

Figure 14.15 Labour costs (1929 = 100, 2007 = 100).

Source: Nominal unit labour costs from Eurostat (accessed online). Nominal wages in the 1930s are average wages in agriculture (male) from Maluquer de Motes and Llonc (2005).

War I. As to the stock exchange, there was a sharp fall in 1929–31, much of it, we surmise, due to domestic causes. In any case, a 50% fall from peak to trough was much smaller than that in the United States and the recovery soon came.

The Bank of Spain intervention in the crisis: A successful lender of last resort to preserve confidence in the currency

The fall of Primo de Rivera in January 1930 and the end of the expansionary fiscal policy associated with his governments created uncertainty in the large industrial and banking sectors. In fact, economic policy changed drastically in 1930 and Argüelles, the new Treasury Secretary, conducted a deliberately restrictive fiscal policy to cut public spending and stop the growth of the budget deficit and the debt. One of the main policy tasks the last cabinets of the monarchy set themselves was the stabilization of the parity of the peseta in relation to gold standard currencies: a new economic program involving significant public spending cuts.[12] Interest rates also increased (see Table A14.2, Appendix).[13] This policy change was so abrupt that the resulting massive suspension of public investment led in 1930 to the first budget surplus in almost 30 years. The negative effects of that sudden fiscal contraction were immediately evident, especially in the construction sector, which had relied on the expansionary government plans in the previous decade. As shown in Figure 14.6, value added indices in this sector fell sharply for the first time in a decade, and so did profits. This more orthodox policy also threatened the traditional coalition of interests between businessmen and bankers.

When the Second Republic unexpectedly arrived in April 1931 (as Palafox [1980a,b] stresses) political uncertainty, coming on top of the budget cut and the deepening international financial crisis, caused a further deterioration of business sentiment. A run on liquidity resulted: both current and savings accounts showed a significant reduction and capital fled abroad. The amounts withdrawn from bank accounts in 1931 amounted to 20% of current accounts and 14% of longer term accounts. Moreover, these were not mere short run reactions, as the amount of capital placed in savings and current accounts did not return to their 1930 level until 1934 and 1935 respectively. Money supply contracted by –2.5% in 1931. A fall in the Spanish general price level ensued, resulting in a –2.5% deflation over the following two years. Due to the significant reduction in their deposits, commercial banks cut their investments (–9%) and credits (–29%) in 1931, with the expected negative effects on businesses.

However, this 'credit crunch' originated in a lack of confidence in the Spanish economy, and the accompanying monetary restriction induced a deflation that cannot be attributed to deliberate Bank of Spain policy; quite the contrary. Far from conducting a deflationary policy, the Bank of Spain had been increasing the monetary base since 1927, reaching 10% growth in 1931, the very same year of the credit contraction (see Table 14.3).

Thus, the Bank of Spain acted decisively as *lender of last resort* for the banks of its club by providing extraordinary funds to the members of the 'Consejo Superior Bancario' – around 1.1 billion pesetas (Martín Aceña 1984). At the same time, the Government relaxed the Bank of Spain restriction to issue notes, which also helped increase the liquidity in the market. Accordingly, the higher level of interest rates in Spain in the late twenties, compared to those in the countries of reference (United Kingdom, United States or France), should not be interpreted as the sign of a relatively more restrictive monetary policy: the interest rate spread can be explained by the risk premium associated with a non-gold standard currency as Spain had to finance successive public deficit abroad.

Carner's exchange rate policy: Short but successful

Monetary and fiscal policy in the first year of the Second Republic did not tally with the avowed aim of stabilizing the peseta proclaimed by the new chancellor Indalecio Prieto. As Martín Aceña (1984) remarks, a strong peseta would have been attainable only if both monetary and fiscal policies had been restrictive. However, monetary policy was focused on alleviating bank illiquidity; and the government ran a public deficit again in 1931. Thus, unwittingly Spain was spared a financial crisis and a prolonged contraction.

After the resignation of the helpless socialist finance minister Prieto, the new Treasury Secretary under Prime Minister Azaña, Jaume Carner (1867–1934) was the only politician of that period to abandon the ideal of returning the currency to the gold standard at the 1868 parity and consciously allowed the peseta to float during the worst time of the Great Depression. During his very short term of office (December 1931–February 1933), monetary, fiscal and exchange policies were for once aligned and properly designed to protect Spain from the contagion of worldwide depression. The Bank of Spain had come to the rescue of banks with liquidity injections and with an expanded circulation of banknotes. The discount rate was slightly reduced in 1932. The peseta was allowed to depreciate against the franc and the dollar, the gold standard currencies. Carner rightly considered a freely floating currency as a lifeboat in the heavy seas of the international financial crisis. Indeed, by that time the United Kingdom had left the gold standard. Carner's policies clearly acted as a temporary stimulus for the sluggish Spanish economy (see Tapia 1998).

However, Spanish governments soon reverted to exchange rate stabilization: from 1933 to 1935 the parity of the peseta was briefly fixed to the French franc, still on the gold standard. This led to an appreciation of the peseta regarding the currencies that had left the gold standard, mainly the British pound and the US dollar (see Figure 4.7). However, new cuts in discount rates (a reduction of 100 basis points in two years), a money supply that either mirrored economic growth or rose above output (see Figure 4.9) and persistent public deficits soon offset the effects of the restrictive exchange rate policy.

The possible effects of world recession in Spain

The world crisis did not cause a deep recession in Spain. The primary sector marched on regardless. Construction did fall steeply but we have argued that this was mainly due to a cut in the public works programme. Services and industry soon recovered from the relatively slight contraction of 1931.

It may be interesting to analyse the evolution of the economy from the point of view of the return on equity in different sectors of the economy (Table 14.4). For the consumption goods sector the return on equity was impervious to the recession. In fact, as Palafox (1980a) remarks, from 1931 to 1933 one of the defining policies of the new republic was a general rise in wages, which must have had a positive impact on consumption. Using data from Maluquer and Llonc (2005), this deliberate income policy resulted in a 15% increase in real wages in the primary sector between 1930 and 1933. By contrast, producers of capital goods suffered a sharp fall in profitability in the early 1930s. Banking fared better though its performance was lacklustre, maybe due to the noted retraction of investment linked with the change of political regime. In any case there seems to be no evidence of a general contraction in the business sector in the years of the Great Depression.

There are no figures at all for unemployment before 1933 and not very reliable ones thereafter. Employment in the construction sector must have suffered a notable deterioration after the commented drastic economic policy change in 1930, but not the country generally. Even though unemployment increased from 1933 to 1936, as shown in Table 14.5, it did not do so on the catastrophic scale of Britain, Germany or the United States. The difficulty to find work did increase as the months went by after the proclamation of the Second Republic and one must not forget that the labour market was disrupted by one or more anarchist uprising per year, repeated strikes organized by the Socialist Union and even a botched attempt at full scale revolution in 1934.

As to the foreign sector, Spanish exports suffered the consequences of world trade contraction but to a lesser extent than the rest of the developed economies. As shown in Table 14.6, exports declined from 1931 onwards but the reduction of the exports did not reach the dramatic figures of the leading economies.

Our thesis can be tested with our estimation of the deviation from trend of the Spanish economy (the so-called 'output gap'). To go back to Figure 14.3: from the middle of the 1920s an active fiscal policy placed the economy above its long-term trend – a deviation of more than 7% in 1929. That growth pattern was not sustainable, as can be seen in the large disequilibria of the late twenties. The budget and trade deficits resulted in excessive money growth and finally in a modicum of inflation in 1930. The new restrictive fiscal policy implemented in that year brought the economy sharply back to its long-term path. Only in 1934 was there another short-lived spike in inflation. Anyhow, both the decline in GDP growth and the negative deviation from trend of the early thirties were smaller than those of the 1915 and 1919 recessions, and smaller than in most developed countries.

A comparison with the euro crisis

The comparison of the effect of the recent financial crisis (2008–09) with the years of the Great Depression must be made with caution. While not intending to provide an exhaustive analysis on the differences between these two major crises, we highlight how much a different monetary regime may affect the length of a crisis, as well as the type of policies more suitable to overcome them, especially in a quite rigid economy such as the Spanish one both at that time and, to a lesser extent, in our days.

Figures 14.12–14.17 should not be taken to imply a mono-causal correlation between the recession and the two monetary regimes prevailing in the Spanish economy then and now. The milder reaction in the thirties must also have been due to the smaller weight of the foreign sector in the economy and thus to the lesser exposure to the international crisis.[14]

As to the fall of economic activity, Figure 14.12 shows that the decline in GDP has been similar in both episodes but in the 1930s aggregate production resumed pre-crisis GDP levels after five years (in 1935) whereas the GDP is still (2017) well below its 2008 peak. In fact, it is only in 2014 that the Spanish economy started to grow again.[15] Regarding unemployment rates (Figure 14.13), there was exponential growth since 2008 and the current rate (higher than 16% at the end of 2017) still doubles the pre-crisis rate of unemployment of around 8%. Unfortunately, the comparison with the rise in unemployment in the 1930s cannot be very accurate as there are no estimates of unemployment rates available until 1933. Anyhow, both the level and the increase in unemployment in the 1930s were lower than today.

We may well find an explanation for the persistence of the current crisis by analysing the economic policy options available for a country having adopted an 'irrevocable' exchange rate with the euro since 1999 and consequently having lost its monetary sovereignty. Under this institutional setting, an economy in crisis can only rely on policies aimed at reducing its costs in order to increase its competitiveness in international markets: i.e. requires a fiscal contraction in the midst of a crisis as well as wage cuts.

Nominal unit labour costs have declined in Spain since 2009 whereas in the Great Depression years (nominal) wages rose from 1930 on. However, the reduction in labour costs after 2009 (an accumulated 7–8% fall from 2010 to 2013) seems still insufficient if compared to the extent of the devaluation of the peseta in the 1930s: from 1929 to 1932, the peseta depreciated against the pound sterling more than 60%. In consequence, this sharp nominal adjustment of the parity of the currency avoided the need for deep cuts in other prices (in goods, services and wages). In contrast, in the recent crisis the euro appreciated against the US dollar (see Figure 14.16) in 2008, 2011 and 2013, making Spanish exports more expensive.

A final comment on money supply growth during both crises. As shown earlier in the chapter, in the absence of exchange rate commitments, the *Banco de España* could intervene actively and on time in 1931 to provide extraordinary lending to the banks and thus prevent the collapse of the Spanish financial system. This was followed by a rather stable and consistent rate of growth of money from 1931 onwards. On the contrary, since 2009 the growth of a broad monetary aggregate such as M3 has collapsed in Spain, with a cumulative fall of more than 8 percentage points in four years (see Figure 14.16). The contraction in the supply of money has been a key factor explaining the persistence of the current crisis (Congdon 2014) and in particular in Spain (Cendejas *et al.*

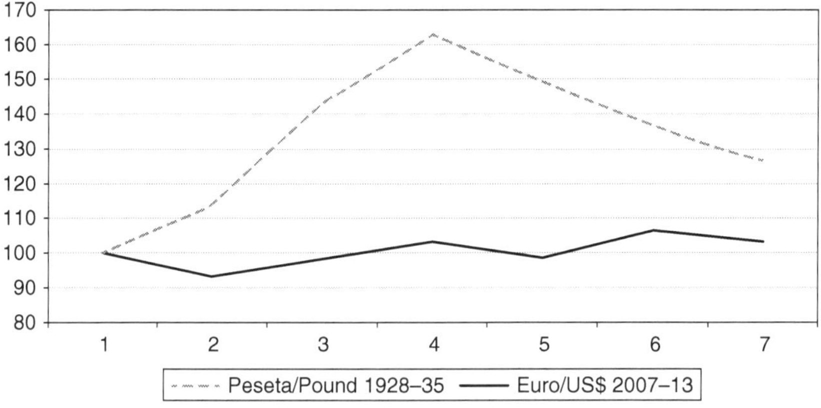

Figure 14.16 Exchange rate peseta versus pound sterling (1929 = 100, 2007 = 100).

Source: Exchange rate Euro/US$ (Eurostat, accessed online). Exchange rate peseta/pound sterling from Fernández Baños (1930) as quoted by Tena (2005).

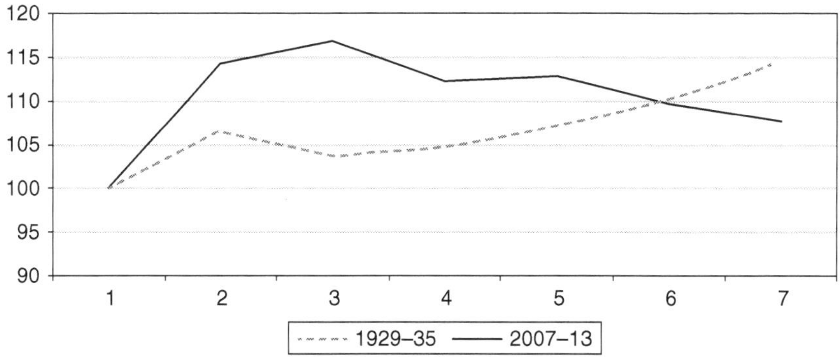

Figure 14.17 Broad money (volumes; 1929 = 100, 2007 = 100).

Source: Contribution of Spain to M3 (2007–2013) from the Bank of Spain data set (accessed online). Broad money growth in Spain in the 1930s from Aceña and Pons (2005).

2014), where the fall of money supply has been particularly sharp. Surprisingly, this has happened despite the injection of 43 billion euros in the Spanish financial sector by Brussels.

Conclusion

As shown in this chapter, the recession of the 1930s in Spain was neither of the same nature nor similar in depth to that of other developed countries. Spain's relative isolation from the world economy, along with a still important primary sector and a *de facto* floating currency, protected it from outright catastrophe. Whatever contraction there was can be attributed to fiscal stabilization policy and to social tensions fanned by politics.

Even though exports and finance were affected by the contraction of international trade and credit, the greater part of Spanish activity was impervious to the Great Depression. In this quite isolated and oligopolistic economy, increases in public spending plans, especially from 1927 to 1929, and the exceptional wheat harvests of 1929, 1932 and 1934 led to moderate GDP growth during the deep international recession.

Finally, the active intervention of the Bank of Spain in the 1931 financial crisis avoided a massive collapse of the Spanish financial system and contributed to bringing the economy back on course. Acting as a lender of last resort, the Bank of Spain prevented the seizure of the payment system. It was able to do that despite the growing need to accommodate the demands for funds of the treasury because it was free from the constraints of a fixed exchange rate. However, the Bank of Spain moderated inflationary pressures by its prudent issue policy and its refusal to monetise its gold reserves: the Bank did not overstep the limits of prudence and conducted a monetary policy based on sound financial criteria. Surprisingly in such fraught times, both price inflation and national bankruptcy were avoided.

It is clear that in the short run a flexible exchange rate makes for a lesser loss of welfare when a country is forced to adapt to a financial crisis. However, currency devaluation does not automatically force structural change in a country suffering from low productivity. Such structural changes only come if the devaluation is accompanied by changes in budgetary and labour policy to avoid having to devalue again in a short time. By contrast, the internal devaluation demanded by a fixed exchange rate forces structural reform, as we have seen has happened in Spain after the euro crisis. There is an added advantage to resisting devaluation and sticking by the exchange anchor: the currency does not lose purchasing power and maintains its long run stability.

Appendix 14.1 Tables on monetary effect on the real economy

Table A14.1 Rates of growth of public and private investment (year on year, %)

	Public Investment	*Private Investment*		*Public Investment*	*Private Investment*
1920	69.5	1.88	1928	46.78	15.05
1921	15.01	15.46	1929	3.71	16.01
1922	15.01	–1.07	**1930**	**- 46.74**	12.47
1923	–9.37	12.56	1931	7.77	–37.22
1924	42.77	16.17	1932	23.8	–23.12
1925	–18.81	1.25	1933	27.8	1.94
1926	–30.04	29.33	1934	4.22	–4.31
1927	124.77	–6.6	1935	–21.91	18.24

Source: Data from Prados (2003).

Table A14.2 Bank of Spain official interest rates

	Discount rate	*Guaranteed rate on public bonds*		*Discount rate*	*Guaranteed rate on public bonds*
1920	6	4.5	1928	5.5	4.5
1921	6	4.5	1929	5.5	4.5
1922	5.5	4.5	1930	6	5
1923	5	4.5	1931	6.5	5
1924	5	4.5	1932	6	5
1925	5	4.5	1933	6	5
1926	5	4.5	1934	5.5	4.5
1927	5	4.5	1935	5	4

Source: Data from Martin Aceña and Pons (2005).

Table A14.3 Ordinary least squares estimation results. Estimated equation: (DL) Money Supply (t) = C + (DL) Money Supply (t–1) + (DL) Public borrowing (t) + (DL) Reserves (t)

Sample: (1920–1935)		
Variable	*Coefficient*	*t-Statistic*
Constant	0.01	1.42
(DL) Money Supply (t–1)	**0.47**	2.46
(DL) Public Borrowing (t)	**0.10**	4.29
(DL) Reserves (t)	**0.46**	2.76
R-squared	0.65	

Source: Underlying data of broad money supply from Martín Aceña and Pons (2005), public borrowing from IEF (1976) as quoted by Comín and Diaz (2005). As to reserves, data comes from the League of Nations Statistical Yearbooks for 1927–1935 and silver stocks between 1920 and 1926 from the Royal Commission for re-establishing the Gold Standard (1929, p. 34).

Note: All variables in first differences (D) of the logarithm (L). All variables are significant at a 5% significance level, except the constant. Reserves include silver and gold kept at the Bank of Spain.

Table A14.4 Granger causality test results

Sample: 190020131936. Lags: 2		
Null Hypothesis:	*F-Statistic*	*Probability*
(DL) Money Supply does not Granger Cause (DL) Public Borrowing	0.03	0.96
(DL) Public Borrowing does not Granger Cause (DL) Money Supply	**4.19**	**0.02**

Source: Underlying data of money supply from Martín Aceña and Pons (2005), public borrowing from IEF (1976) as quoted by Comín and Diaz (2005).

Notes

1 The authors thank Mr. Jorge Jiménez de Cisneros for his help in the research for this chapter and Prof. Pedro Tedde de Lorca for his helpful suggestions in the early stages of the work. We also want to thank Profs. Fraile, Tortella, Prados and Novales for their comments and suggested readings, as well as Profs. Capie and Wood for their comments on previous versions of the work, and finally the comments made by the participants of the conference held at the Vrije Universiteit in Amsterdam, 12–13 December 2014 where a previous version of this chapter was presented.

2 Among them is Hugh Thomas 1976, chapter 12: 'La economía durante la República'. Thomas is also wrong about Jaume Carner's financial policy as Treasury Secretary in the early thirties, when he let the peseta float, see below.

3 Palafox (1980a, b) and Comín and 21Martín Aceña (1984) were the first to suggest that the Spanish recession of the thirties was caused by domestic rather than international factors; and Tortella and Palafox (1983) underlined the isolation of the Spanish economy and a floating peseta as a protection from international deflation and recession. Further, Tortella and Palafox also stressed that the Spanish financial sector remained quite stable

in the thirties, in contrast with widespread collapses all over the developed world. This goes against those who, like Sardá (1948), criticized a supposed restrictive monetary policy of the central bank. We go further in the criticism of Sardá when we show that the central bank injected the necessary amount of liquidity when the danger of a bank run loomed.

4 Curiously, the political and monetary establishment always hankered after the gold standard and hoped that someday the peseta would join the club of respectable currencies. Repeated efforts were made to go back to gold at the 1868 parity but they were never successful. When the peseta went into steep decline after World War I compared with currencies on the gold standard, an official Commission was formed in 1929 to examine the pros and cons of moving to gold but it all came to nothing. Spain remained a silver country and so avoided the 1929–33 international monetary contraction and thus deflation.

5 Both the Basque region, with its strong Socialist movement, and Catalonia, where working class anarchism was endemic, were in constant turmoil.

6 Keynes (1936, ch. X: 3) on foreign trade and the multiplier.

7 Gold reserves in 1913 were close to 700 million pesetas: just after World War I they reached 2,500 million pesetas (1920).

8 Martín Aceña's (1984: 173) goes a little too far when he says that the economic growth of the late twenties was the result of an unanticipated monetary expansion due to the quick depreciation of the currency, rather than the result of the fiscal policy of the government.

9 This is a broad measure of money supply, which consists of cash in circulation, sight deposits, as well as saving and time deposits (see further details on it in 1Aceña and Pons 2005: 699, table 9.16).

10 Government borrowing from the Bank of Spain shows a positive but lower than 1 elasticity. Also, according to our results, a 1% increase of the reserves would be followed by a 0.5% money growth. These results should be interpreted with caution as the residual term might entail a systematic component not included in the estimated equation (see Table A14.3, Appendix 14.1); which would imply the need to incorporate other variables in further research that could be useful to explain money growth. Our estimation is confirmed by running a standard *Granger causality test* (see Table A14.4, Appendix 14.1), which shows that state borrowing from the Bank of Spain is a useful variable to explain money growth and not vice versa.

11 As Martín Aceña (1984) says, the Bank of Spain, with the aim of stabilizing the currency, ran a deflationist policy in 1920 and 1921 similar to that conducted in other European countries.

12 According to Prados (2003), the government cut public investment by 50% from 1929 to 1930.

13 Bank deposits continued their expansion and so did money supply along the same trend of the previous three years. (See Table 14.3 and 21Martín Aceña 1984 for a more detailed explanation of this episode).

14 In order to make the series comparable, we have taken 1929 and 2007 as the base years in both crises. Thus, the vertical axis will show the value of the index and the horizontal axis the year since the base year, either 1929 in the case of the Great Depression or 2007 in the case of the recent financial crisis.

15 The GDP started to grow again in the second quarter of 2014 (0.7%).

References

Aceña, M. and Pons, M. A. (2005). 'Sistema monetario financiero', in Carreras and Tafunell (eds.) (2005, Volume 2): 645–706.

Balcells, A. (1971). *Crisis Económica y Agitación Social en Cataluña de 1930 a 1936*. Barcelona: Instituto Católico de Estudios Sociales.

Barciela, C., Giráldez, J. and López, I. (2005). 'Sector agrario y pesca', in Carreras and Tafunell (eds.) 2005 (I): 245–356.

Carreras, A. and Tafunell, X. (eds.) (2005). *Estadísticas Históricas de España. Siglos XIX y XX*. Volumes I–III. Madrid: Fundación BBVA

Cendejas, J., Muñoz, F. and Castañeda, J. (2014). 'When money matters: Some policy lessons from the business cycle in Spain, 1998–2013', *World Economics*, 15 (29): 77–110.

Cole, H. and Ohanian, L. (2007). 'The great UK depression: A puzzle and possible resolution', in Kehoe T. and Prescott E. (eds.), *Great Depressions of the Twentieth Century*, Minneapolis, MN: Federal Reserve Bank of Minneapolis: 59–84.

Comín, F. and Martin Aceña, P. (1984). 'La política monetaria y fiscal durante la Dictadura y la Segunda República', in *Papeles de Economía Española*, 20: 236–265.

Comín, F. and Díaz, D. (2005). 'Sector público administrativo y estado del bienestar', in Carreras and Tafunell (eds.) 2005 (II): 873–966.

Congdon, T. (2014). 'What were the causes of the Great Recession? The mainstream approach vs the monetary interpretation', in *World Economics*, 15 (29): 1–32.

Feinstein, C. H. (1972). *National Income, Expenditure and Output of the United Kingdom*. Cambridge: Cambridge University Press.

Fernández Baños, O. (1930). *Estudio de Las Fluctuaciones del Cambio de La Peseta*. Santiago de Compostela: Ed. El Eco Franciscano.

Grupo de Estudios de Historia Rural (GEHR) (1991). *Estadísticas Históricas de La Producción Agraria Española*. Madrid: Ed. Ministerio de Agricultura, Pesca y Alimentación.

Hernández Andreu, J. (1986). *España y La Crisis del 29*. Madrid: Espasa Calpe.

Hoyo, A. (2001). 'La evolución de la bolsa y las fluctuaciones de la economía española en el siglo XIX', in Sudrià, C. and Tirado, T. (eds.), *Peseta y Protección. Comercio Exterior, Moneda y Crecimiento Económico en La España de la Restauración*, Barcelona: Edicions Universitat de Barcelona: 261–80.

Instituto de Estudios Fiscales (1976). *Datos Básicos para La Historia Financiera de España (1850–1975)*. Vol. II. Madrid: IEF.

Keynes, J. M. (1936). *The General Theory of Employment, Interest, and Money*, London: MacMillan Press; New York: St. Martin's Press. Repr.: New York: Harcourt, Brace and World (1953).

Maluquer de Motes, Y. and Llonc, M. (2005). 'Trabajo y relaciones laborales', in Carreras and Tafunell (eds.) 2005 (III): 1155–1245.

Martín Aceña, P. (1984). *La Política Monetaria en España. 1919–1935*. Madrid: Instituto de Estudios Fiscales.

Martín Aceña, P. and Pons, M. (2005). 'Sistema monetario y financiero', in Carreras and Tafunell (eds.) 2005 (II): 645–706.

Mitchell, B. (2003). *International Historical Statistics: Europe 1750–1970*. Basingstoke and New York: Palgrave Macmillan.

Nicolau, R. (2003). 'Población, salud y actividad', in Carreras and Tafunell (eds.) 2005 (I): 77–154.

Officer, L. and Williamson, S. (2014). 'The price of gold, 1257–present', Accessed 2014 online at MeasuringWorth (http://www.measuringworth.com/gold/).

Palafox, J. (1980a). 'La gran depresión de los años 30 y la crisis industrial española', *Investigaciones Económicas*, 11: 5–46.

Palafox, J. (1980b). 'La crisis de los años 30: sus orígenes', *Papeles de Economía Española*, 1: 30–42.

Prados de la Escosura, L. (2003). *El Progreso Económico de España (1850–2000)*. Madrid: Fundación BBVA.

Royal Commission for re-establishing the Gold Standard (1929). *Dictamen de la comisión nombrada por real orden de 9 de enero de 1929, para el estudio de la implantación del Patrón Oro*. Chairman of the Comisión, Antonio Flores de Lemus, Madrid: Consejo Superio Bancario.

Sardá, J. (1948). *La Política Monetaria y Las Fluctuaciones de La Economía Española en el Siglo XIX*. Madrid: CSIC.

Tafunell, X. (2000). 'La rentabilidad financiera de la empresa española, 1880–1981: Una estimación en perspectiva sectorial', *Revista de Historia Industrial*, 18: 69–112.

Tafunell, X. (2005). 'Empresa y bolsa', in Carreras and Tafunell (eds.) 2005 (II): 707–834.

Tapia, J. (1998). *La II República y la Quimera de la Peseta: La Excepción Carner*, Barcelona: Real Academia de Ciencias Económicas y Financieras.

Tena, A. (1992). 'Protección y competitividad en España e Italia, 1890–1960', in Prados de la Escosura, L. and Zamagni, V. (eds.), *El Desarrollo Económico en La Europa del Sur. España e Italia en Perspectiva Histórica*, Madrid: Alianza: 321–355.

Tena, A. (2005). 'Sector exterior', in Carreras and Tafunell (eds.) 2005 (II): 573–644.

Thomas, H. (1976). *La Guerra Civil Española (1936–1939)*. Buenos Aires: Grijalbo. [A revised translation of *id.: The Spanish Civil War. 1936–1939*. New York: Kraus Reprint Co. (1975)].

Tortella, G. and Palafox, J. (1983). 'Banca e industria en España, 1918–1936', *Investigaciones Económicas*, 20: 33–64.

15 Money

The long twentieth century

Alessandro Roselli[1]

The gold standard versus bimetallism

The twentieth century marked an unprecedented shift in monetary history: the abandonment of a largely commodity standard in favour of a 'fiat money' system, where the creation of money is submitted to the sole will, or discretion, of the sovereign. To be sure, we have examples of fiat money in earlier periods (think of the 'Assignats' of the French Revolution), but these appear as a sort of aberration from well consolidated, commodity-based, schemes, to be restored as circumstances would permit the return to orderly monetary conditions. In this regard, it is interesting to observe that, even in the past century, in the long transitional period that started with the crisis of the gold standard and led to fiat money currencies, the debasement of a currency was often seen as a temporary measure that would be later phased out, when a commodity standard could be safely reinstated. In the same way, the Bretton Woods system (1944–1971) can be seen as an updated form of gold exchange standard (gold *dollar* standard would be a more appropriate denomination). Gold, not anymore used as a medium of exchange or a store of value in domestic private transactions, has continued to be used as international reserve. It has worked as unit of account in the financial statements of the Bank for International Settlements of Basel (the 'central bankers' bank') until 2002.

In order to understand why that shift occurred, and to try to answer the important question about whether the fiat money system is more conducive to the societal well-being (irrespective of definition), a description of the commodity (metallic) standard that pre-existed the new system is necessary. This description brings us back to the nineteenth century, when the gold standard was firmly established, and will lead us to that very peculiar form of fiat money that is the euro, which has become fully operational (as paper money) in the twenty-first century.[2]

We may start by describing the 'model' of the gold standard, and then try to answer another intriguing question: whether the actual behaviour of policy-makers was coherent with that model. In this regard, we shall consider three countries: The United States, as a country with an important, long-lasting surplus in its foreign accounts; Italy, as a latecomer to the gold standard, but affected by a weak foreign position; and Britain which, as we shall see in some detail, enjoyed a privileged status – a 'seigniorage'[3] – at the centre of the international monetary system.

The gold standard model is based on the assumption that there is a basic link between the quantity of money (money supply) and the price level. This relation has been formalized well after the inception of the standard through the 'quantity theory of money', in particular by the American economist Irving Fisher in 1911, but it's worth mentioning this theory, because any gold standard monetary regime implicitly rests on its assumptions. If money (M) is held only for transaction purposes, if prices (P) are perfectly flexible, and if the physical volume of goods and services produced in a certain period of time (Q) remains unchanged, any change in M – the theory holds – causes a change in P. In addition, even if M and Q (quantity) are unchanged, prices P can vary following a change in the amount of transactions (of money against goods/services) carried out within that period of time, that is a change in the transaction 'velocity' of money (V). All this is expressed by the basic identity MxV = PxQ, which means P = MxV/Q: prices are higher when the money supply is higher and/or money changes hand more frequently; and/or when less goods are available.

In the classical gold standard (gold *specie* standard), the country's money supply is exclusively made of gold and the value of its monetary unit is determined by law as the value of a specific quantity of gold. If a second country is also on the gold standard, the exchange rate between their currencies is determined by their respective 'parity', that is their gold content.[4] The parity is a price expressing exactly the relative quantities of gold in the two units. The free coinage of gold implies that the gold coin is simply an ingot of gold whose weight and fineness are certified by the Mint; coins can be freely brought to the Mint to be melted, and gold bullions can be brought to the Mint to obtain coins. The country's economy is open to foreign transactions to be settled in gold. A one-to-one correspondence exists between gold lost because of a trade deficit, and a reduction of the money supply. Now, let us suppose that, for some reason (a poor harvest, for instance), the quantity of goods available in country A – its national product – falls. The price level has to increase, according to that identity. This will induce its foreign trade partner, country B, which is also on gold standard, to decrease its imports from country A. A deficit will emerge in its trade balance and an outflow of gold will occur to pay for the imbalance.[5] This outflow of gold will reduce its money supply, which is made only of gold. According to the above-mentioned identity, the price level will consequently fall, while, for the same reason (an inflow of gold), the price level will increase in the partner country B, thus restoring the competitiveness of country A. Trade will be again balanced, and the original disequilibrium will be offset by inverse flows of goods and gold. In a model like this, the system is perfectly symmetrical: country A deflates and country B inflates, to restore the competitiveness of the deficit country A.

This model has two relevant features: it works without any government intervention, and this appeals to political and economic liberals, who attribute the greatest relevance to individual economic freedom, and believe that an efficient allocation of resources requires no interference by policy-makers. The second feature is that the flexibility of prices (a decrease in price level, as described earlier for the deficit country A) implies a corresponding flexibility (decrease) of wages, an 'internal devaluation' which causes a lower – if temporary - standard of living. But is that lower standard of living really temporary and socially acceptable? As pointed out by Herbert Grubel,[6] the worsening conditions in country A are mainly due, in a Keynesian perspective, to the fall in aggregate demand following the poor harvest. A more limited price and wages flexibility, as observed in increasingly unionized societies, creates layoffs through the economy, while output is reduced, and imports fall. The trade balance is restored through a permanent import decrease, and gold outflows are more limited, but with a lower level of income and employment.

This is, in essence, the political divide that was at the roots of the gold standard demise. To the reduced price and wages flexibility and stronger trade unions, and wider political suffrage, we should add increasing monetization of large government debts that made gold standard unsustainable.[7]

This form of gold standard is highly impractical and, probably, seldom existed. In the real world, we have various 'substitutes' for gold. Paper currency is compatible with the gold standard if its quantity is strictly backed by an equivalent amount of gold. The authority – treasury or central bank – is committed to issue paper currency only within the amount of gold in reserve. Such a circulation of paper currency allows a more efficient management of the country's gold stock, in particular in relation to the potential outflow of gold due to a trade deficit. A further dissuasion to gold coin circulation is given in a regime of gold *bullion* standard, where private gold holdings are legally permitted, but made inconvenient by maintaining the Mint's commitment to buy and sell gold on demand at a fixed price, but in bullion only.

This is not the only evolution of the standard. In an economy provided with a banking system, the most important substitute for gold is 'banking money', that is means of payment created by banks through demand deposits and bank credit. In order to clarify this point, we may think of the following sequence: an exporter obtains gold coins as payment of his exports, those gold coins are deposited at a bank, in exchange for a banknote, paper currency, which increases 'circulation'. The bank, in turn, transfers that gold coin to the central bank, adding to the country's gold reserve. The central bank opens an account in the name of that bank, which is a credit towards the central bank (a 'central bank balance'). Banks use that balance to extend credit. The central bank may also grant credit to the banking system through discounts and advances. 'Central bank balances' and 'circulation' are the components of the 'monetary base', so called because its increase can result, through bank lending, in a much larger increase in bank deposits, and thus in the country's money supply. Two points are however critical from a quantitative point of view: the central bank must stand ready to redeem money with gold, and banks must stand ready to redeem deposits on demand. Consequently, a certain ratio is defined, by law, between the amount of money supply (or of the 'monetary base', or of 'circulation', depending on the aggregate that the legislator considers as the most critically relevant to maintain convertibility) and the amount of gold in the official reserve ('fractional reserve gold standard'). And a certain percentage of deposits must be kept by each bank in reserve, in the form of cash or equivalent, as determined by custom, prudence or regulation ('fractional reserve banking system'). Together, these two 'fractional systems' portray a sort of inverted pyramid, with three layers: gold at the basis, paper currency at an intermediate level, and bank deposits at the top. The orthodoxy of central bankers – maintaining gold convertibility – required that the weight of the inverted pyramid, concentrated at the top, did not crash on the small base below. It has been observed that '[t]he rise of checking accounts [of banking money] was not well understood for decades [...] The conundrum of the market economy is that there is a need for bank money, but the private sector cannot create riskless collateral to back the money'.[8] An excessive expansion of deposits was the primary source of financial panics, particularly in countries provided with large banking systems. Other countries, with rudimentary financial structures, kept a closer eye on banknote circulation.

If a certain ratio of money supply to gold has to be maintained, even relatively small changes in the gold stock are capable of producing much greater changes in the money supply. The deflationary effect of a gold reserve loss is therefore powerful.[9]

The substitutes of gold that we have so far mentioned break the identity gold = money supply. They increase the money supply and potentially make conversion into gold more difficult to attain. In a third form of gold standard (in addition to the *specie* and the *bullion* standards), the gold *exchange* standard, convertibility is made easier by allowing the convertibility of a currency not directly into gold, but into a foreign currency which is itself preserved at parity with gold. This foreign currency is therefore added to the country's reserve.

We have so far described a classical model of gold standard and its variations stressing the lack of government intervention, that is the automatism of the system. But we have just seen that government may intervene by changing the two critical ratios (between money supply and gold reserve, and between deposits and banking reserve). Moreover, discretionary policies may greatly affect its working, mostly in three ways: by changing the gold content of the currency unit, the money supply, the interest rate.

In fact, when we move from the model description to the historical experience, we shall note that the first device, changing the gold parity of a currency, was one of the most controversial issues in international finance in the first half of the past century. Suffice it to say now that, contrary to a widespread view, the gold standard is compatible with parity changes. The second type of government intervention is also an object of debate about the symmetry, or asymmetry, of the standard: If a country that is experiencing an inflow of gold as a consequence of a trade surplus, sterilizes the expansion of its money supply by offsetting open market operations, the increase in the money supply and prices would not occur and its trade would not be rebalanced. The third device is related to international capital flows: an interest rate increase by a deficit country may stem the gold loss through an inflow of foreign capital. However, the increase in the cost of credit makes the economy less competitive, while a debit position arises vis-à-vis foreign countries and, beyond a certain level, may make its reimbursement unsustainable. If the trade deficit is structural, the interest rate increase cannot be other than a temporary measure.

Before moving to the experience of those three countries with the gold standard, we should mention the relevance of silver as a currency, and explain the reasons of its demise or, better, its reduction to subsidiary money. Two issues are related to bimetallism: the variable ratio of gold and silver respective values, and the need for 'change' in small retail transactions. The first arises because the ratio between the two metals determined by law may not coincide with the market ratio. If, for instance, a relevant increase in the supply of one metal causes a fall in its price relative to the other metal, it is obviously convenient to buy coins of the appreciating metal at the legal ratio, to melt them and to purchase on the market a bigger amount of coins of the depreciated metal. Specifically, a fixed ratio between the two metals was established by law: for a while, in continental Europe 15.5 units of silver against one unit of gold were seen as reflecting the market value of the two metals. If a divergence occurred, for example because the discovery of new mines of gold made gold cheaper against silver, and if the legal ratio remained unchanged, it would be convenient to purchase silver coins at the legal ratio, melt them, and with the same weight of silver in bullion, to buy on the market a higher quantity of gold coins. The idea that substitution between monetary and non-monetary uses of gold and silver would bring the market ratio of gold to silver again into equilibrium with the Mint ratio clashed with actual experience. Coins of the appreciating metal would disappear from circulation (the 'Gresham law'),[10] and the only standard – that is, the only metal used as money – would be the depreciated currency (gold, in our example). The double standard – bimetallism – would make place for the single standard – monometallism.

The second issue is related to the fact that the use of gold coins is totally impractical for retail transactions, so that a single standard would generate an unsatisfied want of small coins. John Stuart Mill praised the 'considerable perfection' of bimetallism, but added that this system left an open question regarding the 'mode' in which smaller payments could be carried out: 'Though the qualities necessary to fit any commodity for being used as money are rarely united in any considerable perfection, there are two commodities which possess them in an eminent, and nearly an equal degree: the two precious metals, as they are called: gold and silver [...]. There is an obvious convenience in making use of the more costly metal for larger payments, and the cheaper one for smaller; and the only question relates to the mode in which this can best be done'.[11] Silver coins were too heavy also for small payments. The solution, the 'mode', was found by issuing silver coins at a premium over their metal content, that is, with a face value higher than their intrinsic silver value. These coins had a limited legal tender and controlled supply, and silver was effectively reduced to a subsidiary role.

The potential instability of a bimetallic standard did not deter the imaginative mind of Irving Fisher from going beyond that, or any metallic standard, at the same time revealing what he called the 'money illusion', the idea that gold (or silver) can be an anchor of stability. Writing in the post-World War I years, he observes a notable increase in the price level, even though the United States is on the gold standard. This means a reduction of the purchasing power of the dollar, that is – if the dollar is defined by a certain gold content – a reduction of the gold price in terms of goods to be purchased. He paradoxically writes that to link the dollar to an alloy of gold and silver would be a better solution, because their divergent movements (which, as we have seen, had brought the demise of bimetallism) might compensate for each other. Still better, however, would be to enlarge the basket of metals that would back the dollar or, by the same token, to adopt the widest possible basket of goods and commodities, and to state by law that 'the dollar represents a composite of those very goods in general'. A general price index would secure a dollar constant in purchasing power. The gold dollar would remain, but it would correspond in value to a 'composite goods-dollar', that is, it would be equivalent to such a market-based dollar. In this way, gold would continue being a medium of exchange, but not a standard of value.

In order to reach this result – Fisher writes – we should vary at short intervals the gold content of the dollar (its gold weight). When the statistical office registers an increase in the price index, the gold brought to the Mint to obtain dollars ('gold certificates') should give a correspondingly smaller amount of them. The reduced amount of dollars would tend to reduce prices to the pristine level. This is not automatic, warns Fisher, but that result may be achieved by gradual adjustments of the dollar's gold weight, that is, by trial and error, like driving a car in a curve when you have to adjust gradually the steering wheel to remain on the road.[12] If all countries simultaneously adopted this 'compensated dollar', fixed exchange rates, one of the benefits of the gold standard, could be maintained.

This idea was not accepted, nor to my knowledge widely discussed as a policy issue, but the link of a currency to a basket of 'values' resurfaced much later, in the 1970s, when Special Drawing Rights (SDRs) were introduced (see the section on the Bretton Woods system), with the not negligible difference that Fisher thought of physical goods, while international bankers linked the SDRs at first to gold, and then to a basket of currencies.

The experiences of three countries up to the First World War

At the outbreak of the First World War, the main countries were on the gold standard. But, in examining the monetary history of specific countries, it is better to get rid of the certainties offered by the classic and somewhat abstract model mentioned earlier, and to try to understand a reality certainly more complex and diversified. Italy is a case in point, given its recent birth as a unitary state, its weak balance of payments, its difficulties in obtaining foreign credit and the changing schemes of its international political alliances.

Soon after the birth of the Kingdom of Italy (1861), in 1865 Italy joined France, Belgium and Switzerland in the creation of the Latin Monetary Union. It should be remembered that, as a consequence of the French political pre-eminence during the First Empire and its trade hegemony in continental Europe, this area had similar currency arrangements, based on bimetallism. The Union, in fact, 'must be regarded as no great leap forward to form what they called a union – a currency union was in effect already in place'.[13] The silver–gold ratio adopted was the 15.5:1 that we have mentioned earlier.[14] Bimetallism, however, suffered the instability of the market values of the two metals. When a divergence between market and legal ratios arose, the divergence only favoured speculative trades, and indicated that a bimetallic standard ended up, alternatively, in a monometallic gold standard and a monometallic silver standard.[15] The discovery of new gold mines in America made gold cheaper, while silver tended to disappear from circulation (along the 'Gresham law' sequence described earlier). While the most obvious outcome might have been the adoption of the gold standard, France insisted on keeping the bimetallism at the same ratio of 15.5:1. Being this ratio not coherent with the market value, it was necessary to reduce the intrinsic value of silver coins (to reduce their silver content), and to limit their use to retail payments only.[16] An opposite trend started in the 1870s, with a strong increase in the production of silver that made convenient the demonetization of gold: another evidence of monetary instability generated by the discrepancy between market and legal ratios. The ascent of Germany as a world power after the victory on France in the war of 1870, followed by huge French reparations paid in gold, made possible the establishment of the gold standard in Germany, and a clear general trend toward the prevalence of this standard in several countries.[17]

In reference to Italy, it should be remembered that, in addition to all the difficulties of a young state, the balance of payment was almost constantly characterized by a trade deficit, while the surplus of the invisibles (mainly, emigrant remittances) was often not sufficient to balance the accounts.[18] The European financial crisis that started immediately after the Latin Union's inception, with the collapse of the British bank Overend Gurney in 1866, forced Italy to adopt the *corso forzoso* (forced legal tender), denying convertibility. Several initiatives were taken in the following years to restore convertibility, and ceilings were introduced to the banknote circulation;[19] however, a plurality of banks maintained the privilege of issue (a legacy of several independent states in the Italian peninsula before the unification).

Only in 1881 a law (the 'Magliani law') abolished the *corso forzoso*, perhaps encouraged by a favourable trend in the balance of payments, which closed in surplus in the years 1880–83: the government took the commitment to establish a metallic reserve through the proceedings of an international loan.[20]

Foreign investors participating in this operation in the years 1881–82 were, interestingly, not only French, who were still feeling the brunt of the dramatic defeat in the French–German war, but also British, who tended to resume the role of support of the Italian government they had assumed during the Risorgimento and, later, German banks, strengthened by the huge French war reparations, and linked to Italy by the new Triple Alliance.[21] Convertibility was restored in 1883 and, thanks to the building of a metallic reserve, the Italian banks of issue were able to expand their paper circulation, previously limited to their own capital, provided that any paper currency beyond it would be covered by that reserve.

A deep financial crisis occurred in the early 1890s. The banks of issue were reorganized and only three survived: the newly established Bank of Italy, Banco di Napoli and Banco di Sicilia. It became again necessary to suspend convertibility, that was made official by law in 1894. From the point of view of reserve management, the most important development, following a law of 1893, was the build-up of a foreign exchange reserve, to be added to the bimetallic component. This, again, sounded as a further detachment from the French sphere of influence. Several countries were at that time moving to the gold standard, and they 'started building around their gold reserve a *cordon sanitaire* made of currencies, to be employed as first line of defence of that same reserve'[22] (this was happening well before the Genoa conference of 1922, which would have given an international blessing to the regime of gold *exchange* standard: see later in this section). The first decade of the new century was generally characterized by a surplus in the balance of payments, which helped a substantial build-up of the Bank of Italy's official reserve. The following table (Table 15.1) reports the amount and composition of the reserve of the Bank of Italy (the most important and, by 1926, the only bank of issue), and the amount of the 'monetary base' (circulation and central bank balances) in 1894 (when the Bank started its operations) and 1914 (at the outbreak of World War I). An increase in the

Table 15.1 Amount and composition of the reserve of the Bank of Italy and the amount of the "monetary base" (circulation and central bank balances) in 1894 and 1914

Italy, m. lire	*1894*	*1914*
Bank of Italy, gold	293	924
—,silver	68	18
—, foreign exchange in reserve	22	118
Tot A	383	1060
Circulation	826	1874
Central bank bank balances	76	220
Tot B	902	2094
A/B	42%	51%

Source: Banca d'Italia (1993). Circulation: Mitchell (1981).

reserve/monetary base ratio, the decreasing importance of the reserve's silver component and the increasing relevance of foreign exchanges will be noted.

The Italian lira, in the period between the unification of the country and the First World War, went in and out of convertibility. It has been observed that in practice, during phases of convertibility, the banks of issue recurred to various expedients to avoid requests of conversion of banknotes at the official parity, while, on the contrary, even in a situation of inconvertibility, at certain times and particularly in the period 1900–1914, when, as just mentioned, Italy's foreign accounts were mostly in surplus, the exchange rate of the Italian lira was maintained around the formal parity, thanks to a particularly abundant metallic reserve.[23] Concluding on this point, it is evident that the rules of play of the gold standard, as described in the model earlier, were clearly violated or at least circumvented, so that 'managed money' would be a more appropriate definition for the monetary system in the years preceding the Great War, at least in reference to the Italian monetary policy.

Would that definition, 'managed money', be correct in the case of the United Kingdom? This country is considered as the prototype of the gold standard model. The history of monetary legislation in Britain between the second half of the nineteenth century and the early twentieth century, in comparison to Italy's, is so simple to the point of non-description. '[T]he only alteration in the system 1870–1914 was the open acceptance by the Bank of England of the role of lender of last resort.'[24] All the legislative debate on convertibility raged before that phase, in the first decades of the 1800s, when, after the victorious but very costly war to Napoleon, the pound was defined again in terms of gold by the Gold Standard Act of 1816,[25] and was made fully convertible into gold in 1821. The Act of 1816 was based on the findings of the Bullion Committee Report of 1810, heavily influenced by David Ricardo, which held that the value of notes used as currency depends on the quantity issued (a meaningful anticipation of Fisher's quantitative theory), and the quantity of notes must be automatically regulated as to maintain their value at par with, and convertible into, gold.[26] This is only part of the story because, more than in other, less developed, countries, Britain was developing a banking system where, as we noted earlier, deposits tend to become a substantial part of the money supply. People started to realize the relevance of bank deposits and credit, in addition to circulation, in assessing the adequacy of the gold reserve. An apparently sterile debate arose between the 'currency school', which held that money consisted of coins and notes, and the 'banking school', which limited the definition of money to coins only. This debate seems, *prima facie*, even for those times, antiquated, because banking money was out of the quarrel. But the real debate went beyond: the banking school critically observed that currency crises were not due just to an over-issue of notes, or coins for what matters, but rather to the excessive expansion of bank credit. The 'currency school' won the debate, and the Peel Act of 1844 stated that the Bank of England could issue notes backed by government securities up to 14 million, while all notes beyond this threshold must be backed by gold to 100%.

As a result, if we look at the Bank of England's balance sheet,[27] we notice that the Act was fully complied with, and the amount of circulation was limited to the value of gold in reserve. But the expansion of the banking system, and the rise of London as an international financial centre, meant that the 'bank balances at the central bank', the other component of the monetary base, could swell to high levels, posing a potential danger to pound convertibility. 'The rise of the overseas banks in London had raised both London's assets and London's liabilities as banker to a wide sterling area [...] The pure international gold standard [...] was pivoted in London as the great free gold market and the great international lender.'[28] In front of the enormous amount that could be drawn from the Bank [...] 'the reserve was *fantastically* small [italics added]'.[29] Walter Bagehot in his Lombard Street, referring to the enormous 'liabilities to the public' (deposits and circulation) of the central bank, was concerned about potentially huge withdrawals, particularly from foreign institutions,[30] and observed that the proportion of reserve to those liabilities should not fall below a 'minimum apprehension' limit.[31] But an alternative solution to the inadequacy of gold reserves was found: the weapon of the official interest rate ('Bank Rate'). Here we come to the privileged position of the United Kingdom, whereby British banks, and foreign institutions having accounts at British banks, refrained from asking conversion of their sterling balances into gold. If a trade deficit emerged, a small increase in the interest rate by the central bank would be sufficient to maintain foreign confidence, stem gold outflows and avoid deflation.[32] We might add, however, that the ultimate protection of the British money supply rested, until the First World War, on a solid current account (where the trade deficit was constantly more than balanced by a surplus in the invisibles), and on a foreign investment position that was positive and acted as an implicit support to the pound.[33]

The convoluted monetary history of the United States in the nineteenth century is marked by a gradual shift from bimetallism to the gold standard, a long period of inconvertibility during the Civil War due to an over-issue of depreciated paper, and the absence of a central bank until the very eve of the First World War. A law of 1837 defined a silver to gold ratio of 16:1, however with a reduced gold fineness of 900.[34] As in other countries, the issue with bimetallism was the instability in the relative values of the two metals, at first – around the mid-century – due to the discovery of gold mines, and then – around the 1870s – to overproduction of silver (the silver mining interests were particularly powerful: the free coinage of silver and the exchange of silver coins against gold coins at the above-mentioned ratio would have displaced gold from circulation, placing the country, in practice, on a silver standard).[35] A compromise led to maintaining silver coinage, but only for limited quantities. This made gold coins necessary, in order to maintain a circulation of an adequate amount. In the end, the Gold Standard Act of 1900 placed the country unequivocally on the gold standard[36] with silver having only a limited legal tender.[37]

The monetary disorder was enhanced by the American peculiarities in regard to paper money creation, with a large number of private banks issuing paper currency; as mentioned earlier, only in 1914 was the Federal Reserve established. Private banks issuing money were not a unique feature of the United States. This system was well entrenched in Scotland in the eighteenth century. The competitive advantages of such a system (banks competed for custom by providing reliability and stability), notwithstanding the ever-present possibility of bank failures, had not brought the Scottish banking system to bank panics and had efficiently supported the local economy, better than the banking system of the southern cousins of England.[38]

According to the American system of Free Banking (1837–1863), each bank, if chartered by its state, issued its own notes, that the bank was obliged to honour in gold and silver on demand; the interesting point here is that those notes were not necessarily backed by gold/silver, but by government – mostly state - securities, to be deposited at the state's competent office. Several factors might therefore contribute to notes' inconvertibility: generally, absence of legal requirements to hold a minimum of specie reserve; but also, an over-issue of notes, related to abundant availability of state bonds (free banking offered the states a good way to raise revenue by promoting the demand for state debt); a falling price of these state bonds (which were of course not risk-free); no effective limit to credit expansion. Bank notes depreciated as a consequence – an uneven depreciation, due to the fragmentation of the banking system - and specie convertibility had to be suspended. In addition, convertibility might by suspended by initiative of the same states, and this fact stimulated an over-expansion of bank credit and failures. State behaviour might generate financial instability.[39] The result was that the banking system was highly unstable. Banking panics (runs on deposits) occurred in 1837, 1839, 1857 and during the Civil War. During some of these panics, convertibility of bank notes into coin had to be suspended. Perhaps the financial exuberance of the American bankers contrasted with the austerity of Scottish capitalists.

With the National Banking Acts of 1863–64, the federal government took over the production of paper money. Only national banks, chartered by a federal office (the Comptroller of the Currency) could issue legal tender notes, backed by US Treasury bonds, and national notes replaced private notes.[40] Thousands of state banks were eliminated. But the problem remained. Any huge credit expansion might generate financial panics and difficulty to observe convertibility. The 'panic of 1907' was at the root of the Federal Reserve establishment in 1913.[41] After that, Federal Reserve notes prevailed, but still in the 1930s national bank notes and Treasury notes were in circulation.

The First World War brought everywhere to the suspension of gold convertibility, caused by the enormous expansion of paper currency to finance the war, and a dramatic increase in inflation followed. The notable exception was the United States, which entered the war late, in 1917, and suspended only external convertibility (a gold embargo, soon lifted in 1919). The large surplus of its balance of payment, thanks to an extremely favourable foreign trade, had permitted the accumulation of net assets abroad, and the United States was a huge lender to the Allies – mostly to the United Kingdom, France and Italy – both during and after the war.

The central issue for any government in the immediate post-war years was not whether to return to gold convertibility, an objective that was given for granted, but at which parity (gold content) to re-enter the gold standard. The theme was extremely sensitive, because economic factors, linked to the price level and the country's competitiveness, intermingled with political considerations, related to national prestige and assertion of power. If, to reinstate gold convertibility, a certain ratio of gold to central bank's liabilities had to be re-established (the 'minimum apprehension' level, in Bagehot's wording), it might imply either a policy of deflation, a contraction of the money supply (greatly expanded during and after the war) or an increase in the gold reserve, made thinner by war financing. This problem was more deeply felt by countries, such as France or Italy, which had suffered extremely high inflation rates and, to a lesser extent, by the United Kingdom. The United States was instead in the enviable position of having experienced less inflation and an increase in its gold reserve.

The United States was able to keep the old dollar parity (as mentioned, it didn't even have to suspend domestic convertibility). The United Kingdom adopted a policy of deflation, and in 1925 triumphantly announced a return to the pre-war sterling parity. For France and Italy, given their depleted gold reserve (partly pledged to the United Kingdom, in the case of Italy), and the enormous amount of their circulation (an exponential increase, in the case of defeated Germany), a deflationary policy aimed at returning to the old parity with gold would be unthinkable, and at the same time to rely on the relatively small gold reserve would be insufficient. The reserve could be increased in two ways: by taking foreign loans, and by devaluing the currency's gold content. The first remedy was therefore to obtain foreign exchange through international – mostly American – loans. The adoption of the gold *exchange* standard found an international support at the Genoa conference of 1922. It permitted an increase in the official reserve, mostly in sterling, of the 'needy' countries mentioned earlier. The British were the most ardent supporters of this *exchange* standard, which temporarily reaffirmed the role of London as a primary financial centre and of the pound as an international reserve currency, and relieved pressure on their currency and gold reserve. The second remedy was to decrease the gold content of the national currency or, in other words, to increase the gold price in terms of that currency, so enhancing the value of the gold reserve.

In practice, the weaker countries adopted a combination of the three devices, in order to reach a reserve/money supply ratio consistent with the 'apprehension level' and, more importantly, complying with the ratio as defined by national legislation: deflation, increase of the foreign exchange component of the reserve, increase of the value of the gold reserve through devaluation, that is, by defining by law a new, smaller, gold parity.

Here we notice an important difference between Italy and France. Mussolini's Italy, in the name of national pride and prestige, wanted a return of the lira to a gold convertibility at a parity that should be as close as practicable to the old one. A restrictive monetary policy of 'strong lira' was pursued, and in 1927 the currency went back to gold, however with a much smaller gold content.[42] The *Cartel des gauches* heavily influenced the French monetary policy, putting the country on the verge of hyperinflation. A government of national unity followed, restoring confidence in the foreign exchange market. The franc came back to gold in 1926–28 with a bigger devaluation than Italy's.[43] Before the war, the franc-lira parity was 1:1 within the Latin Union; in 1928, 1.33 francs were necessary to buy one lira. The franc had a gold devaluation (even bilaterally, vis-à-vis the lira), and this made the French economy particularly competitive.

The restoration of the gold standard in these countries shows that – as mentioned in the first section of this chapter – the gold standard does not rule out changes in a currency's gold content, that is, changes in parity, set in motion by government intervention. Exchange rates can be adjusted, admittedly in exceptional circumstances of fundamental disequilibria. But, were the actual parity changes (or confirmation of old parities) consistent with fundamental trends in the respective economies? This consistency required a strong effort of international cooperation, which in fact lacked. The answer to this question is therefore negative, and the result was the gold standard collapse.

The gold standard collapse

At the completion of the realignments in 1928, the state of the gold standard in these three countries can be measured on the basis of the ratio between the official reserve and central bank's liabilities (monetary base). As we have mentioned earlier, specific, and changeable, legislations defined for each country the minimum ratio to be observed: for instance, in Italy, and France, the liabilities to be accounted for were circulation and current accounts at the central bank; in Britain, they were notes; in the United States, the different types of notes we have described. At the same time, those liabilities had to be backed by gold and/or other means of payment, mostly foreign exchange. In general terms, and neglecting the differences of specific legal provisions, which also reflected different financial structures, reasons of apprehension might arise if the ratio between reserve and liabilities went below 40% (in other terms, if those liabilities were more than 2.5 times the reserve assets). Table 15.2 shows, among the sampled countries, that Britain was in the worst position, due to an overvalued pound. The United States, without devaluation and a reserve made of gold only, was well below the threshold of 2.5. Italy, thanks to the important foreign exchange component of its reserve and to the huge lira devaluation in 1927, was in an apparently comfortable position (and so was France).

France, which had accumulated a large foreign exchange reserve in pounds, thanks also to a competitive franc parity, 'at the beginning of 1929 [...] reversed its policy. It started reducing its holdings of foreign exchange, and brought it down [...]. Thereupon began that tremendous inflow of gold that

Table 15.2 Ratio between the official reserve and central bank's liabilities (monetary base) in 1928

	Italy, m. lire	*UK, m. pounds*	*US, m. dollars*
Gold	4,952	153.8	3854.0
Foreign exchange	5,950		
Tot A	10,902		
Bank balances	2,541	69.5	2389.0
Circulation	17,295	393.0	4800.0
Tot B	19,836	462.5	7189.0
A/B	1.82	3.01	1.87

Source: Banca d'Italia (1993); circulation: Mitchell (1981); Carter *et al.* (2006).

continued with occasional intervals up to the crisis of 1931'.[44] France asked for the conversion of its pound holdings into gold, thus moving from a gold exchange standard towards a pure gold standard. Britain, whose economy was made uncompetitive by a too high pound parity, started suffering a serious haemorrhage of gold. Under pressure from the domestic crisis and loss of gold, the United Kingdom was the first important country to abandon the standard in 1931.

It is always difficult to find a single motivation for epochal events, but there is no doubt that one relevant explanation of why the United Kingdom was driven out of the gold standard, is the choice of a wrong parity for the pound, aimed at restoring that world supremacy that the war had unquestionably moved to the other side of the Atlantic. The devaluation was adopted out of necessity, not as an option. The same cannot be said for the United States.

One should expect that the United States, as a surplus country, with a solid current account and an investment position largely positive, and with the highest gold reserve, should have behaved symmetrically, by adopting an easy monetary stance that might have impressed a stimulus to its own and other countries' economies, and a revaluation of its currency, aimed at rebalancing its foreign accounts, that is, reducing its surplus. Quite the contrary: prompted by the necessity to curb the stock market speculation (have central banks to keep in check financial assets?), the United States raised the interest rate, making the dollar more attractive and contributing to the strengthening of its already huge gold reserve. Moreover, in 1933, at the World Economic Conference in London, called to correct the increasing international imbalances, Roosevelt, with a comfortable surplus in US foreign accounts, amazingly announced the most competitive devaluation possible: the abandonment of the dollar gold parity, which was followed by the definition of a much smaller gold content of the dollar,[45] together with domestic inconvertibility of its currency. The Italian representative at the London conference was literally stunned by Roosevelt's announcement,[46] which was a heavy blow to all the countries (France and Italy in particular) that had remained stuck to the Gold Bloc. The creditor position of the United States obliged other countries to generalized deflation.

In fact, countries like Italy that had relied on fixed parities after the realignments of the late 1920s, barely living with a currency that, although devalued in terms of gold, was characterized by an uncompetitive parity, felt the pinch of these devaluations. The Bank of Italy had already suffered heavy losses on its holdings in sterling after the pound devaluation in 1931; the dollar devaluation of 1933–34 was a further blow to a country that was already in trouble because of the overvalued lira. Financing the Ethiopian war in 1935 was the last straw. The lira had to devalue and was made inconvertible in 1936.[47] France followed suit in the same year, when the Popular Front government of Léon Blum introduced a social programme that led to capital flights abroad (as noted by Goodhart in reference to much more recent events, the hegemonic creditor country pressurizes the surrounding countries to deflate or to exit [the system]).[48]

A sort of truce in this money war was reached in that same year, when a tripartite agreement between the United States, the United Kingdom and France recorded a *modus vivendi*, according to which the respective exchange rates were stabilized at their current level; the US Treasury would provide a market for gold at 35 dollars per ounce, while in other countries, whose currencies were inconvertible into gold, the market price of gold was determined by the exchange rate of the dollar, in a sort of gold *dollar* standard.

At this point, it sounds like a paradox that the only big country with a formally unchanged gold parity remained Germany, which had suffered in 1919–23 a dramatic hyperinflation, and had stabilized in 1924 thanks to important foreign capital inflows. Germany had been later hit by inverse capital flows and by the World Depression, and – even though its huge war reparations had been cancelled - a substantial foreign debt had remained on its shoulders. But Germany avoided devaluation thanks to strict capital controls, a close-knit network of trade arrangements ('clearings') and to the financial tricks of Hjalmar Schacht, the 'Hitler magician'.[49]

The Bretton Woods system

The gold standard had collapsed, but – as we have stressed at the outset of this chapter – the quest for stability could not totally dismantle gold of its monetary role. Summarizing the state of the question in the 1980s, Milton Friedman and Anna Schwartz pointed to 'the emergency of a monetary system that is [...] unprecedented: a system in which essentially every currency in the world is, directly or indirectly, on a pure fiat standard – directly, if the exchange rate of the currency is flexible though possibly manipulated; indirectly, if the exchange rate is effectively fixed in terms of another fiat-based currency'. They add that this system emerged gradually after the First World War: their reference is possibly to the gold exchange standard and later to the aforementioned tripartite agreement, but it should be added that in both the final backing was gold. Friedman and Schwartz belittle that gold reference: '[M]uch of the world was effectively on a dollar standard, while the US, though ostensibly on a gold standard (except for a brief interval in 1933-34), was actually on a fiat standard combined with a government program for pegging the price of gold'.[50]

The Bretton Woods agreements of 1944 led to the establishment of a gold exchange standard, where the 'exchange' component was the US dollar, convertible into gold at 35 dollars per ounce, while the other countries declared the fixed parity of their currencies against the dollar. From this viewpoint, the Bretton Woods system was remarkably similar to the tripartite agreement of 1936, which was in this way 'globalized'. Not by chance, it has been stated that 'the International Monetary Fund [at the centre of the new system] was essentially designed to deal with the problems of the past'.[51] The United States had emerged from the Second World War with an overwhelmingly dominant economy, the highest reserves in gold, and an unprecedented political and military power. The country took over the world financial leadership from the United Kingdom. And the dollar inherited the seigniorage previously enjoyed by Britain. While, in the interwar period, the hegemonic power was no longer in London, and not yet in Washington,[52] the war made it clear where that power would stay. Until it lasted, the 'rest of the world' was willing to rely on dollar holdings that would give an interest and could be freely exchanged into gold. Therefore, the role of gold in this phase, up to the dollar inconvertibility in 1971, should not be dismissed.

The position of the hegemonic country is always problematic. If it runs a surplus, the rest of the world has to deflate in order to regain competitiveness; if it runs a deficit, the seigniorage of its currency avoids the necessity to deflate its economy, it exports inflation to the rest of the world. In addition, in the first case there is a squeeze on the international liquidity (dollars go back home – are transferred to the hegemonic creditor – and subtracted from the international liquidity); in the second case, the international liquidity soars (dollars go and remain abroad, with the risk of an imbalance between the hegemonic country gold stock and the increasing amount of its foreign obligations).

Robert Triffin famously argued in 1960 that an imbalance between the American gold stock and the stock of its dollar obligations would fuel a crisis of confidence in US liquidity.[53] The rest of the world would become aware that dollar obligations were not a riskless asset. Symmetry, which was so missed under the gold standard, was again absent. The hegemonic country, although in deficit, was reluctant to put in order its foreign accounts; surplus countries, Germany for instance and sometimes Italy, were equally reluctant to revalue their currencies. This awareness, and the political will to assert independence, prompted some countries to convert part of their reserve into gold, a road pursued particularly by De Gaulle's France[54] (and, to an extent, by Italy, under the central bank's governorship of Guido Carli).[55] The international liquidity was heavily affected by these transactions – as mentioned, any repatriation of US dollars was equivalent to a decrease of that liquidity. In the 1960s, ideas and proposals were advanced regarding new reserve instruments that would include a fiduciary component, whose creation would not be linked to the vicissitudes of any specific country, but internationally regulated in coherence with the need for an appropriate level of world liquidity. This would require, as often stressed by the proponents, a rebalance of US foreign payments.

The weakness of the Bretton Woods system became evident through an increasing demand for gold that central banks could meet only at the cost of losing reserves, being its price fixed at 35 dollars per ounce. In 1961, a consortium was created by the main central banks to maintain that price (the Gold Pool), while the idea of an increase in its official price was totally rejected. The Pool incurred heavy losses. This development led first, in 1968, to the establishment of a short-lived 'two-tier gold market' (the Washington agreement), where that gold price would be maintained for inter-central bank transactions,[56] while it could freely float on the market; and then to the abandonment by the United States of the 35 per ounce dollar convertibility, in August 1971.[57] In December, a general pegged rate system (the 'Smithsonian Tunnel')[58] followed: the gold price was raised to 38 dollars per ounce, but convertibility was not resumed and confidence was not restored. In 1973, new exchange rates were set. The dollar price of gold was raised further to 42.22 dollars, leaving unchanged the gold value of other currencies. The International Monetary Fund (IMF)'s official gold price was abolished. Then, powerful forces that reflected the specific concerns of any single country drove currencies towards a generalized regime of floating – free, or 'dirty', to mean that foreign exchange intervention by the authorities might, if desirable, alter the rate resulting from the interplay of market forces. Fiat money was unbound, at least in principle, by external constraints.

In 1974, in order to unfreeze gold in official transactions, central bank governors and finance ministers of the main industrial countries (the 'Group of Ten') agreed that gold might be used in settlement of debit positions between monetary authorities, or as a collateral of bilateral credits, at a price derived from its market price. Italy was among the first to seize this opportunity. Hit by a deep balance of payments deficit, in September the country had to ask a large loan from Germany. It took the form of a cross-deposit between the central banks of the two countries: a deposit in US dollars would be put by the Bundesbank at the disposal of the Bank of Italy, against an opposite deposit of Italian gold earmarked to the Bundesbank. The gold – around 20% of the Italian gold reserve – was valued at 149 dollars an ounce (derived from the *gold fixing* in London).

In the meantime, the quest for a stable reserve currency had gone to fruition, and a new instrument was created in 1969, but it did not respond to the ambitious objectives of its proponents. The Special Drawing Rights (SDRs) had originally a one-to-one ratio to the US dollar, valued at 35 dollars per ounce (when, in December 1971, the gold price was increased to 38 dollars, the SDR's value was correspondingly raised to 1.0857 dollars, in order to maintain its value in terms of gold: that is, 35 SDRs per ounce). Since 1974, coherently with the abolition of the gold official price, the SDR has been linked to a basket of currencies, whose components change from time to time to take into account their relative importance in international trade.

The evolution of the SDR's value looks like a monetary micro-history of the twentieth century: from its definition in terms of gold dollar, to a changeable basket of currencies that reflects the floating rate regime and the relative importance of each currency. The amount of SDRs issued has been, however, limited: the need for international reserves is inversely proportional to the exchange rate flexibility; in addition, that need has been mostly met by foreign exchanges, thanks to the growth of international capital markets (SDRs are at present the unit of account of the International Monetary Fund).

What about gold, now?

The fiat money standard has not displaced gold from its role of international reserve. Table 15.3 gives some information about the amount of physical gold held in reserve at 'World' level, and its value at market prices. It will be noted that the stock of gold has not greatly changed between 1971 and 2014 (3rd q): slightly more than one billion of troy ounces; the market value has however increased by around 19 times, calculated in SDRs.[59] The same Table 15.3 reports the value of total reserves, including gold at market price. The gold component has a declining share of total reserves.

According to the World Gold Council, over half (54.6%) of the gold reserves are owned by the 'G-7' countries (the United States, Germany, Italy, France, Japan, the United Kingdom and Canada, in order of their respective gold holdings). The Euro Area (including the ECB), owns around one third (33.7%) of the gold reserves.[60]

Reserves in foreign currencies are mostly held by emerging economies. As of October 2014, the following countries have reserves in foreign exchange in excess of 200 billion SDRs: Japan (815), Saudi Arabia (493), Switzerland (323), Russia (251), Brazil (248), Korea (239) and China (220).[61]

Macrotrends[62] provides a useful set of graphs regarding gold trends. Figure 15.1 shows a century of gold prices, in nominal and real terms (adjusted to the American consumer price index [CPI])[63]. Figure 15.2 compares gold and silver prices, in real terms, over that period. It is interesting to observe a certain correlation between them. Figure 15.3, in particular the 5-year moving average, seems to indicate that the gold to silver price ratio moves in ample waves, which appear to favour gold in the very long run. Figure 15.4 compares

Table 15.3 World reserves of gold in 1971 and 2014

World reserves	*December 1971*	*September 2014*
Gold, troy ounces	1,175.91m	1,032.28m
Gold, market price, SDR	47,254.56m	847,012.68m
Total reserves in SDR, including gold at market price, SDR	134,799.11m	9,066,017.02m

Source: IMF, International Financial Statistics.

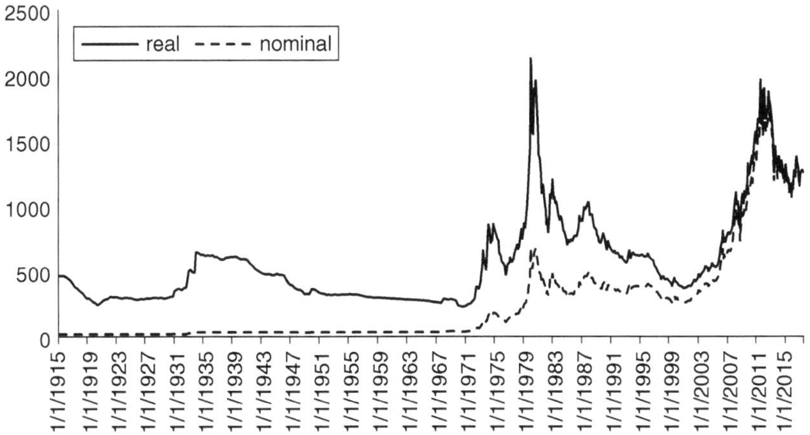

Figure 15.1 100 years of real and nominal gold prices.

Source: http://www.macrotrends.net/1333/historical-gold-prices-100-year-chart

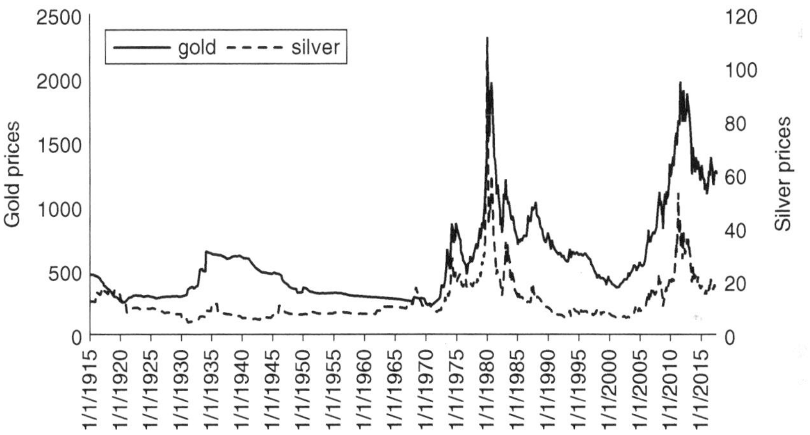

Figure 15.2 Real gold and silver prices.

Source: http://www.macrotrends.net/1333/historical-gold-prices-100-year-chart and http://www.macrotrends.net/1470/historical-silver-prices-100-year-chart

percentage changes in gold prices and CPI changes (10-year rolling percentage changes) since 1951: there is an evident correlation between the two, even though the consolidation of a stable and low inflation in the last few years appears to discourage gold investors. The price of gold rises in periods of financial instability. As Figure 15.4 shows, the high inflation of the 1970s and the financial turmoil of 2007–2011 are both marked by a jump in real gold prices. A final general observation is that dollar and gold prices are inversely related. The recent resurgence of the dollar coincides with a notable decline in gold

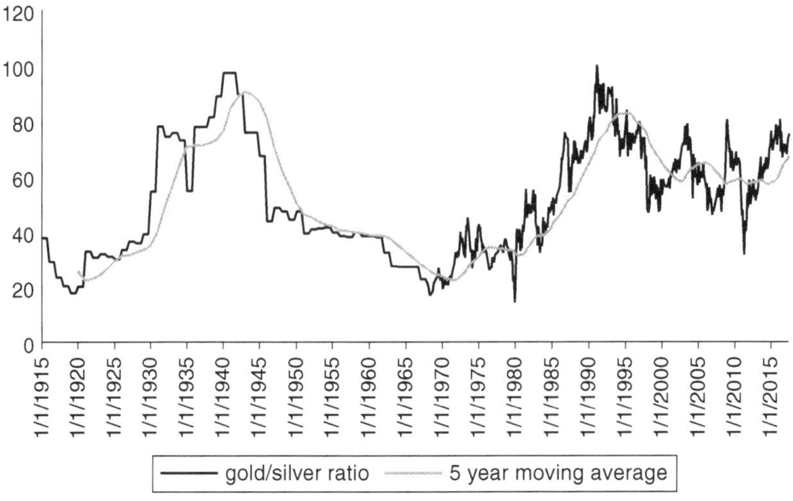

Figure 15.3 Real gold to silver ratio with 5-year moving average.

Source: http://www.macrotrends.net/1333/historical-gold-prices-100-year-chart and http://www.macrotrends.net/1470/historical-silver-prices-100-year-chart

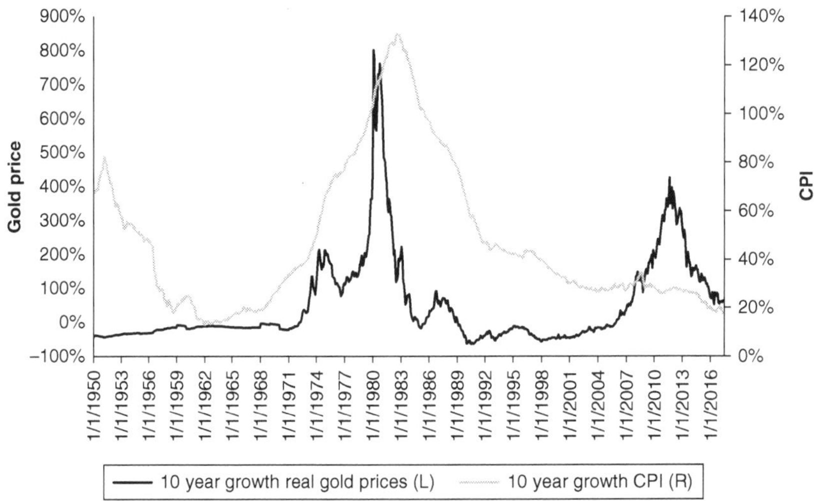

Figure 15.4 Percentage changes in nominal gold prices and CPI changes since 1950.

Source: http://www.macrotrends.net/1333/historical-gold-prices-100-year-chart

prices. In summary, in more recent years, a combination of dollar strength and low or nil inflation creates an environment inimical to the 'gold bugs'.

Why maintain a certain amount of gold as an official reserve? And why have some countries sold not negligible quantities, while others have considerably increased the gold portion of their reserve? The answers may be several, and changeable over time. Different from previous periods, nobody is thinking today of a return to some form of gold standard, even though the instability of exchange rates in a world of fiat money raises still unanswered questions regarding what a stable money should be. Observing the gold market price of around 600 dollars an ounce in 1980, a former governor of the Bank of Italy ironically remarked: 'Using the language of the 19th century, we might say that the gold reserve of the Bank of Italy is more than double the amount of circulation. This means that it would be possible, given the current gold price, to restore the convertibility of banknotes into gold: by using less than half of the Bank's reserve, the banknotes in circulation might be replaced by gold in bars or metallic coins'.[64]

In general, gold as a contingency reserve, against unforeseeable negative developments both in the currency market and the real economy, seems to be the underlying theme below any initiative concerning gold, or lack of it.[65]

For a while, gold transactions by the authorities (Treasury or central bank) may have responded to their view about the prospective role of gold in the international monetary system, by changing the reserve composition accordingly. In addition to this 'strategic view' about gold as an international currency, five seem to be the prevailing motivations behind gold transactions carried out by the authorities: concerns about their national currency; rebalancing a country's negative foreign position; addressing an imbalanced government budget (however, central banks have been sometimes reluctant to this use of their gold reserve, a national asset, as a shortcut to balancing the budget by avoiding painful measures of budget adjustment); using gold transactions for monetary policy purposes, protecting official reserves against exchange rate fluctuations, in particular fluctuations in the value of the dollar against other leading currencies. Gold transactions were sometimes advocated as a form of open market operations, to change the liquidity in the economy: an increased demand for gold by the market, fulfilled by the central bank through an open market sale, reduces the size of the central bank's balance sheet, however without affecting the government securities market, as a common open market operation would do, and the trade balance, as it would happen if gold had to be imported.

We may find one or more of these motivations in various initiatives undertaken by the authorities. Their gold transactions are sometimes made public, other times are hidden in secrecy, and only *ex post facto* details may be made publicly available.

It should be also remembered that the purpose of making the gold reserve profitable is behind a number of different transactions carried out by the authorities, as gold lending to facilitate hedging by gold producers of their future output; location swaps to make profit from changes in gold demand in different places; trading on the spot and future markets.

The issuance of gold-backed bonds has also been proposed, to enable Sovereign funding at high levels of interest rates to reduce meaningfully the cost of debt servicing while at the same time preserving the ownership of gold reserves. Again, objections would be possibly raised by the central bank whose gold would be used as guarantee.

The euro

Let us suppose that the international monetary system is made of a network of fixed exchange rates involving a certain number of countries. Let's also assume that these countries do not want a common standard based on gold, discredited by historical experience and often by economic theory, and that, at the same time, they are well aware of the shortcomings of a standard based on a single currency issued by one specific country: they want to avoid the seigniorage that accrues to that country (as seen in the section on the Bretton Woods system). The only available solution, in order to maintain the stability of certain defined exchange rates, is that each country should either adjust its fiscal and monetary policies to the requirements of its balance of payments, or impose trade restrictions and capital controls. If trade and capital movements are by agreement liberalized, unless disequilibria in its foreign payments are of a very temporary nature, a foreign accounts deficit implies restrictive policies, and a surplus implies accommodative policies. This consequence is inescapable, both under a commodity standard, and in a fiat money system. A fiat money system is indeed consistent with any sort of policy, but if fixed exchange rates are agreed, any discretion is limited. And if foreign accounts are not temporarily, but structurally unbalanced, the final option is either to devalue, or to revalue, the national currency.

Any system of fixed exchange rates implies therefore the adoption of domestic economic policies aimed to avoid a fundamental disequilibrium, through symmetry of behaviour of surplus and deficit countries. Under the gold standard, this symmetry was not followed, as we have seen earlier. The important surplus countries were France and, primarily, the United States. By adopting a restrictive monetary stance, and by devaluing the dollar, the United States consolidated its growing hegemonic position but, by so doing, gave an important contribution to the gold standard collapse, as we have seen earlier in the section on the Gold Standard collapse. 'The US Federal Reserve of the 1920s simply did not follow the cardinal rule of the gold standard – that is, to expand credit conditions when gold flowed in, and contract them when gold flowed out'.[66] The Bretton Woods system, based on fixed rates, was born out of the idea of Keynes that adjustments between creditor and debtor nations should be symmetric. However, the United States – at that time, again, the most powerful creditor nation – did not accept a system that would force it to adjust. The system had a lack of symmetry embedded in it, and it worked mainly as a mechanism of adjustment of deficit countries, even though the text of the Articles of Agreement[67] of the IMF speaks of 'fundamental disequilibrium' as the trigger of changes in parity rates, without distinction between surplus and deficit countries. When the United States shifted to the position of a deficit country, it again refused symmetry. By taking profit of its seigniorage, the deficit position in its foreign accounts was not accompanied by coherent fiscal, monetary and exchange rate policies.[68] There was a divergence between the hegemonic political and military positions of the United States, which supported its right of seigniorage, and its weakening currency, which made the seigniorage economically unjustified. The increasing divergence between the market price and the official price of gold was the evidence of the impending collapse of the system, as discussed earlier in the section on the Bretton Woods system.

In an abstract world, if we make the historically unforgivable mistake of depriving the Bretton Woods system of its characteristic feature, that of being gold-dollar based (the *gold dollar standard*), we might perhaps say that the wisdom of its begetters (reference is mainly to John Maynard Keynes, not to the American Harry Dexter White) conceived the best solution possible for an international system based on reciprocal cooperation: a system characterized by fixed rates, symmetrical adjustments, changes of parities if adjustments proved unfeasible. The creation of an artificially created reserve instrument – the 'bancor', to use Keynes's words – to support the availability of international liquidity when necessary, was banned exactly because the idea of a gold-dollar standard prevailed.[69]

The unviability of the Bretton Woods system ushered in the road to the prevalence of national interest and dysfunctional international cooperation for a long time, and we still live within this environment. To be sure, it has its important advantages. Exchange rates can be continuously adjusted according to domestic needs of economic and social nature, and demand management tailored to those needs becomes the main instrument of economic policy. Freedom of trade and capital movements are perfectly compatible with this non-system, and flourishing economies can well be the result. I guess that no definitive study has been made, attesting the prevalence of a system of fixed – or quasi-fixed – exchange rates over floating rates, or vice versa, from the very general point of view of the societal well-being (to return to a question we raised at the start of this chapter).

We can now move to the experience of Europe, starting from the post-Bretton Woods years and the regime of floating rates that anywhere prevailed. Of course, it would be reductive to look at the European common currency only as a technical development of exchange rate arrangements, overlooking the political attempts towards a closer intra-European integration which characterized most of the twentieth century, since the First World War and its aftermath. 'Horror at the four-year blood-bath caused by "civilized" European nations and at the decline which it portended, led in every country [...] to a passionate debate on how peace could be safeguarded by institutions using supranational legal sanctions'.[70] It is no wonder that this debate continued in the interwar period. But, within a loosely organized League of Nations that would incorporate non-European nations, a prospective union of Europe fell victim of a clash between federalist and democratic left-wing liberals, and a prevailing nationalist Right, and of the difficulty to recognize a common Franco-German destiny. In 1929, a mutual understanding emerged between the foreign ministers of France, Briand, and Germany, Stresemann, according to which a new European Federal Union would overcome bilateral concerns related to a French-German block at the continent's centre. Stresemann even spoke of a European currency. This project clashed however with the view of the German chancellor, Bruning, who saw Briand's idea as an intention to appease Germany and to stabilize the status quo in Europe, and in opposition to the German demand for an adequate 'living space' in Central Europe.[71]

The political organization of Europe continued however, over the years, to be seen as a prerequisite of any monetary agreement. The design of a common currency remained vague in any successive debate about European integration, even when, in the post-Second World War years, forms of economic integration started to take shape. We have to wait until the end of the Bretton Woods era to observe attempts at a closer monetary cooperation.

A period of 28 years elapsed between the demise of the Bretton Woods system (1971) and the adoption of the euro (1999). It is beyond this chapter's scope to give a description of the stages that preceded the single currency. Suffice it to say that in the early 1970s, with increasing frequency, a coordination of the economic policies of the European Community's member states was discussed. They embarked on a process of creating a narrower pegged system (the 'Snake') and an ineffective European Fund for monetary cooperation (Fecom) was established. Divergent economic policies remained well entrenched in the European countries, and tensions emerged between the European currencies inside the Snake, whenever it tended to appreciate against the dollar. The Snake proved unsustainable and ended up as something different: a small group of central European currencies, with the Deutsche mark at its centre.

In 1979, the Exchange Rate Mechanism (ERM) came into force, based, again, on the idea of fixed exchange rate margins among the participating European currencies: a semi-pegged system with the goal to narrow exchange rate variability and achieve monetary stability in view of the introduction of the single currency. In 1992, on the basis of a report prepared by the European Commission (Delors report, 1989), the European Council agreed in Maastricht to create a monetary union and introduce the euro at the end of a convergence period, in 1999.[72] Paradoxically, later that year (September 1992), the ERM collapsed, under heavy speculation against the weak rings of the chain; the British pound and the Italian lira. The two countries had suffered recession to save their exchange rates against the Deutsche mark. It was at that point that Milton Friedman wrote his famous article 'Déjà vu', which concluded: 'How many more fiascos will it take before responsible people [...] are finally convinced that a system of pegged exchange rates is not a satisfactory financial arrangement for a group of large countries with independent political systems and independent national policies?'[73] Is the Euro Area a 'déjà vu'?

It is sometimes discussed whether the Euro Area can be considered as an 'optimum currency area', along the lines described first by Robert Mundell and few others. This implies an attempt to define the features of such an area where an optimal trade-off exists between economic efficiency and the ability to react to local, sub-area shocks (as correctly observed: 'Somewhere between one currency for the entire world and one for each city'),[74] and check if the European Union fits into this uncertain framework. We shall not enter this minefield; we shall just note that behind the motivations that finally led to the monetary union were two main concerns: the need to recreate in Europe a certain stability of exchange rates, lost because of the uncooperative behaviour of the hegemonic country; and a vague, generally undefined need to respond to a basic cultural identity of the peoples of the European continent, torn by a never-ending series of internecine wars. With this broadly political background of a widely shared feeling of 'Europeanness', and some scepticism of European central bankers, the French–German bargain of unifying Germany inside a unified Europe played a decisive role. As observed, the correct question of whether the European Monetary Union (EMU) is an optimum currency area is, eventually, an issue of feasibility rather than optimality.[75]

From what we have said earlier, being an adjustment of exchange rates ruled out by definition in a monetary union, the disequilibria between countries of the Euro Area should be faced by coherently symmetric domestic policies, 'internal' devaluations or revaluations. In abstract, these adjustments should be as rigid as those imposed by the gold standard, because of the irrevocability of the currency arrangement that is at the basis of the Union.

Can these adjustments take place through fiscal or monetary measures? Both types of measures are hindered by legal and political constraints. The recourse to fiscal policy for demand management would not be in line with the Maastricht Treaty, which imposes a period of fiscal consolidation in most countries that have to reach narrow targets of deficits and debt. A balanced budget principle, which makes deficit spending difficult even for investments, has been introduced in some countries by a constitutional amendment. Are the surplus countries inside Europe, Germany in the first place as the hegemonic country, making efforts to rebalance their economies towards more domestic consumption? 'Germany regards its net surplus as an indication of the virtuous qualities of its policies, to which all other countries should aspire by mimicry of Teutonic self-denial',[76] and even Germany has constrained itself through the balanced-budget rule. Therefore, any serious expansionary fiscal policy is precluded. Peripheral Europe seems condemned to adjust through austerity.

Concerning monetary policy, the difficulty of implementing a flexible monetary management is in the first place related to the guidelines that attribute a priority to price stability and stress the long run neutrality of money (according to which the central bank cannot enhance growth by expanding the money supply). We have recently noticed a radical change of tack in the ECB's policy, but this change still meets substantial opposition in Germany, being seen as inconsistent with the ECB's mandate. Moreover, by definition a single monetary policy means that 'one size fits all', and here is the usual problem that it is related to countries that are, structurally and cyclically, in pretty different situations. Just to cite an example, the official rates of the ECB, in the period preceding the big financial collapse of 2007–2008, greatly encouraged real estate speculation and the final collapse of the Irish banking system and its economy. Was that rate appropriate to the Irish economy? Vice-versa, are today's extremely low interest rates consistent with the German growth rates?

Since proactive macroeconomic policies of adjustment within the Euro Area seem to be largely precluded by legal devices and political resistance, and since an integration of the area through supply side measures (the adoption of 'reforms') cannot go ahead other than through trial and error and difficult social conflicts, the way out of this conundrum is, paradoxically, the sort of policies that are discussed at the time of writing (April 2015), amid harsh political confrontation: essentially, an economic governance that allows a transfer of resources, where the surplus country(ies) agree to reduce the credit component, in favour of cooperation and assistance. In other words, a fiscal transfer from the strong to the weak country. A pooling of resources, aimed at favouring the poorest regions of the area, would be an unequivocal, if timid, sign of the necessary jump ahead towards political integration. Without it, the Monetary Union cannot survive in the long run. We have historical precedents: to bail-out backward regions in order to integrate them into larger political areas. The only cautionary note would be that the transfer of resources be an expression of cooperation and not of political exploitation. The most extreme experience, according to Capie and Wood, was the Great Depression of the 1930s, when the federal government of the United States developed federally funded transfer programmes in favour of the most deeply affected regions, deemed essential to the union's survival.[77] Whether the European Union ends up being a 'déjà vu' or not will depend on the willingness of that 'group of large countries' to give up their 'independent political systems and policies'.

What 'money' is and why crypto-currencies are not 'money'

A certain attention is currently devoted to 'crypto-currencies', defined as 'a digital representation of value that can be digitally traded and functions as (1) a median of exchange; and/or (2) a unit of account; and/or (3) a store of value, but does not have legal tender status in any jurisdiction'.[78] It is legitimate to ask which might be their role in an increasingly electronically connected society. They can be included in the wider category of 'private currencies', and an appropriate question is whether these currencies can be qualified as 'money'. This is not a purely terminological question – it is ultimately related to our broader vision of the main functions of a body public, and the answer may be different, depending on whether we see a wide role of the state or, on the contrary, we tilt towards a libertarian view, according to which 'money is after all what we accept as money',[79] or to the extreme, towards a quasi-anarchical perspective. It is worthwhile to remember that two basic approaches to what can be considered as 'money' have been identified: the first – the 'Metallist' view - focuses on money as a medium of exchange, which in the past derived its value mostly through a link to a precious metal; the second – the 'Chartalist' one – puts an emphasis on the link between money and legal tender laws, which require normally that the State's own currency must be accepted.[80] 'To-day', Keynes wrote, 'all civilised money is, beyond the possibility of dispute, chartalist'.[81]

As observed by an authoritative book on crypto-currencies, 'A persistent and complex theme of historical private money systems is their, often uneasy, relationship with the state. The state had a dual role towards them. In most cases it has been a destroyer [...] But, in other cases, it has been a creator of sorts, or at least an unwilling midwife. On the one hand, the typical response of the state has been to stamp out private money [...] In other cases, private money emerged to fill a market niche that the state itself had created'.[82]

As a postulate, I assume that *money* is – as national defence, justice, police, education and few others – a 'public good', which, being a duty of the state[83] to pursue and maintain, cannot be delegated, or can be delegated within very narrow boundaries only. Failure of the state to comply with one of these duties means a serious disturbance, or possibly a collapse, of the social compact upon which the state's authority rests. The integrity of money, and of other public goods as well, is a precondition for an ordinate working of the society. These (I admit) rather clear-cut, and broadly political, propositions – well consistent with the chartalist view – give us a sort of watershed that enables us to find out cases when private currencies are upgraded to 'money'.

An IOU – a credit relationship between private subjects – is not money, even if credit is fully collateralized and transferable, accepted by third parties, as some authors seem to believe. The reason is that it lacks the government guarantee. As the recent financial crisis has amply demonstrated, the government only is able to provide completely riskless collateral: any claim created within the private sector is of uncertain value.[84] The notion that money, as a state debt, is fully collateralized should not be misunderstood. The collateral is not necessarily a physical commodity, as in the gold standard (which, not by chance, imposed to the state a strict legal ratio currency/commodity in reserve) or, as it was the case with the Rentenmark in the early Weimar republic, the very land of Germany: it can just be, as within a regime of 'fiat money', the sovereign's 'full faith and credit': the government's unlimited pledge to discharge the money holder of any of his debts. If we accept the notion of money as a credit fully backed by the state, the crucial question is to what extent this backing is given. In other words, among the billions of credit contracts that characterize at any moment a modern economy, where does the money stop?

This is an intriguing question, but only by relying on a firm demarcation of that boundary may we give a concrete meaning to the concept from where we started, of money as a 'public good'. Money ceases to be a public good when the benefit of its creation is lower than the public/social cost involved in the government guarantee. For instance, bank deposits, as we have seen in the first section, represented, even in a gold standard regime, a rapidly developing 'private currency', a typical case of money creation by private entities (the banks). To what extent can they be considered as 'money'? To the extent that the government unconditionally guarantees the depositors' credit, exactly in the name of that public good that the state has to protect. The public purpose is here identified with the economic stability and growth, and the well-being to which the banking system should be instrumental. The uncertainty of the border, in reference to bank liabilities, is a consequence of the uncertainty and equivocal behaviour of the authorities, as in the recent financial crisis. Governments, with 'constructive ambiguity', had left pretty undetermined the reach of their backing. The more the government backing is extended – i.e., the more inclusive what we call *money* – the higher the risk that the government will have to honour its guarantee, being the cost borne by that general community (the public, the taxpayer) it has to represent and protect. The idea of money as a *public* good becomes blurred and, in the end, defeated.

Do bitcoins – the most talked-about crypto-currency – respond to the 'public good' criteria that are intrinsic to the nature of money?[85]

We shall not enter the technicalities of their creation,[86] but try to respond according to their purposes, as described in the aforementioned book. Why use bitcoins as a medium of exchange, unit of account, store of value? Their purposes are so defined by Dowd: 'Bitcoin has the potential to restore financial privacy and create a peaceful crypto-anarchic social order that operates beyond government control [...] it is increasingly used for both legal and illegal transactions, the latter thanks to its potential to achieve a very high degree of transaction anonymity [...] its price [is] very uncertain and created a bubble-burst cycle'.[87] Elsewhere in the book, the author says: 'The designers of crypto-currencies sought to create not just a new currency, but a new anarchist social order.' Whatever the founders' purpose, 'the anonymity of bitcoin also suggests a demand for bitcoin for tax evasion, escaping capital controls, money laundering and similar purposes, and a store of value in which people use bitcoins to escape financial repression by their own governments'.[88]

It is hard to believe that in some way the public interest would be enhanced in such circumstances. The author adds, as a final consideration: 'The appropriate government response to private money is to allow competition on a level playing field between alternative forms of money'.[89] This is a perfectly plausible standpoint if the 'liberal' view of the body politic is assumed, but one wonders whether the aforementioned features of bitcoins may be consistent even with a society inspired by liberal values. Finally, if we complain about the instability of public money, it is worth remembering that since its inception in 2009, the bitcoin value moved to a peak of almost $215 in April 2013, to collapse few days later to $63, to climb to around $1,200 in November, falling again to $923 in January 2014.[90] In April 2015, it stands at $210. Even the gyrations of the most volatile commodity could not be compared to this seesaw. Advocates of crypto-currencies see a general enforceability of their contracts in courts as a useful reform, but it is doubtful that this reform would pass the test of a cost/benefit analysis.

It may sound like a paradox that while the need for increased transparency is stressed as a way to restore confidence in the financial system, a wider role should be sought for crypto-currencies.

Notes

1 I am grateful to Juan Castañeda, John Chown, Oliviero Pesce, Ronnie Phillips and Geoffrey Wood for their comments.
2 This explains the title of the chapter. The twentieth century has been elsewhere defined as the 'short century', in political terms.
3 By seigniorage we mean, in modern terms, the international acceptability of a currency, even when the issuing country is running a balance of payments deficit.
4 For instance, if the gold content of the Italian lira was 290.322 milligrams of fine gold, and if the gold content of the British pound was 7.322382 grams of fine gold (as in the pre-WW1 world), the exchange rate corresponding to the gold parity was 25.2 lire per pound.
5 The outflow actually occurs only when the exchange rate deviates above or below parity by a certain percentage (around 1% or 2%, the 'gold points' that represent the cost of insurance and shipping gold). If the exchange rate remains within the gold points, it is not worthwhile to transfer gold.
6 Grubel (1969: 96–97).
7 Toniolo (2010).
8 Gorton (2012: 22 and 28).
9 If a ratio of, say, 40% must be maintained, a gold reserve of 100 can support a money supply of 250. But a decrease of the gold stock to 90 implies a reduction to 225 of the money supply (25>10).
10 To Thomas Gresham, a sixteenth-century merchant, is due the famous phrase: 'bad money drives out good'.
11 Mill (1920: 507).
12 Fisher (1920: 81–97).
13 Capie and Wood (2012: 267).
14 One lira equalled 4.5 grams of fine silver and 290.322 milligrams of fine gold, and of course, 1 French franc, within the Union (4.5: 0.290322 = 15.5)
15 Schwartz (1987: 397).
16 De Cecco (1990: 10).
17 Ibid. (5–16).
18 Mitchell 1981, Table K3.
19 755 million in 1874, of which 450 million for the Banca nazionale nel Regno, the biggest bank of issue (Pick and Sédillot 1971: 296).
20 Galanti (2012: 31).
21 De Cecco (1990: 32–39).
22 Ibid. (20).
23 Ibid. (44).
24 The policy of support of illiquid but solvent banks advocated by Walter Bagehot. See Capie and Wood 2012: 71.
25 1 pound = 7.322382 grams of fine gold.
26 Harrod (1969: 26–28).
27 Sheppard (1971, Tab. (A) 1.12).

28 Sayers (1957: 9).
29 Ibid., italics added.
30 He was fearful of the German government, in a historical phase that was witnessing the rise of the German power under Bismarck: 'this part of the bankers' balances is at the mercy of the German government when it chooses to apply for it' (Bagehot 1931: 292).
31 Bagehot (chapter XII, in particular, p. 105, and Appendix I).
32 In technical terms, 'Britain enjoyed an exceedingly high interest rate elasticity of private capital flows, so that a slight change in the discount rate was sufficient to alter the balance of payments by significant amounts' (Grubel 1969: 100).
33 For the current account, see Mitchell (1981, table K3); for the foreign investment position, Feinstein (1976, T 110, Table 50). Sayers (1967: 138) observed that the position of Britain as leader of the Industrial Revolution had 'given her an inherently strong balance of payments throughout the period of London's rise as an international financial centre'. However, it is De Cecco's view that in the final decades before the World War I the special position of London was based on a trade surplus with its colonies, having Britain lost its technological edge to the countries of continental Europe and the United States.
34 One dollar was made equal to 1,504.656 milligrams of fine gold.
35 Laughlin (2000: 174–189).
36 Hawtrey (1931: 73).
37 The gold content of 1504.656 milligrams was confirmed, but with a higher fineness. This content remained unchanged until 1933.
38 Capie and Wood (2001).
39 Dowd (1992), Gorton (2012: 11–17).
40 A federal excise tax on notes issued by state-chartered banks made their issue unprofitable.
41 Gorton (2012: 10–25).
42 The devaluation of the gold content of the lira was 72.47 %. The new parity was 79.19 milligrams of fine gold.
43 The franc devaluation in terms of gold was 79.69%. The new parity of the *franc Poincaré* (from the prime minister's name) was 58.95 milligrams of fine gold.
44 Hawtrey 1931: 122–123.
45 35 dollars per ounce (from 20.67), that is one dollar equals 888.6706 milligrams of fine gold.
46 According to his written testimony.
47 The new parity was fixed at 46.77 milligrams of fine gold, equivalent to a devaluation of 40.94%.
48 Goodhart and Tsomocos (2014).
49 The title of a polemic book by Norbert Muhlen (1939).
50 Friedman and Schwartz (1987: 290).
51 Grubel (1969: 135).
52 Toniolo (2010), who quotes Kindleberger.
53 See on this point Grubel (1969: 137).
54 This French policy may remind one of a similar policy adopted by the French against the pound in the interwar period, which led to the pound collapse in 1931 (see *supra*, section on the gold standard collapse).
55 The foreign exchange component of the Bank of Italy's reserve abruptly decreased from 12.5% to 0.2% in just one year (1965). See Banca d'Italia (1993: 555).
56 As a matter of fact, being the official price so below the market price, gold transactions between central banks were frozen.
57 The 'two-tier gold market' was formally abolished only in 1976.
58 Named after the building in Washington where the agreement was signed.
59 The official value of gold remains at 35 SDRs per ounce. No calculation is based on a basket of currencies. For the purposes of calculating the value of gold based on a common standard across all countries, the IMF multiplies the gold volume – in millions of

fine troy ounces – by the London gold price (US dollars in fine troy ounces) and then applies the USD per SDR exchange rate (end of period) to arrive at the value of gold in millions of SDRs (information given to the author by the Statistical Department of the International Monetary Fund).
60 www.gold.org
61 International Monetary Fund (various issues).
62 www.macrotrends.net
63 All data are in US dollars.
64 Carli (1988: 77). Carli was no fan of the gold standard, but in his words, there was a certain yearning for its 'discipline effect'.
65 Ben Bernanke, the former chairman of the Federal Reserve, told at a Congressional hearing on July 13, 2011 that gold is held as 'a protection against tail risks, very bad outcomes'.
66 Steil (2013: 139).
67 Art. IV, Sec. 5.
68 See on this point Goodhart and Tsomocos (2014).
69 Steil (2013).
70 Lipgens (1982: 36).
71 Salmon and Nicoll (1997: 9–10); Lipgens (1982: 41).
72 To be followed by the actual circulation of euro-denominated banknotes in 2002.
73 Friedman (1992).
74 Capie and Wood (2012: 258).
75 Ibid. (257).
76 Goodhart and Tsomocos (2014).
77 Capie and Wood (2012: 269).
78 Financial Action Task Force (FATF) (2014: 4).
79 Capie and Wood (2001).
80 Wray (2014: 2).
81 The first pages of his Treatise contain a most clear description of why 'money is peculiarly a creation of the State'. See Keynes (1965, vol I, chapter 1).
82 Dowd 2014: 3–4.
83 I am using this term in the European way, as a synonym of government (I will use these two terms as interchangeable).
84 Gorton (2012: 28).
85 Virtual currencies of any kind must be distinguished from 'e-money', which is a digital representation of fiat currency used to electronically transfer value denominated in fiat currency.
86 There is a brilliant description of them in Dowd (2014, chapter 4, in particular pp. 38–45). On the supply side, a 'miner' finds bitcoins by solving a number of computational problems, being in fact rewarded with bitcoins he can spend. On the demand side, the bitcoin is acquired by a person if he believes it will be accepted as payment; bitcoins may be accepted only if it has some alternative non-monetary use. This alternative use is stimulated by the anonymity of bitcoin. As explained later, this anonymity is mostly connected to illegal purposes (Dowd 2014: 45).
87 Ibid. (xv).
88 Ibid. (38 and 45).
89 Ibid. (xv).
90 Ibid. (46).

References

Bagehot, W. (1931, first published in 1873). *Lombard Street: A Description of the Money Market*. London: John Murray.

Banca d'Italia (1993). *I Bilanci degli Istituti di Emissione, 1894-1990.* Roma and Bari: Laterza.

Capie, F. and Wood, G. (2001). 'Monetary problems, monetary solutions and the role of gold', World Gold Council Research Study 25. London: Centre for Public Policy studies. https://www.scribd.com/document/67793000/Role-of-Gold (accessed 2017-08-08).

Capie, F. and Wood, G. (2012). *Money Over Two Centuries.* Oxford: Oxford University Press.

Carli, G. (1988). *Pensieri di un ex Governatore.* Pordenone: Studio Tesi.

Carter, S., *et al.* (ed.) (2006). *Historical Statistics of the United States.* New York: Cambridge University Press.

De Cecco, M. (1990). *L'Italia e il sistema finanziario internazionale 1861–1914.* Bari: Laterza.

Delors, J. *et al.* (1989). Report on economic and monetary union in the European Community. Presented April 17, 1989 (commonly called the Delors Report). By Committee for the Study of Economic and Monetary Union. [EU Commission - Working Document] http://aei.pitt.edu/1007/

Dowd, K. (1992). 'US banking in the "free banking period"', in Dowd, K. (ed.), *The Experience of Free Banking*, London: Routledge: 206–240.

Dowd, K. (2014). *New Private Monies. A Bit-Part Player?* London: The Institute of Economic Affairs.

Federal Reserve System (1943). *Banking and Monetary Statistics 1914–1941.* Washington, DC: Board of Governors of the Federal Reserve System.

Feinstein, C. (1976). *Statistical Tables of National Income, Expenditure and Output of the UK 1855–1965.* Cambridge: Cambridge University Press.

Financial Action Task Force-FATF (2014). *Virtual Currencies. Key Definitions and Potential AML/CFT Risks.* Paris: FATF/OECD. http://www.fatf-gafi.org/media/fatf/documents/reports/Virtual-currency-key-definitions-and-potential-aml-cft-risks.pdf (accessed 2017-08-08).

Fisher, I. (1920). *Stabilizing the Dollar. A Plan to Stabilize the General Price Level Without Fixing Individual Prices.* New York, NY: Macmillan.

Friedman, M. (1992). 'Déjà vu in currency markets', *Wall Street Journal*, 22 September 1992.

Friedman, M. and Schwartz, A. (1987). 'Has government any role in money?', in Schwartz, A. (ed.), *Money in Historical Perspective*, Chicago, IL: The University of Chicago Press: 289–314.

Galanti, E. (2012). 'Le banche', in Galanti E., D'Ambrosio R., and Guccione A. (eds.), *Storia della Legislazione Bancaria Finanziaria e Assicurativa. Dall'Unità d'Italia al 2011*, Venezia: Marsilio: 3–13.

Goodhart, C. and Tsomocos, D. (2014). 'International monetary regimes', *Capitalism and Society* 9 (2): Article 2.

Gorton, G. (2012). *Misunderstanding Financial Crises, Why We Don't See Them Coming.* Oxford and New York: Oxford University Press.

Grubel, H. (1969). *The International Monetary System.* London: Penguin Books.

Harrod, R. (1969). *Money.* London: Macmillan.

Hawtrey, R. (1931). *The Gold Standard. Theory and Practice.* London: Longmans, Green and Co.

International Monetary Fund. *International Financial Statistics*, various issues. https://www.imf.org/external/pubs/cat/longres.aspx?sk=20095.0 (accessed 2017-08-08)

Keynes, J. M. (1965, first published 1930). *A Treatise on Money.* London: Macmillan.

Laughlin, J. L. (2000). 'The history of bimetallism in the United States (1886)', in White, L. (ed.), *The History of Gold and Silver*, vol. 3, London: Pickering & Chatto: 174–189.

Lipgens, W. (1982). *A History of European Integration.* Vol I. Oxford: Clarendon Press.

Mill, J.-S. (1920, first published in 1865). *Principles of Political Economy with Some of Their Applications to Social Philosophy*. London: Longmans, Green & Co.

Mitchell, B. (1981). *European Historical Statistics*. London: Macmillan.

Muhlen, N. (1939). *Schacht: Hitler's Magician. The Life and Loans of Dr. Hjalmar Schacht*. New York, NY: Alliance Book Corporation.

Pick, F. and Sédillot, R. (1971). *All the Monies of the World – A Chronicle of Currency Values*. New York, NY: Pick Publishing.

Salmon, T. and Nicoll, W. (1997). *Building European Union. A Documentary History and Analysis*. Manchester: Manchester University Press.

Sayers, R. (1957). 'The development of central banking after Bagehot', in Sayers, R. (ed.), *Central Banking After Bagehot*, London: Oxford University Press: 8–19.

Sayers, R. (1967). *Modern Banking*. Oxford: Oxford University Press.

Schwartz, A. (1987). 'Lessons of the gold standard era', in Schwartz A. (ed.), *Money in Historical Perspective*, Chicago, IL: The University of Chicago Press: 391–406.

Sheppard, D. (1971). *The Growth and Role of UK Financial Institutions, 1880–1962*. London: Methuen & Co.

Steil, B. (2013). *The Battle of Bretton Woods. John Maynard Keynes, Harry Dexter White and the Making of a New World Order*. Princeton, NJ: Princeton University Press.

Toniolo, G. (2010). 'What is a useful central bank? Lessons from the interwar period', paper presented to the Norges Bank Symposium, 'What is a Useful Central Bank?', Oslo, 18 November 2010. http://www.bancaditalia.it/pubblicazioni/altri-atti-seminari/2011/paper_Toniolo.pdf?language_id=1 (accessed 2017-08-08)

Wray, L. (2014). 'From the state theory of money to modern money theory: An alternative to economic orthodoxy', Levy Economic Institute, working paper no. 792.

www.gold.org

www.macrotrends.net

16 Conclusion

In search of trust

Bas van Leeuwen and Bert van der Spek

Introduction

This book discussed the phenomenon of money in an exceptionally long historical context: from the third millennium BC to the present. The question was how money came into being, how it functioned in different societies and economies and how it affected, advertently or inadvertently, the economy. What effects did monetary policies have, which monetary policies were effective, and which weren't? The central topic of this book that touches on each of these questions is 'trust', the basis of the good functioning of any money.

The first important point of discussion is the essence of money; is it a commodity (partly argued in Chapter 2, Flynn) or a form of debt (Chapter 3, Bezemer)? In our view, it is reductionist to opt for one of the two. Money has certainly been in the greater part of history a commodity; in most times and places this was silver. Nevertheless, debt has also been an, increasingly important, aspect of money already from the beginning. For example, debt notes played a role as money since third millennium BC Mesopotamia and even in barter trade a good may function as debt money (cf. Chapter 11, Gelderblom and Jonker). In a way, a piece of gold or silver or a coin can even be viewed as a debt note that can be exchanged for a desired good. Although silver is a nice and desirable luxury product by itself, its practical use, especially in antiquity, is limited, so that the silver itself is not the only element that makes it valuable,[1] but also the fact that it is generally accepted as means of exchange, unit of account and store of value, the features that are usually accepted as characteristic for the phenomenon of money.

It need not be that all these characteristics of money function at the same time. In the third and second millennium BC silver was used as means of exchange, but only on a very limited scale. Much more important was the function of unit of account and store of value.[2] Whatever the case: the role of the state is of overriding importance. Although it is conceivable that a form of money exists without intervention by any state (silver probably started to be used as money before the state intervened and in some periods people could go to the mint with their bullion [see Mayhew, Chapter 9]), in actual practice the state (or some authoritative body like the temple or the tribe) was controlling the use of money (see also Roselli, Chapter 15). In ancient Mesopotamia, the state played an important role by accepting silver as payment of debts and taxes and by establishing the measures and weights of the silver (see also the conversion to a silver tax [single whip reforms] in China, Xu and Van Leeuwen, Chapter 13). It could also mark some silver pieces as especially trustworthy (cf. Michael Jursa in Chapter 5). Alternatively, it could force the population to use a certain money by threat of death such as during the Wang Mang reign (AD 9–23) in China. This role of the state in adding value, in the form of trust, to a coin increased over time to such an extent that Mayhew (Chapter 9) claims coins relate more to fiat money than to bullion.

This role of the state in monetary affairs was expanded with the invention of coinage (as opposed to bullion) in the kingdom of Lydia (the seventh or sixth century BC; the date of the first coins is a matter of controversy). In Lydia, however, the coins were primarily used as a gift and as a means to tie kings and war leaders to their retinue and supporters. The real breakthrough of coins with all functions of money took place in the Greek world when, after silver and gold, bronze coins were introduced which far exceeded their nominal value and thus were really fiat money. It is difficult to know why this especially happened in the Greek world. One reason might be that the Greeks lived in city-states, where coins were used in internal political competition among local leaders followed by the wish of the cities to have a distinctive means of exchange as national pride next to their neighbours ('peer polity interaction'), so that the introduction had a political rather than an economic motive. The Persian empire also introduced coinage, but this was especially done in the former Lydian empire as a sign to replace Lydian with Persian kingship. And the later gold darics and silver *sigloi* were exclusively used in the western part of the empire for the payment of mercenaries. And we see it emerge in the Phoenician cities, which, as a matter of fact, display characteristics in some respects similar to the Greek city-states. In the core of the empire, Persia and Babylonia, coins could not drive out bullion silver. The real introduction of coinage came in the Near East only after the conquest of Alexander (331 BC) and the use of silver bullion then soon died out. Here coinage was simply enforced by the kings (Mooring *et al.*, Chapter 6).

In China, the introduction of coins took a different path. Here we observe the use of copper and bronze coins very early, later supplemented by the issue of paper money representing bronze coins. Arguably they had a more important function in small scale transactions by commoners as also follows from the observation that China, contrary to many other countries, already from a very early stage had high levels of deep monetization (Lucassen, Chapter 4). Under the Yuan dynasty (the Mongol domination, 1271–1368) paper money became temporarily the standard form of money. Due to unrestrained issuing of new money, trust in this form of money was faltering and backing by silver became required, until under the Ming dynasty (1368–1644) physical silver became, to some extent, the new means of exchange, especially after the 1430s when the Ming government accepted silver in trade and payments

(Von Glahn, Chapter 12). Indeed, paper money was abolished and bullion silver (as a store of value and unit of account, to a lesser extent means of exchange) was used up to the twentieth century, while bronze coins stayed in use for daily transactions. The preference for silver, partly supported by the state, boosted the flow of silver, especially after the so-called 'Single Whip reform' of the 1570s, from all over the world (Japan; South America via Europe and Manila) to China in exchange for the export of gold (and other luxury products) from China to Europe (cf. Xu and Van Leeuwen, Chapter 13).

This trade-off between gold and silver is another dominant feature within monetary history. Essentially, many systems are bi- or multimetallic, often consisting of gold and silver. We encounter this phenomenon in many historical periods (see e.g. Chapters 8 [Butcher], 13 [Xu and Van Leeuwen] and 15 [Roselli]). Yet, even though, as argued by Léon Walras, bimetalism is more efficient from a monetary point of view, it remains essentially unstable (Friedman 1990). The reason for this instability is the gold–silver price ratio, which is set by the government. Yet, gold and silver are also commodities with their own market price. So, if the market price of silver decreases in relation to gold, while the government provides a higher ratio, investors will demand gold from the government and dispose of their silver. This means there will be a de facto gold standard as was the case after circa 1850 (Chapter 15, Roselli). If the market silver to gold ratio increases versus that of the government, the reverse effect happens. An indirect, but telling, example is provided by Zuijderduijn (Chapter 10), where city authorities, speculating on continued devaluation of silver coins, kept borrowing in gold coins while repaying in the devaluated silver coin. As soon as the coin in which the interest payments occurred was revaluated, this system collapsed. This also applies in international relations: if silver is more expensive in country A than B, silver will be drained from country B and it will end up on a de facto gold standard. Although this is theoretically clear, in practice it is difficult to predict in which direction a bimetallic system will develop as it depends on a great many, often difficult to distinguish, factors such as demand and supply factors, government behaviour, monetary or real shocks, and even culture (see e.g. Kreitner 2011).

This development of money as a commodity became increasingly sensitive over time with a reduction of the amount of specie when the monetary system moved from a specie standard, to a bullion standard, to Bretton Woods (1944). Bretton Woods is essentially a link between fiat currencies, which are backed by other fiat currencies (e.g. Special Drawing Rights) and linked with gold only via their link with the gold dollar. Today we witness some small backing by the central banks while some crypto currencies like the bitcoin have no backing at all, other than that of the 'market'.

This development of money, more importantly the commodity of money, indicates a clear decline of backing by value in favour of backing by trust in the government (see e.g. Mayhew, Chapter 9) or market. Besides this increase in the importance of trust in the basic function of money, it also signals an increasing task in using the stock of money in maintaining a stable economy and combatting economic crisis, tasks which also require a great deal of trust. Available instruments are the creation or the contraction of money, by means of the issuing (or withdrawing) of money (silver bullion, coins), by debasements, by issuing paper money and by creating debt (notes) and ledgers, or by introducing instruments like 'ghost money' to facilitate payments across different currencies (Gelderblom and Jonker, Chapter 11). In all cases the maintenance of trust is essential in any policy and to achieve these efficient institutions (governments, banks, legal institutions, financial instruments) is essential. No policy can work out of the blue. A well-functioning real productive economy is basic. Hence, in the following three sections we deal with each of the three aspects of the use of money, i.e. the rise and complexity of institutions, trust, and monetary policy.

The rise and complexity of monetary institutions

Money has exhibited various forms since the beginning of historical times. As said before, in many cases precious metals provided the money specie. Yet, in the course of time we observe changing roles of the precious metals in use. At first intrinsic value and nominal value were equal, though once a type of precious metal was accepted as money, the value of the metal increased, and in this respect even highly pure metal is in essence fiat money. Trust in this form is not only based on the intrinsic value, but also on the fact that the specie in question was accepted as money. But intrinsic value was somehow basic and hence the silver (or other metal) was weighed and if possible tested for purity. But, of course, certain developments made the step to fiat money clearer. First, the silver could be debased (although this did not happen on a grand scale before the invention of coinage). The invention of coinage in itself was a step in the direction of fiat money. Instead of weighing the money, counting of coins became the rule (though still the weight of the coins played an important role) (cf. Mooring *et al.*, Chapter 6). Coins, however, are more susceptible to manipulation. Coins were debased almost at all times, new metals were introduced, like bronze of which the intrinsic value soon after introduction played no role anymore. Although silver was often the main money specie, gold was always present in the background, and in some periods prominent as in the Kassite period in Babylonia (Late Bronze Age) (Kleber in Chapter 5) and the Later Roman empire. Gold also played a major role as standard for other currencies. In the Roman Empire, an *aureus* stood for four silver *denarii* and the *aureus* remained of higher quality, while the *denarius* was debased (Butcher, Chapter 8), as if the gold *aureus* was an anchor for the debased silver *denarii*, much in the same vein as when in modern times the gold standard was introduced as anchor of the currency (central banks) and the gold dollar (agreement of Bretton Woods). But even after the abolishment of the Bretton Woods agreement in 1971, gold (and to a lesser degree silver) remained important as investors invest in gold and silver in times of insecure economic conditions with weak currencies.

This relative reduction in specie was accompanied by an expansion of non-specie types of money. Debt notes were used as means of payment and exchange from the beginning of writing in Mesopotamia. Over time, also ledgers of merchants together with various other instruments came into existence. Since these are in essence debt for those issuing them, they can be considered debt-type monies. Later in the eighteenth century, banks of issue came up, followed by deposit banks in the nineteenth and twentieth centuries thus significantly enhancing the potential for debt-based money creation.

The debate as to whether money is a good or a debt comes back in the chapters by both Flynn (Chapter 2) and Bezemer (Chapter 3). Yet, no matter who is right, monetary systems arose to facilitate the three functions of money, i.e. means of exchange, store of value, and unit of account. It is not necessary that money exercises all three functions simultaneously. This was clear already in history when bullion was converted into coins. Initially functioning as store of wealth and money of account, the means of payment function was less important. It is in a way ironic that it was exactly those functions (store of wealth and money of account) that were the first to suffer when the monetary institutions deteriorated. For example, moderate inflation already erodes the store of wealth function, while slightly stronger inflation affects money of account function and, eventually, lack of trust will also remove the means of exchange function (Eitrheim *et al.* 2016: 6).

This inflation was exactly the elephant in the room throughout monetary history. Following on from debasement, implementation of bank notes or deposits, the risk of inflation increased. Simplifying, one might argue that up to the eighteenth century coins were dominating with private credit supplied by merchants, e.g. ledgers. In the eighteenth century, banks of issue issued money (especially banknotes) without much state control. In the nineteenth century, it became rule-based (that is, there was no uncontrolled expansion of the money stock anymore) and issuing banks became eventually what are now the national banks. After roughly World War II, deposit banks took over (leading to deposit money creation). This is also pointed out by Edvinsson and Ögren (2014) for Sweden; they find that up to circa 1730 coins made up roughly 100% of total M0 (cash plus deposits). After 1730, it dropped to 30% with 70% being covered by banknotes. Again, a third transition occurred in 1880 when coins became negligible, and notes made up circa 10%, with the remaining 90% being covered by bank deposits.

This reduction of the intrinsic value of money was based primarily on the belief that money was stabilized. Currency stabilization moved from controlling coins and ledgers before the eighteenth century, to trying to control first phase issuing banks in the eighteenth century. Control was further enhanced with the shift to second generation rule-based banks of issue in the nineteenth century. This period also marks the rise of internationalization, which allowed a more deposit bank type of lending, while rules were maintained.

The way of stabilization of these monetary systems varied over time. Before working capital markets, applying a monetary policy of maintaining constant exchange rates was indeed all a government could really do. No rule-based expansion of issuing existed. This changed in the nineteenth and twentieth centuries when the government got a stronger hand again in controlling the national banks and, indirectly, lending via deposit banks. Yet, with increasing international integration, national monetary policies became increasingly limited by international connections, since borrowing could also occur outside one's own country. Hence the coming into existence of the famous trilemma (or Impossible Trinity) in monetary economics, i.e. an expansion of the closed (autarkic) IS-LM model, as outlined in the next section, with open borders governed by exchange rates (Fleming 1962; Mundell 1963). The main consequence of this opening of international trade and capital is that the government can only manipulate two out of three functions of money (foreign exchange rate, interest rate on capital, and monetary expansion). So, there are three options:

1 A stable exchange rate and capital controls, but not an independent monetary policy.
2 An independent monetary policy and capital controls, but a floating exchange rate.
3 Stable exchange rate and a monetary policy, but no free movement of capital.

Whereas the initial aim of international monetary relations was to obtain money via exchange rate and liberated capital flows (i.e. advancement of monetary trade), monetary expansion was not one of them. Indeed, in the nineteenth century, governments in principle used rule-based monetary expansion. Yet, as argued by Bordo and Kydland (1995), during wars it became possible to temporarily halt the rules. Most efficiently this was done for tax smoothing, such as for Britain during the Napoleonic wars. Yet, basically up to the end of Bretton Woods in 1971, rule-based policies remained.

Today, with increasing possibility to circumvent capital controls, basically countries must choose between monetary stabilization policy or reducing currency volatility. The last one is chosen by the European Union (EU) (see e.g. Roselli, Chapter 15). Indeed, because of weak policy integration, all the EU can really do is transfer money from rich to poor countries, something that has also occurred in countries like China and the United States over the past centuries. This seems to be relatively efficient when looking at the coin diffusion within the Eurozone, which, 15 years after its introduction, is based on each country's share in total Euro coinage (see Appendix 2 for the case of the Netherlands). This limits monetary policy, but has the advantage of forcing countries to make structural changes to their economies in times of crisis.

In search of trust

Besides the increasing complexity of financial instruments, a second factor important for maintaining a monetary system is trust, i.e. the confidence that money fulfils its function. Early moneys such as coins could be clipped. It has even been argued this was already happening in the sixth century BC since electrum coins seemingly had a lower percentage of gold than the electrum naturally found in that region (Mooring *et al.*, Chapter 6, and Van Leeuwen *et al.*, Chapter 7). Later, bills of exchange and merchant's ledgers were prone to over-issuing.

This changed in the nineteenth century when, first, issuing of notes became based on rules and made it possible to be paid out in gold or silver. In the interwar period, even though the gold standard broke down, it was nevertheless replaced by Bretton Woods (1944), which was a de facto gold standard until the United States cancelled its convertibility in 1971. Second, money became internationalized (convertible) meaning that debasement and over-issue now had international effects (Eitrheim *et al.*, 2016: 9). Basically, before internationalization, banks could lend based solely on their deposits. With expanding international relations money could be lent based on international money flows.

Obviously, the cancelling of the convertibility, in either the interwar period or, later again in 1971, plus the rise of deposit banking, changed the trust issue. Now not only do people need to trust monetary authorities, fiat money, and national issue banks, but they also need to trust conventional banks, which borrow their money from other persons and then lend it back to the public while at the same time enlarging the money stock.

Monetary policy

The increasing complexity required more trust. But the question is now how these monetary institutions and arrangements affect monetary regimes, that is how the central monetary authority controls the money supply to achieve a target. That target can be multifold. There is no shortage of examples of kings clipping money for their own gain. But in many cases the benefit for the wider population was also kept in mind. That, in this latter case, these targets can be very wide is proven by e.g. the Reserve Bank Act 1959 of Australia, which defines as targets the stability of the currency, maintenance of full employment, economic welfare, and prosperity. That is, the targets relate to both the monetary and real economy. Depending on economic theory, this implies more practical targets such as control on consumer prices.

There are various ways a government may control the money stock. This varies very much depending on one's theoretical background as already pointed out in the introduction to this volume. There is no way we can describe the government control for all various theories, so instead we briefly say a word about the basic IS-LM model. Created by Hicks in the 1930s based on Keynes's theory, this model in fact is an eclectic system that fits (or not) in all theories. The Investment Saving (IS) curve represents the combination of interest rate and GDP, where a lower interest rate implies higher investment and, hence, higher GDP, i.e. the IS curve is downward sloping. The Liquidity preference – Money supply (LM) curve represents a set of combinations of interest rate and GDP, where money supply and demand matches. Where the IS and LM curves intersect, the goods and money market are in balance. In theory, in case of a fiscal policy, a rise in government spending (keeping the interest rate constant), will push the IS curve to the right, i.e. increase GDP. This, in turn, must lead to a higher interest rate to keep the monetary economy in balance (but for an opposite point of view see Flynn, Chapter 2). The same is true for monetary policy, where a rise in the supply of money shifts the LM curve outwards, leading to higher GDP and lower interest rates.

Yet, most economists agree that, even though fiscal policy works in raising GDP, monetary expansion raises wages and prices thus leading the LM curve back to its original position, i.e. monetary policy is neutral in the long-run. The problem though is how far the curve goes back. In addition, in extreme economic circumstances, monetary policy is also not nullified, e.g. if an economy is far below its production frontier with many unemployed, increasing the money stock is not leading to inflation (see e.g. Castañeda, Chapter 14).

As pointed out earlier, investments in the real economy can take place in all societies. Yet, in ancient societies, no real capital market existed, which affected the IS-LM model. Obviously, loans were made, but interest rates were often fixed by tradition and hardly fluctuated based on money in circulation like they do in modern economies. So, any investment may not be undone by lowering saving rates and higher consumption. Therefore, if money entered private society, everything depended on the propensity to save, which was most likely low, i.e. in ancient societies investment in private society is not likely to be undone by the LM curve shifting back. Yet, rather than the state using money to invest in private society, it was more likely that, when the state gained a windfall income in silver, deliberately or not it could start a productive investment in e.g. infrastructure which might raise the investment of the people.

However, four things need to be kept in mind. First, essentially this is just public investment, which can be done in any way (also via fiscal policy, not just monetary expansion), even before the existence of a money economy with e.g. slave labour. So, an increase in the stock of money is not a prerequisite. Indeed, as pointed out in Figure 16.1, government investments may, even today, increase economic growth. Second, it all depends on the type of economy. In low level Malthusian-type economies, economic growth will only lead to increased population numbers which will reduce productivity again (Malthus 1798; but for an opposite view, see Boserup 1965, who argues that population growth stirs investments and improved technology). Third, we have to make clear what we mean by "growth". Certainly, in recent years, in the GDP and Beyond scheme, emphasis has been placed on additional aspects of development besides traditional economic growth, e.g. equality and environmental sustainability. Fourth, if you generate higher productivity via increased money creation, that part that does not generate growth will be destroyed by inflation.

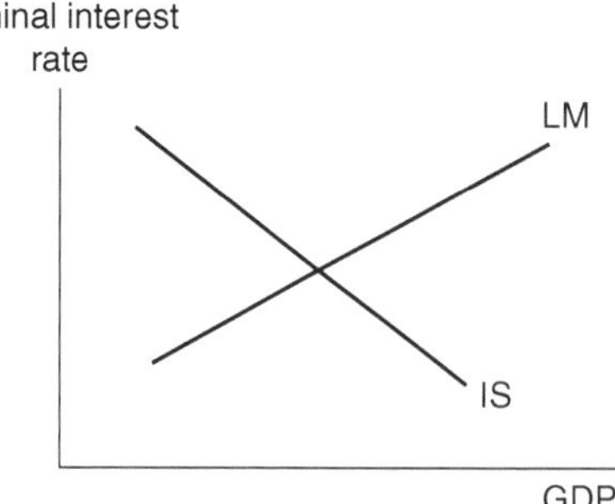

Figure 16.1 Schematic depiction of the real and money markets nominal interest.

If this concerns 100% of the increase in the stock of money, money is neutral in the long run.

The crucial question we return to is again, in case of monetary expansion, how far the LM curve will move backwards over time, i.e. is money indeed completely neutral? That remains to be seen as complete breakdowns in money are rare as they are in nobody's interest (also not in the public interest). A scarce example is Zimbabwe, where the payment of school fees in goats and other items has recently been allowed. Yet, in practice, as pointed out earlier, it is mostly the store of value function that is hurt first, followed by the unit of account function and, finally, means of exchange. It needs, after all, no explanation that countries like Hungary after World War II or Yugoslavia, which knew hyperinflation, still used that money as means of exchange and, to some extent, even as unit of account. It is thus the store of value function that gets hit first and most easily if people expect the value of money to go down and, hence, their accumulated wealth to decline. In practice, this means that protecting past wealth becomes more important than creating new investments in the economy, but this is unlikely to cancel the complete effect of a monetary expansion.

Since, as pointed out in the introduction to this volume, various economic theories have different predictions about the impact of monetary shocks, there really is no way to know for sure other than using empirical analyses. This is true, even though the majority of theories predict no long-run effect (and some even no short-run effect). In general, empirical studies also did not find major effects of monetary indicators on real output (see e.g. Rasche 1998: 88). Yet, Nelson and Plosser (1982) did find a small effect for the United States and so do King *et al.* (1991). Some similar conclusion is reached by Castañeda (Chapter 14) for 1930s Spain, which used monetary policy to partly escape the global economic crisis.

Yet, even though economic growth driven by monetary expansion is possible in principle, it still is subject to various conditions. First, as pointed out earlier, there must be various ways in which the LM curve can be prevented from shifting back to its original position. This can happen if the real economy still has room for expansion, e.g. there must be unemployment and underproduction. Second, as pointed out in e.g. Chapters 14 and 15 by Castañeda and Roselli, the investment needs to be productive and not harm long-run structural changes in the economy.

Especially this last condition makes an expansion of the real economy by means of monetary enlargement difficult since you never know if an investment is good in the long run. One example is provided for 1930s Spain in Chapter 14. Another example is Minitel, a government sponsored French videotext type of service introduced in 1982 that allowed users to send messages, but also place post orders and book train tickets. In 1999, 25 million French people had access to a minitel device. Yet, with the rise of the internet its uses declined until it was abolished in 2012. So, even though deemed profitable at its introduction in 1982, the fast development of the internet made it not only quickly obsolete, but it even hampered the introduction of the internet.

Conclusion

Money fulfils a crucial role in economic development. But over time, it not only got increasingly detached from its intrinsic value, it also got increasingly governed by complex institutions. The initial instruments, such as ledgers, were in the nineteenth century changed to rule-based banks, which would later become the central banks. Yet, this only solved half of the problem since capital could, at this time, also be obtained from abroad, which was less easily controlled by the government. These developments led on the one hand to increasing demand for monetary policy and, on the other hand, to a limit to the extent to which the government could intervene (the Impossible Trilemma).

Given all this uncertainty, why are monetary systems so persistent, i.e. stable? Partly, it is self-interest as nobody benefits from a collapse of the system. Hence, we would like to believe (that is, trust) that these systems are reliable. Indeed, trust appears to be the backbone of any currency in any period in history. We recognize three pillars of trust: intrinsic value, guarantees by the state (preferably of course a strong state), and a well-functioning real economy.

The intrinsic value is all too clear: higher intrinsic value requires less trust. But guarantees by the state are less clear. Obviously, as pointed out by Roselli (Chapter 15), a state may guarantee a coin. He even goes so far as to postulate that backing of the state is part of the definition of 'money'. Yet, also the market may guarantee such a coin such as is the case for e.g. the bitcoin. It is still difficult to assess what the role of the bitcoin will be. A temporary bubble or a real alternative for the present bank- and state-based currencies and credits? Whatever the case, the fact that the number of bitcoins is limited is not helpful for being a worthy instrument of monetary policy. The third pillar, a strong real economy, is also clear as it predicts that monetary expansion must occur or the value of coin increases, lending more trust to the monetary system.

We further considered the question of how monetary policy can be used for generating economic growth. Although neutrality of money is the dominant view, as pointed out, under certain conditions (unemployment and underproduction as well as investment that is beneficial to long-run structural economic changes), monetary change may have an effect on the real economy. Indeed, the real economy can be influenced by monetary actions (inadvertent or not) of the state, for good and for bad. Investments, often accompanied by the creation of money (through *productive* debts, through a *prudent* and *controlled* issue of extra currency or money specie), may further growth. But not all investments are beneficial to the same extent. If invested incorrectly, it may just as well damage long-run growth. It should also be kept in mind that governments often invest, without knowing exactly what they do, or do it for another reason than the advancement of prosperity. The Romans built roads for the armies, but the concomitant benefit for trade was a by-effect. All in all, monetary policy will remain a very sensitive topic that requires a lot of strategy and foresight to be properly implemented.

In sum, in this book we have studied the history of money in comparative perspective over four millennia and very different parts of the world. This should make us wary of making rash conclusions. We should always take the limits of comparison in mind. To take an example, China found a completely different path to money and coinage than the Near East, the Graeco-Roman world, and Europe. They differed very strongly as to the role of silver. After the 1430s, when the Chinese government decided to accept silver for trade and tax payments, comparison is much easier, and as a matter of fact it eased globalization. The fact that both China and the rest of the world after the 1430s, and even more after the 1570s, relied on silver facilitated global trade in all kind of goods, including gold and silver. In the nineteenth century and the early twentieth century, gold became more important, not as means of exchange, but as an anchor in various monetary systems, until finally this also fell down in step with Bretton Woods (1944) and the abandonment of it (1971). Today gold is only used as a kind of reserve for times of need in the vaults of national banks. This falling down of the silver standard and later the gold standard are expressions of the shocks in the rise of the modern economy after the industrial revolution. The accompanying shocks induced shocks in monetary spheres. The present rise of the bitcoin may also be a mark of growing uncertainty about the tenability of the modern monetary economy in view of the expanding technology. After all, the rising internationalization, combined with new communication technologies may lead to fewer government options to control the monetary economy, as is, for example, already the case in the EU, thus implying that additional sources of trust need to be found.

Notes

1 This can also be observed in the case of gold: as today the supply of gold is larger than that of silver, and since silver has more industrial applications, it is remarkable that gold is still more expensive than silver.

2 Flynn (Chapter 2) adds three more functions to the traditional three: standard of value, link money, and measure of relative values and prefers to speak of 'moneys' rather than 'money', as not all functions are applicable at the same time.

References

Bordo, Michael D. and Kydland, F. E. (1995). 'The gold standard as a rule: An essay in exploration', *Explorations in Economic History*, 32: 423–464.

Boserup, E. (1965). *The Conditions of Agricultural Growth: The Economics of Agrarian Change under Population Pressure*. London: George Allen & Unwin LTD.

Edvinsson, R. and Ögren, A. (2014). 'Swedish money supply, 1620–2012', in Edvinsson, R., Jacobson, T. and Waldenström, D. (eds.), *Historical Monetary and Financial Statistics for Sweden*, Volume II: *House Prices, Stock Returns, National Accounts, and the Riksbank Balance Sheet, 1620–2012*), Stockholm: Sveriges Riksbank and Ekerlids: 293–338.

Eitrheim, Ø., Klovland, J. T. and Øksendal, L. F. (2016). *A Monetary History of Norway, 1816–2016*. Cambridge: Cambridge University Press.

Fleming, J. (1962). 'Domestic financial policies under fixed and floating exchange rates', *IMF Staff Papers*, 9: 369–379.

Friedman, M. (1990). 'Bimetallism revisited', *Journal of Economic Perspectives*, 4: 85–104.

King, R. G., Plosser, C. I., Stock, J. H. and Watson, M. W. (1991). 'Stochastic trends and economic fluctuations', *American Economic Review*, 81: 819–40.

Kreitner, R. (2011). 'Money in the 1890s: the circulation of politics, economics, and law', *UC Irvine Law Review*, 1 (3): 975–1013.

Malthus, Th. (1798). *An Essay on the Principle of Population as It Affects the Future Improvement of Society, with Remarks on the Speculations of Mr. Goodwin, M. Condorcet and Other Writers* (1 ed.). London: J. Johnson in St Paul's Church-yard.

Mundell, R. (1963). 'Capital mobility and stabilization policy under fixed and flexible exchange rates', *Canadian Journal of Economic and Political Science*, 29 (4): 475–485.

Nelson, C. R. and Plosser, C. I. (1982). 'Trends and random walks in macroeconomic time series: Some evidence and implications', *Journal of Monetary Economics*, 10: 139–162.

Rasche, R. H. (1998). 'Money and real output', in Wood, G. (ed.), *Money, Prices and the Real Economy*, Cheltenham: Edward Elgar: 82–92.

Appendix 1 Cumulative coinage (million coins) in the Euro zone in December of each year

	The Netherlands	*Germany*	*Belgium*	*France*	*Spain*	*Italy*	*Finland*	*Austria*	*Ireland*	*Greece*	*Luxembourg*	*Portugal*	*other countries*
2015	4,259	36,638	4,377	20,089	20,314	15,676	1,603	6,933	4,798	3,281	791	2,858	2,345
2014	4,201	35,448	4,305	19,381	19,599	15,339	1,579	6,595	4,768	3,212	761	2,747	2,107
2013	4,064	34,441	4,275	18,563	19,204	14,846	1,573	6,155	4,709	3,092	703	2,695	1,903
2012	4,064	33,524	4,149	17,757	18,718	14,448	1,569	6,055	4,601	3,012	659	2,696	1,865
2011	4,055	31,993	3,974	16,856	18,122	13,935	1,537	5,600	4,518	2,903	620	2,595	1,781
2010	4,029	30,644	3,802	15,940	17,451	13,319	1,515	5,164	4,435	2,823	591	2,511	1,617
2009	3,983	29,315	3,645	14,939	16,715	12,596	1,498	4,753	4,316	2,698	546	2,432	1,571
2008	3,942	27,976	3,540	13,739	15,843	12,076	1,484	4,349	4,003	2,518	521	2,236	1,423
2007	3,872	26,359	3,402	12,448	14,654	11,320	1,459	3,924	3,668	2,296	466	2,081	842
2006	3,786	24,744	3,265	11,645	13,575	10,717	1,426	3,488	3,315	2,080	422	1,934	327
2005	3,725	23,379	3,136	10,826	12,180	9,994	1,396	3,212	3,044	1,883	391	1,840	0
2004	3,642	21,509	2,902	10,260	10,607	9,418	1,341	2,888	2,734	1,788	345	1,712	0
2003	3,391	19,480	2,453	9,500	9,179	9,145	1,308	2,465	2,167	1,667	242	1,572	0
2002	3,121	18,187	2,189	8,898	8,191	8,910	1,254	2,122	1,587	1,603	183	1,523	0

Source: Unpublished communication to the European Commission by the member states.

Note: The Eurozone has expanded after 2002 thus increasing the number of countries. New countries include Slovenia (1 January 2007), Cyprus and Malta (1 January 2008), Slovakia (1 January 2009), Estonia (1 January 2011), Andorra (1 July 2011), Latvia (1 January 2014), and Lithuania (1 January 2015).

Appendix 2 Share of coins in the Netherlands by country of origin from January 2002 to July 2017

year	*Month*	*The Netherlands*	*Germany*	*Belgium*	*France*	*Spain*	*Italy*	*Finland*	*Austria*	*Ireland*	*Greece*	*Luxembourg*	*Portugal*	*Other countries*
2017	July	20.1%	35.4%	7.9%	11.0%	10.4%	6.1%	0.6%	0.6%	1.8%	3.0%	1.2%	1.8%	0.0%
2017	June	22.8%	31.6%	8.8%	15.4%	6.6%	5.3%	0.9%	3.5%	0.4%	1.3%	0.0%	1.8%	1.8%
2017	May	18.8%	33.0%	11.2%	11.2%	9.6%	5.6%	1.5%	3.6%	3.0%	0.0%	0.5%	1.0%	1.0%
2017	April	16.2%	37.6%	7.3%	7.7%	9.8%	7.7%	1.3%	4.7%	1.3%	1.7%	0.9%	3.4%	0.4%
2017	March	18.2%	37.2%	14.2%	9.5%	6.1%	8.8%	0.0%	3.4%	0.7%	0.0%	0.7%	1.4%	0.0%
2017	February	18.7%	36.8%	12.3%	7.6%	7.0%	9.4%	1.2%	4.1%	0.6%	0.0%	1.2%	1.2%	0.0%
2017	January	19.1%	28.8%	11.6%	10.7%	11.2%	7.4%	0.5%	2.8%	1.4%	3.3%	1.4%	0.9%	0.9%
2016	December	16.7%	33.8%	14.6%	10.6%	4.5%	8.1%	1.5%	3.0%	1.0%	1.0%	1.5%	1.0%	2.5%
2016	November	19.0%	27.5%	9.5%	11.5%	8.5%	10.0%	2.0%	5.5%	0.5%	2.5%	1.0%	1.0%	1.5%
2016	October	14.5%	27.5%	12.2%	10.7%	12.2%	9.9%	3.4%	3.8%	1.1%	1.5%	1.1%	1.9%	0.0%
2016	September	17.1%	29.5%	9.8%	12.6%	10.1%	9.8%	0.6%	4.8%	2.5%	0.8%	0.3%	0.8%	1.1%
2016	August	20.7%	24.2%	13.2%	13.7%	7.0%	9.3%	1.3%	4.8%	1.8%	2.6%	0.0%	0.9%	0.4%
2016	July	24.0%	27.5%	12.7%	12.4%	8.4%	4.9%	2.9%	2.6%	0.3%	0.3%	1.7%	1.7%	0.6%
2016	June	21.2%	33.2%	12.0%	8.5%	7.0%	6.0%	1.3%	3.2%	2.2%	1.3%	0.9%	0.9%	2.2%
2016	May	20.3%	27.5%	14.2%	12.3%	7.3%	6.0%	0.9%	3.8%	0.9%	1.6%	1.9%	2.5%	0.6%
2016	April	20.6%	27.6%	11.1%	9.5%	10.5%	7.9%	2.9%	2.2%	2.5%	2.2%	0.3%	1.0%	1.6%
2016	March	17.2%	33.2%	11.1%	11.1%	6.9%	6.9%	2.7%	5.0%	1.1%	1.1%	0.8%	1.1%	1.9%
2016	February	23.7%	25.6%	16.2%	7.9%	7.1%	7.5%	1.5%	3.4%	0.8%	1.9%	1.9%	1.9%	0.8%
2016	January	18.2%	31.6%	10.7%	8.6%	11.7%	7.6%	1.7%	3.1%	1.0%	1.7%	2.1%	1.7%	0.3%
2015	December	20.0%	33.9%	11.4%	8.8%	9.3%	6.5%	1.2%	3.9%	1.2%	1.2%	0.7%	1.4%	0.7%
2015	November	18.2%	31.2%	12.3%	14.8%	8.4%	5.9%	0.5%	4.1%	1.3%	0.8%	1.0%	0.8%	0.8%
2015	October	16.3%	31.0%	12.3%	10.9%	10.5%	8.3%	1.6%	2.9%	0.4%	0.9%	0.9%	2.9%	1.1%
2015	September	15.1%	31.2%	15.1%	10.7%	8.7%	8.7%	2.4%	3.3%	0.9%	1.1%	0.4%	1.6%	0.7%

(*continued*)

year	Month	The Netherlands	Germany	Belgium	France	Spain	Italy	Finland	Austria	Ireland	Greece	Luxembourg	Portugal	Other countries
2015	August	17.0%	27.0%	12.7%	14.6%	10.2%	6.7%	1.6%	3.0%	2.2%	1.3%	1.1%	1.9%	0.8%
2015	July	15.1%	26.3%	15.1%	13.1%	10.2%	7.1%	2.2%	4.9%	1.2%	2.4%	0.4%	1.4%	0.4%
2015	June	17.9%	28.0%	12.0%	13.1%	9.8%	6.8%	0.4%	3.9%	1.3%	1.3%	2.4%	2.0%	0.9%
2015	May	17.8%	30.2%	15.7%	10.7%	8.0%	5.9%	1.1%	4.3%	0.4%	0.7%	2.0%	2.8%	0.4%
2015	April	21.8%	26.7%	13.0%	8.6%	10.0%	7.8%	1.7%	4.4%	0.5%	1.0%	1.7%	2.0%	0.7%
2015	March	21.7%	27.7%	10.6%	12.5%	10.4%	7.0%	1.4%	2.9%	1.7%	1.9%	1.0%	0.7%	0.5%
2015	February	23.9%	29.4%	12.3%	9.3%	7.0%	6.8%	2.0%	2.9%	1.1%	1.4%	1.1%	2.0%	1.1%
2015	January	25.5%	27.7%	9.4%	10.6%	8.2%	7.2%	2.8%	3.0%	0.8%	1.8%	1.6%	1.2%	0.4%
2014	December	23.8%	26.7%	13.2%	11.4%	7.9%	5.9%	2.4%	2.7%	1.0%	1.3%	1.3%	1.6%	0.9%
2014	November	18.1%	31.0%	13.5%	10.2%	9.5%	5.8%	2.4%	3.8%	0.7%	1.3%	1.0%	1.7%	1.0%
2014	October	21.2%	25.8%	14.5%	9.1%	11.7%	5.5%	2.4%	2.6%	1.5%	1.3%	1.3%	2.4%	0.8%
2014	September	20.7%	29.5%	12.9%	11.2%	8.1%	5.3%	2.8%	3.0%	1.7%	1.3%	1.4%	1.4%	0.7%
2014	August	20.9%	27.6%	15.5%	11.7%	6.9%	6.3%	1.7%	3.9%	1.2%	0.9%	1.5%	1.4%	0.5%
2014	July	20.6%	27.4%	11.8%	10.7%	8.3%	7.3%	3.8%	2.8%	2.3%	1.7%	1.3%	1.4%	0.7%
2014	June	20.4%	30.0%	13.5%	11.2%	7.6%	5.9%	2.4%	2.5%	1.4%	1.8%	0.9%	1.8%	0.7%
2014	May	22.1%	25.9%	13.8%	10.9%	7.5%	6.6%	4.1%	2.6%	1.3%	1.5%	1.5%	1.1%	1.1%
2014	April	20.5%	27.0%	14.1%	11.9%	8.9%	5.4%	3.5%	3.1%	1.1%	1.3%	1.2%	1.3%	0.8%
2014	March	21.0%	27.3%	12.7%	11.2%	8.6%	5.7%	3.5%	3.2%	2.0%	0.8%	1.6%	1.6%	0.9%
2014	February	20.6%	26.8%	12.0%	11.7%	8.1%	7.0%	3.7%	3.7%	1.5%	1.8%	1.2%	1.1%	1.0%
2014	January	19.0%	28.3%	13.2%	10.4%	8.9%	6.3%	5.0%	2.9%	1.5%	1.4%	1.2%	1.0%	0.7%
2013	December	18.4%	25.3%	14.3%	10.6%	9.7%	5.5%	5.2%	3.1%	2.9%	1.6%	1.4%	1.3%	1.0%
2013	November	18.3%	26.0%	13.8%	9.7%	10.4%	6.9%	3.5%	3.7%	3.5%	1.1%	0.9%	1.5%	0.8%
2013	October	15.7%	32.3%	14.6%	10.4%	8.1%	7.4%	2.6%	3.8%	1.4%	1.1%	1.1%	1.1%	0.4%
2013	September	18.2%	28.1%	13.9%	12.4%	8.1%	6.6%	3.3%	3.3%	1.0%	1.2%	1.0%	1.6%	1.2%
2013	August	22.1%	30.8%	11.1%	10.6%	7.9%	5.9%	2.9%	3.6%	2.2%	0.6%	0.7%	1.1%	0.6%
2013	July	18.2%	28.8%	14.3%	12.6%	7.6%	6.8%	2.6%	3.0%	1.1%	1.4%	1.1%	1.6%	0.7%

2013	June	19.9%	27.8%	12.4%	10.5%	9.1%	7.1%	2.9%	2.9%	1.3%	2.0%	1.5%	1.3%	1.3%
2013	May	22.3%	27.1%	12.7%	11.8%	7.7%	6.1%	2.8%	2.9%	1.3%	1.5%	1.4%	1.5%	0.9%
2013	April	20.3%	26.5%	14.5%	11.8%	8.0%	6.0%	3.6%	3.3%	1.3%	1.2%	1.2%	1.5%	1.0%
2013	March	19.9%	27.6%	13.5%	11.2%	8.0%	5.7%	3.4%	3.8%	1.4%	1.6%	1.4%	1.4%	1.3%
2013	February	21.9%	28.5%	14.4%	10.5%	8.3%	5.6%	2.4%	3.5%	1.2%	1.2%	0.8%	1.3%	0.6%
2013	January	18.7%	28.1%	13.7%	11.4%	7.4%	6.6%	2.9%	3.7%	1.6%	1.8%	1.5%	1.7%	1.1%
2012	December	19.3%	30.0%	14.4%	11.2%	8.2%	6.2%	2.1%	3.0%	1.5%	1.5%	1.1%	1.0%	0.5%
2012	November	18.7%	29.5%	13.5%	11.2%	8.6%	5.7%	2.6%	3.4%	1.5%	1.2%	1.1%	1.8%	1.0%
2012	October	20.5%	25.4%	13.7%	12.0%	8.1%	6.3%	3.4%	2.9%	1.0%	1.1%	1.4%	1.5%	2.8%
2012	September	20.5%	27.2%	12.9%	9.9%	8.5%	5.1%	4.0%	3.6%	0.9%	1.3%	1.3%	1.4%	3.4%
2012	August	19.3%	26.9%	14.9%	10.7%	7.4%	6.4%	3.7%	3.6%	1.2%	1.6%	2.1%	1.1%	1.1%
2012	July	21.1%	28.6%	14.0%	10.0%	7.4%	6.1%	3.1%	3.6%	1.5%	1.3%	1.4%	1.0%	0.9%
2012	June	20.4%	27.0%	13.7%	11.0%	7.6%	6.0%	4.0%	3.1%	1.3%	2.1%	1.5%	1.2%	1.1%
2012	May	22.1%	26.1%	15.0%	11.1%	7.6%	5.9%	2.5%	3.5%	1.1%	1.5%	1.2%	1.5%	1.0%
2012	April	22.4%	28.5%	13.7%	10.6%	7.3%	6.2%	1.6%	3.0%	1.1%	1.4%	1.3%	1.7%	1.2%
2012	March	21.3%	28.5%	16.2%	11.6%	7.5%	5.6%	1.4%	2.7%	1.0%	1.1%	1.1%	1.4%	0.6%
2012	February	21.7%	27.4%	14.7%	10.6%	8.0%	6.1%	2.1%	2.9%	1.4%	1.3%	1.3%	1.5%	0.9%
2012	January	24.5%	26.3%	14.3%	10.1%	7.0%	5.3%	2.6%	2.9%	1.3%	1.4%	1.1%	1.2%	2.1%
2011	December	24.6%	26.3%	14.4%	10.0%	7.2%	5.8%	2.0%	2.8%	1.4%	1.3%	1.0%	2.0%	1.2%
2011	November	25.9%	25.9%	13.2%	10.2%	7.8%	5.0%	1.7%	3.0%	2.2%	1.9%	1.0%	1.3%	0.9%
2011	October	23.1%	25.3%	13.4%	10.3%	7.9%	6.4%	2.3%	3.2%	1.1%	1.4%	1.3%	1.2%	3.2%
2011	September	24.1%	26.0%	15.5%	10.8%	7.6%	6.4%	1.7%	2.7%	1.1%	1.4%	1.1%	1.2%	0.5%
2011	August	24.6%	24.5%	13.9%	10.3%	8.8%	5.6%	2.0%	2.4%	1.4%	1.5%	1.5%	2.6%	1.1%
2011	July	24.4%	26.7%	14.8%	10.4%	7.0%	5.5%	2.0%	3.0%	1.7%	1.8%	1.3%	1.1%	0.5%
2011	June	23.8%	26.2%	14.9%	11.2%	7.2%	5.4%	1.6%	3.1%	1.8%	1.4%	1.1%	1.3%	1.1%
2011	May	26.6%	26.6%	14.5%	10.3%	7.3%	5.8%	1.6%	3.0%	1.0%	1.3%	0.9%	0.7%	0.5%
2011	April	28.8%	25.8%	12.6%	9.8%	7.1%	5.8%	1.6%	3.4%	1.3%	1.0%	1.2%	1.2%	0.5%
2011	March	28.3%	27.0%	14.0%	8.8%	6.6%	6.2%	1.5%	3.0%	0.9%	1.1%	1.1%	1.1%	0.6%
2011	February	28.5%	25.8%	14.4%	9.7%	6.8%	5.7%	1.4%	2.6%	1.2%	1.2%	1.0%	1.0%	0.7%

(continued)

year	Month	The Netherlands	Germany	Belgium	France	Spain	Italy	Finland	Austria	Ireland	Greece	Luxembourg	Portugal	Other countries
2011	January	29.2%	25.1%	13.6%	10.4%	7.6%	5.4%	1.3%	2.6%	1.2%	1.4%	0.8%	0.9%	0.7%
2010	December	25.4%	26.7%	15.8%	9.8%	8.1%	5.6%	1.4%	2.6%	1.1%	1.0%	1.0%	1.0%	0.6%
2010	November	29.1%	22.9%	14.0%	8.2%	7.1%	4.8%	2.3%	2.4%	3.8%	1.0%	1.2%	1.1%	2.3%
2010	October	25.0%	27.3%	13.8%	10.5%	8.5%	5.7%	2.0%	2.8%	1.1%	1.1%	0.8%	1.1%	0.2%
2010	September	25.3%	25.5%	15.1%	11.0%	7.1%	4.9%	1.9%	2.9%	0.9%	1.5%	1.3%	1.0%	1.6%
2010	August	27.3%	26.0%	13.9%	10.1%	6.2%	6.1%	2.2%	3.2%	1.1%	1.0%	1.0%	0.9%	0.9%
2010	July	28.1%	25.9%	15.0%	9.6%	6.7%	5.1%	1.8%	2.5%	1.5%	1.5%	0.9%	0.9%	0.5%
2010	June	23.7%	30.3%	13.7%	10.0%	6.4%	5.4%	2.2%	2.7%	1.8%	1.3%	1.0%	1.0%	0.4%
2010	May	27.0%	27.3%	15.6%	10.1%	7.1%	4.4%	1.4%	2.7%	1.4%	0.9%	0.9%	0.8%	0.4%
2010	April	26.6%	29.2%	13.1%	10.2%	6.9%	5.7%	0.6%	3.0%	1.5%	1.0%	0.9%	0.8%	0.6%
2010	March	31.0%	26.5%	13.8%	10.4%	6.4%	4.9%	0.6%	2.2%	1.0%	1.1%	0.7%	1.0%	0.4%
2010	February	32.8%	26.1%	14.0%	10.4%	6.3%	4.3%	0.3%	2.3%	0.7%	0.8%	0.9%	0.6%	0.4%
2010	January	29.5%	27.6%	14.3%	10.5%	6.6%	4.1%	0.5%	2.6%	0.8%	1.1%	1.3%	0.8%	0.5%
2009	December	30.8%	27.6%	13.7%	9.3%	6.7%	4.8%	0.4%	2.5%	1.2%	0.8%	0.9%	0.9%	0.5%
2009	November	29.8%	27.2%	13.7%	9.1%	6.6%	5.2%	0.5%	3.0%	1.1%	1.3%	1.0%	1.1%	0.5%
2009	October	28.2%	27.7%	13.9%	10.4%	7.0%	5.2%	0.5%	2.4%	1.2%	1.3%	0.8%	1.0%	0.4%
2009	September	32.6%	23.8%	13.5%	8.9%	6.7%	5.1%	0.5%	2.2%	2.5%	1.2%	1.7%	0.6%	0.6%
2009	August	30.2%	25.6%	13.0%	10.7%	6.2%	4.3%	0.6%	2.5%	2.5%	1.3%	0.8%	0.5%	2.0%
2009	July	27.2%	28.0%	15.3%	9.2%	7.2%	4.0%	0.5%	2.6%	2.5%	1.2%	0.8%	1.0%	0.7%
2009	June	33.6%	23.6%	15.2%	8.7%	5.5%	4.5%	0.7%	2.8%	1.1%	1.2%	2.3%	0.7%	0.2%
2009	May	29.1%	25.5%	15.8%	9.7%	7.2%	4.6%	0.5%	2.4%	0.9%	1.9%	1.3%	0.8%	0.3%
2009	April	35.4%	21.6%	14.4%	9.6%	6.0%	4.8%	0.9%	2.8%	1.3%	1.0%	0.9%	0.9%	0.4%
2009	March	33.2%	23.6%	13.4%	9.1%	6.5%	6.0%	0.3%	3.0%	1.4%	0.9%	1.0%	1.2%	0.3%
2009	February	33.0%	24.4%	14.3%	9.9%	7.3%	4.2%	0.5%	2.0%	1.9%	1.0%	0.7%	0.7%	0.2%
2009	January	31.3%	25.9%	14.3%	10.5%	6.5%	4.6%	0.6%	2.2%	1.6%	1.0%	0.7%	0.7%	0.2%
2008	December	39.5%	23.0%	13.2%	8.7%	6.0%	3.6%	0.4%	1.8%	1.2%	0.9%	0.7%	0.6%	0.6%
2008	November	32.2%	25.7%	13.5%	9.9%	6.0%	4.6%	0.4%	2.1%	1.1%	1.0%	0.8%	0.9%	2.0%

2008	October	30.0%	27.9%	13.4%	10.0%	6.9%	4.4%	0.5%	2.6%	1.6%	1.0%	0.9%	0.7%	0.2%
2008	September	33.3%	23.5%	13.2%	10.3%	6.4%	5.3%	0.4%	2.5%	1.9%	0.6%	1.1%	1.1%	0.3%
2008	August	32.7%	23.9%	11.8%	9.8%	5.8%	8.9%	0.4%	2.8%	0.9%	1.0%	0.7%	0.8%	0.6%
2008	July	36.6%	24.0%	14.4%	9.0%	5.4%	3.7%	0.5%	2.4%	0.8%	1.2%	1.0%	0.9%	0.3%
2008	June	38.9%	22.7%	13.2%	8.5%	6.1%	4.4%	0.5%	1.9%	0.8%	1.0%	0.9%	1.0%	0.2%
2008	May	36.7%	24.2%	14.8%	8.6%	6.3%	3.6%	0.4%	2.1%	0.8%	0.9%	0.8%	0.8%	0.2%
2008	April	37.7%	22.7%	14.5%	8.4%	6.5%	4.1%	0.3%	2.1%	1.6%	0.7%	0.6%	0.8%	0.1%
2008	March	38.6%	21.6%	13.7%	8.7%	5.6%	5.8%	0.4%	2.2%	1.0%	0.9%	0.7%	0.8%	0.1%
2008	February	38.9%	23.3%	13.4%	8.6%	6.1%	3.7%	0.3%	2.0%	1.0%	0.7%	0.9%	0.9%	0.1%
2008	January	39.1%	24.1%	13.9%	8.7%	5.0%	3.5%	0.4%	2.1%	0.8%	0.7%	0.8%	0.7%	0.2%
2007	December	37.4%	23.5%	14.5%	9.1%	6.5%	3.2%	0.3%	1.8%	1.2%	0.7%	0.9%	0.9%	0.1%
2007	November	36.0%	23.5%	14.1%	8.8%	6.9%	3.7%	0.8%	2.1%	1.3%	0.9%	0.9%	1.0%	0.0%
2007	October	39.5%	20.6%	13.6%	9.2%	6.2%	3.4%	0.6%	2.0%	2.3%	1.0%	0.7%	1.1%	0.0%
2007	September	37.7%	21.4%	13.3%	9.8%	6.9%	3.9%	0.4%	2.0%	1.0%	1.2%	1.2%	1.2%	0.1%
2007	August	38.9%	23.7%	13.4%	9.2%	5.3%	3.8%	0.4%	2.0%	1.2%	0.6%	0.7%	0.7%	0.1%
2007	July	41.2%	22.1%	13.1%	9.0%	5.1%	3.6%	0.4%	2.2%	0.6%	1.0%	0.9%	0.7%	0.1%
2007	June	38.0%	20.8%	13.2%	8.2%	4.7%	4.1%	0.2%	1.6%	2.6%	5.0%	0.7%	0.7%	0.1%
2007	May	42.4%	21.9%	13.8%	8.7%	4.9%	2.9%	0.3%	1.7%	0.9%	0.8%	1.2%	0.5%	0.1%
2007	April	41.0%	20.9%	14.1%	8.4%	5.6%	3.6%	0.4%	1.8%	2.0%	0.7%	0.9%	0.5%	0.1%
2007	March	42.7%	21.5%	13.9%	9.4%	5.1%	2.9%	0.3%	1.4%	0.5%	0.7%	0.9%	0.7%	0.0%
2007	February	43.2%	20.6%	15.5%	8.1%	4.9%	3.1%	0.2%	1.7%	0.7%	0.8%	0.7%	0.4%	0.2%
2007	January	46.4%	20.3%	12.9%	7.5%	4.9%	2.7%	0.2%	2.1%	1.0%	0.7%	0.9%	0.6%	0.0%
2006	December	43.1%	20.6%	14.2%	8.3%	5.0%	3.1%	0.3%	1.8%	1.1%	0.8%	0.8%	1.0%	0.0%
2006	November	39.7%	22.2%	14.5%	9.4%	4.9%	3.9%	0.4%	1.9%	0.8%	0.9%	0.8%	0.5%	0.0%
2006	October	40.8%	21.1%	13.1%	10.6%	5.9%	3.2%	0.3%	1.8%	0.8%	0.9%	0.8%	0.8%	0.0%
2006	September	39.7%	21.2%	14.1%	10.0%	5.7%	3.1%	0.5%	1.8%	0.7%	0.8%	0.8%	1.7%	0.0%
2006	August	39.0%	21.1%	14.3%	9.4%	5.9%	3.7%	0.5%	1.9%	1.1%	1.0%	1.0%	1.0%	0.0%
2006	July	41.9%	20.7%	13.9%	9.8%	5.5%	3.3%	0.3%	1.3%	1.2%	0.8%	0.7%	0.8%	0.0%
2006	June	42.4%	20.9%	14.8%	9.0%	5.1%	2.9%	0.3%	1.8%	0.6%	0.8%	0.7%	0.7%	0.0%

(continued)

year	*Month*	*The Netherlands*	*Germany*	*Belgium*	*France*	*Spain*	*Italy*	*Finland*	*Austria*	*Ireland*	*Greece*	*Luxembourg*	*Portugal*	*Other countries*
2006	May	41.6%	22.4%	15.2%	8.6%	4.3%	3.6%	0.3%	1.6%	0.8%	0.6%	0.6%	0.6%	0.0%
2006	April	42.4%	22.3%	14.2%	8.6%	4.5%	2.8%	0.4%	2.1%	0.7%	0.7%	0.5%	0.7%	0.0%
2006	March	42.8%	21.3%	14.1%	8.6%	4.9%	2.6%	0.8%	1.8%	0.6%	1.0%	0.8%	0.7%	0.0%
2006	February	44.8%	22.1%	14.3%	7.6%	4.5%	2.8%	0.1%	1.6%	0.7%	0.4%	0.6%	0.6%	0.0%
2006	January	44.1%	21.2%	14.4%	8.4%	4.4%	2.6%	0.4%	1.8%	0.8%	0.9%	0.7%	0.4%	0.0%
2005	December	48.7%	17.1%	11.6%	7.1%	4.0%	3.6%	0.3%	3.4%	1.0%	0.8%	1.6%	0.8%	0.0%
2005	November	44.3%	20.7%	14.1%	8.4%	4.4%	2.6%	0.3%	1.7%	1.3%	0.9%	0.7%	0.7%	0.0%
2005	October	44.7%	20.6%	14.0%	9.0%	4.6%	2.4%	0.3%	1.4%	0.7%	1.0%	0.6%	0.9%	0.0%
2005	September	42.6%	21.7%	13.8%	9.8%	4.5%	2.9%	0.2%	1.6%	0.8%	0.9%	0.7%	0.6%	0.0%
2005	August	45.6%	19.7%	13.7%	9.4%	4.0%	2.9%	0.3%	1.6%	0.9%	0.6%	0.6%	0.7%	0.0%
2005	July	45.5%	20.5%	14.1%	8.1%	4.2%	2.7%	0.3%	1.4%	1.2%	0.9%	0.5%	0.7%	0.0%
2005	June	49.8%	18.8%	12.9%	7.5%	3.7%	2.3%	0.3%	1.3%	0.7%	0.8%	0.9%	0.8%	0.0%
2005	May	47.9%	19.0%	14.5%	8.4%	3.5%	3.0%	0.1%	1.5%	0.6%	0.6%	0.4%	0.6%	0.0%
2005	April	51.3%	17.9%	13.7%	6.9%	3.9%	2.3%	0.2%	1.5%	0.6%	0.7%	0.4%	0.7%	0.0%
2005	March	52.4%	17.7%	13.4%	7.0%	3.5%	2.4%	0.2%	1.6%	0.5%	0.5%	0.5%	0.4%	0.0%
2005	February	52.2%	18.2%	13.3%	7.3%	3.4%	2.2%	0.3%	1.3%	0.6%	0.5%	0.5%	0.4%	0.0%
2005	January	53.0%	18.1%	13.3%	6.8%	3.6%	2.2%	0.2%	0.9%	0.5%	0.6%	0.5%	0.3%	0.0%
2004	December	53.1%	17.5%	12.9%	7.0%	4.1%	2.2%	0.2%	1.1%	0.5%	0.7%	0.4%	0.5%	0.0%
2004	November	55.1%	17.1%	11.9%	7.1%	3.9%	1.9%	0.2%	1.1%	0.4%	0.6%	0.4%	0.4%	0.0%
2004	October	55.8%	16.0%	12.2%	7.1%	3.6%	2.1%	0.3%	0.9%	0.5%	0.5%	0.6%	0.5%	0.0%
2004	September	57.1%	16.0%	10.3%	6.7%	3.4%	2.6%	0.2%	1.3%	0.7%	0.8%	0.4%	0.4%	0.0%
2004	August	55.8%	15.6%	10.7%	7.4%	3.4%	2.3%	0.4%	1.6%	0.5%	0.7%	1.0%	0.5%	0.1%
2004	July	58.4%	15.7%	10.4%	7.3%	3.1%	1.8%	0.3%	0.9%	0.7%	0.4%	0.5%	0.4%	0.0%
2004	June	61.0%	14.7%	11.6%	5.7%	2.6%	1.7%	0.2%	1.0%	0.4%	0.5%	0.4%	0.3%	0.0%
2004	May	61.4%	15.0%	10.9%	5.5%	2.8%	1.7%	0.3%	1.1%	0.3%	0.3%	0.3%	0.3%	0.0%
2004	April	62.4%	14.1%	11.3%	5.8%	2.5%	1.5%	0.2%	0.8%	0.4%	0.4%	0.3%	0.3%	0.0%
2004	March	62.5%	14.4%	11.0%	5.2%	2.8%	1.6%	0.3%	1.2%	0.3%	0.4%	0.3%	0.3%	0.0%

2004	February	63.9%	13.9%	10.5%	5.2%	2.6%	1.5%	0.1%	0.9%	0.3%	0.4%	0.3%	0.4%	0.0%
2004	January	64.8%	13.9%	10.0%	4.8%	2.4%	1.8%	0.2%	1.1%	0.2%	0.2%	0.4%	0.2%	0.0%
2003	December	65.2%	12.9%	10.4%	5.3%	2.6%	1.3%	0.1%	0.8%	0.4%	0.5%	0.3%	0.3%	0.0%
2003	November	65.2%	13.0%	9.9%	4.7%	2.6%	1.4%	0.1%	0.8%	0.4%	1.4%	0.4%	0.4%	0.0%
2003	October	64.7%	13.1%	10.1%	5.2%	2.8%	1.6%	0.1%	0.8%	0.3%	0.7%	0.3%	0.3%	0.0%
2003	September	64.6%	12.4%	9.7%	6.4%	2.4%	1.7%	0.2%	1.1%	0.5%	0.4%	0.2%	0.4%	0.0%
2003	August	64.1%	11.5%	9.5%	6.9%	2.8%	2.1%	0.2%	1.3%	0.5%	0.4%	0.4%	0.4%	0.0%
2003	July	70.7%	10.6%	8.9%	4.2%	2.0%	1.3%	0.2%	0.8%	0.2%	0.6%	0.3%	0.2%	0.0%
2003	June	70.3%	10.9%	9.1%	4.4%	1.7%	1.5%	0.0%	0.7%	0.2%	0.6%	0.2%	0.3%	0.0%
2003	May	70.2%	10.5%	9.1%	4.2%	1.9%	1.3%	0.3%	0.9%	0.3%	0.6%	0.4%	0.3%	0.0%
2003	April	76.2%	8.8%	7.6%	3.7%	1.3%	0.7%	0.1%	0.7%	0.3%	0.2%	0.3%	0.1%	0.0%
2003	March	75.0%	9.1%	8.2%	3.7%	1.7%	0.9%	0.1%	0.6%	0.3%	0.2%	0.2%	0.1%	0.0%
2003	February	76.2%	8.3%	7.9%	3.7%	1.7%	0.8%	0.1%	0.6%	0.3%	0.2%	0.2%	0.1%	0.0%
2003	January	77.2%	8.0%	7.4%	3.3%	1.6%	1.1%	0.1%	0.4%	0.2%	0.2%	0.3%	0.2%	0.0%
2002	December	77.8%	8.0%	6.7%	3.1%	2.0%	1.0%	0.1%	0.4%	0.3%	0.2%	0.1%	0.2%	0.0%
2002	November	76.3%	8.2%	6.9%	3.6%	1.8%	1.0%	0.2%	0.6%	0.4%	0.5%	0.2%	0.2%	0.0%
2002	October	76.5%	7.7%	6.7%	4.3%	1.6%	1.2%	0.1%	0.6%	0.7%	0.3%	0.3%	0.2%	0.0%
2002	September	75.8%	7.6%	6.4%	4.6%	1.9%	1.4%	0.3%	0.6%	0.3%	0.6%	0.3%	0.3%	0.0%
2002	August	76.5%	7.8%	6.4%	4.3%	1.6%	1.0%	0.2%	0.7%	0.4%	0.6%	0.4%	0.2%	0.0%
2002	July	78.8%	6.4%	6.6%	2.9%	1.4%	1.6%	0.1%	0.9%	0.2%	0.4%	0.4%	0.4%	0.0%
2002	June	78.2%	6.0%	5.8%	3.3%	1.7%	1.7%	0.3%	0.9%	0.3%	1.0%	0.5%	0.5%	0.0%
2002	May	83.5%	5.5%	4.9%	2.0%	1.1%	1.0%	0.4%	0.7%	0.4%	0.2%	0.2%	0.2%	0.0%
2002	April	82.7%	5.1%	4.4%	2.6%	1.4%	0.8%	0.2%	1.3%	0.5%	0.2%	0.3%	0.5%	0.0%
2002	March	87.4%	4.1%	3.2%	1.9%	0.8%	0.6%	0.1%	1.2%	0.2%	0.1%	0.2%	0.1%	0.1%
2002	February	90.5%	3.1%	2.1%	1.6%	0.6%	0.5%	0.1%	1.0%	0.2%	0.2%	0.1%	0.1%	0.0%
2002	January	92.1%	3.2%	1.9%	0.8%	0.3%	0.3%	0.0%	0.5%	0.0%	0.0%	0.8%	0.1%	0.0%

Source: Eurodiffusion project & own project.

Note: The Eurozone has expanded after 2002 thus increasing the number of countries. New countries include Slovenia (1 January 2007), Cyprus and Malta (1 January 2008), Slovakia (1 January 2009), Estonia (1 January 2011), Andorra (1 July 2011), Latvia (1 January 2014), and Lithuania (1 January 2015).

Index

Currencies and coins